READINGS IN CROSS-CULTURAL METHODOLOGY

Frank W. Moore
editor

HRAF PRESS • NEW HAVEN

Library of Congress Catalog Number: 61-17325

Preface

During the past few decades a considerable number of works on the theory and method of cross-cultural research have appeared in various journals and compendiums. These works are widely scattered and in many cases the scholar wishing to initiate cross-cultural research finds a key paper practically unavailable.

This situation and the absence of any major single volume on the subject prompted the Human Relations Area Files to undertake the collection of those papers of the past couple decades generally deemed most significant, along with examples of earlier efforts, for publication under a single cover.

Selecting the most widely useful papers from the growing literature proved a difficult task, given the limitations of space. There were enough papers perhaps fully as valuable to fill several volumes. In making the final selections an attempt was made to give a view of the development of cross-cultural comparative studies and to present the basic theoretical and methodological problems involved, together with some discussion of the progress to date in solving these problems.

Arrangement of these studies in a single volume posed additional problems since nearly all the papers partake of several possible rubrics of classification. The same basic criterion used to select the papers was used to classify, namely, usefulness to a potential researcher. Thus the studies have been grouped according to the reason for their selection rather than their total content. A paper included because of a relatively brief but important section on sampling will be found in that section, even though the general theme of the paper may be theoretical.

The publication of this book would have been impossible without the selfless cooperation of the many authors and publishers represented and we wish to add to our citations on the first page of each paper our gratitude for the generous response to our requests for reprint permission.

I wish to thank Professors George P. Murdock, C. S. Ford, and William Davenport for their suggestions and advice. Dr. Harold E. Driver wrote an article especially for this volume and his contribution is greatly appreciated. To my colleagues Dr. Frank LeBar, Director of Research at HRAF, and Mrs. Adelaide Walker, Director of HRAF Press, go special thanks for their labors.

FRANK W. MOORE

New Haven, Connecticut
September 1961

Table of Contents

[illegible]

Contributors

HAROLD E. DRIVER (b. 1907, Ph.D., University of California) is Professor of Anthropology at Indiana University. He has done field research in California and Mexico and has specialized in comparative statistical methodology and culture area classifications. His article, "Introduction to Statistics for Comparative Research," which was written specially for this book, offers an introductory survey of the uses of statistical methods, particularly of chi-square and phi, to indicate correlations between various facets of culture.

FRED EGGAN (b. 1906, Ph.D., University of Chicago), noted authority on social organization, did field research among the American Indians and in the Philippines and is now Professor of Anthropology at the University of Chicago. The emphasis in "Social Anthropology and the Method of Controlled Comparison" is on the history of the theoretical basis of comparative studies, with a consideration of some of the more important problems involved.

CLELLAN S. FORD (b. 1909, Ph.D., Yale University) is Professor of Anthropology at Yale and President of the Human Relations Area Files. His field research has been on the Northwest Coast of America and in the Fiji Islands. His special interests are comparative research and the study of sexual behavior. In "A Sample Comparative Analysis of Material Culture" Ford discusses and demonstrates many possible ways of analyzing information in terms of function, attributes, and form. His other article here, "Society, Culture, and the Human Organism," takes up the problem of measuring cultural behavior on a universal scale for comparative research, particularly in regard to observed versus ideal behavior. The difficulties encountered in converting information as given by the ethnographer into quantifiable data are also discussed.

LEONARD T. HOBHOUSE, GERALD C. WHEELER, and MORRIS GINSBERG made important contributions to the development of sociology and anthropology in England. Hobhouse (1864-1929) was the first professor of sociology at London University, serving from 1907 to his death in 1929. Wheeler (1872- ?) was an authority on Alu and Mono in the Bougainville Straits. Ginsberg (b. 1889), now retired, was Professor of Sociology at the University of London. Their book, *The Material Culture and Social Institutions of the Simpler Peoples*, was an attempt to draw conclusions regarding social evolution from a large-scale comparative study of material culture, government, family, war, and social structure. This study drew heavy criticism for faulty construction of the sample. A related methodological flaw was the failure to achieve a realistic and consistent culture unit classification, a failure that can be attributed at least in part to the extremely uneven area coverage of the literature available at the time. The theoretical base and the methodology of their study are explained in the introductory section reproduced here.

CLYDE KLUCKHOHN (1905-1960, Ph.D., Harvard University) did extensive field research in the American Southwest and was Professor of Anthropology at Harvard. He made lasting contributions to cultural theory and the study of value systems. His article here, "Universal Categories of Culture," is devoted to theoretical discussion of the problems of definition and isolation of universals in cultural materials.

ANDRÉ J. KÖBBEN (b. 1925, Ph.D., University of Amsterdam), Professor of Cultural Anthropology at the University of Amsterdam, did field work in the Ivory Coast and Surinam and is particularly interested in the theory of intercultural comparisons, social change, and prophetic movements. In his article, "New Ways of Presenting an Old Idea: The Statistical Method in Social Anthropology," he reviews the history of comparative studies and techniques with special emphasis on documentation systems and devices. Sharp criticism is offered of several cross-cultural studies, notably those of Murdock, Ford, and Horton.

OSCAR LEWIS (b. 1915, Ph.D., Columbia University) is Professor of Anthropology at the University of Illinois. He has conducted community studies in Mexico and India. In his article, "Comparisons in Cultural Anthropology," which presents a valuable survey of recent trends in comparative research, Lewis classifies comparative studies in eight categories ranging from comparisons within a single local group to comparisons on global or random bases. An exhaustive bibliography of recent studies of each of the eight types is also included.

FRANK W. MOORE (b. 1925, Ph.D., Columbia University), Executive Director of the Human Relations Area Files, did field work in Mexico and has specialized in research in documentation and ethnobotany. His article, "Cross-Cultural Documentation," written especially for this volume, relates special documentation services such as the Human Relations Area Files to conventional methods and points out some of the potential problems for the researcher who uses documentation devices.

GEORGE PETER MURDOCK (b. 1897, Ph.D., Yale University) is Professor of Anthropology at the University of Pittsburgh and a major figure in the field of cross-cultural research. His field research has been mainly in the Northwest Coast of America and Micronesia. He is represented in this volume by three articles. The first, "The Cross-Cultural Survey," examines the basic problems of cross-cultural research. Recognition of these problems led to the founding of the Cross-Cultural Survey and provided the theoretical as well as practical starting point for development of the *Outline of Cultural Materials*. In "World Ethnographic Sample" Murdock considers the problems involved in the selection of a sample of cultural units for use in cross-cultural research, giving information on a sampling of the world's cultures in a series of extensive tables (corrected by the author for this reprinting). The third article, "The Processing of Anthropological Materials," contains a proposed hierarchical classification and definition of culture units. In addition there is much substantive information on research tools and aids.

RAOUL NAROLL (b. 1920, Ph.D., University of California at Los Angeles) is Professor of Anthropology at San Fernando Valley State College. He has done research in comparative culture history and specializes in cross-cultural methodology. The classic problem posed by Galton regarding the historical relationship of the culture units used by Tylor (see below) has concerned comparative researchers ever since, to the extent that some—Boas among them—concluded the method should be abandoned. In "Two Solutions to Galton's Problem," Naroll presents two possible techniques for establishing the degree of relationship of the culture units involved. Galton's original statements will be found in the report of the discussion on Tylor's paper, reprinted here with the paper itself.

EDWARD B. TYLOR (1832-1917, privately educated) was an Oxford professor and a pioneer anthropologist and cultural evolutionist. His article, "On a Method of Investigating the Development of Institutions," is generally acknowledged to be the first effective attempt to quantify, measure, and correlate ethnographic data to scientifically test theoretical postulates. The information available to Tylor was, by today's standards, entirely inadequate, and his methodology has been questioned by many authorities. This does not detract, however, from the singular importance of the study in the evolution of a scientific methodology. The comments by Galton regarding the independence of Tylor's cultural units are also included here.

STANLEY H. UDY, JR. (b. 1928, Ph.D., Princeton University), Assistant Professor of Sociology at Yale, is specializing in comparative sociology. In "Problems and Procedures," taken from his book, *Organization of Work,* Udy details the methodology of this study. Udy's book is of special interest because, though in the classic pattern of "global comparisons," his investigation concerned a subject (labor organization) not previously studied and because the author's training had been almost entirely sociological.

JOHN W. M. WHITING (b. 1908, Ph.D., Yale University) did field research in New Guinea and is now Director of the Laboratory of Human Development at Harvard, specializing in child training studies and comparative research. In his article, "The Cross-Cultural Method," is a detailed treatment of the major methodological problems in cross-cultural research together with an analysis of the potential advantages and pitfalls of this type of research.

Development

On a METHOD *of* INVESTIGATING *the* DEVELOPMENT *of* INSTITUTIONS; APPLIED *to* LAWS *of* MARRIAGE *and* DESCENT.*

By EDWARD B. TYLOR, D.C.L., F.R.S.

FOR years past it has become evident that the great need of anthropology is that its methods should be strengthened and systematised. The world has not been unjust to the growing science, far from it. Wherever anthropologists have been able to show definite evidence and inference, for instance, in the development series of arts in the Pitt-Rivers Museum, at Oxford, not only specialists but the educated world generally are ready to receive the results and assimilate them into public opinion. Strict method has, however, as yet only been introduced over part of the anthropological field. There has still to be overcome a certain not unkindly hesitancy on the part of men engaged in the precise operations of mathematics, physics, chemistry, biology, to admit that the problems of anthropology are amenable to scientific treatment. It is my aim to show that the development of institutions may be investigated on a basis of tabulation and classification. For this end I have taken up a subject of the utmost real as well as theoretical interest, the formation of laws of marriage and descent, as to which during many years I have been collecting the evidence found among

*Reprinted from the *Journal of the Royal Anthropological Institute of Great Britain and Ireland,* Vol. 18 (1889), pp. 245-272, by permission of the Royal Anthropological Institute.

between three and four hundred peoples, ranging from insignificant savage hordes to great cultured nations. The particular rules have been scheduled out into tables, so as to ascertain what may be called the "adhesions" of each custom, showing which peoples have the same custom, and what other customs accompany it or lie apart from it. From the recurrence or absence of these customs it will be our business to infer their dependence on causes acting over the whole range of mankind.

Years since, long before my collection of data approached its present bulk, and could be classified into the elaborate tables now presented, I became naturally anxious to know whether the labour had been thrown away, or whether this social arithmetic would do something to disclose the course of social history. The question was how to make the trial. I remembered a story I had once heard of Horace Vernet, that a friend asked him how he planned out his huge battle-pieces. The painter took the inquirer into his studio and began a picture for him by first touching in a bayonet in one corner of his canvas, then drawing the arm and sabre of the trooper slashing over the bayonet-thrust, and so on from one overlapping figure to the next till he reached the central group. It seemed to me that it would be well to begin thus in one corner of the field. The point I chose was a quaint and somewhat comic custom as to the barbaric etiquette between husbands and their wives' relatives, and *vice versâ*: they may not look at one another, much less speak, and they even avoid mentioning one another's names. Thus, in America, John Tanner, the adopted Ojibwa, describes his being taken by a friendly Assineboin into his lodge, and seeing how at his companion's entry the old father and mother-in-law covered up their heads in their blankets till their son-in-law got into the compartment reserved for him, where his wife brought him his food. So in Australia, Mr. Howitt relates how he inadvertently told a native to call his mother-in-law, who was passing at some little distance; but the blackfellow sent the order round by a third party, saying reproachfully to Mr. Howitt, "You know I could not speak to that old woman." Absurd as this custom may appear to Europeans, it is not the outcome of mere local fancy, as appears on reckoning up the peoples practising it in various regions of the world, who are found to be about sixty-six in number, that is, more than one-sixth of the whole number of peoples catalogued, which is roughly three-hundred and fifty. Thus:—

Avoidance.

Between H. and W.'s Rel.	Mutual.	Between W. and H.'s Rel.
45	8	13

Now, on looking out from the schedules the adhesions of this avoidance-custom, a relation appears between it and the customs of the world as to residence after marriage. This is seen in the following computation of the peoples whose habit is for the husband to take up his abode with the wife's family permanently, or to do so temporarily and eventually to remove with her to his own family or home (the reverse of this does not occur), or for the husband at once to take home the wife.

Residence.

H. to W.	Removal	W. to H.
65	76	141

Now, if the customs of residence and the customs of avoidance were independent, or nearly so, we should expect to find their coincidence following the ordinary law of chance distribution. In the tribes where the husband permanently lives with his wife's family (sixty-five out of three hundred and fifty), we should estimate that ceremonial avoidance between him and them might appear in nine cases, whereas it actually appears in fourteen cases. On the other hand, peoples where the husband at marriage takes his wife to his home (one hundred and forty-one out of three hundred and fifty), would rateably correspond with avoidance between him and her family in eighteen cases, whereas it actually appears in nine cases only. Also, if the thirteen cases of avoidance between the wife and the husband's family were divided rateably among the different modes of residence, two or three cases should come among the peoples where the husband lives with the wife's family, but there are no such cases. On the other hand, five cases should be found among the peoples where the wife lives in the husband's home or family, but actually there are eight. Thus there is a well marked preponderance indicating that ceremonial avoidance by the husband of the wife's family is in some way connected with his living with them; and *vice versâ* as to the wife and the husband's family. Hereupon, it has to be enquired whether the facts suggest a reason for this connexion. Such a reason readily presents itself, inasmuch as the ceremony of not speaking to and pretending not to see some well-known person close by, is familiar enough to ourselves in the social rite which we call "cutting." This, indeed, with us implies aversion, and the implication comes out even more strongly in objection to utter the name ("we never mention her," as the song has it). It is different, however, in the barbaric custom we are considering, for here the husband is none the less on friendly terms with his wife's people because they may not take any notice of one another. In fact, the explanation of this ceremonial cutting may be simpler and more direct than in civilised Europe. As the husband has intruded himself among a family which is not his own, and into a house where he has no right, it seems not difficult to understand their marking the difference between him and themselves by treating him formally as a stranger. So like is the working of the human mind in all stages of civilisation, that our own language conveys in a familiar idiom the same train of thought; in describing the already mentioned case of the Assineboin marrying and taking up his abode with his wife's parents who pretend not to see him when he comes in, we have only to say that they do not *recognise* him, and we shall have condensed the whole proceeding into a single word. In this first example, it is to be noticed that the argument of a causal connexion of some kind between two groups of phenomena brings into view, so far at least as the data prove sound, a scientific fact. But we pass on to less solid ground in assigning for this connexion a reason which may be only analogous to the real reason, or only indirectly corresponding with it, or only partly expressing it, as its correlation with other connexions may eventually show. This important reservation, once stated, may be taken as understood through the rest of the enquiry.

Let us now turn to another custom, not less quaint-seeming than the last to the European mind. This is the practice of naming the parent from the child. When Moffat, the missionary, was in Africa among the Bechuana, he was spoken to and of, according to native usage, as Ra-Mary = father of Mary. On the other side of the world, among the Kasias of India, Colonel Yule mentions the like rule; for instance, there being a boy named Bobon, his father was known as Pabobon. In fact there are above thirty peoples spread over the earth who thus name the father, and, though less often, the mother. They may be called, coining a name for them, *teknonymous* peoples. When beginning to notice the wide distribution of this custom of *teknonymy*, and setting myself to reckon its adhesions, I confess to have been fairly taken by surprise to find it lying in close connection with the custom of the husband's residence in the wife's family, the two coinciding twenty-two times, where accident might fairly have given eleven. It proved to be still more closely attached to the practice of ceremonial avoidance by the husband of the wife's relatives, occurring fourteen times, where accident might have given four. The combination is shown on the diagram, fig. 1, the (appproximate) numbers on which give the means of estimating the probable closeness of causal connection. Were the three customs so distantly connected as to be practically independent, the product of the corresponding fractions

$\frac{132}{350} \times \frac{53}{350} \times \frac{31}{350}$, multiplied into the three hundred and fifty peoples would show that their concurrence might be expected to happen between once and twice in the list of peoples of the world. In fact it is found eleven times. Thus, we have their common causation vouched for by the heavy odds of six to one. Many of the firmest beliefs of mankind rest, I fear, on a less solid basis. In tracing out the origin of the group of customs in conformity with these conditions, it is not necessary to invent a hypothesis, as an account of the proceedings of the Cree Indians will serve as a "luminous instance" to clear up the whole situation. Among these Indians the young husband, coming to live with his wife's parents, must turn his back on

Fig. 1.

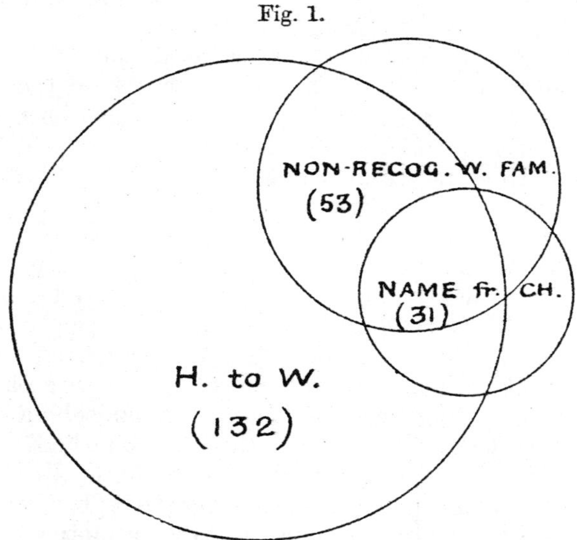

them, not speaking to them (especially not to his mother-in-law), being thus treated as a stranger till his first child is born; whereupon he takes its name, and is called "father of So-and-so," and thenceforth attaches himself to his parents-in-law rather than to his own parents. That is to say, he is ceremonially treated as a stranger till his child, being born a member of the family, gives him a status as father of a member of the family, whereupon they consistently leave off the farce of not recognising him. When I brought this argument to the knowledge of Dr. G. A. Wilken, of Leyden, he pointed out to me that in his series of papers on "Primitive Forms of Marriage,"[1] where he

[1] G. A. Wilken, "Over de primitieve vormen van het huwelijk, &c.," in "Indische Gids," 1880, &c.

gives instances of the naming of fathers from children, he had stated this practice to be an assertion of paternity. Undoubtedly it is so on the father's part, and its being so is quite compatible with its being a recognition of him by the wife's kinsfolk, the two aspects belonging to one social fact.

Taking the connection between residence and ceremonial avoidance to be substantiated by their relative adhesions, it is necessary to notice that there are cases where the husband, although he carries the wife away from the home of her parents, nevertheless goes through the form of avoiding them. This, under the circumstances, seems a motiveless proceeding, but is intelligible as a survival from a time when he would have lived with them. These cases belong mainly to the Malay District and to Australia. In the Malay District the habit of residence in the wife's family is still a notable institution of the country, though being fast superseded by householding on the Arab and European models. In Australia, the native custom is described as being that the husband takes his wife to his own home, while at the same time he carries out the etiquette of cutting his mother-in-law to a ludicrous extreme, with slight traces of the avoidance of the father-in-law. It appeared to me that on the present explanation this must indicate a recent habit of residence on the wife's side, and reference showed a law of the Kurnai tribe of Gippsland,[1] that when a native kills game, certain parts of the meat (of a kangaru, the head, neck, and part of the back) are the allotted share of the wife's parents. As the duty of supplying game to the wife's household when the husband lives there is one of the best-marked points of matriarchal law, I wrote to Mr. Howitt, as the leading authority on Australian anthropology, suggesting that further enquiry would probably disclose evidence hitherto unnoticed as to the maternal stage of society subsisting in Australia. After examination made, Mr. Howitt replied :—"I am now satisfied that your surmises are quite correct," and therewith he sent details bearing on the question, especially an account by Mr. Aldridge, of Maryborough, Queensland, as to the practice of the tribes in his neighbourhood. This I will quote, as being a strongly marked case of residence on the wife's side. "When a man marries a woman from a distant locality, he goes to her tribelet and identifies himself with her people. This is a rule with very few exceptions. Of course, I speak of them as they were in their wild state. He becomes part of and one of the family. In the event of a war expedition, the daughter's husband acts as a blood-relation, and will fight and kill his own blood-relations if blows are struck by

[1] Fison and Howitt, "Kamilaroi and Kurnai," p. 207.

his wife's relations. I have seen a father and son fighting under these circumstances, and the son would most certainly have killed his father if others had not interfered."

The relative positions of the two groups of customs, residence and avoidance, may now be more completely shown, by the aid of the diagram, fig. 2.

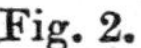

Fig. 2.

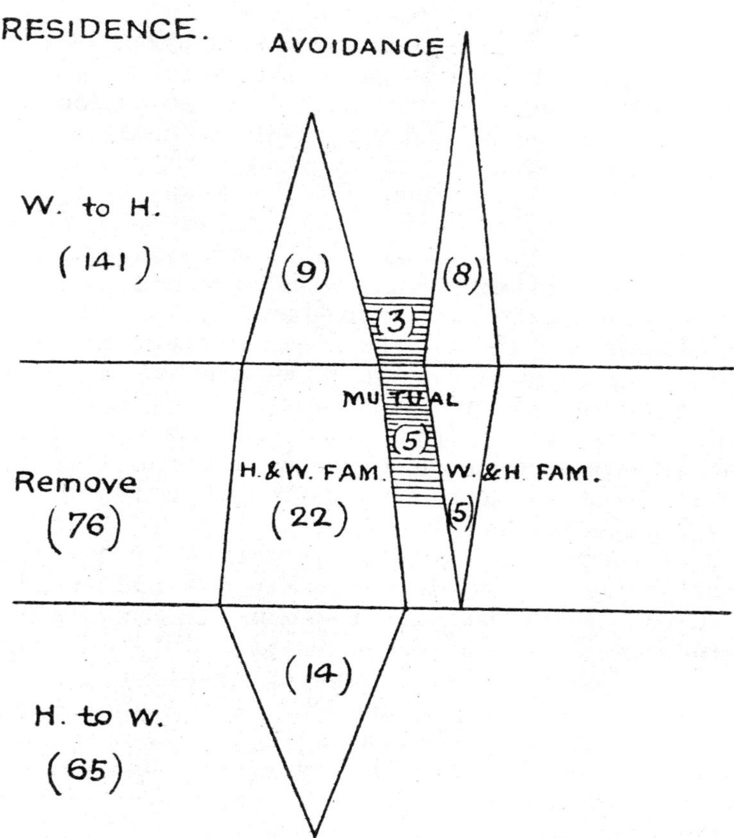

Here the space representing residence is divided into three sections, viz., residence on the wife's side; the transitional stage of removal (where the couple begin married life in the wife's house, but eventually move); residence on the husband's side. According to the previous arguments, the ceremonial avoidance between the husband and the wife's family is taken to have arisen within the periods when he and they lived permanently or temporarily in contact, and to have continued by survival into the period after this co-residence had ceased. There next appear the small group of eight cases of mutual avoidance, at once between the husband and the wife's family, and the wife and the husband's family. These consistently are found in the removal stage, where both kinds of residence meet, surviving into the stage of residence on the husband's side. Avoidance between the wife and the husband's family has the same range, but here the conditions producing it belong to both stages of residence, and there is no question of survival.

From this distribution of the avoidance-customs, it appears that in the parts of the world open to the present inspection, the three stages of residence have tended to succeed one another in the upward order of the diagram. Residence on the wife's side appears earliest, after this the removal stage, and latest, residence on the husband's side. For if it be supposed that the course of society was in the reverse direction, as would be represented by turning the diagram upside down, avoidance between the husband and the wife's family would be represented as arising in the stage when the husband lived away from it, while avoidance between the wife and the husband's family, which ought on this supposition to continue by survival into the stage of residence on the wife's side, is not found there. The avoidance-customs, though practically so trifling, are thus signals showing the direction of a movement, of which we shall more fully see the importance, namely, the shifting of habitual residence from the wife's family to the husband's.

Let us now proceed to apply a similar method to the investigation of the great division of society into matriarchal and patriarchal. In the matriarchal system, descent in the family or clan is reckoned from the mother; authority is mainly on her side, the mother's brother being habitually guardian of the children; succession to rank and office, and inheritance of property, follow the same line passing to the brother or to the sister's son. In the patriarchal system descent is from the father; he has the power over wife and children; succession and inheritance are from him to his offspring. Between these extreme stages lies an intermediate or transitional stage in which their characteristics are variously combined. The terms patriarchal and matriarchal not being quite appropriate, I shall use in preference for the three stages the terms maternal, maternal-paternal, and paternal. The classification is necessarily somewhat vague, but I think will be found to have sufficient precision for the problem of determining the direction in which mankind has tended to move from one of the stages to another. In dealing with this problem certain customs relating to marriage law will be used as indicators.

Among a large proportion of the nations of the world up to the middle levels of culture, the re-marriage of widows is arranged, and more or less enforced, but the regulations are framed on two distinct principles. On the first principle the widow becomes the wife of her husband's brother, or near kinsman, according to some recognized order of precedence of claim. The word "levirate," from *levir* = husband's brother, has become the accepted term for this institution, but its sense must in most cases be extended to take in a series of kinsmen, among whom the brother-in-law only ranks first. Unfortunately, it has seldom been thought worth while to ascertain this precise order, which might throw light on family structure, as in an account drawn up by Mr. Howitt of the practice in Australian tribes where any man is eligible to succeed to the widow, if he stands in the relation of elder or younger brother to the deceased, beginning with actual brothers on the male or female side, according to the rule of descent in the tribe, and extending to tribal brothers who are in our terminology cousins, more or less near. The levirate appears in its various forms among one hundred and twenty peoples in my list, or about one in three in the world. On taking out its adhesions it seems sufficiently accounted for as a custom of substitution, belonging to the period when marriage is a compact not so much between two individuals as between two families, often made when the couple are infants unable to understand it, in fact sometimes before their birth. That the levirate forms part of this family transaction is consistent with other customs more or less associated with it, viz., that when a wife dies or turns out ill her family are bound to replace her by another, a rule which sometimes even holds for betrothal, and that the widow is not allowed to marry out of her husband's family unless by leave of his kinsmen, who have the choice of keeping her, or parting with her, usually for a price. The social distribution of the levirate is shown in fig. 3 to extend through all three social stages. It is in the maternal-paternal stage that it comes into competition with the second principle, unknown in the maternal stage, in which the father's widows pass by inheritance to his sons, especially the eldest son taking his stepmothers. A small but important group of cases forms a bridge between the two principles of levirate and filial succession, combining both in the same nation. This combination is well shown in Africa, where on a chief's death the head wife will pass by levirate to his brother, while her son, the new chief, will inherit a crowd of stepmothers, a less onerous legacy indeed than may seem, as they are practically slaves who hoe and grind corn for their own living. Looking at the distribution of these groups of customs, it is seen to be only compatible with the view that the paternal rule followed the maternal, bringing with it even while its prevalence was but partial, the principle of paternal widow-inheritance.

The quaint custom of the couvade has now to be considered

Fig. 3.

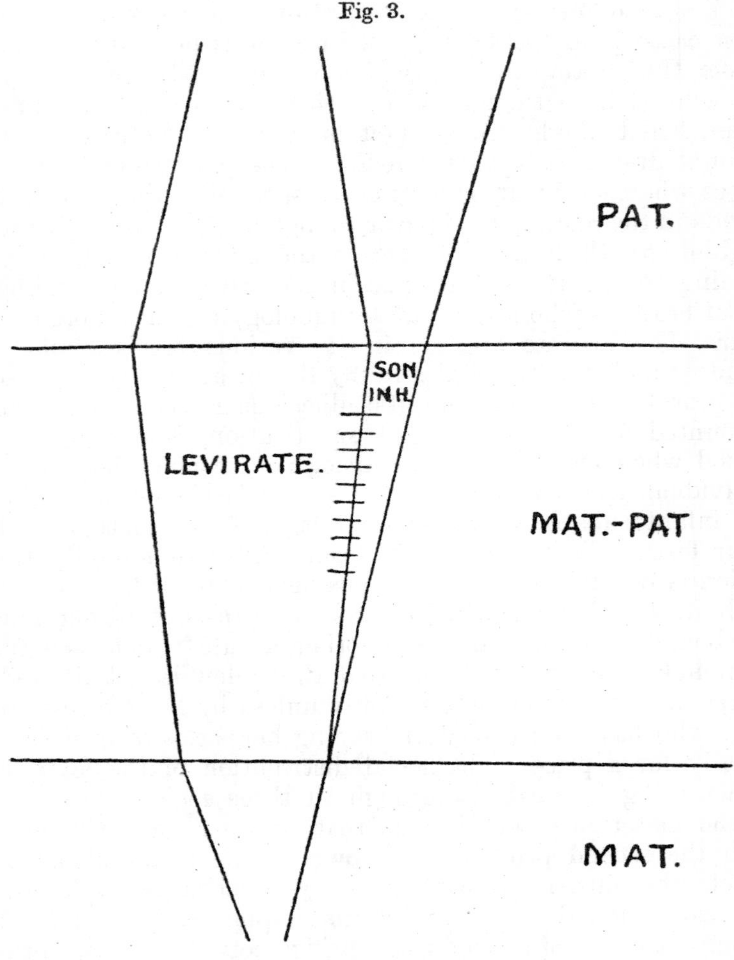

from the same point of view. In this the father, on the birth of his child, makes a ceremonial pretence of being the mother, being nursed and taken care of, and performing other rites such as fasting and abstaining from certain kinds of food or occupation, lest the new-born should suffer thereby. This custom is known in the four quarters of the globe. How sincerely it is still accepted appears in a story of Mr. Im Thurn, who on a forest journey in British Guiana noticed that one of his Indians refused to help to haul the canoes, and on enquiry found that the man's objection was that a child must have been born to him at home about this time, and he must not exert himself so as to hurt the infant. In the Mediterranean district it is not only mentioned by ancient writers, but in Spain and France, in or near the Basque country, it went on into modern times; Zamacola, in 1818, mentions, as but a little time ago, that the mother used to get up and the father take the child to bed. Knowing the tenacity of these customs, I should not be surprised

Fig. 4.

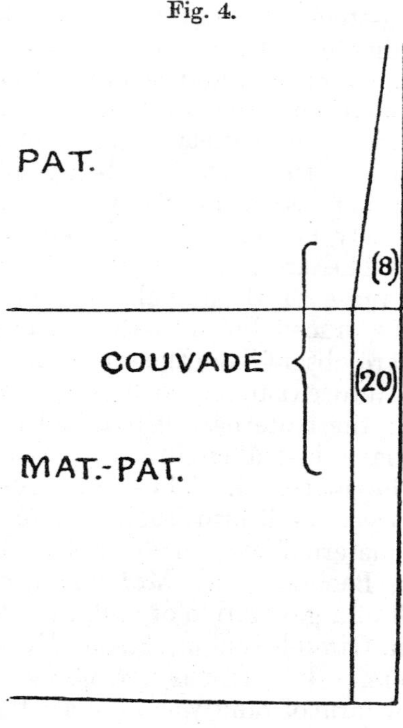

if traces of couvade might be found in that district still. Now examining the distribution of the couvade by the diagram, Fig. 4, we see that this farcical proceeding does not appear in the maternal stage, but arising in the maternal-paternal, at once takes its strongest development of twenty cases; in the paternal the number falls to eight cases, leading to the inference that here it is only kept up in dwindling survival.

Looking at this position, I must now argue that the original interpretation of the couvade given by Bachofen in his great treatise[1] in 1861, and supported by Giraud-Teulon, fits substantially with the facts, and is justified by them. He takes it to belong to the turning-point of society when the tie of parentage, till then recognised in maternity, was extended to take in paternity, this being done by the fiction of representing the father as a second mother. He compares the couvade with the symbolic pretences of birth which in the classical world were performed as rites of adoption. To his significant examples may be added the fact that among certain tribes the couvade is the legal form by which the father recognizes a child as his. Thus this apparently absurd custom, which for twenty centuries has been the laughing-stock of mankind, proves to be not merely incidentally an indicator of the tendency of society from maternal to paternal, but the very sign and record of that vast change.

The distribution of customs in figs. 3 and 4 is only compatible with a tendency of society to pass from the maternal to the paternal systems, the maternal being placed as earliest from the absence of survivals from other stages extending into it, as they freely do into the paternal, which is therefore placed as latest. The argument is a geological one. Just as the forms of life, and even the actual fossils of the Carboniferous formation, may be traced on into the Permian, but Permian types and fossils are absent from the Carboniferous strata formed before they came into existence, so here widow-inheritance and couvade, which, if the maternal system had been later than the paternal, would have lasted on into it, prove by their absence the priority of the maternal. Thus the present method confirms on an enlarged and firm basis the inference as to the antiquity of the maternal system arrived at by the pioneers of the investigation, Bachofen and McLennan, and supported by the later research of a generation of able investigators—Morgan, Lubbock, Bastian, Giraud-Teulon, Fison, Howitt, Wilken, Post, Lippert, and others. By this it is not, however, meant to imply that the maternal form of family as here set forth represents the primitive condition of mankind, but that it is a stage through

[1] J. J. Bachofen, "Das Mutterrecht," pp. 17, 255; Giraud-Teulon, "Les Origines du Marriage," p. 138. In my account of the couvade, "Early History of Mankind," Chap. x, I have laid stress on the magical-sympathetic nature of a large class of couvade rites as implying a physical bond between parent and child; thus an Abipone would not take snuff lest his sneezing might hurt his newborn baby, and a Carib father must abstain from eating sea-cow lest his infant should get little round eyes like it. This motive, which is explicity or implicitly recognised by the savages themselves, certainly forms part of the explanation of the couvade. It is, however, secondary, being due to the connexion considered as subsisting between parent and child, so that these sympathetic prohibitions may be interpreted as originally practised by the mother only, and afterwards adopted by the father also.

which the inhabitants of a great part of the world now in the paternal appear to have passed, and which still continues in force over considerable tracts of every part of the globe except Europe. It seems probable that this maternal system arose out of an earlier and less organised and regulated condition of human life. As to this problem, however, though the present schedules are not devoid of information, I have not been able

Fig. 5.

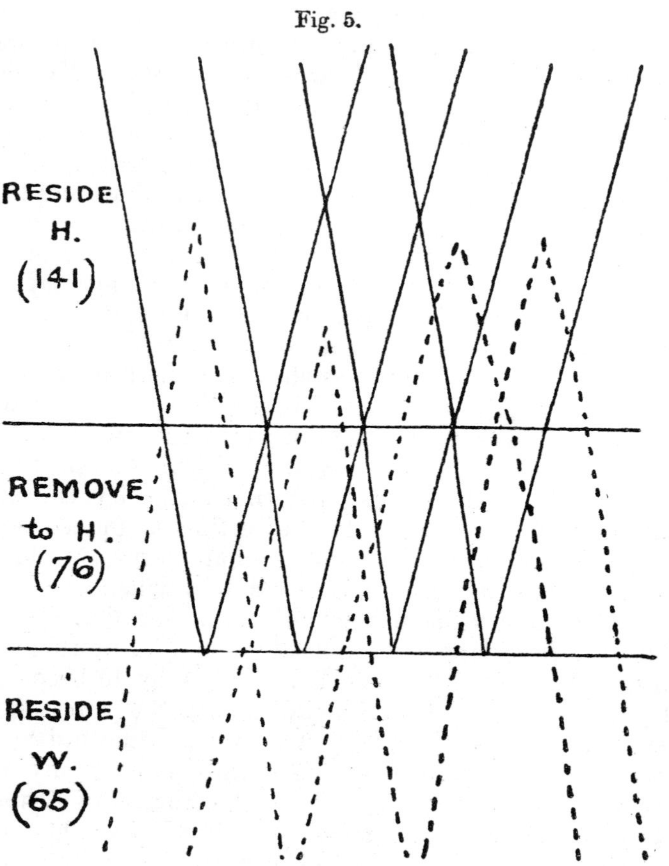

to bring the general evidence into shape sufficiently to justify my offering a theory here.

The analogy has already come into view between the division of society according to residence, and according to the maternal and paternal systems. This relation, the reality of which is evident from mere consideration of the difference as to family life which must ensue from the husband living in the wife's house or the wife living in the husband's, may be corroborated from the schedules. Thus the number of coincidences between peoples where the husband lives with the wife's family and where the maternal system prevails, is naturally large in proportion, while the full maternal system as naturally never appears among peoples whose exclusive custom is for the husband to take his wife to his own home. But as I have pointed out, the maternal and paternal systems are not each a definite institution, but combinations in which more or less strictly the authority, descent, succession, inheritance follow the female or the male side. The imperfection of my schedules makes it desirable for me to postpone an attempt to work out numerically the intricate problem of the mutual relations of these social rules till more perfect data are accessible. I have made, however, a rough sketch illustrative of the hypothesis suggested by the diagrams figs. 3 and 4, namely that in the one simple fact of residence we may seek the main determining cause of the several usages which combine to form a maternal or paternal system. This sketch, fig. 5, is meant to suggest the social movement which the schedules seem to imply. Division according to residence on the female or male side is taken as the fundamental fact, and the lines show the institutions of female descent, avuncular authority, &c., arising in the stage of residence on the female side, and extending into the stages of removal and residence on the male side. Within these two latter stages it is that male descent, paternal authority, &c., arise and extend onward in history. This direction is indeed consistent with what our own knowledge of human nature would lead us to expect. We can well understand how when the man lives in his wife's family his power will count for little against the combined authority of her maternal uncles and brothers, whereas when he takes her to his own home, he is apt to become master of the household; and we should expect the rules of descent, succession, and inheritance to follow the same order. Actual record of such transition is very rare, but at any rate one observer, the Hon. J. W. Powell, of the Bureau of Ethnology at Washington, has had both the opportunity to see and the skill to see what he was seeing, with the result of convincing himself that the transition from maternal to paternal society has in great measure depended on residence. I quote a passage of a letter from him:—"It would seem from such opportunities as I have had to collect facts in the field that hunting and other parties are frequently organised in such a manner that the male members of a clan group proceed together in company with their wives and children. Under such circumstances the control of the family necessarily falls into the hands of the husbands and fathers." This happens among the Pueblo Indians, a matriarchal people with female descent, whose clans, in consequence of the scarcity of water for irrigation in their desert region, are obliged to separate widely for the cultivation of lands at a distance from the central Pueblo. The result is that the control of families and the training of children are temporarily taken out of the hands of their own kin on the mother's side, and with the acquisition of cattle in these new homes comes the tendency to settle there permanently. Observation of these facts led Major Powell to adopt the hypothesis that clanship by female descent passed in this way into clanship by male descent by the segregation of clans for industrial purposes.

The next diagram, fig. 6, throws more light on the great social transformation. It shows the distribution of the practice

Fig. 6.

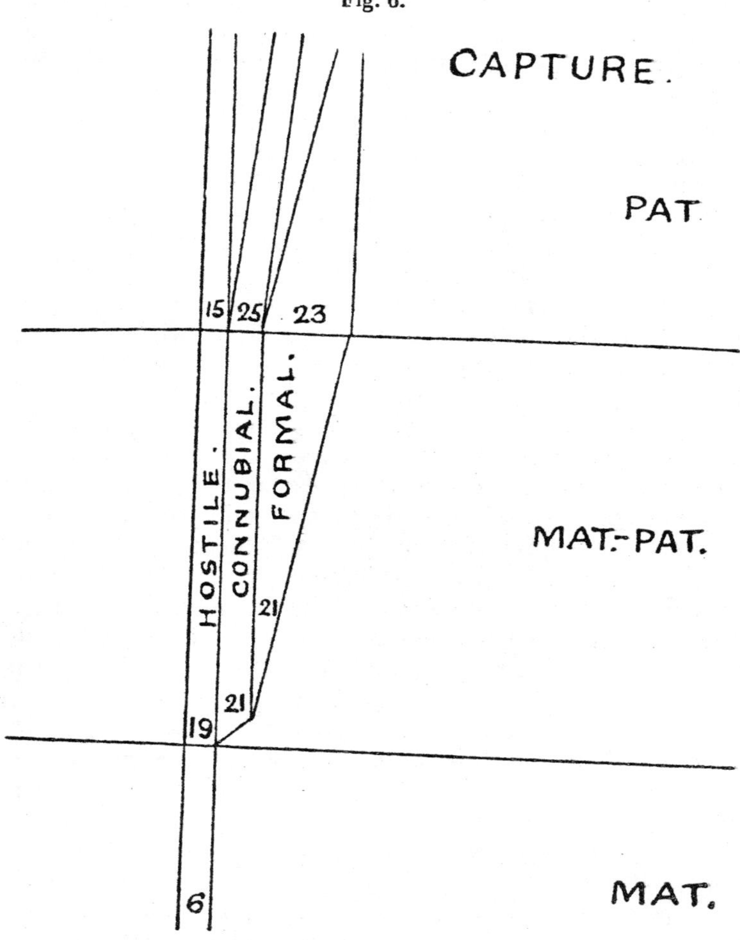

of marriage by capture. When the accounts of national custom are classified they show that capture (which belongs to over one hundred of the peoples scheduled) can be more or less accurately divided into three kinds:—Hostile capture, when warriors of one tribe bring away as captives women of another tribe is a feat of arms praised in history short of the highest levels of culture. There were fierce Indians of the Pampas who held that their god, the Great Eagle, told them to live by making war on all other tribes, slaying their men and carrying off their women and children. The same spirit is heard in the hopes of Sisera's host to divide the spoil, to every man a damsel or two. Looking at hostile capture from the anthropological point of view, we have to notice that it exists equally through the three stages of society, from maternal to paternal. Now it obviously conflicts with full matriarchal institutions that a man should bring in a captive wife, for he cannot take her home to his mother-in-law. To understand such a custom appearing within the range of matriarchy at all, we must remember that a captive has no rights, so that what happens to her does not immediately affect the regular custom of the tribe, which applies to native free women. Yet even here the tendency of capture must always have been to upset the maternal arrangements. When capture comes to be an accepted mode of marriage between or among tribes or clans who live at peace and habitually intermarry, it is evident that such "connubial capture," as it is described on the diagram, can only consist with the paternal system, inasmuch as the husband necessarily carries the wife to his own home, thereby setting on foot a paternal household. This is true also of the cases where the capture has become a merely formal ceremony, accompanying a marriage settled beforehand, for the very form of capture involves the bridegroom coming with his friends to carry the bride to his home. This is the interpretation of the fact, made evident in the diagram, that connubial and formal capture belong only to the intermediate stage where paternal institutions are arising, and to the later stage where they are fully established. The effect of capture in breaking up the maternal system, and substituting the paternal for it, has thus to be taken into account as a serious factor in social development. There is at least one region of the world where the operation may be seen going on at this day—the Malay Islands. To quote the concise description by Riedel of the matrimonial arrangements of the Babar Archipelago:—"The men follow the women, and live in their houses. The children also belong to the wife's family. If a man is rich enough he may marry seven wives, who all remain in the houses of their parents. A man who has many wives is respected. The robbery of a wife from another clan (*negari*) is an honour, and the children follow the father, with or without payment of the fine attached to the deed. Smaller or weaker clans even demand no fine."[1] In the Kisar and Wetar island groups a like state of things appears, the maternal system being the recognised rule, but always liable to pass into the paternal system by capture, which brings wife and children into the husband's hands.

At this point it will be convenient to examine two institutions of early marriage law, namely, exogamy and classificatory relationship. The principle of exogamy was brought prominently into view fifty years ago, by Sir George Grey,[2] when he described the native Australian rule for a man not to marry a woman of the same family name or bearing the same animal-crest or kobong as himself; and called attention to the coincidence of this with the North American system of clans named from totem animals, a man being bound to marry outside his own totem or clan. Mr. J. F. McLennan[3] gave these customs the name of exogamy or "marrying-out," and showed them to belong to "a most widely prevailing principle of marriage law among primitive races." Much information has since then come in, with the result of showing that exogamy has hardly to do with the capture of wives in war between alien nations, but rather with the regulation of marriages within groups of clans or tribes who have connubium; such clans or tribes may be more or less at strife, but they acknowledge ties of kindred and are usually allied by language. It is now also understood that a people may at once practice endogamy or 'marrying-in" within its borders, and exogamy or "marrying-out" of its clans with one another. The situation may be understood among the Hindus, where a man must marry in his caste, but within that caste must not marry in his own gotra or clan. The effect of an exogamic rule is similar whether clanship follows the female or male line of descent. Next, as to the principle of classificatory relationship, an early mention of this is by Father Lafitau,[4] above one hundred and fifty years ago, who states that "among the Iroquois and Hurons all the children of a cabin regard all their mother's sisters as their mothers, and all their mother's brothers as their uncles, and for the same reason they give the name of fathers to all their

[1] Riedel, "De Sluik- en Kroesharige Rassen tusschen Selebes en Papua," p. 351; see 415, 448.

[2] Grey, "Journals of Two Expeditions in N.W. and W. Australia," Vol. II, p. 225.

[3] J. F. McLennan, "Primitive Marriage," pp. 48, 130.

[4] Lafitau, "Mœurs des Sauvages Ameriquains," Paris, 1724, Vol. I, p. 552.

father's brothers, and aunts to all their father's sisters. All the children on the side of the mother and her sisters, and of the father and his brothers, regard each other mutually as brothers and sisters, but as regards the children of their uncles and aunts, that is, of their mother's brothers and father's sisters, they only treat them on the footing of cousins. . . . . In the third generation this changes, the great uncles and great aunts become again grandfathers and grandmothers of the children of those whom they called nephews and nieces. This continues always in the descending line according to the same rule." In our own time, Lewis H. Morgan, living among the Iroquois as an adopted Indian, was struck with this system of relationships, so unlike what he had been brought up among, and which he at first thought to be a peculiar invention of his Iroquois. But finding, on enquiry, that it extended to other North American tribes, he eventually by circulating interrogatories succeeded in collecting a great series of systems of relationship, in which he established the wide prevalence of classificatory systems, as he called them from the relatives being grouped in classes.[1] Under the term classificatory systems, Mr. Morgan included not only those approximating to the Iroquois type, but a much simpler and ruder plan prevalent in Polynesia; it is, however, convenient for me to confine my remarks here to the former group only. This system, as found among the American Indians, Mr. Morgan showed to be closely analogous to that of the Dravidian nations of Southern Hindustan. This latter is a well-known source of perplexity to a newly appointed English civilian, who may be told by a witness that his father was sitting in the house, but presently the same witness mentions his father as coming in from the field; the native is sharply reproved by the judge for contradicting himself, whereupon he explains, it was my "little father," by which he means his father's younger brother.

I am placing together the two institutions, exogamy and classificatory relationship, inasmuch as they are really connected, being in fact two sides of one institution. This was made out eight years ago, by the Rev. Lorimer Fison, in the work on the Kamilaroi and Kurnai tribes of Australia by him and Mr. Howitt.[2] This important explanation is still scarcely known to anthropologists, nor indeed, have I much right to reproach others with neglecting it, for I reviewed Fison and Howitt's book without distinctly realising the bearing of this argument on the theory of exogamy, which only came round to

[1] L. H. Morgan, "Systems of Consanguinity and Affinity of the Human Family" (Smithsonian Contributions, 1871).

[2] Fison and Howitt, "Kamilaroi and Kurnai," 1880, p. 76.

me lately in a way which I had better now describe, as it will enable me to explain shortly and plainly the whole problem. In tabulating the nations of the world, I found a group of twenty-one peoples whose custom as to the marriage of first cousins seemed remarkable; it is that the children of two brothers may not marry, nor the children of two sisters, but the child of the brother may marry the child of the sister. It seemed obvious that this "cross-cousin marriage," as it may be called, must be the direct result of the simplest form of exogamy, where a population is divided into two classes or sections, with the law that a man who belongs to Class A can only take a wife of Class B. Such a division, for instance, is familar in Melanesia. Dr. R. H. Codrington describes it in the Banks Islands, where the natives have two families, called *veve* = mother, which implies that descent follows the mother's side, and a man must marry a wife of the other mother from himself, or as they say, not on his own side of the house but on the other. Thus, taking A, *a*, B, *b*, as males and females of the class A and B, and bearing in mind that the mother's children are of her class, but the father's children of the opposite class to his, we have:—

Fig. 7.

Two sisters, *a*, *a*, their ⋮ ⋮ Children, A, *a*, are of same class = tribal brother and sister = unmarriageable.	Two brothers, A, A, their ⋮ ⋮ Children B, *b*, are of same class = tribal brother and sister = unmarriageable.	Brother and sister, A, *a*, their ⋮ ⋮ Children B, *a*, are of different class = tribal cousins = marriageable.

Having come to this point, it seemed to me that I had seen something like it elsewhere, and on looking back to "Kamilaroi and Kurnai" I found that Fison had thus worked out the origin of the Turanian classificatory system, as Morgan calls that including the above-mentioned systems of North America and India, with others. Fig. 8 puts concisely the main features of the argument as to a man's kin.

Fig. 8.

His

father's brother's child
or
mother's sister's child
} is (tribal) brother or sister,

Therefore

father's brother is (tribal) father,
mother's sister is (tribal) mother,

His

father's sister's child or mother's brother's child } is tribal (cousin).

Therefore

father's sister is (tribal) aunt,
mother's brother is (tribal) uncle.

Though not proposing to enter fully into the deduction of classificatory relationships in all their varieties from the rule of exogamy, it is necessary to point out that the form of exogamy here contemplated is the simplest or dual form, in which a people is divided into two intermarrying classes. Systems of exogamy which are dual in their nature, that is, consisting of two classes or groups of classes, stand in direct connection with cross-cousin marriage and classificatory relationship. But if the number of exogamic divisions is not dual, if there are for instance three clans, and a man of one clan may take a wife of either of the other two clans, it is readily seen that the argument of fig. 7 breaks down. Although at present only prepared to deal with exogamy and classificatory relationship in their dual form, I may notice that the treatment of the problem by the method of adhesions strengthens the view, not wanting in other evidence, that the dual form of exogamy may be considered the original form. In reckoning from the present schedules the number of peoples who use relationship names more or less corresponding to the classificatory systems here considered, they are found to be fifty-three, and the estimated number of these which might coincide accidentally with exogamy were there no close connexion between them, would be about twelve. But in fact the number of peoples who have both exogamy and classification is thirty-three, this strong coincidence being the measure of the close causal connexion subsisting between the two institutions. The adherence is even stronger as to cross-cousin marriage, of which twenty-one cases appear in the schedules, no less than fifteen of the peoples practising it being also known as exogamous. Here, indeed, the relation is not one of derivation, but of identity, the cross-cousin rule being actually a partial form or imperfect statement of the law of exogamy itself. Such adhesions between two or more customs have been already recognised as proving the existence of causal connexion, but it has now to be pointed out that they serve another purpose. The connexion, when proved, reacts on the evidence by which it was proved. When once it has been shown that cross-cousin marriage is part and parcel of exogamy, it may be argued that all the twenty-one peoples practising cross-cousin marriage are to be set down as exogamous. Now as only fifteen of them are expressly recorded to be so, the list of exogamous nations of the world has to be increased by six. So, classificatory relationship being evidence that the peoples practising it are or have been exogamous, this will add some twenty more to the list of nations among whom further investigation will probably disclose record that exogamic society once prevailed or still prevails. Even if no direct record is forthcoming, the indirect proof may with due caution be sufficient for placing them in the exogamous group, which may thus number above one hundred peoples out of the three hundred and fifty of the world. Those who remember the sharp discussion between McLennan and Morgan years ago, and the view that the classificatory relationships were a mere system of addresses, will be struck with the way in which the controversy is likely to end. For myself I hardly know whether I feel more glad or sorry that my old friend McLennan to the day of his death never knew that Morgan and he, who believed themselves adversaries, were all the while allies pushing forward the same doctrine from different sides.

It thus appears that the number of nations who have the system of intermarrying clans is larger than has been known. But even this by no means measures the full importance of exogamy as a factor in the constitution of society. Anthropologists have long had before them the problem of determining how far clan-exogamy may have been the origin of the prohibited degrees in matrimony so variously defined in the laws of nations. The yet larger problem has been opened, how far laws of permission and prohibition of marriage may have led nations to define relationships and give them names, distinguishing for instance uncles from fathers, and cousins from brothers. It may, I think, conduce to the solution of these problems to notice two ways in which the collation of the present tables bears on the meaning and origin of exogamy.

There are conditions of society under which exogamy is found side by side with wife-capture, so that a barbaric marriage often involves both in one and the same act, as when a Tatar and a party of his friends, all armed to the teeth, ride off to the tents of a distant clan, and thence with simulated or even real violence carry off a bride. But on reckoning up the peoples among whom this combination of capture and exogamy is found, the number, though enough to show that they co-exist freely, falls short of what would justify the inference that they are cause and effect.

Moreover, it appears that this co-existence belongs especially to the paternal stage of society, and to the maternal-paternal, in which paternal influence is partly established. This is intelligible enough from what has been already said as to the effect of capture in setting on foot paternal institutions, from its very outset, by bringing the wife into the husband's hands and home. We are thus led to a more fundamental test of the position of exogamy, by enquiring whether it existed in that earliest known stage of the maternal system of society, where the husband lives in the wife's family. The schedules show that there are in different parts of the world twelve or thirteen well-marked exogamous peoples whose habit of residence is for the husband to join the wife's family.[1] This state of things seems to me to prevent our regarding exogamy as a result of capture, it being plain that the warrior who has carried a wife captive from a hostile tribe does not take up his abode in her family. If capture leads to any form of exogamy, this must, I think, be a paternal form, and if it be admitted that the maternal form is earlier, then it follows that capture is inadmissible as the primary cause of exogamy.

More than twenty years ago, in compiling a list of nations practising this custom of marrying out of the tribe or kin, I noticed that in any full discussion of the subject would have to be considered the wish to bind different tribes together in friendship by intermarriage.[2] Compiling the present tables has brought together observations to this effect. Morgan, describing how the alliance of the Iroquois tribes, made up of intermarrying clans, formed a bond of union throughout the national league, writes: "It was the boast of the Iroquois that the great object of their confederacy was peace; to break up the spirit of perpetual warfare, which had wasted the red race from age to age."[3] Another group of North American tribes, the Tinneh, on the Arctic circle, are divided into three castes, their rule being that, for instance, a Chit-sangh may not marry a Chit-sangh. When this does take place, the persons are ridiculed and laughed at, the man is said to have married his sister, even though she may be from another tribe, and there be not the slightest connection by blood between them. Hardisty, who gives these details, remarks:—"One good thing proceeded from the above arrangement, it prevented war between two tribes who were naturally hostile."[4] The Bogos of Abyssinia are exogamous, and of

[1] Kasia, Garo, Menangkabau and Padang, Banks Islands, Mortlock Islands, Chiroki, Delaware, Iroquois, Mandan and Minitari, Moqui, Tlinkit, Arawak.

[2] "Early History of Mankind," p. 286.

[3] Morgan, "League of the Iroquois," p. 91.

[4] "Smithsonian Report," 1866, p. 315.

them Munzinger reports that they are closely bound together by reciprocal marriages, "so that internal war is almost impossible. Blood-quarrels among the Bogos are always settled very quickly, whilst the smallest collision with the adjoining tribes leads to everlasting wars."[1] Du Chaillu writes of Ashango-land, "tribes and clans intermarry with each other and this brings about a friendly feeling among the people. People of the same clan cannot intermarry with each other."[2] Thus, it seems that when Plutarch asks in the "Roman Questions," "Why do they not marry women near of kin?" he has some reason in setting down as one possible answer, "Whether from their wishing to increase friendships by marriages, and to acquire many kinsfolk, giving wives to others and receiving (wives) from them."[3]

On looking at the distinction between endogamy and exogamy from this point of view, it will be seen that there is a period in the growth of society when it is a political question of the first importance. While the vast forest or prairie still affords abundant food for a scanty population, small hordes may wander, or groups of households may be set up, each little tribe or settlement cut off from the rest, and marrying within its own border. But when tribes begin to adjoin and press on one another and quarrel, then the difference between marrying-in and marrying-out becomes patent. Endogamy is a policy of isolation, cutting off a horde or village, even from the parent-stock whence it separated, if only a generation or two back. Among tribes of low culture there is but one means known of keeping up permanent alliance, and that means is intermarriage. Exogamy, enabling a growing tribe to keep itself compact by constant unions between its spreading clans, enables it to overmatch any number of small intermarrying groups, isolated and helpless. Again and again in the world's history, savage tribes must have had plainly before their minds the simple practical alternative between marrying-out and being killed out. Even far on in culture, the political value of intermarriage remains. "Matrimonial alliances increase friendship more than aught else," is a maxim of Mohammed. "Then will we give our daughters unto you, and we will take your daughters to us, and we will dwell with you, and we will become one people," is a well known passage of Israelite history.

Exogamy lies far back in the history of man, and perhaps no observer has ever seen it come into existence, nor have the precise conditions of its origin yet been clearly inferred. Even the

[1] Munzinger, "Sitten und Recht der Bogos," p. 10.
[2] Du Chaillu, "Journey to Ashango-land," p. 427.
[3] "Plutarch, Quæst. Rom.," cviii.

historical relation between exogamy and the system of classes known as totemism is not fully cleared up; whether as Prof. Robertson Smith takes it,[1] totemism supplied the necessary machinery for working a law of exogamy, or whether exogamy itself led to totemism. But as to the law of exogamy itself, the evidence shows it in operation over a great part of the human race as a factor of political prosperity. It cannot be claimed as absolutely preventing strife and bloodshed, indeed, it has been remarked of some peoples, such as the Khonds and the Banks Islanders, that the intermarrying clans do nevertheless quarrel and fight. Still by binding together a whole community with ties of kinship and affinity, and especially by the peacemaking of the women who hold to one clan as sisters and to another as wives, it tends to keep down feuds and to heal them when they arise, so as at critical moments to hold together a tribe which under endogamous conditions would have split up. Exogamy thus shows itself as an institution which resists the tendency of uncultured populations to disintegrate, cementing them into nations capable of living together in peace and holding together in war, till they reach the period of higher military and political organisation. Seen from this point of view, the remarkable fact is more easily understood that exogamy, passing on from the maternal to the paternal stage of society, shifts its prohibitions from the female to the male line of descent, now allowing marriages which it treated formerly as incestuous, while prohibiting others which it formerly allowed without scruple. This transformation has been taking place within recent times among Malay and American tribes, and seems to be even going on still, it making no difference politically whether kinship follows the female or male line, if only marrying-out causes the requisite intermixture of the clans. In this connexion it is worth while to notice that there are a small number of peoples in different parts of the world, who have a rule of exogamy not depending on kinship at all. For instance, Piedrahita[2] relates of the Panches of Bogota, that those of one town did not marry any woman thereof, as all held themselves brothers, and the impediment of kinship was sacred to them, but such was their ignorance that if a sister were born in a different town from her brother, he was not prevented from marrying her. An anthropologist, with the list before him of the peoples who prohibit a man from marrying in his own village, might explain this not as a result of ignorance, but as an extreme case of what may be called "local exogamy."

[1] W. Robertson Smith, "Kinship and Marriage in Early Arabia," p. 184.

[2] Piedrahita, "Historia General de las Conquistas del Nuevo Reyno de Granada," 1688, page 11.

The results here brought forward make no approach to exhausting the possible inferences to be drawn from the tables. These need not even be confined to working out the development of customs found in existence somewhere on the globe, but may in some measure restore the knowledge of forms of society now extinct. Interesting, however, as these problems are, I am more anxious to bring under discussion the method by which they are here treated, how imperfectly I am well aware. The interpretations offered will have to be corrected, the tabulated material improved in quantity and quality, and the principles it involves brought out more justly, yet at any rate it will remain clear that the rules of human conduct are amenable to classification in compact masses, so as to show by strict numerical treatment their relations to one another. It is only at this point that speculative explanation must begin, at once guided in its course and strictly limited in its range by well-marked lines of fact to which it must conform. The key of the position is, as that veteran anthropologist, Prof. Bastian, of the Berlin Museum, is never weary of repeating, that in statistical investigation the future of anthropology lies. As soon as this is systematically applied, principles of social development become visible. Even the diagrams of this paper may suffice to show that the institutions of man are as distinctly stratified as the earth on which he lives. They succeed each other in series substantially uniform over the globe, independent of what seem the comparatively superficial differences of race and language, but shaped by similar human nature acting through successively changed conditions in savage, barbaric, and civilised life.

The treatment of social phenomena by numerical classification will, it must be added, react on the statistical material to which the method is applied. It is in classifying the records of tribes and nations that one becomes fully aware of their imperfect and even fragmentary state. The descriptions happily tend to correct one another's errors, but the great difficulty is blank want of information. As for extinct tribes, and those whose native culture has been re-modelled, there is nothing to be done. But there are still a hundred or more peoples in the world, among whom a prompt and minute investigation would save some fast vanishing memory of their social laws and customs. The quest might be followed up internationally, each civilised nation taking in hand the barbaric tribes within its purview. The future will, doubtless, be able to take care of itself as to most branches of knowledge, but there is certain work which if it is to be done at all, must be done by the present.

Discussion.

The President felt sure that no one would have appreciated Dr. Tylor's memoir more justly, or would have welcomed it more warmly, than Mr. Herbert Spencer, whose efforts to erect a science of sociology upon an inductive basis were well known. Mr. Spencer, as we all remember, went to great cost, and much exerted himself to obtain a collection of the customs of all available nations, savage and civilised, arranged in an uniform and orderly manner for purposes of intercomparison. The result was the publication of an amount of material that filled four very large folio volumes. Unfortunately he had been obliged to delegate to others the task of compilation, and the work was not carried out as accurately as was desirable, or even as completely, notwithstanding its bulk. Much the same may be said of another and a different collection. Dr. Tylor has, on the contrary, collected a mass of well sorted and highly considered information, by means of a sustained and scholarly investigation, extending over many years, and there could be little doubt that a publication of his compact notes, supplemented it might be by the notes of other anthropologists, would be of itself a most valuable and acceptable work. Dr. Tylor's memoir dealt both with a method and with conclusions; it was of the method only that he (Mr. Galton) would now speak. It consisted in ascertaining the degree in which the concurrence of certain customs was exceptionally frequent. He thought that the degree of interdependence, to which the various degrees of exceptional frequency testified, might with advantage be expressed in terms of a scale, in which 0 represented perfect independence, and 1 complete concurrence. By doing so, the values of the various concurrences would become more clear. As an example of what he meant, he would refer to a scale used in certain psycho-physical inquiries and discussed in Fechner's book, where the true significance of the various percentages of success and failure was tabulated.

It was extremely desirable for the sake of those who may wish to study the evidence for Dr. Tylor's conclusions, that full information should be given as to the degree in which the customs of the tribes and races which are compared together are independent. It might be, that some of the tribes had derived them from a common source, so that they were duplicate copies of the same original. Certainly, in such an investigation as this, each of the observations ought, in the language of statisticians, to be carefully "weighted." It would give a useful idea of the distribution of the several customs and of their relative prevalence in the world, if a map were so marked by shadings and colour as to present a picture of their geographical ranges.

Professor Flower remarked upon the great value of Dr. Tylor's paper, congratulating him on the application of a rigid statistical method to a research which had generally been conducted on vague and uncertain lines. It was, however, perfectly obvious that the value of such a method depended entirely upon the units of comparison being of equivalent value, and this seemed to him to be a very great difficulty when dealing with groups of mankind. He had, however, no doubt that Dr. Tylor had taken every means in his power to eliminate the errors which might arise from this source.

Mr. G. Bertin, after remarking that this paper would do a great deal to elevate anthropology, said he thought that, if Dr. Tylor had included in his diagrams one illustrating the primitive state of society in which women were the common wives of the clan or tribe, it would explain everything. This state of things still exists in some parts of Tibet, and traces of it are detected in Ancient Egypt and among the primitive Semites. Women were at first considered like other properties, and in the communist stage they used to belong to each and all; when property was divided women were assimilated to landed properties or estates, and the children took the name of their mother, as in feudal countries they took that of their estate. This is really the origin of the so-called matriarchate, in which the mother had, in fact, no power, but gave her name to her child. It is only with progress and civilisation that the position of women was raised till it tends in our modern times to place them on equal footing with men.

Sir G. Campbell agreed with a preceding speaker that the maternal system does not mean the rule of the female, but only that she is used as the family seed-bed. And he would very much like to obtain information on one point in the history of marriage, viz., who invented or how came about the very peculiar system of monogamy, so prevalent among all Aryan races, and under which a man is not only confined to one wife, but tied to her by indissoluble bonds. The maternal system we understand, under which the women of a family are the brood mares of their own family; the patriarchal system we understand, under which a man rules over his wives, slave girls, and children, and exchanges the former for others when he thinks fit. But the sacramental monogamous marriage, by which a man is tied to one wife for ever, (among the Hindoos the wife is tied to him even beyond the grave), that is very peculiar, and he had never seen it accounted for.

Mr. Bouverie-Pusey remarked that Dr. Tylor's views on the origin of exogamy derived confirmation from an old Hungarian law, according to which the Ishmaelites (Tartars converted from Islam) were commanded to give all their daughters in marriage to Hungarians, and to take none but Hungarian wives for their sons, obviously to prevent their continuing to form a separate nationality.

Dr. Tylor congratulated himself on having been able to place the present method before investigators whose criticism was of such importance, from their thorough appreciation of the points in which such a method has inherent weakness. With the details as yet in an imperfect state, he found it difficult to bring out the results except as a temporary step, which is, however, on the road to permanent settlement. The difficulty raised by Mr. Galton that some of the concurrences might result from transmission from a common source, so that a single character might be counted several times from its mere duplicates, is a difficulty ever present in such investigations, as for instance in the Malay region, where groups of islands have enough differentiation in their marriage systems to justify their being classed separately, though traces of common origin are at the same time conspicuous. The only way of meeting this objection is to make separate clsssification depend on well marked differences, and to do this all over the world. With regard to Professor Flower's caution as to the units of comparison, an answer of somewhat the same kind might be given. When a community or group of communities follows a law of marriage and descent substantially similar, this may be taken as a unit, notwithstanding historical connection and the consequent partial correspondence which may exist between it and other unit systems. If this method be fairly and equably worked over the world, the correspondences brought about by historical connexion tend to set off against one another, leaving the results of general human action more or less clear.

Dr. Tylor added that he had collected much material bearing on the great problem raised by Sir George Campbell, but at present without any result sufficiently definite to be brought forward.

THE MATERIAL CULTURE AND SOCIAL INSTITUTIONS OF THE SIMPLER PEOPLES: AN ESSAY IN CORRELATION. *

L. T. HOBHOUSE, G. C. WHEELER AND M. GINSBERG

INTRODUCTION—THE PROBLEM.

THEORIES of social evolution are readily formed with the aid of some preconceived ideas and a few judiciously selected corroborative facts. The data offered to the theorist by the voluminous results of anthropological inquiry on the one hand, and by the immense record of the history of civilisation on the other, are so vast and so various that it must be an unskilled selector who is unable, by giving prominence to the instances which agree and by ignoring those which conflict with his views, to make out a plausible case in support of some general notion of human progress. On the other hand, if theories are easily made, they are also easily confuted by a less friendly use of the same data. That same variety of which we speak is so great that there is hardly any sociological generalisation which does not stumble upon some awkward fact if one takes the trouble to find it. Anyone with a sense for facts soon recognises that the course of social evolution is not unitary but that different races and different communities of the same race have, in fact, whether they started from the same point or no, diverged early, rapidly, and in many different directions at once. If theorising is easy when facts are treated arbitrarily, a theory which would really grow out of the facts themselves and express their true significance presents the greatest possible difficulties to the inquirer. The data themselves are vast but chaotic, and at every point incomplete. They fall into two main divisions. On the one hand, there is the historical record of the civilisations; upon the other there is the immense field of contemporary anthropology. In both alike the data are equally difficult to ascertain with precision, and when ascertained to reduce to any intelligible order. In the history of civilisation we have full studies of many institutions, and we can learn something, not only of what they were at any one moment, but of their development in time, their genesis, their rise, their maturity, their decay. But even here the information often breaks off short at the most interesting point. Beginnings are frequently matter of conjecture. The nature of institutions, as they appear on paper, may be known to us, while we are left to reconstruct their actual working from casual examples, hints, and references that leave much to the

*Introduction to *The Material Culture and Social Institutions of the Simpler Peoples* (Series of Studies in Economics and Political Science, No. 3 of the Monographs on Sociology), London School of Economics and Political Science, 1930. Reprinted by permission of Morris Ginsberg and the London School of Economics.

imagination. We find them decaying without intelligible cause, and often enough we are faced with the fact that more thoroughgoing inquiry has completely revolutionised our view of an institution which had been taken as thoroughly explored and fully interpreted by earlier schools of historians. So is it also with the anthropological record. Here indeed we have a handful of monographs made by trained and skilled observers in modern times, which leave nothing to be desired excepting that the work had been carried out three or four generations ago before contact with the white man or with other more civilised races had begun to corrupt the purity of aboriginal institutions. Outside these monographs we have a vast mass of travellers' reports, good, bad, and indifferent, data which it is impossible to ignore and yet which can seldom be taken at their face value. Moreover all anthropological data of this kind, however simple the life of the people with which they deal, are modern; with the exception of the few available references that we have to the peoples that surrounded the Greeks and Romans in Herodotus, Tacitus, and other writers of antiquity, the great bulk of anthropological inquiry dates from the last three or four centuries, and it is sometimes forgotten that the peoples of whom they treat must have lived as long, must in a sense have had as extensive a tradition behind them, and to that extent are as far removed from the true primitive as civilised man himself.

Therefore when we are inquiring into development and origins we have to be careful how we take the findings of inquirers among the people of our own day, however simple, as evidence of what must have been in the beginnings of human kind. What ethnographical research yields us is not a history but a number of pictures of given peoples each taken as it were by an instantaneous photograph at a given time. It is a piece of good fortune if in any case we get successive pictures of the same people so full and true that by comparing them we can arrive directly at the actual course of the development of its institutions in a given period. Before the period of civilised influence sets in we have at best only fragments of such history, and in the main our data are descriptive rather than historical. No comparison or classification of these data can tell us offhand how institutions grew, any more than the classification of existing rocks tells the geologist how strata were formed. Yet it is in the main from the actual composition and arrangement of existing strata, assisted by what he knows of permanent physical laws and of recorded or clearly proved physical changes, that the geologist infers the history of the earth's crust, and it is on analogous methods that any scientific theory of social evolution must rely. Such a theory must rest at the outset upon the discovery of some order in the ethnological data. To this end two preliminary steps seem to be necessary. The first consists in taking the main institutions, customs, practices, and beliefs that constitute the structure of social life at any given time, and distinguishing the varieties of form which each institution actually presents in the various peoples among whom we find it. Many institutions can thus be treated from more than one point of view. Taking marriage, for example, we can obviously distinguish monogamy, various forms of polygamy and of polyandry, intermixtures or combinations of these forms, and, some may add, in addition to all some form of group marriage. Again we can treat any of these forms of marriage from the point of view of its rigidity or otherwise. We can inquire how far it is binding, distinguish cases in which it is entered into or dissolved so easily and so entirely at the will of either party that it is doubtful whether the term marriage is strictly applicable; and from this onwards we can trace every sort of gradation in the rigidity of the institution up to indissoluble monogamous marriage. Or again we can exhibit methods by which a partner is obtained, whether it be by free courtship, by child-betrothal, by the exchange of women or of gifts, or by presents to the parents or relations, by sheer purchase, by capture, and so forth. And so carrying this method through the whole field of inquiry relating to marriage, we can set up a system of forms all of which shall be illustrated somewhere in the light of human society; and in general, we can so arrange them as to show transitions from any one form to another of such a kind that we can very easily conceive an institution beginning at one end and passing through these transitional forms until it reaches the most extreme point in the opposite direction. What may be called a social morphology of this kind, that is to say, the ascertaining and classification of the actual forms of any institution known to exist may be regarded as the first step towards the introduction of order into the field of comparative sociology.[1]

But beyond this lies a second and far more difficult step. We have spoken of the form of an institution passing by gradations from one stage to another, very remote from it perhaps. It is one thing to exhibit and even to illustrate possible gradations of such a kind, and another thing to show that actual institutions do pass along such a scale of development. In some cases no doubt we can historically trace a line of change, but it would be exceedingly difficult to maintain that the line of change had always been the

1. The chief danger in forming any social classification is that of over-rigidity in definition. Customs and institutions vary continuously, and the lines of demarcation which any classification must draw are apt to be artificial and unreal. Moreover what is on the surface the same institution may have a different content at different stages of social development. A certain elasticity of interpretation must therefore be allowed in order to adapt any scheme of classification to the facts without forming them into unreal categories.

same in all cases, and quite impossible, we think, at the present stage of our knowledge to lay down that any given institution must take its rise in one form and must pass through a series of graded changes in a uniform direction. If indeed we could make any assumption of this kind, the process of sociological inquiry would be enormously simplified. We should have as it were a scale of development, the direction of which would be definitely known. We should be able to assign to any form of institution credibly reported in any given society, its particular place in that scale. We should know that it had never been further on in the scale, nor yet that it had reached its particular place by any roundabout road. We should be able to infer that it had passed through the earlier phases and no other, and we could in fact treat all differences to be found in social institutions as due to a single comprehensive cause —the difference in the rate of development. In point of fact inquiry lends no countenance to any such simplicity of view. A single instance from the institution that has already been mentioned may suffice to explain this point. We commonly think of strict monogamy as the product of a high civilisation, though not necessarily the highest civilisation, and it is true that we find polygamy associated upon the whole with the lower civilisations and with the peoples whom we do not regard as civilised at all. But apart from the fact that, for fairly obvious reasons, the majority of men in all races live with one wife at a time, we find quite a number of instances in which a rigid monogamy is the established rule among some of quite the rudest races of mankind. By whatever road the Veddas, or the Semang, or the Karok, or the Dyaks have arrived at monogamy, we may be pretty sure that it was by a road quite different from that which established this system in mediæval Europe. Nor can we even infer from the fact that nations of European culture agree with the Veddas, the Semang, and the Karok, any far-reaching identity in ethical views as to the relations of the sexes, or in fact in any other social and moral customs or ideas which in many races stand closely associated with the monogamic rule. We have to recognise from the outset that two societies, as widely divergent as possible in almost every respect, may exhibit close agreement on some one or more points, and we have to learn accordingly that to infer from any single institution a general state of development is to fly in the face of the anthropological facts.

If then we cannot assume any single line of development, what use are we to make of our morphology? Let us consider where we stand. We suppose ourselves to have ascertained the forms which any given institution assumes. We have now recognised that in different societies an institution may arrive at the same form by completely different paths, and that agreement in respect of any one institution is no evidence for agreement in other respects. We cannot lay down any absolute order of development, nor can we maintain as a strict generalisation that any given form of any given institution is to be found only in some determinate stage of the development of society. Sociology in fact is not a science of rigid generalisations. Where rigid generalisation fails science resorts to statistical methods, and the question arises whether this is possible in sociology. On the practical difficulties of applying statistics to the study of social institutions, we shall speak in the next section. But if we suppose for a moment that these are not insuperable, let us see what might be gained. We might begin with any two institutional forms, A and B and find on inquiry that in 90 per cent. of the cases where we have A we also find B, and that in 80 per cent. of the cases where we have B we also find A. If that is so we can infer some connection, though probably an indirect one, between A and B, and perhaps research may show that the residual instances where we have B but not A are associated with the presence or absence of a third institution C. This would throw considerable light on the connection of these forms, and by multiplying such conditions we might obtain considerable insight into the inter-connexion of certain groups of institutions. This was in fact the method applied by Dr. Tylor to the study of certain marriage customs some twenty years ago, and it is to be regretted that little has been done in the interval to extend the method to other problems.

What we propose to ask is whether it is possible to apply this line of inquiry to elucidating the changes of institution which accompany the growth of civilisation, the most important feature of social evolution. The first difficulty that occurs here is the vagueness as to the term civilisation, which, as generally used, implies elements of material, religious, artistic, and intellectual culture. If all these elements are insisted on and civilisations are judged in accordance with the level attained, not in one respect but in all, we shall of course find, if we find anything, that the most civilised race is that which has developed furthest in all these directions. We shall, in fact, achieve a purely identical proposition. The real question is how far these different developments imply one another. To attack this problem with any hope of a fruitful issue it is necessary to find some one characteristic which would be generally regarded as essential to civilisation, as possessing real significance in the life of a people, and as advancing in some determinate direction, which can be recognised and measured with some facility, and of which tangible evidence can be obtained. It will then be possible to follow other lines of development and observe the correlation of various forms of institution with successive stages in this advance. It may always be objected that we have not chosen the most essential point as the basis of our inquiry, but of that the results of the inquiry themselves will afford some test. At any rate, on these lines, if the work can be carried through, we may expect to learn something of the correlation of different elements in social growth.

The development which seems best to serve this purpose is that of material culture, the control of man over nature as reflected in the arts of life. It may be objected that this implies too materialistic a view of human society, and is too superficial a criterion of general progress. It may be replied to the latter point, in the first place that we do not use it as a criterion of general progress, but propose to inquire how far progress or (if the word be disliked) change in any definite direction is in fact associated with advance in the control over the forces of nature. On the former point it may be remarked that material culture is a fair index of the general level of knowledge and, if we may use a more general term, of mentality. The desire for comfort in his material surroundings is, with few exceptions, common to man. How much energy he will put into the business of securing it, how much organising capacity he can apply, what ideas, what knowledge, and what imagination he can bring to bear on it, what fears or scruples deter him from using all his available powers are questions which have different answers for different people, and on the answer depends in general the level of his material culture. Hence this culture does, roughly, though no more than roughly, reflect the general level of intellectual attainment. Moreover, in this case it is fairly easy to agree on the meaning of what in other instances is a very disputable term—the meaning of progress. The control of man over nature is a definite conception, and it is generally easy to recognise any advance on this particular line, while it is also the fact that it is on this particular line that the people that we call civilised show the most palpable advance over those to whom we deny the term. In the history of mankind as a whole the advance in this direction, though neither universal nor continuous, is probably more widespread and more continuous than in any other, and in modern civilisation it becomes more continuous and far more rapid. Finally the question whether there is any correlation between advance on this line and any particular movement on other sides of human life is perhaps the most important question for the general theory of social evolution. Does the advance of human knowledge which in relation to the understanding and control of natural forces seems unlimited, carry with it any distinct movement in morals, law, religion, the general organisation of society? Does it make for progress in these directions, or the reverse, or is it indifferent to them?

We do not here attempt to deal with these problems in general.

To grapple with them at all would involve to begin with a definition of progress which lies outside our immediate sphere. We offer only a preliminary contribution. We do not, in fact, deal with " civilised " peoples at all, but confine ourselves to the classification of those less fortunate races which range from the lowest known *Naturmenschen* to the confines of the historic civilisation. We seek within these limits first to distinguish the advancing grades of material culture, and, secondly—without any systematic inquiry as to what constitutes " progress " or the reverse—to determine how far various forms of political and social institutions can be correlated with each grade.

The Possibility of Sociological Correlation.

We have next to inquire how far it is actually possible to establish any correlations between social and political institutions on the one hand and stages of economic culture on the other, and to what extent ordinary statistical methods can be made available to forward this result. It must be replied at once that in view of the peculiar nature of the subject, and in particular of the data on which we have to rely, statistical methods can only be employed with certain reserves. All results must be rough. All are open to certain special causes of error, and any inference based on a comparison of numbers alone is dangerous. On the other hand, numerical results in combination with close analysis of accompanying conditions, are of high utility, both in checking generalisations and in measuring the value of data. This will be better understood if we study the actual difficulties which confront the inquirer who endeavours to apply the test of numbers to sociological facts.

(1) *The Character of the Data.*

If we confined ourselves to monographs compiled by skilled observers, there would be comparatively little difficulty with the data themselves, but unfortunately, as already remarked, such monographs are few and they would not in the aggregate prove sufficient to warrant any statistical calculations. Moreover, so to limit our vision would be to leave out of sight a vast amount of material which contains valuable evidence, even if the ore is sometimes difficult to sift from the dross. We are therefore forced to take account of the ordinary materials of anthropology—reports of travellers, missionaries, explorers, and casual observers, and it need hardly be said that in all such reports the problem of inferring from the statements of the observer the precise nature of the facts which he means to report, is not one which admits of an easy and straightforward solution. In particular when one endeavours to classify forms of institutions under heads, which is the necessary presupposition of any attempt at correlation, we must bear in mind that no observer has the scheme of classification in his mind, and there is considerable opportunity for error in reducing the contents of his report to the heads of any classification, however wide we may cast our net. Over and above these well-known difficulties in anthropology, there are all the sources of error, obscurity and confusion which arise from the intermixture of cultures, the rise or decay of institutions under the influence of foreigners, and in particular of the white immigrants themselves, to whom the reporter may belong, and there is always the probability that the peoples whom the reporter comes in contact with are precisely those specimens of the tribe who lie nearest to the white man or to other civilised people, and are most influenced thereby. All this, however, is common matter to anthropologists and not much of it presents any difficulty to our inquiry as compared with others.

(2) *The Unit.*

It is otherwise when we pass to the question of the unit which we must take as the basis of our calculations. Every rigid statistical inquiry supposes that the phenomena with which it deals can be stated in terms of some unit which is constant throughout its field. What is the unit social group? Let us consider a people occupying a certain area, the natives of Australia, let us say, or the Algonquin Indians. There are certain features common to the culture of these peoples, but within them there are a great many tribes and even groups of tribes. Not all that is true of one tribe will be true of others even within the same group, and certainly not all things true of a group would be true of all the Algonquins or all the Australians. And lastly, within what is called the tribe itself, there are often clans, local groups, and even sub-tribes, and even these are not always alike in all their institutions.

Now the reports of ethnographers sometimes deal with tribes, sometimes with divisions or branches of a tribe, and sometimes with groups of two or three, a dozen, or even a score of tribes taken together. We might be inclined to take the tribe as the unit. But the term tribe is used with the utmost variety of meaning by our reporters. Some apply the name to the smallest group of people living together, others to the loose unity which extends over a great area and covers all groups using a common dialect and recognising a certain affinity which distinguishes them from the rest of the world. In this wider sense tribes differ greatly in extent—one may contain a dozen or a score of subordinate groups; another may contain one or two only. And moreover, the limitations of the tribe sometimes seem to be assigned rather by the purview of the traveller or by the chance extent to which a dialect has spread than by clearly marked divisions separating it off socially or politically from its neighbours. Indeed a population which is treated as a "tribe" by one writer might be regarded as a collection of many tribes by another. Thus the statements which form our data refer to populations of different magnitude, and there is no discoverable means of reducing these to units of equal magnitude. But in fact no such reduction is necessary for our purpose. What we are examining is the correlation of social institutions with grades of economic culture. For this purpose we wish to know the number of separate social groups at any given grade possessing a given institution, and for this purpose the population or the number of subordinate bodies contained by any given social group is of secondary importance. The real question is, what constitutes a separate social group? In the higher grades of social development political independence supplies a fairly definite criterion. Yet even here it must be remembered that independence may be partial, as well as absolute, and that it might be legitimate and even necessary to count a population as forming one society for certain purposes and two or more for certain other purposes. Be this as it may, on the lower levels political unity is a much vaguer conception, and when the observer finds fundamental similarity of type and custom, uninterrupted intercourse and, in particular, free intermarriage extending over a certain area he will generally treat that area as one, whether the population corresponds to what he calls one tribe or not. In this he will not be far wrong, for the customs and institutions of such a collection of people in all probability have a common origin. They arise and flourish and decay in the main from the same causes and in close interconnection. In general we have no alternative but to follow the reporter, and take each institution that he reports as one case of the existence of that institution. Of course in so doing we are trusting to the judgment of our witness. It may be that he ought to have drawn distinctions and demarcations, and these may in fact appear when we compare his account with that of another observer, while sometimes it becomes apparent through internal evidence. In such a case we should in fact divide the group in our tables and count each of its parts as one. But in so far as groupings and divisions have been made by original observers with judgment and knowledge, it is reasonable to treat as a single instance a homogeneous population living in a continuous area enjoying regular intercourse throughout and not divided by clear lines of racial, social, or political difference.[1] The mere difference in size of these units need not greatly disturb our calculations.

On the other hand, we must recognise that the judgment of observers is not equally to be depended on in all cases, and that

1. In a few cases our units are in strictness too large for this definition Our reasons for attempting to divide them are indicated below.

sometimes mere chance or the bare impossibility of obtaining detailed information as to separate communities has led our reporters to treat as one peoples who might very possibly be distributed into many distinct sections as the result of further enquiry. We note in their place certain possibilities of error in calculation that arise from this source, and throughout, as will be explained presently, we so limit our inferences as to guard against this danger in cases where its presence may have passed unnoticed.

At the same time it may be pointed out that on this side the very defects in our reports tend to cancel one another. Close inspection shows that statements made about a group of tribes are in reality based often enough on the one or two members of the group with whom the reporter has had close personal contact. Hence different reports about the same group often prove to be inconsistent and the explanation of the inconsistency not infrequently is that both are true, one of some members of the group and the other of others. Sometimes we are able to fix the exceptions, sometimes we can only table the statements as true, one of "some" members of the group and the other of "some other" members. But the repeated experience of discrepancies of this kind reduces the value of large generalisations and tends to equate the statistical value of the units with regard to which we may conceive ourselves to possess trustworthy information.

Further, it must be remembered that when we are comparing peoples at much the same level of general culture, whatever irregularity there is in our units will be pretty evenly distributed. Suppose we are dealing with two opposite customs, both found pretty frequently among hunting tribes. Let us say that we have 100 cases of the one and 50 of the other. The 100 will no doubt contain large groups and small, but so also will the 50. If we know of one group of special magnitude and importance, we note the fact and give it due weight in our summing up. But in general there is no reason to think that there will be any aggregation of the larger instances on one side rather than on the other. There is nothing to weight the scale, and if our numbers were sufficiently great, we might find in this consideration alone a solution of the problem so far as it depends on the inadequacy of our reports.

But in many cases our numbers are not great enough to justify us in trusting to the impartiality of chance. The probable error would be high, and we should often be unable to draw any inference at all. We therefore base no inference on small differences. The fact that a given custom is to be found, say in 55 per cent. of the instances obtained at a given level of culture, and an opposite custom in 45 per cent. must be taken as in itself insignificant. It can only mean that, roughly, there is no clear tendency to the one or the other at that stage. Such a proportion as that of 55 : 45

can be of value only if it is a link in a chain, *e.g.*, if, at a lower level the figures were 70 : 30, and at a higher one 30 : 70. It is otherwise when we have a 2 : 1 preponderance. This is not likely to be a mere chance. But even here it is well not to be content with the gross numerical result, but also to examine the constitution of our majority and minority. Such a check is desirable, not only in view of doubts as to the equal value of our units, but to obviate a second difficulty, which has now to be examined.

This difficulty is in a manner the exact converse of the last. It may be asked whether in any cultural area—in any territory, that is, where the conditions of life are very similar, and where, though it is too large for direct intercourse between its parts, there is opportunity for institutions to propagate themselves in the course of generations by social contact—we ought to reckon distinct cases at all. Institutions and customs tend to propagate themselves indefinitely, and if we find, say, a certain form of marriage all over a sub-continent, it may be that it has had a single origin, and ought on our principles to be accounted one case rather than many. Thus we find a certain amount of polygamy—very variable it is true—common apparently, with one doubtful exception, to all Australian tribes. Shall we count this as upwards of thirty instances, or is it in reality only one instance? The reply is that whatever the degree of cultural unity among the Australian aborigines, it did not prevent their marriage customs from differing in many essential respects from one another. If that is so it seems fair to take as a unit each area which observers have, in fact, recognised as homogeneous and interconnected, and if in the matter of descent, or of capture, we get a great variation of custom as between one area and another, while in regard to the permission of polygamy we get uniformity, to let this result have its due weight by entering each instance of polygamy separately in our tables. The result at least shows that a certain degree of polygamy is suited to the conditions of Australian culture generally, while other incidents of marriage vary greatly within the limits of their culture. If an institution has, in fact, propagated and maintained itself over a great area, even though its origin be in some unitary cause, we cannot regard its extensive prevalence as unimportant or insignificant. The fact that it prevails so widely is evidence of its suitability to the conditions of life among the peoples in question, and this correlation is as suitably expressed as any other in the number of separate instances which will be counted.

If such an institution is found in all or most of the various regions of the world occupied by people of a certain industrial grade, we may fairly sum up the instances and treat the result as a measure of the correlation between that institution and the level of economic culture in question. But if all, or the great majority of instances in which it appears, are drawn from one region, it is different. To show how dangerous a simple enumeration might be in such a case we may pursue this particular instance taken a little further. When we compare the Australians with others of the same economic grade we find, for example, that the Wild Semang are monogamous. Now the Wild Semang are only entered in our table as one group. But they are very numerous and scattered, and they count as one only, because they are not sufficiently known for any one to make divisions among them. In order to compare the prevalence of monogamy and polygamy among the Lower Hunters, we cannot crudely set down the Australians as thirty cases on the one side and the Semang as one on the other. In such a case we must consider our figures from more than one point of view. We must cross-classify, and group them not only by the economic but by the geographical order. If all, or the majority of cases of any given institution come from one part of the world, we must note this fact and take it into account before drawing any inferences as to the correlation of that institution with any particular grade of culture as such. This necessity has been kept in mind, and while our geographical grouping has necessarily been rough in this experimental inquiry, we have throughout kept the different continents separate in our tables, and within these certain regions of culture contact are sufficiently apparent. Racial unity is a more problematical matter, which no doubt would explain many identities and differences if we could know all the facts, but to rely on this explanation would constantly have taken us into controversial questions, and we have been compelled for the time being to leave it aside. Meanwhile our plan is, whenever we find an accumulation of instances in a particular area to note the fact as a deduction from any generalisation that might be founded on those instances, and, if necessary, to seek some alternative method of presenting the results. For example, in the particular case referred to above, we present the totals as to polygamy and monogamy arrived at, first by taking the Australians as so many separate instances, and then by treating them as a single cultural group equated with a corresponding cultural type in Asia and Africa. This method—the details of which must vary in accordance with the nature of the concrete case—yields upper and lower limits of error, which often express the nearest approximation that we can make to the truth.

We have then two difficulties to keep in mind. The first is the imperfect precision of our units; the second is the deduction from the value of separate units to be made on account of the influence of culture contacts. Fortunately these two difficulties tend to cancel one another, for the influence of culture-contact diminishes the value of the large area relatively to the smaller. But we cannot disregard them, and to guard against them we must refrain from basing any inference on small preponderances, while if we have large differences, we must first examine the constitution of our majority and minority. When these in combination have been observed we shall in fact find that various positive results emerge.

Our general method then will be as follows. We take as a unit each group which we find so treated in our authorities. Where the treatment is not clear or where different authorities dealing with the same area make different divisions, we are forced to deal with each case on its merits, deciding by the concrete evidence whether to enter one instance or more in our tables. What is "one instance" for one purpose is, of course, one instance for all,[1] and minor variations are met by the entry of "some" or "occasional" if one particular point is true only of certain members of a group.[2] But we do not break up a group which our authority reckons as one unless his own evidence compels us to do so by showing that it presents clear variations of type in the relation in which it is being examined.

There remains a technical difficulty which is much greater than would be supposed by anyone who has not actually tried to grapple with it—that of identifying and defining the reference of a reporter's statement. There is first the difficulty of knowing whether a statement is general or particular. When a writer tells us something of "the Australian native," are we to attach any importance to it, and if so, how are we to table the result? In this particular case the importance is probably very small. The writer most likely knows one or perhaps two tribes fairly well, and he generalises from them. If we can identify his tribes, we refer his statement to them and neglect the generalisation. When we have

1. In a very few instances difficulties in identifying the references of different authorities have led us to enter different group names in different tables.

2. In comparison such instances are reckoned as ½. The same value is given to cases which are entered with a query as probable though not quite certain. It might seem safer to omit such instances altogether, but it must be remembered that in our investigation we are generally comparing this frequency of institution A with that of institution B. If we were considering A alone we might well confine ourselves to the certain cases, but when we are comparing it with B to ignore several probable instances of A may be to exaggerate the preponderance of B. The least error therefore is to reckon the probable case on a reduced value. This has the further justification that the incomplete or imperfect statement will very often reflect a partial development or a decadent condition of the institution, so that the half value may be claimed as nearest to an accurate representation of the facts. It must be borne in mind throughout that a ? in these tables does not mean uncertainty, but either probable evidence for the existence of the institution or positive evidence of its partial existence.

an observer like Grey, who travelled in South, West and North-west Australia, and makes all his statements in general terms, but seems to know quite clearly what he is talking about, we cannot ignore his statement, nor can we pin it down to a single tribe. In this case we have compared several authorities, and we formed for ourselves rough groups of West Australians, those about Perth, those inland on the Swan River, and those of King George's Sound, for each of which we have independent testimony. When we have an account which seems sound but lacking in definiteness of reference, we adopt the device of tabling as true of "some Victorian tribes," "some New South Wales tribes," etc. Sometimes we have general statements about a group which seem worthy of record, but are not borne out by individual cases within the group for which we have independent information. At first sight this may seem simply to discredit the more general statement, but it is also possible, and in some instances it appears to be the fact, that the detailed description lays stress on the exceptions to a rule, and if it is so, the existence of the rule ought not to escape recognition. In such instances we have preserved the general statement again by attributing it to "some" of the group in question.

One of the most serious difficulties in this connection arises from the want of fixity in nomenclature. Some writers refer to savage peoples geographically, others by a name given them by the whites, others by their own name for themselves. A single tribe may figure under half a dozen names which we identify with some difficulty, and sometimes after identifying them discover that there is a local difference. Thus while some writers seem to treat the Loucheux and the Kutchin as the same people under two names, we find a couple of articles in a single report which deal with them separately, and conclude that the Loucheux are a branch of the Kutchin, whose precise limits in the end we have not satisfactorily made out. In Australia the Narrinyeri spread from the mouth of the Murray over Encounter Bay. Yet in the same volume we have two writers treating of the Narrinyeri and of the Encounter Bay tribes as though they were distinct.[1] A margin of error in our identifications undoubtedly remains, and we should welcome detailed corrections on such points.

There must also be some overlapping. For example, the Kamilaroi occur in a group of New South Wales tribes which we enter. But they also occur independently because we have some information about them which does not wholly consort with the

1. In this case detailed comparison shows that the "Encounter Bay" tribes of the one writer correspond to four local groups of the other writer's "Narrinyeri."

statement which we have as to the group. This fact, however, does not prove that the latter statements are untrue. They probably hold of some members of the group, and therefore are correctly recorded of "some" New South Wales tribes. In general the critic must bear in mind that it is more important for our purpose to note that some tribe of a given culture possesses a certain custom than to determine whether it is the Kamilaroi or another, and the statements when put together may give an approximately accurate account of a level of culture as a whole, although wrong in some of the details of reference. The greatest care has been taken under that head, but only criticism and revision can carry the matter further.

Such being our data our method of treatment must be such as to allow for the elements of uncertainty and irregularity which they present. As already mentioned we shall, to begin with, draw no inference from small variations. But if as we ascend the economic scale we find a continuous and marked increase in the numerical preponderance of a certain institution, if, for example, we find such an institution only in one case out of four at the lowest levels and in four cases out of five at the highest, we shall infer a true correlation between it and the level of economic culture. We should still bear in mind the constituent elements of which our groups are composed, and if all or the great majority of the cases on one side should be drawn from a single group, we should call attention to the fact and discount the result accordingly. In several cases we shall in fact see that when due weight has been given to all grounds of doubt, the broad fact of correlation may be fairly taken as established. On the other hand, there are cases in which the proportions remain remarkably constant at all grades, and we may as fairly maintain that the frequency of a given institution is constant at all levels of industrial culture within our limits. Lastly, there are cases in which the variations are irregular, and no inference can be drawn.

THE CROSS-CULTURAL SURVEY *

GEORGE PETER MURDOCK

FOR A NUMBER of years, the Institute of Human Relations at Yale University has been conducting a general program of research in the social sciences, with particular reference to the areas common to, and marginal between, the special sciences of sociology, anthropology, psychology, and psychiatry. In 1937, as one of the specific research projects on the anthropological and sociological side of this program, the Cross-Cultural Survey was organized.[1]

A year of previous experience in collaborating with other social scientists in research and discussion had made it clear to the anthropologists associated with the Institute that the rich resources of ethnography, potentially of inestimable value to workers in adjacent fields, were practically inaccessible to them. Working in the laboratory, the clinic, or the community, the psychologists, sociologists, and others made frequent requests of the cultural anthropologists for comparative data on various aspects of behavior among primitive peoples. Sometimes they wanted perspective, sometimes suggestions, sometimes a check on their own scientific formulations. In trying to assist them, the anthropologists found that they could usually cite a limited number of cases from their own knowledge and give an impressionistic judgment as to the general status of ethnography on the question. For scientists, however, this was often not enough. What guarantee was there that the remembered cases were representative, or the impressions valid? What was needed was access to a dependable and objective sample of the ethnographic evidence. Only rarely was it possible to refer the seeker to an adequate summary of the evidence; in the great majority of instances, he could satisfy his scientific curiosity only by resorting to the vast descriptive literature itself and embarking on a research task of discouraging magnitude.

An actual example will illustrate the difficulty. Several years ago, a group of physiologists, working in the laboratory, had come to a series of conclusions with respect to the relationship between periodicity of eating and bodily health as reflected in measurements of weight, stature, etc. It occurred to them that the literature of anthropology should contain data by which their conclusions might be independently tested, and they referred to the author for advice. He was able to tell them that ethnographers customarily report the relevant data on eating habits—the number of meals

---

[1] Based on a paper presented to the American Anthropological Association in Chicago, Dec. 28, 1939. For further information on the research program of the Institute of Human Relations, and upon the relation of the Cross-Cultural Survey thereto, see M. A. May, "Report of the Director of the Institute of Human Relations for the Academic Years 1937–1938, 1938–1939," *Bulletin of Yale University*, series 35, XXVII (1939), 1–35.

---

*Reprinted from the *American Sociological Review*, Vol. 5, No. 3 (June 1940), 361-370, by permission of the author and the American Sociological Association.

per day, their temporal spacing, the degree of regularity or irregularity in eating, etc.—and that physical anthropologists present the pertinent somatological information. Since the material had been gathered, it could be assembled and the crucial correlations drawn. To have done so, however, would have required several months of research, since the data had nowhere been summarized and it would have been necessary to ransack an immense amount of descriptive literature to assemble it. Understandably enough, the physiologists were discouraged from undertaking this promising but formidable task.

Other sciences have systems of abstracts, bibliographical aids, and quantities of secondary collections, by means of which the researcher can quickly track down the pertinent data and acquaint himself with previous research on any subject. With a few notable exceptions,[2] anthropology lacks such aids. Its materials are widely scattered in descriptive reports, an immense number of which must be scanned if adequate information is desired on any particular topic. The factual data of sociology are in a similarly chaotic condition. It became apparent, therefore, that if these sciences were to be brought to bear effectively in the coöperative research program of the Institute, a representative sample of the cultural materials on the various societies of the world needed to be organized for ready accessibility on any subject. The Cross-Cultural Survey was developed, in part to fill this need, in part to facilitate a distinctive type of scientific research which will be described below.

The first problem was to devise a standard system of classification for the arrangement and use of the collected materials. After six months of preliminary research, with the aid of helpful suggestions from about a hundred anthropologists, sociologists, and other specialists, the author and five collaborators published the *Outline of Cultural Materials*. Although this manual has proved of some incidental utility in field research, it was in no sense designed for such a purpose. It was written solely as a guide for organizing and filing our abstracted cultural materials, and for facilitating reference to the data already classified and filed.

Since the publication of the manual, in 1938, the staff of the Cross-Cultural Survey has been engaged in the actual assembling of materials. To date, the descriptive data on nearly a hundred cultures have been abstracted, classified, and filed. It is hoped ultimately to assemble and organize all the available cultural information on several hundred peoples,

[2] Useful for special purposes are the massive collections of Frazer, Sumner and Keller, Thurnwald, and Westermarck, such classic monographic studies as those of Hahn on domestic animals, Nieboer on slavery, Schurtz on age groupings, and Steinmetz on punishment, and such recent special treatises as that of Clements on theories of disease. These compilations, however, do not lend themselves to the determination of "adhesions" in Tylor's sense, i.e., correlations within a culture indicative of functional relationships, and thus have but limited use in the testing of scientific hypotheses.

who will be adequately distributed with regard to geography and fairly representative of all major types and levels of culture. Although primitive cultures will preponderate numerically, because they reveal the widest range of human behavioral variations, there will be a fair representation of the historical civilizations of the past, of modern folk cultures, and of the communities studied by contemporary sociologists.

For each of the cultures analyzed, the entire literature is covered, including manuscript materials when available. In some instances, more than a hundred books and articles have been combed for a single tribe or historical period. All material in foreign languages has been translated into English. The information, if of any conceivable cultural relevance, is transcribed in full—in verbatim quotations or exact translations. The object has been to record the data so completely that, save in rare instances, it will be entirely unnecessary for a researcher using the files to consult the original sources. Mere abstracts are deemed unsatisfactory and are resorted to only in exceptional cases, when the information is excessively detailed or technical. The *Outline of Cultural Materials* is not a "trait list," nor are the files confined to data on the items listed in it. These items are merely suggestions as to the kinds of material to be filed—or sought—under a particular heading, and they make no pretense of being exhaustive. Special pains are taken to preserve intact the functional relationships of the data. Wherever division according to the categories of the manual would be arbitrary, or would destroy the context, the original account is preserved intact and is filed in one place, with a carbon copy or a cross-reference slip under each other category to which the information is pertinent. Each file, moreover, contains a short synopsis of the total culture to which any note can be referred for context.

The collection of organized and classified materials in the files of the Cross-Cultural Survey should prove useful in nearly every type of research which anthropologists and other social scientists have hitherto pursued. If an investigator wishes to study a particular culture, he will find all the data, from whatsoever source, organized conveniently for his use. If he is interested in a topic, he can run through the material under one or more headings for as many cultures as he likes, and secure his information in a mere fraction of the time required to comb the sources for himself. If he desires to test an hypothesis, he can similarly examine the material under two or more categories and obtain a quantitative check in the form of a correlation. A cross-cultural test of the physiologists' hypothesis on the periodicity of eating, alluded to above, could, for example, probably now be made with not more than two days of research. Even regional or distributional studies are possible for areas, like the Gran Chaco of South America, on which the files approach completeness. The Cross-Cultural Survey, in short, should prove useful in a wide variety of scientific researches for which ready access to a body of organized cultural data is needed. It is intended, of course, to make the material generally available on a coöperative basis. Recent users of the files include—to cite but a few examples—a sociologist analyzing social classes, a psychologist interested in adolescent problems, and a psychiatrist seeking a cultural definition of insanity.

In addition to its practical objective of facilitating diverse forms of social science research, the Cross-Cultural Survey has a special theoretical objective. It is organized so as to make possible the formulation and varification, on a large scale and by quantitative methods, of scientific generalizations of a universally human or cross-cultural character. Sociologists and most other social scientists regard the establishment of generalizations or "laws," i.e., verified statements of correlations between phenomena, as their primary aim, but anthropologists tend to shy away from theory, as Kluckhohn[3] has pointed out, and to confine themselves to historical rather than scientific interpretations of their subject matter. Nevertheless, it seems premature to conclude that anthropology cannot be made a science until, using all known safeguards, we have made at least one serious and systematic attempt to formulate scientific generalizations about man and culture which will withstand a quantitative test. Anthropology has many objectives. That envisaged by the Cross-Cultural Survey is not intended to supplant the others, nor does it lay claim to greater importance. It is simply regarded as legitimate, promising, and opposed by no insuperable theoretical obstacles.

The plan rests, at bottom, on the conviction that all human cultures, despite their diversity, have fundamentally a great deal in common, and that these common aspects are susceptible to scientific analysis. Its theoretical orientation may be expressed in a series of seven basic assumptions. These are not claimed to be original, since many of them are shared by all social scientists, and all of them by many.

1. *Culture Is Learned.* Culture is not instinctive, or innate, or transmitted biologically, but is composed of habits, i.e., learned tendencies to react, acquired by each individual through his own life experience after birth. This assumption, of course, is shared by all anthropologists outside of the totalitarian states, but it has a corollary which is not always so clearly recognized. If culture is learned, it must obey the laws of learning, which the psychologists have by now worked out in considerable detail. The principles of learning are known to be essentially the same, not only for all mankind but also for most mammalian species. Hence, we should expect all cultures, being learned, to reveal certain uniformities reflecting this universal common factor.

2. *Culture Is Inculcated.* All animals are capable of learning, but man

[3] C. Kluckhohn, "The Place of Theory in Anthropological Studies." *Philosophy of Science*, VI (1939), 328–344.

alone seems able, in any considerable measure, to pass on his acquired habits to his offspring. We can housebreak a dog, teach him tricks, and implant in him other germs of culture, but he will not transmit them to his puppies. They will receive only the biological inheritance of their species, to which they in turn will add habits on the basis of their own experience. The factor of language presumably accounts for man's preëminence in this respect. At any rate, many of the habits learned by human beings are transmitted from parent to child over successive generations, and, through repeated inculcation, acquire that persistency over time, that relative independence of individual bearers, which justifies classifying them collectively as "culture." This assumption, too, is generally accepted by anthropologists, but again there is an underestimated corollary. If culture is inculcated, then all cultures should show certain common effects of the inculcation process. Inculcation involves not only the imparting of techniques and knowledge but also the disciplining of the child's animal impulses to adjust him to social life. That there are regularities in behavior reflecting the ways in which these impulses are thwarted and redirected during the formative years of life, seems clear from the evidence of psychoanalysis, e.g., the apparent universality of intrafamily incest taboos.

3. *Culture Is Social.* Habits of the cultural order are not only inculcated and thus transmitted over time; they are also social, that is, shared by human beings living in organized aggregates or societies and kept relatively uniform by social pressure. They are, in short, group habits. The habits which the members of a social group share with one another constitute the culture of that group. This assumption is accepted by most anthropologists, but not by all. Lowie,[4] for example, insists that "a culture is invariably an artificial unit segregated for purposes of expediency. . . . There is only one natural unit for the ethnologist—the culture of all humanity at all periods and in all places . . . ." The author finds it quite impossible to accept this statement. To him, the collective or shared habits of a social group—no matter whether it be a family, a village, a class, or a tribe—constitute, not "an artificial unit" but a natural unit—a culture or subculture. To deny this is, in his opinion, to repudiate the most substantial contribution which sociology has made to anthropology. If culture is social, then the fate of a culture depends on the fate of the society which bears it, and all cultures which have survived to be studied should reveal certain similarities because they have all had to provide for societal survival. Among these cultural universals, we can probably list such things as sentiments of group cohesion, mechanisms of social control, organization for defense against hostile neighbors, and provision for the perpetuation of the population.

4. *Culture Is Ideational.* To a considerable extent, the group habits of which culture consists are conceptualized (or verbalized) as ideal norms or

[4] R. H. Lowie, *The History of Ethnological Theory*, 235–236, New York, 1937.

patterns of behavior. There are, of course, exceptions; grammatical rules, for example, though they represent collective linguistic habits and are thus cultural, are only in small part consciously formulated. Nevertheless, as every field ethnographer knows, most people show in marked degree an awareness of their own cultural norms, an ability to differentiate them from purely individual habits, and a facility in conceptualizing and reporting them in detail, including the circumstances where each is considered appropriate and the sanctions to be expected for nonconformity. Within limits, therefore, it is useful to conceive of culture as ideational, and of an element of culture as a traditionally accepted idea,[5] held by the members of a group or subgroup, that a particular kind of behavior (overt, verbal, or implicit) should conform to an established precedent. These ideal norms should not be confused with actual behavior. In any particular instance, an individual behaves in response to the state of his organism (his drives) at the moment, and to his perception of the total situation in which he finds himself. In so doing, he naturally tends to follow his established habits, including his culture, but either his impulses or the nature of the circumstances may lead him to deviate therefrom to a greater or lesser degree. Behavior, therefore, does not automatically follow culture, which is only one of its determinants. There are norms of behavior, of course, as well as of culture, but, unlike the latter, they can be established only by statistical means. Confusion often arises between anthropologists and sociologists on this point. The former, until recently, have been primarily preoccupied with ideal norms or patterns, whereas sociologists, belonging to the same society as both their subjects and their audience, assume general familiarity with the culture and commonly report only the statistical norms of actual behavior. A typical community study like *Middletown* and an ethnographic monograph, though often compared, are thus in reality poles apart. To the extent that culture is ideational, we may conclude, all cultures should reveal certain similarities, flowing from the universal laws governing the symbolic mental processes, e.g., the worldwide parallels in the principles of magic.

5. *Culture Is Gratifying*. Culture always, and necessarily, satisfies basic biological needs and secondary needs derived therefrom. Its elements are tested habitual techniques for gratifying human impulses in man's interaction with the external world of nature and fellow man.[6] This assumption is an inescapable conclusion from modern stimulus-response psychology. Culture consists of habits, and psychology has demonstrated that habits

[5] From the point of view of behavioristic psychology, of course, an idea is merely a habit of a special sort, a tendency to react with implicit linguistic or symbolic behavior rather than with overt muscular responses. The underlying mechanisms, e.g., of learning, are similar if not identical. Fundamentally, therefore, our fourth assumption should be subsumed under our first—that culture is learned—as a special case thereof. In view of the importance of symbolic, especially linguistic, behavior in man, however, it has seemed advisable to segregate the ideational point for separate exposition.

[6] The only exceptions are partial and temporary ones, with respect to elements of culture in the process of dying out or being supplanted.

persist only so long as they bring satisfaction. Gratification reinforces habits, strengthens and perpetuates them, while lack of gratification inevitably results in their extinction or disappearance. Elements of culture, therefore, can continue to exist only when they yield to the individuals of a society a margin of satisfaction, a favorable balance of pleasure over pain.[7] Malinowski has been insisting on this point for years, but the majority of anthropologists have either rejected the assumption or have paid it but inadequate lip service. To them, the fact that culture persists has seemed to raise no problem; it has been blithely taken for granted. Psychologists, however, have seen the problem, and have given it a definitive answer, which anthropologists can ignore at their peril. If culture is gratifying, widespread similarities should exist in all cultures, owing to the fact that basic human impulses, which are universally the same, demand similar forms of satisfaction. The "universal culture pattern" propounded by Wissler[8] would seem to rest on this foundation.

6. *Culture Is Adaptive.* Culture changes; and the process of change appears to be an adaptive one, comparable to evolution in the organic realm but of a different order.[9] Cultures tend, through periods of time, to become adjusted to the geographic environment, as the anthropogeographers have shown, although environmental influences are no longer conceived as determinative of cultural development. Cultures also adapt, through borrowing and organization, to the social environment of neighboring peoples. Finally, cultures unquestionably tend to become adjusted to the biological and psychological demands of the human organism. As life conditions change, traditional forms cease to provide a margin of satisfaction and are eliminated; new needs arise or are perceived, and new cultural adjustments are made to them. The assumption that culture is adaptive by no means commits one to an idea of progress, or to a theory of evolutionary stages of development, or to a rigid determinism of any sort. On the contrary, one can agree with Opler,[10] who has pointed out on the basis of his Apache material, that different cultural forms may represent adjustments to like problems, and similar cultural forms to different problems. It is probable, nevertheless, that a certain proportion of the parallels in different cultures represent independent adjustments to comparable conditions.

The conception of cultural change as an adaptive process seems to many anthropologists inconsistent with, and contradictory to, the conception of

---

[7] Culture is gratifying, of course, not in an absolute but in a relative sense. To a slave, for example, the submission and drudgery demanded by his status are not actually pleasant; relative, however, to the painful alternative of punishment or death for rebellious behavior, observance of the cultural requirements of his status is gratifying or "reinforcing." Agricultural labor, again, may not be enjoyable in itself, but it is gratifying because it brings rewards, e.g., in food.

[8] C. Wissler, *Man and Culture*, 73–79, New York, 1923.

[9] See A. G. Keller, *Societal Evolution*, New York, 1915.

[10] M. E. Opler, "Apache Data concerning the Relation of Kinship Terminology to Social Classification," *Amer. Anthropol.*, n.s., XXXIX (1937), 207–208.

cultural change as an historical process. To the author, there seems nothing inconsistent or antagonistic in the two positions—the "functional" and the "historical," as they are commonly labeled. On the contrary, he believes that both are correct, that they supplement one another, and that the best anthropological work emerges when the two are used in conjunction. Culture history is a succession of unique events, in which later events are conditioned by earlier ones. From the point of view of culture, the events which affect later ones in the same historical sequence are often, if not usually, accidental, since they have their origin outside the continuum of culture. They include natural events, like floods and droughts; biological events, like epidemics and deaths; and psychological events, like emotional outbursts and inventive intuitions. Such changes alter a society's life conditions. They create new needs and render old cultural forms unsatisfactory, stimulating trial and error behavior and cultural innovations. Perhaps the most significant events, however, are historical contacts with peoples of differing cultures, for men tend first to ransack the cultural resources of their neighbors for solutions to their problems of living, and rely only secondarily upon their own inventive ingenuity. Full recognition of the historical character of culture, and especially of the role of diffusion, is thus a prime prerequisite if a search for cross-cultural generalizations is to have any prospect of success. It is necessary to insist, however, that historical events, like geographic factors, exert only a conditioning rather than a determining influence on the course of culture. Man adjusts to them, and draws selectively upon them to solve his problems and satisfy his needs.

7. *Culture Is Integrative.* As one product of the adaptive process, the elements of a given culture tend to form a consistent and integrated whole. We use the word "tend" advisedly, for we do not accept the position of certain extreme functionalists that cultures actually are integrated systems, with their several parts in perfect equilibrium. We adhere, rather, to the position of Sumner[11] that the folkways are "subject to a strain of consistency with each other," but that actual integration is never achieved for the obvious reason that historical events are constantly exerting a disturbing influence. Integration takes time—there is always what Ogburn[12] has called a "cultural lag"—and long before one process has been completed, many others have been initiated. In our own culture, for example, the changes wrought in habits of work, recreation, sex, and religion through the introduction of the automobile are probably still incomplete. If culture is integrative, then correspondences or correlations between similar traits should repeatedly occur in unrelated cultures. Lowie,[13] for example, has pointed out a number of such correlations.

---

[11] W. G. Sumner, *Folkways*, 5–6, Boston, 1906.

[12] W. F. Ogburn, *Social Change*, 200, New York, 1922.

[13] R. H. Lowie, *Primitive Society*, New York, 1920.

If the seven fundamental assumptions outlined above, or even any considerable proportion of them, are valid, then it must necessarily follow that human cultures in general, despite their historical diversity, will exhibit certain regularities or recurrences which are susceptible to scientific analysis, and which, under such analysis, should yield a body of scientific generalizations. A primary objective of the Cross-Cultural Survey is to formulate and test generalizations of this sort.

The first methodological step will be the logical elaboration of hypotheses. From whatever source derived—from generalizations advanced by anthropologists and sociologists, from psychological theory, or from leads found in the material—the hypotheses will be subjected to rigorous logical analysis and worked over into a series of basic postulates and testable theorems. By this procedure, the most effective of scientific methods, all logical or deductive operations are performed prior to the empirical test; there remain no fallible logical steps to be taken after the inductive labor is completed—a weakness which has vitiated much comparative anthropology.

The second step will be the verification of the theorems. A postulate can stand only if every theorem derived from it checks with the facts; if even a single one fails in this test, the postulate falls. The verification will be quantitative. In scientific anthropology, it would seem, there is safety in numbers. Only if one deals with a large number of cases can one expect to encompass all the significant causal factors, occurring in various permutations and combinations, estimate by statistical means their relative efficacy, and segregate by their quantitative preponderance the universal or cross-cultural factors from the local or historical ones. In testing each theorem, it is intended to use an adequate number of cases, preferably at least two hundred tribes if possible, selected from the files as the fairest sample feasible of all known cultures. In so far as possible, they will be chosen in equal numbers from all continents and all culture areas, including a representative selection of historical and modern civilizations. Each theorem will be posed to all the cases in terms of an anticipated correlation between two traits or aspects of culture, and the positive and negative results will be tabulated and expressed in terms of some reliable statistical coefficient. If, for each of a set of theorems, the coefficients obtained are positive in sign and significant in quantity, the postulate in question will be regarded as tentatively verified.

The third step will be a critical analysis of the results from an areal or distributional point of view. A valid cross-cultural hypothesis should hold true in any area. If, however, some areas are discovered to yield negative coefficients, while other areas with a larger total number of cultures yield positive coefficients, it must be concluded that the apparent statistical confirmation of the hypothesis is fictitious and accidental, and the hypothesis must either be rejected entirely or modified and tested again. To survive, therefore, any generalization will have to pass two tests—a quantitative statistical one and an analytical historical one.

The fourth step will be a detailed examination of all exceptional or negative cases. To a valid scientific principle, there are no exceptions; apparent exceptions are always due to the intrusion of another countervailing principle. Thus, water always obeys the law of gravity, which causes it to flow downhill. In all cases where water moves in the opposite direction, as in osmosis, capillary attraction, evaporation, the siphon, and the hydraulic ram, the law of gravity is still in operation but its influence is counteracted by some other force or principle. Similarly, a valid cultural principle should have no real exceptions. This makes it important to examine carefully all seeming exceptions. If countervailing factors are not found, the principle becomes suspect. One example may be cited from ethnography. The functional association of an Omaha type of kinship system with patrilineal sibs appears to be a valid cultural principle, yet Wagner[14] has reported an Omaha system for the Yuchi, who are known to have had matrilineal sibs. Eggan cites evidence, and Speck[15] agrees with him, that the Yuchi formerly possessed a Crow type of kinship system, which is functionally associated with matrilineal sibs, and that they shifted to an Omaha system only in relatively recent times in consequence of close contacts with Central Algonkian tribes like the Shawnee, who are patrilineal and possess kinship systems of Omaha type. Presumably, the Yuchi have changed too recently for the integrative process to have run its course. Thus, the apparent exception is not a real one, and the principle is not negated. An hypothesis, all of whose seeming exceptions can be explained in some such fashion as this, may be regarded as finally validated—subject always, of course, to correction as new evidence comes in.

The Cross-Cultural Survey, it may be said in conclusion, is designed to contribute in several ways to scientific research in the disciplines concerned with cultural phenomena. It can answer specific questions of fact with a minimum of time-wasting labor. It can reveal gaps in the ethnographical record and thus suggest what groups should be restudied and what hitherto unreported data should be gathered in the field. It can subject existing theoretical hypotheses about collective human behavior to a quantitative test, and can be used to formulate and verify new social science generalizations. In short, it should prove helpful in nearly every type of research requiring an organized and classified body of cultural materials.

---

[14] G. Wagner, "Yuchi," *Handbook of American Indian Languages*, III, 339–340, New York, 1934.

[15] F. G. Speck, "Eggan's Yuchi Kinship Interpretations," *Amer. Anthropol.*, n.s., XLI (1939), 171–172.

Comparisons in Cultural Anthropology *

OSCAR LEWIS [1]

Dr. Lewis has been Professor of Anthropology at the University of Illinois since 1948. Previously he was Field Representative for Latin America, Office of Indian Affairs; Social Scientist for the United States Department of Agriculture; and Visiting Professor at the University of Havana, Cuba. During 1952–1954 he was a Consulting Anthropologist in India for the Ford Foundation. His field research has been conducted in the United States, Cuba, Mexico, Spain, and India. He is author of: On the Edge of the Black Waxey: A Cultural Survey of a Texas County, 1948; and Life in a Mexican Village: Tepoztlán Restudied, 1951.

INTRODUCTION

IT is part of the thesis of this paper that there is no distinctive "comparative method" in anthropology, and that the persistence of this expression has led to unnecessary confusion and artificial dichotomies in much of the theoretical writing on this subject. Thus, we prefer to discuss comparisons in anthropology rather than the comparative method. This simple semantic change makes a difference, for it highlights the fact that the method of a comparison is only one aspect of comparison, other relevant aspects being the aims or objectives, the content, and the location in space of the entities compared. Our subject at once becomes broader than most considerations of "the comparative method" and includes comparisons within a single society as well as cross-cultural comparisons, comparisons over time as well as in space.

The unfortunate tendency to identify "the comparative method" with a particular type of research design or anthropological school of thought, dates back to 1896 when Boas identified the comparative method with the early evolutionists. His juxtaposition of his "historical method" against the comparative method of the evolutionists obscured what is fundamental for our purpose, namely, that both used comparisons toward the end of arriving at general laws. Of course, Boas was not against comparisons or comparative method. He wanted to improve it and specifically referred to his historical method as an improved comparative method. What we should like to emphasize is that the differences in anthropology are not between approaches which use comparisons and those which do not. All approaches—functionalism, diffusionism, kulturkreis, or evolutionism—make use of comparisons, but in different ways and for different ends.

Comparison is a generic aspect of human thought rather than a special method of anthropology or of any other discipline. Laymen as well as scientists make comparisons. The major difference between common-sense, everyday comparisons by the layman and those by the scientist, is that the latter, in their systematic study of similarities and differences, strive for a greater degree of control by utilizing the methods of correlation and co-variation.

It does not follow, however, that those

[1] We are grateful to the Behavioral Sciences Division of the Ford Foundation for a grant in aid, a portion of which was used for research assistance in the preparation of this study.

*Reprinted from William L. Thomas, Jr. (ed.), *Current Anthropology: A Supplement to Anthropology Today* (Chicago, University of Chicago Press, 1956), pp. 259-292.

studies which use quantification and express co-variation statistically are the only valid, useful, or scientific studies. Nor must all comparisons necessarily be directed toward testing hypotheses or arriving at general principles of societal development, worthwhile as these objectives are. Comparisons may have other values, depending upon the nature of the data and the objectives of the study. And so long as cultural anthropology feels a sense of kinship with the humanities as well as with the natural sciences, comparisons which increase our general understanding shall have their rightful place.

Most anthropological writing contains comparisons. Even the monographs which are primarily descriptive generally make comparisons with earlier literature, and many have a final comparative chapter. Textbooks use comparisons as illustrations, theoretical articles compare methods, points of view, and schools of thought, or review the literature of an area in a comparative manner. There are comparisons between single culture traits, between institutions, between subcultures, between areas, nations, and civilizations. There are synchronic and diachronic comparisons, controlled and uncontrolled, localized and global, formal and functional, statistical and typological. The kinds of comparisons made by anthropologists seem to be of an endless variety indeed.

This paper attempts to classify and analyze comparisons found in the literature for the five year period 1950–1954 in order to determine the major types of comparisons, their objectives, methods, research designs, and the location in space and time of the entities compared. References to earlier comparative studies will be made only when necessary for background purposes. The scheme used for the classification of comparisons will be presented later. Here let us first examine some of the highlights of recent theoretical articles on comparative method.

Within the past five years there have appeared an unusually large number of theoretical writings dealing with comparative method in anthropology.[2] In addition, an equally large number of books and articles have touched upon problems of comparative method indirectly or in passing. In all, probably more has been written on this subject within the past five years than within any comparable period since Boas published his famous piece of 1896. It is noteworthy that many of the authors cited above refer back to Boas, accepting, modifying, or rejecting his position. This concentration of interest in comparative method is probably a reflection of the growing maturity of anthropology as a science, the ever-increasing concern of anthropologists with problems of theory and method, and the accumulation of great masses of data which cry out for systematic comparative analysis.

A review of the literature cited above suggests a number of observations. Many of the theoretical discussions still use the phrase "the comparative method" as if it were a unitary and distinctive method of anthropology. For example, Ackerknecht (1954), who uses the expression "the comparative method" over thirty times in his short piece without once defining it, treats it almost as if it were a culture trait. He attempts to trace its introduction into anthropology from the biological and natural sciences and finally concludes that it was probably a case of convergence, if not of independent invention! He writes of the method as being "abandoned" by the functionalists and cites (p. 117) the publication of Murdock's *Social Structure* in 1949 as a sign of "a renaissance of the comparative method." Kroeber (1954, p. 273), in commenting on Ackerknecht's article, quite properly points out that ". . . the comparative method has never gone out, it has only changed its tactic."

The titles of some of the papers on comparative anthropology are in themselves revealing. Thus Radcliffe-Brown (1951), like Ackerknecht, follows the old tradition

[2] Murdock, 1950a, b; Steward, 1950; Evans-Pritchard, 1951; Nadel, 1951; Radcliffe-Brown, 1951; Köbben, 1952; Ackerknecht, 1954; Kluckhohn, 1953, 1954; Lowie, 1953; Schapera, 1953; Eggan, 1954; Herskovits, 1954; and Whiting and colleagues, 1954.

and calls his paper "The Comparative Method In Social Anthropology." He gives two major purposes of comparisons, the reconstruction of history, which he identifies with ethnology, and the discovery of regularities in the development of human society, which he identifies with social anthropology. He frankly defines the comparative method as a library method of "arm-chair anthropologists" and calls for more rather than less armchair anthropology. He writes (1951, p. 15):

> At Cambridge sixty years ago Frazer represented armchair anthropology using the comparative method, while Haddon urged the need of intensive studies of particular societies by systematic field studies of competent observers. The development of field studies has led to a relative neglect of studies making use of the comparative method. This is both understandable and excusable, but it does have some regrettable effects. The student is told that he must consider any feature of social life in its context, in its relation to the other features of the particular social system in which it is found. But he is often not taught to look at it in the wider context of human societies in general.

Singer's summary (1953, p. 362) of the discussion on Schapera's paper, titled "Some Comments on Comparative Method In Social Anthropology," is germane here. He writes,

> Schapera's original paper which was circulated before the conference was entitled 'Some Thoughts on the Comparative Method in Social Anthropology.' . . . dropping the 'the' from the title of the revised paper is perhaps the most eloquent, if inconspicuous, testimony of the impact of the conference: for Schapera and the other participants agreed that there is no single method of comparison in anthropology, that method is largely determined by problem, and that a method appropriate for the comparison of kinship systems is not necessarily most appropriate for other types of cross-cultural comparisons.

Eggan's excellent paper "Social Anthropology and the Method of Controlled Comparisons" (1954) gets away from "the comparative method" in the title and speaks instead of methods of comparisons. But even Eggan lapses again and again into the older terminology. He writes (p. 747), "In the United States . . . the comparative method has long been in disrepute, and was supplanted by what Boas called the 'historical method.' In England, on the other hand, the comparative method has had a more continuous utilization." Or again, he writes (p. 749) that most of Boas' students were predisposed against "the comparative method" and "hence against any generalizations which require comparisons." The use of the term "the comparative method" makes the above statements confusing. It is doubtful that the Boas students were against all comparisons. Certainly they have contributed their share of comparative studies. Rather, they objected to what they thought were uncontrolled comparisons, comparisons out of context.

Murdock (1954) and Whiting (1954) think of the comparative method almost exclusively in terms of the testing of hypotheses on a global scale with a heavy reliance upon statistics. Schapera (1953) tends to identify the comparative method with the intensive study of limited areas as a prerequisite to testing regionally derived general propositions in other areas. Eggan recognizes the validity and usefulness of a wide range of comparisons from those within a single community to global comparisons, but prefers the more limited and controlled comparisons to the more global and less controlled.

Lowie (1953) and Nadel (1951) take exception to the trend of identifying "the comparative method" with a particular school or approach in anthropology. Lowie challenges the meaningfulness of equating the old dichotomy of historians versus generalizers with that between the ethnographers and social anthropologists, as suggested by some British anthropologists. He makes the point that comparisons are just as important in an intensive study or descriptive integration of a single community as they are in cross-cultural analysis, and sees the two as part of a single continuum of comparisons. An intensive study of a single community "implies cognizance of correlated phenomena and thereby precludes erroneous inferences due to the currency of the same labels. . . . Complete description involves a *global* survey of correlations because only such a global survey guarantees accurate definition of the cultural phenomenon under discussion in relation to its real or apparent equivalents elsewhere." (p. 532).

Nadel offers us by far the most systematic and comprehensive treatment of comparative method. He defines it in terms of the systematic study of similarities and differences through the use of correlation and co-variation. It is therefore not a distinctive method of anthropology, but one shared by all the sciences. Following Durkheim, he distinguishes (1951, p. 226) three applications of the method of co-variation: (1) in the study of broad variations in particular modes of action or relationships within a single society; (2) in the study of the same society at different periods of time or of several essentially similar societies which differ only in certain respects; (3) in the study of numerous societies of a widely different nature. Nadel does not regard these three applications "as separate and independent lines of inquiry." Moreover, he believes that regularities can be derived from all three applications, the major differences being that the regularities derived from "narrow-range applications," i.e., within a single society, "are themselves of narrow applicability; they would exhibit specific phenomena present in only a limited number of societies. . ." (p. 227).

While Nadel recognizes the value of cross-cultural comparison and its distinctive place in anthropology as compared with other disciplines, he would not define anthropology exclusively in terms of cross-cultural studies. Indeed, he takes exception to a statement of Radcliffe-Brown which suggests that a study of a single society cannot "demonstrate" co-variations but can only lead to hypotheses which have to be tested in other societies. Nadel writes (1951, p. 240):

> Though this conclusion undoubtedly often holds, I do not think it applies invariably. Thus, if we include time perspective and cultural change in our enquiry, the necessary co-variations will be available, too, in societies sufficiently differentiated to exhibit the "broad" variations in the behavior of different group sections we spoke of before. Furthermore, in any society, . . . inasmuch as cultural elements 'hang together' in their own institutional setting, they do so by means of co-variations; the standardized, predictable patterns of behavior which are the elements of social existence mean nothing else.

Many of the recent writings on comparative methods and problems in anthropology express the particular theoretical preferences of the authors but they do not provide us with a systematic examination and analysis of contemporary comparative research. In this sense, the theoretical writing has lagged behind the field work. Steward (1950) reviews a good sample of community studies and older ethnographic studies and points to difficulties in comparability due to the uneven coverage which seems to depend largely upon individual interests. But he does not deal with the vast number of comparative studies in the literature. Similarly, Kluckhohn (1953) raises important theoretical problems in connection with the comparability of anthropological data and reports on the comparability of anthropological monographs based upon the examination of the table of contents of ninety monographs, but does not deal extensively with comparative studies as such. The single article within the past five years which makes some attempt at an evaluation of comparative research is the excellent piece by Köbben (1952), titled "New Ways of Presenting an Old Idea: The Statistical Method in Social Anthropology," in which he critically reviews *one type* of comparative study. His work will be cited later.

ANALYSIS AND CLASSIFICATION OF COMPARISONS

A total of 248 writings dealing with comparisons, within the period 1950–1954, were examined in the preparation of this paper.[3] These include 52 books, 173 articles, and 23 dissertations. Twenty-eight of these

[3] I am grateful to Dr. Ruth Landman for bibliographical research assistance in preparation of this paper.

writings deal primarily with theory and method in comparative anthropology and have been summarized earlier. The remaining 220 writings (45 books, 152 articles, and 23 dissertations) are reports of comparative research. The 152 articles with which we will be concerned were found after an examination of 23 scientific journals, including most of the major anthropological journals which are concerned with cultural or social anthropology. While the coverage is not exhaustive, it probably represents about ninety per cent of the comparative writings in the past five years.[4] Only a few of the dissertations cited were available to the writer. The analysis of most of the dissertations is based primaly upon published abstracts and is therefore partial and tentative.

In the light of recent discussions as to whether British or American anthropologists were more vitally concerned with comparative studies, it is interesting to note that 40, or seventeen per cent, of the 220 writings, were British publications. This is a high proportion in view of the relatively small number of British anthropologists. However, it demonstrates that American anthropologists are also active in the field of comparative studies. Our survey of the major French and German anthropological periodicals yielded very few comparative studies for the period covered.

In our analysis and classification of the above writings five broad dimensions of comparisons were considered: (1) the location in space of the entities compared, (2) the content, (3) the aims of the comparisons, (4) methods of obtaining data, and (5) research design. These dimensions were, in turn, subdivided so that each comparative study was judged against a check list of numerous items. (See Table 1.)

The geographical distribution of the comparative studies is shown in Table 2 (note that Ie and If have been combined, and Ib divided as between continents or nations or as within one continent): It can be seen that the greatest number of studies occur in North America and Latin America, the smallest number in Europe and Oceania; Africa and Asia hold an intermediate position. Although the location of the entities to be compared may seem like a relatively unimportant consideration, we find that it correlates significantly with the other major categories, but especially with methods. Comparative studies within a single culture area seem, by and large, to be interested in controlling the greatest number of variables and in relatively modest and limited goals. Global comparisons generally have more ambitious goals, and seek world-wide typologies or evolutionary sequences.

The relationship between methods used and the location of the entities compared can be seen in Table 3.

One of the most striking conclusions to be drawn from the data in Table No. 3, is that comparative studies in anthropology can no longer be defined as library studies. Each of the three methods, library comparisons, library plus field work, and primarily field work comparisons, are used about equally.

As we move from the global and larger categories to the smaller ones, we find an increasing reliance upon field work. Conversely, as we go from the smaller to the larger categories (Table 4) we find an increasing use of library comparisons.

The inverse relationship is most striking when we compare the two extremes of our geographical categories, i.e., global or random comparisons as over against comparisons within a single local group or culture (Column I versus VI in Table 3). In the former, there is a complete absence of comparisons based primarily upon field work and a predominance of library comparisons. In the latter, there are no library comparisons and a large number of studies based on field work. The zero scores in Column I and Column VI, Table No. 3, though understandable in terms of the nature of the research, are by no means inevitable. As comparative field research designs organized on a world-wide basis increase (for example, the Cornell Project

[4] Unfortunately the two major Indian anthropology journals were not available to the writer and so articles and books on India are not well covered.

TABLE 1

Outline For the Classification and Analysis of Comparative Studies

I. Location in space of the entities compared [5]
   - a. comparisons of cultures or aspects thereof selected randomly over the globe, i.e., global comparisons
   - b. comparisons of societies or aspects thereof located in different nations or major civilizations
   - c. comparisons within a nation
   - d. comparisons within a single culture area (for example, the Plains or Southwest in the U.S.)
   - e. comparisons of local groups within a single culture (for example, different bands within a single tribe, or between two Blackfoot Indian tribes)
   - f. comparisons within a single local group (band, village, or other type of localized settlement)

II. Content of comparisons
   - a. material culture
   - b. settlement pattern
   - c. ecology
   - d. technology
   - e. economics
   - f. social organization
   - g. political organization
   - h. religion
   - i. mythology
   - j. art
   - k. warfare
   - l. personality and culture
   - m. life cycle
   - n. sex
   - o. disease
   - p. relations with other communities
   - q. acculturation and culture change
   - r. race relations
   - s. law
   - t. values
   - u. total culture

III. Aims of the comparisons
   - a. establish general laws or regularities
   - b. document range of variation in the phenomena studied
   - c. document distribution of traits or aspects of culture
   - d. reconstruction of culture history
   - e. test hypotheses derived from Western society
   - f. test hypotheses derived from non-Western societies

IV. Methods of obtaining data
   - a. library comparisons
   - b. comparisons based upon library data plus field work
   - c. comparisons based primarily upon field work

V. Research design
   - a. statistical comparisons
   - b. broad typological comparisons
   - c. descriptive, functional analyses of one or more aspects of culture
   - d. descriptive and analytic comparisons of total cultures
   - e. restudies by the same investigator
   - f. restudies by different investigators

[5] Most of the geographical categories under I. above are self-explanatory. Categories Ic. and Id. are intended to distinguish between tribal studies of peasantry, rural, and urban groups. The culture area is taken as the frame of reference of the former, the nation for the latter

TABLE 2

Location of Studies

	Oceania	Asia	Africa	Europe	Latin America	North America	TOTAL
Random or global comparisons (34)	–	–	–	–	–	–	–
Comparison between continents or nations (20)	2	9	2	6	8	6	33 (13 repeat)
Comparison within one continent (31)	1	5	8	0	8	9	31
Comparison within one nation (31)	0	9	1	3	10	8	31
Comparison within one culture area (70)	10	2	17	0	14	27	70
Comparison within one group or culture (34)	7	3	2	0	9	13	34
Total	20	28	30	9	49	63	

TABLE 3

Distribution of Methods by Category of Comparison

Method	I. Random or global comparisons (34)	II. Comparison between continents or nations (20)	III. Comparison within one continent (31)	IV. Comparison within one nation (31)	V. Comparison within one culture area (70)	VI. Comparison within one group or culture (34)	Total number of cases
Library comparison	28	6	20	3	23	0	80
Comparisons based upon field work and library data	6	6	7	6	37	9	71
Comparison based primarily upon field work	0	8	4	22	10	25	69

TABLE 4

Distribution of Methods of the Three Larger Categories Compared with That of the Three Smaller Categories

Method	Large groups (I, II, III)	Small groups (IV, V, VI)
Library comparisons	63.5%	19.2%
Comparisons based on field work plus library data	22.3%	38.5%
Comparisons based primarily upon field work	14.1%	42.2%

on the effects of technological change and the Whiting field study of socialization in five cultures, now under way), the zero scores will disappear. Similarly, with the increase of restudies of local communities by the same or different investigators, library comparisons within this category will be possible.

Another interesting aspect of the relationship between method and geographical categories can be seen by comparing the distribution of methods in the one nation category (peasantry and rural studies) with the culture area category (tribal studies). See Columns IV and V, Table 3. Seventy-one per cent of the studies in the former as compared to only fourteen per cent in the latter are based primarily upon field work. Moreover, twenty-nine per cent of the comparisons within a nation based primarily upon field work, were done cooperatively by research teams, rather than by a single investigator, as over against one per cent within a single culture area. Since the comparative study of peasantry is a much more recent trend in anthropology than comparative tribal studies, it is here that we find the greatest concentration of field work and cooperative research. However, comparisons based upon tribal studies still outnumber the others by more than two to one.

The distribution of content in the 220 studies examined shows that the bulk of comparative work is being done in six fields, social organization, 68; culture change and acculturation, 65; total culture, 39; economics, 30; religion, 27; culture and personality, 21. Studies of social organization and culture change each constitutes approximately thirty per cent of the total number of studies. The relatively high number of total culture comparisons is a tribute to the holistic approach of many anthropologists. The fields in which we find the fewest comparative studies are race relations, 1; law, 2; relations with other communities, 3; sex, 3; life cycle, 4; mythology, 5; warfare, 5; settlement patterns, 7; and art, 8.

It will be seen (Table 3) that sixty-one per cent of all the studies are within the three smaller categories and thirty-nine per cent in the three larger categories. If we assume that the comparisons within small geographical areas give one greater control than widespread comparisons, we might interpret the above distribution to mean that contemporary comparative anthropology has moved a great distance toward the limited and controlled comparisons which Eggan and others have called for. Studies of social organization and culture change are concentrated in the smaller geographical categories. Thirty-five per cent of all the studies of culture change and acculturation are found concentrated in the category of a single community or culture.

The classification of the writings in terms of the theoretical aims of the comparisons proved extremely difficult because of the lack of any explicit statement in so many of the writings. The categories we have listed in our outline must therefore remain as items for future analysis of comparative studies. However, some general findings can be given here. Approximately forty per cent of the studies are descriptive, functional, comparative analyses of one or more aspects of culture, which seek to establish the relationship between variables, either for the purpose of establishing typologies or refining existing types. Approximately thirty per cent of the studies deal with acculturation and culture change. The culture change studies are generally historical reconstructions intended to show the direction of change. Only a few studies explicitly formulate developmental hypotheses. Approximately eighteen per cent of the studies are concerned primarily with demonstrating the range of variation in the phenomena studied; another eight per cent are straight distribution studies, and three per cent are attempts to delineate or redefine the nature of culture areas. Let us now examine the studies in more detail.

GLOBAL OR RANDOM COMPARISONS

Twelve books, 18 articles and 4 dissertations making a total of 34 out of 220 writings examined, fall into this category. All have in common the comparison of societies selected either at random or in accord with some special sampling design, but in no case limited to a single culture area, region, nation, or continent. Twenty-seven are library comparisons, and 10 are library plus field work comparisons.

The content covers a wide range, seventeen of our twenty-one content categories (see Table 1). The largest number are studies of social organization (8 cases), followed by economics (4), technology (4), religion (4), socialization (4), disease (4), etc. Seven studies deal with culture change and/or acculturation.

The objectives of these writings show a wide range, from the tracing of single trait distribution, to the testing of one or more hypotheses and to the reconstruction of stages in the history of human society. However, the writings can be divided into sub-groups in terms of a combination of methods and general research design: 1. *Statistical Comparisons* (10 cases),[6] 2. *Broad Typological Comparisons* (6 cases),[7] 3. *Functional Cross-cultural Analysis of One or More Aspects of a Culture* (7 cases),[8] 4. *Simple Distribution Studies* (3 cases),[9] and 5. *Case Books and Texts* (8 cases).[10]

[6] For example, Murdock and Whiting, 1951, "Cultural Determination of Parental Attitudes"; Ford and Beach, 1951, *Patterns of Sexual Behavior;* Charles, 1953, "Drama in Shaman Exorcism"; McClelland and Friedman, 1952, "A Cross-Cultural Study of the Relationship between Child-training Practices and Achievement Motivation Appearing in Folk-Tales"; Whiting and Child, 1953, *Child Training and Personality: A Cross Cultural Study.*

[7] For example, Redfield, 1953, *The Primitive World and Its Transformations;* Meggers, 1954, "Environmental Limitations on the Development of Culture"; Fried, 1952, "Land Tenure, Geography and Ecology in Contact of Cultures."

[8] For example, Freedman and Ferguson, 1950, "The Question of 'Painless Childbirth' in Primitive Cultures"; Aberle, 1952, "'Arctic Hysteria' and Latah in Mongolia"; Erikson, 1950, *Childhood and Society;* James, 1952, "Religion and Reality."

[9] For example, Anderson and Cutler, 1950, "Methods of Corn Popping and Their Historical Significance"; Balfour, 1951, "Ritual and Secular Uses of Vibrating Membranes as Voice Disguisers."

[10] For example, Spicer (ed.), 1952, *Human Problems in Technological Change;* Hoebel, 1954, *The Law of Primitive Man: A Study in Comparative Legal Dynamics;* Goode, 1951, *Religion among the Primitives,* Herskovits, 1952, *Economic Anthropology.*

The Spicer volume deserves special mention because many of the cases have come out of the Cornell Project in Applied Anthropology, one of the few centrally organized comparative research projects with field stations in major ethnographic areas of the world.

Limitation of space permits us to discuss only two of the five sub-categories above, namely, the statistical and the typological approaches.

Statistical Comparisons

All ten statistical studies are based in part or in whole upon the Cross-Cultural Files and the Human Relations Area Files at New Haven. The strengths and weaknesses of this type of study have received much discussion in the literature. Perhaps the fullest evalution of this approach is to be found in the lengthy discussion of Murdock and Whiting's paper (1951) on "The Cultural Determination of Parental Attitudes," by a panel which included, among others, Escalona, Erikson, and Lee. More recently Köbben has provided a searching analysis in his paper, "New Ways of Presenting An Old Idea: The Statistical Method in Social Anthropology."

The use of the physical sciences as a model, the testing of hypotheses derived primarily from Freudian or Hullian thinking, faith in quantification and large numbers of cases, optimism about the possibility of arriving at general laws, and the definition of the cross-cultural method as the statistical method, are characteristics of some of the writings of members of this group. Whiting (1954, p. 528) for example, in his article on "The Cross-Cultural Method," generalizes the steps he used in his own study on *Child Training and Personality* (1953) to define *the* cross-cultural method. Murdock, repeatedly identifies the cross-cultural method with the statistical method based upon the cross-cultural files. He writes;

> We believe that the day is past when we can depend upon an analysis of single cases or single societies to give us scientific answers. We feel that hypotheses suggested by the exploratory

> studies of individual societies should be tested by quantitative methods in a large number of societies. (Murdock and Whiting 1951, p. 32).

Murdock (1949, p. 183) believes that "the data of culture and social life are susceptible to exact scientific treatment as are the facts of the physical and biological sciences. It seems clear that the elements of social organization, in their permutations and combinations, conform to natural laws of their own with an exactitude scarcely less striking than that which characterizes the permutations and combinations of atoms in chemistry and of genes in biology." Murdock (1954, p. 30) optimistically writes that anthropology "if it rises to the occasion, may ultimately become the final arbiter of the universality of social science propositions."

While Köbben's discussion deals primarily with the cross-cultural studies published prior to our limiting date of 1950 (i.e., Horton, 1943; Ford, 1945; Murdock, 1949) much of his criticism applies also to the studies covered in our present review. Köbben notes (1952) that the "Grand Design" of the cross-cultural files is not novel and lists as direct precursors the works of Steinmetz, 1898; Tylor, 1889; Hobhouse, Wheeler and Ginsburg, 1930; Niebohr, 1910; and Unwin, 1934. Köbben finds that in some ways the work of these precursors was methodologically more rigorous than the later studies; it was also more meaningful, in that they attempted to deal with the interrelationships between various institutions or aspects thereof, in contrast to the more limited problems posed by the recent studies. For example, they sought answers to the question: How do systems of social organization vary with economic systems or modes of production? On the other hand, by limiting his problem, Murdock arrived at a useful typology of social structures, albeit largely in terms of kinship systems and residence rules. Moreover, Murdock's broad interest in general laws, his concern with evolutionary problems, and his striving for scientific rigor in comparative studies, is a salutary trend in contemporary anthropology.

The questions raised by Köbben and others about the statistical type of study are many and serious, and might be summarized as follows: The units compared are not always truly independent; the conclusions would be changed considerably if the size of the sample were increased; the items compared are taken out of context and are therefore not truly comparable; the items compared are frequently atomized traits rather than functioning wholes; questions asked of the materials are frequently beyond what the data can answer (this applies better to the culture-personality studies than to Murdock's *Social Structure*). The study of Whiting and Child (1953) raises an additional question by its use of a presumed modal or average custom as the basic unit of comparison. It thereby maximizes one of the weaknesses of anthropological reporting of the past, namely, the assumption of an underlying homogeneity in the customs of so-called primitive peoples. We have here indeed a curious combination of sophisticated statistical techniques applied to poor materials in such a way as to eliminate by definition the possibility of studying the range of behavior or custom within any of the societies examined.

Murdock and Whiting (1951) and Whiting (1954) among others, are not unaware of the problems posed by the criticism, and when pressed, have admitted to some crucial weaknesses. For example, when Erikson (1950, p. 38), in discussing the 1951 paper by Murdock and Whiting, suggested that most anthropological data on parental attitudes and child training was extremely uneven and unsystematic and rarely distinguished between observed behavior, ideal patterns, or projections of the investigators' stereotypes, Murdock replied (pp. 40–41):

> "The points he (Erikson) made raise very serious problems. . . . In justification of our method, we can only say that in our selected societies, in general, what the sources report is what the informants said was supposed to be the case, so that the comparisons are generally between two supposed or ideal patterns. We have to assume, to make these results valid, that the difference between the ideal pattern and the

manifest behavior is approximately the same from society to society, which is a very questionable assumption, I grant."

Granting limitations in the data and the methods used, many social scientists find the hypotheses themselves stimulating and suggestive. In this connection it appears to the writer that of all the recent cross-cultural studies of a statistical nature done on the grand scale, Murdock's is the most original and creative in the sense that he is not simply testing Freudian or Hullian hypotheses derived from the data of western societies, but that he comes up with original general propositions derived from the data of non-Western societies.

To this writer one of the contributions of the studies by Whiting is to reveal the serious gaps in anthropological data on culture and personality for cross-cultural comparative purposes and the need for planned comparative field research. Whiting and colleagues are now engaged in such a project, "Field Guide for a Study of Socialization in Five Societies," 1954. The detailed directions and questions to field workers recently prepared by Whiting and colleagues to insure greater comparability of data is evidence of the lessons learned from working with library materials.

Broad Typological Comparisons

The outstanding item is the book by Redfield on *The Primitive World and Its Transformations,* which is a comparison on a vast scale, of mankind all over the world before "civilization," i.e., before the growth of cities, with that after the growth of cities. While recognizing the wide range of cultural differences among precivilized (prior to 6000 B. C.) and contemporary primitive peoples, both of whom are treated together, Redfield (1953, p. 1) attempts to go beyond cultural relativism and asks the question: What do these peoples have in common, irrespective of "whether they lived in the arctic or in the tropics, whether they hunted, fished, or farmed," which sets them apart from civilized man? His findings are stated in terms of the now familiar characteristics of the folk society, namely, isolation, homogeneity, the predominance of the moral order, etc. However, Redfield's major concern is with the broad problem of culture change, of evolution, and of the transformation of the folk societies into other kinds of societies, peasant and urban.

In terms of the global nature of the design Redfield yields nothing to the statistically oriented studies. But unlike the latter, which suffer from atomism, Redfield, in the great humanist tradition, never loses sight of man as a whole, and maintains the sense of the wholeness of culture by his constructed types. But at the same time, the emphasis upon the similarities within the type and the lumping together of prehistoric peoples with contemporary primitive peoples tend to neglect differences. Perhaps this weakness, if it is a weakness, is inevitable when working on such a high level of abstraction without the controls inherent in the more limited kinds of comparisons to be considered later. Moreover, in a recent paper on "The Cultural Role of Cities," Redfield and Singer (1954) take a long step in the direction of correcting the earlier stereotyped urban category by showing the considerable range in the forms and functions of cities in different historical periods in various parts of the world.

Although Steward's recent work on Puerto Rico is in our category of studies within a single nation, his theoretical approach properly belongs here. It too, is a typological approach of a global nature which cuts across culture areas to seek out the phenomena intended for study. It shares some of the strengths and weaknesses of the Redfield approach. It differs from the latter, however, in that it deals with more limited problems, for it strives for empirically derived, rather than ideal, types; it shows greater concern with developmental sequences; it is more selective in the variables treated; and, on the whole, manifests a materialistic rather than an idealistic philosophical position. The major emphasis is upon productive relations, technology, social structure, and ecology. Values and ethics are given much less weight;

indeed, some would feel they are neglected, and perhaps it is this which makes for a somewhat mechanistic approach.

COMPARISONS BETWEEN CONTINENTS OR NATIONS

Three books, 16 articles and 1 dissertation, or a total of 20 out of 220 writings examined, fall into this category. This category is defined by the fact that the comparisons are either between nations or major civilizations as such, or are between societies or aspects thereof, located in different nations or continents. Six are library studies, six are a combination of library and field work, and eight are based primarily upon field work.

The range of content of these studies is narrower than that of the global studies. Studies of religion (7), total culture (6), economics (5), and social organization (3) account for over ninety per cent of all the studies.[11] The studies in this category fall into the following groups: 1. *Comparisons between One or More Major Civilizations* (4 cases),[12] 2. *Studies of Variants of One Culture, or Aspects Thereof, in Two Continents* (6 cases),[13] 3. *Problem Oriented Studies with Examples from Two Continents or Nations* (8 cases),[14] and 4. *Distribution Studies, Independent Invention vs. Diffusion* (2 cases).[15]

The studies in this category lend themselves to a variety of interesting theoretical problems. On the whole, the studies are of two contrasting types: first, those which compare historically related peoples and attempt to show the re-adaptations and reinterpretations of culture traits or institutions in a new setting; second, those which compare historically unrelated peoples. The latter—which predominate in this geographical category—are especially suitable for pointing up contrasts, for testing the applicability of generalizations formulated on the basis of studies in other areas, and for the formulation of new hypotheses.

Hsu's interesting study (1953) is the fullest total cultural comparison between two nations done by an anthropologist in recent years. He contrasts the American "individual-centered" way of life with the Chinese "situation-centered" way of life and examines the manner in which these key concepts are reflected in child training, marriage, economics, government, religion, ethics, art, alcoholism, suicide, etc. The book is based primarily upon library sources, plus insights which have come to Hsu from living in two cultures. Hsu paints with a big brush, combines psychoanalytic and anthropological interpretations, and is often closer to the literary than the scientific tradition.

The studies by Bascom (1950, 1952) and Foster (1951, 1953) share the advantage of first-hand comparative field research in their respective areas. This, combined with the controls inherent in the historical research design, gives their work a fresh quality and lends weight to their findings. Foster's ethnographic research in Spain throws new light on the difficult problem of what is Indian and what is Spanish in Mexico and Latin America. His paper on *cofradia* and *compadrazgo* illustrates the differential role of a common trait or institution in two or more cultures, as well as the differential solution in two cultures to a basic need of both. Bascom's comparison of Cuban worship of African deities with the Yoruba practice of rituals involving stones, blood, and herbs, shows the reinterpretation of a trait cluster in a new setting. Moreover, it shows how a study of Cuba can throw light on the native African institutions, which could not be derived

11 Some of these studies cover two or three fields and are therefore listed more than once.

12 For example, Hsu, 1953, *Americans and Chinese;* Patai, 1954, "Religion in Middle Eastern, Far Eastern, and Western Culture."

13 For example, Bascom, 1950, "The Focus of Cuban Santeria"; Mintz and Wolf, 1950, "An Analysis of Ritual Co-Parenthood (Compadrazgo)"; Foster, 1953, "*Cofradia* and *Compadrazgo* in Spain and Spanish America."

14 For example, Lewis, 1954, "Peasant Culture in India and Mexico: A Study in Contrasts"; Steward and Murphy, 1954, "The Mundurucu and the Algonkians: A Parallel in Processes of Acculturation"; Needham, 1954, "Siriono and Penan: A Test of Some Hypotheses."

15 Erasmus, 1950, "Patoll, Pachisi, and the Limitation of Possibilities"; Hatt, 1951, "The Corn Mother in America and Indonesia."

from a contemporary study of Africa alone. In the same sense, it may be possible to learn much of sixteenth-century Spain by a study of contemporary Mexican societies, which could not be learned by a direct study of contemporary Spain. The study by Mintz and Wolf (1950), though not based on comparative field work in the regions compared, relies heavily upon historical controls, and is of a high caliber of scholarship.

Lewis's detailed comparison between a Mexican and a north Indian village (1954), based upon field work in each village, covers social organization, economics, politics, and other aspects of culture. He found that despite similarities in their economic base, the two villages had strikingly different systems of social organization. This suggests that we need to restudy the whole problem of peasant communities in greater detail, and within nations and regions, before we can venture broader generalizations about peasantry as a whole.

Goldschmidt's fascinating comparisons (1951) between the Protestant ethic of sixteenth-century Europe with the values of the Hurok-Hupa and other California tribes raises important critical questions about our traditional assumptions as to the relationship between economy, social structure, and value systems. Steward and Murphy, concerned more with structure than culture content, show (1954) how the fur-trapping Montaignais and the rubber-tapping Mundurucu develop similar types of social organization in reaction to a market economy.

Needham (1954), drawing upon a field study of the forest Penan of Borneo offers both confirmatory and contradictory findings on Holmberg's seventeen hypotheses derived from his study of the Siriono of Bolivia. Holmberg's hypotheses were intended to apply to societies "where conditions of food insecurity and hunger frustration are comparable to those found among the Siriono." Penan meets these conditions admirably. However, Needham was able to confirm only five of seventeen hypotheses; two could not be tested, and ten were patently contradicted. Space permits only two examples of the latter. One of Holmberg's hypotheses is that "Aggression will be expressed largely in terms of food: if not, such aggression will be so severely punished that it will be almost entirely repressed." However, Needham writes (p. 230):

> Aggression in Penan society cannot be expressed in terms of food. They do not fight and quarrel about food, do not manifest a strong reluctance to share food, and do not lie about food. On the contrary, they are extremely punctilious about sharing equally in all circumstances . . . .
>
> Penan are born into a culture lacking these aggressive features, and there are no sure signs that it is only severe disapproval of them which represses the assumed aggressive desires. The reaction of Penan culture to food insecurity is not individualistic aggressiveness but scrupulously exact sharing.

Another hypothesis of Holmberg was that "There will be a tendency to kill, neglect, or otherwise dispose of the aged, the deformed young, and the extremely ill. If not, such dependents will occupy a favored status in the society."

To this Needham writes (p. 232):

> This is completely false of the Penan, in conception and action. The old, deformed, and extremely ill are cared for in every way known to the Penan. The group changes or postpones its movements for their sake, even to the considerable detriment of its members. No suggestion so horrifies the Penan as that they might kill, abandon, neglect, or otherwise dispose of such individuals. On the other hand, these are recognized for the burdens they are on the group, and in no way occupy a favored status.

COMPARISONS WITHIN ONE CONTINENT

Three books, 24 articles and 4 dissertations, a total of 31 out of 220 writings, fall in this group, which is defined by the fact that the entities compared, be they single traits, institutions, cultures, or culture areas, are within a single continent.[16] Twenty studies are purely library comparisons, seven combine library and field work, and four are based primarily upon field work.

[16] Note our inclusion of Latin America within this category.

The content covers a wide range, 19 out of 21 content categories. The greatest concentration is in social organization (13 cases), followed by total culture (7), acculturation (4), economics (4), art (3), etc.

These studies fall into four groups: 1. *Culture Area Studies* (5 cases),[17] 2. *Typological Studies* (6 cases),[18] 3. *Problem Oriented Studies Comparing One or More Aspects of a Culture* (9 cases),[19] and 4. *Distribution Studies* (9 cases).[20]

The studies in this category, though preponderantly library comparisons are, on the whole, of high quality, and capitalize upon the controls inherent in the study of continuous geographical areas which, though large, have usually been subject to common historical influences. It should be noted that most of the comparative studies of culture areas are found here. Space permits brief consideration of only three studies.

Lowie's paper (1952) "The Heterogeneity of Marginal Cultures" is critical of the traditional typology which distinguishes sharply between food-collectors and food-producers because, among other reasons, it tends to overlook important differences among the cultures within each type. Lowie stresses the wide range of variation in the culture of food-collectors, in ecological adaptation, social organization, and religion, and emphasizes the creativity of such peoples.

Foster's paper (1952), "Relationships Between Theoretical and Applied Anthropology: A Public Health Program Analysis," reports on a study of the operation of a health program in seven Latin American countries, sponsored by the Health and Sanitation Division of the Institute of Inter-American Affairs. It is one of the few comparative analyses in the field of applied anthropology. This cross-cultural study of "folk medicine" and the nature of interpersonal relationships between patients and doctors revealed a number of basic similarities in all the countries and suggested (p. 16) that regularities are of sufficiently wide validity to supply useful guide lines for health programs in other Latin American countries and in other parts of the world where similar culture types exist.

Wolf's paper (1955), "Types of Latin American Peasantry: A Preliminary Discussion," raises the interesting question of the differential effects of the industrial revolution and the growing world market upon peasantry. He distinguishes seven types of peasantry in Latin America. Two of these—the "corporate type" and the "open type"—are treated in detail. The "corporate type" of the highland areas is characterized by location on marginal land, use of a traditional technology, limited production (primarily for subsistence), reliance upon a variety of occupations to supplement income from agriculture, a strong sense of community defined in terms of the politico-religious system, the predominance of the nuclear family, conspicuous consumption geared to religiously oriented communal ends rather than individual maximation, a "cult of poverty" based upon the need to restrict expenditures, and institutionalized envy.

The "open type," located in the tropical humid lowlands, is characterized by production of a cash crop (sugar cane, bananas, coffee, etc.) for the world market, dependence upon outside capital, the private ownership of land, an alternating cycle between reliance upon subsistence crops and reliance upon cash crops, a greater emphasis upon individualism, a weaker sense of community solidarity, the accumulation and display of wealth, and greater social and economic mobility.

[17] For example, Naroll, 1950, "A Draft Map of the Culture Areas of Asia"; Murdock, 1951, "South American Culture Areas"; Lange, 1953, "A Reappraisal of Evidence of Plains Influences among the Rio Grande Pueblos."

[18] For example, Smith, 1951, "American Indian Warfare"; Bacon, 1954, "Types of Pastoral Nomadism in Central and Southwest Asia"; Wolf, 1955, "A Typology of Peasantry for Latin America."

[19] For example, Flannery, 1952, "Two Concepts of Power"; Goldfrank, 1952, "The Different Patterns of Blackfoot and Pueblo Adaptation to White Authority"; Lowie, 1952, "The Heterogeneity of Marginal Cultures"; Foster, 1952, "Relationships between Theoretical and Applied Anthropology."

[20] For example, Collins, 1951, "Antiquity of the Pineapple in America"; Riley, 1952, "The Blowgun in the New World"; Spinden, 1952, "Power Animals in American Indian Art."

COMPARISONS WITHIN ONE NATION

Three books, 27 articles, and 1 dissertation, a total of 31 writings out of 220, are in this category, in which we find for the first time that the greatest proportion of the comparative studies are based primarily upon field work. Twenty-two studies are based primarily upon field work, six upon a combination of library work and field work, and only three are purely library comparisons.

While there is a considerable range in the content of these studies—15 of our 21 content categories, there is a marked clustering: acculturation (10), economics (8), social organization (7), total culture studies (6), personality and culture (3), etc.

The studies can be divided conveniently into three groups: 1. *Comparisons of Regions, Sub-cultures, or Total Communities* (8 cases),[21] 2. *The Documentation of Range of Variation* (10 cases),[22] and 3. *Culture Change* (14 cases).[23]

Taken as a whole, the category of comparisons within a nation contains some of the most interesting studies, in terms of content, competence, and originality of research design. The study of Puerto Rico by a few research teams under the direction of Steward is a case in point. In line with his concept of socio-cultural levels of integration, Steward stresses the need to distinguish between what is local and what is national in community and regional studies. Viewing Puerto Rico as a socio-cultural whole characterized as a tropical island with a long history of colonial dependency, "part of a capitalistic world," depending upon cash, credit, an export crop, and importing nearly all of its manufactured goods and about half its food, an attempt was made to formulate and test hypotheses which would hold for Puerto Rico and similar "socio-cultural wholes" anywhere in the world. Critical of national character studies and assuming that no single community was Puerto Rico in microcosm, detailed field studies were organized in four rural communities to sample some of the major crop and community types on the island. In addition, a study was made of prominent upper-class families. Although Steward uses the term "sociocultural" the greatest emphasis is clearly upon economic variables, such as methods of production technology, crops, cash, credit, markets, etc. Moreover, the emphasis is upon structural analysis rather than culture content.

Another very interesting study is the comparison of a highland and lowland Totonac village in Mexico, based upon first-hand field work in each (Viqueira and Palerm, 1954). This is one of the few comparative studies in Mexico since Redfield's *Folk Culture of Yucatan* (1941). Eloxochitlan, the highland community, has an economy of scarcity, population pressure, production primarily for subsistence, strong political controls, community solidarity against the outside, collective labor, monogamy, and the predominance of the nuclear family. The world is viewed as hostile, and sorcery and black magic are all pervasive. Tajin, the lowland community, has an economy of relative abundance, an important cash crop in vanilla, the predominance of the extended family, polygyny, an almost Apollonian sense of order and restraint, and the absence of sorcery. Against this background the authors contrast the differential role of alcoholism. In the highland village, drinking is frequent, generalized, socially sanctioned, and drunkenness is common but inoffensive, leading to social cohesion and euphoria. In the low-

[21] For example, Ryan, 1950, "Socio-Cultural Regions of Ceylon"; Fried, 1952, "Chinese Society: Class as Sub-culture"; Viqueira and Palerm, 1954, "Alcoholismo, Brujeria y Homocidio en dos Comunidades Rurales de México"; Manners and Steward, 1953, "The Cultural Study of Contemporary Societies: Puerto Rico."

[22] For example, Wagley, 1952, *Race and Class in Rural Brazil;* Wolf, 1952, "Growing Up and Its Price in Three Puerto Rican Subcultures"; Sanders, 1953, "Village Social Organization in Greece."

[23] For example, Raper, 1951, "Some Recent Changes in Japanese Village Life"; Du Wors, 1952, "Persistence and Change in Local Values of Two New England Communities"; and Zen Sun, 1952, "Results of Culture Contact in Two Mongol-Chinese Communities"; Caudill, 1952, *Japanese-American Personality and Acculturation;* Van der Kroef, 1954, "Disorganization and Social Change in Rural Indonesia."

land village, drinking is infrequent, drunkenness rare, but when it occurs it almost inevitably leads to violence and homicide.

COMPARISONS WITHIN A SINGLE CULTURE AREA OR REGION

This category is defined in terms of comparisons within a single culture area or attempts to treat the area as a unit. It is by far the largest category, with a total of 70 studies: 12 books, 45 articles, and 13 dissertations. Twenty-three are library comparisons, thirty-seven library plus field work, and ten primarily field work. The content coverage is extremely broad, including 19 out of our 21 content categories, with only sex and mythology absent. The greatest concentration, however, is in studies of social organization (30 cases), followed by total culture (11), religion (9), economics (5), technology (5), settlement patterns (4), etc.

The 70 studies of this category can be grouped as follows: 1. *Reviews of Research Trends on One or More Aspects of an Area* (4 cases),[24] 2. *Definitions and/or Reconstruction of Culture Areas* (6 cases),[25] 3. *Detailed, Intensive, Functional Analyses of One or More Aspects of Culture in a Small Number of Societies* (14 cases),[26] 4. *Survey Studies of a Single Aspect of Culture among a Larger Number of Societies* (15 cases),[27] 5. *Studies Concerned Primarily with Culture Change, either in Terms of Acculturation or Internal Development (Evolution) or Both* (12 cases),[28] 6. *Studies of Relations between Communities* (3 cases),[29] and 7. *Single-trait Distribution Studies* (5 cases).[30]

Before commenting upon some of the exemplary studies of this category, it should be noted that, within the past few years, a number of anthropologists have reaffirmed the earlier Boasian position on the methodological advantages possible by careful studies within the context of a single culture area. Kluckhohn (1954) quotes the Boas statement that a primary requirement for valid comparison is that the phenomena compared be derived "psychologically or historically from common causes. . . ." Kluckhohn writes (p. 693):

> "One of the main rewards of intensive study of a culture area . . . is that such study eventually frees investigators to raise genuinely scientific questions—problems of process. Once the influences of various cultures upon others in the same area and the effects of a common environment (and its variant forms) have been reasonably well ascertained, one can then operate to a first approximation under an 'all other things being equal' hypothesis and intensively examine the question: why are these cultures and these modal personality types still different in spite of similar environmental stimuli . . . and access over long periods to the influence of generalized area culture or cultures. We are ready now, I believe, for such studies, but no one is yet attempting them seriously."

[24] Evans-Pritchard, 1952, "Nilotic Studies"; Elkin, 1953, *Social Anthropology in Melanesia;* Kluckhohn, 1954, "Southwestern Studies of Culture and Personality"; Keesing, 1953, *Social Anthropology in Polynesia.*

[25] For example, Kirchhoff, 1952, "Meso-America"; Smith, 1952, "Culture Area and Culture Depth: With Data from the Northwest Coast"; Read, 1954, "Cultures of the Central Highlands, New Guinea."

[26] For example, Eggan, 1950, *Social Organization of the Western Pueblos;* Richards, 1950, "Some Types of Family Structure amongst the Central Bantu"; Nadel, 1950, "Dual Descent in the Nuba Hills"; Nadel, 1952, "Witchcraft in Four African Societies: An Essay in Comparison"; Smith, 1953, "Secondary Marriage in Northern Nigeria."

[27] For example, Paul and Paul, 1952, "The Life Cycle"; Fischer, 1950, "The Concept of Incest in Sumatra"; Hogbin and Wedgewood, 1953, "Local Grouping in Melanesia"; Berndt, 1951, "Ceremonial Exchange in Western Arnhem Land"; Wisdom, 1952, "The Supernatural World and Curing."

[28] For example, Tax, 1952b, "The Sixteenth Century and the Twentieth"; Lystad, 1951, "Differential Acculturation of the Ahafo-Ashanti of the Gold Coast and the Indenie-Agni of the Ivory Coast"; Leacock, 1954, *The Montagnais Hunting Territory and the Fur Trade;* Secoy, 1953, *Changing Military Patterns on the Great Plains;* Wagley, 1951, "Cultural Influences on Population: A Comparison of Two Tupi Tribes."

[29] Honigmann, 1952, "Intercultural Relations at Great Whale River"; Starr, 1954, "Levels of Communal Relations"; Underhill, 1954, "Intercultural Relations in the Greater Southwest."

[30] For example, Riesenfeld, 1951, "Tobacco in New Guinea and Other Areas of Melanesia"; Suttles, 1951, "The Early Distribution of the Potato among the Coast Salish"; Lemert, 1952, "Stuttering among the North Pacific Coastal Indians."

Schapera (1953, p. 359) claims at least three advantages for the intensive study of single regions as over against global or random comparisons, namely, it eliminates the need for sampling (since all the peoples of an area should be studied), it solves the problem of what is the proper unit for comparative study, and eliminates the need to deal with large numbers of societies. Instead, the method relies heavily upon typologies. Once types have been established for a region, they can be tested in adjoining regions and later in distant regions.

Eggan (1954, p. 746), too, prefers "the utilization of the comparative method on a smaller scale and with as much control over the frame of comparison as it is possible to secure. It has seemed natural to utilize regions of relatively homogeneous culture or to work within social or cultural types, and to further control the ecology and the historical factors as far as it is possible to do so."

Goldman has given us a forceful statement (1955) on the value of the intensive study of culture areas, especially for arriving at generalizations concerning cultural evolution. He writes (p. 1):

> "Cultural evolution, to rephrase Maitland's classic remark, will be history or nothing. If it is to be history its proper focus is the culture area, or to be more precise, the comparative study of culture areas. A culture area comprises historically related societies each showing significant variations from a common pattern. In these variations—their nature, origin and direction—are revealed the basic processes of cultural development in the area—that is, its cultural evolution. From a comparison of culture areas rather than from the comparative study of historically unrelated societies may emerge the more general and more meaningful laws of development."

Despite the recognition of the great potentialities for deriving scientific generalizations by the intensive study of culture areas, there is still a surprising paucity of adequate and well rounded area studies. Kluckhohn (1954, p. 757) and Eggan (1954, p. 689) independently have pointed this out. This impression is confirmed further by our review of the comparative writings of the past five years. The single attempt at a developmental interpretation of a culture area, seeking broad generalizations, and covering most aspects of the culture, is Goldman's study (1955) on "Status Rivalry and Cultural Evolution in Polynesia"—all the more striking as an example of what can be done by purely library research, given an adequate theoretical frame of reference.

Goldman classifies eighteen Polynesian societies into three types: traditional (10 societies), where social status is based primarily upon seniority of age or lineage and social mobility is limited; open (4 societies), "paying lip service to hereditary rank, (they) reserved their honors for outstanding achievement in war and tribal politics. . . . Social mobility was, accordingly, very high and status gradations were uneven"; and stratified (4 societies), where the distinctive feature was "the fundamental cleavage between the landed and the landless." These three types represent stages of social, economic, political, and religious complexity and are due primarily to an evolutionary process of internal development within Polynesia rather than to diffusion, as is evidenced by the fact that single societies seem to recapitulate the development of the entire area. Goldman then summarizes the fundamental changes in the Polynesian status systems in a series of thirty-eight general developmental propositions covering religion, authority, property, social organization, warfare, etc. These propositions serve as hypotheses which can be tested in other areas. One of the distinctive aspects of this work is the central role it gives to value systems; in the case of Polynesia it is status rivalry, and the manner in which it relates changes in value systems to changes in other aspects of culture.

While most of the studies in a single culture area deal with more limited problems than those considered by Goldman, many are models of controlled comparisons approaching very close to experimental studies. Nadel's study (1952) of witchcraft is a model of this type in which a large number of factors are controlled so that a single variable can be tested. In Nadel's study of witchcraft each of the two pairs of societies shows wide cultural similarities with only a few differences, chief of which is the role of witchcraft or its absence. Nadel demonstrates how the witchcraft beliefs are causally related to specific anxieties in social life, in Nupe due to marriage relations, in Mesakin due to relations between mother's brother and sister's son. He stresses the role of adult experiences in addition to infantile experiences in the formation of anxieties in the societies examined, and attempts to test a Freudian hypothesis in terms of his findings.

The research model of Wagley's paper (1951) on differential population trends among two Tupi tribes under the influence of white contact, is much the same as Nadel's, although the problem here is culture change. The tribes examined share many cultural similarities as well as a common language, but are shown to have differed, even in aboriginal times, in the attitudes toward family size, which in turn was related to other differences between them.

COMPARISONS WITHIN A SINGLE LOCAL GROUP OR CULTURE

Twenty-two articles and twelve books, a total of thirty-four items, fall into this category. The range of content is fairly wide, touching upon 15 of our 21 content items. However, the greatest concentration is in studies of culture change and acculturation (22), followed by social organization (8), total culture (7), personality and culture (6), values (4), economics (4), etc. As we have noted earlier, 25 studies are based primarily upon field work and 9 upon a combination of field work and library research.

As a group these studies are fresh and reflect some of the most sophisticated methodological trends, both in field work and research design, to be found in contemporary anthropology. Most of the studies are theoretically eclectic, combining a number of interests and approaches, chief of which is the concern with culture change, functional and historical analysis, restudies, the use of quantification and the documentation of range of variation within a single community, and finally, the control of as many variables as possible so as to approach the experimental method.

It is difficult to classify these studies into sub-groups without considerable overlapping. However, the following sub-divisions may serve for our purpose: 1. *Studies Dealing with Research Methods* (4 cases),[31] 2. *Restudies by the Same Investigator* (3 cases),[32] 3. *Restudies by Different Investigators* (4 cases),[33] 4. *Studies Showing Range of Variation in Culture Forms or Personality* (9 cases),[34] 5. *Acculturation Studies* (6 cases),[35] and 6. *Historical Reconstructions Based upon Library and/or Field Work* (9 cases).[36]

The pros and cons of restudies, both in providing a baseline for the study of culture change and as a test of the reliability of anthropological reporting, have been discussed by Lewis (1951, 1953). However, studies dealing with range of variation, for

[31] For example, Barnes, 1951, "Measures of Divorce Frequency in Simple Societies"; Goldschmidt and Spindler, 1952, "Experimental Design in the Study of Culture Change"; Colson, 1954, "The Intensive Study of Small Sample Communities."

[32] Redfield, 1950, *A Village that Chose Progress: Chan Kom Revisited;* Mead, 1954, "Manus Restudied: An Interim Report"; and Firth's restudy of Tikopia.

[33] For example, Lewis, 1951, *Life in a Mexican Village: Tepoztlán Restudied;* Firth, 1952, "Notes on the Social Structure of Some South-Eastern New Guinea Communities"; Nett, 1952, "Historical Changes in the Osage Kinship System."

[34] For example, Roberts, 1951, *Three Navaho Households;* Vogt, 1951, *Navaho Veterans, A Study of Changing Values;* Fenton (ed.), 1951, *Symposium on Local Diversity in Iroquois Culture;* Hart, 1954, "The Sons of Turimpi"; Mandelbaum, 1954, "Form, Variation and Meaning of a Ceremony"; and Tremblay, Collier, and Sasaki, 1954, "Navaho Housing in Transition."

[35] For example, Barnouw, 1950, *Acculturation and Personality among the Wisconsin Chippewa;* Hallowell, 1952, "Ojibwa Personality and Acculturation"; Spindler, 1952, "Personality and Peyotism in Menomini Indian Acculturation."

[36] For example, Bascom, 1950, "Ponape: The Cycle of Empire"; Kaplan, 1951, "Changing Functions of the Huanancha Dance at the Corpus Christi Festival in Paracho, Michoacán," México; Hogbin, 1951, *Transformation Scene: The Changing Culture of a New Guinea Village;* Marriott, 1952, "Social Change in an Indian Village"; Schmidt and Schmidt, 1952, *Wichita Kinship: Past and Present.*

which Herskovits (1954) has suggested the term "microethnography," deserve further comment.

These studies are a much needed corrective to the tendency of anthropologists in the past to assume the essential homogeneity of the culture of folk societies or little communities. The demonstration by some of the articles cited above of a wide range in personality, in family life, and in ceremonial forms, within relatively simple and homogeneous societies, highlights the difference between real and ideal culture patterns, leads to a search for more refined concepts than the catch-all of basic personality and culture, and focuses upon the role of additional factors—personal, social, situational, environmental, accidental, etc. The studies by Vogt (1951), Roberts (1951), Voget (1952), Hart (1954), and Mandelbaum (1954) illustrate some of these points.

Despite a presumed Navaho basic personality, Vogt is more impressed by the range of variation in the reactions of twelve Navaho veterans to army life experiences, than by the common elements. He relates the differential changes in attitudes and values to specific life experiences before entering the army as well as to army experiences. As a result we get a picture of acculturation in terms of understandable human beings rather than as stereotypes and averages.

Mandelbaum's vivid and detailed description of a funeral ceremony and its variations within a single community with a population of 1,200, leads him to suggest a typology of variations in terms of invariant patterns, alternative patterns, contingent patterns, elective patterns, patterns of neutral variation, optative patterns, weighted alternatives, and compulsive alternatives. He then discusses the meaning of the modal statements of anthropologists in the light of these variations.

CONCLUSIONS

One of the distinctive characteristics of cultural or social anthropology has been its simultaneous concern with the intensive and holistic study of small societies and their cultures and with the comparative analysis of these same societies and cultures over the entire world. Traditionally, the former has been based upon field work and comparative analysis, the latter upon library studies, with or without the statistical manipulation of large masses of data.

Our survey of the comparative studies over the past five years reveals an important trend in the relationship between these two aspects of our discipline. Comparative anthropology no longer can be defined as a library method and is becoming increasingly based upon field work. Comparisons based upon library research alone constitute only one-third of all the studies examined. Moreover, most anthropologists have had first-hand experience both in the intensive study of small communities and in comparative cross-cultural analysis.

By the traditional definition of comparative anthropology as cross-cultural comparisons, the many comparisons within a single community or culture which we have cited would have been excluded. However, there is a need to broaden our view of comparative anthropology to include the latter type studies, for our theoretical writing has lagged behind the actual field work. We have included such studies, therefore, as a legitimate part of comparative anthropology because they can make an important contribution in their own right toward the formulation of general principles, and in addition can help establish a more solid basis for cross-cultural comparisons by their careful definition of types and their increasing use of quantification. In short, now that anthropology has achieved its historic task of documenting the wide range of variation in the cultures of the world, we can join our sociological brethren and take a closer and more careful look at individual small societies. The numerous studies and restudies of "microethnography" which we have cited reflect this trend. These studies also reveal a much wider range of variation than might have been expected from our earlier overplaying of homogeneity, and this variation, in turn, serves as a basis for comparative analysis.

The trend toward comparisons based upon first-hand field work in more than one society holds great promise for improving the quality of comparative studies. Field work by the same investigator in the societies compared assures greater comparability of data and leads to more refined insights than is generally possible in working with library data alone. It is important that anthropologists become more aware of the advantages inherent in this kind of comparative study. We suspect that many who have done field work in more than a single society have not given us the benefit of their comparative experience, in terms either of their field problems or of detailed comparative analysis of their data.

On the whole, first-hand field experience in different societies is of greatest value for comparative analysis when the societies compared are on the same general socioeconomic level. For example, Lewis' study (1942) of the Blackfoot Indians of Canada, a tribal reservation people, was of little help in his later study (1951) of the peasant village of Tepoztlán, Mexico. On the other hand, the study of Tepoztlán was of enormous help in his later studies of peasantry in Spain, Cuba, and India. If this observation is confirmed by the experiences of others, it has some implications for training programs and planning field research for students. For a marked improvement in comparative anthropology, it might be wise to encourage our students to specialize either in tribal, peasant, or rural societies.

Comparative studies in anthropology might be grouped into two broad types: first, comparisons of historically related societies, in which common history, language, and culture serve as controls against which variables may be tested; and second, comparisons of historically unrelated societies in which similarities in form, structure, and process are a basis for establishing typologies or causal relationships between various aspects of culture. These two approaches clearly are reflected in our earlier grouping of studies by the location in space of the entities compared. On the whole, the three smaller spatial categories, i.e., comparisons within a single community or culture, comparisons within a single culture area, and comparisons within a single nation, contain examples of the first approach, while the three larger categories, i.e., comparisons within a continent, between nations and continents, and global comparisons, contain examples of the latter. The major exceptions are the relatively few studies of Africanisms in the New World and of Spanish influences in Latin America.

While highly competent and interesting studies are to be found in each approach, it seems that each has its distinctive strengths and weaknesses. Some of the advantages of the former are: (1) a large proportion of the studies are based upon first-hand comparative field research, (2) there is a greater certainty about the comparability of the data, (3) the wholeness of culture is maintained and aspects of culture are seen in context, (4) a larger number of variables can be studied functionally, and (5) the objectives generally are of limited scope and the research designs more closely approximate those of the experimental method. Certainly the bulk of our model, small-scale, comparative studies are found in this approach. Perhaps the single greatest weakness to be noted is the lack of broad developmental hypotheses and the paucity of intensive comparative analyses of culture areas as wholes.

The comparative studies based upon historically unrelated societies are, as a whole, more ambitious, seek broader generalizations on a wider scale, in terms either of universals, world-wide typologies, or evolutionary sequences, and are based primarily upon library studies rather than field work. Here we must distinguish between the statistical studies which rely upon a large number of cases, control only a few variables, and tend to atomize culture, and the broader typological studies which seek to maintain the wholeness of culture by establishing types based upon form, structure, content, and process. Though lacking many of the controls inherent in the more limited studies, many of these studies seem more daring and give the satisfaction which comes from painting with a big brush and searching for general laws.

One of the problems of contemporary anthropology is to develop a strategy of research which will combine the strengths of each of the two major approaches outlined above. The quality and reliability of comparative cross-cultural analysis can hardly be better than that of the original field data upon which it is based. As the intensive studies of particular societies improve, they make possible more meaningful and higher quality comparative studies. Similarly, comparative studies point up the weaknesses or lacks in data, confirm or refute favorite hypotheses, and help thereby to guide further field research. Some anthropologists prefer to wait for better data from single societies before attempting world-wide comparisons. Others utilize whatever data is now available on the ground that we cannot afford to lose time. Others would change the research design and employ more limited and controlled comparisons. Finally, still others place their greatest faith in organizing comparative field research projects around specific problems of limited scope.

In conclusion, our survey of the literature of the past five years has revealed a remarkably large number of comparative studies of high quality, a broad coverage of subject matter, a variety of methods and approaches, a wide range of objectives, and a healthy eclecticism which speaks well for anthropology and its future.

REFERENCES

THEORETICAL WRITINGS

ACKERKNECHT, ERWIN H.
1954 "On the Comparative Method in Anthropology," pp. 117–125 in Spencer, Robert F. (ed.), *Method and Perspective in Anthropology*. Minneapolis: University of Minnesota Press. 323 pp.

BECKER, HOWARD
1954 "Anthropology and Sociology," pp. 102–159 in Gillin, John (ed.), *For A Science of Social Man*. New York: The Macmillan Company. 289 pp.

BIDNEY, DAVID
1954 "The Ethnology of Religion and the Problem of Human Evolution," *American Anthropologist*, Vol. 86, No. 1, Feb., pp. 1–18.

BRAM, JOSEPH
1953 "The Application of Psychodrama to Research in Social Anthropology," *Transactions of the New York Academy of Sciences*, Vol. 151, No. 7, pp. 253–257.

EGGAN, FRED
1954 "Social Anthropology and the Method of Controlled Comparison," *American Anthropologist*, Vol. 56, No. 5, Pt. 1, pp. 743–763.

EVANS-PRITCHARD, E. E.
1951 *Social Anthropology*. London: Cohen and West. 134 pp.

FIRTH, RAYMOND
1951a "Contemporary British Social Anthropology," *American Anthropologist*, Vol. 53, No. 4, Pt. 1, pp. 474–489.
1951b *Elements of Social Organization*. New York: Philosophical Library. 257 pp.

GOLDSCHMIDT, WALTER
1950 "Social Class in America—A Critical Review," *American Anthropologist*, Vol. 52, No. 4, Pt. 1, pp. 483–498.

HALLOWELL, IRVING A.
1954 "Psychology and Anthropology," pp. 160–226 in Gillin, John (ed.), *For A Science of Social Man*, New York: The Macmillan Company. 289 pp.

HENRY, JULES
1953 "Direct Observations and Psychological Tests in Anthropological Field Work," *American Anthropologist*, Vol. 55, No. 4, pp. 461–480.

HERSKOVITS, MELVILLE J.
1954 "Some Problems of Method in Ethnography," pp. 3–24 in Spencer, Robert F. (ed.), *Method and Perspective in Anthropology*. Minneapolis: University of Minnesota Press. 323 pp.

HILGER, SISTER M. INEZ
1954 "An Ethnographic Field Method," pp. 28–42 in Spencer, Robert F. (ed.), *Method and Perspective in Anthropology*. Minneapolis: University of Minnesota Press. 323 pp.

KLUCKHOHN, CLYDE
1953 "Universal Categories of Culture," pp. 507–523 in Kroeber, A. L. and others, *Anthropology Today*. Chicago: University of Chicago Press. 966 pp.
1954 "Southwestern Studies of Culture and Personality," *American Anthropologist*, Vol. 56, No. 4, Pt. 1, pp. 685–697.

KÖBBEN, A. J.
1952 "New Ways of Presenting an Old Idea: The Statistical Method in Social Anthropology," *Journal of the Royal Anthropological Institute of Great Britain and Ireland*, Vol. LXXXII, Pt. 2, pp. 129–146.

KROEBER, A. L.
1954 "Critical Summary and Commentary," pp. 273–299 in Spencer, Robert F. (ed.), *Method and Perspective in Anthropology*. Minneapolis: University of Minnesota Press. 323 pp.

KROEBER, A. L. and KLUCKHOHN, CLYDE
1952 *Culture: A Critical Review of Concepts and Definitions*, Papers of the Peabody Museum of American Archaeology and Ethnology, Harvard University, Vol. XLVII, No. 1). Cambridge, Mass. 223 pp.

LEVY, MARION J., JR.
1952 *The Structure of Society*. Princeton, N. J.: Princeton University Press. 584 pp.

LEWIS, OSCAR
1953 "Controls and Experiments in Field Work," pp. 452–475 in Kroeber, A. L. and others, *Anthropology Today*. Chicago: University of Chicago Press. 966 pp.

LOWIE, ROBERT H.
1953 "Ethnography, Cultural and Social Anthropology," *American Anthropologist*, Vol. 55, No. 4, Oct., pp. 527–534.

MURDOCK, G. P.
1949 *Social Structure*. New York: Macmillan. 387 pp.
1950a "Feasibility and Implementation of Comparative Community Research," *American Sociological Review*, Vol. 15, No. 6, pp. 713–720.
1950b *Outline of Cultural Materials*. 2nd ed. New Haven: Yale University Press. 56 pp.
1954 "Sociology and Anthropology," pp. 14–32 in Gillin, John (ed.), *For A Science of Social Man*. New York: The Macmillan Company. 289 pp.

NADEL, S. F.
1951 *The Foundations of Social Anthropology*. Glencoe, Ill.: The Free Press. 426 pp.

RADCLIFFE-BROWN, A. R.
1951 "The Comparative Method in Anthropology," *Journal of the Royal Anthropological Institute of Great Britain and Ireland*, Vol. 81, No. 1, pp. 15–22.

RAY, VERNE F.
1952 "Techniques and Problems in the Study of Human Color Perception," *Southwestern Journal of Anthropology*, Vol. 8, No. 3, pp. 251–259.

SCHAPERA, I.
1953 "Comparative Method in Social Anthropology," *American Anthropologist*, Vol. 55, No. 3, pp. 353–361.

SINGER, MILTON B.
1953 "Summary of Comments and Discussion" (of I. Schapera, "Some Comments on Comparative Method in Social Anthropology"), *American Anthropologist*, Vol. 55, No. 4, pp. 363–366.

SMITH, BREWSTER M.
1954 "Anthropology and Psychology," pp. 32–66 in Gillin, John (ed.), *For A Science of Social Man*. New York: The Macmillan Co. 289 pp.

SMITH, MARIAN W.
1952 "Different Cultural Concepts of Past, Present, and Future, A Study of Ego Extension," *Psychiatry*, Vol. 15, No. 4, pp. 395–400.

STEWARD, JULIAN H.
1936 "The Economic and Social Basis of Primitive Bands," pp. 331–350 in Lowie, R. H. (ed.), *Essays in Anthropology*. Berkeley: University of California Press. 433 pp.

STEWARD, JULIAN H.—Cont'd
1950 *Area Research: Theory and Practice* (Social Science Research Council Bulletin 63). New York: Social Science Research Council. 164 pp.
1951 "Levels of Sociocultural Integration: An Operational Concept," *Southwestern Journal of Anthropology*, Vol. 7, No. 4, pp. 374–390.

WHITING, JOHN W. M.
1954 "The Cross-Cultural Method," pp. 523–531 in Lindzey, G. (ed.), *Handbook of Social Psychology*. Cambridge: Addison-Wesley. 2 vols.

WHITING, JOHN W. M. and colleagues
1954 "Field Guide for a Study of Socialization in Five Societies" *(manuscript)*.

GLOBAL OR RANDOM COMPARISONS

ABERLE, DAVID F.
1952 " 'Arctic Hysteria' and Latah in Mongolia," *Transactions of The New York Academy of Sciences*, Series II, Vol. 14, No. 7, May, pp. 291–297.

ANDERSON, EDGAR and CUTLER, HUGH C.
1950 "Methods of Corn Popping and Their Historical Significance," *Southwestern Journal of Anthropology*, Vol. 6, No. 3, pp. 303–308.

BALFOUR, HENRY
1951 "Ritual and Secular Uses of Vibrating Membranes as Voice Disguisers," *Journal of the Royal Anthropological Institute of Great Britain and Ireland*, Vol. LXXVIII, Pts. 1 & 2, pp. 45–70.

BARNETT, H. G.
1953 *Innovation: The Basis of Cultural Change*. New York: McGraw-Hill. 462 pp.

BOHANNAN, L. M.
1951 "A Comparative Study of Social Differentiation of Primitive Society" (Doctoral dissertation). University of Oxford.

BROWN, JULIA S.
1952 "A Comparative Study of Deviation from Sexual Mores," *American Sociological Review*, Vol. 17, No. 2, pp. 135–146.

CHARLES, LUCILLE H.
1951 "Drama in First-Naming Ceremonies," *Journal of American Folklore*, Vol. 64, No. 251, pp. 11–36.
1953 "Drama in Shaman Exorcism," *Journal of American Folklore*, Vol. 66, No. 260, pp. 95–122.

ERIKSON, ERIK H.
1950 *Childhood and Society*. New York: Norton. 397 pp.

FORD, CLELLAN S. and BEACH, FRANK A.
1951 *Patterns of Sexual Behavior*. New York: Harpers. 307 pp.

FREEDMAN, LAWRENCE Z. and FERGUSON, VERA M.
1950 "The Question of 'Painless Childbirth' in Primitive Cultures," *American Journal of Orthopsychiatry*, Vol. 20, No. 2, pp. 363–372.

FRIED, MORTON
1952 "Land Tenure, Geography and Ecology in Contact of Cultures," *American Journal of Economics and Sociology*, Vol. 11, No. 4, July, pp. 391–412.

GOODE, W. J.
1951 *Religion Among the Primitives*. Glencoe, Ill.: The Free Press. 321 pp.

HEIZER, ROBERT F.
1953 "Aboriginal Fish Poisons," *Bureau of American Ethnology Bulletin No. 151*, pp. 225–283.

HERSKOVITS, MELVILLE J.
1952 *Economic Anthropology: A Study in Comparative Economics*. New York: Knopf. 551 pp.

HOEBEL, ADAMSON E.
1954 *The Law of Primitive Man: A Study in Comparative Legal Dynamics*. Cambridge, Mass.: Harvard University Press. 357 pp.

JAMES, E. O.
1952 "Religion and Reality," *Journal of the Royal Anthropological Institute of Great Britain and Ireland*, Vol. LXXX, Pts. 1 & 2, pp. 25–36.

MCCLELLAND, D. C. and FRIEDMAN, G. A.
1952 "A Cross-Cultural Study of the Relationship between Child-Training Practices and Achievement Motivation Appearing in Folk-Tales," pp. 243–249 in Swanson, G. E.; Newcomb, T. M.; and Hartley, E. L. (eds.), *Readings in Social Psychology*. New York: Henry Holt & Co. 680 pp.

MEGGERS, BETTY J.
1954 "Environmental Limitation on the Development of Culture," *American Anthropologist*, Vol. 56, No. 6, pp. 801–824.

MURDOCK, GEORGE P.
1950 "Family Stability in Non-European Cultures," *Annals of the American Academy of Political and Social Sciences*, Vol. 270, November, pp. 195–201.

MURDOCK, GEORGE P. and WHITING, JOHN W. M.
1951 "Cultural Determination of Parental Attitudes: The Relationship between the Social Structure, Particularly Family Structure and Parental Behavior," pp. 13–34 in Senn, M. J. E. (ed.), *Problems of Infancy and Childhood* (Transactions of the Fourth Conference, March 6–7, 1950). New York: Josiah Macy, Jr. Foundation. 181 pp.

PAUL, BENJAMIN D. (ed.)
1955 (In press) *Medicine and Social Science: A Casebook*. New York: Russell Sage Foundation.

PITKIN, DONALD S.
1954 "Land Tenure and Family in an Italian Village" (Doctoral dissertation). Harvard University.

QUEEN, STUART A. and ADAMS, JOHN B.
1952 *The Family in Various Cultures*. Philadelphia: Lippincott. 280 pp.

RADIN, PAUL
1953 *The World of Primitive Man*. New York: Henry Schuman. 370 pp.

REDFIELD, ROBERT
1953 *The Primitive World and Its Transformations*. Ithaca: Cornell University Press. 185 pp.

REDFIELD, ROBERT and SINGER, MILTON
1954 "The Cultural Role of Cities," *Economic Development and Cultural Change*, Vol. 3, No. 1, pp. 53–73.

SPICER, EDWARD H. (ed.)
1952 *Human Problems in Technological Change: A Casebook*. New York: Russell Sage Foundation. 301 pp.

STEWART, OMER C.
1954 "The Forgotten Side of Ethnography," pp. 221–248 in Spencer, Robert F. (ed.), *Method and Perspective in Anthropology*. Minneapolis: University of Minnesota Press. 323 pp.

VELSEN, J. VAN
1951 "Delict in Primitive Law" (Doctoral dissertation). University of Oxford.

WHITING, BEATRICE B.
1950 "A Cross Cultural Study of Sorcery and Social Control," pp. 82–91 in Whiting, Beatrice B., *Paiute Sorcery* (Viking Fund Publications in Anthropology, No. 15). New York: The Viking Fund, Inc. 110 pp.

WHITING, JOHN M. and CHILD, IRVING L.
1953 *Child Training and Personality: A Cross-Cultural Study*. New Haven: Yale University Press. Vol. 1, 353 pp.

WRIGHT, G. O.
1952 "Projection and Displacement: A Cross-Cultural Study of the Expression of Aggression in Myths" (Doctoral dissertation). Harvard University.

YAP, M. A.
1951 "Mental Disease Peculiar to Certain Cultures: A Survey of Comparative Psychiatry," *Journal of Mental Science*, Vol. XCVII, No. 407, pp. 313–327.

COMPARISONS BETWEEN CONTINENTS OR NATIONS

BASCOM, W. R.

1950 "The Focus of Cuban Santeria," *Southwestern Journal of Anthropology*, Vol. 6, No. 1, pp. 64–68.

1952 "Two Forms of Afro-Cuban Divination," pp. 169–179 in Tax, Sol (ed.), *Selected Papers of the XXIXth International Congress of Americanists*, Vol. 2. Chicago: University of Chicago Press. 339 pp.

BOUTEILLER, MARCELLE

1950 *Chamanisme et Guerison Magique*. Paris: Presses Universitaires. 337 pp.

COMAS, JUAN

1954 "Influencia Indigena en la Medicina Hipocratica, en la Nueva Espana del Siglo XVI," *America Indigena*, Vol. 14, No. 4, October, pp. 328–361.

DREWS, R. A.

1952 "The Cultivation of Food Fish in China and Japan: a study disclosing contrasting national patterns for rearing fish consistent with the differing cultural histories of China and Japan" (Doctoral dissertation). University of Michigan.

ERASMUS, CHARLES JOHN

1950 "Patolli, Pachisi, and the Limitation of Possibilities," *Southwestern Journal of Anthropology*, Vol. 6, No. 4, pp. 369–387.

FIRTH, RAYMOND

1951 "Religious Belief and Personal Adjustment," *Journal of the Royal Anthropological Institute of Great Britain and Ireland*, Vol. LXXVIII, Pts. 1 & 2, pp. 25–43.

FOSTER, GEORGE M.

1951 "Report on an Ethnological Reconnaissance of Spain," *American Anthropologist*, Vol. 53, No. 3, pp. 311–325.

1953 "*Cofradia* and *Compadrazgo* in Spain and Spanish America," *Southwestern Journal of Anthropology*, Vol. 9, No. 1, pp. 1–28.

GOLDSCHMIDT, WALTER

1951 "Ethics and the Structure of Society. An Ethnological Contribution to the Sociology of Knowledge," *American Anthropologist*, Vol. 53, No. 4, Pt. 1, pp. 506–524.

HATT, GUDMUND

1951 "The Corn Mother in America and Indonesia," *Anthropos*, Vol. 46, pp. 853–914.

HSU, FRANCIS L. K.

1952 *Religion, Science and Human Crises; A Study on China in Transition and Its Implications for the West*. London: Routledge & Kegan Paul. 142 pp.

1953 *Americans and Chinese, Two Ways of Life*. New York: Henry Schuman. 457 pp.

LEVY, MARION J., JR.

1953 "Contrasting Factors in the Modernization of China and Japan," *Economic Development and Cultural Change*, Vol. II, No. 3, pp. 161–197.

LEWIS, OSCAR

1954 "Peasant Culture in India and Mexico: A Study in Contrasts," *Transactions of The New York Academy of Sciences*, Series II, Vol. 16, No. 4, pp. 219–223.

MINTZ, SIDNEY W. and WOLF, ERIC R.

1950 "An Analysis of Ritual Co-Parenthood *(Compadrazgo)*," *Southwestern Journal of Anthropology*, Vol. 6, No. 4, pp. 341–368.

NEEDHAM, RODNEY

1954 "Siriono and Penan: A Test of Some Hypotheses," *Southwestern Journal of Anthropology*, Vol. 10, No. 2, pp. 228–232.

PATAI, RALPH

1954 "Religion in Middle Eastern, Far Eastern and Western Culture," *Southwestern Journal of Anthropology*, Vol. 10, No. 3, pp. 233–254.

STEWARD, JULIAN H. and MURPHY, ROBERT F.

1954 "The Mundurucu and the Algonkians: A Parallel in Processes of Acculturation," Paper given at Annual Meeting of the American Anthropological Association, December, 1954.

WELTFISH, GENE
1952 "The Study of American Indian Crafts and Its Implication for Art Theory," pp. 200–209 in Tax, Sol (ed.), *Selected Papers of the XXIXth International Congress of Americanists,* Vol. 3. Chicago: University of Chicago Press. 410 pp.

COMPARISONS WITHIN ONE CONTINENT

ARMSTRONG, ROBERT C.
1952 "State Formation in Negro Africa" (Doctoral dissertation). University of Chicago.

BACON, ELIZABETH E.
1954 "Types of Pastoral Nomadism in Central and Southwest Asia," *Southwestern Journal of Anthropology,* Vol. 10, No. 1, Spring, pp. 44–65.

BARBEAU, MARIUS
1952 "The Old-World Dragon in America," pp. 115–122 in Tax, Sol (ed.), *Selected Papers of the XXIXth International Congress of Americanists,* Vol. 3. Chicago: University of Chicago Press. 410 pp.

BEALS, RALPH L.
1952 "Social Stratification in Latin America," *American Journal of Sociology,* Vol. 58, No. 4, pp. 327–339.

BEATTIE, J. H. M.
1951 "Checks on the Abuse of Political Power: A Comparative Study of the Social Factors Acting in Restraint of the Abuse of Such Powers by Indigenous Political Authorities in Certain Native Societies of Africa" (Doctoral dissertation). University of Oxford.

BEKKER, KONRAD
1951 "Historical Patterns of Culture Contact in Southern Asia," *Far Eastern Quarterly,* Vol. XI, No. 1, pp. 3–15.

COLLINS, J. L.
1951 "Antiquity of the Pineapple in America," *Southwestern Journal of Anthropology,* Vol. 7, No. 2, pp. 145–155.

EISENSTADT, S. N.
1954 "African Age Groups, A Comparative Study," *Africa,* Vol. 24, No. 2, pp. 100–113.

ELMENDORF, W. W.
1952 "Soul Loss Illness in Western North America," pp. 104–114 in Tax, Sol (ed.), *Selected Papers of the XXIXth International Congress of Americanists,* Vol. 3. Chicago: University of Chicago Press. 410 pp.

FLANNERY, REGINA
1952 "Two Concepts of Power," pp. 185–189 in Tax, Sol (ed.), *Selected Papers of the XXIXth International Congress of Americanists,* Vol. 3. Chicago: University of Chicago Press. 410 pp.

FOSTER, GEORGE M.
1952 "Relationships between Theoretical and Applied Anthropology, a Public Health Program Analysis," *Human Organization,* Vol. II, No. 3, Fall, pp. 5–16.

GLUCKMAN, MAX
1950 "Kinship and Marriage among the Lozi of Northern Rhodesia and the Zulu of Natal," pp. 116–206 in Radcliffe-Brown, A. R. and Forde, Daryll (eds.), *African Systems of Kinship and Marriage.* Oxford: Oxford University Press 399 pp.

GOLDFRANK, ESTHER S.
1952 "The Different Patterns of Blackfoot and Pueblo Adaptation to White Authority," pp. 78–79 in Tax, Sol (ed.), *Selected Papers of the XXIXth International Congress of Americanists,* Vol. 2. Chicago: University of Chicago Press. 339 pp.

KAPLAN, B.
1954 *A Study of Rorschach Responses in Four Cultures* (Papers of the Peabody Museum of American Archaeology and Ethnology, Harvard University, Vol. 42, No. 2). Cambridge, Mass. 44 pp.

LANGE, CHARLES H.
1953 "A Reappraisal of Evidence of Plains Influences among the Rio Grande Pueblos," *Southwestern Journal of Anthropology,* Vol. 9, No. 1, pp. 212–230.

LOWIE, ROBERT H.
1952 "The Heterogeneity of Marginal Cultures," pp. 1–8 in Tax, Sol (ed.), *Selected Papers of the XXIXth International Congress of Americanists,* Vol. 3. Chicago: University of Chicago Press. 410 pp.

MILLER, ROBERT J.
1953 "Areas and Institutions in Eastern Asia," *Southwestern Journal of Anthropology,* Vol. 9, No. 2, pp. 203–211.

MÜLLER, A. R.
1951 "A Study of the Social Organization of Indian Tribes of South America" (Doctoral dissertation). University of Oxford.

MURDOCK, GEORGE PETER
1951 "South American Culture Areas," *Southwestern Journal of Anthropology,* Vol. 7, No. 4, pp. 415–436.

NAROLL, RAOUL S.
1950 "A Draft Map of the Culture Areas of Asia," *Southwestern Journal of Anthropology,* Vol. 6, No. 2, pp. 183–187.

PATAI, RAPHAEL
1951 "Nomadism: Middle Eastern and Central Asian," *Southwestern Journal of Anthropology,* Vol. 7, No. 4, pp. 401–414.

PHILLIPS, ARTHUR
1953 *Survey of African Marriage and Family Life.* New York: Oxford University Press. 462 pp.

RADCLIFFE-BROWN, A. R. and FORDE, DARYLL (eds.)
1950 *African Systems of Kinship and Marriage.* New York: Oxford University Press. 399 pp.

RILEY, CARROLL L.
1952 "The Blowgun in the New World," *Southwestern Journal of Anthropology,* Vol. 8, No. 3, pp. 297–319.

RUBIO ORBE, GONZALO
1953 "Aculturaciones de Indigenas de los Andes," *America Indigena,* Vol. XIII, pp. 187–222.

SCHUSTER, CARL
1952 "V-Shaped Chest-Markings: Distribution of a Design-Motive in and around the Pacific," *Anthropos,* Vol. 47, pp. 99–118.

SELIGMAN, BRENDA Z.
1950 "The Problem of Incest and Exogamy: A Restatement," *American Anthropologist,* Vol. 52. No. 3, pp. 305–316.

SMITH, MARIAN W.
1951 "American Indian Warfare," *Transactions of The New York Academy of Sciences,* Series II, Vol. 13, No. 8, pp. 348–364.

SPINDEN, HERBERT J.
1952 "Power Animals in American Indian Art," pp. 195–199 in Tax, Sol (ed.), *Selected Papers of the XXIXth International Congress of Americanists,* Vol. 3. Chicago: University of Chicago Press. 410 pp.

TEGNAEUS, HARRY
1952 *Blood Brotherhood: An Ethno-Sociological Study of the Institution of Blood-Brotherhood with Special Reference to Africa.* New York: Philosophical Library. 181 pp.

WOLF, ERIC
1955 (In press) "Types of Latin American Peasantry: A Preliminary Discussion," *American Anthropologist,* Vol. 57.

COMPARISONS WITHIN ONE NATION

BELTRAN, GONZALO AGUIRRE
1952 "El Gobierno Indìgena en México y el Proceso de Aculturación," *America Indigena,* Vol. XII, No. 4, October, pp. 271–297.

CARRASCO, PEDRO
1951 "Las Culturas Indígenas de Oaxaca, México," *America Indigena,* Vol. XI, No. 2, April, pp. 99–114.

CAUDILL, WILLIAM
1952 *Japanese-American Personality and Acculturation* (Genetic Psychology Monographs, Vol. 45). Provincetown, Mass.: Journal Press. 102 pp.

DU WORS, RICHARD E.
1952 "Persistence and Change in Local Values of Two New England Communities," *Rural Sociology*, Vol. 17, No. 3, September, pp. 207–217.

ERASMUS, CHARLES JOHN
1952 "Changing Folk Beliefs and the Relativity of Empirical Knowledge," *Southwestern Journal of Anthropology*, Vol. 8, No. 4, pp. 411–427.

FRANCIS, E. K.
1952 "The Adjustment of a Peasant Group to a Capitalistic Economy: The Manitoba Mennonites," *Rural Sociology*, Vol. 17, No. 3, September, pp. 218–228.

FRIED, MORTON H.
1952 "Chinese Society: Class as Sub-culture," *Transactions of The New York Academy of Sciences*, Series II, Vol. 14, No. 8, pp. 331–336.

LANDMAN, RUTH
1954 "Mexican Acculturation, Compared with Jewish and Japanese Immigrant Acculturation." Paper given at the Annual Meeting of the American Anthropological Association, December, 1954.

MANNERS, ROBERT A. and STEWARD, JULIAN H.
1953 "The Cultural Study of Contemporary Societies: Puerto Rico," *American Journal of Sociology*, Vol. 59, No. 2, pp. 123–130.

MUKHERJEE, R. K. and GIRLING, F. K.
1950 "Breton Family and Economic Structure," *Rural Sociology*, Vol. 15, No. 1, March, pp. 49–62.

OLMSTEAD, DAVID L.
1951 "Two Korean Villages: Culture Contact on the 39th Parallel," *Human Organization*, Vol. 10, No. 3, pp. 33–36.

OPLER, MARVIN K.
1950 "Two Japanese Religious Sects," *Southwestern Journal of Anthropology*, Vol. 6, No. 1, pp. 69–78.

OPLER, MORRIS E. and SINGH, RUDRA DOTT
1952 "Two Villages of Eastern Uttar Pradesh (U.P.), India: An Analysis of Similarities and Differences," *American Anthropologist*, Vol. 54, No. 2, Pt. 1, pp. 179–191.

PAINTER, NORMAN W. and MORRISON, PAUL C.
1952 "Rural Population Stability, Central District of Turrialla Canton, Costa Rica," *Rural Sociology*, Vol. 17, No. 4, December, pp. 356–366.

PATAI, RAPHAEL
1953 *Israel Between East and West: A Study in Human Relations*. Philadelphia: The Jewish Publication Society. 348 pp.

PATERSON, T. T. and WILLET, F. J.
1951 "An Anthropological Experiment in a British Colliery," *Human Organization*, Vol. 10, No. 2, pp. 19–25.

PEDERSEN, HAROLD A.
1951 "Cultural Differences in the Acceptance of Recommended Practises," *Rural Sociology*, Vol. 16, No. 1, March, pp. 37–49.

RAPER, ARTHUR F.
1951 "Some Recent Changes in Japanese Village Life," *Rural Sociology*, Vol. 16, No. 1, March, pp. 3–16.

ROOKSBY, R. L.
1951 "Ritual and Society in Selected South Indian Societies" (Doctoral dissertation). University of Oxford.

RYAN, BRUCE
1950 "Socio-Cultural Regions of Ceylon," *Rural Sociology*, Vol. 15, No. 1, March, pp. 3–18.
1952 "The Ceylonese Village and the New Value System," *Rural Sociology*, Vol. 17, No. 1, March, pp. 9–28.

SANDERS, IRWIN T.
1953 "Village Social Organization in Greece," *Rural Sociology*, Vol. 18, No. 4, December, pp. 366–375.

STEWARD, JULIAN H. and collaborators
1955 *The People of Puerto Rico.* Urbana: University of Illinois Press.

TAYLOR, GORDON D.
1953 "Some Crop Distributions by Tribes in Upland Southeast Asia," *Southwestern Journal of Anthropology*, Vol. 9, No. 3, pp. 296–308.

VAN DER KROEF, JUSTUS M.
1954 "Disorganization and Social Change in Rural Indonesia," *Rural Sociology*, Vol. 19, No. 2, June, pp. 161–173.

VAZQUEZ-CALCERRADA, P. B.
1953 "A Research Project on Rural Communities in Puerto Rico," *Rural Sociology*, Vol. 18, No. 3, September, pp. 221–233.

VIQUEIRA, CARMEN and PALERM, ANGEL
1954 "Alcoholismo, Brujeria y Homocidio en dos Comunidades Rurales de México," *America Indígena*, Vol. 14, No. 1, January, pp. 7–36.

VOGT, EVON Z. and O'DEA, THOMAS F.
1953 "A Comparative Study of the Role of Values in Social Action in Two Southwestern Communities," *American Sociological Review*, Vol. 18, No. 6, pp. 645–654.

WAGLEY, CHARLES
1952 *Race and Class in Rural Brazil.* New York: Columbia University Press. 160 pp.

WOLF, KATHLEEN L.
1952 "Growing Up and Its Price in Three Puerto Rican Subcultures," *Psychiatry*, Vol. 15, No. 4, pp. 401–433.

ZEN SUN, E-TU
1952 "Results of Culture Contact in Two Mongol-Chinese Communities," *Southwestern Journal of Anthropology*, Vol. 8, No. 2, pp. 182–210.

COMPARISONS WITHIN A SINGLE CULTURE AREA OR REGION

BAILEY, F. G.
1951 "The Political Organization of the Plains Indians" (Doctoral dissertation). University of Oxford.

BELLAH, ROBERT N.
1952 *Apache Kinship Systems.* Cambridge, Mass.: Harvard University Press. 151 pp.

BERNARDI, B.
1952 "The Age-System of the Nilo-Hamitic Peoples," *Africa*, Vol. 22, No. 4, pp. 316–332.

BERNDT, RONALD M.
1951 "Ceremonial Exchange in Western Arnhem Land," *Southwestern Journal of Anthropology*, Vol. 7, No. 2, pp. 156–175.

BROKENSHA, D. W.
1951 "The Political Institutions of Some Southern Nguni Tribes" (Doctoral dissertation). University of Oxford.

BROWN, P. S.
1950 "A Study in Authority in Indigenous West African Societies" (Doctoral dissertation). University of London.

BURRIDGE, K. O. L.
1951 "Aspects of Rank in Melanesia" (Doctoral dissertation). University of Oxford.

BUTT, A. J.
1951 "The Social Organization of the Central and Eastern Eskimo" (Doctoral dissertation). University of Oxford.

CAMARA, FERNANDO
1951 "Religious and Political Organization," pp. 142–164 in Tax, Sol (ed.), *Heritage of Conquest.* Glencoe, Ill.: The Free Press. 312 pp.

DE LA FUENTE, JULIO
1952 "Ethnic and Communal Relations," pp. 76–94 in Tax, Sol (ed.), *Heritage of Conquest.* Glencoe, Ill.: The Free Press. 312 pp.

DRUCKER, PHILIP
1951 *The Northern and Central Nootka Tribes* (Bureau of American Ethnology Bulletin 144). Washington, D. C.: Smithsonian Institution. 480 pp.

EGGAN, FRED
1950 *Social Organization of the Western Pueblos.* Chicago: University of Chicago Press. 373 pp.

ELKIN, A. P.
1950 "The Complexity of Social Organization in Arnhem Land," *Southwestern Journal of Anthropology,* Vol. VI, No. 1, pp. 1-20.
1953 *Social Anthropology in Melanesia.* London: Oxford University Press. 166 pp.

ELLIS, FLORENCE HAWLEY
1951 "Patterns of Aggression and the War Cult in Southwestern Pueblos," *Southwestern Journal of Anthropology,* Vol. VII, No. 2, pp. 177–201.

ESTERMANN, C.
1952 "Clans et alliances entre clans dans le sudouest de l'angola," *Anthropos,* Vol. 47, pp. 587–606.

EVANS-PRITCHARD, E. E.
1952 "Nilotic Studies," *Journal of the Royal Anthropological Institute of Great Britain and Ireland,* Vol. LXXX, Pts. 1 & 2, pp. 1–6.

FALLERS, L. A.
1953 "Bantu Bureaucracy: A Study of Role Conflict and Institutional Change in the Soga Political System" (Doctoral dissertation). University of Chicago.

FISCHER, H. T.
1950 "The Concept of Incest in Sumatra," *American Anthropologist,* Vol. 52, No. 2, pp. 219–224.

GARIGUE, PHILIP
1954 "Changing Political Leadership in West Africa," *Africa,* Vol. 24, No. 3, pp. 220–232.

GIBSON, GORDON D.
1952 "The Social Organization of the Southwestern Bantu" (Doctoral dissertation). University of Chicago.

GILLIN, JOHN
1952 "Ethos and Cultural Aspects of Personality," pp. 193–212 in Tax, Sol (ed.), *Heritage of Conquest.* Glencoe, Ill.: The Free Press. 312 pp.

GOLDMAN, IRVING
1955 (In press) "Status Rivalry and Cultural Evolution in Polynesia," *American Anthropologist,* Vol. 57.

GUIART, JEAN
1951 "Forerunners of Melanesian Nationalism," *Oceania,* Vol. 22, No. 2, pp. 81–90.

GUITERAS HOLMES, CALIXTA
1952 "Social Organization," pp. 97–108 in Tax, Sol (ed.), *Heritage of Conquest.* Glencoe, Ill.: The Free Press. 312 pp.

HAWLEY, FLORENCE
1950 "Big Kivas, Little Kivas, and Moiety Houses in Historical Reconstruction," *Southwestern Journal of Anthropology,* Vol. 6, No. 3, pp. 286–302.

HOGBIN, H. IAN and WEDGEWOOD, CAMILLA H.
1953 "Local Grouping in Melanesia," *Oceania,* Vol. 23, No. 4, pp. 241–276; Vol. 24, No. 1, pp. 58–76.

HOLAS, B. and DEKEYSER, P. L.
1952 *Mission dans l'est Liberien* (Memoires de l'Institut Français d'Afrique Noire, No. 14). Dakar. 566 pp.

HONIGMANN, JOHN J.
1952 "Intercultural Relations at Great Whale River," *American Anthropologist,* Vol. 54, No. 4, pp. 510–522.

HOWELL, P. P.
1950 "A Comparative Study of Customary Law Among Cattle-Owning Tribes of the Southern Sudan (Doctoral dissertation). University of Oxford.

JAMES, ALICE

1950 "Village Arrangement and Social Organization Among Some Amazon Tribes" (Doctoral dissertation). Columbia University.

KEESING, FELIX M.

1953 *Social Anthropology in Polynesia; A Review of Research.* London: Oxford University Press. 126 pp.

KIRCHHOFF, PAUL

1952 "Meso-America," pp. 17–30 in Tax, Sol (ed.), *Heritage of Conquest.* Glencoe, Ill.: The Free Press. 312 pp.

1954 "Gatherers and Farmers in the Greater Southwest: A Problem in Classification," *American Anthropologist,* Vol. 56, No. 4, Pt. 1, pp. 529–560.

KLUCKHOHN, CLYDE

1954 "Southwestern Studies of Culture and Personality," *American Anthropologist,* Vol. 56, No. 4, Pt. 1, pp. 685–697.

KURATH, GERTRUDE P.

1952 "Dance Acculturation," pp. 233–242 in Tax, Sol (ed.), *Heritage of Conquest.* Glencoe, Ill.: The Free Press. 312 pp.

LANE, BARBARA S.

1953 "A Comparative and Analytic Study of Some Aspects of Northwest Coast Religion" (Doctoral dissertation). University of Washington.

LEACH, E. R.

1954 *Political Systems of Highland Burma.* Cambridge, Mass.: Harvard University Press. 323 pp.

LEACOCK, ELEANOR

1954 *The Montagnais Hunting Territory and the Fur Trade* (Memoir 78, American Anthropological Association). 59 pp.

LEMERT, EDWIN M.

1952 "Stuttering Among the North Pacific Coastal Indians," *Southwestern Journal of Anthropology,* Vol. 8, No. 3, pp. 420–441.

1954 *Alcohol and the Northwest Coast Indians* (University of California Publications in Culture and Society, Vol. 2, No. 6). Berkeley: University of California Press. 103 pp.

LÉVI-STRAUSS, CLAUDE

1952a "Kinship Systems of Three Chittagong Hill Tribes (Pakistan)," *Southwestern Journal of Anthropology,* Vol. 8, No. 1, pp. 40–51.

1952b "Les Structures Sociales dans le Brésil Central et Orientales," pp. 302–310 in Tax, Sol (ed.), *Selected Papers of the XXIXth International Congress of Americanists,* Vol. 3. Chicago: University of Chicago Press. 410 pp.

LYSTAD, R. A.

1951 "Differential Acculturation of the Ahafo-Ashanti of the Gold Coast and the Indenie-Agni of the Ivory Coast" (Doctoral dissertation). Northwestern University.

MASON, J. ALDEN

1952 "Notes and Observations on the Tepehnan," *American Indigena,* Vol. 12, No. 1, January, pp. 33–53.

MCCONNELL, URSULA H.

1950 "Junior Marriage Systems: A Comparative Survey," *Oceania,* Vol. 21, No. 2, pp. 107–143.

NADEL, S. F.

1950 "Dual Descent in the Nuba Hills," pp. 333–359 in Radcliffe-Brown, A. R. and Forde, Daryll (eds.), *African Systems of Kinship and Marriage.* New York: Oxford University Press. 399 pp.

1952 "Witchcraft in Four African Societies. An Essay in Comparison," *American Anthropologist,* Vol. 54, No. 1, pp. 18–29.

NEWCOMB, W. W.

1950 "A Re-examination of the Causes of Plains Warfare," *American Anthropologist,* Vol. 52, No. 3, pp. 317–330.

PAUL, BENJAMIN D. and PAUL, LOIS

1952 "The Life Cycle," pp. 174–192 in Tax, Sol (ed.), *Heritage of Conquest.* Glencoe, Ill.: The Free Press. 312 pp.

PETTERSSON, OLOF

1953 *Chiefs and Gods: Religious and Social Elements in South Eastern Bantu Kinship* (Studia Theologia Lundensia, No. 3). Lund: C. W. K. Glerrup. 405 pp.

POCOCK, D. F.

1951 "A Comparative Study of Social Organization Among the Nilotic People" (Doctoral dissertation). University of Oxford.

READ, K. E.

1954 "Cultures of the Central Highlands, New Guinea," *Southwestern Journal of Anthropology,* Vol. 10, No. 1, pp. 1–43.

RICHARDS, A. I.

1950 "Some Types of Family Structure Amongst the Central Bantu," pp. 207–251 in Radcliffe-Brown, A. R. and Forde, Daryll (eds.), *African Systems of Kinship and Marriage.* New York: Oxford University Press. 399 pp.

RIESENBERG, SAUL H. and GAYTON, A. H.

1952 "Caroline Island Belt Weaving," *Southwestern Journal of Anthropology,* Vol. 8, No. 3, pp. 342–375.

RIESENFELD, A.

1951 "Tobacco in New Guinea and other Areas of Melanesia," *Journal of the Royal Anthropological Institute of Great Britain and Ireland,* Vol. LXXXI, Pts. 1 & 2, pp. 69–103.

SAUER, JONATHAN D.

1950 "Amaranths as Dye Plants Among the Pueblo Peoples," *Southwestern Journal of Anthropology,* Vol. 6, No. 4, pp. 412–415.

SECOY, FRANK RAYMOND

1953 *Changing Military Patterns on the Great Plains (Monographs of the American Ethnological Society,* Vol. 21). New York: J. J. Augustin. 112 pp.

SMITH, MARIAN W.

1952 "Culture Area and Culture Depth: With Data from the Northwest Coast," pp. 80–96 in Tax, Sol (ed.), *Selected Papers of the XXIXth International Congress of Americanists,* Vol. 3. 410 pp.

SMITH, M. G.

1953 "Secondary Marriage in Northern Nigeria," *Africa,* Vol. 23, No. 4, pp. 298–323.

STARR, BETTY W.

1954 "Levels of Communal Relations," *American Journal of Sociology,* Vol. 60, No. 2, September, pp. 125–135.

STEVENSON, H. N. C.

1951 "Religion and Society Among Some Tribes of Chota-Nagpur (Doctoral dissertation). University of Oxford.

SUTTLES, WAYNE

1951 "The Early Distribution of the Potato Among the Coast Salish," *Southwestern Journal of Anthropology,* Vol. 7, No. 3, pp. 272–288.

TAX, SOL

1952a "Economy and Technology," pp. 43–75 in Tax, Sol (ed.), *Heritage of Conquest.* Glencoe, Ill.: The Free Press. 312 pp.

1952b "The Sixteenth Century and the Twentieth," pp. 262–281 in Tax, Sol (ed.), *Heritage of Conquest.* Glencoe, Ill.: The Free Press. 312 pp.

THOMPSON, LAURA

1951 *Personality and Government: Findings and Recommendations of the Indian Administration Research.* Mexico, D.F.: Instituto Indigenista Inter-Americano. 229 pp.

UNDERHILL, RUTH

1954 "Intercultural Relations in the Greater Southwest," *American Anthropologist,* Vol. 56, No. 4, pp. 645–662.

VAN DER KROEF, JUSTUS M.

1952 "Some Head-Hunting Traditions of Southern New Guinea," *American Anthropologist,* Vol. 54, No. 2, Pt. 1, pp. 221–235.

WAGLEY, CHARLES

1951 "Cultural Influences on Population: A Comparison of Two Tupi Tribes," *Revista do Museu Paulista,* Vol. 5 *n.s.,* pp. 95–104.

WISDOM, CHARLES
1952 "The Supernatural World and Curing," pp. 119–134 in Tax, Sol (ed.), *Heritage of Conquest*. Glencoe, Ill.: The Free Press. 312 pp.

COMPARISONS WITHIN A SINGLE LOCAL GROUP OR CULTURE

BARNES, J. A.
1951 "Measures of Divorce Frequency in Simple Societies," *Journal of the Royal Anthropological Institute of Great Britain and Ireland*, Vol. LXXIX, Pts. 1 & 2, pp. 37–62.

BARNOUW, VICTOR
1950 *Acculturation and Personality Among the Wisconsin Chippewa* (Memoir 70, American Anthropological Association). 152 pp.
1954 "The Changing Character of a Hindu Festival," *American Anthropologist*, Vol. 56, No. 1, pp. 74–86.

BASCOM, WILLIAM R.
1950 "Ponape: The Cycle of Empire," *Scientific Monthly*, Vol. LXX, No. 3, pp. 141–150.

COLSON, ELIZABETH
1954 "The Intensive Study of Small Sample Communities," pp. 43–59 in Spencer, Robert F. (ed.), *Method and Perspective in Anthropology*. Minneapolis: University of Minnesota Press. 323 pp.

FENTON, WILLIAM N. (ed.)
1951 *Symposium on Local Diversity in Iroquois Culture* (Bureau of American Ethnology, Bulletin No. 149). Washington, D. C.: Smithsonian Institution. 187 pp.

FIRTH, RAYMOND
1952 "Notes on the Social Structure of Some South-Eastern New Guinea Communities," *Man*, Vol. 52, No. 5, pp. 65–67; No. 6, pp. 86–89.

FRIED, JACOB
1953 "The Relation of Ideal Norms to Actual Behavior in Tarahumara Society," *Southwestern Journal of Anthropology*, Vol. 9, No. 3, pp. 286–295.

GOLDSCHMIDT, WALTER and SPINDLER, GEORGE
1952 "Experimental Design in the Study of Culture Change," *Southwestern Journal of Anthropology*, Vol. 8, No. 1, pp. 68–83.

HALLOWELL, A. IRVING
1950 "Values, Acculturation and Mental Health," *American Journal of Orthopsychiatry*, Vol. 20, No. 4, pp. 732–743.
1952 "Ojibway Personality and Acculturation," pp. 106–112 in Tax, Sol (ed.), *Selected Papers of the XXIXth International Congress of Americanists*, Vol. 2. Chicago: University of Chicago Press. 339 pp.

HART, C. W. M.
1954 "The Sons of Turimpi," *American Anthropologist*, Vol. 56, No. 2, Pt. 1, pp. 242–261.

HENRY, JULES
1951 "The Economics of Pilaga Food Production," *American Anthropologist*, Vol. 53, No. 2, pp. 187–219.

HOGBIN, IAN
1951 *Transformation Scene: The Changing Culture of a New Guinea Village*. London: Routledge and Kegan, Paul. 326 pp.

KAPLAN, BERNICE A.
1951 "Changing Functions of the Huanancha Dance at the Corpus Christi Festival in Paracho, Michoacán, México," *Journal of American Folklore*, Vol. 64, No. 254, pp. 383–396.

LEWIS, OSCAR
1950 "An Anthropological Approach to Family Studies," *The American Journal of Sociology*, Vol. LV, No. 5, pp. 468–475.
1951 *Life in a Mexican Village: Tepoztlán Restudied*. Urbana: University of Illinois Press. 512 pp.

MANDELBAUM, DAVID G.
1954 "Form, Variation and Meaning of a Ceremony," pp. 60–102 in Spencer, Robert F. (ed.), *Method and Perspective in Anthropology*. Minneapolis, University of Minnesota Press. 323 pp.

MARRIOTT, MCKIM
1952 "Social Change in an Indian Village," *Economic Development and Cultural Change*, No. 2, June, pp. 145–155.

MEAD, MARGARET
1954 "Manus Restudied: An Interim Report," *Transactions of The New York Academy of Sciences*, Ser. II, Vol. 16, No. 8, pp. 426–432.

NETT, BETTY R.
1952 "Historical Changes in the Osage Kinship System," *Southwestern Journal of Anthropology*, Vol. 8, No. 2, pp. 164–181.

REDFIELD, ROBERT
1950 *A Village that Chose Progress: Chan Kom Revisited.* Chicago: University of Chicago Press. 187 pp.

REICHEL-DOLMATOFF, GERARDO
1953 "Actitudes hacia el Trabajo en una Población Mestiza de Colombia," *America Indigena*, Vol. XIII, No. 3, July, pp. 165–174.

ROBERTS, JOHN M.
1951 *Three Navaho Households* (Papers of the Peabody Museum of American Archaeology and Ethnology, Vol. 40, No. 3). Cambridge, Mass. 84 pp.

SCHMIDT, KARL and SCHMIDT, OSANAI IVA
1952 *Wichita Kinship, Past and Present.* Norman, Okla.: University Book Exchange. 72 pp.

SPINDLER, GEORGE D.
1952 "Personality and Peyotism in Menomini Indian Acculturation," *Psychiatry*, Vol. 15, No. 2, pp. 151–159.

STOUT, D. B.
1952 "Persistent Elements in San Blas Cuna Social Organization," pp. 262–265 in Tax, Sol (ed.), *Selected Papers of the XXIXth International Congress of Americanists*, Vol. 3. Chicago: University of Chicago Press. 339 pp.

TREMBLAY, MARC-ADELARD; COLLIER, JOHN, JR.; and SASAKI, TOM T.
1954 "Navaho Housing in Transition," *American Indigena*, Vol. 14, No. 3, pp. 187–220.

TUMIN, MELVIN M.
1952 *Caste in a Peasant Society: A Case Study in the Dynamics of Caste.* Princeton: Princeton University Press. 300 pp.

WALLACE, ERNEST and HOEBEL, E. ADAMSON
1952 *The Comanches, Lords of the South Plains* (Civilization of the American Indian Series, No. 34). Norman, Okla.: University of Oklahoma Press. 381 pp.

WATSON, JAMES B.
1952 *Cayuá Culture Change: A Study in Acculturation and Methodology* (Memoir 73, American Anthropological Association). 144 pp.

VOGET, FRED
1952 "Crow Socio-Cultural Groups," pp. 88–93 in Tax, Sol (ed.), *Selected Papers of the XXIXth International Congress of Americanists*, Vol. 2. Chicago: University of Chicago Press. 339 pp.

VOGT, EVON Z.
1951 *Navaho Veterans, A Study of Changing Values* (Papers of the Peabody Museum of American Archaeology and Ethnology, Vol. 41, No. 1). Cambridge, Mass. 223 pp.

Theory

Universal Categories of Culture[1] *

By CLYDE KLUCKHOHN

THERE ARE two interrelated problems: Are there fairly definite limits within which cultural variation is constrained by panhuman regularities in biology, psychology, and the processes of social interaction? Do these limits and also the accompanying trends toward similarities in form and content make for categories of culture which are universal in the sense of being both invariant points of reference for description and comparison and, perhaps, substantive uniformities or near-uniformities? This paper will move back and forth between these two slightly different, but closely connected, frames of reference. First, various aspects of the two problems and their implications must be stated in slightly more expanded form.

There is a certain paradox in recent and contemporary anthropological thinking. Radcliffe-Brown and other British anthropologists have characterized social anthropology as "comparative sociology." American anthropologists of late have stressed the cross-cultural approach, and some of us have justified our sometimes rather imperialistic claims to being the *scientia scientiarum* of human studies on the grounds that only anthropologists transcend the limitations of the categories of their own cultures. Yet genuine comparison is possible only if nonculture-bound units have been isolated.[2]

In fact, linguistics alone of the branches of anthropology has discovered elemental units (phonemes, morphemes, and the like) which are universal, objective, and theoretically meaningful. Even physical anthropology, which deals with the biological givens in a single order, is just beginning to grope its way beyond common-sense concepts such as "nose," "young," "middle-aged," and "old." The whole history of science shows that advance depends upon going beyond "common sense" to abstractions that reveal unobvious relations and common properties of isolable aspects of phenomena. Anthropologists, above all, should realize this because "sense" becomes "common" only in terms of cultural convention, particularly in terms of the conventions of implicit culture.

Cultural anthropology has followed two paths, neither of which makes possible a true and complete comparison. A few anthropologists have organized their descriptions largely along the dimensions recognized by the culture being described. The categories chosen

1. The research assistance of Nathan Gould is gratefully acknowledged.

2. The broad tripartite classification of "cultural" (relation of man to nature, man to man, and "subjective aspects"), upon which there has been a large measure of convergence, does not help us much for comparative purposes. For a detailed discussion see Kroeber and Kluckhohn (1952). Perhaps the "seven major facets" of culture elements used in the 1950 edition of Murdock *et al.*, *Outline of Cultural Materials*, see pp. xix ff., takes us a bit further.

are those which appear explicitly in the native language. This method, in the favorable case, gives a view of experience as it appears consciously to the people studied and avoids the distortions that inevitably result when a culture is dismembered and reassembled arbitrarily according to the classifications familiar to Western thought. On the other hand, no approach which neglects the tacit premises and cryptocategories of the implicit culture really presents a unique cultural world in its totality. Moreover—and more to the point for the present discussion—this path represents untrammeled cultural relativism at its extreme. Each distinct culture becomes, indeed, a self-contained monad which can in the nature of the case be compared with others only vaguely, "intuitively," "artistically."

The second path is the one followed, with numerous variations and compromises, by the overwhelming majority of ethnographers. The selected categories are the well-known ones of the "standard" monograph, typically: physical environment; techniques, economic and technological, for coping with this environment; social organization; religion; sometimes language; more recently, "life-cycle" or methods of childhood training and the like. In the first instance these were common-sense concepts corresponding to nineteenth-century Western notions of the all-pervasive framework of human life. They have been slightly modified in accord, on the one hand, with the empirical generalizations summed up under Wissler's "universal culture pattern" and, on the other hand, with changing theoretical fashions (for example, recent attention to nursing habits, toilet training, etc.).

On the whole, these categories have been crudely serviceable and have made certain meaningful comparisons possible. In broad form, though not in content, they represent rough empirical universals into which descriptive data can conveniently be grouped. Comparative analysis is aided by more truly scientific concepts, purposefully created by anthropologists: Linton's "item," "trait," and "activity"; his "form," "function," "use," and "meaning"; his "universals," "alternatives," and "specialties"; Kroeber's three types of patterns; Opler's "themes"; and Herskovits' "focus." But the data obtained in the field which must serve as our materials for a comparative science continue to be perverted, slightly or greatly, by the prescientific nature of our basic categories. The technical processes of farming or weaving (though not the symbolic accretions of these activities) can be compared with relatively little distortion because of their objectivity and of the limiting "givens" of nature. Our concepts, however, of "economics," "religion," and "politics" have a large element of cultural arbitrariness. Probably the main reason that anthropologists have written so little about "political behavior" is the circumstance that they have felt intuitively uncomfortable, unable to isolate in many cultures an order of phenomena strictly comparable to our category of "government."

In cultural anthropology we are still too close to the phase in linguistics when non-European languages were being forcibly recast into the categories of Latin grammar. We can discover and recognize similarities due to historical connection, but nonhistorically derived similarities, other than the most gross and obvious ones, elude us because our frame is too culture-bound and so insufficiently abstract that we can compare only in terms of specific content. The Human Relations Area Files are admirable in intent and decidedly useful in many ways as they stand. Yet it is the testimony of many who have worked intensively with these materials that the Files bring together much which is conceptually distinct, and separate much that ought to be together. An altogether adequate organization of comparative data must await a better working-out of the theory of the universal categories of culture,[3] both structural principles and content categories. Present methods obtain, organize, and compare in ways that beg questions which are themselves at issue. This is the contemporary paradox of the so-called "comparative" science of cultures.

The present paper cannot hope to resolve this paradox. It can at best state the problem more clearly, focus the central issues, indicate some clues as to the lines along which resolution may eventually take place. First, the state of affairs in a sample of recent monographs will be briefly summarized. There will follow a short historical sketch of anthropological thinking about universal categories. Finally, some aids from biology, psychology, and sociology will be mobilized.

An examination was made of the tables of contents of ninety ethnographic monographs published in English within the last twenty years. Of these, four were works on the cultures of contemporary industrial societies. Studies limited to or focused upon single topics were not examined. Rather, the sample was restricted to general accounts of a people and their culture.

Findings may be summarized as follows: There is a stereotyped scheme with numerous but comparatively minor variations upon it; genuine innovation is exceedingly rare; reports in the second decade of our sample tended strongly to show more conscious theoretical orientation. Variations reflect, in part, shifting conceptual fashions, in part the interests and presumably the temperaments of individual workers.[4]

Avoidance of explicit theoretical frames of reference is particularly marked in certain series, such as *Anthropological Records* and the Bishop Museum publications. However, the majority of studies which have appeared since World War II exhibit a striving toward problem-centered research and toward (sometimes strained) theoretical sophistication. There is also a greater awareness of the dangers of imposing the categories of the anthropologist's culture upon cultures outside the Western tradition. Honigmann, for example, uses "ideational culture" and avoids "religion" in his treatment of the Kaska.

Expectably, comparability is best where description treats of the satisfaction of basic physical needs or por-

3. Murdock *et al.* (1950, p. xix), state that "they have attempted to group inherently related categories in the same section and they have arranged the sections in an order that is not wholly without logic. Beyond this, however, they insist that the classification is wholly pragmatic. . . . Through trial and error . . . the categories have come to represent a sort of common denominator of the ways in which anthropologists, geographers, sociologists, historians, and non-professional recorders of cultural data habitually organize their materials."

4. Commenting on the comparability of community studies of contemporary societies, Steward (1950, p. 25) states: "In a *comparative approach* to contemporary communities, the problems which are studied in one community—or at least the cultural perspectives acquired in any study—are utilized in the investigation of other communities. Ideally, there is some comparability of research projects that have common purposes, problems, and methods. The widely differing characteristics of communities naturally dictate some differences in approach; but individual interests, purposes, and methods have produced even greater differences, and community studies have little in common beyond the fact that they purport to use a cultural approach."

Commenting on the "more purely ethnographic studies," Steward (1950, p. 26; see illustrations of this, pp. 26–27) states: "These show considerable disparity of emphasis because of varied individual interests. The general chapter headings may be more or less similar, but there is a great difference in purpose and problem."

trays customs directly related to the life-cycle or departs from other biologically or physically given points of reference. The proportion of space given to various topics reflects, of course, theoretical orientation and personal interests.[5] In general, the distribution of attention appears somewhat more "objective" or better balanced in the monographs of the pre–World War II period when theory was less explicit. Reading of prefaces and introductions makes it clear that exigencies of the field situation were also important in influencing the kind and amount of data collected. Finally, there are the technical problems and limitations which Herskovits has discussed.[6]

In short, careful examination confirms an initial impression that the data recorded in recent anthropological monographs are only roughly, loosely, and for certain purposes comparable. About 1939 Malinowski began to publish what he later called his "universal institutional types."[7] What is substantially a revision of this has recently been presented by Nadel (1951, pp. 135 ff.). However, no ethnography has yet been published which organizes its materials in accord with this theoretical system. Similarly, Leslie White has discussed universal categories of a Morgan-Engels-Marx sort, but his published studies of cultures follow the traditional pattern. The situation remains as Evans-Pritchard described it (1940, p. 261): "These weighty volumes generally record observations in too haphazard a fashion to be either pleasant or profitable reading. This deficiency is due to absence of a body of scientific theory in Social Anthropology."

---

5. Steward (1950, p. 28), who analyzed the relative amount of space accorded different subjects in community studies to determine differences of emphasis, states in summary: "The amount of space devoted to a subject depends somewhat, of course, upon its functional importance in the community. *Nonetheless, even substantially similar communities are given quite unlike treatment, which reflects individual purposes and methods even more than differences in facts*" (my italics).

Discussing "the more purely ethnographic studies" of community life, Steward states that "even these show considerable disparity of emphasis because of varied individual interests. The general chapter headings may be more or less similar, but there is a great difference in purpose and problem. The Lynds' studies of Middletown [1929, 1937] are concerned with how economic factors and changes affect community life, which is described in most of its aspects. West's *Plainville* [1945], Yang's Chinese Village [1945], and Hsu's study of a Chinese community [1948] are interested in the interrelation of culture and personality, and following the current approach to this problem, they accord considerable space to the 'life cycle'—the development of the individual in the culture. Parsons' Mexican [1936] and Ecuadorian [1945] studies have the very different purpose of determining the native Indian and Spanish elements in the culture of her communities. Redfield's study of Yucatan [1941], though dealing with folk cultures not unlike those recorded by Parsons, is preoccupied with the transformation of folk societies under urbanizing influences. And Fei's monographs on Chinese peasants [e.g., Fei and Chang, 1945], through reporting on people who are similar to those studied by Yang and Hsu, are concerned with rural economy in its relationship to community types and show no interest in culture and personality."

6. "It is impossible for any study of a culture . . . to describe more than a portion of the aspects of the life of a single people. Even those whose aim is to give the most rounded portrayal possible find certain limits which, for technical reasons of time, space and competence they cannot exceed. In practice, language is left to the specialist, and so is music. If any attempt is made to include expressions of the literary arts, this material must commonly be reserved for separate treatment because of its bulk. Some aspects of culture are rarely studied as such; forms of dramatic expression, for instance, since in non-literate societies drama is customarily a part of ritual. The dance, also, has too rarely been analyzed, because of the technical difficulties it presents in the way of valid recording" (1948, p. 238).

7. For his final version see *A Scientific Theory of Culture* (1944, pp. 62 ff.).

Many of the earlier anthropologists were certain that there were universal categories[8] for culture or universal categories which underlay all cultures. Witness the "stages" of the evolutionists and the "elementary ideas" of Bastian. Boas[9] called chapter VI of the 1911 edition of *The Mind of Primitive Man* "The Universality of Culture Traits" and says:

> We may therefore base our further considerations on the theory of the similarity of mental functions in all races. Observation has shown, however, that not only emotions, intellect, and will-power of man are alike everywhere, but that much more detailed similarities in thought and action occur among the most diverse peoples.

But, in general, from about this time on, the attention of anthropologists throughout the world appears to have been directed overwhelmingly to the distinctiveness of each culture and to the differences in human custom as opposed to the similarities. The latter, where recognized, were explained historically rather than in terms of the common nature of man and certain invariant properties of the human situation. In the case of the United States, there was the added factor of the antitheoretical bias of American anthropologists for at least a generation.

Between roughly 1910 and roughly 1940 the only significant anthropological advance[10] in formulating the basic principles upon which all cultures rest appears to be represented by Wissler's discussion of the universal culture pattern, in 1923.[11] However, workers in other disciplines were attempting to establish regularities in human response which transcended cultural difference. Durkheim, Mauss, and other French sociologists propounded their famous principles of collective representations, reciprocity, and the like. Simmel looked for social regularities of a somewhat different type. Birkhoff in his *Aesthetic Measure* tried to develop panhuman canons of artistic response.[12] Zipf discovered the *k*-constant, applied the harmonic principle to social behavior, and, a little later, enunciated his so-called "law of least effort." The psychoanalysts tried to show the universality of the Oedipus complex, sibling rivalry, and certain sorts of fantasy and symbolic processes. Human geography, in France and elsewhere, abandoned simplist "environmental determinism" in favor of the view that there was a high correlation between certain aspects of culture, especially types of social organization, and certain ecological situations.

These and other movements had an impact upon anthropology. There was probably also within the profession an increasing skepticism of the tautology that culture alone begets or determines culture and of the proposition that culture is purely and solely the precipitate

8. For brief discussions of the history of theories of the universal culture pattern see Murdock (1945) and Herskovits (1948).

9. In the 1938 edition of the same work Boas (p. 195) says: "There is no reason why we should accept Bastian's renunciation. The dynamic forces that mould social life are the same now as those that moulded life thousands of years ago. We can follow the intellectual and emotional drives that actuate man at present and that shape his actions and thoughts."

10. Linton's *Study of Man* (1936) did significantly advance some theoretical aspects. For example, he discusses "the universal reactions of man," such as the dependence of human beings upon emotional responses from one another—a factor to which William James had directed attention.

11. In a sense, as Mr. Gould has pointed out to me, enumerative definitions of culture, of which Tylor's is the classical illustration, may be viewed as statements of the categories of the universal pattern.

12. Cf. a recent statement by Raymond Firth (1951): "I believe that there are universal standards of aesthetic quality, just as there are universal standards of technical efficiency." Such standards are based on "similar psychological impulses."

of the accidents of history.[13] At all events Radcliffe-Brown led off an anthropological search for "universal social laws" in the English-speaking world. Chapple and Arensberg, stimulated alike by Simmel, Radcliffe-Brown, and Malinowski, attempted to establish quantitatively invariant properties of social interaction. Murdock, departing from the Sumner-Keller sociological tradition and from Wissler and other American anthropologists, likewise initiated quantitative work with the aim of factoring out the specifically historical and establishing cross-cultural trends and tendencies. His founding of the Cross-cultural Survey in the thirties appears to have been largely a means to this end.[14] Roheim and other psychoanalytically oriented anthropologists put Freudian theory to the test of field work. Leighton, an anthropologically experienced psychiatrist, formulated, in *The Governing of Men* and *Human Relations in a Changing World,* some principles about raw or subcultural human nature. Forde, Richards, and others in British anthropology and Steward and others in American anthropology put the search for the environmental determinants of culture upon a new and more sophisticated basis. Steward's 1938 paper, "Ecological Aspects of Southwestern Society," was a particularly notable demonstration of certain relationships between forms of social organization and geographical situation.

Two cross-disciplinary papers in which each team of writers included an anthropologist attempted to sketch out the more abstract foundations for a system of categories that would permit true cross-cultural comparability. A quotation from the first of these is appropriate because the present paper represents essentially a modification and a development of the same point of view:[15]

13. The most impressive theoretical statement by an anthropologist signalizing a return to universal processes and factors is contained in A. V. Kidder's paper "Looking Backward" (1940):

"In both hemispheres man started from cultural scratch, as a nomadic hunter, a user of stone tools, a palaeolithic savage. In both he spread over great continents and shaped his life to cope with every sort of environment. Then, in both hemispheres, wild plants were brought under cultivation; population increased; concentrations of people brought elaboration of social groupings and rapid progress in the arts. Pottery came into use, fibres and wools were woven into cloth, animals were domesticated, metal working began—first in gold and copper, then in the harder alloy, bronze. Systems of writing were evolved.

"Not only in material things do the parallels hold. In the New World as well as in the Old, priesthoods grew and, allying themselves with temporal powers, or becoming rulers in their own right, reared to their gods vast temples adorned with painting and sculpture. The priests and chiefs provided for themselves elaborate tombs richly stocked for the future life. In political history it is the same. In both hemispheres group joined group to form tribes; coalitions and conquests brought preeminence; empires grew and assumed the paraphernalia of glory.

"These are astonishing similarities. And if we believe, as most modern students do, that the Indians' achievement was made independently, and their progress was not stimulated from overseas, then we reach a very significant conclusion. We can infer that human beings possess an innate urge to take certain definite steps toward what we call civilization. And that men also possess the innate ability, given proper environmental conditions, to put that urge into effect. In other words, we must consider that civilization is an inevitable response to laws governing the growth of culture and controlling the man-culture relationship."

14. In "The Cross-cultural Survey" (1940, p. 366), Murdock remarks: "To the extent that culture is ideational, we may conclude all cultures should reveal certain similarities, flowing from the universal laws governing the symbolic, mental processes, *e.g.*, the worldwide parallels in the principles of magic."

15. Lynd (1939, p. 124) provides the same clue: ". . . the error lies in seeking to derive the laws of social science from study of sequences observed in a single set of historically conditioned *institutions, qua institutions,* rather than from study of the *full range of*

The following model is intended to cut across . . . specialized and narrow abstractions. It does not rest on . . . assumptions about "human nature" but abstracts immediately from the concrete behavior of men in social systems. . . . Variations in the patterning of different social systems are indefinitely numerous. The principle on which the present outline has been built up is, however, that these variations are grouped about certain *invariant points of reference*. These are to be found in the nature of social systems, in the biological and psychological nature of the component individuals, in the external situations in which they live and act, in the nature of action itself, in the necessity of its coordination in social systems. In the orientation of individuals these "foci" of structure are never ignored. They must in some way be "adapted to" or "taken account of." The . . . three main classes of patterns [situational, instrumental, and integrative] are coherently grouped because of their relation in each case to a related group of these foci of patterning. In the first case it is certain facts about the situation in which men are placed, their biological nature and descent, their psychological nature. In the second it is the content of the differentiated functional roles by virtue of which a system of interdependent units becomes possible. In the third, finally, it is certain necessities of the coordinated functioning of a social system as a whole.[16]

The second paper, "The Functional Prerequisites of a Society" (Aberle *et al.*, 1950), refines and elaborates one aspect of the conceptual scheme just referred to. The theoretical takeoff is as follows:

A comparative social science requires a generalized system of concepts which will enable the scientific observer to compare and contrast large bodies of concretely different social phenomena in consistent terms. A promising social analysis is a tentative formulation of the functional prerequisites of a society. Functional prerequisites refer broadly to the things that must get done in any society if it is to continue as a going concern, *i.e.*, the generalized conditions necessary for the maintenance of the system concerned. The specific structural arrangements for meeting the functional prerequisites differ, of course, from one society to another and, in the course of time, change in any given society. Thus all societies must allocate goods and services somehow. A particular society may change from one method, say business enterprise, to another, say a centrally planned economy, without the destruction of the society as a society but merely with a change in its concrete structures.

Florence Kluckhohn (1950), combining sociological and anthropological thinking and conclusions, has provided a frame for comparing the profiles exhibited by different cultures with respect to their premises, tacit and overt, about five universal human problems: "what are the innate predispositions of man? what is the relation of man to nature? what is the significant time dimension? what is the direction in time of the action process? what type of personality is to be most valued? what is the dominant modality of the relationship of man to other men?" Assuming that "all societies find a phraseology within a range of possible phraseologies of basic human problems," she notes: "The problems as stated are constant; they arise inevitably out of the human situation. The phraseology of them is variable but variable only within limits."

Human biology sets limits, supplies potentialities and drives, provides clues which cultures neglect or elaborate.[17] This is standard anthropological doctrine at present, and it may turn out that this is about all there is to it. Yet

behavior around the functional cores these institutions express."

16. J. F. Dunlop, M. P. Gilmore, C. Kluckhohn, T. Parsons, and O. H. Taylor, "Toward a Common Language for the Area of Social Science" (mimeographed, 1941). The above quotation appears in the portion of the complete memorandum printed in T. Parsons (1949).

17. For a recent review see Bergman (1952).

when one learns that the introduction of an electric needle into a certain cortical area of one species of monkey results in these monkeys thereafter defecating upon their own kind, whereas previously they would defecate only upon strangers, one wonders if, after all, there may not be specific biological bases for certain of our social habits.[18] At all events, there is general recognition of the social and cultural implications of such elementary biological facts as the existence of two sexes, the ordinary human life-span, the dependency of human infants (of which the psychoanalysts have made so much). Those features of human cultures such as family life which have their counterparts in lower primates and other mammals presumably have a rather definite biological base. This assumption has recently been discussed by Marston Bates (1950, p. 162 and *passim*) and by Ford and Beach (1951, pp. 3 ff.). Allee's (1951) studies of patterns of social co-operation among animals are also highly suggestive both for biological and for social determinants of universal categories of culture.

The biological leads easily into the psychological. The ways, for instance, in which biological dependency is transformed into psychological dependency have often been discussed. Dreaming, which has surely given rise to many cultural parallels, is both a biological and a psychological process. And the biological nature of man plus his psychological capabilities and predispositions interact with certain universalities in man's social interactions and other features of his environing situation. As Bates and others have shown, the sheer territorial dimension of human existence has its effects upon culture. In various studies Steward has generalized some of these. Given the principle of limitation of possibilities, independent parallel developments have occurred again and again. As Steward (1949) says, for example:

> In densely settled areas, internal needs will produce an orderly interrelationship of environment, subsistence patterns, special groupings, occupational specializations, and overall political, religious, and perhaps military integrating factors. These interrelated institutions do not have unlimited variability, for they must be adapted to the requirements of subsistence patterns established in particular environments; they involve a cultural ecology.

In psychological language the generalization is that human beings are so constituted that, particularly under conditions of extreme stress, they will often react in roughly similar ways to the same pressures. Nativistic movements constitute a case much studied of late by anthropologists. Details vary widely in accord with the pre-existing cultures, but the broad patterns are very much alike. Marie Bonaparte (1947) has demonstrated that at the time of the fall of France in 1940 a tale with the same general theme ("the myth of the corpse in the car") was told over widely separated areas within such a brief period that the possibility of diffusion must be ruled out. There is considerable evidence of parallelisms in fantasy productions arising over long periods and under "normal" conditions among peoples who cannot be presumed to have had direct or indirect historical contact within a relevant time range. Rank (1914), for instance, has demonstrated remarkable similari-

18. Current experiments at the Orange Park primate laboratory are also interesting. Give chimpanzees an incomplete circle, and they will fill it in, and they will draw a cross to complete the symmetry of a design. This and Schiller's work on perceptual completion suggest a specific biological basis, shared by humans and other primates, for certain tendencies toward closure manifested in human cultures. The facts are well established that such behavior as nursing and walking are dependent more on the myelination of the relevant nerve tracts and less on sociocultural factors than had previously been thought.

ties in widespread myths of heroes. In spite of the fact that many psychoanalytic writers have run Freudian theories of panhuman sexual symbolism into the ground, there remain arresting and irreducible resemblances among such symbolisms in the most historically diverse cultures.

Throughout, one can recognize the empirical convergences without necessarily accepting the psychoanalytic interpretations. Thus one can pay due regard to Bonaparte's data without allegiance to her "human sacrifice" explanation. Nevertheless I should like to repeat what I have recently written about psychoanalysis and anthropology (Kluckhohn and Morgan, 1951):

> I still believe that some of the cautions uttered by Boas and others on the possible extravagances of interpretations in terms of universal symbolism, completely or largely divorced from minute examination of cultural context, are sound. But the facts uncovered in my own field work and that of my collaborators have forced me to the conclusion that Freud and other psychoanalysts have depicted with astonishing correctness many central themes in motivational life which are universal. The styles of expression of these themes and much of the manifest content are culturally determined, but the underlying psychologic drama transcends cultural difference.

This should not be too surprising—except to an anthropologist overindoctrinated with the theory of cultural relativism—for many of the inescapable givens of human life are also universal. Human anatomy and human physiology are, in the large, about the same the world over. There are two sexes with palpably visible differences in external genitalia and secondary sexual characteristics. All human infants, regardless of culture, know the psychological experience of helplessness and dependency. Situations making for competition for the affection of one or both parents, for sibling rivalry can be to some extent channeled this way or that way by a culture but they cannot be eliminated, given the universality of family life. The trouble has been —because of a series of accidents of intellectual and political history—that the anthropologist for two generations has been obsessed with the differences between peoples, neglecting the equally real similarities—upon which the "universal culture pattern" as well as the psychological uniformities are clearly built.

A. V. Kidder[19] some time ago put the general case cautiously but wisely:

> The question . . . is: does culture, although not biologically transmitted, develop and function in response to tendencies—it is perhaps too connotative to call them law—that are comparable to those controlling biological evolution? There seems to be evidence that, in some degree at least, it does. All over the world and among populations that could apparently not possibly have come into contact with each other, similar inventions have been made and have been made in a seemingly predetermined order. Extraordinary similarities are to be observed in the nature and order of appearance among widely separated peoples of certain social practices and religious observances.
>
> These are likenesses, not identities; history, to reverse the proverb, never repeats itself; different environments and differing opportunities have seen to that. But they do seem to indicate that there are definite tendencies and orderlinesses, both in the growth of this compelling force and in man's responses thereto. It is therefore the task of the disciplines concerned with man and his culture—genetics, history, archaeology, sociology, the humanities—to gather and to correlate information which may enable us more fully to understand these now dimly perceived trends and relationships.

Anthropologists have been rightly criticized by sociologists and certain psychologists for neglecting the universalities in interaction processes, the common elements in the structuring of social action. To some extent, as suggested earlier, this has been corrected in recent years by the work of the Brit-

19. Mimeographed document from the Carnegie Institution, quoted in Steward (1950, p. 118).

ish social anthropologists and such Americans as Chapple and Arensberg. It does appear that groups as such have certain basic properties. One may instance Lewin's concept of quasi-stationary equilibrium (cf. Wilson, 1951). A philosopher (Riezler, 1950) has just published a penetrating study of the constant and the variable in human social life which raises many issues too often overlooked by anthropologists.

My colleague, Professor George Homans, has investigated, with the aid of his seminar, the relations between mother's brother and sister's son, father's sister and her brother's son, and brothers and sisters in a considerable range of nonliterate societies. Homans operates upon the hypothesis that there are discoverable structural laws for social conduct in all human societies, but he informs me that this investigation only partially bore out this hypothesis. For the first two relationships there appeared to be patterns that transcended cultural differences. These relationships evidenced considerable regularity, but the relations between brothers and sisters were irregular in the same societies. In some, stringent avoidance was enjoined; in others, brothers and sisters were permitted to be what Lévi-Strauss has called "chaste companions of the bed." The difference seemed to be traceable not to principles of social structure but rather to cultural values, specifically the varying emphasis upon internal as opposed to external controls for moral behavior. I suspect that this work of Homans[20] may represent a broader paradigm: some aspects of culture take their specific forms solely as a result of historical accidents; others are tailored by forces which can properly be designated as universal.

20. Homans has been strongly influenced by Chapple, Arensberg, and other anthropologists who have tried to limit themselves to observable social interaction analyzed in terms of a few simple concepts (cf. 1950).

It is possible, of course, to follow Kroeber (1949)[21] and regard cross-cultural likenesses as being subcultural—as the limits and conditions of culture:

> Such more or less recurrent near-regularities of form or process as have to date been formulated for culture are actually mainly sub-cultural in nature. They are limits set to culture by physical or organic factors. The so-called "cultural constants" of family, religion, war, communication, and the like appear to be biopsychological frames variably filled with cultural content, so far as they are more than categories reflecting the compartments of our own Occidental logico-verbal culture. Of processes, diffusion and socialization are both only psychological learning, imitation, and suggestion under special conditions. Custom is psychobiological habit on a social scale and carrying cultural values.

But the universals are part of cultures in the sense that they are incorporated and socially transmitted. Moreover, the "so-called 'cultural constants'" are not mere empty frames. In the case of language, for instance, there are also striking resemblances within the frame. Every phonology is a system, not a random congeries of sound-classes. The differentiating principles of a phonetic system are applied with some consistency to sounds produced in more than one position. In a study just published Jakobson and others (1952) assert: "The inherent distinctive features which we detect in the languages of the world and which underlie their entire lexical and morphological stock amount to twelve binary oppositions." All languages are made up of "vowels" and "consonants." Meaningful utterances in all languages arise from combining morphemes, and there are certain other generalized properties of morphophonemics. All languages exhibit a high degree of flexibility with

21. For a reply to Kroeber's often expressed view that categories, like "sacrifice," are "fake universals" see Lévi-Strauss, *Twentieth Century Sociology*, pp. 523 ff.

respect to the meanings that can be expressed. The subject-predicate form of expression is universal so far as extended and connected discourse is concerned. Possession or the genitive is expressed in all languages. This list could be considerably extended.[22]

It can be argued that even these congruences in content reflect subcultural "limits." That is, the facts that the range of number of phonemes in human languages is narrow and that all languages appear to embrace between five and ten thousand morphemes can be interpreted as reflecting only certain limits of human anatomy and physiology which, assuming the principle of economy or "least effort," make a language based upon forty thousand combinations of two phonemes most unlikely (since the human nervous system is not equipped to "code" and "decode" that fast). The same argument can be advanced as regards the limited range of variation in number of kinship terms and the fundamental contrasts in principles of kinship systems which Murdock has published. However, it is not important whether these phenomena be regarded as universal categories *of* culture or universal categories *for* the comparison of cultures. They reflect, admittedly, "limits" or "conditions" and are in this sense "subcultural."

But it should be noted in passing that features which no one would dispute as cultural are also limiting conditions to other aspects of culture. Thus Boas (1940) has said: "We may . . . consider exogamy as the condition on which totemism arose." Fortes (1949) and Firth (1951) have asserted:

> The hypothesis that all kinship institutions derive from the facts of sex, procreation, and child-rearing is acceptable if the emphasis is laid not on their biological and utilitarian value but on the moral values attached by society to these facts, and perpetuated through the social relationships brought into being by their conjunction. . . . The existence of a social system necessitates, in fact, a moral system for its support.

In any case, the crucial point is this: *biological, psychological, and sociosituational universals afford the possibility of comparison of cultures in terms which are not ethnocentric, which depart from "givens," begging no needless questions.*

Most anthropologists would agree that no constant elemental units like atoms, cells, or genes have as yet been satisfactorily established with culture in general.[23] Many would insist that within one aspect of culture, namely, language, such constant elemental units have been isolated: phonemes[24] and morphemes. It is arguable whether such units are, in principle, discoverable in sectors of culture less automatic than speech and less closely tied (in some ways) to biological fact.[25]

22. While most of the points in this and the following paragraph have been familiar to me and used in my lectures for some years, this statement in its present form owes much to a lecture delivered by Dr. Joseph Greenberg in April, 1952, to the staff of the Laboratory of Social Relations, Harvard University. I am grateful to Dr. Greenberg for this help and stimulation.

23. Much of the remaining portion of this paper is drawn, in slightly modified form, from a monograph (*Culture* ["Papers of the Peabody Museum of Harvard University"], in press) by A. L. Kroeber and C. Kluckhohn. While most of the paragraphs utilized here were originally drafted by Kluckhohn, they have been improved by Dr. Kroeber, to whom gratitude is expressed for permission to reuse in this form.

24. R. Jakobson (1949) remarks: "Linguistic analysis with its concept of ultimate phonemic entities signally converges with modern physics which revealed the granular structure of matter as composed of elementary particles."

25. Wiener (1948) and Lévi-Strauss (1951) also present contrasting views on the possibilities of discovering lawful regularities in anthropological data. Wiener argues (*a*) that the obtainable statistical runs are not long enough and (*b*) that observers modify the

Kroeber feels that it is highly unlikely that any such constant elemental units will be discovered. Their place is on lower, more basic levels of organization of phenomena. Here and there suggestions have been ventured that there are such basic elements: the culture trait, for instance, or the small community of face-to-face relations. But no such hints have been systematically developed by their proponents, let alone accepted by others. Culture traits can obviously be divided and subdivided and resubdivided at will, according to occasion or need. Or, for that matter, they are often combined into larger complexes which are still treatable, in *ad hoc* situations, as unitary traits and are, in fact, ordinarily spoken of as traits in such situations. The face-to-face community, of course, is not actually a unit of culture but the supposed unit of *social* reference or frame for what might be called a "minimal culture." At that, even such a social unit has in most cases no sharply defined actual limits.

As for the larger groups of phenomena like religion that make up "the universal pattern"—or even subdivisions of these such as "crisis rites" or "fasting" —these are recurrent indeed, but they are not uniform. Anyone can make a definition that will separate magic from religion; but no one has yet found a definition that all other students accept: the phenomenal contents of the concepts of religion and magic simply intergrade too much. This is true even though almost everyone would agree in differentiating large masses of specific phenomena as respectively religious and magical—supplicating a powerful but unseen deity in the heavens, for instance, as against sticking a pin into an effigy. In short, concepts like religion and magic have an undoubted heuristic utility in given situations. But they are altogether too fluid in conceptual range for use either as strict categories or as units from which larger concepts can be built up. After all, they are in origin common-sense concepts, like "boy," "youth," "man," "old man," which neither physiologists nor psychologists will wholly discard but which they will also not attempt to include among the elementary units and basic concepts upon which they rear their sciences.

This conclusion of Kroeber's is akin to what Boas said about social-science methodology in 1930: "The analysis of the phenomena is our prime object. Generalizations will be more significant the closer we adhere to definite forms. The attempts to reduce all social phenomena to a closed system of laws applicable to every society and explaining its structure and history do not seem a promising undertaking" (Boas, 1930, p. 268). The significance of generalizations is proportional to the definiteness of the forms and concepts analyzed out of phenomena—in this seems to reside the weakness of the uniformities in culture heretofore suggested; they are *indefinite*.

A case on the other side is put as follows by Julian Steward (1949) in his important paper: "Cultural Causality and Law: A Trial Formulation of the Development of Early Civilization":

> It is not necessary that any formulation of cultural regularities provide an ultimate

---

phenomena by their conscious study of them. Lévi-Strauss replies that linguistics at least can meet these two objections and suggests that certain aspects of social organization can also be studied in ways that obviate the difficulties. It may be added that Wiener has remarked in conversation with one of us that he is convinced of the practicability of devising new mathematical instruments which would permit of satisfactory treatment of social-science facts. Finally, note Murdock's (1949, p. 259) finding: "Cultural forms in the field of social organization reveal a degree of regularity and of conformity to scientific law not significantly inferior to that found in the so-called natural sciences."

explanation of culture change. In the physical and biological sciences, formulations are merely approximations of observed regularities, and they are valid as working hypotheses despite their failure to deal with ultimate realities. So long as a cultural law formulates recurrences of similar inter-relationships of phenomena, it expresses cause and effect in the same way that the law of gravity formulates but does not ultimately explain the attraction between masses of matter. Moreover, like the law of gravity, which has been greatly modified by the theory of relativity, any formulation of cultural data may be useful as a working hypothesis, even though further research requires that it be qualified or reformulated.

Cultural regularities may be formulated on different levels, each in its own terms. At present, the greatest possibilities lie in the purely cultural or superorganic level, for anthropology's traditional primary concern with culture has provided far more data of this kind. Moreover, the greater part of culture history is susceptible to treatment only in superorganic terms. Both sequential or diachronic formulations and synchronic formulations are superorganic, and they may be functional to the extent that the data permit. Redfield's tentative formulation that urban culture contrasts with folk culture in being more individualized, secularized, heterogeneous, and disorganized is synchronic, superorganic, and functional. Morgan's evolutionary schemes and White's formulation concerning the relationship of energy to cultural development are sequential and somewhat functional. Neither type, however, is wholly one or the other. A time-dimension is implied in Redfield's formulation, and synchronic, functional relationships are implied in White's. . . .

The present statement of scientific purpose and methodology rests on a conception of culture that needs clarification. *If the more important institutions of culture can be isolated from their unique setting so as to be typed, classified, and related to recurring antecedents or functional correlates, it follows that it is possible to consider the institutions in question as the basic or constant ones, whereas the features that lend uniqueness are the secondary or variable ones.* For example, the American high civilizations had agriculture, social classes, and a priest-temple-idol cult. As types, these institutions are abstractions of what was actually present in each area, and they do not take into account the particular crops grown, the precise patterning of the social classes, or the conceptualization of deities, details of ritual, and other religious features of each culture center.

There are, admittedly, few genuine uniformities in culture content unless one states the content in extremely general form—e.g., clothing, shelter, incest taboos, and the like. There are mainly what Kidder has called "likenesses rather than identities." The seventy-two items listed by Murdock (1949, p. 124) "which occur, so far as the author's knowledge goes, in every culture known to history or ethnography" are mainly blanket categories of the "universal ground plan," though a few, such as "modesty concerning natural functions," approach a certain kind of specificity. This list could doubtless be extended. Hallowell[26] in an unpublished paper has suggested self-concepts. Even the most exhaustive list, however, would have to be purged of culture-bound or partially culture-bound categories before it could serve more than the rough heuristic utility suggested by Herskovits' (1948, p. 239) comment on the organization of a "rounded study of a culture":

> The assumptions that underlie the progression of topics in such a presentation is that of most descriptive studies. They derive from a logic that proceeds from the consideration of those aspects that supply the physical wants of man, to those that order social relations, and finally to the aspects which, in giving meaning to the universe, sanction everyday living, and in their aesthetic manifestations afford men

26. "The Self and Its Behavioral Environment." To appear in: Geza Roheim (ed.), *Psychoanalysis and the Social Sciences*, Vol. IV.

some of the deepest satisfactions they experience.

A few rather specific content universals have been mentioned earlier. A few others could also be mustered. As Murdock has shown, the nuclear family is universal either as the sole prevailing form or as the basic unit from which more complex familial forms are compounded. Boas (1911) remarked that "the three personal pronouns—I, thou, and he—occur in all human languages."[27] Unilateral preferential cross-cousin marriage takes rather consistently different forms in matrilateral than in patrilateral societies. Institutionalized female homosexuality appears to be largely, if not completely, absent in matrilateral societies.

But, in general, one, *of course*, expects uniqueness in detail—this follows from the very essence of culture theory. As Steward remarks in the passage just quoted, the secondary or variable features of culture naturally exhibit distinctiveness. After all, the *content* of different atoms and of different cells is by no means identical. These are constant elemental units of *form*. Wissler, Murdock, and others have shown that there are a considerable number of categories and of structural principles found in all cultures. Fortes (1949) speaks of kinship as an "irreducible principle of Tale social organization." It appears to be an irreducible principle of all cultures, however much its elaboration and the emphasis upon it may vary. When Fortes also says that "every social system presupposes such basic axioms," he is likewise pointing to a constant elemental unit of each and every culture.

The inescapable fact of cultural relativism does not justify the conclusion that cultures are in all respects utterly disparate monads and hence strictly noncomparable entities. If this were literally true, a comparative science of culture would be *ex hypothesi* impossible. It is, unfortunately, the case that up to this point anthropology has not solved very satisfactorily the problem of describing cultures in such a way that objective comparison is possible. Most cultural monographs organize the data in terms of the categories of our own contemporary Western culture: economics, technology, social organization, and the like. Such an ordering, of course, tears many of the facts from their own actual context and loads the analysis. The implicit assumption is that our categories are "given" by nature—an assumption contradicted most emphatically by these very investigations of different cultures. A smaller number of studies have attempted to present the information consistently in terms of the category system and whole way of thought of the culture being described. This approach obviously excludes the immediate possibility of a complete set of common terms of reference for comparison. Such a system of comparable concepts and terms remains to be worked out and will probably be established only gradually.

In principle, however, there is a generalized framework that underlies the more apparent and striking facts of cultural relativity. All cultures constitute so many somewhat distinct answers to essentially the same questions posed by human biology and by the generalities of the human situation. These are the considerations explored by Wissler under the heading of "the universal culture pattern" and by Murdock under the rubric of "the least common denominators of cultures." Every society's patterns for living must provide approved and sanctioned ways for dealing with such universal circumstances as the existence of two sexes; the helplessness of infants; the need for satisfaction of the elementary biological requirements such as food, warmth, and sex;

27. For a fuller discussion of the implications of this and related facts, see Riezler (1950).

the presence of individuals of different ages and of differing physical and other capacities. The basic similarities in human biology the world over are vastly more massive than the variations. Equally, there are certain necessities in social life for this kind of animal, regardless of where that life is carried on or in what culture. Co-operation to obtain subsistence and for other ends requires a certain minimum of reciprocal behavior, of a standard system of communication, and, indeed, of mutually accepted values. The facts of human biology and of human gregariousness supply, therefore, certain invariant points of reference from which cross-cultural comparison can start without begging questions that are themselves at issue. As Wissler pointed out, the broad outlines of the ground plan of all cultures are and have to be about the same because men always and everywhere are faced with certain unavoidable problems which arise out of the situation "given" by nature. Since most of the patterns of all cultures crystallize around the same foci, there are significant respects in which each culture is not wholly isolated, self-contained, disparate but rather related to and comparable with all other cultures.

Valid cross-cultural comparison could best proceed from the invariant points of reference supplied by the biological, psychological, and sociosituational "givens" of human life. These and their interrelations determine the likenesses in the broad categories and general assumptions that pervade all cultures because the "givens" provide foci around which and within which the patterns of every culture crystallize. Hence comparison can escape from the bias of any distinct culture by taking as its frame of reference natural limits, conditions, clues, and pressures. Cultural concepts are human artifacts, but the conceptualization of nature is enough bound by stubborn and irreducible fact so that organisms having the same kind of nervous system will at the very least understand one another, relatively free from arbitrary convention. Hartmann, Kris, and Lowenstein (1951, pp. 13–14) have well joined the various kinds of determinants in this statement from a (tempered) psychoanalytic viewpoint:

> The "ubiquity" of certain symbols, particularly of sexual symbols, seems accountable if we keep in mind how fundamentally similar every human infant's situation in the adult world is; how limited the number of meaningful situations is which the infant invests with affect; how typical and invariant the infant's anxieties are, and finally how uniform some of his basic perceptions and bodily sensations are bound to be. The fact that most sexual symbols are related to parts of the body and their function has repeatedly been pointed out. These functions are familiar from a large number of experiences of the child and these experiences themselves are organized in the image of the body, one of the apparatus of the ego. However far the differentiation of human behavior by environmental influences may go, the basic relationship of precepts to parts of the body, of movements to the impulses to caress or hurt, to eliminate or to include, to receive or to retain—at least to these—not only form the basis for the formation of symbols but are equally the basis for the universality of nonverbal communication . . . not only the body is "human"; the fact that the personality is structured, that verbalization is part of the function of the apparatus of all men, that the transition from primary to secondary processes in the child's development, etc., are universal, is bound to influence the formation of symbols. . . . We expect to find "limits" of ubiquity and cultural variations and superimposed symbolic meanings around an ubiquitous core.
>
> . . . Propositions dealing with the oedipus complex imply similar assumptions: the fetalization of the human and the extraordinary dependence of the infant on adult (maternal) care and protection, the development of impulses of a genital order at a time when the child lives among adults, is attached to them and at the same

time still totally dependent on them, is the nucleus of a conflict situation which we believe to be universal.

The next step is to organize data and write an ethnography within the framework of the invariant points of reference. The first serious trial will not be easy, but it should be rewarding.

In conclusion, it should be explicitly recognized that this procedure, like any other scientific method, has its cost as well as its gain. In this case, however, the cost would not be greater than in most current practice. This involves abstraction and relative neglect of how the events or patterns described appear or "feel" from the standpoint of participants (cf. Riezler, 1950). It is a question of what MacLeod (1947)[28] has called "the sociological bias," analogous to the stimulus-receptor bias in the field of perception:

> This bias in its most common form involves the acceptance of the structures and processes of society as defined by the sociologist as the true coordinates for the specification of behavior and experience. From this point of view, *e.g.*, the church or the political party in which the individual possesses membership, is regarded as an institution of society, possessing the manifold properties and functions which a many-sided sociological investigation reveals, rather than as the church or political party as it is apprehended and reacted to by the individual. The process of social adjustment, of socialization or of attitude formation thus becomes defined in terms of a set of norms which have reality for the scientific observer, but not necessarily for the individual concerned.

28. Quoted in Hallowell, *op. cit.*

REFERENCES

Aberle, D.; Cohen, A.; Davis, A.; Levy, M.; and Sutton, F. 1950. "The Functional Prerequisites of a Society," *Ethics*, LX, No. 2, 100–111.

Allee, W. C. 1951. *Cooperation among Animals: With Human Implications.* New York: Henry Schuman.

Bates, Marston. 1950. *The Nature of Natural History.* New York: Charles Scribner's Sons.

Bergman, R. A. M. 1952. "The Biological Foundations of Society," *Civilisations*, II, No. 1, 1–15.

Boas, Franz. 1911. *Mind of Primitive Man.* New York: Macmillan Co.

——. 1940. "The Origin of Totemism." In his *Race, Language, and Culture*, pp. 316–23. New York: Macmillan Co.

Bonaparte, Marie. 1947. *Myths of War.* London: Imago Publishing Co.

Evans-Pritchard, E. E. 1940. *The Nuer.* Oxford: Clarendon Press.

Fei Hsiao-tung and Chang Chih-i. 1945. *Earthbound China: A Study of Rural Economy in Yünnan.* Chicago: University of Chicago Press.

Firth, Raymond. 1951. *Elements of Social Organization.* New York: Philosophical Library.

Ford, Clellan S., and Beach, Frank A. 1951. *Patterns of Sexual Behavior.* New York: Harper & Bros.

Fortes, Meyer. 1949. *The Web of Kinship among the Tallensi.* London: Oxford University Press, for the International African Institute.

Hartmann, Heinz; Kris, Ernst; and Lowenstein, Rudolph M. 1951. "Some Psychoanalytic Comments on 'Culture and Personality.'" In *Psychoanalysis and Culture*, pp. 3–31.

Herskovits, Melville. 1948. *Man and His Works.* New York: A. A. Knopf.

Homans, George. 1950. *The Human Group.* New York: Harcourt, Brace & Co.

Hsu, Francis L. K. 1948. *Under the Ancestors' Shadow: Chinese Culture and Personality.* New York: Columbia University Press.

Jakobson, R. 1949. "On the Identification of Phonemic Entities," *Travaux du Cercle linguistique de Copenhague*, V, 205–13.

Jakobson, R.; Fant, C.; and Halle, M. 1952. *Preliminaries to Speech Analysis.* ("MIT Acoustics Laboratory Technical Reports," No. 13.)

KIDDER, A. V. 1940. "Looking Backward," *Proceedings of the American Philosophical Society*, LXXXIII, No. 4, 527–37.

KLUCKHOHN, CLYDE, and MORGAN, WILLIAM. 1951. "Some Notes on Navaho Dreams." In *Psychoanalysis and Culture*, pp. 120–31.

KLUCKHOHN, FLORENCE. 1950. "Dominant and Substitute Profiles of Cultural Orientations," *Social Forces*, XXVIII, 376–93.

KROEBER, ALFRED L. 1949. "The Concept of Culture in Science," *Journal of General Education*, III, 182–88.

KROEBER, A. L., and KLUCKHOHN, C. 1952. *Culture*, Part III. ("Papers of the Peabody Museum of Harvard University.")

LÉVI-STRAUSS, C. 1951. "Language and the Analysis of Social Laws," *American Anthropologist*, n.s., LIII, No. 2, 155–63.

LINTON, RALPH. 1936. *The Study of Man*. New York: Appleton-Century-Crofts, Inc.

LYND, R. S. 1939. *Knowledge for What?* Princeton: Princeton University Press.

LYND, ROBERT S. and HELEN M. 1929. *Middletown*. New York: Harcourt, Brace & Co.

——. 1937. *Middletown in Transition: A Study in Cultural Conflicts*. New York: Harcourt, Brace & Co.

MACLEOD, ROBERT B. 1947. "The Phenomenological Approach to Social Psychology," *Psychological Review*, LIV, 193–210.

MALINOWSKI, BRONISLAW. 1944. *A Scientific Theory of Culture*. Chapel Hill: University of North Carolina Press.

MURDOCK, G. P. 1940. "The Cross-cultural Survey," *American Sociological Review*, V, No. 3, 361–70.

——. 1945. "The Common Denominator of Cultures." In LINTON, R. (ed.), *The Science of Man in the World Crisis*, pp. 123–42. New York: Columbia University Press.

——. 1949. *Social Structure*. New York: Macmillan Co.

MURDOCK, G. P., *et al.* 1950. *Outline of Cultural Materials*. New Haven: Human Relations Area Files, Inc.

NADEL, S. F. 1951. *The Foundations of Social Anthropology*. Glencoe, Ill.: Free Press.

PARSONS, ELSIE C. 1936. *Mitla: Town of the Souls, and Other Zapoteco-speaking Pueblos of Oaxaca, Mexico*. Chicago: University of Chicago Press.

——. 1945. *Peguche, Canton of Otavalo, Province of Imbabura, Ecuador: A Study of Andean Indians*. Chicago: University of Chicago Press.

PARSONS, T. 1949. *Essays in Sociological Theory*. Glencoe, Ill.: Free Press.

RANK, OTTO. 1914. *The Myth of the Birth of the Hero*. New York: Journal of Nervous and Mental Disease Publishing Co.

REDFIELD, ROBERT. 1941. *The Folk Culture of Yucatan*. Chicago: University of Chicago Press.

RIEZLER, K. 1950. *Man Mutable and Immutable: The Fundamental Structure of Social Life*. Chicago: Henry Regnery.

STEWARD, JULIAN. 1949. "Cultural Causality and Law: A Trial Formulation of the Development of Early Civilization," *American Anthropologist*, n.s., LI, No. 1, 1–27.

——. 1950. *Area Research: Theory and Practice*. (Social Science Research Council Bull. 63.)

WEST, JAMES. 1945. *Plainville, U.S.A.* New York: Columbia University Press.

WIENER, N. 1948. *Cybernetics*. New York: Technology Press, John Wiley & Sons.

WILSON, A. T. M. 1951. *Some Aspects of Social Process*. (*Journal of Social Issues*, Supplementary Ser., No. 5.)

YANG, MARTIN C. 1945. *A Chinese Village: Taitou, Shantung Province*. New York: Columbia University Press.

Social Anthropology and the Method of Controlled Comparison* **

FRED EGGAN
University of Chicago

I

THE contemporary student of anthropology is in a difficult position in attempting to achieve a sound orientation in our rapidly changing and developing discipline. Nowhere is this more true than in the general field of cultural anthropology, where there is an apparent schism between those who call themselves ethnologists and the newer group of social anthropologists. Ethnology, which has had its major development in the United States, has been concerned primarily with culture history and culture process; social anthropology, on the other hand, is primarily a product of British anthropology and has emphasized social structure and function as its major concepts. These differences in emphasis and interest have led to considerable misunderstanding on both sides. As one who has had a foot in both camps for some two decades I may perhaps be permitted some observations on this situation, along with some suggestions as to a common meeting-ground.[1]

Since World War II rapid changes have taken place in all branches of anthropology. Genetics and the experimental method, plus a host of new fossil finds from Africa, are revolutionizing physical anthropology; archeology, with the aid of radiocarbon dating and other new techniques, is beginning to achieve a world-wide chronology and is turning to cultural anthropology for further insight into cultural development; linguistics, with structural methods well established, is returning anew to historical problems and re-examining the relations of language and culture. But ethnology, one of whose tasks it is to synthesize and interpret the conclusions reached by its sister disciplines, is lagging behind.

It is not clear how long anthropology can remain partly a biological science, partly a humanity, and partly a social science. As we shift from the descriptive, data-gathering phases of anthropology to analysis, interpretation and theory, it is inevitable that realignments will come about. My predecessors in the presidency during the postwar period have sketched some of these new developments and realignments as they have seen them.[2] It is highly probable that the forces for fusion will prevail over the tendencies to fission in the near future, so far as the United States is concerned; in England the forces are more nearly balanced, and the outcome is more uncertain.[3] In the long run we may or may not follow the patterns set by other disciplines.

Turning to the field of cultural anthropology, one of the important developments of the last few years has been the series of articles and books defining, denouncing, or defending "social anthropology." Murdock, in the most out-

* Presidential paper, 1953, American Anthropological Association.

** Reprinted from the *American Anthropologist,* Vol. 56, New Series, No. 5 (October 1954), 743-763, by permission of the author and the American Anthropological Association.

spoken attack, notes that: "For a decade or more, anthropologists in other countries have privately expressed an increasingly ambivalent attitude toward recent trends in British anthropology—a curious blend of respect and dissatisfaction" (1951:465). His analysis of the strengths and weaknesses of British social anthropology, as revealed in current productions, and his diagnosis of the social anthropologists as primarily "sociologists" have led to replies and counterreplies.

At the International Symposium on Anthropology sponsored by the Wenner-Gren Foundation a special session was devoted to "Cultural/Social Anthropology," in which various scholars presented the usages current in their respective countries. Tax's (Tax and others 1953:225) summary of the consensus is to the effect that we ought to "use the words 'cultural' and 'social' anthropology interchangeably and forget about the question of terminology"; but Kroeber in his "Concluding Review" (1953:357–76) returns to the problem of society and culture and finds distinctions. If these distinctions were merely a question of factional dispute or of alternate terms for similar activities, we could agree, with Lowie (1953:527–28), on some neutral term such as "ethnography"—or allow time to make the decision in terms of relative popularity.

But the distinctions being made are not merely a matter of British and American rivalry or of terminology, and it is essential that we realize that there is a problem and that it is an important one. After accepting contemporary British social anthropologists as "true ethnographers" interested in the realities of culture, Lowie (1953:531) goes on to unequivocally reject Fortes' contention that "social structure is not an aspect of culture but the entire culture of a given people handled in a special frame of theory" (Fortes 1953*a*: 21). However, many British social anthropologists would go even further than Fortes! In general they make a clear distinction between the concepts of *society* and *culture* and think of social anthropology as concerned primarily with the former. Murdock's (1951:471) startling conclusion that the Britishers are sociologists was anticipated by Radcliffe-Brown (1931*a*) and recently reaffirmed by Evans-Pritchard: "I must emphasize that, theoretically at any rate, social anthropology is the study of all human societies. . . . Social anthropology can therefore be regarded as a branch of sociological studies, that branch which chiefly devotes itself to primitive societies" (1951:10–11). In contrast, the current Americanist opinion subsumes social structure as one aspect of culture, following Tylor (Lowie 1953:531), or separates the two but gives primacy to the concept of culture.

Before we read our British brethren out of the anthropological party, however, it might be wise to see whether we may not have taken too narrow a view of cultural anthropology. Lowie, who, along with many American anthropologists, takes his cultural text from Tylor, defines the aim of ethnography as "the *complete* description of all cultural phenomena everywhere and at all periods" (1953:528, italics Lowie's). It may be both possible and useful to view the "capabilities and habits acquired by man *as a member of society*" under the heading of social structure, despite the fact that Lowie finds it inconceivable. We might wait for the remainder of Fortes' materials on the Tallensi before rendering a verdict. And if we look more closely at Tylor's famous definition it seems clear that anthropology should be concerned with *both* society and culture, as they are interrelated and reflected in human behavior. We need a complete description and interpretation of both social and cultural phenomena, not to mention those concerned with the individual, if we are going to think in global terms. I would agree with Hallowell that society, culture, and personality may "be conceptually differentiated for specialized types of analysis and study. On the other hand, it is being more clearly recognized than heretofore that society, culture and personality cannot be postulated as completely independent variables" (1953:600). We can wait until we know more about each of these concepts before we rank them as superior and inferior.

More important, we cannot afford to ignore the contributions of the British social anthropologists to both theory and description. In the last thirty years they have been developing a new approach to the study of man in society, which is currently producing significant results. Is is no accident that many of the best monographs of the postwar period have come out of the small group of British social anthropologists. Reviewing *African Systems of Kinship and Marriage,* Murdock states (1951:465) that "the ethnographic contributions to the volume reveal without exception a very high level of professional competence in field research and in the analysis of social structural data, equalled only by the work of the very best men in other countries." What some of these contributions are has been recently pointed out by Firth (1951*a, b*), Evans-Pritchard (1951), and Fortes (1953*a, b*), among others. While Fortes recognizes that they lack the wide and adventurous sweep of American anthropology, "the loss in diversity is amply balanced by the gains we have derived from concentration on a limited set of problems" (1953*a*:17). Most American anthropologists are inclined to attribute the relative excellence of these contributions to good field techniques or perhaps to superior literary abilities, considering the British theoretical approach as rather barren and lifeless. But this seems to me to be a mistake. The structural point of view makes possible a superior organization and interpretation of the cultural data, and good monographs may well be related to this point of view. If we are to meet this competition (particularly in view of Firth's [1951*a*] account of their new directions) we need to do more than label our British colleagues as "comparative sociologists" or invoke the magical figures of Tylor and Franz Boas.

If I may venture a prescription based on my own experience, we need to adopt the structural-functional approach of British social anthropology and integrate it with our traditional American interest in culture process and history. For the weaknesses of British social anthropology are in precisely those aspects where we are strong, and if we can develop a way of relating the two approaches we can perhaps save ethnology from the destiny to which Kroeber has assigned it—"to a premature fate or a senescent death as one may see it"

(1953:366). I feel encouraged in this attempt because I have a genuine interest in both culture and social structure and because Murdock believes I have succeeded "in fusing functional analysis with an interest in history and an awareness of process in a highly productive creative synthesis" (1951:469).

In contrast to most of my contemporaries I arrived at this synthesis without too many conflicts. My early anthropological education was in the Boas tradition as interpreted by Cole, Sapir, and Spier—with additions from Redfield. But before the mold had hardened too far I came under the influence also of Radcliffe-Brown. The early thirties was a period of intense excitement among graduate students at Chicago, enhanced by debates between Linton and Radcliffe-Brown and heated arguments about functionalism. Redfield's (1937) account gives something of the flavor of this period, as well as a brief characterization of Radcliffe-Brown's contributions to anthropology. And Linton's *Study of Man* (1936) shows definite evidence of the impact of the structural and functional points of view on his thinking: culture and society are clearly differentiated, though they are mutually dependent, and concepts such as social system, status and role, integration and function are intermixed with the more usual cultural categories. But *The Study of Man*, while widely admired, was little imitated by Linton's colleagues—though it has had important effects on social science as a whole and on some of his students.

Once we were in the field, however, some of us discovered that the alternatives about which we had been arguing were in reality complementary. We found that the structural approach gave a new dimension to the flat perspectives of American ethnography and allowed us to ask new kinds of questions. Functionalism gave us meaningful answers to some questions and enabled us again to see cultures as wholes. But we also maintained an interest in cultural regions and a concern for culture process and cultural development. The resulting data were utilized for a variety of purposes. Some students prepared "descriptive integrations" which approximated to that complex reality which is history. Others were attracted to the formulation of general propositions as to society or culture. I, myself, began by working in limited areas on problems of kinship and social structure, utilizing comparison as a major technique and attempting to see changes over time. When Radcliffe-Brown went to Oxford in 1937 we put together some of these studies under the ambitious title, *Social Anthropology of North American Tribes*.

The distinction between society and culture, far from complicating the procedures of analysis and comparison, has actually facilitated them. Generalization requires repeatable units which can be identified, and social structures, which tend to have a limited number of forms, readily lend themselves to classification and comparison. Cultural data, on the other hand, tend to fall into patterns of varying types which are more easily traced through time and space. Social structures and cultural patterns may vary independently of one another, but both have their locus in the behavior of individuals in social groups. Depending on our problems one or the other may be central in our analysis, and we may utilize one or another of the basic methods of investigation—history or science. I would agree with Kroeber (1935:569) that these latter need differentiation, "precisely because we shall presumably penetrate further in the end by two approaches than by one," but I see no reason why we should not use the two approaches together when possible.

The crucial problem with regard to generalization, whether broad or limited, is the method of comparison which is used. In the United States, for reasons which I will mention later on, the comparative method has long been in disrepute and was supplanted by what Boas called the "historical method." In England, on the other hand, the comparative method has had a more continuous utilization. Nadel (1951:222–55) discusses the techniques and limitations of the comparative method and the nature of the results which may be obtained from its application. As Radcliffe-Brown has stated: "It is only by the use of the comparative method that we can arrive at general explanations. The alternative is to confine ourselves to particularistic explanations similar to those of the historian. The two kinds of explanation are both legitimate and do not conflict; but both are needed for the understanding of societies and their institutions" (1952*a*:113–14).

The particular adaptation of the comparative method to social anthropology which Radcliffe-Brown has made is well illustrated in The Huxley Memorial Lecture for 1951, where he begins with exogamous moiety divisions in Australia and shows that the Australian phenomena are instances of certain widespread general tendencies in human societies. For him the task of social anthropology is to "formulate and validate statements about the conditions of existence of social systems . . . and the regularities that are observable in social change" (1951:22). This systematic comparison of a world-wide variety of instances, while an ultimate objective of social anthropology, is rather difficult to carry out in terms of our present limited knowledge of social systems. We can make some general observations about institutions such as the family; and the war between the sexes in aboriginal Australia has some interesting parallels with the world of Thurber. But I am not sure, to give one example, that the "Yin-Yang philosophy of ancient China is the systematic elaboration of the principle that can be used to define the social structure of moieties in Australian tribes" (1951:21), though Radcliffe-Brown's analysis and wide experience give it a certain plausibility.

My own preference is for the utilization of the comparative method on a smaller scale and with as much control over the frame of comparison as it is possible to secure. It has seemed natural to utilize regions of relatively homogeneous culture or to work within social or cultural types, and to further control the ecology and the historical factors so far as it is possible to do so. Radcliffe-Brown has done this with great skill in *The Social Organization of Australian Tribes* (1931*b*). After comparing the Australian moiety structures and finding their common denominators, I would prefer to make a comparison with the results of a similar study of moiety structures and associated practices of the Indians of Southern California, who approximate rather closely the Australian sociocultural situation. The results of this comparison could then be matched against comparable studies of Northwest Coast and other similar moiety systems, and the similarities and differences systematically examined by the method of concomitant variation. I think we would end up, perhaps, with Radcliffe-Brown's relationship of "opposition," or the unity of opposites, but we would have much more, as well, in the form of a clearer understanding of each type or subtype and of the nature of the mechanisms by which they are maintained or changed. While I share Radcliffe-Brown's vision of an ultimate science of society, I think that we first have to cultivate more intensively what Merton (1949:5) has called the middle range of theory. I suggest the method of controlled comparison as a convenient instrument for its exploration, utilizing covariation and correlation, and avoiding too great a degree of abstraction.

Before examining the ramifications and possible results of such exploration it may be useful to glance at selected aspects of the history of anthropology to see how certain of the present differences between American and British anthropologists have come about. We are somewhere in the middle of one of Kroeber's "configurations of culture growth," and it is important to see which patterns are still viable and which are close to exhaustion.

II

The early developments in American cultural anthropology have been delineated by Lowie (1937) and parallel in many respects those which were occurring in England. In addition to Morgan, Bandelier, Cushing, J. O. Dorsey, Alice Fletcher, and others were among the pioneers whose work is today largely forgotten in the United States. For with the advent of Franz Boas a major break was made with the past, resulting not so much from his program for cultural anthropology as in its selective implementation. Boas in "The Limitations of the Comparative Method" (1896) outlined a program which included two major tasks. The first task involved detailed studies of individual tribes in their cultural and regional context as a means to the reconstruction of the histories of tribal cultures and regions. A second task concerned the comparisons of these tribal histories, with the ultimate objective of formulating general laws of cultural growth, which were psychological in character (1940:278–79). This second task, which Boas thought of as the more important of the two, was never to be fully implemented by his students.

Boas formulated this program in connection with a destructive criticism of the comparative method as then practiced in England and America. After stating as a principle of method that uniformity of processes was essential for comparability, he goes on to say: "If anthropology desires to establish the laws governing the growth of culture it must not confine itself to comparing the results of growth alone, but whenever such is feasible, it must compare the processes of growth, and these can be discovered by means of studies of the cultures of small geographical areas" (1940:280). He then compares this "historical method" with the "comparative method," which he states has been remarkably barren of results, and predicts that it will not become fruitful until we make our comparisons "on the broader and sounder basis which I ventured to outline." The requirement that only those phenomena can be compared which are derived psychologically or historically from common causes, valuable as it may have been at that time, has had the effect of predisposing most of Boas' students against the comparative method—except in linguistics where genetic relationships could be assumed—and hence against any generalizations which require comparison. And the processes which Boas sought in a study of art and mythology on the Northwest Coast proved more difficult to isolate than was anticipated. Kroeber notes that though Boas was "able to show a multiplicity of processes in culture, he was not able—it was impossible in his day and perhaps is still—to formulate these into a systematic theory" (1953:368).

In the "Formative Period"[4] of American ethnology, from 1900 to 1915, these were minor considerations. There were the vanishing Indian cultures to study, and it was natural for the students of Boas to concentrate on the first portion of his program. They wrote theses, for the most part, on specific problems, or to test various theories which had been advanced to explain art, or myth, or ritual, generally with negative results. This clearing of the intellectual air was essential, but it also led to excesses, as in Goldenweiser's famous study of totemism (1910). It also resulted in the ignoring of earlier anthropologists and even contemporaries. Alice Fletcher's *The Hako: A Pawnee Ceremony* (1904) excellently describes and interprets a ritual but was never used as a model.

The major attention of the early Boas students was devoted to the task of ordering their growing data on the American Indian in tribal and regional context. During this and the following periods many important monographs and studies were published, which formed a solid base for future work. The climax of this fact-gathering revolution was reached with the culture-area concept as crystallized by Wissler (1914, 1922), and in the studies by Boas on the art, mythology, and social organization of the Northwest Coast.

The period which followed, from 1915 to 1930, was a "Florescent Period" in American ethnology. The culture area provided a framework for the analysis and interpretation of the cultural data in terms of history and process. Sapir opened the period with his famous *Time Perspective* (1916), which began: "Cultural anthropology is more and more rapidly getting to realize itself as a strictly historical science. Its data cannot be understood, either in themselves or in their relation to one another, except as the end-points of specific sequences of events reaching back into the remote past." Wissler, Lowie, Kroeber, Spier, Benedict, and many others provided a notable series of regional studies utilizing distributional analyses of cultural traits for chronological inferences—and for the study of culture process. Wissler developed the "law of diffusion" and then turned his attention to the dynamic factors underlying the culture area itself. In *The Relation of Nature to Man in Aboriginal America* (1926) he thought that he had found them in the relationship of the culture center to the underlying ecology. The great museums dominated this period, and American anthropology shared in the general prosperity and optimism which followed the first World War.

One result of these distributional studies was that chronology tended to become an end in itself, and some ethnologists became so preoccupied with seeking time sequences that they did not pay much attention to culture as such. The analysis of culture into traits or elements and their subsequent treatment often violated principles of historical method by robbing them of their context. The normal procedure of historians of basing their analysis on chronology was here reversed—the chronology resulted from the analytic study. The generalizations as to process which were formulated were used as short-cuts to further historical research.

Another important result of these studies was the conception of culture which gradually developed. Culture came to be viewed as a mere aggregation of traits brought together by the accidents of diffusion. Here is Benedict's conclusion to her doctoral dissertation: "It is, so far as we can see, an ultimate fact of human nature that man builds up his culture out of disparate elements, combining and recombining them; and until we have abandoned the superstition that the result is an organism functionally interrelated, we shall be unable to see our cultural life objectively, or to control its manifestations" (1923: 84–85).

The revolt against this mechanical and atomistic conception of culture came both from without and from within. Dixon (1928) criticized both Wissler's procedures and his conceptions of the processes of culture growth, as well as his formulation of the dynamics of the culture area. Spier (1929:222) renounced historical reconstruction as misleading and unnecessary for understanding the nature of the processes of culture growth, advocating in its place a consideration of the actual conditions under which cultural growth takes place. Benedict was soon engaged in the study of cultural patterns and configurations, and her *Patterns of Culture* (1934) represents a complete reversal of her earlier position—here superstition has become reality.

During this period there was little interest in social structure as such, even though Kroeber, Lowie, and Parsons all studied Pueblo life at first hand. The shadows of Morgan, McLennan, Spencer, and Maine still loomed over them, and sociological interpretations were generally rejected in favor of psychological or linguistic ones. Lowie, however, began to develop a moderate functional position and sociological orientation with regard to social organization, perhaps best exemplified in his article on "Relationship Terms" (1929).

The "Expansionist Period" which followed, 1930–1940, was a time of troubles and of transition for American ethnology. The old gods were no longer omniscient—and there was an invasion of foreign gods from overseas. The depression brought the great museums to their knees and temporarily ended their activities in ethnological research; the center of gravity shifted more and more to the universities, as the social sciences grappled with the new social problems. This was a period of considerable expansion for cultural anthropology, much of it in terms of joint departments with sociology. Archeology also experienced a remarkable expansion during the decade, partly as a by-product of its ability to utilize large quantities of WPA labor. The chronological framework that resulted, based on stratigraphy and other techniques, further emphasized the inadequacy of the reconstructions made from distributional analyses alone.

In the meantime *Argonauts* and *The Andaman Islanders* had been published but had made relatively little impression on American scholars. Malinowski's field methods were admired, and his functional conception of culture struck some responsive chords; as for Radcliffe-Brown, his "ethnological appendix" was utilized but his interpretations of Andamanese customs and beliefs were largely ignored. Soon afterwards, however, Malinowski began developing social anthropology in England on the basis of the functional method and new techniques of field research. Brief visits by Malinowski to the United States, including a summer session at the University of California, plus the work of his early students in Oceania and Africa, led to a considerable increase in his influence, but during the 1930's he was largely preoccupied with developing a program of research for Africa.

In 1931 Radcliffe-Brown, who had been first in South Africa and then in Australia, brought to this country "a method for the study of society, well defined and different enough from what prevailed here to require American anthropologists to reconsider the whole matter of method, to scrutinize their objectives, and to attend to new problems and new ways of looking at problems. He stirred us up and accelerated intellectual variation among us" (Redfield 1937: vii).

As a result of these and other forces American ethnologists began to shift their interests in a variety of directions. Kroeber re-examined the relationship between cultural and natural areas in a more productive way and formulated the concept of culture climax to replace Wissler's culture center. He also explored the problem of culture elements more thoroughly, in the course of which he organized the Culture Element Survey; at the other end of the cultural spectrum he wrote *Configurations of Culture Growth* (1944). Herskovits, who had earlier applied the culture-area concept to Africa, developed a dynamic approach to the study of culture (1950) which has had important results. Redfield, in the meantime, was beginning the series of studies which resulted in *The Folk Culture of Yucatan* (1941)—a new and important approach to the study of social and cultural change.

During this period, also, Steward was beginning his ecological studies of Great Basin tribes, Warner was applying social anthropological concepts and methods to the study of modern American communities, and Sapir was shifting his interests in the direction of psychiatry. Linton, with his perception of new and important trends, had put them together with the old, but his interests also shifted in the direction of personality and culture. Acculturation became a respectable subject with the Redfield, Linton, and Herskovits' "Memorandum on the Study of Acculturation" (1936), and applied anthropology secured a foothold in the Indian Service and in a few other government agencies.

These developments, which gave variety and color to American ethnology, also tended to leave a vacuum in the center of the field. We will never know for sure what might have developed out of this interesting decade if World War II had not come along.

The "Contemporary Period"—the decade since the war—is difficult to characterize. In part there has been a continuation of prewar trends, in part a carry-over of wartime interests, and in part an interest in new problems resulting from the war and its aftermath. There is a growing interest in complex cultures or civilizations, such as China, Japan, India, and Africa, both at the village level and at the level of national culture and national character, and new methods and techniques are in process for their study and comparison.

One postwar development of particular interest in connection with this paper has been the gradual but definite acceptance in many quarters in this country of social anthropology as a separable but related discipline.[5] Of even greater potential significance, perhaps, is the growing alliance between social psychology, sociology, and social anthropology as the core groups of the so-called "behavioral sciences," a relationship also reflected in the Institute of Human Relations at Yale and in the Department of Social Relations at Harvard, as well as elsewhere.

Perhaps most important of all the postwar developments for the future of anthropology has been the very great increase in the interchange of both students and faculty between English and American institutions, including field stations in Africa. The Fulbright program, the Area Research Fellowships of the Social Science Research Council, the International Symposium on Anthropology of the Wenner-Gren Foundation, and the activities of the Carnegie, Rockefeller, and Ford Foundations have all contributed to this increased exchange. I am convinced that such face-to-face contacts in seminar and field represent the most effective way for amalgamation of techniques and ideas to take place. The testimony of students back from London or Africa is to the general effect that our training is superior in ethnography and in problems of culture history but is inferior in social anthropology: kinship, social structure, political organization, law, and so on. There are exceptions, of course, but we would like the exceptions to be the rule.

III

For the details of the complementary developments in England we are indebted to Evans-Pritchard's account in *Social Anthropology* (1951) and to Fortes' inaugural lecture entitled *Social Anthropology at Cambridge Since 1900* (1953*c*). There are differences in emphasis between the Oxford and Cambridge versions, but in general the developments are clear.

In England cultural anthropology got off to a fine start through the efforts of Tylor, Maine, McLennan and other pioneers of the 1860's and 1870's, but their attempts to construct universal stages of development ultimately fell afoul of the facts. The nineteenth-century anthropologists in England were "armchair" anthropologists; it wasn't until Haddon, a zoologist by training, organized the famous Torres Straits expedition of 1898–1900 and converted an assorted group of psychologists and other scientists into ethnologists that field work began. But from this group came the leaders of early twentieth-century British anthropology: Haddon, Rivers, and Seligman. According to Evans-Pritchard, "This expedition marked a turning point in the history of social anthropology in Great Britain. From this time two important and inter-connected developments began to take place: anthropology became more and more a whole-time professional study, and some field experience came to be regarded as an essential part of the training of its students" (1951:73).

During the next decade a gradual separation of ethnology and social anthropology took place, culminating, according to Radcliffe-Brown (1952*b*:276), in an agreement to use "ethnography" for descriptive accounts of nonliterate peoples, "ethnology" for historical reconstructions, and "social anthropology" for the comparative study of the institutions of primitive societies. The institutional division of labor also took a different organization which has led to different views as to how anthropology should be constituted.

Sir James Frazer dominated social anthropology in the early decades of this century, and the conceptions of evolution and progress held sway long after they had given way in American anthropology. But Fortes notes that, while anthropologists had a magnificent field of inquiry, the subject had no intrinsic unity: "At the stage of development it had reached in 1920, anthropology, both in this country and elsewhere, was a bundle-subject, its data gathered, so to speak, from the same forest but otherwise heterogeneous and tied together only by the evolutionary theory" (1953*c*:14).

Ethnology flourished for a period under Haddon, Rivers, and Seligman, but with the advent of Malinowski and Radcliffe-Brown "social anthropology has emerged as the basic discipline concerned with custom and social organization in the simpler societies" (Fortes 1953*c*:16). From their predecessors the latter received their tradition of field research and the principle of the intensive study of limited areas—a principle that Malinowski carried to its logical conclusion.

Beginning in 1924 Malinowski began to train a small but brilliant group of social anthropologists from all parts of the Commonwealth in the field techniques and functional theory that he had developed from his Trobriand experience, but his approach proved inadequate for the complex problems encountered in Africa. This deficiency was remedied in part by the advent of Radcliffe-Brown, who returned to the newly organized Institute of Social Anthropology at Oxford in 1937 and proceeded to give British social anthropology its major current directions. Evans-Pritchard discusses this period with the authority of a participant, and I refer you to his *Social Anthropology* for the details—and for a summary of what a social anthropologist does.

The postwar developments in England have been largely a continuation of prewar developments together with a considerable expansion stimulated by government support of both social anthropological and applied research. Unlike the situation in the United States there is no large established group of sociologists in England, and social anthropology has in part filled the gap. Major theoretical differences as to the nature of social anthropology as a science or as a humanity are developing, but these differences are subordinate to a large area of agreement as to basic problems, methods, and points of view. Just as the American ethnologists of the 1920's had a common language and a common set of problems, so do the British social anthropologists today.

One important key to the understanding of British social anthropology resides in their conception of social structure. The contributions in this field with regard to Africa have been summarized by Fortes in "The Structure of Unilineal Descent Groups" (1953*a*). Here he points out that the guiding ideas in the analysis of African lineage organization have come mainly from Radcliffe-Brown's formulation of the structural principles found in all kinship systems, and goes on to state that he is not alone "in regarding them as among the most important generalizations as yet reached in the study of social structure" (p. 25). For Fortes the social structure is the foundation of the whole social life of any continuing society.

Not only have the British social anthropologists produced an outstanding series of monographs in recent years but they have organized their training programs in the universities and institutes to insure that the flow will continue. In the early stages of training there is a more concentrated program in social anthropology in the major British universities, though the knowledge demanded of other fields is less, and linguistics is generally conspicuous by its absence. Only the top students are given grants for field research. As Evans-Pritchard (1951:76–77) sketches the ideal situation, the student usually spends at least two years in his first field study, including learning to speak the language of the group under observation. Another five years is allotted to publishing the results, or longer if he has teaching duties. A study of a second society is desirable, to avoid the dangers of thinking in terms of a single society, but this can usually be carried out in a shorter period.

Granted that this is the ideal procedure, it still offers a standard against which to compare our American practices. My impression is that our very best graduate students are approximating this standard, but our Ph.D. programs in general require considerably less in terms of field research and specific preparation. We tend to think of the doctorate as an earlier stage in the development of a scholar and not a capstone to an established career.

This proposed program, however, has important implications for social anthropology itself. If each anthropologist follows the Malinowskian tradition of specializing in one, or two, or three societies and spends his lifetime in writing about them, what happens to comparative studies? Evans-Pritchard recognizes this problem: "It is a matter of plain experience that it [the comparative study] is a formidable task which cannot be undertaken by a man who is under the obligation to publish the results of the two or three field studies he has made, since this will take him the rest of his life to complete if he has heavy teaching and administrative duties as well" (1951:89).

In place of the comparative method he proposes the "experimental method," in which preliminary conclusions are formulated and then tested by the same or other social anthropologists on different societies, thus gradually developing broader and more adequate hypotheses. The old comparative method, he says, has been largely abandoned because it seldom gave answers to the questions asked (1951:90).

This concentration on intensive studies of one or two selected societies has its own limitations. The hypotheses advanced on such a basis can often be modified in terms of studies easily available for comparison. Thus Schneider (1953:582–84) points out that some of Evans-Pritchard's generalizations about the Nuer could well have been tested against the Zulu data. The degree to which comparison may sharpen hypotheses is well illustrated by Nadel's study of "Witchcraft in Four African Societies" (1952). There is a further reason for this lack of interest in comparative studies on the part of Evans-Pritchard in that he thinks of social anthropology as "belonging to the humanities rather than to the natural sciences" (1951:60) and conceives of his task as essentially a historical one of "descriptive integration." His colleagues are currently disagreeing with him (Forde 1950; Fortes 1953*c*).

Schapera (1953) has recently reviewed a number of studies utilizing some variation of the comparative method and finds most of them deficient in one respect or another. The comparative approach he advocates involves making an intensive study of a given region and carefully comparing the forms taken among the people of the area by the particular social phenomena which are under scrutiny, so as to classify them into types. These types can then be compared with those of neighboring regions. "Social anthropology would benefit considerably, and have more right to claim that its methods are adequate, if in the near future far more attention were devoted to intensive regional comparisons" (p. 360).

One difficulty in the way of any systematic and intensive comparison of African data is being remedied by the Ethnographic Survey under the direction of Daryll Forde. The absence of any interest in linguistics is a major criticism of a group who advocate learning a language to carry out researches in social structure but who ignore the structure in the languages which they learn. Lévi-Strauss (1951) has pointed out some of the problems in these two fields, and it is difficult to see why they are neglected.

Ultimately the British anthropologists will discover that time perspective is also important and will encourage archeology and historical research. The potentialities of Greenberg's recent genetic classification of African languages, and the subgrouping of Bantu languages through shared correspondences and lexico-statistical techniques, are just beginning to be appreciated. And for those who demand documents there are the Arab records and historical collections such as the Portuguese records for Delagoa Bay. That the same tribes speaking the same languages are still in this region after four hundred years suggests that there is considerable historical material which needs to be utilized. For our best insights into the nature of society and culture come from seeing social structures and culture patterns over time. Here is where we can distinguish the accidental from the general, evaluate more clearly the factors and forces operating in a given situation, and describe the processes involved in general terms. Not to take advantage of the possibilities of studying social and cultural change under such relatively controlled conditions is to do only half the job that needs to be done.

IV

These brief and inadequate surveys indicate that cultural anthropology has had quite a different development in the United States and England and suggest some of the reasons for these differences. They also suggest that the differences may be growing less. In the United States ethnology began with a rejection of Morgan and his interest in the development of social systems, and an acceptance of Tylor and his conception of culture. Tylor's views by-and-large still prevail, though since the 1920's there have been many alternative definitions of culture as anthropologists attempted to get a more *rounded* view of their subject. In England, as Kroeber and Kluckhohn (1952) have pointed out, there has been more resistance to the term "culture"; on the other hand, Morgan is hailed as an important forerunner, particularly for his researches on kinship. Prophets are seldom honored in their own country.

Both Kroeber (1953) and Redfield (1953) have recently reviewed the role of anthropology in relation to the social sciences and to the humanities and have emphasized the virtues of a varied attack on the problems that face us all. With Redfield, I believe we should continue to encourage variety among anthropologists. But I am here particularly concerned with cultural anthropology, and I am disturbed by Kroeber's attitude toward ethnology: "Now how about ethnology?" he writes in his Concluding Review of *Anthropology Today*, "I am about ready to abandon this baby to the wolves." He goes on to detail some of the reasons why ethnology appears to be vanishing: the decrease in primitives, the failure to make classifications and comparisons, and the tendencies to leap directly into large-scale speculations (1953:366–67). His solution is to merge ethnology with culture history and, when that is soundly established, to extricate the processes at work and "generalize the story of culture into its causal factors." This is a return to the original Boas program.

My own suggested solution is an alternate one. While there are few "primitives" in our own back yard, there are the new frontiers of Africa, India, Southeast Asia, Indonesia, and Melanesia to exploit. Here is still a complete range in terms of cultural complexity and degree of culture contact. Africa alone is a much more challenging "laboratory" in many respects than is the American Indian. And for those who like their cultures untouched there is interior New Guinea.

The failure to make adequate classifications and comparisons can in part be remedied by borrowing the methods and techniques of the social anthropologists or by going in the directions pioneered by Murdock (1949). Social structure gives us a preliminary basis for classification in the middle range while universals are sought for. Steward's "sociocultural types" are another step in the directions we want to go.

The tendency to leap directly into large-scale speculations is growing less and will be further controlled as we gradually build a foundation of well-supported hypotheses. Speculations are like mutations in some respects—most of them are worthless but every now and then one advances our development tremendously. We need to keep them for this reason, if for no other.

If we can salvage cultural anthropology in the United States, I do not worry too much about the "anthropological bundle" falling apart in the near future. As a result of the closer co-operation among the subdisciplines of anthropology in this country new bridges are continually being built between them, and joint problems, and even new subfields, are constantly being generated. So long as our interaction remains more intensive than our relations with other disciplines, anthropology will hold together.

One thing we can do is to return to the basic problems American ethnologists were tackling in the 1920's and 1930's, with new methods and points of view and a greater range of concepts. I have elsewhere (1952:35–45) discussed the potential contributions that such a combined approach could achieve, and for the Western Pueblos I have tried to give a specific example (1950). But in terms of present possibilities, not one single region in North America has had adequate treatment. Nor are the possibilities of field research in North America exhausted. The Cheyenne, for example, are still performing the Sun Dance pretty much as it was in Dorsey's day. But despite all the studies of the Sun Dance we still do not have an adequate account giving us the meaning and significance of the rituals for the participants and for the tribe. One such account would enable us to revalue the whole literature of the Sun Dance.

The Plains area is now ripe for a new integration which should be more satisfying then the older ones. In addition to Wissler's and Kroeber's formulations, we now have an outline of cultural development firmly anchored in stratigraphy and radiocarbon dates, and a considerable amount of documentary history as well as a series of monographs on special topics. By centering our attention on social structure, we can see the interrelations of subsistence and ecology, on the one hand, and political and ritual activities, on the other. For those interested in process we can ask: Why did tribal groups coming into the Plains from surrounding regions, with radically different social structures, tend to develop a similar type? The answer is not simply diffusion (Eggan 1937*a*). Once this new formulation of the Plains is made, new problems will arise which will require a more complex apparatus to solve.

Another type of comparative study which has great potentialities is represented by the investigation of the Southern Athabascan-speaking peoples in the Plains and the Southwest. Here the same or similar groups have differentiated in terms of ecology, contacts, and internal development. Preliminary studies by Kluckhohn, Opler, Hoijer, Goodwin, and others suggest the possibilities of a detailed comparative attack on the problems of cultural development in this relatively controlled situation. Bellah's (1952) recent study of Southern Athabascan kinship systems, utilizing Parsons' structural-functional categories, shows some of the possibilities in this region.

In the Southwest I have attempted to work within a single structural type in a highly integrated subcultural area and to utilize the archeological and historical records, which are here reasonably complete, to delimit and interpret the variations which are found (1950). Clyde Kluckhohn looks at the Southwest from a broader standpoint and with a different but related problem: "One of the main rewards of intensive study of a culture area such as the Southwest is that such study eventually frees investigators to raise genuinely scientific questions—problems of process. Once the influence of various cultures upon others in the same area and the effects of a common environment (and its variant forms) have been reasonably well ascertained, one can then operate to a first approximation under an "all other things being equal" hypothesis and intensively examine the question: Why are these cultures and these modal personality types still different—in spite of similar environmental stimuli and pressures and access over long periods to the influence of generalized area culture or cultures? We are ready now, I believe, for such studies—but no one is yet attempting them seriously" (1954:693).

The Ramah Project, directed by Kluckhohn, has been planned so as to furnish a continuous record of a series of Navaho from childhood to maturity and of the changes in their culture as well. This project is in its second decade, and a variety of participants have produced an impressive group of papers. So far Kluckhohn's major monograph has concerned *Navaho Witchcraft* (1944), which he has interpreted in both psychological and structural terms and which breaks much new ground. A newer project in the same region involves the comparison of the value systems of five groups: Navaho, Zuni, Mormon, Spanish-American, and Texan, but the results are not yet available.

Comparative studies can also be done on a very small scale. The few thousand Hopi are divided into nearly a dozen villages, each of which differs in significant ways from its neighbors in terms of origins, conservatism, contacts, independence, degree of acculturation, and specific sociocultural patterns. And on First Mesa the Hano or Hopi Tewa, who came from the Rio Grande around A.D. 1700, still maintain their linguistic and cultural independence despite biological assimilation and minority status—and apparently differ significantly in personality traits as well. Dozier's (1951) preliminary account of this interesting situation suggests how valuable this comparison may eventually be.

How much can be learned about the processes of social and cultural change by comparative field research in a controlled situation is illustrated by Alex Spoehr's researches in the Southeast. Here some preliminary investigations by the writer (1937*b*) had led to tentative conclusions as to the nature of changes in kinship systems of the Creek, Choctaw, Chickasaw, and other tribes of the region after they were removed to reservations in Oklahoma. Spoehr (1947) not only demonstrated these changes in detail but has analyzed the historical factors responsible and isolated the resulting processes.

Here Redfield's (1941) comparative study of four Yucatecan communities in terms of progressive changes in their organization, individualization, and secularization as one moves from the tribal hinterland through village and town to the city of Merida should also be mentioned. The significance of its contributions to comparative method has been largely overlooked in the controversies over the nature of the "folk society" and the usefulness of ideal types.

We can also begin to study particular social types wherever they occur. Murdock's *Social Structure* (1949) demonstrates that similar social structures and kinship systems are frequently found in various parts of the world. We can compare matrilineal social systems, or Omaha kinship systems, in different regions of the world without restricting ourselves to the specific requirements originally laid down by Boas. Thus Audrey Richards' (1950) comparison of matrilineal organizations in Central Africa will gain in significance when set against the Northwest Coast data. When variant forms of matrilineal or patrilineal social systems are compared from the standpoint of structure and function, we will have a clearer idea of the essential features of such systems and the reasons for special variants. The results for matrilineal systems promise to give quite a different picture than Lowie originally drew of the "Matrilineal Complex" (1919), and they will help us to see more clearly the structural significance of cultural patterns such as avunculocal residence and cross-cousin marriage.

These and other studies will enable us ultimately to present a comprehensive account of the various types of social structure to be found in the regions of the world and to see the nature of their correlates and the factors involved in social and cultural change. It is clear that new methods and techniques will need to be developed for the evaluation of change over time; quantitative data will be essential to establish rates of change which may even be expressed in statistical terms.

I have suggested that there may be some virtues in combining the sound anthropological concepts of structure and function with the ethnological concepts of process and history. If we can do this in a satisfactory manner we can save the "ethnological baby" from the fate to which Kroeber has consigned it—what we call the infant when it has matured is a relatively minor matter. In suggesting some of the ways in which comparative studies can be made more useful I have avoided questions of definition and ultimate objectives. This is only one of the many ways in which our science can advance, and we have the personnel and range of interests to cultivate them all.

After this paper was substantially completed the volume of papers in honor of Wilson D. Wallis entitled *Method and Perspective in Anthropology* (Spencer 1954) became available. Much of what Herskovits says with regard to "Some Problems of Method in Ethnography" is relevant to points made above, particularly his emphasis on the historical approach and the comparative study of documented change (1954:19) as well as on the importance of repeated analyses of the same phenomena. And Ackerknecht's scholarly survey of "The Comparative Method in Anthropology" emphasizes the importance of the comparative method for cultural anthropology: "One of the great advantages of the comparative method will be that in a field where the controlled experiment is impossible it provides at least some kind of control." He sees signs of a renaissance: "In whatever form the comparative method may reappear, it will express the growing desire and need in cultural anthropology to find regularities and common denominators behind the apparent diversity and uniqueness of cultural phenomena" (p. 125).

Kroeber, in commenting on the papers in this volume, subscribes" whole heartedly to Ackerknecht's position. My one criticism is that he doesn't go far enough. He sees the comparative method as something that must and will be revived. I would say that it has never gone out; it has only changed its tactic" (1954:273). He goes on to point out that all science ultimately seeks knowledge of process, but that this must be preceded by "description of the properties of the form and substance of the phenomena, their ordering or classification upon analysis of their structure, and the tracing of their changes or events" (pp. 273–74). These are the essential points that I have tried to make with reference to cultural anthropology.

On both sides of the Atlantic there is an increasing willingness to listen to one another and a growing conviction that the varied approaches are complementary rather than competitive. We can agree, I think, with Radcliffe-Brown: "It will be only in an integrated and organized study in which historical studies and sociological studies are combined that we shall be able to reach a real understanding of the development of human society, and this we do not yet have" (1951:22). It seems to me that it is high time we made a start—and indeed it is well under way.

In time we may be able to simplify and further order our conceptual schemes in terms of direct observations on human behavior. Sapir, in perhaps a moment of insight, once defined culture "as a systematic series of illusions enjoyed by people." But culture, like the "ether" of the nineteenth-century physicists, plays an essential role today and will do so for a considerable time to come. The distant future is more difficult to predict—I think it was Whitehead who remarked that the last thing to be discovered in any science is what the science is really about!

NOTES

[1] The publication of this paper has been delayed through no fault of the editors. The opportunity to attend the Eighth Pacific Science Congress in Manila in November, 1953, plus the competition afforded by the Apache Crown Dancers at our Tucson meetings made it easy to follow the precedent, begun the year before by President Bennett, of not reading a presidential address. I have written this paper rather informally, however, and have attempted to give a somewhat personal interpretation of social and cultural anthropology as practiced in the United States and in Great Britain. I have addressed myself primarily to my American colleagues, since there are a number of recent addresses directed toward British anthropologists; and I have omitted many important contributions from here and abroad through reasons of space and competence. Several friends have been kind enough to make suggestions for improvement, notably Edward Bruner, David Schneider, and Milton Singer. I would also like to thank the editors for their forbearance.

[2] See, particularly, Benedict (1948), Hallowell (1950), Beals (1951), Howells (1952), and Bennett (1953).

[3] With regard to the general problem of the integration of anthropological studies Daryll Forde, in his recent presidential address (1951) to the Royal Anthropological Institute, emphasized the importance of this integration and suggested the concept of ecology as a possible common point of reference for all the varied fields of anthropology.

[4] For the limited purposes of this paper I have utilized the terms which Bennett applied to the Andean area in his presidential paper of last year, though I am sure better terms can be found.

[5] The term "social anthropology" has been used by American anthropologists in the past: both Wissler and Radin wrote textbooks under that title, but these involved no new points of view. Chapple and Coon's *Principles of Anthropology* (1942) did present a new point of view, even dispensing with the concept of culture, but has not been widely accepted in the United States.

REFERENCES CITED

ACKERKNECHT, ERWIN H.

1954 On the comparative method in anthropology. *In:* Method and Perspective in Anthropology, ed. R. F. Spencer. Minneapolis.

BEALS, RALPH

1951 Urbanism, urbanization, and acculturation. American Anthropologist 53:1–10.

BELLAH, R. N.

1952 Apache kinship systems. Cambridge, Harvard University Press.

BENEDICT, RUTH

1923 The concept of the guardian spirit in North America. Memoirs of the American Anthropological Association No. 29.

1934 Patterns of culture. Boston and New York, Houghton Mifflin Co.

1948 Anthropology and the humanities. American Anthropologist 50:585–93.

BENNETT, WENDELL C.

1953 Area archeology. American Anthropologist 55:5–16.

BOAS, FRANZ

1896 The limitations of the comparative method in anthropology. Science, n.s. 4:901–8.

1927 Primitive art. Instittutet for Sammenlignende Kulturforskning, Series B, No. VIII. Oslo.

1940 Race, language and culture. New York, The Macmillan Co.

CHAPPLE, ELIOT and CARLETON COON

1942 Principles of anthropology. New York, Henry Holt.

DIXON, R. B.

1928 The building of cultures. New York, Scribners.

DOZIER, EDWARD P.

1951 Resistance to acculturation and assimilation in an Indian pueblo. American Anthropologist 53:56–66.

EGGAN, FRED

1937*a* The Cheyenne and Arapaho kinship system. *In:* Social Anthropology of North American Tribes, ed. Fred Eggan. Chicago, University of Chicago Press.

1937*b* Historical changes in the Choctaw kinship system. American Anthropologist 39:34–52.

1950 Social organization of the Western Pueblos. Chicago, University of Chicago Press.

1952 The ethnological cultures and their archeological backgrounds. *In:* Archeology of the Eastern United States, ed. J. B. Griffin. Chicago, University of Chicago Press.

EGGAN, FRED (ed.)

1937 Social anthropology of North American tribes. Chicago, University of Chicago Press.

EVANS-PRITCHARD, E. E.

1951 Social anthropology. London, Cohen & West Ltd.

FIRTH, RAYMOND

1951*a* Contemporary British social anthropology. American Anthropologist 53:474–89.

1951*b* Elements of social organization. London, Watts and Co.

FLETCHER, ALICE

1904 The Hako: a Pawnee ceremony. 22nd Annual Report, Bureau of American Ethnology. Washington, D. C.

FORDE, DARYLL

1947 The anthropological approach in social science. Presidential Address, Section H, British Association for the Advancement of Science. London.

1950 Anthropology, science and history. Man, 254.

1951 The integration of anthropological studies. Journal of the Royal Anthropological Institute 78:1–10.

FORTES, MEYER

1953*a* The structure of unilineal descent groups. American Anthropologist 55:17–41.

1953*b* Analysis and description in social anthropology. Presidential Address, Section H, British Association for the Advancement of Science. London.

1953*c* Social anthropology at Cambridge since 1900, an inaugural lecture. Cambridge University Press.

GOLDENWEISER, A. A.

1910 Totemism: an analytic study. Journal of American Folklore 23:1–115.

HALLOWELL, A. IRVING

1950 Personality, structure, and the evolution of man. American Anthropologist 52:159–73.

1953 Culture, personality and society. *In:* Anthropology Today, by Alfred L. Kroeber and others, pp. 597–620. Chicago, University of Chicago Press.

HERSKOVITS, MELVILLE J.

1950 Man and his works, the science of cultural anthropology. New York, A. A. Knopf.

1954 Some problems of method in ethnography. *In:* Method and Perspective in Anthropology, ed. R. F. Spencer. Minneapolis.

HOWELLS, W. W.

1952 The study of anthropology. American Anthropologist 54:1–7.

KLUCKHOHN, CLYDE

1944 Navaho witchcraft. Papers of the Peabody Museum of Harvard University XXII, No. 2.

1949 The Ramah project. Papers of the Peabody Museum of Harvard University XL, No. 1.

1954 Southwestern studies of culture and personality. American Anthropologist 56:685–97.

KROEBER, ALFRED L.

1935 History and science in anthropology. American Anthropologist 37:539–69.

1939 Cultural and natural areas of native North America. Berkeley, University of California Press.

1944 Configurations of culture growth. Berkeley and Los Angeles, University of California Press.

1953 Introduction (pp. 1–4) and Concluding Review (pp. 357–76). *In:* An Appraisal of Anthropology Today, ed. Sol Tax and others. Chicago, University of Chicago Press.

1954 Critical summary and commentary. *In:* Method and Perspective in Anthropology, ed. R. F. Spencer. Minneapolis.

KROEBER, ALFRED L. and CLYDE KLUCKHOHN

1952 Culture, a critical review of concepts and definitions. Papers of the Peabody Museum of Harvard University XLVII, No. 1.

KROEBER, ALFRED L. and others

1953 Anthropology today, an encyclopedic inventory. Chicago, University of Chicago Press.

LÉVI-STRAUSS, CLAUDE

1951 Language and the analysis of social laws. American Anthropologist 53:155–63.

LINTON, RALPH

1936 The study of man. New York, D. Appleton-Century Co.

LOWIE, ROBERT H.

1919 The matrilineal complex. University of California Publications in American Archaeology and Ethnology XVI:29–45.

1929 Relationship terms. Encyclopedia Britannica, 14th ed.

1937 The history of ethnological theory. New York, Farrar & Rinehart, Inc.

1953 Ethnography, cultural and social anthropology. American Anthropologist 55:527–34.

MALINOWSKI, B.

1922 Argonauts of the western Pacific. London, Routledge.

MERTON, R. K.

1949 Social theory and social structure. Glencoe, The Free Press.

MURDOCK, GEORGE PETER

1949 Social structure. New York, The Macmillan Co.

1951 British social anthropology. American Anthropologist 53:465–73.

Nadel, S. F.

1951 The foundations of social anthropology. Glencoe, The Free Press.

1952 Witchcraft in four African societies: an essay in comparison. American Anthropologist 54:18–29.

Radcliffe-Brown, A. R.

1931*a* The present position of anthropological studies. Presidential Address, Section H, British Association for the Advancement of Science. London.

1931*b* The social organization of Australian tribes. Oceania Monographs, No. 1.

1933 The Andaman Islanders. Reprinted with additions. Cambridge. (1st ed., 1922.)

1951 The comparative method in social anthropology. Huxley Memorial Lecture. London.

1952*a* Structure and function in primitive society, essays and addresses. London, Cohen and West Ltd.

1952*b* Historical note on British social anthropology. American Anthropologist 54:275–77.

Radcliffe-Brown, A. R. and Daryll Forde (eds.)

1950 African systems of kinship and marriage. London, Oxford University Press.

Redfield, Robert

1937 Introduction to: Social Anthropology of North American Tribes, ed. Fred Eggan. Chicago, University of Chicago Press.

1941 The folk culture of Yucatan. Chicago, University of Chicago Press.

1953 Relations of anthropology to the social sciences and to the humanities. *In:* Anthropology Today, by Alfred L. Kroeber and others, pp. 728–38. Chicago, University of Chicago Press.

Redfield, Robert, Ralph Linton and Melville J. Herskovits

1936 Memorandum on the study of acculturation. American Anthropologist 38:149–52.

Richards, Audrey I.

1950 Some types of family structure amongst the Central Bantu. *In:* African Systems of Kinship and Marriage, ed. A. R. Radcliffe-Brown and Daryll Forde. London, Oxford University Press.

Sapir, Edward

1916 Time perspective in aboriginal American culture: a study in method. Canada, Department of Mines, Geological Survey, Memoir 90, Anth. Ser. 13. Ottawa.

Schapera, I.

1953 Some comments on comparative method in social anthropology. American Anthropologist 55:353–62.

Schneider, D.

1953 Review of: Kinship and Marriage among the Nuer, by E. E. Evans-Pritchard. American Anthropologist 55:582–84.

Spencer, R. F. (ed.)

1954 Method and perspective in anthropology, papers in honor of Wilson D. Wallis. Minneapolis, University of Minnesota Press.

Spier, Leslie

1929 Problems arising from the cultural position of the Havasupai. American Anthropologist 31:213–22.

Spoehr, Alexander

1947 Changing kinship systems. Anthropological Series, Chicago Natural History Museum, Vol. 33, No. 4.

Tax, Sol and others (ed.)

1953 An appraisal of anthropology today. Chicago, University of Chicago Press.

Wissler, Clark

1914 Material cultures of the North American Indian. American Anthropologist 16:501 ff.

1922 The American Indian. 2nd ed. New York, Oxford University Press.

1926 The relation of nature to man in aboriginal America. New York, Oxford University Press.

SOCIETY, CULTURE, AND THE HUMAN ORGANISM* **

Institute of Human Relations, Yale University

C. S. Ford

Traditionally, the social sciences encompass many special fields of investigation. Sociologists, anthropologists, and psychologists have so defined the object of their study as to develop relatively independent disciplines. When a somewhat naïve and untutored person discovers this categorization in social science he fails to see its validity or importance, and becomes confused by the apparently artificial barriers separating these special fields of inquiry. After all, do not these studies concern themselves with human behavior? Why should sociologists choose to study one aspect of humanity and exclude from their sphere of interest many of the contributions to social science furnished by other specialists? The many reasons, historical and practical, which might answer this question need not be discussed in detail here. Suffice it to remark that such specialization exists, and that it has its shortcomings as well as its advantages.

Sociologists, for the most part, recognize that culture and history would be different if human beings were some other kind of animal. How different life might have been were men equipped with wings instead of arms, or endowed with the ability to live without food and drink! Sociologists seldom lose sight of the fact that man is an animal with specific needs and limitations. They generally overlook, however, the effectiveness of this knowledge as a tool of research. Since peoples live in such varied fashion, under such diverse codes of morality, and with such different ideals and interests, some students conclude that the needs and limitations of human beings are rather unimportant to the study of societies. Cultural relativity, a significant discovery of anthropology, has encouraged some sociologists to disregard the human organism. Others have either left the consideration of man's organic characteristics to the physiologist and psychologist or have been content with crude and unsatisfactory assumptions about human nature. These points of view do less than

*Recommended for publication by Mark May, and received in the Editorial Office on April 27, 1938.

** Reprinted from the *Journal of General Psychology*, Vol. 20 (1939), 135-179 by permission of the author and the Journal Press, Provincetown, Massachusetts.

justice to the fact that human societies are composed of men, women, and children.

To visualize human beings as mere individual units which compose a group is to inhibit a functional understanding of social phenomena. On the other hand, alertness to the organic characteristics of mankind gives new life to a science of society. Organic is used here to denote the animal aspect of human behavior; it is assumed that all human acts are organically based. A man punching another in the nose, an infant crying for the breast, a woman menstruating, and a dictator striving for power are examples of organic facts. In this sense, organic is not limited to those aspects of human behavior which are purely instinctive and remain unmodified by experience. Some of man's organic characteristics will be more significant and important to societies than others. Hunger, for example, presumably plays a rôle in social life more consequential than the knee-jerk. The present study is an attempt to determine those organic traits, characteristic of mankind, which are generally crucial to societies. Specifically its objective is to identify those manifestations of human behavior which are commonly subject to societal control. It purposes to infer organic facts from cultural materials, to study comparatively a number of different societies with the aim of discovering the behavior which their cultures regulate. While its conclusions are confessedly tentative, they are presented in the hope that they will prove suggestive and that they will indicate the probable fruitfulness of similar research.

The objective of this study may be more clearly understood if its underlying assumptions are made explicit. Human beings are driven to behave as they do by impulses that demand gratification and by tendencies to avoid pain. An individual, severely thwarted in his attempts to satisfy impulses and minimize pain, will break down, or, if the frustrations are excessive, will die. Human animals characteristically struggle to survive in association. A group of human beings, living in close proximity, and achieving the maintenance and reproduction of life through coöperative effort, constitutes a society. Within a society, integrated (though not mutually exclusive) groups of individuals are organized about these and other aspects of life. Any human being, therefore, lives as a member of society, and of certain subgroups, gratifying impulses and avoiding pain through behavior which utilizes an environment including other human beings.

Human behavior is predominantly acquired through a learning process based on experience; unconditioned and unmodified instinctive behavior plays a negligible rôle. For the most part, human beings learn by inculcation and example from other human beings, and their behavior, therefore, primarily proceeds from the accumulated experience of others, namely, culture. Any culture represents a compromise between the interests and needs of the individual and those of the society. Inasmuch as the members of a society gratify their impulses and avoid pain chiefly through learning actions which are derived from a common cultural heritage, their behavior is limited and blocked by the conditions necessary for the existence and effectiveness of the society. The endurance of a society depends upon the survival of the majority of its members. When death or emigration depletes the ranks of the living, new individuals to replace the missing must be obtained. To gain new individuals, however, is not sufficient; the raw recruits must become members of the society. For this reason the young must be socialized. Furthermore, internal organization must be effective in providing for the existence of society, especially under conditions of group conflict. These and other requirements for the endurance of society impose, through culture, limits and checks upon the activities of human beings.

This approach to social phenomena emphasizes the organic aspect of human beings and the pressing problems involved in societal life. Individuals, for the most part, overcome the difficulties encountered in their attempts to utilize the environment in patterned ways which they inherit as members of a society from the experience of past generations. They are forced to attain these ends in ways which, at the same time, contribute to the solution of societal problems. The requisites for a society's endurance are accomplished through the activity of its members; in no other way can the problems facing a society be solved. The members of a society are forced to gratify impulses, avoid pain, and iron out their individual difficulties in ways which are in adjustment to the existence needs of that society. Culture, in the form of regulations governing human behavior, provides solutions to societal problems. These rules are sanctioned by reward and punishment, and justified by the experience and wisdom of the ancestors. When the members of a society, for instance, find themselves in conflict they ordinarily refrain from attempting to kill each other and resolve their difficulties in traditionally patterned and socially accepted ways, e.g., by recourse to law. Murder cannot be permitted as a method of resolving individual difficulties; an individual who rejects the cultural ways of solving his difficulties and vents his anger by killing a fellow member, is ordinarily punished with death. The law against murder, together with the ways offered to individuals for the resolution of their conflicts, is regarded here as a way of meeting the need to suppress destructive activity within a society.

The concept of culture as outlined above harmonizes with the folkways and mores as they are elaborated by Sumner.[1] Folkways are the customs characteristic of the members of a society. Folkways become mores, or taboos, when there is associated with them the conviction that they are not only right and true, but also so necessary to societal welfare that departure from them will involve disaster. The mores of a society prescribe and restrict the activity of its members. The sanctions and judgments attached to them reveal the dynamic nature of the behavior which they control. Since human beings, apparently, must be coerced to conform to the mores, it is likely that a society will tend to maintain, over a period of time, only those mores which are necessary for its existence. Some

---

[1]"The struggle to maintain existence was carried on, not individually but in groups. Each profited by the other's experience; hence there was concurrence towards that which proved most expedient. All at last adopted the same way for the same purpose; hence the ways turned into customs and became mass phenomena. . . . The young learn them by tradition, imitation and authority. The folkways, at a time, provide for all the needs of life then and there. They are uniform, universal in the group, imperative, and invariable.

"When the elements of truth and right are developed into doctrines of welfare, the folkways are raised to another plane. They then become capable of producing inferences, developing new forms, and extending their constructive influence over men and society. Then we call them mores. The mores are the folkways, including the philosophical and ethical generalizations as to societal welfare which are suggested by them, and inherent in them, as they grow. . . . The mores necessarily consist in large part, of taboos, which indicate the things which must not be done. In part these are dictated by mystic dread of ghosts who might be offended by certain acts, but they also include such acts as have been found by experience to produce unwelcome results, especially in the food quest, in war, in health, or in increase or decrease of population. . . . The primitive taboos correspond to the fact that the life of man is environed by perils. . . . The taboos carry on the accumulated wisdom of generations, which has almost always been purchased by pain, loss, disease, and death. Other taboos contain inhibitions of what will be injurious to the group" (5, p. 2, pp. 30-31).

mores will be necessitated by local and historically limited conditions; others will correspond to fundamental social needs and will be widespread or universal. To eliminate the former and discover the latter, it is necessary to use information from a number of geographically separated and culturally divergent societies.

The present paper utilizes materials from 25 societies, selected on the basis of geographical location and fullness of information. North America is represented by the Blackfoot, Huron, Ingalik, Kwakiutl, Navaho, Omaha, and West Greenland Eskimo; Africa by the Ashanti, Azande, BaThonga, BaVenda, Nama Hottentot, and Tuareg; Eurasia by the Ainu, Chukchee, Hebrews of the period of Deuteronomy, Sema Naga, and Toda; Oceania by the Andamanese, Aranda, Ifugao, Kiwai Papuans, Samoans, and Trobrianders; and South America by the Jivaro of Western Amazonas. These societies were canvassed for their mores with the anticipation that by a process of elimination there might ultimately be obtained a list of mores common to all or the greater portion of the groups studied. The resulting sample of widespread or universal mores could then form the basis for a tentative statement of the organic characteristics universally the subject of direct societal control. These results should also reveal, to some extent, the problems commonly facing societies, which necessitate the widespread control of human behavior.

Certain problems were encountered during the course of collecting the information. If the mores of one society were to be matched against those of another society, the information had to be in comparable form. The statements of ethnographers were not useful without being subjected to analysis. Ethnographers often encompass within a single sentence a description of many diverse items of behavior. The conclusion of the puberty rites for girls among the BaVenda, for example, is given in the following sentence:

> The last morning, when the girls are taken to the river, they are washed from head to foot and their bodies smeared with fat, and their heads shaved into the usual crown and smeared with red ochre (4, p. 109).

Were analysis not resorted to, the information, imbedded in crude lumps of fact, could not be subjected to the direct comparisons which such a study as this requires.

A further problem was encountered in attempting to distinguish mores from other cultural data. If, for instance, the ethnographer states merely that the natives never eat a certain species of fish, or that they always crouch in the presence of a chief, it is difficult to tell whether a mos is being described or not. Another obstacle to the project resulted from an inconsistent usage of various concepts by ethnographers. Where actual behavior is cited to illustrate the meaning of a concept, direct comparison with other concepts similarly defined was possible. Unfortunately, however, many ethnographers neglect to establish the meaning of such terms as "avoidance," "cowardice," "indolence," and "unnatural vice." The assumption that these concepts carry the same connotations for all ethnographers was belied by those instances in which illustrative cases are given and the meanings attached to the concepts are then found to be quite different.

A brief résumé of the specialized technique developed in adjustment to these problems will clarify the results of the research. Ethnographies vary in the elaboration and emphasis accorded to the various aspects of society. By and large, ethnographers consistently include two kinds of information, first, what their informants have told them is proper and correct conduct in that society, and second, what the people actually do. An anthropologist going to a functioning society, one which has not yet seriously disintegrated in the face of modern acculturation, may observe first of all what the members of that society do, i.e., how they act. He may make a statistical statement correlating human beings and their behavior with conditions. Thus, he might record his observations that 90 per cent of the adults are married, that the age of first menstruation for girls is between 12 and 14 years, and that women never participate in house-building activities.

He may then question the natives about the behavior which he has observed. From a careful investigation of this sort he might find the opinions consistently expressed that men and women should get married soon after the age of puberty and that the ones who do not get married will soon become ill and die, that menstruation is the result of impregnation by a spirit and is a necessary precondition to marriage, and that women should never touch a house while it is being built lest she be killed for thus endangering the welfare of the community. During the course of this investigation he might also find the natives consistently agreeing that no married woman should commit adultery on pain of death, that no native should steal, and that all the members of the society must be hospitable to strangers. These statements about what the members of the society should and should not do may direct his attention to behavior which he had not previously noticed. Reinvestigation of behavior might reveal that the great majority of wives do not commit adultery and that the exceptions are severely punished, that over half the natives steal and that few are ever punished, and that hospitality as practiced differs strikingly from its description. By thus comparing actual behavior with native statements about appropriate behavior he can determine the degree of conformity between what the people actually do and what they say they should do. He may find further that people commonly threaten to do what they apparently want to do, but dare not do.

Most ethnographers, however, are not so complete in their reports and there are many reasons for this. An anthropologist investigating a culturally disintegrated American Indian group is retarded from making such a complete report because he has little strictly aboriginal behavior to observe and because he relies upon his informants for statements of how the natives lived in the old days. On the other hand, the sociologist probing into modern conditions, where certain forms of behavior may be recorded statistically, is often baffled in an attempt to determine what the members of the community traditionally hold to be ideal conduct. Traditional rules given by informants are not commonly differentiated in the literature from normal behavior noted by the observer.[2] But for the purposes of this study it becomes vitally necessary not only to realize the existence of these two kinds of information, but also to distinguish carefully between them. We are attempting here to infer societally relevant organic facts from cultural materials. The validity of this approach depends, in part, upon the assumption that a society will maintain, over a period of time, only those restrictions of human behavior which are necessary for its existence. Therefore, the traditional rules which characterize a society must be clearly identified. Normal be-

[2]For the purpose of contrasting biologically derived and socially derived behavior, these two types of information apparently need not be distinguished. Without utilizing this distinction comparative anthropology has established the relative importance of traditional learned behavior in contrast to instinctive behavior in the study of human societies.

havior of the members of society may or may not reveal long-established rules. The inference of traditional patterns from average behavior involves unjustified assumptions and its results should be accepted with extreme caution.

To clarify the distinction between observed behavior and the traditional ideals and beliefs characterizing a society, let us consider a sample of information as it is given to us by an able ethnographer.

> When a new member of the tribe is expected, when the mother begins to feel the pangs of childbirth (*ku lunwa*), the father sends word to the midwives of the neighborhood and all of them come at once. . . . The place chosen for the delivery (*Phuluka*) is generally the back of the hut (*nahosi*) where the pregnant woman lives. Some mats are brought and hung up in such a way as to form a small enclosure. This is done to protect the woman from indiscreet onlookers. Should there be enough bush to hide her, mats are not used. A big wooden mortar is given to her to lean against during her pains. . . . Should the birth be difficult, the divinatory bones will probably be consulted and the woman will be removed to another place, inside the hut or somewhere else. . . . *during the whole labor, it is taboo for the mother to eat or drink anything; she would kill the child if she did so.* Of course no man must attend the birth; nor must girls come near. A newly married woman may be allowed to enter the enclosure in order to "be taught." It is also forbidden for the female relations of the woman, her sisters, even her mother to come . . . , they might be ashamed if their relative behaved badly and "broke her child" (2, pp. 36-37, italics added).

In this quotation description of average behavior lies intertwined with statement of traditional beliefs and rules.[3] The attempt to analyze this information clarifies the difference between the two types of information. Analyzing the first sentence into its component parts, we obtain the following result:

a) When a new member of the tribe is expected
When the mother begins to feel the pangs of childbirth
b) The father

[3]It is quite possible that Junod is actually reporting throughout upon behavior which he knows to be traditionally patterned, and that the way in which he has phrased the information is expository and quite immaterial from his point of view.

> Sends word to the midwives of the neighborhood
> And all of them come at once.

Giving names to *a, b, c,* and *d,* we have the following factors: (*a*) the conditions, (*b*) the person, (*c*) the behavior, (*d*) the resultant behavior. By examining more cases of behavior, we would find other factors occasionally occurring, for example, affect displayed by the person in *b* when performing *c,* and rationalizations given by the person in *b* to explain his behavior.

The examination of the italicized sentence results somewhat differently:

> *a*) During the whole labor
> *b*) It is taboo
> *c*) For the mother
> *d*) To eat anything, or drink anything
> *e*) She would kill the child if she did so.

This analysis differs from the one which was made of the first sentence by the addition of the two new statements, namely, "it is taboo," and "she would kill the child if she did so." If a woman actually abstaining from food and drink were asked why she behaved in such a fashion she might reply, "It is taboo; it would kill the child if I did so." In this way she would include these additional statements in one of the factors previously mentioned, namely, the rationalization. The woman, in this case, would support her performance by voicing a traditional rule. Rationalizations are not always, however, thus related to rules; they may be justifications supplied by the individual which have no obvious derivation. These two statements, the one concerning behavior and the other concerning a rule of behavior, are incomplete as set forth by the ethnographer. In the first no rationalization is supplied as to why the father sends for the midwives, and there is no way of relating the behavior to rules of conduct traditionally held by the natives. In the second no behavior is described, and it is not stated that women in labor actually follow the rule which has been expressed. Unfortunately, most ethnographies are incomplete in this sense.

Ethnographers, moreover, have failed to distinguish clearly between actual information and their own assumptions. Many of them apparently assume that statements of rules indicate average behavior. There are, however, many illustrations denying the validity of these assumptions. Rattray, for example, makes this commendable observation among the Ashanti:

> *Adultery.* This is, of course, a ground for divorce, and if proved will entitle the husband, besides divorcing the woman, to recover the customary damages, in addition to all his marriage expenses, i.e., "bride-price" and any sum of money he had paid to liquidate a debt of his wife's family. Very often, however, the offense will be condoned and the couple will continue to live together (3, p. 98).

Furthermore, ethnographers, on the basis of the behavior which they observe, infer certain traditional patterns which may or may not be recognized by the natives. The following example will make this clear:

> *Gulad,* or intent, is probably the greatest single factor in determining penal responsibility. Thus: A deed committed without intent, and without carelessness, is excused. One has not, usually, even to make restitution for the injury done. Thus, in the case of a bolo flying out of a man's hand, and putting out the eye of another, no damages were assessed. An enormous number of men, every year, are injured in the free-for-all scrambles over sacrificed carabaos. Many of these injuries result in stiff joints; some of them in deaths. In no case, not even in the case of death, is a payment demanded. Suppose that in the chase a number of hunters have surrounded a wild boar. The boar charges one of them. This man leaps backward, and, at the same time, draws back his spear to throw it at the boar. In so doing, he stabs a companion behind him with the shod end of the spear handle. This is not an uncommon accident. The others of the party are witnesses that the killing was purely accidental (*naloktat*). No fine is assessed; but the killer, to show that he is sorry, usually assists in the funeral feast. Of course, if there were no witnesses, and if there were a possible motive to complicate matters, the ending of the case might not be so happy. Suppose that a number of men are throwing at a target with their spears. A child runs in the way and is killed. One-half the usual fine for manslaughter is assessed on the ground that the thrower was careless in that he did not make sure before he threw the spear that such an accident could not occur. In this case there was an absence of intent; but carelessness was present. A man kills a neighbor at night, acting under the impression that he

> is killing an enemy seeking his life. He is subjected to a much heavier fine than if he had killed him through carelessness, since there is present both the intent to kill, although not criminal, and carelessness in that he did not make sure at whom he was casting his spear (1, pp. 65-66).

In this paragraph Barton has offered the differentiating features which explain, to his satisfaction, a correlation of behavior with certain circumstances. The configuration which he has hypothecated may or may not be traditional. Native terminology closely parallels his hypothesis, strongly implying traditional recognition of these rules. Nevertheless, the points of agreement and disagreement are left to the reader to decide. Barton may have determined what the natives have actually formalized to be reasons for distinguishing between these cases, or what they have not formalized but actually follow unconsciously, or he may have made a misinterpretation, i.e., a statement which fits all his cases but which is not functionally correct. These examples make explicit the necessity of distinguishing between behavior and traditional rules. Rules stated by informants do not necessarily reveal normal behavior; actual practice may violate the tradition. Similarly, configurations hypothecated by an observer to explain customary behavior may not accord with the rules actually followed by the natives.

A careful inspection of the data exposes a further distinction between behavior and tradition. Human actions may be classified into two types, varying in extensiveness, by selecting the common elements in each action. Or, on the other hand, each specific act may be differentiated from all other actions. Thus, for example, the act of a man murdering another may be differentiated from all similar actions by concentrating upon the individual characteristics of the man and the way in which he committed the murder. The characteristics differentiating individual acts are in great part due to the history of the component parts, i.e., the individual history of the person performing the action and that of the various substances entering into the action. Extreme analysis would resolve all objects into individual units, each one differentiated from all others. Rules, however, cannot be individualized to the same extent because tradition has already selected the significant component parts and defined each object. Thus, for example, a rule may prescribe sexual abstinence for a widow during the year following the death of her spouse. In such a case tradition has selected the characteristics of human beings which are significant, and all other details remain unimportant. The age and beauty of the widow are irrelevant. Behavior itself may be treated by a process of abstraction and acts classified into types. Such abstraction, however, must be sharply distinguished from the abstractions which the members of a society, over the course of time, have themselves established.

Many anthropologists tend to limit their descriptions to the more formal aspects of native culture and custom. Purely descriptive accounts of forms of behavior and thought represent extreme abstractions from reality and neglect both the human beings who exhibit them and the dynamic qualities of motivation. Similarly, the picture of a gun represents merely its form and fails to portray either the material of which it is made or its potentialities as an effective weapon. Such abstractions impress the sociologist as inadequate data for a science of society. The sociologist has a feeling of incompleteness after attempting to study primitive societies through the eyes of the cultural anthropologist. This paper, except in default of more dynamic information, will not be concerned with abstract culture forms.

The view taken here is that traditional beliefs, rules, and behavior are not to be ruthlessly torn from their human setting. This does not mean, however, that descriptions in dynamic terms cannot apply to the average members of a society. For example, an adolescent boy in a primitive tribe may display intense fear of circumcision rites which, nevertheless, he repeatedly announces his willingness to undergo because, as he puts it, "being circumcised will make a man." If the majority of such boys in that society also display the same anxiety and apparent willingness, this can be stated as a characteristic of the *adolescent boy* in that society. Such statistical abstraction in contrast to a formal description of initiation rites in that society emphasizes the emotional investment of the behavior and gives life to threadbare habit forms.

The term *culture,* although it seems to connote to some writers only descriptive forms of behavior, is most widely accepted in the sense defined by Tylor: "that complex whole which includes knowledge, belief, art, morals, law, custom, and any other capabilities and habits acquired by man as a member of society" (6, p. 1). In accordance with the last part of this definition, culture is often used to distinguish non-biologically transmitted behavior from that which is purely instinctive or biologically transmitted. Historically, *culture* has been serviceable in this sense as a weapon against racialism, instinctivism, and other biological theories of social phenomena. However, the distinction is more effective in crude judgments than in refined analyses. When a specific item of behavior, e.g., sneezing, is closely examined, it becomes difficult to determine the degree to which the behavior has been non-biologically rather than biologically transmitted. In this discussion, the term *acquired behavior* is employed to define behavior which is learned, either in whole or in part, by man as a member of society. Behavior may be acquired through a conditioning process on the basis of either undirected experience, as by trial and error learning or the application of intelligence, or directed experience, as by example or inculcation, ultimately derived from the experience of others. The accumulated and transmitted experience of human beings, in the form of traditional beliefs and rules of conduct characterizing the members of a society, constitutes *culture,* as we shall use this term. Culture, in this sense, consists of *beliefs* and *rules.* Rules and beliefs are usually, though probably not invariably, formalized and can be stated by an informant. Though rules may be inferred from sample cases of behavior, they must be verified by independent investigation. Thus, in practice, the ethnographer asks questions, the answers to which will give him the basis for determining the relevance of observed behavior to culture. Actual behavior which is characteristic of the members of a society is termed *custom.* Custom, in this sense, denotes that behavior in which the members of a group show wide concurrence. Exhibiting mingled horror and anger when the American flag is insulted by the members of a foreign nation, wearing glasses as an aid to sight, and listening to the radio are samples of custom exhibited by the members of many groups in the United States. A segment of custom which corresponds to or follows a rule is a *way.* Conformance to rules forbidding incest or adultery, for example, are ways in our society. A segment of custom which varies from a rule is a *deviant.* Thus, in the preceding quotation from Rattray, the observable fact that "very often the offence will be condoned and the couple will continue to live together" is a deviant. A segment of custom which is not known either to follow or to deviate from a rule, i.e., whose relationship to culture has not been determined, is termed a *norm*. By way of illustration, the facts presented in the preceding quotation from Barton are termed norms until the relationship of the behavior to rules recognized by the natives has been established.

Neither rules nor ways enjoy an independent existence apart from the members which make up the society. No individual member exemplifies the total culture and custom of his society. Rules and ways are differentially distributed among the members of a society as habits of thought and action. Some segments of culture and custom are manifested by all the members of a society, others are exhibited by certain groups, and others are scattered throughout the society apparently in accordance with the accidents of individual life histories. Rules and ways are inculcated into the members of a society by other members. This process of socialization perpetuates culture and custom from one generation to another. During the course of this important, if imperfectly understood, process, which is begun soon after birth and continues throughout life, the members of the society incorporate from their socializing agents segments of culture and custom. Probably in some relationship to the manner of socialization each individual member invests with emotion the segments which he exemplifies. The emotion attached to the various segments of culture and custom by one individual apparently differs in intensity from that attached to the same items as manifested by other members of the society. Further, rules may differ with respect to the average or normal emotion with which they are invested by the members of society. Reflections of this appear in the ethnographer's statement that rules are differentiated by the degree of compulsion or prohibition stated to apply. It is probably the average intensity of feeling attached to a rule which enables the ethnographer to say that an Ashanti subject *must not* commit adultery with the King's wives. Each particular informant whom he interviews will have emphasized the prohibition in accordance with the emotion which he attaches to it. In the course of a comparative gathering of information he will attempt to determine the average emotional investment and then to convey his findings in the literature by some phrase to describe the normal feeling which characterizes this particular pattern. This emotional investment he may, or may not, have modified by his observations of behavior.

The distinction between culture and custom here employed must be kept clearly in mind if the following method is to be fully understood. The method of analysis developed for this project pertains to rules as an aspect of culture. This does not necessarily imply that any sample of human behavior may be analyzed according to this method.

Close inspection of rules as they are given in the literature reveals formal properties which characterize them. Certain factors are discernible in every rule of behavior. First of all there is the *person* to whom the rule applies. The person may be every member of the society or certain specified individuals. Thus, the rule may apply to each and every member of the society, to the members of a certain subgroup, or to one particular member of the society. When the rule does not apply to every member of the society, the person is definable in terms of his biological and social characteristics. For example, the person to whom a certain rule applies may be an adult male with a specified status in the society such as that resulting from marriage, an infant cutting his first tooth, or an unmarried woman who finds herself pregnant.

Another factor, closely related to the social characteristics of the person, is the *condition* under which the rule applies. This may vary from any and all circumstances to certain social, temporal, and spacial conditions, i.e., the rule may apply all the time and under any circumstance, or at specified times and occasions. For example, the rule may be applicable to the married adult male mentioned above only "early in the morning before he sets out on a hunting expedition."

Another factor is the emotional investment which indicates the importance of each rule as a device for controlling behavior. This is the *emphasis*[4] placed upon the rule in the society. The emphasis as reported in the literature may vary from a complete prohibition to a complete compulsion, i.e., from *must not* through various degrees of *should not, ought not,* and the like to *may do, should do,* and *must do.*

Emphasis relates to the *behavior* with which the rule is concerned. This behavior may be relatively simple and derived directly from bodily activity, e.g., coughing or sneezing, or complicated in various

[4]Emphasis has been divorced from *sanction* with which it seems logically connected because it is so presented in the literature. Often no sanction is supplied, the ethnographer stating merely that the natives "must not" perform a certain act.

ways through the introduction of material or human objects, e.g., the prohibition that a man may not manufacture bark cloth. Both relatively simple and more complex behavior may be made still more involved by the addition of qualifications such as "in a specific manner" or "using certain artifacts." It is obvious that in such complicated actions there are involved many factors which are subject to isolation. For our purpose an analysis of the behavior itself would be too unwieldy for use. Throughout this study, therefore, behavior is described in the following terms: the simple bodily action whenever stated by the ethnographer, along with the name of the entire process, the general type of materials or persons involved, and an abbreviated statement of the technique or qualifying phrases involved. Thus an action is stated in such terms as "sneeze," "eat vegetable foods," "eat vegetable foods with a fork," "speak to his wife."

Closely related to the emphasis and behavior is the *sanction* which is traditionally associated with the rule. The sanction is both *positive* and *negative*, and is that part of the rule concerned with the results attendant upon conformity and nonconformity thereto. A positive sanction is the theoretical result of conformity to the rule; a negative sanction is the theoretical result of nonconformity to the rule. The positive sanction may be concerned with the raising of the status of the person, the removal of disabilities, and the like. The negative sanction may be, for example, an automatic supernatural punishment, the liability to punishment, restitution, or fine, or deprivation of privileges. By way of example, a married adult male, early in the morning before setting out to hunt, must not speak to his wife in order to be successful and lest he be killed by the beasts he hunts. Accompanying the sanction there is often an agent responsible for enforcing conformity and punishing nonconformity. Such a person may not necessarily be specified.

Finally, there is the *meaning* traditionally associated with the manner of acting and the objects, material or human, entering into the behavior. The meaning is in part gathered from beliefs and may pertain to any of the factors given above. Ability to understand a rule apparently increases with the knowledge of what the behavior and the objects attaching to it mean to the natives. The recognition that looking at a person is a way of making a sexual advance makes more understandable an avoidance of staring at one's mother-in-law.

Similarly, if it is realized that the shark is believed to be the manifestation of a departed ancestor, taboos on eating the shark are more readily understood. These factors may be summarized in the following outline:

FACTORS IN RULES

1. *Person.* The person involved as perpetrator of *the action,* and defined by biological and social characteristics.

2. *Condition.* The occasion and circumstances related to the action and defined by social, temporal, and spacial conditions.

3. *Emphasis.* The importance of the action and its patterning, e.g., compulsive, permissive, and prohibitive.

4. *Behavior.* The action itself, which, when they are present, may be described in terms of (*a*) the bodily action, (*b*) the materials and objects involved, and (*c*) the technique (including motor habits) specified as a qualifying factor.

5. *Sanction.* (*a*) *Positive:* rewards and the like associated with conformity together with the agent designated as responsible for enforcement.

(*b*) *Negative:* punishments and the like associated with nonconformity together with the agent designated as responsible for inflicting the penalty.

6. *Meaning.* The meaning attached to the person, circumstances, action, and objects involved and the relationship which this rule is conceived to bear to other parts of culture. Often the meaning will be distributed among the above factors.

The above summary may be clarified by example:

1. *Person.* Any married man in the society.
2. *Condition.* At any time and in any place.
3. *Emphasis.* Must not.
4. *Behavior.* Speak to his mother-in-law.
5. *Sanction.* (*a*) *Positive:* thus respecting his mother-in-law.
   (*b*) *Negative:* lest he become ill.
6. *Meaning.* Speaking is a sign of intimacy and to be intimate with one's mother-in-law is shameful; relationship: must not be intimate with mother-in-law.

The action restricted by this prohibition can be pinned to a certain rather specific category of behavior, namely, talking. A number of such specific actions may define a complex of behavior described as intimacy on the part of a man with his mother-in-law. On the whole, however, this is rather exceptional in the literature. More often the ethnographer gives us the statement that a man must not be intimate with his mother-in-law, thus indicating the complex behavior without specifying the particular actions of which it is composed; in other words the concept of "being intimate" is reported without an accompanying definition relating it to the specific instrumental behavior. In many cases, doubtless, the specific actions which would define such a complex are too numerous for the ethnographer to mention, as is conceivably the case when it is stated that a man must "avoid" his mother-in-law. Avoidance here may actually mean keeping away from her altogether. In such cases what probably exists is a blanket prohibition so extensive that definition in other terms would involve far too many specific actions to be conveniently recorded. If some term were reserved for those cases alone, much confusion could be eliminated and the concept would be useful in the description of societies. In this paper *pattern* is reserved for aspects of culture concerned with complex behavior and *rules* for those concerned with relatively simple actions. In the above instance, for example, the prohibition on speaking is termed a rule, whereas the restriction on intimacy of which this rule forms a component part is termed a pattern.

Notably missing from the above example is the term *function.* There are two reasons for this omission. In the first place, the function of any pattern is seldom, if ever, given as a part of the factual information. In other than relatively clear-cut cases of material culture the function is highly speculative. Because of the questionable validity of assumptions concerning function they are not included as factual formal properties of rules. A second reason for this omission is that in most cases function is relatable not to a specific rule but rather to groups of them which seem to serve a function or use only in combination. Thus the function of a specific rule would be a part of the function of a pattern of which the particular rule is merely a constituent part. Function is regarded here as the relationship which a pattern or rule bears to a specific problem or problems. A rule or pattern may be considered to be functional only if it provides at least a partial solution to an individual or social problem. Rules may form a problem solution in combination; when thus related those rules compose a pattern. Patterns, in addition, may contribute to the solution of a common problem; a group of patterns thus interrelated may be considered as a complex pattern. In recognition of this complexity, attempts were made throughout the project to hypothecate the function of each specific rule and the pattern of which it formed a part. This speculation yielded many valuable suggestions, and in some cases evidence could be adduced to indicate a strong possibility that the hypotheses were correct. The line between such tentative conclusions and the factual data was strictly kept, however, and all hypotheses were labeled as such to prevent confusion. The following "function" might be hypothecated in the example given above:

> 7. *Tentative Function.* A part of an avoidance pattern which may function to support the pattern against sexual intercourse between a man and his mother-in-law, and which may be necessary primarily because the mother-in-law would be an eligible sex-object were it not for the fact that he had married her daughter, to reduce rivalry between the man's wife and her mother, to emphasize and strengthen group coöperation, to prevent expressions of aggression between these members of society.

Societies appear to be characterized by a traditional heritage of beliefs and patterns, i.e., culture. When the information is supplied, patterns may be defined in terms of specific rules. Patterns are interrelated in two ways. First, patterns may be connected by a specific rule which forms a component part of each pattern. Second, patterns are interrelated if together they compose a more complex pattern, i.e., if together they furnish a solution to a common problem. This interrelationship, in part, illustrates the extreme complexity of culture and explains, to some extent, the difficulty of distinguishing mores from other data.

When one writes of the mores of a society the effort is made to limit the description by concentrating upon the more important rules of conduct and ways of life. One speaks, for example, of the mos against murder, but of the folkway, in our society, of men tipping their hats to women. This distinction, however, is somewhat confused by the probability that the folkway in this case supports the mos demanding that men respect women in our society. Furthermore, mos is used ambiguously to denote both the rule or pattern and the conduct which follows it. Mos is not formally distinguished from folkway in terms of rule versus behavior, but rather by its relatively greater importance. For the purposes of this study the problem of distinguishing mores becomes clearer if the differentiation between culture and custom is applied to the mos concept. The term *mos* is a collective term which includes both the behavior and the rule to which the behavior corresponds. These two aspects of mos are differentiated here as *mosway* and *mosrule* or *mospattern,* e.g., abstention from murder is a mosway which follows a mosrule against murder. Similarly, *folkway* is distinguished from *folkrule* or *folkpattern,* e.g., the folkway of men tipping their hats to women in our society follows a folkrule that men should thus respect women. By making these distinctions the problems of selecting mores is resolved into that of selecting those rules and patterns which are of sufficient importance to be termed mosrules or mospatterns.

Of the formal factors which characterize rules, the emphasis and sanction directly reveal relative importance. Those rules characterized by "must" and "must not" or sanctioned by the threat of death are without question extremely important. The meaning of the action may also shed light on the importance of the rule. If, for example, it is stated by the natives that a man should not look at his mother-in-law and if looking at her is a sexual advance which in other forms is strictly prohibited and punishable by death, there is good reason for assuming the restriction to be critical. The meaning of the action relates a particular rule to the pattern of which it forms a part. In our example, the rule of behavior which forbids looking at one's mother-in-law is a part of the pattern against in-law incest and is one of many actions which together define the meaning of the pattern against in-law incest in the particular society.

A further way of determining the importance of a rule is to discover the proportion of people in the community who are affected and the proportion of their life span during which the rule is applicable. A pattern against murder, which applies to all persons throughout their lives, is in this sense more important than a pattern against killing women on the battlefield. In the latter case it is only the warrior who is restricted—and then only on the battlefield and with respect to women alone. On the other hand, this latter restriction may be looked upon as a special case of a larger pattern than murder, i.e., a complex pattern against specified kinds of killing, of which murder is one and killing women on the battlefield is another. It thus appears that each of the factors into which a rule may be analyzed bears upon its importance and the legitimacy of terming it a mosrule. No clear-cut distinction is possible. Degrees of importance shade imperceptibly into one another. They resemble a spectrum, where the fringes of each color intergrade with their neighbors although the major bands of color stand out. Thus, complex mospatterns seem fairly distinct, whereas the individual rules of behavior of which they are composed merge together and diminish in importance as their relevance to major mospatterns decreases.

To differentiate relatively important from relatively unimportant rules and patterns is admittedly difficult and often inevitably arbitrary. Nevertheless, selection is a necessity in research and its validity rests upon its usefulness for the purpose at hand. For the present study, rules and patterns were selected as important if, in the first place, they were given by the ethnographer as compulsions or prohibitions, i.e., positive or negative mosrules or mospatterns, and also if, as in a few cases, the meaning attached to the action or some other indication suggested that the rule or pattern formed part of a complex mospattern. The following examples will illustrate the range of rules and patterns which were selected: The Omaha mother, after giving birth to her child, must bathe twice a day for about a week and is not permitted to carry or cut wood for two or three days; a menstruating woman, among the Kiwai Papuans, must not go near a sick person for he would become afflicted with running sores, or bathe in the sea when others are out in their canoes because to do so would cause a storm; small Samoan children should keep their scant loin cloths at least nominally fastened to their persons and if they do not are greeted with cuffings and shoutings; among the Chukchee, a man who has expressed a desire to die must do so within a day or two because the spirits who have listened to the promise would severely retaliate at any failure to fulfill it and his whole family would be exterminated by the revengeful spirits.

The various rules and patterns were roughly quantified as to their importance in the society on the basis of (*a*) the number of persons affected in respect to the total population, and (*b*) the number of circumstances when these persons were affected throughout their lives. Four quantitative categories were employed, as follows:

1. (*a*) One person to a very few members of the society. (*b*) Rather seldom in their lives (or, in case of one person, often).
2. (*a*) Few people to roughly half the members of the society. (*b*) Seldom to often.
3. (*a*) Most members of the society. (*b*) Seldom to often.
4. (*a*) Most to all members. (*b*) Often to all the time.

In cases where actual behavior was given, contrasting with the rule or pattern, allowance was made in the quantification, but not to the extent of excluding the pattern from the survey. A comparative absence of such concrete material was greatly deplored, but there was nothing to do under the circumstances except to adjust to the situation. If the reader is disappointed with the part played by actual behavior in this study, his quarrel is with the point of view of the many ethnographers whose interest centers rather in the formal aspects of culture patterns than in the dynamic aspects of social life. In those cases where customary behavior was cited without additional information as to the corresponding patterns, inferences were made as to the patterning wherever the probability of their correctness seemed high on the basis of supplementary information.

After the collection, analysis, and rough quantification of the data, as above described, the information had to be reduced and organized so as to bear upon the primary problem of determining the socially relevant organic facts. Many possible ways of classifying the material presented themselves. The information could be grouped in accordance with any one of the major factors of each pattern, or any combination thereof. Each possibility was carefully weighed, and sample tests were made to determine which seemed to lead most directly to the socially relevant organic facts. It developed that some organic facts would be likely to emerge if the material were organized in one way, e.g., on the basis of behavior, and others if it were classified differently, e.g., on the basis of the person or circumstances. A decision had to be reached. The behavior controlled by rules and patterns was chosen as the basis of classification, because this organization promised to reveal those aspects of human activity subjected to direct societal regulation.

The information had then to be tabulated for each society. In this process, the factors other than behavior, as well as most of the phrases and objects qualifying the behavior, were omitted. Two reasons account for this rather abrupt and drastic abstraction. In the first place, factors were considered extraneous to the objective of the classification unless they were of cross-cultural relevance. Thus, whether a man was prohibited from eating a bit of roast pork or a certain kind of fish seemed of little cross-cultural relevance; the common denominator susceptible of comparison from society to society is the restriction upon eating food.

However, during the tabulation, it was found necessary to classify rules in more than one place because two additional factors found in nearly all rules, namely, a meaning and sanction, do have cross-cultural significance. Let us consider a specific case. A BaThonga male must not go near a sick man who stands in a particular relationship to him. To do so would mean that he wanted to make him sicker. Furthermore, it was believed that if he did approach the sick man the latter would die and he himself would subsequently become ill. This pattern may therefore be classified either in three categories—(*a*) to go near another; (*b*) to cause another to die; (*c*) to make oneself sick—or in one compound category: (*d*) to go near another thus causing another to die and ultimately making oneself ill. Category *d* as it stands is obviously too complicated to use for comparative purposes. On the other hand, although *a, b,* and *c* are all important, they nevertheless represent three different orders of things. The "going near another" is the physical action controlled. This action, "going near," however, means causing another to die. This is the native's reason for inhibiting the action and relates the particular rule to the mospattern against harming others.[5] Furthermore, becoming ill is the automatic punishment believed to follow transgression of *a* and *b*. These three aspects of this particular rule seemed to have importance for the survey.[6] Since each

[5]It is of course true that the meaning attached to the action by the native may be a form of rationalization not actually connected in fact with the real reason why the action is prohibited. Nevertheless, the fact that the meaning is given as an explanation indicates that any action meaning what this one is believed to mean would be restricted. In other words, whether or not *a* and *b* are actually related other than by an associated rationalization, there is little question about the presence in the society of a mospattern against b, especially if it appears in other forms throughout the society as this one does.

[6]Furthermore, on the basis of certain hypotheses as to function it would be possible in many cases to include any specific pattern under a great many categories. This was done in a few cases with a symbol to indicate that the rule had been inferred. This method of filling out the charts was narrowly restricted, however, to those cases where the probability that the inference was correct seemed very high.

aspect had to be differentiated for cross-cultural purposes a system of tabulation was devised which would automatically distinguish these aspects of each rule. A sample of the tabulation of information for individual tribes is given in Figure 1.

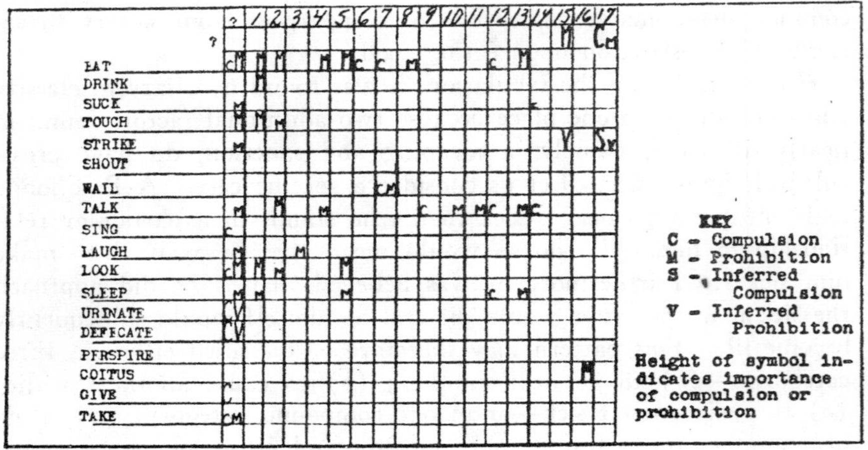

FIGURE 1

A Sample of the Data Tabulated for the Kwakiutl

1. lest harm self
2. thus hindering food quest
3. thus hindering manufacturing processes
4. thus inviting bad luck
5. thus harming another
6. thus curing self
7. thus mourning
8. thus neglecting to mourn
9. thus protecting self
10. thus being intimate with others
11. thus insulting another
12. thus facilitating delivery
13. thus making delivery difficult
14. thus curing another
15. thus murdering another
16. thus committing adultery
17. thus killing animals

This method of tabulation differentiates two aspects of behavior. Down the left-hand column behavior is defined in its elementary physiological aspects; horizontally across the page it is defined in terms of the meanings and sanctions which reinforce the rules. Thus, in one aspect, physical acts like eating and talking are forbidden under certain circumstances, and, in the other, these and other actions are prohibited if they are believed to bring harm to oneself or to others. The items entered along the top of the page are not definable with reference to activity on the part of the human organism. Insulting another, for example, is not cross-culturally definable in terms of the actions which a person exhibits when insulting another. A comparative study of societies reveals that insults can be expressed in such diverse ways as thumbing one's nose, biting one's finger nails, staring, or turning one's back. If acts interpreted as insulting vary from group to group, the concept "insult another" cannot be defined in terms of specific behavior. This accords with the distinction previously made between rules and patterns. Some of the behavior items listed along the top of the page are, to be sure, partially definable by reference to a specific activity of the human organism. Adultery would be a good example. Nevertheless, the acts included under the term adultery may vary from society to society. Looking at the genitals of another man's wife or stepping over a woman's legs, for instance, may be interpreted in a specific society as adulterous behavior and punished with as much severity as if actual coitus had taken place.

Differentiation between these aspects of behavior raises the query as to the relationship which cross-culturally exists between them. To determine this relationship it is necessary to discover the interpretations which accompany such physical acts as eating and talking. This is impossible in many instances due to the inadequacy of the information. Many ethnographers, for example, state "insulting another" is prohibited, without identifying the kinds of behavior which are deemed insulting. It is possible, however, to indicate by an example how the various biologically defined actions are interpreted in our 25 societies.

Relationship between Eating and Associated Concepts

(The following tribes have prohibitions on eating accompanied by these interpretations:)

Thus reducing breast milk. Tribe 1.
Thus assuming the rôle of the opposite sex. Tribe 1.
Thus stealing. Tribe 2.
Thus inviting bad luck. Tribe 14.
Thus expressing selfishness. Tribe 24.
Thus insulting others. Tribes 1, 17.

Thus hindering course of war. Tribes 14, 21.
Thus hindering manufacturing. Tribes 8, 18.
Thus being intimate with others. Tribes 19, 20, 25.
Thus expressing greediness. Tribes 4, 14, 20.
Thus inducing abortion. Tribes 6, 7, 8, 18.
Thus hindering food quest. Tribes 8, 12, 14, 19, 20.
Thus polluting food. Tribes 1, 2, 3, 6, 18, 19, 20.
Thus assuming another's prerogatives. Tribes 1, 2, 3, 4, 9, 12, 14, 18, 25.
Thus neglecting to mourn. Tribes 6, 8, 9, 12, 14, 17, 18, 19, 23, 24, 25.
Thus harming others. Tribes 1, 2, 3, 5, 6, 8, 10, 13, 14, 18, 19, 20, 21, 22, 24.
Lest harm self. Tribes 1, 2, 3, 6, 7, 8, 11, 12, 13, 14, 15, 17, 18, 20, 21, 23, 24, 25.

(The following tribes specify that the following foods must not be eaten:)

Condiments. Tribe 1.
Human beings. Tribes 1, 2, 4, 6, 8, 10, 12, 14, 15, 16, 18, 22, 23, 24, 25.

(The following tribes have compulsions to eat accompanied by these interpretations:)

Thus producing breast milk. Tribe 2.
Thus pacifying others. Tribe 7.
Thus purifying others. Tribe 4.
Thus mourning. Tribe 13.
Thus protecting others. Tribes 1, 3.
Thus atoning for crime. Tribes 4, 15.
Thus aiding food quest. Tribes 12, 14.
Thus facilitating delivery. Tribes 14, 15, 22.
Thus inducing fertility. Tribes 2, 3, 17.
Thus purging self. Tribes 8, 14, 17, 19.
Thus curing self. Tribes 4, 12, 14, 15, 18.
Thus purifying self. Tribes 1, 3, 4, 17, 18, 20.
Thus protecting self. Tribes 1, 3, 5, 13, 15, 18, 21.

The diversity of interpretations associated with eating contrasts strikingly with the consistency of those associated with whistling. The five tribes which prohibit whistling (Tribes 1, 11, 17, 24, 25), despite their widely separated geographical location, offer the same interpretation, namely, that whistling would summon evil spirits and thus automatically result in harm to other members of the society. The cases of eating and whistling illustrate the two extremes of relationship between biologically defined behavior and its social interpretation.

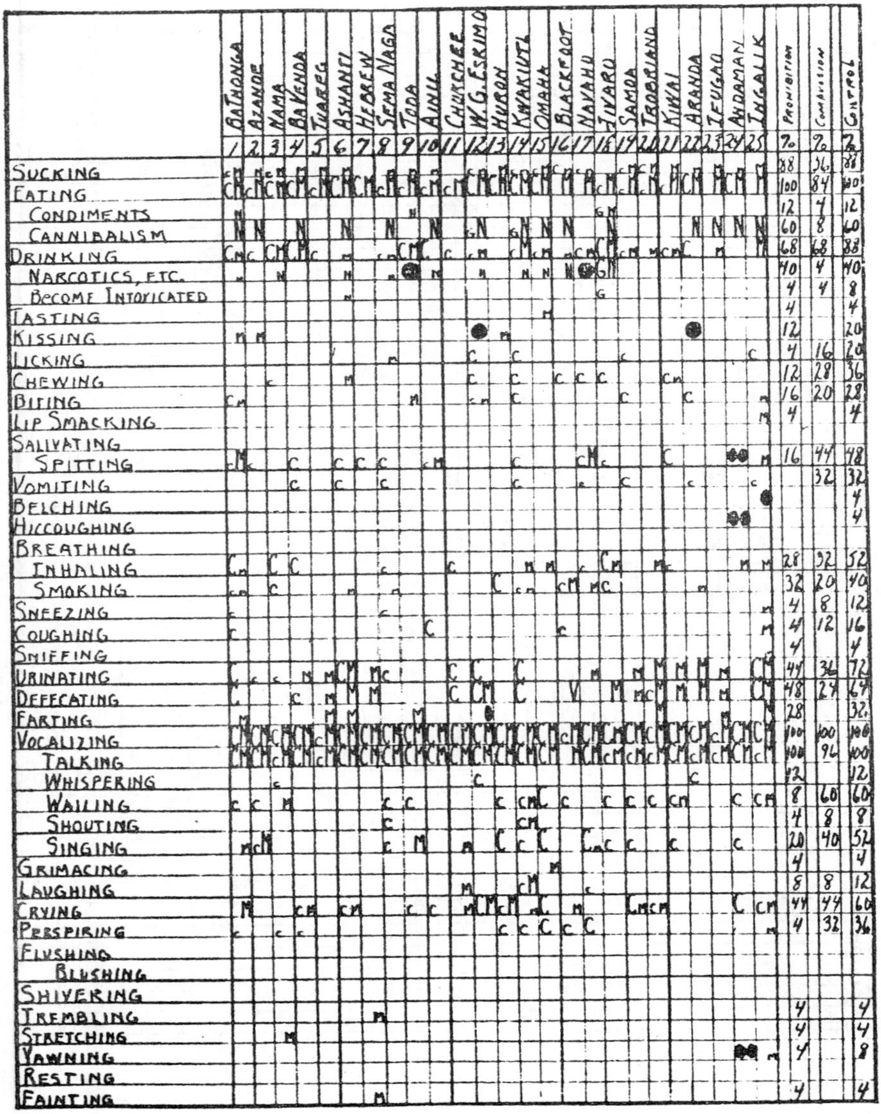

	BaThonga 1	Azande 2	Nama 3	BaVenda 4	Tuareg 5	Ashanti 6	Hebrew 7	Sema Naga 8	Toda 9	Ainu 10	Chukchee 11	W.G. Eskimo 12	Huron 13	Kwakiutl 14	Omaha 15	Blackfoot 16	Navaho 17	Jivaro 18	Samoa 19	Trobriand 20	Kiwai 21	Aranda 22	Ifugao 23	Andaman 24	Ingalik 25	Prohibition %	Commission %	Control %
SUCKING	cM	Mc	cM	M	M	M		M	M	M		cM	Mc	cM	M	Cc	c		cM	CM	M	M	M	M	M	88	36	88
EATING	CM	cM	CM	CM	cM	CM	CM	cM	cM	cM	cM	CM	CM	CM	CM	M	M	cM	cM	cM	M	CM	M	CM	M	100	84	100
CONDIMENTS	M								M									GM								12	4	12
CANNIBALISM	N	N		N		N		N		N		GN		GN	N	N		N				N	N	N	N	60	8	60
DRINKING	CM	c	CM	CM	c	M		cM	CM	C	c	cM		cM	cM	m	CM	CM	cM	m	CM	C	M		M	68	68	88
NARCOTICS, ETC.	M		M			M		m	●	M		M		N	N	N	●	GM								40	4	40
BECOME INTOXICATED						M												G								4	4	8
TASTING															M											4		4
KISSING	M	M										●	M									●				12		20
LICKING						/		M				C		C					c						C	4	16	20
CHEWING			c			M						C		C		C	C	C			CM					12	28	36
BITING	CM								M			cM		C					C			C			M	16	20	28
LIP SMACKING																									M	4		4
SALIVATING																												
SPITTING	cMc			C		C	C	C		cM				C			cMc				C			●●	M	16	44	48
VOMITING				C		C		C						C			c		C			c			c		32	32
BELCHING																									●			4
HICCOUGHING																								●●				4
BREATHING																												
INHALING	CM		C	C				c			C			M	M		c	CM			Mc			M	M	28	32	52
SMOKING	cM		C			M		M					C	cM		cM		MC				M				32	20	40
SNEEZING	c							c																	M	4	8	12
COUGHING	C									C						c									M	4	12	16
SNIFFING																										4		4
URINATING	C	c	c	M	M	CM	Mc				C	C		C			M		M	M	M	M	M		CM	44	36	72
DEFECATING	C			c	M	M	M				C	CM		C		V		M	Mc	M	M	M	M		CM	48	24	64
FARTING	M				M	M			M			●								M			M		M	28		32
VOCALIZING	CM	CM	cM	CM	cM	CM	CM	CM	CM	CM	CM	CM	CM	CM	CM	cM	CM	CM	CM	cM	CM	CM	cM	CM	CM	100	100	100
TALKING	CM	CM	cM	CM	cM	CM	CM	CM	CM	CM	CM	CM	CM	CM	CM		M	CM	cM	cM	CM	cM	cM	CM	cM	100	96	100
WHISPERING			c									C										C				12		12
WAILING	c	c	M					c	c				c	cM	C	c		c	c	c	CM			C	CM	8	60	60
SHOUTING								C						CM												4	8	8
SINGING	Mc	M						c	M		M		C	c	C		CMC		c		c			c		20	40	52
GRIMACING															M											4		4
LAUGHING											M			cM			c									8	8	12
CRYING	M			CM		CM			c	c	M	CM		cM	C	M			C	MCM				C	CM	44	44	60
PERSPIRING	c		c	c									c	c	C	c	C								M	4	32	36
FLUSHING																												
BLUSHING																												
SHIVERING																												
TREMBLING							M																			4		4
STRETCHING			M																							4		4
YAWNING																								●●	M	4		8
RESTING																												
FAINTING							M																			4		4

FIGURE 2

	1	2	3	4	5	6	7	8	9	10	11	12	13	14	15	16	17	18	19	20	21	22	23	24	25	%	%	%
SLEEPING	cM	CM	M	CM		cM		CM	M			M		cM	C	CM	cM	CM	M	CM	M		CM	M	M	72	48	76
DREAMING						M					c	M	C			c		C								8	16	24
SLEEP WALKING																									M	4		4
SLEEP TALKING																									M	4		4
THINKING	M						M																			8		8
MENSTRUATING																												
CONCEIVING	M						c						c		c								c			4	32	36
GIVING BIRTH		cM																								4	4	4
SUCKLING	cM		CM	M											c				CM						M	20	16	24
ERECTION																												
ORGASM																												
NOCTURNAL EMISSION																												
MASTURBATION	●		●			M													●	●					M	8		8
HOMOSEXUAL MASTURBATION											C						M	●	●	M		●				8	4	12
HETEROSEXUAL MASTURBATION			●			M													●			●				4		4
FELLATIO																						M				4		4
SADISM																			●									
MASOCHISM																			●									
COITUS	CM	M	MC	M	cM	M	M	Mc	M	M	M	MC		M	M	M	M	M	M	Mc	M	MC	M	M	M	100	36	100
MARITAL	CM	M			c								Mc	M						c						20	16	24
PREPUBERTAL	M			M	M	M		c		M	M				M			M	M	●		M				36	4	40
PREMARITAL	M			M	M	●	M	M		M		●	M		M	M		M	M	●	cMC			●	●	52	8	52
ADULTERY	M	M	M	M	M	M	M	M	M	M		M	M		M	M	M	M	M	M	M	M	M	M	M	92		92
BETROTHAL ADULTERY		M		M		M	M											M					M			24		24
EXTRAMARITAL											c									c							8	8
PROSTITUTION					M		M								M							M				16		16
INCEST	cM	M	M	M	M	M	M	M	M	M	M	M	M	M	M	M	M	M	M	M	M	M	M	M	M	100	4	100
INLAW INCEST	M	M	M	M		M	M	M	M	M	M	M	M	M	M	M	M	M	M	M	M	M	M		M	92		92
SEDUCTION				M		M																				8		8
RAPE		M	M			M	M							M			M		M				M			32		32
INTERRUPTUS	C																										4	4
SODOMY	●		M												M		M			MC					●	16	4	20
BESTIALITY			M																	M					●	8		8
EXHIBITIONISM																				M						4		4
STANDING				M															M	M			M			16		16
ASSUMING POSTURE																												
CROUCHING			c					c																			8	8
SITTING	cM		M	CM					M		M	M		cM	M	M		c	M	CM	MC			c		48	32	56
LYING		c	c									C				c					c						20	20
CRAWLING			c																								4	4
WALKING	M		M											M	M	M			M	M	M	cM				36	8	36
REMAINING	cM		c								c			c	c					CM						8	24	24
APPROACHING	M	M	M	M		M		M	M		M			M	M	M	M	M			M	M	M		M	68		68
ENTERING	cM	cM	cM	cM		cM	cM	cM	cM	cM	cM	cM	CM	cM	cM	cM	cM	cM	cM	cM	cM	cM	cM	cM	M	96	92	96
ACCOMPANYING			M			M		M							M				M				—			20		20
AVOIDING	C													c	c	c		C			C						24	24
RUNNING			c			M										c										4	8	12
JUMPING	c		c																								8	8
KICKING																												
STEPPING ON	M								M	M				M		M	M				M					28		28
DANCING	c		c									C	c			Cm	C		Mc	M	M		c			16	36	44
SWIMMING															M											4		4
CLIMBING																										4		4

FIGURE 2 (*continued*)

	1	2	3	4	5	6	7	5	9	10	11	12	13	14	15	16	17	18	19	20	21	22	23	24	25	%	%	%
Grasping	m					M	m										M									16		16
Taking	M	m	cM	m	M		M	m	M	M	m	M		M	M	m	M	m	M	M	M	M	M	M	m	92	4	92
Carrying	cM	c	c			m								M					c	CM		M				20	20	32
Placing	CM	CM	C	CM	C	C	CM	CM	CM	C	CM	CM	C	CM	CM	C	C	CM	C	CM	CM	C	CM	CM	C	60	100	100
Giving	C	C	C	Cm	C	C	C	C	C	C	C	C	C	C	Cm	C	C	C	C	C	C	C	C	C	C	8	100	100
Touching	M	m	cM	m	M		M	m	M	M	m	M		M	M	m	M	m	M	M	M	M	M	M	m	92	4	92
Massaging	c	c	C		c					C				C			C			C		C			c		40	40
Tickling																									M	4		4
Striking	V	M	VMc	V	cV	M	cV	V	VM	V	M	V	V	VM	V	cVM	VM	V	V	V	VM	V	V	V	M	100	16	100
Handclapping				C																							4	4
Pointing	M										M			M	m					M		●			m	24		24
Scratching											m			CM			m								cM	16	8	16
Looking	M	M	m	M	M	M			m	M		M	m	cM		m	M	m	M	M	M	M	m		M	80	4	80
Blinking																												
Winking																									m	4		4
Hearing						c	C									C		C		●		m				4	16	20
Hating															M											4		4
Fearing	m						Cm									m		M								16	4	16
Being Obstinate																M										4		4
Being Jealous	M																						m			8		8
Being Angry E	N	N	N			N						GN	cM		m	M	M		M	N	M			NM	m	56	8	56
Being Sulky																			M							4		4
Being Lazy	N										N	M			M	N	N						M	M	m	36		36
Being Selfish																												
Being Greedy				N			N							N	M					N						20		20
Being Sex Greedy																				M			m			8		8
Being Irresponsible																M										4		4
Being Dependent						M																				4		4
Being Independent	G	G	G		G			G																			20	20
Being Curious																												
Being Kind		G	c													C					C		CM			4	20	20
Being Loving										C																	4	4
Being Just, Honest						c								C													8	8
Being Industrious														C													4	4
Being Thrifty														C													4	4
Being Dignified		C		C	C																						12	12
Marrying	Mc	Mc	Mc	Mc	MC	Mc	M	M	Mc	MC	Mc	MC	MC	MC	Mc	M	MC	M	Mc	Mc	MC	Mc	MC	M	M	100	84	100
Divorcing				M			M					●	M						●	●			C●			12	4	16
Transvestitism	m						W	W		C							C									12	8	20
Inducing Barrenness	M		m			M	W	W		WM		M									M				M	36		36
Inducing Fertility	G	G	G	G					C	G						C											28	28
Facilitating Delivery	G	G		G					G		G		G	G			G		G		G						40	40
Hindering Delivery												N		N						N		N	N		M	24		24
Increasing Breast Milk	G							G		G			G								G						20	20
Removing Breast Milk	G	G													M											4	8	12
Encouraging Sucking													G														4	4
Discouraging Sucking	G	G																G		G							16	16
Helping Others	Ƨ	C	Ƨ	C	S	S	S	S	S	Ƨ	SM	CM	C	Ƨ	S	Ƨ	Ƨ	S	Ƨ	C	CMƧ	C	C	Ƨ		12	68	76
Being Hospitable				G	C		CM					G	G	G	G	G			G	G	G		C	C		4	52	52
Greeting Others	G	G																				G					12	12

FIGURE 2 (*continued*)

	1	2	3	4	5	6	7	8	9	10	11	12	13	14	15	16	17	18	19	20	21	22	23	24	25	%	%	%
BEING INTIMATE	N			N			N	N	N	N	N		N		N	N	N	N	N	N	N	N	N	GN	N	76	4	76
BEING FRIENDLY		nG	GN					GN						G			G				G					12	32	36
BEING FORMAL	G	G	G	G	G	G	G	G	G	G	G	G	G	G	G	G	G	G	G	G	G	G	G	G	G		100	100
RESPECTING OTHERS	C	G	C	C	C	C	CM	G	G	C	C	C			C	C	C	G	C	G				G	G	4	80	80
OBEYING OTHERS	C	C		C	C	C	C			C			C		C	C	C	C	C	G	C	C		C	C		72	72
ASKING PERMISSION				G		G												C									12	12
PACIFYING OTHERS		G	G	C		G	G		G	G			G					G									36	36
PAYING OTHERS	G	G	G	G	G	G		G						G	G		G	G	G	G			G	G			60	60
THANKING OTHERS		G		G		G	G			C			G		G				G								32	32
BEGGING PARDON	G																										4	4
TEACHING OTHERS	C			C	C	G	G			C		C								C		C	C				40	40
LEARNING	C	C	C	C	C	G	G	G		C						G		C			C						48	48
NAMING OTHERS	GN	G	G	G	G	G	G	GN	G	G	G	G		G	G		GN	GM		G	G	G	G			12	80	80
BEING NAMED	G	G	G	G	G	G	G	G	G	G	G	G	G	G	G	G	G	G	G	G	G	G	G	G	G		100	100
CLOTHING OTHERS	G	G	G	G	G	G		G	G		G	G	G	G				G	G	G	G	G					68	68
CLOTHING SELF	GN	GN	G	GN	G	G	GN	GN	GN	G	GN	GN	G	GN	GN	G	G	GN	G	GN	G		GN	GN	G	56	96	96
ORNAMENTING OTHERS	G										G							G			G						16	16
ORNAMENTING SELF	G	G	G					G	G	G						G		G		G	G	G					44	44
CONCEALING SELF	G	G	G	G	G	G	G										G										52	52
CONCEALING GENITALIA		G	G	G				G											G	G		G	G				32	32
CLEANSING OTHERS	G	G	GN	G	C	CM						G		C			C	C	C	C	G				G	8	56	56
CLEANSING SELF	CM	C	C	C		CMG		G	G	CM	MG	NG		G		NG	NC	M	G	CM	G			MC	G	40	80	92
PURGING SELF	C		O	G				G						G			G		G				G				28	28
CURING OTHERS				G				C		C			G	G	G		G	G		G			G		G		44	44
CURING SELF	G		G	G		G		G			G	G	G	G	G		G		G		G	G		G			60	60
PURIFYING OTHERS	G	G		G																G	G						20	20
PURIFYING SELF	G	G	G	G		G	G	G	G	G		G		G			G	G	G	G	G		G				72	72
AVOIDING RETALIATION	G	G	G	G		G	G	G	G		G	G	G	G			G	G			G	G					64	64
PROTECTING OTHERS	G	G	G	G		G			G	G	G	G	G	G	G		G	G		G	G	G	G		G		76	76
WARNING OTHERS														G									G				8	8
PROTECTING SELF	G	G	G	G	G	G	G	G	G	G	G	G		G	G	G	G	G			G	G	G				80	80
SECLUDING SELF	G	G	G	G		G	G	G	G	G	G		G	G	G	G		G		G	G	G					72	72
CONFINING SELF	G	G							G	G										G							20	20
EXPRESSING GRIEF	G	G		G		G		G	G						G	G		G				G			G		44	44
MOURNING	GN	G	G	G	G	G		nG	G	G	G	GN	GN	GN	G	G	G	G	G	G	GN	G	G	G	G	24	96	100
EXHIBITING COWARDICE		M		M	M	M	M	W				W	M		M	M	M								M	48		48
EXHIBITING BRAVERY	G													G	C	C		C	C			C					28	28
EXPRESSING PAIN				N							N		N		N			N	N							24		24
EXHIBITING DISGUST																				M						4		4
RIDICULING OTHERS											N				N		M								M	16		16
BOASTING																							N			4		4
DECEIVING OTHERS			N	N		N	N				N					N	N	N							N	36		36
BETRAYING OTHERS	N			GM		GN															N	N				20	8	20
ANGERING OTHERS	N	N		N		N		N			N			W												28		28
FRIGHTENING OTHERS																					G						4	4
BEING FRIGHTENED																					G						4	4
BEWITCHING OTHERS	M	M	M	M		M	M					M	M				M					M	M			44		44
DISRESPECTING OTHERS	N		N	N		N				N	N	N	N	N	N	N	N		N		N	N	N	N	N	72		72
DISOBEYING OTHERS			N	N		N	N		M		M				N			M	N		M					40		40
INSULTING OTHERS	N	N	N	N	N	N			N	N		N	N	N	N		N	N	N		N		N		N	72		72

FIGURE 2 (*continued*)

	1	2	3	4	5	6	7	8	9	10	11	12	13	14	15	16	17	18	19	20	21	22	23	24	25	%	%	%
Being Obscene	N	n	N			N		n					N						N	n			N		n	40		40
Stealing	n	N	N	N	N	N	N	N	N	N		N	N	N	N	N	N	N	N	N	N	N	N	N	N	96		96
Plundering					C		M																			4	4	8
Assuming Prerogatives	N	n	n	N		N			N			N		n				n	N		N	N				48		48
Quarrelling (Ingroup)	M		M	M		M			m			M	M		M				m		m	CM	M			48	4	48
Fighting (Outgroup)				C	C		CM					M	C	c	CM	C		c			CM		C			16	40	44
Committing Treason			M	M		M							M			M										20		20
Hindering War				n										N				N	N	n	N					24		24
Punishing Others		C	C	C		cM	Cm				c	CM	C		cm	c	m	cm			Cm	Cm	Cm	mC		40	60	68
Punishing Self		G	G		G		G	G			G		G	G		G			G								44	44
Atoning for Crime		G											G		G												12	12
Confessing Guilt	G	G		G		G						G							G		G		GM		•	4	32	36
Mutilate Others (Without Pain)															CM							C	C			4	12	12
Mutilate Self (Without Pain)	m	c	c	C		Cm	m		cm	cM		cm	c	c	c	c		c		c	c			cm	c	28	64	72
Mutilate Others											C				C		C					C					16	16
Mutilate Self	C	C	C	C	c	c	M	C	C	c	c	c	c	C	C	c		cm	C	c	C	C	c	c	c	4	96	96
Harm Others	N	GN	GN	GN	GN	GN	GN	N	cN	N	GN	GN	GN	N	GN	GN	GN	GN	N	N	GN	GN	GN	N	N	100	64	100
Harm Self	GW	GW	GW	GW	G	GW	GW	GW	GW	GW	GW	GW	GW	GW	GW	GW	W	GW	GW	GW	GW	GW	W	GW	W	96	88	100
Kill Others																												
Murder	M	M	cM	cM	M	cM	cM	M	•	M	M	M	M	M	M	M	M	cM	M	M	M	M	M	M	M	96	16	100
Accidental Homicide	M	M	M	M		M	M								M						M		•			32		36
Abortion				M		W		W		M			W					m	•			•				24		32
Infanticide		•							c	Mc	c	c			M	M		C	•			c•		•		12	30	32
Warfare				m	cm	M	C	m				M					m	C							m	28	12	36
Kill Self	m					M					WC			m	m		W							•		28	4	28
Playing		m		CM				M			C				M		M		C	M	M	M				32	12	48
Working	M	Cm	cm	CM	Cm	M	Mc	M	cm	c	Cm	CM		CM	CM	cm	C	c	CM	C	m		CM	m	cm	72	72	92
Hunt, Fish, Till, Etc.	c		c							m	m	CM	Cm	M	Cm	cm		m		C	M	cM	m	m		48	36	60
Aid Food Quest												G	G	G	G						G	G					24	24
Kill Animals	cM	cM	mc		M		M		C	C	C	Cm				cM	m	M	m	M	m	m	m	Cm	m	64	32	76
Hinder Food Quest	N	N	N	n		N	n	N		N	N	N	N	N	N	n		N	N	N	N	N	N	N	n	88		88
Pollute Food	N	N	N	N		N	N	N	N	n	N	N	N	N	N	n	N	N	N	N	N	N			n	88		88
Manufacturing	m		c	m			M					c		c			cm	cM								20	20	32
Hinder Manufacturing	N	N	N	N		N		N	N		N			N	N	N	N	N	N	N	N					64		64
Destroy Goods	cM	cM		N			M	M										C					N	M		28	12	32
Arson				M																			M			8		8
Invite Bad Luck	W	W	w		W	W	W		W	W	w			N			N								N	48		48
Violate Rules	m			M		M				M	m	M														24		24

FIGURE 2 (*continued*)

Organized in this way, the data suggest interesting possibilities. Is it true, for example, that some actions such as whistling are similarly interpreted among all the societies prohibiting them? Interesting and important though it might be to pursue such questions, they are not an integral part of the present study. No attempt is here made to compare compulsions and prohibitions in terms of the relationship of their physiological and social aspects. The data are arranged in a two-dimensional chart (Figure 2), which reveals only the aspects of behavior directly or indirectly controlled in our 25 societies without showing the relationship between the behavior restricted and either its meaning or its sanction. Although the relationship is ignored, the information itself is retained and is differentiated as to type by the use of different symbols, viz., *C* or *M* for the direct subject of the pattern or rule, *G* or *N* for the interpretation given to the behavior and commonly expressed by *thus* (e.g., thus stealing), *Q* or *W* for the sanction commonly expressed by *lest* (e.g., lest harm befall self), and *S* or *V* for inferential or otherwise questionable information. The symbols *C, G, Q* and *S* indicate compulsions; *M, N, W* and *V* prohibitions. A solid dot when placed in the left of a block indicates a stated absence of compulsions; when placed in the right a lack of prohibitions. If a solid dot is placed in the center the behavior itself was stated to be absent.

A word is needed to explain the grouping of items in the chart. A satisfactory classification of what appear to be rather miscellaneous actions is difficult without considerable insight. In the classification adopted, actions were grouped in the ways which seemed most useful after working with the information. Since it was not of primary importance to evolve a refined classification, little effort was expended in that direction. A more thorough study, embracing a larger number of tribes, would doubtless lead to a more satisfactory classification.

Each restriction or compulsion was given a quantitative value as to its importance in the society. This importance, or strength, is roughly indicated by the height of the symbol, e.g., a completely filled square signifying that the pattern or rule is of great importance.

Perhaps the most noticeable feature of the chart is the high proportion of blank spaces. That this is not an accurate representation of the facts is extremely probable. Defecating, urinating, masturbating, raping, and being cowardly, for example, are very likely controlled by more societies than is indicated in the chart.

The proportion of tribes which are reported to prohibit or compel the action is given at the extreme right of the chart. Thus, the percentage of tribes prohibiting the behavior occurs in the first column; that of tribes compelling the behavior in the second; and that of tribes controlling the behavior in the third.

If the behavior items are grouped by the percentage of tribes which control them the following result is obtained:[7]

100% eat, vocalize, talk, coitus, (erection), (orgasm), incest, give, (strike), marry, be formal, be named, mourn, harm others, harm self.

96% enter, clothe self, steal, mutilate self, murder.

92% adultery, in-law incest, take, cleanse self, touch, work.

88% suck, drink, hinder food quest, pollute food.

80% look, respect others, name others, protect self.

76% sleep, help others, be intimate, protect others, kill animals.

72% urinate, premarital coitus, obey others, purify self, seclude self, disrespect others, insult others, mutilate self without pain.

68% approach, clothe others, punish others.

64% defecate, avoid retaliation, hinder manufacturing.

60% cannibalism, wail, cry, pay others, cure self, hunt, fish, till, etc.

56% sit, cleanse others, be angry.

52% inhale, sing, be hospitable, conceal self.

48% learn, cowardice, assume prerogatives, quarrel, play, invite bad luck.

44% spit, perpubertal coitus, dance, ornament self, cure others, express grief, bewitch others, fight, punish self.

40% smoke, massage, facilitate delivery, teach others, disobey others, be obscene.

36% chew, perspire, conceive, walk, be lazy, induce barrenness, be friendly, pacify others, deceive others.

32% consume narcotics, vomit, rape, thank others, conceal genitalia, carry, confess guilt, accidental homicide, abortion, infanticide, manufacture, destroy goods.

28% bite, fart, marital coitus, step on, point, divorce, induce fertility, purge self, exhibit bravery, anger others, kill self.

24% dream, suckle, betrothal adultery, remain, avoid, hear, hinder delivery, express pain, hinder war, aid food quest, violate mores and taboos.

20% lick, whistle, sodomy, lie, accompany, be greedy, be independent, be kind, transvestitism, increase breast

---

[7]The behavior items are given in parentheses if the information is inferential or otherwise questionable.

milk, purify others, confine self, betray others, commit treason.

16% cough, prostitution, stand, grasp, scratch, fear, discourage sucking, ornament others, ridicule others, mutilate others.

12% eat condiments, kiss, sneeze, whisper, laugh, homosexual masturbation, run, be dignified, remove breast milk, greet others, ask permission, atone for crime, mutilate others without pain.

8% become intoxicated, shout, think, masturbation, extramarital coitus, seduction, bestiality, crouch, jump, be jealous, be sex greedy, be just, warn others, plunder, arson.

4% taste, smack lips, sniff, grimace, tremble, stretch, faint, sleep walk, sleep talk, give birth, heterosexual masturbation, fellatio, coitus, interruptus, exhibitionism, crawl, swim, climb, tickle, hand clapping, wink, hate, be obstinate, be sulky, be irresponsible, be dependent, be loving, be industrious, be thrifty, encourage sucking, beg pardon, exhibit disgust, boast, frighten others, be frightened.

0% salivate, belch, hiccough, breathe, flush, blush, shiver, yawn, menstruate, nocturnal emission, sadism, masochism, kick, blink, be curious.

The behavior items controlled in more than 50 per cent of our societies constitute a tentative summary of human activities subject to widespread societal control. Such a list follows:

50 to 100% suck, eat, cannibalism, drink, vocalize, talk, wail, cry, sing, inhale, defecate, urinate, coitus, (orgasm), (erection), incest, adultery, in-law incest, premarital coitus, touch, (strike), give, take, sit, enter, approach, look, sleep, marry, be formal, be named, name others, clothe self, cleanse self, protect self, protect others, purify self, clothe others, respect others, help others, be intimate, seclude self, avoid retaliation, pay others, cure self, be hospitable, conceal self, mourn, harm self, mutilate self without pain, work, hunt, fish, till, etc., be angry, hinder manufacturing, hinder food quest, harm others, steal, murder, pollute food, kill animals, disrespect others, insult others, punish others.

An additional group was obtained by critically considering each of the remaining items and selecting those which met one of the following conditions: (*a*) if it seemed probable that the relevant information was not usually given in the literature and if, in those societies on which relevant information was supplied, the behavior was harshly controlled, as in the case of farting, which is strongly tabooed in seven tribes; (*b*) if the behavior was universally reported to occur but was actually mentioned as compulsory in only a few of the tribes, as in the case of teaching, and, conversely, if the behavior seemed universally to be avoided although seldom specifically mentioned as prohibited; and (*c*) if the number of tribes in which an item of behavior was prohibited added to those in which its direct opposite was compelled exceeded 50 per cent of the total, as in the cases of be cowardly and be brave. This list, when combined with the previous one, yields a more complete, though still tentative, summary of the forms of behavior which are subject to widespread societal control. This list is given here in three groups as follows: (1) behavior items which are both prohibited and compelled, (2) behavior items which are generally prohibited, and (3) behavior items which are generally compelled.

1. Behavior Items Both Prohibited and Compelled

Eating, drinking, vocalizing, talking, defecating, urinating, placing, marrying, working, harming others, harming self.

2. Behavior Items Prohibited

Sucking, cannibalism, biting, crying, hearing, seeing, coitus, incest, adultery, in-law incest, rape, prepubertal coitus, marital coitus, suckling, sleeping, touching, grasping, taking, placing, striking, farting, walking, approaching, murdering, stealing, assuming, another's prerogatives, harming food, hindering food quest, hindering manufacturing, hindering course of war, inviting bad luck, violating mosrules, being intimate, disrespecting others, insulting others, being angry, killing animals, quarrelling, bewitching, defying others, being obscene, deceiving others, angering others, committing suicide, betraying others, destroying goods, committing treason, being jealous, being irresponsible, hating, becoming barren, playing, being lazy.

3. Behavior Items Compelled

Wailing, weeping, sleeping, giving, entering, being formal, being named, mutilating self, mutilating self without pain, mourning, naming others, respecting others, cleansing self, protecting self, protecting others, obeying others, purifying self, being secluded, helping others, learning, avoiding retaliation, curing self, paying, cleansing others, avenging, being hospitable, concealing parts of body, concealing genitalia, being punished, facilitating delivery, teaching others, curing others, expressing grief, fighting outgroup, pacifying others, being friendly, thanking others, being fertile, participating in food quest, purging self, being brave, avoiding bad luck, ensuring good luck, aiding food quest, being generous, being kind, manufacturing, being industrious.

This tentative list of behavior items generally controlled by societies serves the purpose of furnishing a target toward which future research may be aimed. Doubtless further study will delete some of these behavior items and add many others to the list. In all probability, however, future investigation will substantiate those actions controlled in at least 80 per cent of our 25 societies. These behavior items are given here accompanied by exceedingly brief explanatory remarks.

Sucking

Primarily it is the infant whose sucking behavior is controlled; the infant is forced to give up the breast as a source of nourishment. All societies, apparently, are faced with the problem of weaning. Weaning methods vary from one society to another, the most popular being that of smearing the nipple with some bitter or peppery substance which effectively discourages the infant from sucking the breast. In many of our societies sucking is compelled in blood-letting or in removing objects which are considered to be the cause of illness.

Eating

Societies regulate what their members eat. No member of our societies escapes specific food taboos. In most cases individuals, as members of groups within the society, must abstain from certain flesh foods. Furthermore, cannibalism is commonly prohibited. Even in those societies where war or ceremonial cannibalism is permitted or enjoined, members do not commonly eat their fellows. Furthermore, societies determine when, where, and with whom food may be eaten. There are circumstances in the lives of a society's members when fasting is obligatory for varying periods of time. Mourning, for example, is characteristically marked by compulsory renunciation of food.

There are also occasions when certain foods must be eaten. A specific diet, for example, is commonly prescribed for the sick person, for the nursing mother, and for children.

Drinking

Though somewhat less commonly regulated in our sample of societies than eating, drinking is often the object of societal control. Intoxicants and narcotics, too, are in certain societies prohibited to many members on grounds of prestige and are as commonly enjoined as a magical means of protection or purification. Medicines are characteristically administered in liquid form, and this is especially true of emetics and purgatives.

Vocalizing

A collective term used here to include all forms of vocal expression. Talking (see below) is the form of vocalization most commonly controlled.

Talking

Talking is strictly controlled in our twenty-five societies. This scarcely seems surprising inasmuch as language is a universal means of communication for human beings. Many thoughts are commonly suppressed in their verbal form, e.g., insults, sexual overtures, and expressed intentions to harm other members of society. Many of the actions which people wish to perform cannot be expressed, even symbolically, in speech. The evidence suggests that to permit even the verbal expression of some desires is dangerous to society. On the other hand, talking is often compulsory under certain circumstances. Praying, begging another's pardon, and formally addressing others are widespread examples.

(*Erection*) (*See coitus*)

(*Orgasm*) (*See coitus*)

Coitus

Societies regulate the sexual activity of their members. In the main, coitus is forbidden rather than enjoined. Primarily, members of society are restricted and limited in their selection of sex-objects. Incest, in-law incest, and adultery, in particular, are strictly prohibited and cruelly sanctioned. A possible reason for these restrictions is the rivalry, or sex-jealousy, generated by competition for sex-objects, which is obviously disruptive to coöperation and ingroup solidarity. Adultery, for example, is commonly regarded as a violation of property rights. Sexual intercourse is often employed magically as a means of purification. Abstention from sexual intercourse is commonly enjoined as a renunciation which will ensure success in hunting or in war.

(*Striking*)

Though not commonly specified as the means employed, striking has been inferred to be the action by which the destruction of life is effected in our twenty-five societies. (See ***murder*** below.)

Touching

Touching is commonly prohibited by societies when property rights are threatened. To touch something apparently carries the implication of desire to appropriate. Furthermore, touching as a sign of intimacy is commonly forbidden. To touch a person is often considered to be a forerunner of sexual activity and is prohibited where intercourse is also forbidden.

(*Grasping*)

An elemental action inferred to occur as an integral part of many acts, e.g., taking.

Taking

Societies regulate what their members may take, or appropriate. To take for oneself any article often involves the interests of fellow members. Thus, taking as a means of violating property rights (see ***stealing***) is commonly forbidden.

Giving

Giving is strongly enjoined in many of our societies as a way of repaying others for goods or services rendered, thus reinforcing group coöperation. Gifts are often made to propitiate the gods or to pacify outraged fellow members. Some gift frequently accompanies marriage. When death has occurred offerings are commonly made in order to appease the ghost. Similarly, a gift is often made to pacify the spirit of a slain animal.

Entering

To go into, or enter, certain structures or enclosures is commonly forbidden. It is in this form that the rambling activities of a society's members are most often controlled. Places are protected, apparently, thus ensuring the protection of persons and things. Property rights and notions of secrecy, intimacy, and privacy are involved, apparently, when men enter the house of another or when women seek to attend the boys' initiation ceremonies.

Marrying

Each of our twenty-five societies is characterized by rules governing the persons one may marry. (See also *coitus,* and restrictions on incest.) Furthermore, certain marriages are often enjoined. This is especially true in the case of widows who are often compelled to marry specified relatives of the deceased spouse.

Being formal

Compulsions to be formal and to avoid treating others with undue familiarity are widespread. This seems to be a way of emphasizing and reinforcing many important rules such as avoiding sexual intimacy, jealousy, and rivalry. Formality stresses deference to others (see also *respecting others*). Granting prestige in one form or another is enforced in all our societies. Formality continually emphasizes and reinforces the rules which define social relationships.

Being named

The members of all our twenty-five societies are required to have a name. In many societies some specific relative has the duty of naming the child. The identification of individuals by a name seems to be a widespread expedient without which the functioning of a society would be severely handicapped; it is a realistic necessity in social coöperation.

Mourning

The dead must be mourned. Though mourning customs vary from one society to another, rules regulate the procedure of surviving members in all our twenty-five tribes. A common expression of grief at death is wailing which is compulsory in many of these societies. Abstention from food, self-mutilation, and various purificatory rites are commonly enjoined as a sign of mourning. Death is a painful, mystifying, and apparently terrifying event. The loss of a group member cannot go unnoticed. Social ties are broken and social relationships must be readjusted.

Harming others

Many actions are prohibited on the ground that they will automatically result in harm to other members of the society. Continually reinforced at every turn, this prohibition finds direct expression as a mosrule against murder.

Murdering

"Thou shalt not kill" as applied to the members of one's own group is generally sanctioned by the threat of death. Vengeance is almost sure to follow the violation of this rule. There are indications, however, of an interesting exception. Murder within a very small and closely knit ingroup is sometimes condoned, as for example, among the Jivaro where murder within the household is permitted to go unavenged. In all such cases thus far examined the rationalization is that the group has already suffered a loss and cannot afford to sustain another.

Stealing

The violation of property rights in this form is commonly forbidden. To take another person's property is a provocative act which commonly results in bloodshed. This seems reasonable since to steal another's property is to cheat him of his labor, i.e., to steal his work. Like murder, stealing seems to threaten the solidarity of the society, and is one of the first rules taught to children.

Clothing self

Though to wear clothing is not universally compelled in our sample of tribes, clothes of some sort, usually concealing the genitalia, are worn by the members of most of them. Interestingly, among the Aranda who do not clothe themselves, strict etiquette governs concealment of the genitalia. Words designating that part of the garments which covers the genitals are often tabooed, a fact which indicates that clothing serves more than the utilitarian function of protecting people from cold or the sun's rays.

Mutilating self

To mutilate oneself or to submit to mutilation at the hands of an experienced operator is surprisingly common. Puberty rites and other initiation ceremonies are often accompanied by mutilations as though the importance of the occasion had to be indelibly engraved upon the skin of the neophyte. As mentioned above, self-mutilation is prevalent as a sign of mourning. The result of mutilation is often conceived to be ornamental and also, many times, a mark of ingroup membership.

Working

The members of all our societies with but rare exceptions are obliged to work. Only by work, of course, can mankind exploit the environment and win subsistence. The widespread presence of rules forbidding work is not so easy to understand. Such prohibitions become somewhat more reasonable if it is realized that the food quest and processes of manufacturing are somewhat precarious for primitive peoples and that working is forbidden when to do so is conceived likely to increase the probability of failure. The hunter who goes to hunt alone, for example, and frightens away the game, may even be killed as punishment for making the food quest more difficult for his fellows.

Hindering food quest

Societies commonly prohibit any activity which is deemed likely to reduce the efficiency of the methods of procuring food (see *working* above).

Polluting food

Pollution of food seems to be a widespread possibility attendant upon a state of impurity which must be carefully avoided. During menstruation, for example, a woman is often forbidden to touch food with her fingers and is required to eat with a skewer or fork so that the food will not be contaminated.

Respecting others

Compulsion to respect others and associated prohibition on the expression of insults are strongly insisted upon by our twenty-five societies. Death is not an uncommon punishment meted out to the disrespectful person; this is especially true where chiefly status is involved (see also *being formal, stealing*).

Cleansing self

The necessity of cleansing oneself seems in our societies to be related more to the removal of blood and ritual contamination than to the removal of dirt. Menstruation and childbirth, for instance, are common occasions accompanied by admonitions to cleanliness. Cleansing is also prevalent as a method of purification as, for example, after the death of a near relative.

Protecting self

The members of our societies commonly undergo ceremonies which are designed to protect them from harm. Most often, perhaps, as children they are forced to participate in activities designed to prepare them for the hardships which will await them in adult life. Common, too, are protective rites preceding hunting and war expeditions. Protection from ill health and disease is mandatory for the members of these societies. To preserve the life and health of its individual members is apparently of extreme importance to the welfare of a society.

Harming self

Harming oneself is practically never prohibited or enjoined directly. That the members of society are commonly forced to submit to the infliction of pain is apparent from the widespread rules compelling self-mutilation. "Lest you harm yourself" is a common sanction which deserves attention here.

The behavior which has been considered here is only one dimension of the socially relevant organic factors. Notably missing from this study are many physiological states. The fact that all women menstruate, for example, is not included in the list of human behavior controlled in these societies. This results from the fact that menstruation is not directly prohibited or compelled in these societies, but indirectly controlled by the association of many rules with this physiological state. The association of rules with physiological conditions appears to be an important aspect of social phenomena which deserves detailed investigation.

During the course of investigation many questions suggested themselves which are as yet unanswered. For example, how do different societies deal with human behavior which tends to exceed limits imposed by societal needs? Do different societies employ similar techniques to solve problems arising from conflicts between human impulses and societal needs? How do societies socialize their young so they fit smoothly into the grooves which as adults they must follow? What are the sanctions which are generally successful in suppressing behavior?

One group of interesting suggestions derives from the discovery that rules and patterns vary with respect to the extent of their application. A rule prohibiting incest, for example, is less general in its application than a rule which permits coitus only under the conditions of monogamous marriage. It is likely that the more generalized the rule the less necessity there will be for coincidental specific rules. A case in point appears to be the comparative absence, in our society, of avoidance rules governing in-law relationships. The validity of this suggestion could be tested on a cross-cultural level. In societies where mother-in-law avoidance is strictly enjoined it might be found, for example, that the mother-in-law is not included in any generalized prohibition on sexual intercourse. The tendency for important rules to be continuously reinforced appears to be working against this principle and must be applied as a corrective factor. In nearly all our societies, for example, the generalized pattern governing acts which are harmful to ingroup members is frequently emphasized and reinforced. Almost any action which can be interpreted as harmful to others is specifically stated in those terms, apparently as a continuous reminder of the importance of the prohibition. The natural and logical extension of this study will be to pursue these and other suggestions.

The specialized technique developed for investigating cultural materials exposes a fundamental difficulty involved in making cross-cultural comparisons. Culture consists of traditional beliefs and rules of conduct. The rules vary as to the sanction reinforcing them. Although it is comparatively easy to estimate the relative importance of varying sanctions when dealing with a specific society, difficulties arise when cross-cultural comparisons of sanctions are attempted. For example, it is difficult to equate a fine of rice among the Ifugao with a sanction of ridicule among the West Greenland Eskimo.

Furthermore, rules vary as to their complexity. Complex rules, or patterns, may be defined, when the information is supplied, in terms of the segmental rules which compose them. These component rules may be identified cross-culturally when the object of control is defined in biological terms. A pattern against intimacy, for instance, may be reduced to rules against looking at, talking to, touching, and the like. The actions thus controlled, however, seem in most cases to be merely instrumental, i.e., the means by which it is thought a specific result will be attained. In such instances, a pattern may be defined by the anticipated result of the behavior controlled. Thus, a pattern against praising an infant in one society might be judged similar to a pattern against naming a newly born child in another society. The basis for comparison is that both patterns are apparently directed against an intention to injure the child. Difficulties arise in attempting to use this method because information concerning intent is rarely included in the literature. A further possible way of defining a pattern is in terms of another pattern which is more easily identified. For example, a pattern against sorcery might be defined in terms of its relationship, in a particular society, to a pattern against murder. Finally, a pattern may be defined in terms of the problem which it appears to solve. Such a method of definition, however, depends for its validity upon the competence of the investigator who judges the function of the pattern. Some combination of these or other methods of identifying patterns for cross-cultural comparison must be rigorously employed if valid generalizations in social science are to be made.

The importance of research directed toward a more complete understanding of the relationship between human beings and society deserves to be emphasized. Human impulses, tendencies to avoid pain, and the conflicts which arise when human beings attempt to utilize the environment pose societal problems. Further problems arise when individuals in their striving to gratify impulses and avoid pain fall short of satisfying societal needs. Solutions to their problems are afforded by culture which controls human behavior and imposes rewards and punishment.

When social scientists are able to establish a finite list of human characteristics which are commonly subject to societal control, investigations can be directed toward an understanding of the reasons underlying this widespread similarity of societies. When the specifications imposed by common societal needs are accurately determined, it will be possible to isolate those problems which are peculiar to each individual society. Societies will then be characterized by the problems which they have and have not adequately solved.

What do all societies have in common? To this, the first question which the sociologist must ask, a naïve traveller would not hesitate to answer: "Men, women, and children." Naturalists, anthropologists, and sociologists would add many other common elements, e.g., climate, flora, fauna, culture, change, and a history. Though these factors do not have the same content for every society, they are, nevertheless, characteristic of all human societies. To state merely that these are common to all societies, however, scarcely supplies an adequate answer to the question posed above. The true significance of these factors will be achieved only through careful and detailed investigation. Until the universal characteristics of societies have been precisely delineated sociologists will be unable to progress beyond their initial task of defining a society. Why societies are similar will be determined before conclusive theories as to dissimilarities are established. Quantification in social science will await the answer to this question. The common denominator is lacking in social science, and the first task of its students is to establish one.

References

1. Barton, R. F. Ifugao Law. *Univ. Cal. Pub. Amer. Arch. & Eth.*, 1919, **15**, 65-66.
2. Junod, H. A. The Life of a South African Tribe. London: 1927.
3. Rattray, R. S. Religion and Art in Ashanti. Oxford: Oxford Univ. Press, 1927.
4. Stayt, H. A. The BaVenda. London: 1931.
5. Sumner, W. G. Folkways. Boston: Ginn, 1906.
6. Tylor, E. B. Primitive Society. London: 1871.

Institute of Human Relations
Yale University
333 Cedar Street
New Haven, Connecticut

NEW WAYS OF PRESENTING AN OLD IDEA:

THE STATISTICAL METHOD IN SOCIAL ANTHROPOLOGY[1] *

Curl Prize Essay for 1952

BY ANDRÉ J. KÖBBEN

University of Amsterdam

It has been remarked that it is almost impossible to overestimate the significance of sex in human affairs, but that this impossibility Freud has achieved. In much the same sense, one may say that it is almost impossible to overestimate the significance of refined statistical procedures for social sciences but that some current researches are achieving that impossibility (Robert S. Lynd, *Knowledge for What?*).

Since 1937 certain American scholars have been at work on a Grand Design in the field of social anthropology: an inventory is being made of "all known cultures, primitive, historical and contemporary" (Murdock *et al*, 1950, p. xii) or, at least, of a representative sample of them. Almost a hundred and fifty tribes and peoples have already been dealt with, and others are to follow. This notable enterprise, the Cross-Cultural Survey, initiated by the Institute of Human Relations at Yale University, is conspicuous for its systematic planning, for its numerous learned contributors and for the large ancillary staff engaged in it. The importance with which it is regarded is shown by the fact that even during the second world war its progress was uninterrupted.

Now, before this American scheme is further discussed, the question should be asked whether it is entirely novel in conception. To that the answer must be "No". The same idea, namely a catalogue of world tribes and cultures, was put forward at the end of the last century by the Dutch anthropologist and sociologist S. R. Steinmetz in the following terms:

> "... de chaque peuple on devrait donner les qualités sociales les plus importantes et d'une manière systematique. Par example le nom du peuple, le caractère de sa vie économique ... le caractère de son gouvernement, de sa composition sociale, de l'organisation de la famille, de la propriété, sa situation démographique, sa phase intellectuelle et religieuse, etc." (Steinmetz, 1898, p. 208).

The author's aim was near completeness, although he believed that his catalogue would be of service as soon as it comprised from a thousand to fifteen hundred tribes and phases of culture (p. 209).

It seems worth while to compare these two projects, lying as they do nearly fifty years apart, in regard to their plan, to the intellectual climates from which they originated, and above all, to the use made of them in anthropological literature. Steinmetz knew exactly what he intended to achieve by his catalogue. In the first place it would furnish him with a weapon to attack his arch-enemies, the *raisonneurs*, whom he did not hesitate to belabour severely:

> "... en déduisant un peu, on construit toute une série de lois en quelques heures. C'est très amusant et cela ne fatigue que le lecteur. Cette tendance de l'esprit est encore renforcée par le besoin économique d'obtenir de grand résultats à peu de frais. On désire des verités larges, éternelles, valables pour toute l'humanité, comme prix de quelques heures de spéculation somnolente. ... Toute cette race de spéculateurs paresseux doit etre extirpées de notre science ...." (p. 100).

Quantitative studies, based on material in his catalogue, would, he thought, *prove* the rashness of mere theorizing; and he also hoped that evidence of the kind it provided would deter the spinners of theories from their activities. Scholars would no

[1] The writer wishes to express his thanks to Miss M. R. Hulleman, of Amsterdam, who assisted in the translation of the Dutch original, and to Dr. J. C. Trevor, of Cambridge, who revised the English version for press. He further wishes to acknowledge the help of Dr. D. R. Cox, also of Cambridge, in clarifying certain points relating to statistical nomenclature. None of the persons named, of course, must necessarily be supposed to agree with the opinions contained in the text, which are the writer's own.

*Reprinted from the *Journal of the Royal Anthropological Institute of Great Britain and Ireland*, Vol. 82 (1952), 129-146, by permission of the author and the Royal Anthropological Institute.

longer dare restrict themselves to purely deductive reasoning if they knew that thereby they ran the risk of exposure. The catalogue would *compel* induction:

" . . . elle forcera les intelligences le plus recalcitrantes à l'induction véritable,[2] parce qu'elle montrera qu'il y a des groupes différents de types sociaux, que ce qui est vrai pour l'un n'est pas vrai pour l'autre " (p. 207).

Another of Steinmetz' objectives was to discover and proclaim the gaps in ethnographical writings.

" Il ne suffit pas d'indiquer [les] lacunes; il faut les exposer et les fixer dans notre esprit d'une façon plus intensive. C'est ce résultat que peut être obtenu par le catalogue que je vais proposer " (p. 207).

But more remained: running like a golden thread through the whole of his argument was the idea that, when once the inductive method had been fully applied in the manner he suggested, the results obtained would be irrefutable: the " true Truth " would have been found. In a few places this is explicitly stated by him, for example:—

" Elle [the statistical method] nous aidera à atteindre cet idéal, que toute contribution qui comptera parmi les vrai adeptes sera vraiment une contribution a notre savoir positive, *veritable* " (p. 109; present writer's italics).

Buoyed up by such a fresh and vigorous optimism, Steinmetz felt able to begin his task. And he did so in a way which it might be claimed was typical of him: he did not enlist the aid of any learned society but, apart from a few lady helpers whom he employed to file source books and periodicals, he set to work alone. It is hardly surprising that his ambitious venture could not be realized to the full. What he did achieve, however, constitutes an impressive piece of documentation that fills a whole cabinet with large manuscript (not typewritten) files.

If unquestionably a pioneer, Steinmetz was not the first to embark on such a scheme as he had tried to accomplish. A predecessor, from whom he borrowed the idea, was Herbert Spencer. Spencer's System of Synthetic Philosophy, comprising *First Principles*, the *Principles of Biology*, the *Principles of Psychology*, the *Principles of Sociology* and the *Principles of Ethics*, was completed in 1896, seven years before he died. What he had begun in 1867 (Spencer, 1904, II, pp. 173, 261, 351) but did not succeed in finishing while alive, was another large-scale project, the *Descriptive Sociology*, although eight parts of it, all in royal folio, appeared between 1873 and 1881. After a loss of from £3,000 to £4,000[3] Spencer had to abandon the venture, for which he could not furnish any more money. " Even had there been shown considerable appreciation of the work," he observes with understandable bitterness, " it would have been out of the question to continue it . . ."[4]

Because too few primitive societies had been included in them, Steinmetz refrained from using Spencer's previous compilations (1898, p. 208). He was, of course, ignorant of the fact that further parts of the *Descriptive Sociology* were to be published after its inceptor's lifetime by trustees with funds from his estate and that as late as 1930 there would be a reissue of one of them, *African Races*, which boasted a high degree of completeness.[5]

A second precursor of Steinmetz was Tylor. On 13 November 1888, in an address (remarkable for its time) to the Anthropological Institute of Great Britain and Ireland, entitled " On a Method of Investigating the Development of Institutions; applied to Laws of Marriage and Descent," Tylor stated the results of a study of " between three and four hundred peoples, ranging from insignificant savage hordes to great cultured nations " (1889, p. 246). While it is clear that, within the limits of this lecture, he could not deal adequately with all the evidence considered by

---

[2] That in this respect Steinmetz was far too sanguine need scarcely be insisted upon.

[3] *Ibid.*, pp. 351–2. The higher figure is given by Tillett (1939, p. 24).

[4] Spencer, 1904, p. 351. It is nevertheless curious that a little later incessant demands were being made for an ethnographical thesaurus, championed among others by Arnold van Gennep (Gerretson, 1911, p. 83). Somló, like Dürkheim, recommended the inductive and comparative method as that of the " indirect experiment " but pointed out that its realization depended entirely on the existence of a complete and systematically arranged corpus of knowledge, to the duty of compiling which he summoned all his colleagues (Somló, 1909, *passim*).

[5] Spencer (1930). This was No. 13, for which the compiler, Emil Torday, had made extracts from over three hundred books and articles. If not so comprehensive as might have been wished, it remains a reliable collection of sources which even nowadays has lost none of its value as a work of reference. Nos. 9–13 and 15 (the last issued, in large quarto, in 1934) were edited for Spencer's Trustees by H. R. Tedder and T. W. Hill. No. 14 not being published. Four additional volumes, in demy octavo, appeared under Hill's editorship between 1931 and 1934. The winding up of the Trust and the question whether or not a fifth book (Rumney, 1934) could be considered as part of the Descriptive Sociology series aroused some controversy, one aspect of which is given in Tillett (1939).

him, one wonders why Tylor also failed to publish it later (Lowie, 1937, p. 79). Even the precise number of societies of which he took account is not known. His findings will be referred to again below, but here it is enough to say that he, too, was of Bastian's opinion " that in statistical investigation the future of anthropology lies " (Tylor, 1889, p. 269). Tylor, however, was more cautious than Steinmetz and did not expect the truth to crystallize automatically from such a process. While claiming that the rules of human conduct are amenable to classification in compact masses so as to show, by strict numerical treatment, their relations to one another, he added: " *It is only at this point* that speculative explanation must begin . . ." (1889, p. 269; present writer's italics). As noteworthy as Tylor's lecture itself was the warning uttered, in the subsequent discussion, against the dangers of the statistical method by the chairman, Galton, the greatest English authority on statistics of his day:

" It was extremely desirable for the sake of those who may wish to study the evidence for Dr. Tylor's conclusions, that full information should be given as to the degree in which the customs of the tribes and races which are compared together are independent. It might be, that some of the tribes had derived them from a common source, so that they were duplicate copies of the same original. Certainly, in such an investigation as this, each of the observations ought, in the language of statisticians, to be carefully 'weighted' " (Tylor, 1889, p. 270).

The first to tread the way Tylor had indicated did so with the aid of the " Steinmetz Tables " and were in fact the Dutchman's pupils. The works of some of them and that of the authors of an English book in the same vein, will now be submitted to a critical examination, more especially as regards the methods used. They are: Nieboer's *Slavery as an Industrial System*, in which an attempt is made to discover " constants " in that phenomenon; van der Bij's *Ontstaan en eerste Ontwikkeling van de Oorlog* (*Origin and Earlier Development of War*); Ronhaar's *Women in Primitive Mother-right Societies*; Tijm's *Die Stellung der Frau bei den Indianern der Vereinigten Staaten und Canada's*; and Hobhouse, Wheeler and Ginsberg's *The Material Culture and Social Institutions of the Simpler Peoples*. The aim of the last is to discover whether " the advance of human knowledge carries with it any distinct movement in morals, law, religion, the general organisation of society " (1930, p. 6), and this it attempts to do by correlating social institutions with certain methods of production. Apart from some minor differences, its classification of tribes is borrowed from Nieboer (pp. 16–29).

All these studies are characterized by the fact that they consider one element of culture, or a group of such elements, in as many tribes and over as large a geographical range as possible, thus attempting to identify associated variables that transcend the vagaries of historical contact and local conditions. Following Gonggrijp (van der Bij, 1929, p. 15), this method may be called the *hologeistic*.[6] The authors themselves stress the fact that they use the inductive and statistical method,[7] as if this term automatically entailed the method outlined above. This is by no means correct, however, for the word " method " in " statistical method " is of an entirely different order from that in " functionalist method " or " culture-historical method ". In the last instance it refers to the object of an investigation, for example determining the manner in which a culture or a culture-element spreads. The statistical method, on the other hand, is no more than a particular way of tackling a problem: it is a technique, a means, and may therefore be applied equally well to an evolutionary problem like that discussed by Tylor and to an historical one, an instance of which will be given below. But it is undoubtedly true that the statistical technique is best suited to, and has most often been applied in conjunction with, the hologeistic or cross-cultural method. Criticism will consequently be directed to this aspect of its use in particular.

The optimism, one might almost say touching faith in progress, encountered in the work of Steinmetz's pupils is much the same as, or sometimes even greater than, that of their master. Thus van der Bij believes that induction will compel students to leave an erroneous path (1931, p. 47), and

---

[6] From the stem of the Greek *hólos*, " whole," and *gé*, " earth." The phrase " cross-cultural method " is also applicable here.

[7] Not all are inclined to use the word " statistical," however. Ronhaar says that his method is inductive but not statistical, because he does not discuss *all* matrilineal societies. Nieboer and van der Bij also prefer to avoid " statistical " since, for one thing, the units are not strictly comparable *inter se* owing to the difference in the quality of the sources. The first remarks: " Instead of stating: slavery in such a group exists in many cases, it is much more accurate to state: slavery exists in, say, 80 cases " (Nieboer, 1910, p. xviii). Yet since his laws are based on numbers and he uses no other than these quantitative criteria, it appears impossible to regard his approach as being made from a standpoint other than that of statistics, simple statistics, it is true, and applied with much care, but statistics all the same.

Ronhaar speaks of it as the method " which does lead to results " (1931, p. 47), adding significantly as the motto of his book: " Our aim is not to prove some theory or another, but to arrive at the Truth." To this last statement may be opposed another, by Professor Norman Smith, which affords a better insight into the relative value of every scientific method: " The history of human thought . . . is the record, not of a progressive discovery of truth, but of our gradual emancipation from error " (1919, p. 14). Of course no single technique, inductive, statistical or any other, guarantees the attainment of truth, as can be shown by the fact that different authorities may arrive at entirely discordant results even when applying similar methods with equal scrupulousness. Thus Tylor in the paper he published in 1889 " proved " statistically his evolutionary theories, while sixty years later Murdock, by the same technique, showed them to be wrong (1929, *passim*). Reasoning on inductive lines, van der Bij concluded that most primitive tribes are peaceful (1929, pp. 262–3), and Friederici that they are aggressive (Fahrenfort, 1931, p. 576).

Hobhouse, Wheeler and Ginsberg adopt a more critical attitude towards their own procedures and conclusions, remarking that: " All results must be rough, all are open to certain special causes of error, and any inference based on a comparison of numbers alone is dangerous " (1930, p. 7). There are indeed " special causes of error " inherent in the method used, and these will now be reviewed. The first objection to it, which has already been encountered in Galton's concisely formulated criticism of Tylor's lecture, may be designated *culture-historical*.[8] This can be exemplified by asking whether from the point of view of the argument it would not be senseless to consider, say, ten tribes as the same number of independent units if their institutions could be referred to a single source. Would it not be better, by according proper " weight " to the fact of historical contact, to count them not as ten but as one ? Here Lowie's observations on the occurrence of the daughter-in-law taboo among a dozen Siberian tribes are particularly apposite:

" If the Siberian cases represented twelve instances of the taboo arising independently from antecedent patrilocal residence, we should admit at once that they completely outweighted the [sole] negative testimony of the Blackfoot data. But if there has been historical connection, the twelve Siberian units are reduced to a single one for our purposes and we have one case of connection harmonizing with Tylor's theory and one case contravening it. . . " (1947, p. 95).

That Hobhouse, Wheeler and Ginsberg pay heed to this historical objection is clear from the following comments made by them:

" . . . we must consider our figures from more than one point of view. We must cross-classify and group them not only by the economic, but [also] by the geographical order. If all or the majority of cases of any given institution come from one part of the world, we must note this fact and take it into account " (1930, p. 95).

They put their principles into effect, for example, when pointing to the fact that the social position of women shows hardly any association with economic criteria (methods of production) but is related to various culture-areas, which the authors indicate very roughly by continents (1930, p. 170–4).

Nieboer does not touch on the question until almost at the end of his book, where he states that while nearly all slave-owning tribes have had experience in the slave trade with Western Europeans, slavery has not occurred where trade remained unknown (1910, p. 411). Only here does he pause and ask himself whether he ought not to have started with such a premise, in other words, if historical contact with Western Europe has not contributed far more to the origin of slavery than have factors which are peculiar to the societies investigated and which up to then he had always held responsible for it. He dismisses the subject with the remark that " tribe slavery is an institution playing a great part in native life " (p. 414). Nieboer's inference is that the actual need of slaves mattered more than the fact that it could have been filled through historical contact alone. In this he is probably right, but conversely it is quite possible that slaveless societies had as great a need of slaves which was unsatisfied only through lack of contact with Western Europe. If such is the case then his theory of the intrinsic causes of slavery, which seemed to be established, is again to some degree in doubt.

A related problem is the choice of the statistical unit. To take the tribe as such would seem to be an obvious solution. Unfortunately, however, ethnographers disagree over the exact meaning of that word. For example, Hobhouse, Wheeler and Ginsberg regard the Australians as more than thirty tribes and the Semang as one, although the latter are numerous and live in scattered bands like the Australians; but nobody knows them well enough to enumerate the various groups into which they are divided (1930, p. 12). These authors devote much space to the

[8] In the same sense in which the term is used by the Austro-German school of that name.

question, but in the end find no alternative to allowing themselves to be guided by ethnographers in the hope that the law of averages will rectify their mistakes (pp. 8–11). To those who protest that this is too simple an answer, it may be said that, with the exception of van der Bij, the other writers mentioned do not trouble about the problem at all.

So much for the culture-historical objections to the statistical method. Attention will now be turned to criticism of it from a standpoint which may be called *functionalist.*[9] The quantitative approach is also strongly analytical: it notes certain phenomena in a society and isolates them from their cultural context, thereby conveying an entirely different impression from the one they make when studied within this context. To illustrate the point, Lowie can again be cited. After having given a synthetic and typological account of the religion of the Crow and the Ekoi, he says:

> " Most of the phenomena that occur in either tribe are also found in the other, *but they are quite differently weighted.*[10] For example, the individual psychic experience that looms so large in Crow life is not lacking among the Ekoi. Nevertheless it remains true that they are far from having the universal and pivotal, because socially standardized significance attaching to them in the plains of North America . . . merely to catalog the occurrence of such and such beliefs and observances is a futile enterprise. When we know that a tribe practises witchcraft, believes in ghosts, recognizes the mysterious potency resident in inanimate nature . . . we know precisely nothing concerning the religion of the people concerned " (1948, p. 53).

To cite another example: in their tables Hobhouse, Wheeler and Ginsberg show that among the Shingu Indians wives occupy an inferior position and have no functions in the political organization (1930, pp. 190–1). This does indeed tally with the facts given by von den Steinen who studied them, but the whole matter takes on an entirely different aspect if one knows that the ethnographer concluded his discussion of it with these words: " Er war ihr [*i.e.* the woman's] Herr und Gebieter . . . und that was sie wollte " (1907, p. 287). It is extremely difficult, if not impossible, to take proper account of remarks of this kind in statistical tables where inclusion must be restricted to the formal or what can be laid down in rules. But if only laws are shown, the result is a picture without light and shade of a community bound by rules that are never transgressed and composed of robots instead of living people. It is like trying to satisfy a request for information about Dutch society with a copy of the Netherlands civil code !

In extreme cases the adoration of the " inductive " and statistical method leads to a mere enumeration of facts which is at most entitled to the epithet " laundry-list science," so little has it to do with the real thing. An example of this is the book by Tijm, in which a central problem is all but lacking, and to which it is therefore permissible to apply Lynd's apothegm: " If the problem is wizened, the data are but footnotes to the insignificant " (1945, p. 202), a harsh judgment but a true one. It is unfair, however, to condemn a method on the evidence of any but its strongest adherents. By going more deeply into the matter where general rules were not applicable in order to explain the exceptions to them, Nieboer in his excellent work met more than half way the functionalist objections to statistical procedures.[11] Thus he argues that a slave cannot generally be used as a hunter; but when later on he comes across a case of hunting slaves, he examines the significance of hunting in the particular society and the role it plays both in methods of production as a whole and in social institutions and so tries to account for the exception (1910, pp. 195, 215–6). It is evident that Nieboer's standards demand such a phenomenal acquaintance with literature and mastery of subject that there are not many who have followed consistently in his path.

The statistical method can also err by a failure to recognize the specificity of phenomena which it treats as if they were identical. This may be instanced as follows. In discussing marriage customs, Hobhouse, Wheeler and Ginsberg consider whether or not the woman's wishes are taken into account as regards the choice of a prospective husband. They reach the conclusion that in 103 cases her consent is sought and that in 81½ it is not. In a footnote they offer some illustrations of how their plus (permission necessary) and minus (permission unnecessary) values were obtained:

> " Among some Victorian tribes, according to a narrative, it would appear as though a girl might succeed in maintaining her refusal of a man and then an exchange would be necessary. This is a borderline case which we table as ' consent required.' Among the Yerkla Mining on the other hand, if the betrothed husband claims his wife, the dispute is settled by a regulated

---

[9] In the sense in which the ethnographical writings of Malinowski are functionalist.

[10] The italics are Lowie's.

[11] Since the first edition of the book appeared as long ago as 1900 the meaning of " functionalist " in its Malinowskian connotation was naturally unknown to him.

fight. This we think is 'consent not required.' Among the Hidatsa and Dakota elopements occurred, but were not strictly honorable, marriage being properly arranged with the parents. In such cases we take consent as being not required . . ." (1930, p. 144).

Now this peep into the authors' statistical kitchen, where one can observe the mixing of different ingredients to form a single monotonous dish, is most instructive. At the same time it illustrates a grave danger, for people are tempted to adopt altogether too mechanical explanations of social phenomena when these present an over-simplified appearance through being lumped together as statistical tables and their local peculiarities are insufficiently taken into account.

Attention may finally be drawn to a study which stands somewhat apart from the rest, the late Dr. J. D. Unwin's *Sex and Culture*, perhaps the most curious book of them all. Curious because the author boldly asserts that he has discovered a regularity that holds good in all cases, in all societies; in other words he contends that he has found a real " law " among the social sciences, one without any exceptions and strictly comparable to the laws of the natural sciences. It can be formulated thus: the cultural condition of a society is determined by the limitations of sexual opportunity that operate within it, or, in Unwin's words:

" If the social regulations forbid direct satisfaction of the sexual impulses the emotional conflict is expressed in another way, and what we call 'civilisation' has always been built up by compulsory sacrifices in the gratification of innate desires " (1934, p. vii).

The method employed by the author is certainly worth scrutiny. He first assesses the cultural condition of eighty primitive societies and then examines the opportunities for sexual contact of their members. The criterion for cultural condition (" high " or " low ") is seen in their rites. In the highest group he classifies societies which are *deistic*, *i.e.*, have temples and priests. Under them are ranged the *manistic* peoples, those who pay some kind of post-funeral attention to their dead. These he subdivides into two: one (whose ritual attitude towards the dead is that of *do ut des*) is described as having a manistic " cult," and the other (among whom the attitude of *do ut abeas* predominates) as having a manistic " tendance." The lowest group is formed of societies which neither erect temples nor pay any form of post funeral attention to their dead: the cultural condition of all such societies is *zoistic*. Now, according to Unwin, the following correlation exists: all deistic peoples insist that their women should be *virginae intactae* when marrying and that the tokens of their chastity are visible on the nuptial mat. On the other hand, premarital license exists among all zoistic peoples, while the manistic occupy an intermediate position, demanding only occasional or irregular sexual freedom[12].

Several doubts arise on reading Unwin's exposition. In the first place, are his criteria for " high " and " low " cultures well chosen, is it possible to find them and is it legitimate to make the distinction he does? Again, can the sexual opportunities open to a society be adequately measured by the habits of its nubile women? And, thirdly and lastly, supposing that a correlation can be established between sexual opportunity before marriage and cultural condition, does this mean that one is the consequence of the other, that sex is the causal factor of the level of culture, as the author contends?[13]

These are all legitimate and important questions, a more extended treatment of which, however, would lead too far afield. It is enough to point out that Unwin himself does discern the problems mentioned and has advanced some weighty arguments in favour of the method adopted by him. Comment will be restricted to a single point: whether he has succeeded in establishing that his law always holds good for all cases. He himself is convinced that it does, remarking: " If the sexual relations of some uncivilised societies with which I am unfamiliar are related . . . I am ready to prophesy the general pattern of their culture and to abide by the result " (1934, p. 35). If the author is correct, it is clear that culture-historical objections to statistical procedures are not valid here. But is he right? One feels bound to admit distrust on this point, not because one is among " those whose temperaments are opposed to the meaning of [Unwin's] induction " (1934, p. 236), but because such a law would accord ill with all one's experience up to the present of regularities in the field of the social sciences. He has admittedly done his best to preserve a spirit of detachment with regard to the material he uses, and proof of his critical sense can be found on each page of his book. The truth may also be conceded of Unwin's statement that when embarking upon his researches he " sought to establish nothing,

[12] A further difference occurs between manistic peoples opportunities being more restricted among those having a " cult " than among those with a " tendance."

[13] A detailed discussion of this problem appears in an article reviewing Unwin's book by Morant (1935, pp. 38-9).

and had no idea of what the result would be " (p. vii). Nevertheless he appears to have been to some extent carried away by a number of cases that accorded perfectly with his argument, so that later he was not always able to avoid the danger of *Hineininterpretierung*, despite his insistence that " we cannot bask in the sunsine of theory before we have plunged into the cold waters of fact " (p. 2). To lay such an accusation at the door of a man no longer alive on the basis of *a priori* reasoning alone would be quite unpardonable, and an illustration of this *Hineininterpretieren* will therefore be given.[14] This is taken from the author's treatment of premarital sexual relations among the Trobriand Islanders and the Thonga.

From Malinowski's widely read works we know that Trobriand boys and girls were initiated into the mysteries of sexual life at an early age and that not long afterwards they were indulging in regular amours. On the other hand a girl who gave birth to a child before her marriage was regarded with disfavour, although not punished. The situation may be compared with that among the Thonga where the institution called *gangisa* existed. According to *gangisa*, each girl was required to choose her mate and apparently could not refuse to do so. Here, too, prenuptial pregnancy was frowned upon: " If this happens, the parents will say to the lover: ' You have spoiled our daughter, you must buy her in marriage ' " (Junod, 1927, I, p. 97). The compulsion thus implied is unlikely to have been a general characteristic of Thonga life, however, as the man could refuse, in which case nothing further seems to have happened.

On this point the institutions of the two societies appear to correspond with each other, although Unwin classifies them differently. He defends his position by remarking of the Thonga: " . . . it would be strange if a society which regarded prenuptial pregnancy as the ' spoiling ' of a girl did not have a recognized punishment for the man who was responsible: but M. Junod does not seem to have inquired into the economic details."[15] This is an instance in which one cannot help doubting the correctness of the author's classification. Also it strikes one that even where he himself admits that the material is indecisive he fits the societies concerned into the scheme so as to harmonize with his theory, sometimes even without a note of interrogation.[16]

Following this all-too-cursory review of *Sex and Culture*, some space will be accorded the consideration of a different type of quantitative approach to ethnological questions, as an example of which Driver and Kroeber's monograph (1932) will be taken. These authors also use statistical methods, but their study is entirely different as regards both its plan and purpose from those already discussed. Whereas in the other cases the writers' efforts were always directed towards determining the intrinsic connection between *elements* of culture, independently of coincidence of historical contact, Driver and Kroeber wish to investigate the degree of relationship between the component sub-cultures *within one culture-area*, and at the same time to ascertain the way in which cultural transference has occurred. They achieve this end by assuring themselves which typical culture elements are common to each pair of subcultures, which are absent in both and which are mutually opposed (p. 212).

It is clear that the functionalist objection to the use of statistical methods cannot hold good in the present instance because of the far more modest plan of the study. Neither does the culture-historical one, for the purpose of the writers is precisely that of tracing historical contact. Here, then, we meet with a diffusion study in *optima forma*, to which the statistical technique has been applied, and very elegantly at that, and which proves that this need by no means be the monopoly of one school or method in social anthropology, but may be made subservient to every trend in it.

Driver and Kroeber wrote their essay with the particular aim of testing the usefulness of the statistical method in such cases, to which end they included a number of problems previously discussed by eminent

---

[14] Strangely enough, Unwin's work is almost unknown on the Continent, at least in the Netherlands, and only a short time before the present writer's manuscript went into proof was his attention drawn to *Sex and Culture*. While the text stands sufficiently high in his esteem for a detailed analysis to be made of it, the book came into his hands too late for such a purpose to be realized.

[15] Unwin, 1934, p. 150. How detailed a description of Thonga life Junod provides is, of course, well known. Moreover in discussing *gangisa* he mentions a case in which becoming pregnant is really taboo for a girl, *i.e.*, where she has had relations with her lover inside her parents' village. In this the necessary purification rites are duly observed and the " economic details " are mentioned, in other words the fine the boy has to pay (Junod, *loc. cit.*).

[16] Thus his comment on the Tahitians " . . . the descriptions of the rites are meagre and vague . . . the evidence is scattered, confused and conflicting " (Unwin, 1934, p. 219).

scholars.[17] They reached the conclusion that statistics are no more than a tool—" statistical results can never be better than the ethnographical data " (1932, p. 255)—but a very useful tool indeed. Their own results accorded well with those derived from non-quantitative studies, which they express more precisely but, from the point of view of accuracy, also enable larger or smaller corrections to be made to these. The authors have also taken pains to appraise the usefulness of various formulæ and suggest a few which are relatively simple from a technical point of view and the implications of which may be grasped by social anthropologists not well versed in the minutiæ of statistics.

While a valuable piece of work has been accomplished by Driver and Kroeber, it may be suggested that their method is applicable only to a few restricted cases, a condition for its use being exhaustive and detailed knowledge of an area, such as is only too seldom found in ethnographical monographs. Nevertheless the authors have found several adherents, among them Klimek, in whose memoir " The Structure of California Indian Culture " the statistical approach of Driver and Kroeber is applied but with some refinements.[18] Klimek was able to classify groups of tribes which had similar lists of culture traits, and groups of traits which had a similar distribution. The first corresponded to cultural provinces in California and the second represented cultural strata. Now although California is one of the best known culture-areas of the world, additional fieldwork was necessary to make Klimek's investigation possible.[19] Whatever its potentialities, however, these studies have shown that for scrupulous exactness the culture-historical school need not be inferior to any method in social anthropology.

Steinmetz published his " Classification des types sociaux et catalogue des peuples " in 1898–99, and the last work written in accordance with the hologeistic method he advocated appeared in 1933, immediately before he retired from his chair (Tijm, 1933, p. 7). It seems no mere coincidence that the date marks the end of such studies. These already bore signs of being slightly antiquated, in spite of their permanent merit of having furnished social anthropology with a more solid foundation of preciseness on which alone it could rise from the causerie-level to that of a science. The method, then, appeared to be a closed chapter in the history of our discipline, one which, if it had not revealed the " true Truth," had nevertheless helped the work of the next generation; for each new generation discards the methods of its predecessors at the same time as it assimilates them.

But the chapter is not yet concluded; on the contrary! The hologeistic method has lately experienced a revival which bids fair to outshine the glory of the first period, with the difference that the field of activities has shifted from Europe to the U.S.A.; and as the studies of Steinmetz's disciples were based on his catalogue of peoples, so the modern American project depends on the new inventory mentioned in the first lines of this essay. A closer examination of the system it follows is therefore necessary. This has been made possible by the publication of the *Outline of Cultural Materials*, which serves as its basis. Essentially, the *Outline* is no more than an extraordinarily comprehensive decimal classification covering the whole field of the material, social and spiritual (or ideological) aspects of culture and so arranged that a place can be found for each item relating to any people or any trait whatever. That the extent of the scheme requires a book to encompass it is characteristic of the thoroughness with which the work has been undertaken. The authors describe the purpose of the survey as " testing cross-cultural generalizations, revealing deficiencies in the descriptive literature and directing corrective fieldwork."[20] Because the object corresponds down to details with that of Steinmetz half a century earlier, this essay has been entitled " New Ways of Presenting an old Idea," but it deals with a presentation which has been infinitely perfected and which (possibly the greatest difference of all) is the fruit of collaboration among a considerable number of scholars.

What is the *modus operandi* of the American scheme? When once the decision has been taken to include a

[17] Namely, cultural connections between Polynesia and North-East Peru and the North-West coast of North America, as well as the diffusion of the Sun Dance.

[18] For example, he employs the " *Q*6 " formula and reminds us that as early as 1911 Czekanowski had recommended the use by ethnologists of Yule's even simpler coefficient of association (Klimek, 1935, pp. 17–18).

[19] Klimek, 1935, pp. 9–10. As far as the writer is aware, the most recent work of this nature is that of Milke (1949), who provides maps with *cultural isopleths*, namely, curves linking all tribes which have the same " coefficient of similarity " in relation to a certain tribe selected as a reference point. Similar studies have been made by Klimek and Milke 1935) and by Milke (1935).

[20] Murdock *et al.*, 1950, p. vii. As a further aim, Murdock (1940) gives the making of ethnographical literature more easily accessible to students of other sciences.

book or paper in the "Human Relations Area Files" (H.R.A.F.), the contents are transcribed on 5 x 8-in. index-cards. No more than about ten lines of text appear on a card, and since as a rule these relate to more than a single category of the *Outline* it is generally necessary for several cards to be made in order that one may appear under each appropriate heading. For example, a card concerning shamans among the Kazaks will be annotated as follows:—

4 : 57—Castagné	1930	Kazak
116, 158, 756, 776, 787		

"4 : 57—Castagné 1930 Kazak" indicates that the excerpt below was published by Castagné in 1930 and has been taken from page 57 of the fourth item in the bibliography on the Kazaks. The numbers 116, 158 etc., denote the various categories under which the card is filed, namely, 116 "Texts";[21] 158 "Personality Disorders"; 756 "Psycho-therapists"; 776, "Spirits and Gods" and 787 "Revelation and Divination."[22]

By 1943 the details of some 150 groups, including such historical entities as the Roman Empire and Elizabethan England, had been recorded in this fashion on half a million cards,[23] the ultimate purpose being to catalogue a representative sample of 10 per cent. "of all the cultures known to history, sociology and ethnography" (Murdock, 1949, p. viii). During the second world war this collection was repeatedly put to practical use. For example, nine United States *Military Government Handbooks*, relating to various Japanese-occupied islands of which the invasion was planned, were published with its help. Since 1949 an inter-university organization has been formed under the title of Human Relations Area Files, Incorporated, which is supported financially by the Carnegie Corporation. One of its main tasks will be to duplicate the existing files of the Cross-Cultural Survey for the members and to distribute additional data obtained by the Survey among them.

The great value of such carefully and methodically assembled material to social anthropology is beyond dispute. In fact, one ought to ask oneself whether it is not inevitable that, without this help, we in Western Europe shall fall behind the Americans. It is impossible for us to make a similar archive because of the sad fact that we have little enough money at our disposal and should moreover have much difficulty in securing the collaboration needed for such a purpose. It may be possible, however, for Western Europeans to obtain one or more copies of the Human Relations Area Files and action directed towards this end deserves serious consideration.

As far as the present essay is concerned, however, the interest aroused lies more particularly in the use made of this catalogue of tribes. Have its users succeeded in avoiding the errors of Steinmetz's disciples, or has the material provided by it perhaps been treated in an entirely different way by them? As an answer to this question, a number of works written with the aid of the files will be examined. Attention will chiefly be devoted to *Social Structure* by Professor G. P. Murdock, who until 1949 played the leading part in the cross-cultural survey project and whose book has aroused much interest in American professional circles. Further the doctoral thesis of Murdock's pupil Horton, "The Functions of Alcohol in Primitive Societies", and Ford's *Comparative Study of Human Reproduction* will be considered. Finally attention will be given to *The Role of the Aged in Primitive Society* by Professor L. W. Simmons, also of Yale, who, although he too applies the statistical method, makes no use of the files or at any rate does not mention them.

In his *Social Structure* Murdock occupies himself with kinship relations. He analyses and classifies them carefully, noticing the factors that determine kinship terminology and the way in which one kind of kinship structure arises from another. Eventually he discusses the social regulation of sexual relations. To this end he subjects to several hundred calculations the data on kinship relations for 250 tribes and peoples, his information for 89 of them being obtained from the files of the Cross-Cultural Survey and that for the rest from library research in the traditional fashion. Horton on his part attempts to discover the more profound, psychical, causes of excessive indul-

[21] Under this heading a full set of the excerpts from each source is arranged in page order, so that the context of any particular excerpt can be found, the sets appearing in the numerical order of the sources. A source is usually transferred to cards in its entirety, and only wholly irrelevant parts are omitted.

[22] A number of sub-categories appear in several of these, No. 756 including, for example, both shamans and modern clinical psychologists (Murdock *et al.*, 1950, pp. xvi–xvii).

[23] In 1952 only about 20 cultures had been treated under the new more elaborate system, as provided by the 3rd revised edition of the *Outline of Cultural Materials* (personal communication).

gence in alcohol. He studies 56 tribes which he regards as so many statistical units and he grades them as either positive or negative according to whether their drinking habits are or are not excessive. These data he then correlates with a large number of social phenomena which he uses as an index of the psychological condition of the group members. Simmons sets to work in the same way: he correlates the status and position of the aged in 71 societies with series of different social data, so as to establish their inherent connections. The conclusion is inevitable that these modern Americans not only apply statistical techniques but also work on hologeistic lines just as Steinmetz's disciples did many years ago. From the point of view of method, therefore, they are fully comparable.

A similar optimism pervades their activities. This is especially true of Murdock, who repeatedly contends that by the use of statistics he has reached the same standard of exactness in social anthropology as is found in the natural sciences, and, it would seem, lays claim to be the first to write an anthropological treatise worthy of the designation "scientific" (1949, pp. 183, 259, 283). While in the Introduction to *Social Structure* Murdock discusses various trends in anthropology, behaviourist psychology, and psycho-analysis, all of which he states have influenced him deeply, he does not include his predecessors in the statistical method at all. Yet he is well aware of some of them, for elsewhere in his book he refers to Tylor's 1888 lecture as well as to Hobhouse, Wheeler and Ginsberg's work in footnotes (pp. 17, 206), and he also mentions Steinmetz and Nieboer in an article published by him in the *American Sociological Review* (1940, p. 361). Now, Tylor's method is essentially the same as Murdock's, apart from the fact that the statistical techniques employed by the American are more refined.[24] For example, Murdock devotes the entire seventh chapter of *Social Structure* to showing how kinship terminology is determined by kinship structure, or, as he puts it:

Postulate 1: The relatives of any two kin-types tend to be called by the same kinship terms, rather than by different terms, in inverse proportion to the number and relative efficacy of (a) the inherent distinctions between them and (b) the social differentials affecting them, and in direct proportion to the number and relative efficacy of the social equalizers affecting them (1949, p. 138).

Although one wonders whether the game is worth the candle, one cannot but admire the methodical way in which Murdock sets about his task. He does not consider himself free from it until he has demonstrated statistically the correctness of thirty theorems and propositions, of which the first and simplest reads thus:

Theorem 1: When secondary or tertiary relatives of any kin-type are called by a kinship term used to denote a primary relative, the daughters of such secondary or tertiary relatives tend to be called by the same kinship term as the daughter of the primary relative (p. 139).

Its verification is given in tabular form as follows, coefficients of association being denoted by the symbol Q:[25]

Pairs of relatives[26]	Parent called "mother"		Parent called otherwise		
	Child called "sister"	Child called otherwise	Child called "sister"	Child called otherwise	—
FaSi—FaSiDa	18	22	42	156	0·50
MoSi—MoSiDa	110	16	62	34	0·58
FaBrWi—FaBrDa	85	9	50	24	0·64
MoBrWi—MoBrDa	17	10	29	113	0·74

[24] Thus he always calculates Yule's coefficient of association (Q) and also the X^2 test, which is a measure indicating whether a certain result is likely or unlikely to be due to mere chance (Murdock, 1949, pp. x–xi).

[25] This is part of Murdock's Table 15 (*loc. cit.*), very slightly modified to conform to customary usage.

[26] The abbreviations below the heading stand for "father's sister," "father's sister's daughter," etc.

All the values of Q are significant at the 0·1 per cent. level, *i.e.*, there is a very small probability indeed, one in a thousand, of the association being due to chance.

Murdock's procedure may be compared with that used by Tylor in showing the connection between the mother-in-law taboo (on the part of the man) and matrilocality. Such a taboo was present in 45 out of the 350 societies Tylor examined, and he remarks:

" Now, if the customs of residence and the customs of avoidance were independent or nearly so, we should expect to find their coincidence following the ordinary law of chance distribution. In the tribes where the husband permanently lives with his wife's family (sixty-five out of three hundred and fifty) we should estimate, that ceremonial avoidance between him and them might appear in nine cases, whereas it actually appears in fourteen cases. On the other hand, peoples where the husband at marriage takes his wife to his home (forty-one out of two hundred and fifty), would correspond with avoidance between him and her family in eighteen cases, whereas it actually appears in nine cases only " (1889, p. 247).

Clearly this is the same method expressed in simpler terms, and the more refined techniques that Murdock uses are therefore fully applicable to the problems considered by Tylor, as can be shown when Tylor's data are presented in the form of a contingency table:

Type of residence	Mother-in-law taboo		Totals
	present	absent	
Matrilocal	14	51	65
Patrilocal	9	132	141
Other	22	122	144
Totals	45	305	350

From this it is found that $X^2 = 10 \cdot 3$, which is significant at the 1·0 per cent. but not at the 0·1 per cent. level, *i.e.*, there is only a small probability (between one in a hundred and one in a thousand) that the association noted by Tylor is fortuitous.[27]

It must be admitted that Murdock's—and Horton's—views are in one respect sounder than those of the earlier authors. Whereas the latter stressed the fact that they used the statistical-*inductive* method, the Americans talk about the statistical and *postulational* method. The adjective " postulational " implies that one starts from a hypothesis, a postulate, so that " all logical or rational operations are performed prior to the final empirical and statistical test " (Murdock, 1949, p. 127). Now, the inductive method is not necessarily incompatible with this way of tackling a problem, for in its essence " induction " means no more than that laws or rules are not formulated until every individual case has been examined, but it does not imply that the holding of a provisional hypothesis is prohibited before the research proper is begun. The last view, however, does not seem to be universally held by adherents of the inductive method: they would prefer an investigator's mind to be a *tabula rasa* when collecting his material,[28] as if such could ever be the case in genuinely scientific work. In this connection the controversy between van der Bij and Fahrenfort in *Mensch en Maatschappij* over van der Bij's book on war is very instructive. Fahrenfort utters a warning against expecting too much of the inductive method and particularly of the idea that the " facts " lead automatically to the truth. He asks whether van der Bij when he started his inquiry, did not, from a desultory reading of ethnographical literature, already hold the opinion that most primitive tribes lacked pugnacity, and adds that he believes this to be so, " and it is the only natural thing to expect " (Fahrenfort, 1931, p. 574). Van der Bij, who in his book had argued that the purely inductive scholar does not start from a presupposed theory (1929, p. 9), later admitted that there could be no objection to a provisional opinion, *alias* hypothesis, after the initial induction (1931, p. 323). The moot point can then be worded as follows: according to the earlier investigators one is *allowed* to base one's views on a postulate, according to their American successors one *must* do so. Naturally the latter are right. How does one create order out of the apparent chaos of facts—which is, after all, the investigator's task—if some well-defined postulate is not formed? In the work of Tijm already cited we have met with an example of a book without a central problem. Ford's study of human reproduction, and to some extent Simmons's work on the role of the aged, might be regarded as its American counterparts. The first contains hardly anything but data from 64 tribes on menstruation, conception, pregnancy, birth and parenthood which the author had

[27] See Hagood, 1947, pp. 500–22.

[28] This is not valid for Nieboer, who asserts in his book on slavery: " We shall never be able to arrive at a true understanding of the facts without the help of leading ideas. The facts do not arrange themselves spontaneously; we must try to account for them by hypotheses, which seem *a priori* plausible."

collected from the files of the Institute of Human Relations; explanations of his findings are, if given at all, of a most superficial nature.[29] Of course, he informs us of a number of disconnected facts which are interesting in themselves, but he does not do anything with them, and for those who have access to the files, the book must be superfluous. It is instructive, however, in so far as it shows that from a scientific standpoint excellent source material does not necessarily produce excellent results. The same applies, although in a lesser degree, to Simmons. In seeking to ascertain, for example, on what the prestige of the aged in society depends, he correlates " prestige " with a large number of other factors and so obtains several important results, one being that " aged men have been much more likely to enjoy prestige as the constancy of the food supply increased but such prerogatives have not been equally shared by aged women, indeed with them the coefficients of correlation were very significantly negative " (Simmons, 1945, pp. 79–80). Now, instead of trying to explain this remarkable fact, he merely states it. Elsewhere he presents as causes what are rather effects, or characteristics, and then expresses surprise at the high positive coefficients of correlation (p. 80).

Unlike their predecessors, Murdock and his followers have no intention of discussing all the tribes in the world but, like Unwin, content themselves with representative samples of these. Yet are they in fact representative ? The number of samples ranges from 56 with Horton to 250 with Murdock, whose choice may be examined from this aspect. There is little doubt that he has been guided more by the presence of good sources than by the proportional representation of each culture-area. Also he has not troubled himself with the question of whether too many peoples with the same mode of subsistence, *e.g.*, hunting and collecting, occur in his list, which in fact contains no fewer than 70 North American Indian tribes.[30] The value of the material may be tested by a comparison with that of others. Thus, Hobhouse, Wheeler and Ginsberg find among their 643 tribes a proportion of ten with a matrilocal to thirteen with a patrilocal system (1930, p. 151). In Murdock's work this ratio is at best as one to two (1949, p. 17). With Nieboer the proportions of slave-keeping to slaveless tribes are about equal and with Murdock, again, one to two (Nieboer, 1910, p. 166; Murdock, 1949, p. 87). Further suspicion of the unsatisfactory nature of Murdock's sampling is provided by a passage from his own book where he discusses two different explanations of the same phenomenon by Lowie and Kroeber respectively.[31] When he had treated 221 societies out of his 250, Murdock believed that in view of his figures something more was to be said for Kroeber's theory than for Lowie's. Nevertheless, study of the remaining 29 societies was able to make him change his conclusion. What, then, would remain of his theories if he undertook to deal with 643 tribes like Hobhouse, Wheeler and Ginsberg ? One is all the more inclined to ask oneself this question if one realizes that some of Murdock's results have a coefficient of association no higher than + 0·20 and that Murdock himself points out that any negative coefficient would necessitate the invalidation of a theorem unless the index of reliability (determined by the X^2 test) were very low (1949, p. 129). On the other hand, one cannot but admit the value of many of his statistical results, since, as he points out, all the 120 coefficients of association calculated by him are positive, a result that can hardly be due to mere chance (1949, p. 178).

It is astonishing, however, that despite Murdock's preciseness here, in other chapters he repeatedly makes the same kind of unscientific assertions against which he fulminates so strongly. Thus he maintains, without a shade of proof, that " grandparent and grandchild are drawn together by the fact that each can expect from the other an unconscious sympathy for his own dissatisfactions with the intervening relative " (1949, p. 278). This statement is not meant to reflect the situation in a single tribe but as a general rule,[32] and there are still more instances of Freudian theory that one would be inclined to call into question (*e.g.* Murdock, 1949, p. 294).

Do the two objections to the statistical approach so

[29] See, *e.g.*, Ford, 1945, pp. 56–7.

[30] Murdock, 1949, pp. viii–ix. Of the other authors, Simmons least deserves this reproach, for he takes account not only of different methods of production but also of different climates and races.

[31] Murdock, 1949, pp. 164–5, where it is pointed out that in a matrilineal society the mother's sisters are usually denoted by the same term as is the mother, whereas the father's sister is called by a different name (bifurcate merging). Lowie attributes this to the exogamous character of the matri-sibs, Kroeber to unilinear descent *per se*.

[32] The relationship between grandparents and grandchildren does not lend itself to formulation as a series of general rules, if only because of the fact that with many, but not nearly with all, primitive peoples it is the grandparents rather than the parents who educate the children.

far advanced, the culture-historical and the functionalist, also apply to these modern American authors ? Only the first would seem to affect Murdock, who refers to "the curious paradox that kinship terminology and the forms of social organization often differ precisely where historical connections are indisputable and show resemblances where historical relations are inconceivable "(1949, p. 116). And he uses this as specific disproof " that historical connections significantly affect the forms of social organisation " (1949, p. x), a very bold assertion indeed and one which it would not be very difficult to refute. Yet later it appears as if that was not his meaning: social organization indeed reacts to historical influences, but as Murdock points out (1949, pp. 177–222), in a very special way, namely indirectly. If, for example, a tribe under influence of a more powerful culture accepts a new method of production, its rule of residence will soon change, for this is the first to respond to altered conditions. Now a new kinship structure will occur only by internal re-adjustment to this new rule of residence; it is thus the result of a secondary process alone and so need not become the same as that of the influencing culture, as may be exemplified by the formerly matrilineal and matrilocal Jukun, who, under strong influence from the patrilocal Fulani, " adopted bilocal residence and bilateral descent as a compromise between opposing forces" (1949, p. 209). As far as Murdock's treatment of kinship is concerned, then, the culture-historical objection to the statistical method has been partly disposed of.[33] It nevertheless applies fully to Horton's inquiry into the function of alcohol in primitive societies, as this author's denial of the relevance to his problem of historical contact with Western civilization is extremely disputable. What are the facts ? Finding that alcoholic excesses are most common among the higher acculturated societies studied by him, Horton attributes the fact to the feelings of insecurity, and therefore of anxiety, which are always powerful when such societies are in transition. He therefore regards the phenomenon as further evidence in support of his proposition that anxiety is the cause of excessive drinking. But it can be contended that another factor is also responsible, at least to a high degree, that it is precisely these acculturated groups who find it easiest to procure the desired liquor, and in many cases it is even thrust upon them by the whites.[34] As to historical contact as the cause, Horton will have none of it, although he himself informs us that primitive tribes mostly obtain their spirits from the whites who have also taught them the process of distillation.[35]

There remain to be considered the functionalist objections to the approach of these American scholars, and unfortunately they are as weighty as with the earlier authors mentioned.[36] Murdock's book may be taken as an illustration. What purpose is gained by spending years of labour in order to establish statistically the connection between kinship relations and kinship terminology ? Surely, it would be of greater interest to discover whether a connection exists and, if so, what it is, between kinship relations and way of life, method of production, technical developments, property, political organization, population size and so on. Then one would no longer entertain the idea that kinship relations are something *Freischwebendes*, a *bündige Form* as Freyer has it (1930, *passim*), but would realize that they constitute part of an integrated social whole. And what does Murdock himself say to this ?

> " A special investigation of the factors predisposing a society towards one or another type of family structure would doubtless yield illuminating results. Unfortunately the present study can shed little light directly upon this subject, since evidence was not gathered on exploitative techniques, division of labour, property, and other aspects of basic economy which presumably play a decisive role " (1949, p. 36).

It must not be held against him as lack of industry that he has not gathered data on these subjects: the mass of material which he has incorporated in his work is large enough as it is. Given a world-embracing, hologeistic method, he simply could not cover them as well. Again, he found it impossible to elaborate the

[33] Partly but not wholly, for the traits of social organization, far from turning out to have an " almost random distribution " (Murdock, 1949, p. 196), show statistically significant patterning. This has been aptly demonstrated by Wilson, who gives a theory to account for the patterning which accords with Murdock's views, although it remains a theory and not a proof (Wilson, 1952, p. 135).

[34] The present writer does not intend to deny the existence of anxiety in such societies, but he does deny its being the cause of the fact that they are more given to alcoholic excesses than is usual elsewhere. This is at least not proved.

[35] Horton, 1943, p. 269. There are, of course, fermented beverages as well, which are not nearly so intoxicating as the distilled.

[36] Least, however, for Simmons, who writes: " When a problem is defined a liberal selection of concrete cases is represented. . . . This material is used solely to demonstrate the range of adaptation, to point up the issues more concretely, and to illustrate them amply " (Simmons, 1945, p. 18).

information on a number of tribes with which he dealt, owing to his choice of sources that were too succinct for the purpose. Thus out of the 250 societies, 10 are drawn from Meek's *Tribal Studies in Northern Nigeria*, where the Daka are dealt with in 18 pages, of which more than half are word-lists, and the Ndoro in ten (Meek, 1931, I, p. 394; II, pp. 589–605).

The worst feature of phenomena abstracted from their context is that it leads to positive mistakes, as, for instance, where Murdock discusses the avoidance of a wife's brother's wife which occurs in 12 out of his 250 cases. He offers an extremely tortuous explanation of this which amounts to supposing that the reciprocal attitude of reserve between a man and his brother-in-law (a questionable general fact, it may be observed) is transferred to the brother-in-law's wife, the attitude itself arising from the fact that the same woman was allowed to have sexual relations with one of the two, her husband, and not with the other, her brother. Since Murdock considers only a single factor, sex, he is apt to hold this responsible for the phenomenon observed without further probing into the matter. But Junod, discussing a similar law of avoidance among the Thonga, succeeds in making it plausible that an economic factor, the *lobola* or bride-price, is involved in the case (1927, I, pp. 239–43).

A consequence of Murdock's insufficiently functional approach is that his product often amounts to no more than mere classifying. Where he enters into the minutiæ of a problem, as occasionally happens, his argument at once becomes more lively and interesting.[37] More often, however, he simply formulates rules or produces columns of figures. A Dutch sociologist once called a certain book " a work without a heart," and in reading Murdock's *Social Structure* one is constantly reminded of this description. Of course, the author may well protest that what he writes has gained in exactness what it lacks from a functional point of view and that a functional treatment is hardly compatible with mathematical precision. Now every effort to be exact is welcome in our discipline, which certainly does not suffer from an overdose of this tonic, but it must be real and not *quasi*-exactness. Can quasi-exactness be denied if different phenomena are placed in the same category and treated as though strictly comparable when in fact they are not ? Horton's study in particular exhibits such shortcomings, an example of which may be cited. Horton postulates that " the primary function of alcoholic beverages in all societies is the reduction of anxiety." [38] At the same time he does not believe that the strength of the drinking habit is directly proportional to the strength of the anxiety drive in a given case, for he considers that the reduction of anxiety by the use of alcohol permits formerly inhibited sexual or aggressive responses to take place and, if these are punished, the act of drinking may itself elicit fresh (or counter-) anxieties. Horton argues that, if his reasoning is correct, the following proposition must hold good: wherever peoples are given to excessive indulgence in alcohol, there is *ceteris paribus*, little sexual anxiety and vice versa. He measures the existence or non-existence of sexual anxiety by the respective non-existence or existence of premarital sexual freedom, and consequently endeavours to discover whether excessive drinking and premarital sexual freedom are associated in his sample to a greater extent than could be accounted for by chance alone.

Serious objections may be raised to these arguments, in fact to the entire nature of the reasoning that underlies them, but Horton silences all would-be critics by revealing with a *voilà* the mathematical proof (or its semblance) of his proposition in the following table, headed "Association between premarital sexual freedom and insobriety when societies in which strong anxiety, due to subsistence hazards, competes with sexual anxiety, are eliminated " (1943, p. 277):

Premarital sexual freedom	Insobriety strong	Insobriety moderate or slight
Strongly restricted and moderately restricted	4	8
Relatively unrestricted	20	4

From this it is found that $X^2 = 9$, which is significant

[37] As when discussing his own field work among the Haida (1909, pp. 72–3).

[38] Horton, 1943, p. 223. On the danger of excessive simplification, Aldous Huxley has written: " In its impatience to understand, its hunger and thirst after explanation, the intellect tends to impose more rationality upon the given facts than those facts will bear, tends to discover in the brute diversity of phenomena more identity than really exists in them . . . Man is a double being and can take, now the god's-eye view of things, now the brute's-eye view. For example, he can affirm that chalk and cheese are both composed of electrons . . . Such reduction of the diverse to the identical may satisfy our hunger for explanation; but we have bodies as well as intellects, and these bodies have a hunger for Stilton and a distaste for chalk " (1938, p. 13).

at the 1·0 per cent. but not at the 0·1 per cent. level, *i.e.*, it is unlikely that the association is fortuitous, or in other words, what has been postulated is true (assuming that the author has correctly entered his cases in the table). He omits to reproduce in his text the ethnographical data on which the conclusions are based, and indeed it would hardly have been possible for him to do so.

Now, to check the accuracy of entries in each "cell" in the table is a tedious and time-consuming business which, it will be understood, one does not readily undertake. Nevertheless an attempt will now be made to check part of the contingency table reproduced above. In the top right-hand cell of this Horton includes eight societies with moderate drinking habits among whom premarital sexual freedom is stringently or moderately restricted. Now, Ford, and Ford and Beach—on the basis of exactly the same material, it should be noted—class two of them, the Lango and the Balinese, with those having almost complete sexual freedom. "Among the Lango," Ford remarks, "premarital sexual intercourse is free and the normal route by which a couple learns to care enough for each other to marry" (1945, p. 20). Of the Balinese, Ford and Beach state that incest rules are the only major restriction on the sexual activities of adolescents (1951, p. 190).

Are these authors right? The immediate source of both Ford's and Horton's information on the Lango does indeed mention the frequent occurrence of premarital sexual intercourse among them but adds that it is not permissible in all instances and that illegitimate intercourse with an unmarried woman entails a fine (Spencer, 1930, p. 47). As far as the Balinese are concerned, however, Ford and Beach are undoubtedly correct. Covarrubias, consulted by them as well as by Horton, reports of the ordinary Balinese villages: "There, matters of sex are not solemn mysterious prohibitions, and it is natural that in coming of age they should continue to have sexual relations that started in the character of play, incompletely of course, in childhood."[39] This statement is indeed borne out by another authority to a remarkable degree.[40]

[39] Covarrubias, 1937, pp. 136–7. See also *ibid.*, p. 140.

[40] Jacobs, 1883, pp. 133–4. Horton must incur some censure for often consulting no more than one ethnographical work, a practice which renders him susceptible to a double source of error: in the first place the ethnographer may have made a mistake and in the second the author may misinterpret the ethnographer.

But the inclusion in the top right-hand cell of Horton's table of two more tribes, the Azande and the Tanala, is also susceptible of criticism. Concerning the Azande, the Seligmans note that "with the institution of European rule there has been a weakening of the sanctions enforcing chastity; to-day there is no penalty for sexual intercourse between unmarried persons, . . . love-affairs, both with married and unmarried girls are therefore more frequent" (1932, p. 576). From this one would infer that *in the past* premarital sexual intercourse entailed some form of punishment, but, as Horton expressly states, he is concerned with drinking habits and sexual intercourse *at the present time*. With the Tanala of Madagascar, girls are usually chaste before marriage, at least according to some authors.[41] Not that chastity in itself is valued or increases a girl's desirability, but "girls are told that intercourse at a too early age, and especially promiscuity, are likely to lead to sterility" (Linton, 1933, p. 297). Yet this does not apply to young men: "Premarital chastity on the part of a youth would be taken as a confession of impotence and he would find it difficult to find a wife." Since Horton is interested in the drinking habits of the *men*, the appearance of the Tanala in the place they occupy in his table does not seem to be very felicitous, even if sexual intercourse with unmarried girls is forbidden among them.

As the result of the check, then, one would be justified in stating of three societies at least, and probably even of four, that prenuptial sexual freedom was "relatively unrestricted" rather than "moderately restricted."[42] If these are taken into account, the table may be amended to read as follows:

Premarital sexual freedom	Insobriety strong	Insobriety moderate and slight
Strongly restricted and moderately restricted	4	(5) (4)
Relatively unrestricted	20	(7) (8)

[41] "Les filles Antanala d'Ikongo sont également respectées jusqu'à leurs fiançailles" (Grandidier, 1914, pp. 136–7). See also Linton, 1933, p. 297. On the other hand, there is the following assertion: "Sakalava, Betsileo, Tanala . . . . l'adolescent cohabite avec la fille à laquelle l'a conduit son désir" (Lebland, 1907, p. 145).

[42] The vagueness of this distinction as a basis for mathematical treatment may be contrasted with Unwin's far more rigorous criterion.

From this $X^2 = 2{\cdot}6$ or $1{\cdot}2$, according to which set of figures is taken. In neither case, however, is its value significant at the 10·0 per cent. level, so that the correlation is quite possibly spurious and the postulate from which Horton started, and which forms a cornerstone of his argument, remains unverified.

In 1947 Lowie, in the preface to the new edition of his *Primitive Society*, wrote that he "would like to resume Tylor's statistical approach." "In recent years," he adds "it has actually been cultivated by Professor G. P. Murdock and his colleagues at Yale, but to date not enough has been published to permit an assessment of the results" (p. ix). Some time has now passed since that assertion, and in the interim a number of new publications by Murdock and his associates have come from the press which enable a provisional estimate to be made of them. It is small wonder that such a task appealed to one who is a Dutchman, for in these works is to be found a striking resemblance to a procedure once followed by the school of Steinmetz in the Netherlands, even if now abandoned there as obsolete.[43] But more than a remarkable historical coincidence provided the impulse for the inquiry: Murdock may be counted among America's most prominent social anthropologists, and his method is making headway; one might almost speak of an American school, which, together with personality studies, may assume a leading position and . . . pass for something new in the United States! Finally the fact that, up to a short while ago, Murdock was responsible for the Cross-Cultural Survey and apparently believes his method of using this precious material to be the best, provided yet another reason for supposing that a critical analysis would not be inopportune.[44]

Are the objections to the statistical technique perhaps so weighty as to make one advise against its use in all cases? Certainly not. Not only the culture-historical studies of Driver and Kroeber and their followers show impressive results but, in a hologeistic sense, statistics should be able to render valuable service, on condition that less ambitious goals are chosen and more care is used in applying them. There would seem to be two ways in which quantitative methods can most profitably be used. In the first place, as a means of detecting certain regularities, which would have to be accounted for by thorough functional examination of a number of representative societies. And, secondly, as a means of finding out whether peculiarities observed in one society also occur in others, and how often and in what way. This point may be illustrated from some remarks made by Malinowski who, after having given an account of the system of reciprocal obligations among his Trobrianders, says: "*I venture to foretell* that reciprocity . . . will be found to be [one of] the main factors in the binding machinery of primitive law," and "*there must be* in all societies a class of such rules."[45] With the aid of a statistical technique the degree of correctness of such statements could be ascertained.[46] To some extent these ideas are met with in the work of Horton, the writing of whose book derived its inspiration from two studies by Hallowell and Bunzel on the role of alcohol in primitive societies and who regards his own research as complementary to them (Horton, 1943, pp. 298–302).

In this way a fruitful collaboration may be established between two methods in social anthropology, the hologeistic and the *Gestalt*, which seem at first glance to be absolutely contradictory. Both will profit from it, the hologeistic by achieving depth, and the functional and *Gestalt* by the possibility of a systematic comparison of phenomena observed in one society with those in others. Whoever shares the opinion that social anthropology has to be comparative or nothing at all will also believe the advantage far from small and predict a flourishing future for this aspect of the statistical approach.

[43] The present writer hastens to explain that this does not mean that he agrees with superficial gossip on the part of many Europeans about the superficiality of American scientific methods.

[44] To avoid misunderstanding, it is necessary to state expressly the present writes's opinion that most of the works discussed have their very real merits. Because of his objections to the authors' methods, however, an appreciation of much that is excellent in them does not come to light. He believes further that the unfavourable criticism of Murdock's *Social Structure* by Steiner (1951) is far too harsh and in some places quite unjust.

[45] Malinowski, 1947, p. 68, and *ibid.*, p. 67 (present writer's italics).

[46] It is certain that Malinowski would not have been against a similar testing of the views he had formed from a study of one society. Curiously enough, this functionalist *pur sang* thought highly of Steinmetz's school as can be seen in his introduction to Hogbin, 1934, p. xxxiv, and in Malinowski, 1933, pp. 154–5.

References

Bij, T. S. van der .. .. 1929 *Ontstaan en eerste ontwikkeling van de oorlog (Origin and Earliest Development of War)*. Groningen.

——— .. .. 1931 "Methode en classificatie in de ethnologie" (Method and classification in ethnology), *Mensch en Maatschappij*, 7.

Covarrubias, M. .. .. 1937 *Island of Bali*. New York and London.

Driver, H. E., and Kroeber, A. L. .. 1932 "Quantitative expression of cultural relationships," *Univ. Cal. Publ. Amer. Arch.*, **31**.

Fahrenfort, J. J. .. .. 1931 "Ook een enkel woord over de methode in de ethnologie" (A few more words concerning method in ethnology), *Mensch en Maatschappij*, 7.

Ford, C. S. .. .. 1945 "A comparative study of human reproduction", *Yale Univ. Publ. Anthrop.*, **32**.

——— and Beach, F. A. .. .. .. 1951 *Patterns of Sexual Behavior*. New Haven.

Freyer, H. .. .. 1930 *Soziologie als Wirklichkeitswissenschaft*. Leipzig.

Gerretson, C. .. .. 1911 *Prolegomena der Sociologie*. Haarlem.

Grandidier, A. .. .. 1914 *Ethnographie de Madagascar*. Paris.

Hagood, M. J. .. .. 1947 *Statistics for Sociologists*, 2nd imp. New York.

Hobhouse, L. T., Wheeler, G. C., and Ginsberg, M. 1930 *The Material Culture and Social Institutions of the Simpler Peoples*. London.

Hogbin, H. I. .. .. 1934 *Law and Order in Polynesia*. London and Gloucester.

Horton, D. .. .. 1943 "The functions of alcohol in primitive societies," *Q.J. Stud. Alcohol*, **4**.

Huxley, A. .. .. 1938 *Ends and Means*. London.

Jacobs, J. .. .. 1883 *Enige Tijd onder de Baliërs* (Some Time among the Balinese).

Junod, H. A. .. .. 1927 *The Life of a South African Tribe*, 2nd ed., 2 vols. London.

Klimek, S. .. .. 1935 "The structure of Californian Indian culture," *Univ. Cal. Publ. Amer. Arch.*, **37** (1).

——— and Milke, W. .. .. .. 1935 "An analysis of the material culture of the Tupi peoples," *Amer. Anthrop.* (n.s.), **37**.

Lebland, M. A. .. .. 1907 *La grande île de Madagascar*. Paris.

Linton, R. .. .. 1933 "The Tanala, a hill tribe of Madagascar", *Field Mus. Anthrop. Ser.*, **22**.

Lowie, R. H. .. .. 1937 *The History of Ethnological Theory*. New York.

——— .. .. 1947 *Primitive Society*, 3rd imp. New York.

——— .. .. 1948 *Primitive Religion*. New York.

Lynd, R. S. .. .. 1945 *Knowledge for What ?*, 4th ed. Princeton (N.J.).

Malinowski, B. .. .. 1933 "The work and magic of prosperity in the Trobriand Islands", *Mensch en Maatschappij*, **9**.

——— .. .. 1940 *Crime and Custom in Savage Society*, 3rd ed. London.

Meek, C. K. .. .. 1931 *Tribal Studies in Northern Nigeria*, 2 vols. London.

Milke, W. .. .. 1935 *Süd-Ost Melanesien, eine Ethnostatistische Analyse*. Würzburg.

——— .. .. 1949 "The quantitative distribution of cultural similarities and their cartographic representation," *Amer. Anthrop.* (n.s.), **51**.

Morant, G. H. .. .. 1935 "Cultural anthropology and statistics", *Man*, **35**.

Murdock, G. P. .. .. 1940 "The Cross-Cultural Survey," *Amer. Sociol. Rev.*, **5**.

——— .. .. 1949 *Social Structure*. New York.

———, Ford, C. S., Hudson, A. E., Kennedy, R., Simmons, L. W., and Whiting, J. W. M. 1950 *Outline of Cultural Materials*, 3rd rev. ed. New Haven.

Nieboer, H. J. .. .. 1910 *Slavery as an Industrial System*, 2nd ed. The Hague.

Ronhaar, J. H. .. .. 1931 *Woman in Primitive Mother-right Societies*. Groningen and London.

Rumney, J. .. .. 1934 *Herbert Spencer's Sociology*. London.

Seligman, C. G., and Seligman, B. Z. .. 1932 *Pagan Tribes of the Nilotic Sudan*. London.

Simmons, L. W. .. .. 1945 *The Role of the Aged in Primitive Society*. New Haven.

Smith, N. K. .. .. 1919 *The Present Situation in Philosophy*. Edinburgh. Reprinted (1920) in *Philos. Rev.*, **29**.

Somló, F. .. .. 1909 *Zur Gründung einer beschreibenden Soziologie*. Berlin and Leipzig.

Spencer, H. .. .. 1904 *An Autobiography*, 2 vols. London.

——— .. .. 1930 *African Races*, 2nd fully rev. ed. by E. Torday. London.

Steinen, H. von den .. .. 1907 *Unter den Naturvölkern Zentral Brasiliens*. Berlin.

Steiner, F. .. .. 1951 Review of G. P. Murdock's *Social Structure*. *Brit. J. Sociol.*, **2**.

STEINMETZ, S. R. .. .. 1898–99 " Classification des types sociaux et catalogue des peuples ", *Année sociol.* Reprinted (1930) in S. R. Steinmetz, *Gesammelte Kleinere Schriften*, 2 vols. Groningen.

TJIM, J. .. .. 1933 *Die Stellung der Frau bei den Indianern der Vereinigten Staaten und Canada's*. The Hague.

TILLETT, A. W. .. .. 1939 *Herbert Spencer Betrayed.* London.

TYLOR, E. B. .. .. 1889 " On a method of investigating the development of institutions; applied to the laws of marriage and descent," *J. Anthrop. Instit.*, **18**.

UNWIN, J. D. .. .. 1934 *Sex and Culture.* London.

WILSON, T. R. .. .. 1952 " Randomness of the distribution of social organization forms," *Amer. Anthrop.* (n.s.). **54**.

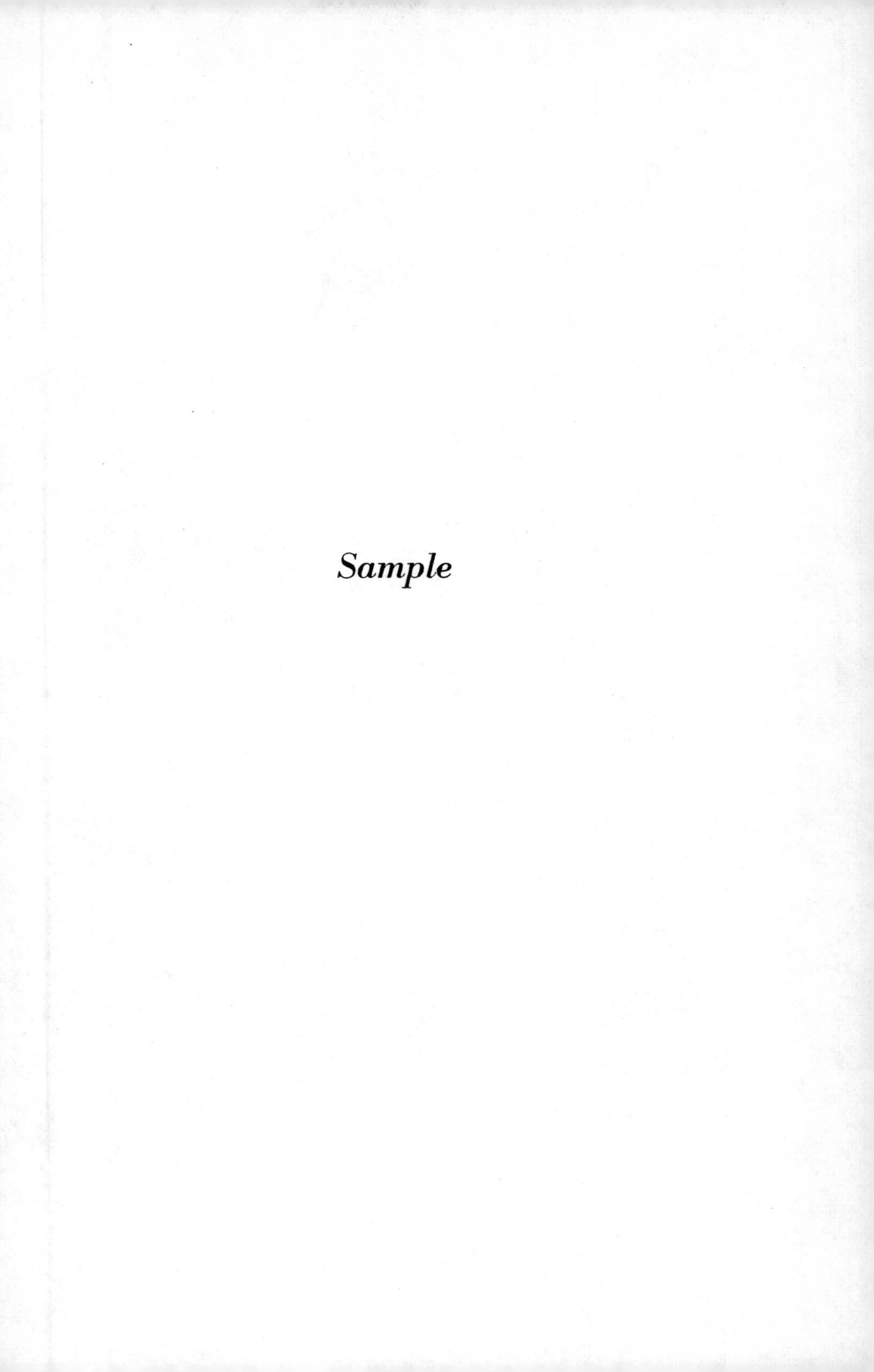

Sample

World Ethnographic Sample *

GEORGE PETER MURDOCK
Yale University

THIS paper has two primary objectives: (1) to present a carefully selected sample of all the cultures known to history and ethnography, and (2) to classify each selected culture according to certain standard ethnographic categories. The sample is specifically designed to be as representative as possible of the entire known range of cultural variation, so that it may serve alike as a rough indication of the quantitative incidence of the tabulated traits among mankind as a whole, as a guide to their distribution by geographical regions and areas, and as an aid in the testing of scientific hypotheses.

Regional surveys and the now somewhat outmoded world ethnographies tend to stress the distinctive features of particular culture areas without reference to universal standards of comparison. Theoretical works, on the other hand, typically emphasize the definition and illustration of crucial distinctions without recording their actual cross-cultural incidence and geographic distribution. The aim here is to combine the distributional and classificatory approaches.

The tabulated data are mainly from fields in which typological classification has become relatively standardized, namely, basic economy, settlement patterns, and social and political organization. To achieve uniformity of judgment the author has read and assessed all ethnographic sources himself, with the exception of a few classroom reports done by graduate students under close supervision. Besides covering the descriptive sources in the languages which he himself can use (Dutch, English, French, German, Italian, and Spanish), he has had access to a number of important sources in Chinese, Japanese, and Russian translated by the Human Relations Area Files.

The most serious problem has been the selection of the sample. At one time the author believed that an adequate sample might be obtained merely by selecting a large number of cultures from a wide geographic range and avoiding excessive representation of any particular areas. A test conducted recently in a graduate class convinced him that this is not sufficient. In this test the major statistical correlations of *Social Structure* (Murdock 1949) were recalculated from two worldwide samples of 300 cultures each, one completely unselected and the other carefully chosen to give precisely equal representation to all the culture areas of the world. Though no startling reversals appeared, the results from the two samples differed so markedly in enough instances to demonstrate the imperative need for a much more systematic sampling procedure.

Random sampling of all the world's known cultures must unfortunately be excluded for several reasons. In the first place, this would result in the inclusion of many cultures for which the descriptive information is very incomplete and in the exclusion, through chance, of a substantial proportion of the richest and most dependable ethnographic literature. In the second place, it

---

*Reprinted from the *American Anthropologist,* Vol. 59, New Series, No. 4 (August 1957), 664-687, by permission of the author and the American Anthropological Association.

would yield only a percentage of all the world's cultures without reference to their distribution by types. Areas like Europe and the Far East with a few large and culturally homogeneous nations, for example, would tend to be heavily under-represented as compared with areas like aboriginal Australia with hundreds of discrete but not notably divergent tribal cultures. The sample selected by Hobhouse, Wheeler, and Ginsberg (1915) came to grief on precisely this point. Third, purely random sampling would inevitably omit many of the truly unique cultures of the world, each the sole known representative of a distinctive type, e.g., the Ainu of Japan, the Dorobo of East Africa, the Guanche of the Canary Islands, the Inca of Peru, the Tasmanians, the Toda of India, and the Yahgan of Tierra del Fuego.

A truly satisfactory ethnographic sample must obviously be adapted both to the quality of the descriptive literature and to the structure of the particular universe, which is the known range of cultural variation. It must give representation to every distinctive cultural type and subtype for which information is available, even where these include only a single known example. It must similarly represent all the culture areas and subareas of the world. It must include examples of recorded ancient civilizations, of the contemporary complex civilizations of Europe and Asia, of European and African cultures transplanted to other continents, and of acculturated native peoples on the same basis as indigenous ethnographic cultures, i.e., approximately in proportion to their degree of cultural diversity. All this we have attempted to do.

Care must be taken, however, to prevent multiplication of examples of any particular type. We have thus chosen very sparingly from transplanted Europeans (one example for each of the five major colonizing nations), from transplanted Africans (the Black Carib, Bush Negroes, and Jamaicans), and from strongly acculturated indigenous peoples (the Chamorro, Chorti, Paez, and a few others). There are also examples of native cultures which, at the time of their first description, had already adopted and integrated important elements from European sources, e.g., the horse among the American Indians of the Plains and Pampas. In general, however, the data on nonliterate societies have been presented as of the earliest date for which information is available. European cultures, unless another date is indicated, are categorized for some period of political independence during the present century.

Since the purpose of the tabulation of data is to reveal associations within cultures, i.e., what Tylor (1889) called "adhesions," care has been exercised to record only elements occurring together at the same period of time. A complication arises in certain cases where the descriptive information is available only for a community or other small segment of a larger culture-bearing society. Here the author has recorded the information on settlement pattern, division of labor by sex, marriage, kin-group organization, and kinship as reported for the particular locality but has indicated the economy, social stratification, and political organization prevailing for the larger society on the assumption that these aspects of a national culture normally form part of the actual social context even in the local situation.

Our sample is intentionally large enough to enable users with other criteria to eliminate, by random or other means, enough cases to produce a sample conforming to their own specifications and still large enough for reliable statistical treatment. For their guidance we must make our own criteria of selection explicit.

The world was first divided into six great regions. Anthropologists customarily recognize five such regions: Africa, Eurasia, North America, Oceania, and South America. Of these, however, Africa and Eurasia are characterized by a much larger land surface and a considerably greater diversity of cultures than the other three. We therefore reduced them to comparable proportions by creating a sixth region, the Circum-Mediterranean, and transferring to it the northern portion of Africa and the western portion of Eurasia, including Europe, the Caucasus, and the Near East. This new area corresponds roughly to the core of the Christian and Islamic worlds. Moslem countries east of Iraq, however, were not thus transferred, for to have done so would have made the new area unduly large and the rest of Asia unduly small. We thus arrived at the following six approximately equivalent ethnographic regions:

Africa, excluding Madagascar and the northern and northeastern portions of the continent.

Circum-Mediterranean, including Europe, Caucasia, the Near East, and northern and northeastern Africa.

East Eurasia, excluding Formosa, the Philippines, Indonesia, and the area assigned to the Circum-Mediterranean but including Madagascar and other islands in the Indian Ocean.

Insular Pacific, including all of Oceania and areas like Australia, Indonesia, Formosa, and the Philippines that are sometimes but not always counted as part of Oceania.

North America, including the indigenous cultures of this continent as far south as the Isthmus of Tehuantepec.

South America, including the Antilles, Central America, and Yucatan.

Each of these regions was next divided into ten smaller areas. Insofar as feasible, boundaries between recognized culture areas were observed, but where a region included fewer than ten culture areas the larger and more culturally heterogeneous ones were split in two, and where more than ten, smaller and relatively similar ones were combined. The resulting 60 areas are equivalent in only a very approximate sense, for it was considered preferable to reconcile their differences in size and complexity by permitting a certain flexibility in the number of cultures chosen from each area. Though a quota of ten cultures per area was set as a rough ideal, this number was reduced for areas that are small, or culturally homogeneous, or deficient in adequate ethnographic descriptions, and expanded for those that are relatively large or heterogeneous. In no case, however, was the number of cultures selected for an area alloweb to exceed fifteen or to fall below five.

Within each area, the selection of representative cultures followed very explicit criteria. The ethnographic literature was ransacked for cases meeting the following specifications, and a needed example was omitted only if the search failed to uncover any society which both met the specifications and was sufficiently well described to merit inclusion.

1. The most populous society in the area, or, in default of reliable population data, the society occupying the greatest expanse of territory.
2. The best described culture in each of the other recognizable cultural subareas.
3. An example of each basic type of economy (agricultural, pastoral, fishing, or hunting and gathering) and of each major rule of descent (matrilineal, patrilineal, double, or bilateral) represented in the area, even though there might be only a single and otherwise unimportant case.
4. One example from each linguistic stock or major linguistic subfamily found in the area.
5. Additional cultures which appeared for any reason to be relatively distinctive within the context of the entire area.

Besides these positive criteria, two negative criteria were adopted to prevent duplication of essentially similar cultures. The mere fact of historical relatedness does not disturb the author, for the evidence now seems clear that societies borrow from one another, much as they invent for themselves, cultural elements for which they have a need and which are at least reasonably consistent with preexisting usages, and that borrowed like invented and traditional elements undergo a continual process of integrative modification leading to the emergence of new independent configurations. Diffusion negates the independence of two cultures only if it has occurred too recently for the integrative process to have run its course. To guard against the inclusion of such duplicate cases, we have wherever possible avoided the selection of two cultures from the same area that are either (a) geographically contiguous or (b) characterized by mutually intelligible languages unless they reveal such major differences in either their basic economy, their social organization, or in the former instance their languages, as to assure that they have achieved independent integration. This has made it necessary to eliminate one culture in such well described pairs as Arapaho-Cheyenne, Bena-Hehe, Bontoc-Ifugao, Kwakiutl-Nootka, and Swazi-Zulu. Since linguistic relationships are assumed to constitute the most reliable index of historical relatedness, we set for all areas an absolute maximum of ten societies belonging to the same linguistic subfamily. Any area represented by more than ten cultures is consequently characterized by linguistic as well as cultural diversity.

Application of the above criteria has resulted in a total world sample of 565 cultures distributed as follows: Africa 116, Circum-Mediterranean 78, East Eurasia 85, Insular Pacific 99, North America 110, and South America 77.

Cultural data for so large a sample of human societies can obviously be presented, within our limitations of space, only by means of a table and a system of symbols. In Table 1 the selected societies are grouped by regions, within the latter by areas, and alphabetically under each area. Societies are in some instances further identified by an alternative name, a date, or an indication of the particular subgroup described, shown in parentheses, and each is located geographically to the nearest even degree of longitude and latitude in the first two columns. Other columns, numbered from 1 to 15, present thirty items of cultural information for each society in the form of classificatory categories represented by symbols. A period or dot indicates lack of information. Other symbols consist of capital and lowercase letters, a pair to each column, which are defined in the following key:

Column 1: Cultivated Plants and Domesticated Animals

C Cereal grains, e.g., maize, millet, rice, wheat, the principal crops or at least as important as any other type of crop.
G Agriculture absent, unimportant, or recent, but gathering important.
O Agriculture absent, unimportant, or recent, and gathering unimportant.
R Roots or tubers, e.g., manioc, sweet potatoes, taro, yams, the principal crops or as important as tree fruits and more important than cereal grains.
T Tree fruits or starches, e.g., bananas, coconuts, dates, sago, the principal crops.
l Large domestic animals, e.g., buffaloes, cattle, horses, mithun, reindeer, kept aboriginally in at least moderate numbers, but not milked.
m Large domestic animals kept aboriginally in appreciable numbers, and milked.
o Domestic animals (as defined under l and s) absent or unimportant.
r Domestic animals (as defined under l and s) not aboriginal but introduced through European contact and important and well integrated at the period as of which the culture is described.
s Smaller domestic animals, e.g., donkeys, goats, llamas, pigs, but not larger ones, kept aboriginally in appreciable numbers. Lesser domestic animals, e.g., cats, dogs, fowl, guinea pigs, are ignored.

Column 2: Agriculture

C Codominant, i.e., sharing the position of principal subsistence activity with another such activity.
D Dominant, i.e., the principal subsistence activity.
I Important, though not the major subsistence activity.
O Absent, insignificant, or sporadic as a subsistence activity.
P Present but relatively unimportant as a subsistence activity.
a Standard division of labor by sex, i.e., men clear the land and women do the cultivation [in Column 3, men herd and women milk; in Column 4, men do the major fishing and/or marine hunting and women do the minor shore or reef fishing and/or shellfishing; in Column 5, men hunt and women gather]. For any other distribution of sex participation in a subsistence activity the following symbols are employed to indicate the relative importance of the sexes in the total activity.
b Both sexes participate approximately equally in the activity.
f Females conduct the activity, male participation being negligible.
g Both sexes participate, but the female share is appreciably greater.
m Males conduct the activity, female participation being negligible.

n Both sexes participate, but the male share is appreciably greater.

o The activity is absent, unimportant, or recent.

s The activity is conducted mainly by slaves or members of servile castes.

Column 3: Animal Husbandry [symbols the same as in Column 2]

Column 4: Fishing, Shellfishing, and Marine Hunting [symbols the same as in Column 2]

Column 5: Hunting and Gathering [symbols the same as in Column 2]

Column 6: Settlement Pattern and Community Organization

B Bands, i.e., migratory or nomadic communities.

C Compound settlements consisting of a nuclear village or town and outlying homesteads or satellite hamlets.

F Fixed or sedentary settlements whose precise pattern is unreported.

H Clusters of separated hamlets.

N Neighborhoods of dispersed homesteads.

S Seminomadic communities, i.e., life in nomadic bands during certain seasons of the year and in fixed settlements at other seasons.

V Compact villages or towns.

a Agamous communities without reported localized clans and without any marked tendency toward either local exogamy or local endogamy.

b Exogamous barrios, wards, hamlets, or localized lineages where a community normally includes several such and is not itself an exogamous unit.

c Clan-communities, i.e., communities which are themselves essentially localized exogamous lineages or sibs.

d Demes, i.e., communities which reveal a marked tendency toward local endogamy without being composed of localized exogamous units.

e Exogamous communities, i.e., those revealing a marked tendency toward local exogamy without having the specific structure of clans.

o Absence of localized clans in default of specific evidence on local endogamy or exogamy.

Column 7: Family and Household

E Extended families, regardless of whether housed in one or more dwellings, where they constitute definite corporate units and are large in size, i.e., normally comprising the families of procreation of at least two siblings or cousins in each of at least two adjacent generations.

I Independent families, i.e., familial groupings which do not normally, or other than temporarily, include more than one nuclear or polygamous family.

L Lineal families, i.e., small extended families normally comprising the families of procreation of only one individual in the senior generation but of at least two individuals in the next generation.

S Stem families, i.e., minimal extended families normally consisting of only two related families of procreation (disregarding polygamous unions), particularly of adjacent generations.

c Communal households, i.e., occupancy of a single large dwelling by all the families of a settlement or a sizeable segment thereof.

e Extended family households, i.e., normal occupancy of a single dwelling by an entire large extended family.

l Lineal family households, i.e., normal occupancy of a single dwelling by an entire lineal (small extended) family.

m Mother-child households, i.e., normal occupancy of a single dwelling by one married woman and her children, especially in societies practicing polygyny where co-wives typically occupy separate dwellings.

n Nuclear family households, i.e., normal occupancy of a single dwelling by one married couple and their children, including monogamous societies and those practicing limited polygyny for which the residence arrangements for co-wives are not specifically reported.

p Polygamous family households, i.e., normal occupancy of a single dwelling by an entire polygynous or polyandrous family in cases of plural marriages.

q Qualified polygynous family households, i.e., where co-wives occupy a single dwelling if they are sisters, separate dwellings if they are not sisters.

s Stem family households, i.e., normal occupancy of a single dwelling by a stem (minimal extended) family.

Column 8: Marital Residence [capital letters in the first column indicate normal societal profiles; the same symbols in lower case in the second column indicate patterned alternatives occurring with sufficient frequency to suggest either the survival of an earlier rule or the incipient emergence of a new one; the capital letter is repeated in lower case where no such alternatives are reported; a dot in the second column indicates that the residence profile is incompletely reported or inferential]

A Avunculocal, i.e., normally with or near the husband's male matrilineal kinsmen.

B Bilocal, i.e., either patrilocal or matrilocal with about equal frequency.

D Duolocal, i.e., without establishment of a common residence, both spouses continuing to reside with or near their own kinsmen.

M Matrilocal, i.e., normally with or near the wife's female matrilineal kinsmen.

N Neolocal, i.e., normally in a new household whose location does not depend on the kinship ties of either spouse.

P Patrilocal, i.e., normally with or near the husband's male patrilineal kinsmen.

R Duopatrilocal, i.e., normally patrilocal after an initial period of duolocal residence.

S Sororilocal, i.e., residence with or near the husband's female matrilineal kinsmen. Since such residence can occur only in individual cases and cannot prevail throughout a society, this symbol appears only in the second column.

U Uxoripatrilocal, i.e., normally patrilocal after an initial period with or near the wife's kinsmen.

V Uxoravunculocal, i.e., normally avunculocal after an initial period with or near the wife's kinsmen.

W Uxorineolocal, i.e., normally neolocal after an initial period with or near the wife's kinsmen.

X Uxoribilocal, i.e., bilocal after an initial period with or near the wife's kinsmen.

Y Viravunculocal, i.e., normally avunculocal after an initial period with or near the husband's father.

Z Duoavunculocal, i.e., normally avunculocal after an initial period of duolocal residence.

Column 9: Marriage

G General polygyny, i.e., polygynous unions where they are both preferential and common (incidence over 20 percent) and are not reported to be either exclusively nonsororal or preferably sororal.

L Limited polygyny, i.e., unions of one man with two or more wives where these are culturally favored but relatively infrequent (incidence under 20 percent), e.g., being mainly confined to men of wealth or high status, and are not specifically reported to be preferably sororal.

M Monogamy, plural marriages being either forbidden or nonpreferential and infrequent.

N Nonsororal polygyny, i.e., polygynous unions where they are common but occur exclusively in the nonsororal form.

S Sororal polygyny, i.e., unions of one man with two or more wives who are sisters where polygyny is preferential and exclusively sororal or where it is general and occurs in both forms but preferentially or more commonly in the sororal form.

T Limited polygyny when specifically reported to be preferably sororal.

Y Polyandry, i.e., unions of one woman with two or more husbands where these are culturally favored and involve residential as well as sexual cohabitation.

b Bride-price, i.e., marriages normally involving a material consideration of which the principal element is a substantial property payment by the groom or his relatives to the kinsmen of the bride.

d Dowry, i.e., marriages normally involving a material consideration of which the principal element is a dowry provided for the bride or a substantial payment by the bride's relatives to the kinsmen of the groom.

g Gift exchange, i.e., marriages normally involving a reciprocal exchange of gifts of substantial amount between the relatives of the bride and groom or else entailing a continuing exchange of goods and services in approximately equal amounts between the groom or his kinsmen and the bride's relatives.

o Absence of any significant material consideration in marriage.

s Bride-service, i.e., marriages normally involving a substantial material consideration of which the principal element consists of labor or other service rendered by the groom to the bride's kinsmen.

t Token bride-price, i.e., marriages normally involving only a small or symbolic bride-price as a consideration.

x Exchange, i.e., marriages normally involving a consideration in the form of a sister or other female relative of the groom given in exchange for the bride.

Column 10: Patrilineal Kin Groups and Exogamy

L Lineages, in the absence of specific evidence of larger unilinear kin groups.

M Exogamous moieties.

N Agamous (nonexogamous) moieties.

O Absence of any unilinear kin groups with the rule of descent in question.

P Phratries, moieties being absent.

Q Segmentary lineage organization, i.e., unilinear kin groups of varying generational depth where such are specifically attested.

S Sibs, in the absence of specific evidence of moieties, phratries, and segmentary unilinear organization.

a Marriage with a parallel cousin [FaBrDa in Column 10, MoSiDa in Column 11] allowed but not preferred.

d Marriage with a parallel cousin disapproved but not specifically forbidden.

f Marriage with a parallel cousin forbidden, unilinear exogamy being absent.

l Lineage exogamy, i.e., marriage forbidden with any lineage mate (or with comparable relatives in the absence of lineages) but permitted with remoter unilinear kinsmen.

m Maximal extension of unilinear exogamy, i.e., marriage forbidden with any member of the unilinear kin groups of either parent.

p Preferential marriage with a parallel cousin.

s Sib exogamy, i.e., marriage forbidden with any member of the same sib (or larger unilinear kin group) in the absence of maximal extension.

Column 11: Matrilineal Kin Groups and Exogamy [Symbols the same as in Column 10]

Column 12: Bilateral and Bilinear Kin Group and Exogamy

B Bilateral descent, kindreds being unreported.

D Double descent, kindreds and sections being unreported.

K Bilateral kindreds reported. In such cases, the rule of descent can be determined through examination of Columns 10 and 11.

M Matrilineal descent, kindreds being unreported.

P Patrilineal descent, kindreds being unreported.

S Double descent with bilinear kin groups or sections.

a Cross-cousin marriage allowed symmetrically, i.e., with either MoBrDa or FaSiDa.

c Cross-cousin marriage preferred symmetrically.

d Cross-cousin marriage disapproved symmetrically but not specifically forbidden.

f Cross-cousin marriage forbidden symmetrically.

g Marriage forbidden with any second cousin, cross or parallel, but allowed with at least some remoter cousins.

h Marriage forbidden with any known consanguineal kinsmen, or at least with any third or closer cousin.

m Matrilateral cross-cousin marriage preferred asymmetrically, i.e., unions preferred with MoBrDa, forbidden or unreported with FaSiDa.

n Cross-cousin marriage allowed with matrilateral preference, i.e., unions preferred with MoBrDa, allowed with FaSiDa.

o Matrilateral cross-cousin marriage allowed asymmetrically, i.e., unions allowed with MoBrDa, forbidden or unreported with FaSiDa.

p Patrilateral cross-cousin marriage preferred asymmetrically, i.e., unions preferred with FaSiDa, forbidden or unreported with MoBrDa.

q Cross-cousin marriage allowed with patrilateral preference, i.e., unions preferred with FaSiDa, allowed with MoBrDa.

r Patrilateral cross-cousin marriage allowed asymmetrically, i.e., unions allowed with FaSiDa, forbidden or unreported with MoBrDa.

Column 13: Kinship Terminology [in the case of cousin terms, if the pattern differs by sex of cousins or of speaker, that employed by males for female cousins is indicated]

B Buryat cousin terminology, i.e., paternal cousins (FaBrCh and FaSiCh) equated, and likewise maternal cousins (MoBrCh and MoSiCh), the two pairs being distinguished both from each other and from siblings.

C Crow cousin terminology, i.e., FaSiCh equated with kinsmen of a higher generation and/or MoBrCh with kinsmen of a lower generation.

D Descriptive or derivative, rather than elementary, terms employed for cousins, or at least for cross-cousins.

E Eskimo cousin terminology, i.e., FaBrCh, FaSiCh, MoBrCh, and MoSiCh equated with each other and distinguished from siblings.

F Equivocal Eskimo terminology, i.e., where sources report a term for "cousin" without clearly indicating that Eskimo rather than Iroquois terms are implied.

H Hawaiian cousin terminology, i.e., all cousins equated with siblings or called by terms clearly derived from those for siblings.

I Iroquois cousin terminology, i.e., FaSiCh equated with MoBrCh and both distinguished alike from siblings and parallel cousins.

M Murngin cousin terminology, i.e., FaSiCh distinguished from MoBrCh and both distinguished from siblings and parallel cousins without conforming to either the Crow, the descriptive, or the Omaha pattern.

O Omaha cousin terminology, i.e., MoBrCh equated with kinsmen of a higher generation and/or FaSiCh with kinsmen of a lower generation.

U Unusual cousin terminology in which ortho-cousins (those of Ego's lineage) are equated with siblings or half siblings, all other cousins being differentiated therefrom and equated with one another.

V Unusual cousin terminology in which the children of aunts are equated, and also the children of uncles, both groups being distinguished alike from siblings and from one another.

W Unusual cousin terminology in which paternal cousins are equated with siblings, while maternal cousins are differentiated therefrom and either equated or called by descriptive terms.

X Unusual cousin terminology in which nonmarriageable cross-cousins are equated with siblings, while marriageable cross-cousins are differentiated.

c Bifurcate collateral avuncular terminology, i.e., distinct elementary terms for Fa, FaBr, and MoBr.

d Descriptive or derivative terminology differentiating FaBr and MoBr from Fa and from each other.

g Generation avuncular terminology, i.e., FaBr and MoBr equated with Fa or called by identical terms clearly derived from that for Fa.

l Lineal avuncular terminology, i.e., FaBr and MoBr equated with each other but differentiated from Fa.

m Bifurcate merging avuncular terminology, i.e., FaBr equated with Fa but MoBr differentiated from both.

n Derivative bifurcate merging avuncular terminology, i.e., MoBr called by a distinct term, FaBr by a derivative of the term for Fa, e.g., "little father."

Column 14: Social Stratification

A Formal age-grades without other significant stratification among freemen.

C Complex stratification into three or more social classes or castes (exclusive of slaves).

H Hereditary aristocracy or noble class differentiated from ordinary freemen.

O Absence of significant social stratification among freemen. Purely political and religious statuses, e.g., chiefs or priests, are not treated as classes.

W Wealth distinctions of importance, based on possession or distribution of property, without definite crystallization into hereditary social classes.

h Hereditary slavery, slaves forming a distinct social class.

i Incipient or nonhereditary slavery, i.e., where slave status is temporary and is not transmitted to the children of slaves.

o Absence or near absence of slavery.

s Slavery reported but without indication of whether or not the status is hereditary.

Column 15: Political Integration and Succession [for cross-cultural comparability the rule of succession, indicated in the second column, is that prevailing for the headman of a local community or a near equivalent thereto]

A Autonomous local communities, i.e., politically independent local groups which do not exceed 1500 in average population.

D Dependent societies lacking any political organization of their own, e.g., those forming an integral part of some larger political system and those governed exclusively and directly by agents of another and politically dominant society. Colonial governments operating through indirect rule are ignored.

L Little states, i.e., political integration in independent units averaging between 10,000 and 100,000 in population.

M Minimal states, i.e., political integration in independent units averaging between 1500 and 10,000 in population.

O Absence of any political integration even at the local level, e.g., where family heads acknowledge no higher political authority.

P Peace groups transcending the local community where the basis of unity is other than political, e.g., derived from reciprocal trade relations, defensive military agreements, or a common cult or age-grade organization.

S States, i.e., political integration in large independent units averaging at least 100,000 in population.

a Nonhereditary succession through appointment of headmen by some higher political authority.

b Patrilineal succession where a younger brother is preferred to a son.

c Councils, i.e., absence of true headmen, political authority at the local level being exercised exclusively by a council or other collective body.

e Nonhereditary succession through election or some other method of formal consensus.

i Nonhereditary succession through informal consensus or personal influence.

m Matrilineal succession other than n or y or where preference is unspecified.

n Matrilineal succession where a sister's son is preferred to a younger brother.

o Absence of any indigenous political authority, as in societies lacking political integration even at the local level and in some dependent societies.

p Patrilineal succession other than b or s or where preference is unspecified.

s Patrilineal succession where a son is preferred to a younger brother.

y Matrilineal succession where a younger brother is preferred to a sister's son.

Table 1. Thirty Cultural Characteristics among Sample Peoples

Area and Culture	Location		1	2	3	4	5	6	7	8	9	10	11	12	13	14	15
AFRICA																	
Pygmies & Khoisan																	
Bagielli	12E	2N	Go	Oo	Oo	Ig	Da	Bc	In	Pp	Mb	Ll	Of	Pf	..	Oo	Ap
Bambuti	28E	2N	Go	Oo	Oo	Pf	Da	Bc	Im	Pp	Lx	Ll	Od	Pa	..	Oo	Ap
Bergdama	16E	22S	Gs	Oo	Pm	Pm	Da	Bo	Im	Uu	Ss	Oa	Oa	Ba	Vl	Oi	A.
Hottentot (Nama)	18E	26S	Om	Oo	Da	P.	Ia	Bc	Im	Uu	Ls	Ss	Of	Pa	Im	Wo	Ms
Kindiga	35E	3S	Go	Oo	Oo	P.	Da	Bo	Iq	Pp	Gb	O.	O.	B.	..	Oo	Oo
Kung	21E	20S	Go	Oo	Oo	P.	Da	Be	In	Uu	Ms	Oa	Oa	Ba	El	Oo	As
Naron	21E	22S	Go	Oo	Oo	Oo	Da	Be	Ip	Uu	To	Oa	Oa	Ba	.c	Oo	As
Sandawe	36E	5S	Cm	Da	Im	Pf	Ia	No	In	Pu	Mb	Ss	Of	Pm	Wm	Oo	Ap
Xam	22E	31S	Go	Oo	Oo	P.	Da	Bo	In	Xx	Ls	Oa	Oa	Ba	He	Oo	A.
Southern Bantu																	
Herero	16E	21S	Gm	Oo	Db	Oo	Ia	Bc	Lm	Pa	Gb	Qs	Ss	Dq	Io	Wh	Ab
Lovedu	31E	24S	Cm	Db	Im	Oo	Pa	He	Im	Pp	Sb	Pl	Of	Pn	Ic	Co	Lp
Mbundu	16E	12S	Cl	Da	Im	Pn	Pa	Vc	Im	Pa	Nb	Sf	Lf	Dn	Im	Hh	Lp
Nyaneka	14E	15S	Cm	Cb	Cm	Pb	Pm	No	Lm	Yy	Gb	Of	Ps	Ma	Im	.s	Ln
Poudo	30E	31S	Cm	Cb	Cm	Pa	Pa	Nb	Lm	Pp	Gb	Sm	Of	Pf	Im	Wo	Ss
Shona (Hera)	31E	19S	Cm	Db	Im	Pn	Ia	Hb	Em	Pu	Sb	Pm	Of	Kf	On	Hs	Lb
Sotho	28E	29S	Cm	Ca	Cm	Oo	Ia	Hb	Em	Pu	Sb	Sa	Oa	Pc	In	Ho	Ss
Thonga	32E	24S	Cm	Dg	Im	Pm	Ia	Hb	Em	Pa	Sb	Sl	Of	Pf	On	.o	Lb
Tswana (Kgatla)	27E	24S	Cm	Da	Im	Oo	Im	Cb	Em	Uu	Sb	Sa	Oa	Pn	In	Co	Ls
Zulu	31E	29S	Cm	Ca	Cm	Oo	Im	Nc	Lm	Pp	Gb	Sm	Of	Ph	Im	Co	Ss
Central Bantu																	
Bemba	31E	11S	Cs	Db	P.	In	Pa	Vc	Im	Vm	Ss	Of	Ss	Ko	Im	Hi	Sy
Chokwe	20E	10S	Rs	Da	P.	In	Im	Vc	Im	Aa	Gt	Of	Ss	Mn	In	Hh	Ln
Ila	27E	16S	Cm	Cg	Cm	Im	Ia	Va	Lm	Pa	Nb	Ll	Ss	Dp	Im	Wh	Am
Kongo	14E	6S	Rs	Da	P.	In	In	Vc	Im	Aa	Nb	Of	Ss	Ma	Cm	Hh	Sy
Kuba	22E	5S	Cs	Da	P.	Ib	Pm	Hb	I.	Av	Gb	Of	Ss	Mg	In	Hh	Lm
Lamba	28E	13S	Co	Db	Oo	In	Im	Vc	In	Vu	Ls	Of	Ss	Mn	Im	Hs	Mm
Lozi	23E	15S	Cm	Da	Im	In	In	Ve	Im	Pm	Nt	Of	Of	Kh	Hm	Ch	Sp
Luimbe	18E	12S	Cl	Ia	I.	Dm	Im	Ve	Im	Pa	Gb	Of	Ss	Ma	In	..	Ay
Ngoni (Mpezeni)	33E	12S	Cm	Ia	Dm	Oo	Pm	Va	Im	Pm	Gb	Of	Of	Ba	Im	Hi	Ls
Yao	36E	13S	Cs	Dg	P.	Im	Im	Ha	En	Ms	Lo	Of	Sl	Mc	In	Os	Mn
Northeast Bantu																	
Chagga	37E	3S	Cm	Db	Ib	Oo	Pm	Nc	Im	Pn	Nb	Ss	Of	Pg	Om	Ho	Ma
Gusii	35E	1S	Cm	Da	Im	Oo	Pm	Vc	Im	Pp	Gb	Qm	Of	Ph	.m	Oo	Ao
Hehe (Iringa)	35E	8S	Cm	Dg	Im	P.	Pm	Nc	Im	Pn	Gb	Ss	Of	Pn	In	Hh	Lp
Kikuyu	37E	1S	Cm	Dg	Im	Oo	Oo	Nc	Im	Pp	Gb	Sm	Of	Ph	On	Ao	Ao
Kwere	39E	6S	Cs	Df	P.	Oo	Im	V.	Im	U.	Gb	O.	Ss	M.	In	Os	Ma
Mbugwe	36E	4S	Cm	Cn	Cm	Oo	Im	N.	Ln	Pp	Mb	Ll	Ss	Df	Cn	Wo	Ac
Nika (Digo)	39E	4S	Rm	Dg	Im	I.	Pm	Vc	Im	Pu	Gb	Ll	Ss	Da	In	As	Mc
Nyakyusa	34E	9S	Tm	Dn	Im	Pn	Pm	Ve	Im	Nm	Sb	Of	Of	Kg	Im	Ai	Ma
Safwa	33E	9S	Cm	Dg	Im	I.	Ia	Ve	Im	Pu	Gb	Ss	Of	Pf	.m	Os	M.
Sukuma	34E	3S	Cm	Dg	Im	Oo	Oo	Va	Im	Pn	Nb	Sl	Of	Ph	Cm	Hs	Ma
Equatorial Bantu																	
Babwa	25E	3N	Ts	Da	P.	Pg	Im	He	Em	Pp	Gb	Ss	O.	P.	Hm	Oi	Ms
Fang (Pangwe)	12E	2N	Rs	Da	Pm	In	Pm	Vo	Em	Pp	Gb	Ss	Of	Ph	..	Oo	As
Ganda	32E	1N	Tm	Da	Im	Im	Pm	No	Im	Pn	Gb	Sm	Of	Pf	Im	Hs	Sa
Kpe (Kwiri)	9E	4N	Rl	Dg	I.	Pf	Im	Vb	Im	Pa	Nb	Sl	Ll	Dh	.m	Wi	Ag
Lesa (Sakata)	18E	3S	Rs	Da	P.	Ib	Pm	Ve	Im	Ap	Nb	Of	Sl	Mf	.m	Ob	Mm
Luba (Bena Kalundwe)	26E	8S	Rs	Da	P.	In	In	Vb	Im	Pp	Gb	Ll	Of	Pf	.m	Hs	La
Mongo (Nkundo)	20E	0	Rs	Da	P.	In	Pa	Hc	Em	Pa	Gb	Ss	Ol	Pf	Cm	Ol	Mb
Nsaw	11E	6N	Cs	Dg	I.	Oo	Pm	Vb	Lm	Pp	Gs	Sm	Of	Pf	..	Hs	Lp
Nyoro (Kitara)	32E	2N	Cm	Ca	Cm	P.	Pm	Nb	Im	Pp	Cb	Sm	Of	Pf	On	Hh	Sa
Poto	22E	2N	Os	Pf	P.	Dm	Pm	Ve	E.	Pp	Gb	Lm	Of	Pf	Hm	Wi	Ap

TABLE 1. THIRTY CULTURAL CHARACTERISTICS AMONG SAMPLE PEOPLES (Continued)

Area and Culture	Location		1	2	3	4	5	6	7	8	9	10	11	12	13	14	15
Guinea Coast																	
Ashanti	2W	7N	Rs	Db	P.	Im	Pm	Vb	Lm	Zp	Nb	Sl	Ss	Dn	Dm	Ci	Se
Bete	7W	6N	Rs	Dg	P.	Pb	Im	Vb	Lm	Pp	Gb	Ll	Of	Pf	..	Oo	Ap
Bijcgo	16W	11N	Cl	Dn	I.	Ia	Pm	V.	In	Mm	Mo	Of	Ll	Mf	.g	Os	My
Dahomeans (Fon)	2E	7N	Rl	Dg	Ib	Pm	Pm	Vb	Em	Pm	Gb	Ss	Oa	Pa	Dn	Ch	Sp
Ga	0	6N	Cs	In	P.	Dm	Oo	Cb	E.	Dp	Gb	Ld	Od	Pn	Hl	.s	Ab
Ibibio (Efik)	8E	5N	Rs	Db	Pm	Ib	Ib	Vb	Im	Pp	Nb	Ll	Of	Pf	Dd	Ah	Pp
Ibo (Ezinihite)	7E	6N	Rl	Dg	I.	Pn	Pm	Hb	Em	Pp	Gb	Qm	Of	Ph	Od	Hh	Pe
Igbira (Panda)	7E	8N	Rs	Dn	P.	In	Pm	F.	Em	Pp	Ns	Lm	Ol	Pg	Om	Hs	Lp
Kissi	10W	9N	Cl	Db	Im	Pn	Pm	Vb	Em	Pp	Gb	Sl	O.	Pm	Hm	Oh	Mp
Mende	11W	8N	Cs	Db	P.	If	Im	Cb	Lm	Pm	Nb	Lf	Oa	Km	Hn	Hh	Lp
Serer	17W	14N	Cm	Dn	Ib	Ia	Pm	Na	Em	Pa	Nb	Of	Ss	Mf	.g	Ch	Ly
Tenda (Coniagui)	13W	13N	Cl	Db	Ib	Oo	Ia	Va	Im	Yp	Ls	Oa	Sl	Ma	..	Ao	My
Vai	11W	7N	Cl	Da	I.	P.	P.	Va	Em	Pp	Nb	Sf	Of	Pf	Om	Ws	Al
Yako (Umor)	8E	6N	Rl	Dg	P.	Oo	Im	Vb	Lm	Rz	Nb	Ll	Sl	Dp	Im	Ai	Am
Yoruba (Ibadan)	4E	8N	Rs	Dn	Pg	P.	Pm	Vb	Ee	Pp	Gb	Sm	Of	Pf	Hg	Cl	Sp
Western Sudan																	
Awuna	2W	11N	Cl	Dn	I.	Pb	Pm	Hb	Em	Pp	Gb	Ss	Of	Pf	Hm	Os	Ab
Birifor	3W	10N	Cl	Dn	Im	Pb	Ib	Ne	Ss	Pa	Gb	Ss	Ml	Dq	Cm	Oh	Ap
Bozo	5W	14N	Co	In	Oo	Dm	Pm	Vb	E.	Pp	Nb	Sa	Oa	Pa	.n	A.	Ap
Dogon	3W	15N	Cl	Db	Im	Oo	Ib	Vb	Ep	Pp	Ls	Ll	Of	Pf	In	Oh	Ab
Foutadjalonke	13W	11N	Cm	Cn	Cb	P.	Pm	Cb	Em	Pp	Nb	Lp	Oa	Fa	Im	Ch	Sp
Ka[illegible]re	1E	10N	Cl	Dg	I.	Pm	I.	N.	Im	Pp	Gs	Ll	Of	Pf	..	Oo	Oo
Konkomba	0	10N	Cl	Db	Im	Pn	Pa	Ne	Lm	Pp	Ns	Sl	Oa	Pa	In	Oi	Ac
Lobi	4W	10N	Cl	Dn	Im	Pb	Pa	No	Ip	Pa	Gs	Of	Nl	Mq	Cm	Oi	Am
Malinke (Mandingo)	10W	12N	Cl	Dn	Im	Pm	Pa	Va	Em	Pp	Nb	Sl	Of	Pd	Io	Ch	Mp
Mossi	2W	13N	Cl	Dn	Im	Oo	Ia	Ne	Im	Pp	Nb	Ll	Of	Pg	Mn	Ch	Ss
Senufo	6W	10N	Cl	Dn	P.	Pm	Pa	Vb	Em	Pp	Gb	Sl	Of	P.	..	Oh	Mp
Susu	13W	10N	Cl	Dn	I.	P.	P.	Vb	Em	Pp	Nb	Sl	Of	Pe	Im	Ch	L.
Tallensi	1W	11N	Cm	Dn	Im	Oo	Pa	Ne	Lm	Pp	Nb	Sm	Ol	Pf	Hn	Oi	Ap
Nigerian Plateau																	
Bassakomo	7E	8N	Cl	Dg	I.	Im	Pm	Hb	Lm	Pm	Nx	Sl	Of	Pf	..	Oo	Mp
Chamba (Lekon)	12E	8N	Cs	D.	P.	P.	Pm	Vo	Ln	Pa	Lb	Sl	Ll	Df	Cn	Hs	Mp
Dera	12E	10N	Cl	Db	I.	I.	Pm	Vb	E.	Pa	Gb	Ll	Ll	D.	Hm	H.	Mb
Fulani (Djafun Bororo)	12E	7N	Om	Ps	Db	Oo	Ps	Be	Im	Pr	Gb	Ll	Of	Pe	In	Ws	Ai
Gbari	7E	10N	Cl	Dn	I.	P.	I.	Vb	Em	Pp	Ns	Ll	Of	Pf	On	Hs	Ms
Gure	9E	10N	Cs	Db	P.	Oo	I.	Hb	Ln	As	Lo	Of	Sl	Mg	Hm	Oi	Oo
Jukun	10E	8N	Cs	Db	Im	Im	Im	Vo	Em	Ap	Lb	Od	Od	Kd	Hg	Hi	Lp
Kadara	8E	10N	Cs	Db	P.	Pg	Im	Vb	Lm	Pa	Gs	Sm	Of	Ph	Om	As	Pp
Karekare	11E	12N	Cl	Db	I.	Oo	P.	Hb	Em	Uu	Nb	Ss	Of	Pf	Hn	Hs	M.
Margi (Kilba)	13E	11N	Cl	Db	I.	P.	P.	Hb	Lm	Pa	Nb	Sl	Of	Pg	Hm	Hs	Lp
Matakam	14E	9N	Cs	Db	In	Oo	P.	Ne	Lm	Pp	Lb	Sm	Of	Pf	On	O.	Ap
Mumuye	12E	9N	Cl	Db	I.	Oo	Pm	Hb	Lm	Uu	Nb	Sl	Of	Pf	Hm	Os	Ap
Ndoro	11E	7N	Cs	D.	P.	P.	P.	Va	..	As	Ls	Of	Ll	Mc	Cm	Hs	Am
Tiv	9E	7N	Rs	Db	I.	Pn	Im	Ne	Em	Pa	Nx	Ql	Of	Pf	Hn	Oh	Mp
Wute	12E	5N	Cs	Dg	Pb	Pb	Ia	Ve	Em	Pa	Nb	Sl	Of	Pf	.n	Hh	Mp
Eastern Sudan																	
Azande	27E	5N	Co	Da	Oo	Pg	Im	Ne	Im	Pu	Gb	Sm	O.	Pf	Dm	Hi	Ls
Banda	22E	7N	Cs	Da	P.	Pg	Im	Ne	Im	Pp	Sx	Sm	Of	Pf	Om	Oi	Ab
Baya	16E	6N	Rs	Da	Pf	Ib	In	Ve	Im	Pp	Nb	Ss	Of	Pg	..	Oh	As
Bongo	29E	7N	Cs	Db	P.	Pm	Im	Ve	..	Pp	Gb	Sm	O.	Pf	..	Oo	Ai
Dilling	30E	12N	Cm	Db	In	Oo	Ia	Hb	Im	Rr	Nb	Ss	Of	Pa	Dn	Hh	Mp
Ingassana	34E	11N	Cm	Dm	I.	Oo	Oo	Hd	Ln	Ba	Ms	Of	Of	Kg	Hm	Oo	As
Koma	34E	10N	Cs	Db	P.	I.	Pm	Ve	..	Pp	Lx	Ss	Of	Pf	..	O.	Ap
Lugbara	31E	3N	Cm	Cg	Cm	Oo	Oo	He	Em	Pp	Gb	Ss	Of	Pg	..	Oi	As
Mangbetu	28E	3N	To	Da	Oo	In	Ia	N.	Im	Pn	Nb	Ll	Of	Pf	Hm	Hh	Lb
Mesakin	30E	11N	Cm	Db	In	Oo	Pa	Hd	Im	Ap	Lb	Of	Sf	Mh	Im	Ws	Mm
Shilluk	32E	10N	Cm	Db	Im	I.	Im	Hb	Im	Pr	Sb	Qs	Of	Ph	Dm	Ch	Sp
Tullishi	29E	11N	Cm	Db	In	Oo	Pa	Hd	Im	Pp	Lb	Lf	Sl	Df	Wn	.s	Ap

TABLE 1. THIRTY CULTURAL CHARACTERISTICS AMONG SAMPLE PEOPLES (Continued)

Area and Culture	Location		1	2	3	4	5	6	7	8	9	10	11	12	13	14	15
Upper Nile			Cs	Dn	I.	Oo	Ia	Vo	Im	Pp	Nb	Ss	O.	P.	On	Ao	Ap
Acholi	32E	3N	Cm	Ib	Dn	Oo	Oo	Nb	Im	Pu	Nb	Sm	Of	Ph	Om	Ho	As
Bari	32E	5N	Cm	Ia	Dm	Oo	Im	Hb	I.	Pn	Nb	Ss	O.	P.	..	Ai	As
Didinga	34E	4N	Cm	Ib	Da	Im	Ia	Sb	Im	Pu	Nb	Se	Of	Pg	Dn	Ws	Pi
Dinka	29E	9N	Go	Oo	Oo	Oo	Dn	Bc	Ln	Pp	Mt	Ll	Of	Pf	Om	Ao	Ac
Dorobo	36E	0	Cm	Ca	Cm	Oo	P.	Ve	Sm	Pp	Nb	Sm	Of	Ph	Om	Ai	As
Lango	33E	2N	Cm	Db	Im	Ib	Pm	He	Lm	Pp	Gb	Sm	Of	Pf	Om	Oo	As
Luo	34E	1S	Om	Oo	Da	Oo	Oo	Ba	Im	Pm	Nb	Sm	Of	Ph	Im	Ao	Pc
Masai	36E	2S	Cm	Cg	Cn	Oo	Oo	Na	Im	Pn	Lb	Sl	Of	Kf	Om	Ao	Pc
Nandi	35E	0	Cm	Ib	Da	In	Pa	Sc	Lm	Un	Nb	Qm	Of	Kh	Dn	Oo	Po
Nuer	32E	8N	Cm	Ig	Dn	Oo	Ib	Se	Im	Pn	Gb	Sm	Of	Pf	Om	Ao	Pc
Suk (Plains)	36E	1N	Cm	If	Da	Pm	Ia	Be	Im	Pn	Gb	Sm	O.	Pf	Dm	Ao	Oo
Turkana	35E	4N															
							CIRCUM-MEDITERRANEAN										
Horn & Ethiopia																	
Afar	42E	12N	Om	Oo	Db	P.	Oo	Bc	Lm	Pp	Nb	Ql	O.	Pc	Dc	Hh	Mp
Amhara	38E	12N	Cm	Dn	Ia	Oo	Oo	Ve	In	Pn	Mo	Of	Of	Kh	Vl	Ch	Sa
Beja (Bisharin)	35E	20N	Om	Pf	Dm	Oo	Oo	Sd	Ip	Uu	Lb	Qp	Oa	Pa	D.	Oo	Mp
Bogo	38E	16N	Om	P.	Dm	Oo	Oo	Se	Im	Pp	Lb	..	O.	P.	..	Hh	L.
Galla (Boran)	39E	3N	Om	Oo	Da	Oo	Oo	Bc	Lm	Pp	Gb	Ms	Of	Ph	Dc	As	Mp
Iraku	35E	4S	Cm	Cg	Cm	Oo	P.	N.	I.	Pp	Gb	Ss	O.	P.	Dn	Oo	Ap
Kafa	36E	7N	Rm	D.	In	Oo	P.	No	Ip	Pp	Gb	Ss	Of	Pf	Fn	Ch	Ss
Konso	38E	5N	Cm	Db	In	Oo	Oo	Va	Sm	Pn	Lo	Ss.	O.	P.	..	Ao	Mp
Kunama	37E	15N	Cm	Db	In	Oo	P.	Vo	Im	P.	Lb	Of	Lf	Mg	..	Oi	Ac
Somali (Mijertein)	49E	9N	Om	Oo	Db	Oo	Oo	Bc	Lm	Pp	Nb	Qs	Of	Pf	Dc	Wh	Le
Tigre	39E	16N	Om	P.	D.	Oo	Oo	Sa	E.	P.	Lb	Qa	Oa	Pa	Dn	Hh	Lp
Moslem Sudan																	
Buduma	15E	13N	Cm	I.	C.	C.	P.	F.	I.	Pp	Nb	.a	Oa	Pa	In	Os	A.
Fur	24E	12N	Cm	Db	Ia	Ib	Pm	Va	Em	Mm	Lb	Oa	.f	Mr	Hm	Ca	Ss
Hausa (Kanawa)	9E	12N	Cm	Dn	In	Oo	Pm	Vd	L.	Pn	Nb	Sp	Oa	Pa	Hg	Ch	Sa
Kababish	30E	16N	Om	Oo	Dn	Oo	Oo	Bd	Em	Pu	Nb	Qp	Oa	Pa	Dc	Wb	Lp
Kanembu	14E	14N	Cm	Db	Ia	I.	Pm	Va	I.	Pp	Nb	La	Oa	Pa	.n	Ch	L.
Songhai	1W	17N	Cm	Dn	I.	I.	Pm	Va	In	Pp	Lb	Ld	O.	Pa	In	Ch	Lp
Soninke	9W	15N	Cm	Dn	I.	Oo	P.	Vd	Lm	Pp	Nb	Sa	Oa	Pa	..	Ch	.p
Wolof	17W	15N	Cm	Dn	Ib	Im	Pa	Vc	Lm	Pa	Nb	Ll	Ll	Dc	Hm	Ch	Sp
Zenaga (Mbarek)	7W	16N	Cm	Dm	Im	Oo	Oo	Va	Ln	Pp	Mb	Qa	Oa	Pa	..	Ch	Lp
Sahara																	
Berabish	5W	20N	Om	Oo	Dm	Oo	Oo	Bd	In	Pp	Lb	Qp	Oa	Pa	Dc	Ch	Ms
Mzab	4E	33N	Ts	Dm	Pb	Oo	Oo	Vb	In	Pn	Mb	S.	O.	P.	..	Oa	Mc
Siwans	26E	29N	Tm	Dm	I.	Oo	Oo	Vd	Ll	Pp	Mb	Sa	Oa	Pa	Dc	Ws	Mc
Teda (Tibesti)	17E	21N	Tm	Is	Dn	Oo	Pm	Sc	Lm	Pp	Lb	Ql	Of	Pf	Fl	Ch	Pp
Tuareg (Antessar)	5W	17N	Cm	Is	Dm	Oo	Pm	Bo	In	Pa	Mb	Oa	La	Mc	Id	Ch	Me
North Africa																	
Ancient Egyptians	31E	30N	Cm	Dn	Im	P.	Oo	Vo	In	Np	Mb	Oa	Oa	Ba	..	Ch	S.
Barabra	31E	21N	Cm	Dm	Ib	P.	Oo	Vd	In	Uu	Nb	Qa	Oa	Pa	Dn	Ws	Do
Beraber (Serruchen)	4W	33N	Cm	Im	Da	Oo	P.	Sa	Ln	Pp	Mb	Q.	O.	P.	..	Wo	Mc
Egyptians (Silwa)	33E	25N	Cm	Dm	In	P.	Oo	Vd	Ll	Uu	Lb	Qp	Oa	Pa	Dc	Co	Se
Guanche	16W	28N	Cm	Db	I.	Im	Oo	Vo	Ee	P.	Mb	Oa	..	Ma	..	Ho	Mm
Kabyle	4E	36N	Cm	Db	I.	Oo	Oo	V.	En	Pp	Lb	Qa	Oa	Pa	..	Oi	Lc
Riffians	4W	35N	Cm	Dm	Ib	P.	Pm	Vb	Lp	Pn	Lb	Sl	Oa	Pa	..	Wo	Mo
Shawiya	7E	35N	Cm	Dn	Ia	Oo	Oo	Vd	Ll	Pp	Mb	.p	Oa	Pa	..	..	D.
Shluh (Mountain)	9W	30N	Cm	Dm	Im	Pa	Pa	Vb	Ll	Pp	Mb	Ll	O.	P.	Dc	Oo	Mc
Ulad Nail	5E	34N	Om	Pm	Da	Oo	Pm	Sd	..	Pp	Nb	Qp	Oa	Pa	..	W.	Lp
Southern Europe																	
Albanians (Northern)	20E	42N	Cm	Ib	Dm	Oo	Oo	He	Ee	Pp	Lb	Se	Oa	Ka	Ec	Wo	Ms
Athenians (450 B.C.)	24E	38N	Cm	Dm	I.	Im	Oo	Ca	En	Pn	Md	Pa	Oa	Pa	El	Ch	Se
Basques (Labourd)	1W	43N	Cm	Dn	I.	Im	Oo	Ca	Ss	Bn	Md	O.	O.	B.	El	Co	De

TABLE 1. THIRTY CULTURAL CHARACTERISTICS AMONG SAMPLE PEOPLES (Continued)

Area and Culture	Location		1	2	3	4	5	6	7	8	9	10	11	12	13	14	15
Southern Europe (continued)																	
French (Provence)	4E	44N	Cm	Db	Ig	Im	Oo	Vd	Ss	Pn	Md	Od	Od	Kd	El	Co	Se
Italians (Sicily)	13E	38N	Cm	Db	Im	Im	Oo	Va	In	Pn	Md	Of	Of	Bf	El	Co	Se
Romans (100 A.D.)	12E	42N	Cm	Dm	I	Im	Oo	Va	In	N.	Md	Oa	Oa	Ba	Dn	Cb	Se
Spaniards (Andalusia)	6W	37N	Cm	Dn	Im	Oo	Oo	Va	In	Nn	Mo	Oa	Oa	Ba	El	Co	Sa
Overseas Europeans																	
Americans (New England)	72W	42N	Cm	Dm	Im	Im	Oo	Ca	In	Nn	Mo	Od	Od	Kd	El	Co	Se
Argentinians	62W	32S	Cm	Cm	Cm	Oo	Oo	Ca	Ln	Pn	Md	Oa	Oa	Ka	El	Co	Se
Brazilians (Bahia, 1650)	39W	12S	Rm	Ds	Ps	P.	Pm	Ha	Ll	Pn	Md	Oa	Oa	Ba	El	Wh	D.
French Canadians	72W	47N	Cm	Dn	Ia	Im	Oo	Va	In	Np	Md	Od	Od	Kd	El	Co	De
Transvaal Boers (1850)	28E	16S	Om	Ps	Dm	Oo	Pm	Na	Ln	Pn	Md	O.	O.	B.	El	Wl	Le
Northwest Europe																	
Danes (Lolland)	11E	55N	Cm	Db	Ia	Pm	Oo	Ca	In	Nn	Mo	Oa	Oa	Ba	Ed	Co	Se
Dutch (Anlo)	7E	53N	Cm	Dn	In	Pm	Oo	Va	Ll	Bn	Mo	Oa	Oa	Ka	El	Co	Sc
English (1600 A.D.)	0	52N	Cm	Dn	Ia	Im	Pm	Va	In	Np	Mo	O.	O.	K.	El	Co	Sa
Germans (Prussia)	14E	53N	Cm	Dn	Ia	Pm	Oo	Va	In	Nn	Md	Oa	Oa	Ba	El	Co	Se
Icelanders (1100 A.D.)	20W	64N	Om	Pn	Da	Im	Oo	Na	Ll	Pn	Md	O.	O.	B.	Dd	Hh	Lp
Irish (County Clare)	9W	53N	Rm	D.	Im	Pm	Oo	Ca	Ss	Pn	Md	Of	Of	Kg	Ed	Co	Se
Lapps (Lainiovuoma)	21W	68N	Om	Oo	Db	In	Im	Se	In	Ub	Ms	Od	Od	Kd	Ec	Wo	As
Eastern Europe																	
Bulgarians (Dragelevtsy)	23E	43N	Cm	Db	Ib	Oo	Oo	Va	Ln	Pn	Mo	O.	O.	B.	Dc	Co	S.
Cheremis	48E	56N	Cm	Db	I.	Oo	Pm	Va	In	Np	Md	Of	Of	Bg	..	Wo	D.
Czechs (Hana)	16E	50N	Cm	Db	If	Oo	Oo	Ca	Ss	Pn	Md	Od	Od	Kd	El	Co	Se
Finns	25E	64N	Cm	Dn	Ig	Im	Oo	Na	In	Nb	Mo	Of	Of	Bf	Ec	Co	Se
Hungarians	20E	47N	Cm	Db	I.	Pm	Oo	Nd	Ll	Pp	Mb	Of	Of	Bf	El	Co	S.
Hutsul	24E	49N	Cm	In	Da	Pm	Pm	Nd	In	Np	Md	Of	O.	K.	El	Wo	Do
Lithuanians	24E	55N	Cm	Dn	Ig	Pm	Oo	Va	Ll	Pn	Md	Of	Of	Kf	El	Co	Si
Rumanians	26E	45N	Cm	Db	Im	Pm	Oo	Hd	In	Np	Mo	Of	Of	Bf	El	Co	Sc
Russians (Soviet)	37E	56N	Cm	Dn	Ib	Pm	Oo	Va	In	Nb	Mo	Of	Of	Kf	El	Ci	Sa
Serbs (Orasac)	20E	44N	Cm	Db	Ig	Oo	Oo	Cb	Ll	Pn	Md	Ll	O.	P.	Hc	Co	Sc
Caucasia																	
Armenians	45E	40N	Cm	Dn	Ia	Oo	Pm	Va	En	Pp	Mb	Of	Of	Bf	Es	Co	Se
Chechen	46E	43N	Cm	Cn	C.	Oo	Pm	Vc	Ll	Pp	.b	Ss	O.	P.	..	..	D.
Circassians (Cherkess)	42E	44N	Cm	Cn	C.	Oo	Im	He	Ll	Pp	Nb	Ss	O.	P.	El	Hh	Mp
Georgians	45E	42N	Cm	Db	In	Pm	Pm	Ve	Ll	Pp	Md	Lf	Of	Pf	Ed	Cs	S.
Kalmyk (Baga Dorbed)	46E	46N	Om	Oo	Da	P.	Pa	Bc	En	Pn	Lb	Qs	Of	Ph	On	H.	Lp
Osset	44E	43N	Cm	Ca	C.	Oo	Pm	Vc	Ee	Pp	Lb	Ss	Oa	Pa	..	Hh	Pp
Scythians (150 B.C.)	40E	45N	Om	Ps	Dm	I.	Im	B.	E.	P.	G.	S.	O.	P.	..	Hs	Sa
Svan	43E	43N	Cm	Cn	C.	P.	Im	Vc	Ee	Pp	Mb	Ss	O.	P.	..	H.	Do
Near East																	
Babylonians (2000 B.C.)	45E	32N	Cm	Dm	I.	I.	Oo	Vd	.n	Bn	Mb	O.	O.	B.	..	Ch	S.
Bedouin (Rwala)	37E	33N	Om	Oo	Dm	Oo	Pa	Bd	Ip	Pp	Nb	Qf	Of	Kf	Dc	Wh	Lp
Hebrews (800 B.C.)	35E	32N	Cm	Dn	I.	Pm	Pm	V.	L.	Pp	Nb	Qa	Oa	Pa	Ec	Cs	S.
Kurd (Rowanduz)	45E	37N	Cm	Dn	Ia	Pm	Pm	Vd	Ep	Pp	Lb	Sp	Oa	Pa	Dc	Ho	Mp
Lebanese (Munsif)	36E	34N	Tm	Dm	I.	P.	Oo	Vd	Ln	Pn	Mo	Qf	Of	Pf	Dc	Co	Se
Turks (Anatolia)	30E	38N	Cm	Dn	Ia	Pm	Oo	Vd	Ss	Pn	Lb	Oa	Of	Kr	Dc	Co	Se
									EAST EURASIA								
Middle East																	
Afghan (Pushtun)	68E	33N	Cm	Dm	In	Oo	Oo	Fd	Ll	Pp	Lb	Qp	Oa	Pa	El	Ch	Se
Hazara (Urazgani)	67E	32N	Cm	Cm	Cn	Oo	Oo	Sd	Ll	Pp	Lb	Qf	Oa	Pa	..	Co	Ms
Iranians	52E	33N	Cm	Dn	Ia	P.	Oo	Vd	El	Pn	Lb	.p	Oa	Pa	Dc	Ch	Se
Lur (Bakhtiari)	48E	33N	Om	Pm	Dn	Oo	Pm	B.	..	Pp	Lb	Q.	O.	P.	Dc	Hs	Le

TABLE 1. THIRTY CULTURAL CHARACTERISTICS AMONG SAMPLE PEOPLES (Continued)

Area and Culture	Location		1	2	3	4	5	6	7	8	9	10	11	12	13	14	15
Middle East (continued)																	
Nuri (Kafir)	71E	36N	Cm	Dg	Im	Oo	Pm	V.	Ls	Pp	Gb	Sm	O.	Pf	..	Wh	Ms
Qashgai	52E	30N	Om	Oo	Da	Oo	Pm	Bc	..	Pp	Mb	Q.	O.	P.	..	H.	Sp
Sindhi	68E	25N	Cm	Dm	Ib	Pm	Oo	Vd	Ll	Pp	Lb	La	Oa	Pa	Dn	Ch	Di
Tajik (Mountain)	73E	37N	Cm	Cg	Cn	Oo	Pm	S.	Ll	Pp	Lb	Qa	Oa	Pa	..	Hh	Ms
Central Asia																	
Buryat	104E	52N	Om	Oo	Da	Oo	Ia	Sc	E.	Pp	Lb	Ss	Oa	Po	Bn	Hs	Mp
Dagor (Botaha)	125E	49N	Cm	Dn	Ia	Pm	Im	Vc	Ll	Pp	Mb	Ss	Of	Pd	Ie	Wo	Do
Kazak	70E	48N	Om	Oo	Da	Oo	Oo	Sc	Ll	Pp	Nb	Qs	Of	Ph	Oc	Hh	Sp
Khalka (Narobanchin)	97E	48N	Om	Pm	Da	Oo	Pm	S.	Sn	Pn	Mb	Ql	Of	Kf	On	Ho	Ls
Monguor	100E	39N	Cm	Db	Ia	Pm	Pm	Nb	Ll	Pp	Lb	Ss	O.	Pa	.n	Hs	Ms
Turkmen (Merv)	62E	38N	Cm	Dm	Ia	Oo	Oo	Vc	Ep	Pp	Lb	Ql	O.	Pm	Mc	Hs	Ls
Uzbek (Kongrat)	60E	43N	Cm	I.	Dn	I.	Pm	S.	Ll	Pp	Gb	Qa	Oa	Pc	Oc	H.	L.
Arctic Asia																	
Ainu (Hokkaido)	144E	44N	Go	Oo	Oo	Dn	Ia	Vd	Im	Bn	Go	Oa	Oa	Ba	Fl	Oo	Dp
Chukchee (Reindeer)	177E	66N	Ol	Oo	Dn	Im	Ia	Ba	Im	Um	Ns	Oa	Oa	Ba	El	Wi	Al
Gilyak	142E	53N	Go	Oo	Oo	Dm	Ia	Sa	Ip	Pp	Sb	Ss	Of	Pm	Im	Oo	Oo
Goldi	132E	47N	Os	Pf	P.	Db	Im	Ve	Ll	Rp	.b	Ss	Oa	Po	.c	Os	D.
Ket	90E	62N	Ol	Oo	Pm	Im	Dn	S.	In	Pn	Mb	Ss	O.	P.	..	Oo	Oo
Koryak (Maritime)	164E	62N	Ol	Oo	Im	Dn	Ia	Vo	Ll	Um	Ls	Of	Of	Bf	El	Wi	Al
Ostyak (Southern)	74E	62N	Ol	Oo	Im	Dm	Im	S.	I.	Pp	Gb	Ss	Oa	Pa	O.	Ws	A.
Samoyed (Yurak)	75E	68N	Ol	Oo	Dm	Im	Im	S.	Ip	Pp	Lb	Ss	Oa	Pm	Fl	Wo	A.
Yakut	125E	65N	Ol	Oo	Dn	Im	Im	Sc	Ls	Pp	Gb	Qs	Oa	Pa	On	Ws	Lp
Yukaghir	145E	72N	Oo	Oo	Oo	Im	Dm	Se	Ss	Mu	Ls	Of	Of	Bf	..	Oi	Ai
East Asia																	
Cantonese	113E	23N	Cl	Dn	Ig	Pn	Oo	Vc	Ls	Pp	Lb	Ss	Oa	Pa	Hc	Ci	Di
Chinese (Shantung)	118E	37N	Cl	Dn	Im	Pm	Oo	Vb	Ll	Pp	Md	Ss	Oa	Pa	De	Co	Sa
Ch'i-tan (1000 A.D.)	118E	42N	Om	Pf	Dn	Im	Pm	S.	E.	Pn	G.	Ql	O.	Pc	..	Ch	Sp
Japanese	136E	35N	Cm	Db	In	Im	Oo	Va	Ss	Pn	Mo	Oa	Oa	Ba	El	Co	Se
Koreans	127E	38N	Cl	Db	I.	In	Oo	Ve	Se	Pn	Mo	Ss	Of	Pf	Ec	Ci	Si
Lolo	102E	27N	Cl	Db	Ib	Pb	Pm	Vc	Lm	Pp	Lb	Ss	Of	Pc	Dd	Hh	As
Manchu	126E	45N	Cl	Dn	Ib	Pf	Oo	Vc	Ee	Pp	Mb	Ss	Oa	Pa	Ie	Wi	De
Miao	106E	28N	Cl	Db	If	Pm	Pm	Vb	Ll	Pp	Lb	Sf	Of	Ka	Md	Oo	..
Minchia	100E	26N	Cm	Db	In	Im	Oo	Vd	Ll	Pp	Lb	La	Ca	Pa	Uc	Co	De
Okinawans	128E	26N	R1	Db	If	Im	Oo	Vb	Ss	Pn	Mo	Sf	Od	Ka	El	Ho	De
Himalayas																	
Abor	95E	28N	Cl	Db	I.	Pm	Im	V.	Ip	Pp	Gb	Ns	O.	Po	..	Wh	Ae
Burusho	75E	37N	Cm	Db	Im	Oo	Oo	V.	Ll	Pp	Lt	Sc	Of	Pf	Hm	Co	L.
Dard (Shina)	73E	35N	Cs	Db	Im	Oo	Pm	Va	L.	Pp	Nb	Ss	Of	Pf	In	Co	L.
Lepcha	89E	28N	Cm	Db	I.	Oo	Pa	Ne	Ll	Pp	Mb	Ss	Of	Pg	Hn	Wh	Ds
Nepalese (Kiranti)	87E	27N	Cm	Db	In	Oo	Oo	V.	Em	Pp	Gt	Sl	O.	P.	Ho	Cs	S.
Tibetans (Central)	91E	30N	Cm	Db	Ib	Oo	Pm	F.	Sp	Pm	Yb	Ss	Oa	Pa	Fc	Cs	Sa
North & Central India																	
Aryans (800 B.C.)	75E	30N	Cm	Dg	I.	Oo	Pm	Vc	El	Pp	Gb	Sl	Of	Kg	Hm	C.	Sp
Bengali (Western)	88E	23N	Cm	Dm	Im	Im	Oo	V.	E.	Pp	Lb	Sm	Of	Pg	He	Co	D.
Bhil	74E	22N	Cm	Db	I.	Pb	Pa	Ne	Ip	Pu	Nb	Sm	Of	Pf	..	Co	Ds
Ho	85E	22N	Cm	Dn	I.	I.	Im	Ve	Ep	Pp	Sb	Ss	O.	Pd	Ie	Ho	Sa
Kol	85E	24N	Cm	Dn	In	Oo	Oo	Ve	Ip	Pp	Lb	Of	Of	Bf	He	Co	Di
Oraon	85E	23N	Cm	Dn	In	Pm	Pn	Ve	In	Pp	Lb	Ss	Of	Pf	He	Ci	Me
Santal	87E	24N	Cl	Db	In	Im	Ia	Ve	Ln	Pm	Lb	Sm	O.	Pf	De	Oo	Ms
South India																	
Baiga	81E	22N	Co	Db	Oo	Ib	Ia	Fc	Ip	Pp	Gb	Ss	Of	Pa	Ie	Oo	A.
Bondo	82E	18N	Cl	Db	I.	Pf	Oo	Vc	Ip	Pp	Lb	Ns	O.	Pa	Ie	.o	D.
Chenchu	79E	16N	Go	Oo	Oo	Pm	Db	Se	En	Bb	Mb	Ps	Of	Pn	In	Oo	Ai
Coorg	76E	12N	Cm	Dm	In	Pm	Pm	N.	Ee	Pp	.o	Ss	Of	Pa	Ie	Ch	Sp
Gond (Hill Maria)	80E	21N	Cs	Db	I.	P.	Ia	Vc	Ee	Pp	Sb	Ps	O.	Pc	Ie	Wo	Mp
Kerala (Nayar)	76E	9N	Cm	Ds	Is	Ps	Ps	Va	Ee	Da	Yo	Od	Qs	Ma	In	Ch	Sy

TABLE 1. THIRTY CULTURAL CHARACTERISTICS AMONG SAMPLE PEOPLES (Continued)

Area and Culture	Location		1	2	3	4	5	6	7	8	9	10	11	12	13	14	15
South India (continued)																	
Tamil (Tanjore)	79E	11N	Cm	Ds	Is	Oo	Oo	Va	Ll	Pp	Md	Qs	Of	Pc	Mn	Ch	Se
Telugu (Shamirpet)	79E	18N	Cm	Dn	I.	Oo	Oo	Va	Ll	Pp	Ld	Ss	Of	Pn	Im	Co	Dp
Toda	77E	12N	Om	Oo	Dm	Oo	Oo	Sc	Ip	Pp	Yd	Ss	Ss	Dc	Im	Oo	Ac
Indian Ocean																	
Andamanese (Akar-Bale)	93E	12N	Go	Oo	Oo	Ca	Ca	Sa	In	Bb	Mo	Of	Of	Bf	El	Oo	Oo
Antandroy	45E	25S	Rm	Ig	Dm	In	Oo	V.	Em	Pp	Gb	Sd	Of	Pd	..	Hh	Mp
Merina (Hova)	46E	19S	Cm	Db	Im	Pg	Oo	Vd	Em	Pp	Gt	Sp	Ol	Pd	Hg	Hh	Sa
Nicobarese	94E	7N	Ts	Dn	Pf	Im	Im	Ha	In	Mp	Lo	Of	Of	Bf	El	Wo	Ai
Sinhalese (Kandyan)	80E	7N	Cm	Db	I.	Pm	Oo	Fa	In	Pm	Md	Lf	Of	Pc	In	Co	S.
Tanala (Menabe)	47E	22S	Cm	Db	Im	In	Oo	Vb	Em	Pp	Nt	Sl	Ol	Pc	Id	Hh	Me
Vedda	81E	8N	Go	Oo	Oo	Im	Da	Sc	Ll	Mm	Mo	O.	Ss	Mc	Ic	Oo	A.
Assam & Burma																	
Ao (Chongli)	94E	27N	Cl	Db	I.	Pm	Pm	Vb	In	Pp	Mt	Ps	Of	Pf	Oa	Wh	Oo
Burmese	95E	20N	Cl	Db	I.	Im	Oo	Vd	In	Mn	Md	Oa	Oa	Ba	Hl	Cs	Sa
Chakma	92E	23N	Cl	Db	I.	Oo	Pm	Vo	..	Pu	.b	Ll	Of	Pg	Dc	Hh	Ls
Garo	91E	26N	Cl	Db	Ib	Ib	Pn	Vb	Ss	Mp	Lo	Of	Ms	Mn	Ic	Wo	Mn
Kachin (Jinghpaw)	97E	26N	Cl	Db	I.	Oo	Pa	Vb	Ll	Pp	Lb	Ql	Of	Pm	Om	Hh	Ms
Karen	97E	17N	Cl	Db	I.	Ib	Pm	Va	In	Mm	Mt	Oa	La	Ma	El	Wi	As
Khasi	92E	26N	Cl	Db	I.	P.	Im	Vb	Ls	Mm	Mo	Of	Ss	Md	In	C.	My
Lakher	93E	22N	Cl	Db	I.	Im	Im	Va	In	Pp	Mb	Sd	Oa	Pm	Hm	Hh	Ms
Mikir	93E	26N	Cl	Db	I.	P.	Im	V.	Ll	Pp	Lo	Ps	O.	Pm	.c	O.	Ae
Palaung (Katur)	97E	23N	Cl	Db	I.	Oo	Oo	Va	Ip	Pp	Lb	S.	O.	P.	..	W.	L.
Rengma	94E	26N	Cl	Db	I.	Pm	Im	Vd	Im	Pn	Lb	Ps	O.	Pm	Oc	Wo	Ap
Thado	94E	25N	Cl	Db	I.	I.	Im	V.	.s	Pp	Lb	Ss	O.	Pm	Om	Wi	As
Southeast Asia																	
Akha	100E	21N	Cl	Db	Ib	Pb	In	Va	Ip	Pp	Lo	Ll	Of	Pf	Ic	Oo	Ab
Cambodians	105E	12N	Cl	Db	In	Im	Oo	V.	In	Ww	Lb	Oa	Oa	Ba	El	Ch	Sl
Lamet	101E	20N	Cl	Db	Ib	Oo	Is	Va	Ep	Up	Lb	Ss	Of	Po	Mm	Wo	As
Malay (Trengganu)	103E	5N	Cl	Db	Pb	Im	Oo	Na	Ln	Un	Lb	O.	O.	Ka	Hl	Cl	Sp
Muong	105E	21N	Cl	Db	I.	Ib	Pm	Vc	Ee	Pp	Lb	Sm	Of	Pd	..	Ho	Ms
Selung	98E	12N	Go	Oo	Oo	Dn	Pn	Ba	In	Nu	Mo	O.	O.	B.	Fl	Oo	Oo
Semang	102E	5N	Go	Oo	Oo	Im	Dn	Be	Im	Uu	Lo	Of	Of	Bf	Hl	Oo	Oo
Thai	100E	15N	Cl	Db	Ib	Im	Oo	Vd	Ss	Mm	Lt	Oa	Oa	Ka	Hl	Ch	Se
Vietnamese	107E	17N	Cl	Db	I.	In	Oo	Va	Ll	Pm	Nt	Ss	Of	Pf	Hc	Ch	Se
								INSULAR PACIFIC									
Philippines & Formosa																	
Aeta (Bataan)	120E	15N	Ro	Da	Oo	Pn	In	S.	In	..	Lb	Oa	Oa	Ba	.l	Oo	Oo
Atayal	121E	24N	Cs	Dg	Pf	Pm	Im	Va	In	Pn	Mb	Lf	Of	Pg	Hl	Oi	Ae
Hanunoo	121E	13N	Cl	Db	In	Pn	In	Hd	Ep	Mm	Ts	Of	Of	Kh	El	Oo	Oo
Ifugao	121E	17N	Cs	Df	P.	Pg	Im	Ha	In	Bb	Mb	Of	Of	Kh	Hg	Wh	Oo
Kalinga	121E	18N	Cl	Da	I.	Pn	In	Hd	In	Mp	Mo	Of	Of	Kg	El	Wo	Oo
Manobo	126E	8N	Cs	Dg	P.	P.	Pm	Ne	In	Uu	Lb	Of	Of	Bh	Hl	Oi	Ai
Subanun (Sindangan)	123E	8N	Cs	Db	P.	Oo	Pm	Na	In	Xw	Lb	Oa	Oa	Ka	Hl	Oo	Oo
Tagalog	121E	14N	Cl	Db	I.	In	Oo	Va	In	N.	M.	Of	Of	Bf	Hg	Co	Se
Tagbanua	119E	10N	Cl	Db	I.	Pn	Pm	Cd	Im	Mm	Tt	Od	Od	Kd	Eg	Hi	Pl
Yami	122E	22N	Rs	Db	Pf	Ia	Oo	Va	In	Pp	Mo	Of	Of	Kf	..	Oo	Ac
Western Indonesia																	
Balinese	115E	8S	Cl	Dm	In	Pm	Oo	Vd	Ln	Pm	Lt	Lp	Oa	Pa	Hg	Hl	Le
Batak (Toba)	99E	2N	Cl	Dn	In	Oo	Oo	Va	Ll	Pm	Lb	Ss	Of	Pm	Xg	Oa	Ap
Dusun	117E	6N	Cl	Db	Ib	I.	Pm	Vd	Ic	Up	Mb	Of	Of	Bh	Hl	Wh	Ms
Iban	112E	2N	Cs	Db	I.	In	Pn	Va	Ic	Xb	Ms	Oa	Oa	Ka	Ed	Oh	Al
Javanese	110E	7S	Cl	Db	Im	Im	Oo	Va	In	Bn	Lo	Od	Oa	Ba	El	Ch	Se
Kubu (Ridan)	103E	3S	Go	Oo	Oo	I.	Da	B.	In	Xx	Ls	Of	Of	Bg	..	Oo	A.
Maanyan (Siong)	115E	1S	Cs	Dn	P.	Pm	Pm	Vd	In	Mp	Mo	O.	S.	M.	..	.h	M.

TABLE 1. THIRTY CULTURAL CHARACTERISTICS AMONG SAMPLE PEOPLES (Continued)

Area and Culture	Location		1	2	3	4	5	6	7	8	9	10	11	12	13	14	15
Western Indonesia (continued)																	
Mentawelans (N Pageh)	100E	3S	Rs	Dg	P.	In	Pm	Vb	In	Pp	Ms	Ll	Oa	Pa	Fc	Oo	Oo
Minangkabau	101E	1S	Cl	Db	1.	Pn	Oo	Vb	Ee	Dd	Lo	Of	Ps	Mc	Hm	Wo	Ac
Eastern Indonesia																	
Alfur (W Ceram)	129E	3S	To	Dg	Oo	Oo	Im	V.	In	Pu	Lb	Lf	Of	Po	..	.s	Mp
Alorese (Atimelang)	125E	8S	Cs	Dg	P.	Oo	Ia	Ce	In	Pp	Lb	Of	Of	Bf	H.	Wi	A.
Belu (Mountain)	126E	9S	Cl	Db	Ib	Oo	Oo	Hb	Ep	Mm	Gb	Of	Ss	Mm	Hm	Ch	Mm
Ili-Mandiri (E Flores)	123E	8S	Cs	Db	P.	Ia	Pm	V.	Ll	Pu	Lb	Ss	O.	Pn	..	H.	Sp
Kei Islanders	133E	6S	Rs	D.	P.	1.	Pm	V.	En	Pp	Mb	Ss	O.	Pm	..	Oh	Ap
Macassarese	119E	5S	Cl	Dn	Im	Im	Oo	Hd	In	Mp	Mb	Of	Of	Kf	El	Ch	Lp
Rotinese	123E	11S	Cl	Db	1.	P.	Oc	V.	Ip	Pp	Gb	Ss	Oa	Pc	In	Hs	M
Sumbanese (Eastern)	120E	10S	Cl	Da	1.	Oo	Pm	Nc	Ss	Pp	Lg	Ss	Of	Pm	..	Hh	Mp
Tanimbarese	131E	6S	Rs	Dg	Pf	Im	Im	Va	Ll	Uu	Lb	Ll	Of	Pu	Hm	Hi	As
Tobelorese	128E	1N	Cs	Db	P.	Ia	Pm	Ve	Ee	Pm	Mb	Of	Of	Bf	..	.s	Di
Toraja (Bare'e)	121E	2S	Cl	Db	1.	Oo	Im	Va	Es	Mm	Mb	Od	Od	Bd	Hl	Ws	Ae
Australia																	
Aranda	134E	24S	Go	Oo	Oo	Oo	Da	Bc	Ip	Pp	Sx	Mm	Ms	Sf	Im	Oo	As
Dieri	129E	28S	Go	Oo	Oo	P.	Da	Bc	Ip	Pp	Sx	Ms	Ms	Sf	Im	Oo	Ap
Karadjeri	122E	18S	Go	Oo	Oo	Da	Ia	Bc	1.	Pp	.o	Ms	Ms	So	.m	Oo	A.
Kariera	118E	21S	Go	Oo	Oo	Im	Da	Bc	Ip	Pp	Sx	Ms	Ms	Sc	Im	Oo	Ap
Murngin	136E	12S	Go	Oo	Oo	Ia	Da	Bc	Ip	Uu	Ss	Ms	Ms	Sm	Mm	Oo	As
Tasmanians	146E	42S	Go	Oo	Oo	If	Da	Be	In	P.	L.	..	..	..	..	Oo	Oo
Tiwi	131E	12S	Go	Oo	Oo	Ia	Da	Bd	En	Pm	Gx	Of	Ms	Mr	Mm	Oo	Ai
Wongaibon	146E	32S	Go	Oo	Oo	P.	Da	Bc	In	Pp	Tx	Ms	Ms	Sf	Im	Oo	Ap
Yiryoront	142E	15S	Go	Oo	Oo	Im	Da	Bc	Ip	Uu	So	Ms	Of	Pm	M.	Oo	Ai
Yungar (Pibelman)	115E	34S	Gc	Oo	Oo	In	Da	Bc	Ip	Pp	G.	Ss	Ms	Dc	Im	Oo	A.
New Guinea																	
Arapesh	144E	4S	Rs	Db	Pf	Oo	Pm	Hb	Ip	Pp	Go	Ns	Of	Pf	Oc	Oo	Oo
Banaro	145E	4S	Rs	Dg	P.	Pm	Pm	Hb	In	Pp	Mx	Ss	O.	Pc	Hm	Ao	Oo
Kapauku	136E	4S	Rs	Db	If	Ig	Pm	Vc	Ll	Pp	Gb	Ss	Of	Pf	Im	Wo	Pi
Keraki	142E	9S	Rs	Db	Pf	Pa	Pm	Vc	Ip	Pp	Gx	Ms	Of	Pa	Ic	Oo	Ab
Kiwai	143E	9S	Ro	Db	Oo	Ia	Pm	Vb	Ec	Pp.	Lx	Ss	Of	Pf	Id	Oo	Ac
Kutubu	143E	6S	Ts	Db	Pf	Pa	Pm	Va	Es	Pp	Gb	Sm	O.	Pf	Ic	Oo	Oo
Mailu	149E	10S	Rs	Db	P.	Ia	Pa	Vb	Ll	Pp	Mg	Ss	O.	P.	Mm	Oo	Oo
Miriam	144E	10S	Rs	Df	P.	In	Oo	Vc	Ip	Pp	Lx	Sm	Of	Pf	Um	Oo	Oo
Orokaiva	148E	9S	Rs	Da	Pb	Pa	Pn	Va	Im	Pp	Lb	Ss	O.	Pa	Im	Oo	Ai
Waropen	137E	2S	Ts	Cb	Pm	Cm	Pm	Vb	Ee	Pp	Lg	Sl	O.	Pm	Im	Oi	Oo
Wogeo	144E	3S	Rs	Db	P.	Pm	Pn	Vb	Ip	Pp	Go	Ll	Ms	Dd	1.	Oo	Oo
Micronesia																	
Chamorro (Saipan)	145E	15N	Cr	Db	I.	Oo	Oo	Vo	In	Nn	Mo	Of	Of	Bg	El	Wo	De
Gilbertese (Onotoa)	175E	2S	To	Cb	Oo	Ca	Oo	V.	Ee	Pp	Sb	Ll	Of	Kb	Hg	Wi	Ac
Ifaluk	147E	7N	Ts	Db	P.	Ia	Oo	Vb	El	Mm	Mo	Of	Ss	Kf	Hm	Oo	Ay
Kusaians	163E	6N	To	Dn	Oo	Ia	Oo	No	Im	Pp	Lo	Of	Sl	Ma	Hg	Ho	M.
Marshallese (Bikini)	165E	12N	Ts	Cm	P.	Ca	Oo	Vd	En	Ms	Lo	Of	Ss	Mc	Im	Oo	Do
Nauruans	167E	1S	To	Db	Oo	Ia	Pa	N.	Ll	Mm	Go	Of	Ss	Kc	Im	Hi	Ay
Palauans	135E	7N	Ro	Dg	Oo	Im	Oo	Ve	El	Yp	Lb	Of	Ss	Mh	Hc	Ho	My
Ponapeans	158E	7N	Ro	Dn	Oo	In	Oo	Na	In	Ma	Lo	Od	Ss	Mc	Cm	Ho	Mm
Trukese	152E	7N	Ts	Cb	Pf	Ca	Oo	Hb	Ee	Ms	Mo	Of	Sm	Mf	Cg	Oo	Am
Yapese	138E	9N	Ts	Dg	Pf	Im	Oo	Na	En	Pa	Mo	Ll	Ss	Df	Cm	Co	M.
Western Melanesia																	
Aua	143E	2S	Rs	In	P.	Da	Pn	Va	Im	Dd	So	Oa	La	Ma	..	Oo	Ms
Bougainville (Siuai)	155E	6S	Rs	Db	Pf	Pb	Pm	Hb	Ip	Yb	Gb	Of	Ss	Mn	Hm	Wo	Al
Buka (Kurtatchi)	154E	5S	Rs	Df	P.	Ia	Ia	He	Im	Bb	Sb	Of	Ss	Kg	Im	Ho	An
Dobuans	151E	10S	Rs	Db	P.	Im	Pm	Vc	In	Vm	Mo	Of	Sl	Mf	Im	Oo	Oo
Malaitans	161E	9S	Rs	Db	P.	Ia	Ia	Va	In	Pp	Lb	Of	Of	Bg	Im	Oo	As
Manus	147E	2S	Os	Oo	P.	Dn	Oo	Vb	In	Pp	Mg	Lm	Ll	Df	Cc	Wo	Ap
Nakanai (Western)	151E	5S	Rs	Db	If	Ia	Im	Hb	Ll	Yp	Lb	Of	Nl	Mc	In	Wo	Oo

TABLE 1. THIRTY CULTURAL CHARACTERISTICS AMONG SAMPLE PEOPLES (Continued)

Area and Culture	Location		1	2	3	4	5	6	7	8	9	10	11	12	13	14	15
Western Melanesia (continued)																	
New Ireland (Lesu)	153E	3S	Rs	Cs	Pf	Ca	Pm	Hb	Im	Mm	Lb	Of	Ms	Mf	Im	Oo	Al
Rossel Islanders	154E	12S	Te	Dg	P.	Im	Pm	Vo	In	Pu	Lb	O.	Ss	Mf	Cm	Wo	Ms
Trobrianders	151E	8S	Rs	Db	Pf	Ia	Oo	Vc	In	Ap	Lg	Od	Ps	Mp	Cm	Ho	Mn
Ulawans	161E	10S	Rs	Dg	P.	Im	Oo	Ho	In	Pp	Lb	Of	Of	Kf	Hm	Oo	Ap
Eastern Melanesia																	
Ambrym (Ranon)	168E	16S	Rs	Db	I.	..	Oo	Vb	..	Pp	Tx	Sm	Ms	Sg	Om	Wo	Ac
Banks Islanders (Mota)	168E	14S	Rs	D	In	Im	Oo	Vb	Ip	Ay	Sb	Of	Ms	Mf	Cm	Wo	Al
Espiritu Santo (Tismulun)	167E	16S	Rs	D.	I.	..	Oo	Ve	..	Pp	.b	Of	Ss	Mp	Hm	Wo	A.
Lau Fijians	179E	18S	Rs	Dn	P.	Ia	Pa	Vc	Ll	Pm	So	Sl	O.	Pc	In	Ho	Mb
Loyalty Islanders (Lifu)	167E	21S	Rs	Df	P.	In	Oo	Vc	Em	Pp	Gb	Ss	Of	Pg	Hm	Hs	Ms
Malekulans (Seniang)	167E	17S	Rs	Db	In	Im	Oo	Vc	Ip	Pp	Sb	Sm	Of	Pg	Cn	Wo	Ms
New Caledonians (Ajie)	165E	22S	Rs	Dg	P.	I.	Oo	Vc	..	Pp	Gx	Ss	O.	Pc	Im	Oo	Ms
Rotumans	177E	13S	Rs	Dm	P.	Im	Oo	Vb	I.	Ms	.o	Of	Ll	Mf	Hg	Oo	M.
Tannese (Whitesands)	168E	20S	Rs	Db	P.	P.	Oo	Vc	Ip	Pp	Sb	Ld	Od	Pc	In	Ho	As
Vanua Levu (Nakoroka)	179E	17S	Rs	Dn	P.	I.	Pa	Vc	Ll	Pm	Lo	Lf	Ms	Df	Im	Oo	Mp
Western Polynesia																	
Ellice Islanders	178E	8S	Ts	Cn	P.	Ca	Oo	Vo	Ll	B.	Lo	Of	Of	Kf	Hg	Oo	M.
Kapingamarangi	155E	1N	Rs	Cf	P.	Cm	Oo	Vd	Ln	Bb	Mo	O.	O.	K.	Hg	Oo	As
Ontong-Javanese	160E	5S	To	Cg	Oo	Cm	Oo	Va	Ee	Mp	Lo	Lm	Lf	Dh	Hm	Wo	A.
Pukapukans	166W	11S	Ts	Cf	P.	Ca	Oo	Va	In	Pp	Mo	Lf	Nl	Kg	Eg	Oo	As
Rennell Islanders	161E	11S	Ro	Dn	Oo	Im	Oo	No	En	..	Lo	Of	Of	Bc	In	Ho	As
Samoans (Manua)	170W	14S	Ts	Dg	Pn	Ia	Oo	Va	Ee	Bx	Lo	Of	Of	Kg	Hg	Ho	Ms
Tikopia	168E	12S	Ro	Cg	Oo	Ca	Oo	Ha	In	Pp	Gg	Sl	Of	Kf	Hm	Ho	Ap
Tokelau	172W	9S	Ts	Im	P.	Da	Oo	Vd	En	Mu	Lo	Of	Of	Kg	Om	Oo	Mp
Tongans	174W	20S	Rs	Dn	Pm	Ia	Oo	Va	Ep	Pm	Lo	Of	Of	Kd	Hm	Ho	Ls
Eastern Polynesia																	
Easter Islanders	109W	27S	Ro	Dn	Oo	In	Oo	Vo	Ll	Pm	Lo	Of	Of	Bf	Hg	Hi	As
Hawaiians	156W	20N	Rs	Cm	P.	Ca	Oo	Vo	El	Bb	To	Od	Od	Kd	Hg	Hh	Ls
Manihikians	160W	10S	To	C.	Oo	Ca	Oo	Vo	Ll	Pm	Lo	Oa	Oa	Ka	Hg	Ho	As
Mangaians	158W	22S	Ro	Df	Oo	Ia	Oo	Ne	Ll	Pm	Go	Of	Of	Kg	Hg	Hi	Mb
Maori (North Island)	175E	35S	Ro	Dn	Oo	Ia	In	Va	Ee	Bb	Go	Of	Of	Kf	Hg	Hi	Ms
Marquesans	140W	9S	Ts	Dm	P.	In	Oo	Na	Ip	Pn	Yo	Of	Of	Ko	Hm	Oo	Ms
Raroians	142W	16S	To	Cn	Oo	Ca	Oo	Na	En	Bn	Lo	O.	O.	K.	Hg	Oo	As
Tahitians	152W	18S	Ts	Dn	P.	Ia	Oo	Vo	Ee	Bb	Lo	Of	Of	Kf	Hg	Ho	Ms
NORTH AMERICA																	
Arctic America																	
Aleut	167W	54N	Oo	Oo	Oo	Dn	Ia	Va	Ee	Um	Gs	Oa	Oa	Bs	En	Hb	As
Caribou Eskimo	96W	64N	Oo	Oo	Oo	Im	Dn	Sd	Ip	Pm	Gb	Of	Of	Bf	Ec	Oo	Oo
Carrier (Upper)	124W	54N	Oo	Oo	Oo	Cn	Ca	Sa	Ll	Mu	Sb	Of	Ps	Mc	Ic	Hb	An
Cree (Attawapiskat)	83W	53N	Go	Oo	Oo	Dm	Ia	Sa	Ip	Um	Ss	Of	Of	Bc	Ic	Oo	Al
Kaska	128W	59N	Oo	Oo	Oo	Db	Ia	S.	In	Mm	Ms	Of	Ms	Mm	Cc	Oo	Oo
Kutchin	140W	67N	Oc	Oo	Oo	Cb	Cm	Sd	Ss	Pm	Lo	O.	Ss	M.	Hc	Wi	As
Naskapi (Northern)	70W	58N	Oo	Oo	Oo	I.	Da	Bs	Ip	Bb	Lx	Of	Of	Bc	Ic	Oo	Al
Nunivak Eskimo	166W	60N	Oo	Oo	Oo	Db	Im	Va	Ll	Uu	Lo	Ld	Od	Pa	Ic	Wo	Ai
Polar Eskimo	70W	78N	Oo	Oo	Oo	Dn	In	Sa	In	Bn	Mo	O.	O.	B.	Ec	Oo	Oo
Slave	120W	61N	Oo	Oo	Oo	In	Dm	Ss	Ip	Mm	Ss	Of	Of	Bf	Hc	Oo	Al
Tanaina	144W	62N	Oo	Oo	Oo	Dm	Ia	Va	Ll	Ua	Nb	Of	Ms	Mg	Ic	Ho	As
Northwest Coast																	
Alsea	124W	44N	Oo	Oo	Oo	D.	I.	Ve	Ll	Pm	Lb	Of	Of	Bf	Hc	Hh	Al
Bellacoola	127W	52N	Go	Oo	Oo	Dm	Ia	Va	Ll	Pm	Ng	Of	Of	Kf	Hc	Wh	Ap
Eyak	145W	61N	Oo	Oo	Oo	Dm	Ia	Va	Ll	Va	Gs	Of	Ms	Ma	Ic	Hi	Ay
Haida (Masset)	132W	54N	Go	Oo	Oo	Dm	Ia	Vc	Ll	Va	Ls	Of	Ms	Mq	Cc	Hh	Ay

TABLE 1. THIRTY CULTURAL CHARACTERISTICS AMONG SAMPLE PEOPLES (Continued)

Area and Culture	Location		1	2	3	4	5	6	7	8	9	10	11	12	13	14	15
Northwest Coast (continued)																	
Nootka	125W	49N	Go	Oo	Oo	Dn	Ia	Ve	Ee	Pm	Sg	Of	Of	Bg	Hl	Ch	Ms
Puyallup	122W	47N	Go	Oo	Oo	Cn	Ca	Va	Ee	Pm	Gb	Of	Of	Kf	Hl	Hi	Ai
Quileute	124W	48N	Go	Oo	Oo	Dm	Ia	Ve	Ee	Pp	Gb	Of	Of	Bg	.1	Hs	A.
Stalo (Halkomelem)	122W	49N	Go	Oo	Oo	Dm	Ia	Ve	Ee	Pm	Gg	Of	Of	Bg	Hl	Hh	Ap
Takelma	123W	43N	Go	Oo	Oo	I.	Da	Se	..	Pp	Gb	Of	Of	Bf	Mc	Ws	Oo
Tlingit	134W	58N	Oo	Oo	Oo	Dm	Ia	Sc	Ll	As	Lo	Of	Ms	Mr	Cc	Hh	An
Tolowa	124W	42N	Go	Oo	Oo	Cm	Ca	Sc	Ip	Pm	Gb	Ll	Oa	Po	Ic	Wi	Ai
Yurok	124W	41N	Go	Oo	Oo	Cm	Ca	Ve	Ll	Pu	Gb	Of	Of	Bh	Hl	Wo	Oo
California																	
Atsugewi	121W	41N	Go	Oo	Oo	Im	Da	Se	Ip	Uu	St	Of	Of	Bh	Ec	Wo	As
Diegueno (Southern)	116W	32N	Go	Oo	Oo	Oo	Da	Se	Ip	Pu	So	Ss	Of	Pg	Ic	Oo	As
Luiseno	117W	33N	Go	Oo	Oo	I.	Da	Se	Ip	Pp	Sb	Ll	Of	Pg	Ic	Oo	Ap
Maidu (Mountain)	121W	40N	Go	Oo	Oo	Pb	Dn	Se	Lp	Pu	Ss	Of	Of	Bg	Ic	Wo	Ms
Miwok (Central Sierra)	120W	38N	Go	Oo	Oo	P.	D.	Vc	Ip	Pu	So	Ms	Of	Pf	Om	Oo	As
Pomo (Clear Lake)	123W	39N	Go	Oo	Oo	Im	Da	Va	Ll	Bb	Lo	Of	Of	Bf	Oc	Wo	An
Shasta (Eastern)	123W	41N	Go	Oo	Oo	In	Da	Ve	Ll	Pm	Lb	Of	Of	Bg	Ic	Wi	Mb
Tubatulabal	118W	36N	Go	Oo	Oo	In	Da	Sa	In	Pu	Mb	Of	Of	Bg	Hc	Oo	As
Wappo	122W	38N	Go	Oo	Oo	Im	Dn	Sd	Ll -	Bb	Mo	Of	Of	Bh	Cc	Oo	Ai
Wintun (Nomlaki)	122W	39N	Go	Oo	Oo	In	Da	Vc	In	Uu	Lo	Ss	Of	Pf	Oc	Wo	As
Yana	122W	40N	Go	Oo	Oo	In	Da	Sa	Ll	Up	So	Of	Of	Bg	Ec	Wi	As
Yokuts (N Foothills)	120W	36N	Go	Oo	Oo	Cu	Cn	Sa	Em	Uu	Gb	Ms	Of	Pg	Hc	Wo	Ab
Yuki	123W	40N	Go	Oo	Oo	Cn	Ca	Ha	In	Up	Lo	Of	Of	Bh	Hc	Wo	As
Great Basin & Plateau																	
Havasupai	112W	36N	Co	Dm	Oo	Oo	Ia	Sd	Ep	Uu	Lt	Of	Of	Bg	Ic	Oo	Ap
Hukundika	112W	42N	Go	Oo	Oo	I.	Dn	Sd	Ll	Bb	So	Of	Of	Bh	Hn	Oo	As
Klamath	122W	43N	Go	Oo	Oo	Dn	Ia	Sa	Ll	Pp	Tb	Of	Of	Bh	Hc	Wi	Pi
Kutenai	117W	50N	Go	Oo	Oo	Dm	Ia	So	En	Xx	Lo	Of	Of	Bh	Hc	Oi	Ai
Paiute (Surprise Valley)	120W	42N	Go	Oo	Oo	Pm	Da	Sa	Ip	Xx	Ss	Of	Of	Bh	Hc	Oo	Ap
Shivwits	114W	37N	Go	Oo	Oo	Oo	Da	Sa	Ip	Bb	To	Of	Of	Kg	Hc	Oo	Ai
Shoshone (White Knife)	117W	41N	Go	Oo	Oo	Pm	Da	Se	In	Mp	Lo	Of	Of	Bc	Ic	Oo	Ai
Shuswap (Southeastern)	120W	52N	Go	Oo	Oo	Dn	Ia	Sa	Ll	Pp	Gg	Of	Of	Bg	Hl	Oi	As
Sinkaietk	120W	48N	Go	Oo	Oo	Cn	Ca	Sd	Iq	Bb	So	Of	Of	Kh	Hc	Wo	As
Tenino	121W	45N	Go	Oo	Oo	Dn	Ia	Se	Ss	Pm	Gg	Of	Of	Kg	Hc	Wi	Ps
Ute (Uintah)	110W	40N	Go	Oo	Oo	Ib	Da	Sa	Ip	Mm	So	Of	Of	Bh	Hc	Oo	As
Walapai	113W	35N	Go	Pm	Oo	Oo	Da	Se	Ip	Um	Lo	Of	Of	Ba	Ic	Oo	Ap
Washo	120W	39N	Go	Oo	Oo	Pb	Dn	Sa	In	Mp	Lo	Of	Of	Bh	Hc	Oo	As
Wishram	121W	46N	Go	Oo	Oo	Dm	Ia	Sa	Ll	Up	Go	Of	Of	Bh	Hc	Wh	Pp
Plains																	
Blackfoot (Siksika)	109W	51N	Or	Oo	Im	Oo	Dm	Be	Ep	Pm	Sb	Of	Of	Bh	Hl	Wo	Ai
Cheyenne	104W	39N	Gr	Oo	Im	Oo	Da	Be	Ep	Mp	So	Of	Of	Kh	Hm	Oo	Mi
Comanche	100W	33N	Or	Oo	Im	Oo	Da	Bd	Ep	Bb	So	Of	Of	Bf	Hm	Oi	Pp
Crow	108W	45N	Gr	Oo	Im	Oo	Da	Be	Iq	Pp	So	Of	Pm	Mf	Cm	Oo	Mi
Gros Ventre	109W	49N	Gr	Oo	Im	Oo	Da	Be	Ip	Pu	Sb	Of	Of	Bh	Hm	Oo	Mi
Karankawa	96W	29N	Go	Oo	Oo	Cm	Cn	Bo	In	Uu	Ls	O.	O.	B.	..	Oo	Ap
Kiowa	101W	37N	Or	Oo	Im	Oo	Dm	Be	Ln	Pm	To	Of	Of	Kf	Hm	Wo	Mi
Mandan	101W	47N	Cr	Df	Pm	Im	Im	V.	Ll	Mm	So	O.	Ms	M.	Cm	Ao	Me
Sarsi	110W	54N	Or	Oo	Im	Oo	Da	Be	Ip	Pu	Sb	Of	Of	Bf	Hl	Oo	Mi
Teton	103W	43N	Or	Oo	Im	Oo	Dm	Be	Iq	Um	Sb	Of	Of	Kf	Im	Oo	Pi
Prairie																	
Caddo (Hasinai)	95W	31N	Co	Da	Oo	P.	Ia	Ha	Ll	Mp	Lo	Of	Of	Bg	Hn	Hs	Ms
Fox	89W	45N	Co	Df	Oo	Oo	In	So	Ll	Xx	Ss	Ss	Of	Kh	Om	Os	Ms
Menomini	88W	46N	Go	Pf	Oo	Im	Da	Vc	I.	Pp	Go	Ps	Of	Pf	Om	Os	Pp
Miami	86W	40N	Co	Df	Oo	Oo	Ia	S.	I.	Pp	Sg	Ss	Of	Pf	Om	Os	Mp
Ojibwa (Chippewa)	91W	49N	Go	Oo	Oo	I.	Da	Sa	Ip	Um	Gs	Ss	Of	Pc	Io	Oo	Ai

TABLE 1. THIRTY CULTURAL CHARACTERISTICS AMONG SAMPLE PEOPLES (Continued)

Area and Culture	Location		1	2	3	4	5	6	7	8	9	10	11	12	13	14	15
Prairie (continued)																	
Omaha	96W	41N	Cr	Cg	Pm	Ib	Cm	So	Ip	Mu	To	Ms	Of	Pg	Om	Oo	Mi
Oto	95W	40N	Cr	Ig	Pm	Pm	Dm	Sd	Ip	Um	Tb	Ss	O.	P.	Om	Ho	As
Pawnee (Skidi)	100W	42N	Cr	Df	Pm	Oo	In	Sd	Es	Mu	So	Of	Of	Bf	Cm	Ci	Ms
Shawnee	85W	37N	Co	Df	Oo	I.	In	Va	..	Pp	Lo	Ss	Of	Pg	Om	Oo	Ms
Wichita	98W	34N	Cr	Df	Pm	Oo	Im	Sa	Ll	Mm	So	Of	Of	Kf	Hn	Oo	Mi
Winnebago	88W	44N	Co	Df	Oo	Pm	In	Vb	Ll	Uu	Ts	Ms	Of	Pa	Oc	Oo	Mp
Eastern Woodlands																	
Cherokee	83W	36N	Co	Dg	Oo	Im	In	Vb	In	Mm	Lo	Of	Sm	Mf	Cm	Oo	Lm
Choctaw	88W	33N	Co	Dg	Oo	I.	In	Nd	Im	Mn	To	Of	Ms	Mh	Cm	Oo	L.
Creek	84W	33N	Co	Df	Oo	Ib	Ia	Va	Ep	Mm	So	Of	Ns	Mg	Cn	Oo	Li
Delaware (Munsee)	75W	40N	Co	Df	Oo	Im	Ia	Hb	Ee	Mn	Lo	O.	Ps	M.	Hn	Oo	An
Huron	78W	44N	Co	Df	Oo	Im	Ia	Vb	Ee	Mm	Mo	Of	Ss	Mf	Im	Wo	Mn
Iroquois	77W	43N	Co	Df	Oo	Im	Ia	Vb	Ee	Mm	Mo	Of	Ms	K.	Im	Oo	Lm
Micmac	65W	46N	Oo	Oo	Oo	Ca	Cm	Sa	In	Uu	Ms	Sf	Of	Pg	Hl	Oo	Mp
Natchez	91W	32N	Co	Dg	Oo	Im	In	Vo	Ll	Up	Go	Of	Of	Bg	Ec	Co	Mm
Penobscot	68W	45N	Co	Ig	Oo	I.	Dn	Sa	In	Mu	Ls	Of	Of	Bf	Ec	Oo	M.
Timucua	82W	27N	Co	Da	Oo	I.	I.	V.	Ee	Mm	Lo	O.	Ss	M.	Cn	Ho	M.
Yuchi	86W	36N	Co	Db	Oo	Ib	In	Vo	Ip	Nu	Go	O.	Ss	M.	Cg	Oo	Ae
Southwest																	
Acoma	108W	35N	Co	Dn	Oo	Oo	Pm	Vd	Ee	Mp	Mo	Of	Sm	Mf	Cm	Oo	Am
Chiricahua	108W	31N	Go	Oo	Oo	Oo	Da	Ba	Ep	Mm	So	Of	Of	Bh	Hc	Oo	Ai
Cochiti	106W	36N	Co	Dm	Oo	Pm	Im	Vd	Ll	Mw	Mo	Of	Ss	Mg	Hm	Oo	Ai
Cocopa	115W	32N	Co	Db	Oo	I.	In	No	In	Uu	Ls	Sm	Of	Pg	Ic	Oi	Ai
Hopi	111W	36N	Co	Dm	Oo	Oo	Ia	Va	Ee	Mm	Mo	Of	Sm	Mg	Cm	Oo	Ac
Isleta	107W	35N	Co	Dm	Oo	Oo	Pm	Vd	In	Nn	Mo	Of	Of	Bh	Hl	Oo	Ai
Jemez	107W	36N	Co	Dm	Oo	Oo	Im	Vd	In	Nb	Mo	Of	Sm	Mg	El	Oo	Am
Maricopa	113W	33N	Co	In	Oo	Im	Da	Va	Ip	Pp	Lo	Ss	Of	Ph	Hc	Oo	Mp
Navaho	110W	37N	Cr	Dn	Ib	Oo	Ia	Ha	Em	Mm	So	Of	Sm	Mg	Im	Oi	Ai
Taos	106W	37N	Co	Dm	Oo	Oo	Im	Vd	In	Nw	Mo	Of	Of	Bg	El	Oo	Ae
Tewa (San Ildefonso)	106W	36N	Co	Dm	Oo	Oo	Im	Vd	In	Nn	Mo	Of	Of	Bh	El	Oo	Ae
Western Apache	110W	34N	Co	Ig	Oo	Oo	Da	Sd	Em	Mp	Ts	Of	Ps	Mh	Io	Oo	Am
Zuni	109W	35N	Co	Dn	Oo	Oo	Pm	Vd	Ee	Mm	Mo	Of	Sm	Mf	Cm	Oo	Ac
Northwest Mexico																	
Huichol	104W	23N	Cr	Dn	I.	Pm	Im	Ho	Ep	Bb	Lo	O.	O.	B.	.l	H.	De
Opata	109W	29N	Co	Dn	Oo	P.	I.	Vo	In	..	Mo	O.	O.	B.	Ec	Oi	Ac
Papago	112W	31N	Co	Dn	Oo	Oo	Ia	Se	Ll	Pp	So	Of	Of	Bg	Hc	Oo	Ac
Seri	112W	29N	Go	Oo	Oo	D.	I.	So	En	Pp	Mb	Of	Of	Bf	Hc	Oo	A.
Tarahumara	107W	28N	Cr	Dm	Ib	Oo	Pa	Nd	Ip	Wm	Ts	Of	Of	Kf	Hc	Wo	A.
Yaqui	110W	28N	Co	Dm	Oo	I.	Im	Va	E.	Pp	Lo	Of	Of	Bh	Hl	Oo	Ae
Central Mexico																	
Aztec	99W	19N	Co	Dn	Oo	Im	Pm	Va	Im	Pp	Lo	Of	Of	Bf	Hl	Ci	Ss
Chinantec (Ijitlan)	96W	18N	Cr	Dm	Pf	Oo	Pa	Hd	Ss	Pp	Mo	Ll	Of	Ph	Hd	..	De
Huastec	98W	22N	Co	Dm	Oo	Pm	Im	Va	In	Pp	..	O.	O.	B.	Hn	C.	Mc
Mazatec	100W	20N	Co	Dm	Oo	Oo	Pm	Va	In	Pp	Lo	Of	Of	Bh	Hl	..	D.
Mixe (Western)	95W	17N	Co	Dm	Oo	Oo	Pm	Nd	In	Pu	Mo	O.	O.	B.	Hl	..	..
Popoluca (Sierra)	95W	18N	Cr	Dm	P.	Pm	Im	Vo	Iq	Np	So	Of	Of	Bf	Hl	..	D.
Tarasco	101W	19N	Co	Dm	Oo	I.	Pm	Vo	Ll	Pp	Lo	Oa	Oa	Ba	Dc	H.	Ss
Totonac	97W	20N	Co	Dm	Oo	Im	Im	Vo	..	P.	Lo	Of	Of	Bf	Hl	Cs	Ss
Zapotec	96W	17N	Co	Dm	Oo	P.	P.	Va	Ln	Pp	Lo	Of	Of	Bh	Hc	C.	D.
SOUTH AMERICA																	
Central America																	
Black Carib	89W	16N	Ro	Dg	Oo	Ia	Pm	Vo	In	Nw	Lo	Of	Of	Ba	Im	.o	Da
Cakchiquel	91W	14N	Co	Dn	Oo	P.	Pm	Nb	In	Uu	Ms	Ss	Of	P.	Hm	Ch	Mi
Chorti	89W	14N	Cr	Dm	Pn	Pm	Pm	Cd	Ln	Bb	Ms	Od	Od	Bd	Hl	Ho	Da
Cuna	78W	9N	Co	Dn	Oo	In	Pm	Vd	Ee	Mm	Ms	Od	Od	Bd	Hl	Ws	Me
Guaymi	83W	8N	Ro	Da	Oo	I.	Im	V.	Ee	Mm	Ss	O.	Ss	M.	.l	Hs	M.
Lenca	88W	14N	Co	Dm	Oo	Pm	Im	Vd	Ip	Ww	Go	O.	O.	B.	..	Ho	A.
Maya	90W	18N	Co	Dm	Oo	I.	Im	Ca	In	Un	Ms	Ll	Oa	Po	Hn	Ch	Ms

TABLE 1. THIRTY CULTURAL CHARACTERISTICS AMONG SAMPLE PEOPLES (Continued)

Area and Culture	Location		1	2	3	4	5	6	7	8	9	10	11	12	13	14	15
Central America (continued)																	
Miskito	85W	13N	Ro	Df	Oo	Ib	Im	Va	Ee	Mn	Ls	Of	Of	Bc	.c	H.	Me
Talamanca (Bribri)	83W	9N	Co	Dm	Oo	I.	P.	V.	Ee	Mm	Ls	Of	Ms	M.	Hn	Hs	My
Tzeltal	92W	17N	Co	Dm	Oo	Oo	Im	Vd	Ln	Uu	Ls	Ss	Of	Po	On	..	A.
Caribbean																	
Cagaba	74W	11N	Ro	Db	Oo	Oo	Oo	Vo	Im	Mm	Ls	Of	Of	Bf	Hl	Wo	A.
Callinago	61W	15N	Ro	Ca	Oo	Ca	Pm	No	Em	Mp	Ts	Of	Of	Bp	Im	Oi	Ai
Goajiro	72W	12N	Or	Pf	Da	Oo	Oo	Bc	Im	A.	Gb	Oa	Sl	Ma	Cm	Hh	An
Jamaicans (Modern)	77W	18N	Rm	Dn	Ib	Im	Oo	Va	In	Nb	Mo	Od	Od	Kd	El	Co	Se
Motilon (Iroka)	72W	9N	Ro	Im	Oo	Im	Da	Va	Ep	Mp	Gs	Of	Of	Be	Im	Oo	A.
Taino	75W	19N	Ro	Df	Oo	Im	Pm	Vo	Ee	P.	Lb	O.	O.	B.	..	Hs	Ln
Guiana																	
Arawak (Locono)	57W	6N	Ro	Da	Oo	I.	In	Vo	Ip	Mm	Ts	Of	Ss	Mn	.m	Os	Ai
Bush Negroes (Saramacca)	56W	4N	Ro	Dg	Oo	Im	In	Vb	Im	Am	Gb	Oa	Sl	Mr	Hm	Oo	My
Camaracoto	63W	6N	Ro	Dg	Oo	Im	Ia	Va	I.	Pn	Gb	Oa	Oa	Ba	Hm	Oo	Ai
Carib (Barama River)	59W	5N	Ro	Dg	Oo	In	In	Na	Ip	Wx	Ls	Of	Of	Be	In	Oo	Ai
Guahibo	68W	5N	Go	Oo	Oo	Cm	Ca	Bd	Ep	Mm	Ts	Op	Ll	Mc	Il	Oo	As
Panare	66W	6N	Ro	Dg	Oo	In	Im	So	Ec	Mp	S.	Of	Of	Bn	..	Oo	Ai
Wapishana	59W	3N	Ro	Dg	Oo	I.	Ia	Ve	Ee	Uu	Gs	Of	Of	Bc	In	Oo	A.
Warrau (Winikina)	68W	9N	Ro	Ia	Oo	Cm	Cm	Vd	Ll	Mm	Ss	Oa	Oa	Ba	He	Oo	Ai
Yaruro	68W	7N	Rr	Dm	Pm	Im	Ia	Vd	Ss	Ms	Ls	Of	Of	Bc	Hm	Oo	Ap
Lower Amazon																	
Apalai	53W	0	Ro	Dg	Oo	Im	Im	Ve	Ln	Pp	Mo	Ss	O.	Pp	..	Oo	Ap
Cawahib	60W	9S	Ro	D.	Oo	I.	I.	Ve	Ip	Pp	Lo	Ss	O.	P.	..	Oo	As
Mundurucu	58W	6S	Ro	Db	Oo	I.	Im	Va	Ee	Mu	Ls	Ms	Of	Pe	.m	Oo	Ap
Palikur	51W	1N	Ro	Db	Oo	In	Pm	Fo	In	Xb	Mo	Ss	O.	P.	.m	Oo	Ai
Tapirape	52W	11S	Ro	Dn	Oo	P.	In	Vd	Ee	Mm	Ms	Of	Of	Bf	Hm	Ao	A.
Waica	65W	2N	Oo	Pa	Oo	Cn	Cm	Ba	Ip	Bb	So	O.	O.	B.	..	Oo	A.
Interior Amazonia																	
Cashinawa	73W	8S	Ro	Dg	Oo	Im	Im	Ho	Ec	Mm	L.	O.	O.	Bc	..	Oo	A.
Chama	75W	8S	Ro	Dg	Oo	Im	Im	V.	Ll	Mm	Ss	O.	L.	M.	..	Oi	A.
Cocama	75W	5S	Ro	C.	Oo	C.	P.	V.	Ee	Uu	Ls	Ss	O.	P.	..	Hs	A.
Jivaro	78W	4S	Ro	Dg	Oo	In	Pm	Hd	Ee	Um	Gs	Lf	Oa	Pa	Xm	Oo	Oo
Piro	74W	12S	Ro	Cg	Oo	Cm	Im	Vo	Ip	Mm	To	Of	Of	Ba	.n	Oo	Ai
Siriono	64W	16S	Co	Ib	Oo	Im	Dn	Sd	Ec	Mm	So	Of	Of	Bm	Cm	Oo	As
Tucano (Cubeo)	71W	1N	Ro	Df	Oo	Im	Pa	Vc	Ec	Pp	.x	Ps	O.	Pn	In	Oo	A.
Tucuna	70W	3S	Ro	Cg	Oo	Cm	In	Vc	Ec	Um	Tx	Ms	Of	P.	Ic	Oo	A.
Witoto	73W	1S	Ro	Df	Oo	Im	Im	Vc	Ec	Pp	Ms	Ss	Of	Po	.c	Ol	As
Yagua	72W	3S	Ro	Cg	Oo	Pn	Cm	Vc	Ec	Uu	Ms	Ss	O.	P.	..	Oo	Ae
Andes																	
Aymara (Modern)	69W	16S	Rs	Db	Ig	Im	Oo	Vd	En	Pp	Mo	Ll	Of	Pf	Hn	Wo	Do
Cayapa	79W	1N	Ro	Df	Oo	Im	Ia	No	In	Bn	Mo	Of	Of	Bg	Vg	Oo	As
Chibcha	74W	5N	Co	Db	Oo	P.	Pm	Vo	Ip	P.	Gb	O.	..	M.	En	Hs	Ln
Inca	72W	13S	Cs	Db	Im	Oo	Pm	Vd	In	Pp	Lo	Oa	Oa	Ba	Hm	Co	Ss
Paez	76W	3N	Rr	Db	Im	Oo	Im	No	Ip	Nn	Go	O.	O.	B.	..	.o	M.
Uru	67W	18S	Oo	P.	Oo	Dm	Im	Vd	..	Pn	.o	O.	O.	B.	Ec	Oo	Do
Chile & Patagonia																	
Alacaluf	74W	52S	Oo	Oo	Oo	Da	Im	Ba	In	M.	Lo	Oa	Oa	Ba	..	Oo	Oo
Araucanians (Mapuche)	68W	39S	Cs	Db	Im	Im	Ia	Hb	Ll	Pp	Gb	Ll	O.	Pm	Oc	Wo	Ap
Ona (Shelknam)	69W	54S	Go	Oo	Oo	Ia	Da	Be	Ip	Uu	Gs	Of	Of	Bh	Ec	Oo	Ai
Tehuelche	70W	46S	Gr	Oo	Im	P.	Dn	Bo	In	Pp	Lb	O.	O.	B.	..	Oi	As
Yahgan	69W	55S	Oo	Oo	Oo	Dg	Ia	Be	In	Pp	Ts	Of	Of	Bh	Ee	Oo	Oo
Gran Chaco																	
Abipon	61W	29S	Gr	Oo	Im	Oo	Da	Bo	In	Ww	Mb	Of	Of	Bg	F.	Hh	As
Caduveo	57W	22S	Or	Oo	Im	Im	Dm	Bo	Ll	Mm	Lo	O.	O.	B.	Hm	Hs	M.
Chamacoco	59W	20S	Go	Oo	Oo	Oo	Dn	Bo	In	Mp	Ms	O.	O.	B.	..	Hs	M.

TABLE 1. THIRTY CULTURAL CHARACTERISTICS AMONG SAMPLE PEOPLES (Continued)

Area and Culture	Location		1	2	3	4	5	6	7	8	9	10	11	12	13	14	15
Gran Chaco (continued)																	
Chiriguano	64W	20S	Co	Dn	Oo	Pf	Pm	Vo	Ee	Uu	Ls	O.	O.	B.	..	Oo	Mp
Choroti	62W	22S	Gr	Ps	P.	Im	Da	Ve	In	Mm	Ms	Of	Of	Bf	F.	Oo	A.
Lengua	59W	23S	Go	Pm	Oo	I.	Da	Bo	Ee	Mp	Mo	O.	O.	B.	..	Oo	As
Mataco	63W	24S	Gr	Pf	Pf	Dm	In	So	In	Xx	Lb	Of	Of	Bf	Hl	Oo	A.
Terena	58W	21S	Rr	Cb	Im	I.	Cn	Sa	Ee	Xx	Lo	Of	Of	Bf	Hn	Hh	Ap
Mato Grosso																	
Bacairi	55W	14S	Ro	Dg	Oo	Im	Im	Vd	Ll	Uu	Lo	Of	Of	Ba	Im	Oo	Ai
Bororo	55W	16S	Go	Oo	Oo	P.	Da	Sd	Ee	Mm	Lo	Of	Ms	Ma	Cm	Oo	Am
Camayura	54W	12S	Ro	Cn	Oo	Cm	Ia	Va	Ee	Uu	Ts	Of	Of	Bf	In	Oo	Ap
Guato	57W	18S	Go	Oo	Oo	Im	Dn	So	In	P.	L.	O.	O.	B.	Im	Oo	Ap
Nambicuara	59W	12S	Ro	Ib	Oo	P.	Da	Sa	In	Pu	Lo	Of	Of	Bc	Im	Oo	Ai
Paressi	58W	15S	Co	D.	Oo	P.	I.	Vo	Ee	Mu	So	O.	O.	B.	Im	Oi	As
Trumai	53W	12S	Ro	Dg	Oo	Im	Ia	Va	Ee	Pp	To	Of	Of	Bc	Ic	Oi	As
Umotina	57W	15S	Ro	Dm	Oo	Pb	Ia	Vd	In	Uu	..	Of	Of	Bf	Hg	Oo	As
Eastern Brazil																	
Apinaye	49W	6S	Ro	Db	Oo	Pb	Ia	Vb	Ll	Mm	Mo	Of	Nf	Mf	Cm	Ao	Am
Botocudo	42W	18S	Go	Oo	Oo	P.	Da	Be	Ip	..	So	Oa	Oa	Ba	Hn	Oo	Ai
Caingang (Aweikoma)	50W	28S	Go	Oo	Oo	Pm	Da	Bd	Ip	Bb	Lo	Oa	Oa	Ba	Hg	Oo	Oo
Caraja	50W	12S	Ro	Im	Oo	Dm	Ia	Vd	Ee	Mm	Lo	Oa	Oa	Ba	H.	O.	Ap
Cayua	54W	26S	Ro	Db	Oo	Im	Ia	Hb	Ee	Uu	Ls	L.	O.	P.	Hn	O.	A.
Sherente	48W	9S	Ro	Db	Oo	Im	Ia	Vb	In	Uu	Mo	Ms	Of	Pr	Om	Oo	Mp
Tenetehara	46W	3S	Ro	Db	Oo	P.	Im	Vd	El	Mn	Ls	Of	Of	Bf	Hc	O.	A.
Timbira (Ramcocamecra)	45W	7S	Go	Pg	Oo	Oo	Da	Sb	Ll	Mm	Ms	Of	Ms	Mf	Cm	Ao	Oo
Tupinamba	35W	8S	Ro	Df	Oo	Im	Ia	Vo	Ee	Mu	Gs	O.	O.	Bc	Fn	Wi	Ap

From this tabulation it is possible to calculate the approximate incidence of the tabulated traits for the world as a whole and for particular regions. Thus from Table 2, which does this for forms of marriage, we learn that monogamy is characteristic of about 24 percent of the world's societies, polyandry of 1 percent, and polygyny of 75 percent, and that general polygyny is particularly prevalent in Africa, monogamy in the Circum-Mediterranean, limited polygyny in the Insular Pacific, and sororal polygyny (shown in parentheses) in North America.

TABLE 2. REGIONAL VARIATIONS IN THE INCIDENCE OF PLURAL MARRIAGES

Form of Marriage	Africa	Circum-Mediterranean	East Eurasia	Insular Pacific	North America	South America	Total
Monogamy	8	43	34	23	19	12	135
Polyandry	0	0	3	1	0	0	4
Limited polygyny	16 (1)	17	36	43 (5)	40 (9)	32 (7)	184
General polygyny	92 (9)	17	21 (4)	29 (12)	50 (31)	21 (9)	231

The data may also be organized to test scientific hypotheses. Many of the statistical correlations of the author's previous work (Murdock 1949), for example, can be recalculated on the basis of the new, larger, and more representative world sample. It must suffice, by way of illustration, to present the evidence bearing upon the comparative study by Homans and Schneider (1955) on asymmetrical cross-cousin marriage. Examination of Table 3 will reveal that these authors are correct in ascribing matrilateral preferences primarily to patrilineal societies and patrilateral preferences to matrilineal societies. The worldwide incidence of such preferences, however, is so low as to cast some doubt on the validity of the theoretical interpretation advanced.

TABLE 3. THE RELATIONSHIP OF PREFERENTIAL MARRIAGE TO DESCENT

Rules Governing Cousin Marriage	Matrilineal Descent	Double Descent	Patrilineal Descent	Bilateral Descent	Totals
Preferential marriage with a parallel cousin	0	0	12	0	12
Cross-cousin marriage with patrilateral preference	8	5	2	1	16
Cross-cousin marriage with matrilateral preference	7	5	34	3	49
Symmetrical cross-cousin marriage	21	4	45	18	88
Marriage permitted with any first cousin	2	0	13	30	45
Marriage not approved with any first cousin	33	14	109	121	277
No data available on cousin marriage	13	1	32	31	77
Totals	84	29	247	204	564

The usefulness of Table 1 depends, of course, upon its degree of correctness and completeness. It unquestionably contains many errors—some purely typographical, others resulting from the arbitrariness inherent in any system of classification, and still others reflecting faulty judgment in the categorization of data or failure to utilize important sources. The author craves the indulgence of his colleagues and earnestly requests them to submit to him any corrections or additions which they can supply, as well as data on other cultures which they feel should be added to the sample or substituted for some now included in it. If new and corrected material is provided in sufficient quantity, and if the sample proves sufficiently useful, the author will undertake to publish a revised sample and table with selected bibliographies on the cultures included.

REFERENCES CITED

HOBHOUSE, L. T., G. C. WHEELER, and M. GINSBERG
1915 The material culture and social institutions of the simpler peoples. London.

HOMANS, G. C., and D. M. SCHNEIDER
1955 Marriage, authority, and final causes. Glencoe.

MURDOCK, G. P.
1949 Social structure. New York.

TYLOR, E. B.
1889 On a method of investigating the development of institutions. Journal of the Royal Anthropological Institute 18:245–269.

TWO SOLUTIONS TO GALTON'S PROBLEM* **

RAOUL NAROLL

San Fernando Valley State College

Two solutions are offered to the problem of distinguishing "historical" from "functional" associations in cross-cultural surveys. The underlying logic of the mathematical model is discussed and three kinds of association distinguished: hyperdiffusional or purely "historical" association, undiffusional or purely "functional" association, and semidiffusional or mixed "historical-functional" association. Two overland diffusion arcs constitute the test sample; the relationship of social stratification to political complexity constitutes the test problem. A sifting test establishes a bimodal distribution of interval lengths between like types and sifts out repetitions with a lesser interval length than the second mode. A cluster test shows that for the test problem, the "hits" cluster more than the "misses".

Galton's problem is one of the most important problems of scientific method facing social scientists today. Galton's problem is that of discriminating so-called "historical" from "functional" associations in cross-cultural surveys. By a cross-cultural survey I mean a comparative statistical study in which the "tribe", "society" or "culture" is taken as the unit and samples from a world-wide universe are studied to test hypotheses about the nature of society or culture. *Social Structure*[1] and *Child Training and Personality*[2] are probably the best known recent examples of this kind of study, but there have been dozens of others. The importance of the method may be gauged by the judgement of Levy and Fallers—who in the course of a sharp critique of one of Murdock's basic concepts recently called *Social Structure* "certainly the most extensive and influential comparative study yet undertaken."[3]

Galton's problem is widely considered to be a crucial weakness in the cross-cultural survey method. Galton raised his problem at the meeting of the Royal Anthropological Institute in 1889 which heard Tylor read his pioneer paper introducing the cross-cultural survey method. Tylor showed correlations ("adhesions" he called them) between certain traits; in the discussion which followed, Galton pointed out that traits often spread by diffusion—by borrowing or migration. Since this is often so, how many independent trials of his correlations did Tylor have?[4] Boas, for decades the immensely influential dean of American anthropologists, once told his student Lowie that when he first read Tylor's paper, he became greatly enthusiastic.

* Received July, 1960.

[1] George P. Murdock, *Social Structure* (New York: Macmillan, 1949).

[2] John W. M. Whiting and Irving L. Child, *Child Training and Personality* (New Haven: Yale University Press, 1953).

[3] M. J. Levy, Jr., and L. A. Fallers, "The Family: Some Comparative Considerations," *American Anthropologist* 61 (1959) 648.

[4] Francis Galton in Edward B. Tylor, "On a Method of Investigating the Development of Institutions applied to the Laws of Marriage and Descent," *Journal of the Royal Anthropological Institute*, 18 (1889) 272.

** Reprinted from the *Philosophy of Science*, Vol. 28, No. 1 (January 1961), 15-39, by permission of the author and the Philosophy of Science Association.

This seemed to him an ideal research technique. On reflecting further, however, Galton's objection seemed to him a devastating one; unless there was a solution to Galton's problem, Boas considered the cross-cultural survey method valueless.[5]

This paper demonstrates two solutions to Galton's problem. These solutions offer a proof more rigorous than ever before presented of the widely held belief that social and cultural development proceed in obedience to sociological laws. The proposition chosen for demonstration here is simple and familiar: complexity of social stratification is correlated with complexity of political organization. That such a correlation exists was long ago shown by the sociologists Hobhouse, Wheeler and Ginsburg[6]—the focus of the present paper is on the demonstration of the nomothetic nature of this relationship. Neither these writers, nor anyone else has ever, heretofore, presented any rigorous treatment of the proposition that this correlation, or any of the many others involved in social and cultural development, arises out of the very nature of human society and culture, and not from chance diffusion.

Why do sociologists and anthropologists generally think that social stratification and political complexity tend to develop together? Because they know that most societies with complicated political organizations have complicated social class structures while most societies with simple political organizations have simple social class structures. The question this paper answers is the question of the nature of this correlation. One hypothesis is that these, like other elements of higher civilization, diffused through borrowing and migration from one or two or three or four main centers, so that there are really only one or two or three or four independent tests of the hypothesis that these traits are correlated. If this hypothesis is correct, their association in hundreds of cultures throughout the world can be explained as a mere historical accident, an idiographic association. In this paper, I do not deal with the question of independent invention but rather with the nature of diffusion. To begin with, I take the trouble to establish by formal test what is already generally believed, that no matter how many times these treats have been independently invented, they have often been *spread* by diffusion. Then I get to the main problem. I show that no matter how *few* times these traits have been independently invented, they have tended to diffuse together. Societies which increase the complexity of their political organization are likely to increase the complexity of their social class system; whether these increases are independently invented or spread by borrowing doesn't matter. By showing that these traits tend to diffuse together, I show that there is a nomothetic relationship between them—that their association arises out of the very nature of human society, not out of accident, like the association of bow ties and airplanes.

[5] Robert H. Lowie, "Evolution in Cultural Anthropology: a Reply to Leslie White," *American Anthropologist* 48 (1946) 227, 230.

[6] L. T. Hobhouse, G. C. Wheeler and M. Ginsburg, *The Material Culture and Social Institutions of the Simpler Peoples* (London: Chapman and Hall, 1930).

Anthropologists and sociologists take association of traits in a society as evidence of a "functional" relationship between them where a "functional" hypothesis sounds plausible *a priori*. But the method presented here provides for the first time a method of distinguishing between associations which reflect a "functional" relationship and associations which reflect mere historical accident.

The method I use is generally applicable to all cross-cultural surveys where it is desired to distinguish nomothetic from idiographic relationships. It is well to bear in mind that there are two distinct types of cross-cultural studies which use statistics, taking the "tribe" or society as a unit, and thus compare the characteristics, of a number of societies. First, there is the well-known cross-cultural survey, which seeks to test hypotheses about functional relationships in society and culture.[7] Second, there are regional studies of trait distributions, like the magnificent, but little appreciated, Culture Element Distribution studies of Kroeber and his associates at the University of California a couple of decades ago.[8] The object of the first is to discern "functional" relationships, association of traits arising out of the nature of human personality, human society or human culture. The object of the second is to discern "historical" relationships, associations of traits spread through an area by borrowing or migration. Critics of each of these studies have pointed out that an examination of either phenomenon ("functional" relationship or diffusion) needs to allow for the effect of the other. As already remarked, when Tylor introduced the cross-cultural survey method, Boas at first reacted with keen enthusiasm, seeing it as the answer to all problems; but after he thought more about it, he came to feel that Galton's objection was deadly—if traits spread by diffusion, how many independent trials of the phenomenon did Tylor have? No one knew, and thus his statistics seemed meaningless.[9] Wallis[10] similarly pointed out very early that the existence of a functional relationship between traits involved in a Culture Element Distribution study impeached the validity of its correlations taken as evidence of diffusion, an objection repeated by Kluckhohn[11] and whose cogency with regard to the relationship between the distribution of girls' puberty rites and the distribu-

[7] Andre J. Köbben, "New Ways of Presenting an Old Idea: The Statistical Method in Social Anthropology," *Journal of the Royal Anthropological Institute*, 82 (1952) 129-146; John W. M. Whiting, "The Cross-Cultural Method," *Handbook of Social Psychology*, Gardner Lindzey, ed. (Cambridge, Mass.: Addison-Wesley, 1954 1: 525-31.)

[8] For a review of the many studies of this kind see Clyde Kluckhohn, "On certain recent applications of association coefficients to ethnological data," *American Anthropologist* 41 (1939) 345-377; Harold E. Driver, "Statistics in Anthropology", *American Anthropologist*, 55 (1953) 50 f.

[9] Galton in Tylor, *loc. cit.*, Lowie, *loc. cit.*; Franz Boas, "Anthropology and Statistics," *The Social Science and their Interrelations*, W. F. Ogburn and A. Goldenweiser, eds., (Boston: Houghton Mifflin, 1927) 120 f.

[10] Wilson D. Wallis, "Probability and the Diffusion of Culture Traits," *American Anthropologist* 30 (1928) 94-106.

[11] Clyde Kluckhohn, *op. cit.*, 259 f.

tion of religious cults in California was conceded by Kroeber himself.[12]

As far as I know, nothing has been attempted by authors of trait distribution studies to allow for or measure the extent to which "functional" relationships weaken the significance of correlations as evidence of diffusion. But there have been several attempts to deal with the converse problem of estimating the effect of diffusion on "functional" correlations. To supplement her study of Paiute sorcery,[13] Beatrice Whiting in a cross-cultural survey showed a negative correlation between presence of authoritative political officials and witchcraft attribution; in order to reduce the effect of diffusion, she recomputed her correlation using only one tribe from each culture area, and found the result statistically significant. A similar method was used by her husband, John Whiting, and his collaborator, Irvin Child, in their study of child training and personality;[14] they recomputed their correlations separately for each continent; however, these results did not prove statistically significant. Both these approaches use what I propose we call the *sifting* method, which has as its object the sifting out of duplications reflecting diffusion. These two attempts are vulnerable to the objection that diffusion cannot be assumed to stop at culture area or continental boundaries but on the contrary is known to be often hemispheric or even worldwide in its scope. The distribution of the alphabet as a writing system, of the magic flight motif in folklore, of the bear cult in Siberia and northern North America, of tailored clothing through northern Eurasia and North America, of the wheat-cattle farming complex through most of the Eastern Hemisphere and the maize-beans-squash complex through most of the Western, are often-cited evidences of this tendency.

Another tack has been taken in recent critiques of Murdock's *Social Structure* by Wilson[15] and by Driver[16]. Wilson shows through statistical analysis of continental distributions and Driver through an illuminating set of trait distribution maps that kinship terminology and associated traits are affected by diffusion; both Wilson and Driver share Murdock's view that they are nevertheless "functionally" linked traits but offer no method of testing this hypothesis. However their work, particularly Driver's maps, helps the student to grasp intuitively the nature of the diffusional process.

As I pointed out in an earlier paper, the interesting question usually is not

[12] A. L. Kroeber, "Culture Element Distributions: III Area and Climax," *University of California Publications in American Archeology and Ethnology* 37 (1936) 111 f.

[13] Beatrice Whiting, *Paiute Sorcery*, Viking Fund Publications in Anthropology, No. 15 (New York: Wenner-Gren Foundation, 1950) pp. 88 f.

[14] John W. M. Whiting and Irving L. Child, *Child Training and Personality* (New Haven: Yale University Press, 1953), pp. 184-7.

[15] Thurlow R. Wilson, "Randomness of the distribution of social organization forms: a note on Murdock's *Social Structure*," *American Anthropologist*, 54 (1952) 134-138.

[16] Harold E. Driver, "An Integration of functional, evolutionary and historical theory by means of correlations," *Indiana University Publications in Anthropology and Linguistics*, Memoir 12, (Bloomington, 1956); Harold E. Driver and William C. Massey, *Comparative Studies of North American Indians*, Transactions of the American Philiosophical Society, Vol. 47, Part 2 (Philadelphia, 1957) pp. 421-439.

whether traits have been spread by diffusion but *how* they have been, and *why*.

"Are cultures merely chance agglomorations of traits acquired almost entirely by diffusion or dispersion? Or are they instead functionally interrelated systems which rearrange the raw materials of diffused or dispersed traits into unique patterns"?[17]

Thus, the present problem is a special analysis of a causal relationship between traits, as reflected in a correlation. The concept of cause used here is simple. It involves three elements: an actor, an antecedent event A and a subsequent event B. The actor is presumed to be considering whether or not to produce the antecedent event A; his ability to do so is given; the concept of cause is an element in his decision. In these circumstances, A is defined as a cause of B if the actor by producing event A will increase the probability of the occurrence of effect B. That is the logical definition; since the actor's ability is given, the usefulness of the concept does not depend upon his actually possessing such an ability but can be used as well to apply to purely imaginary situations: given a sufficiently long lever, strength to move it, and a fulcrum, can Archimedes move the world?

It is often said that "correlation does not necessarily prove causation". By this is meant only that the establishment of a correlation between Trait A and Trait B does not necessarily establish that A has caused B or vice versa. Both may be the joint effects of some other factor or factor complex not considered in the study. Thus, there is said to be a correlation between the price of rum in Havana and the salaries of Congregational ministers in New England. Even so, this fact would not prove that either directly causes the other; the correlation would more likely merely reflect the general rise in the prices of everything over the past centuries. But if we consider causation in a more general sense, as a direct or indirect relationship, then I submit that correlation *does* prove some kind of causal connection between the traits, if only that they both are alike effects of some third factor or complex of factors.

I wish to distinguish three types of causal associations between traits shown to be correlated by a cross-cultural statistical study. The first of these is the *hyperdiffusional* association, commonly called "historical relationship" in earlier discussions of this problem. By a hyperdiffusional association, I mean one which reflects no other causal relationship than common historical origin of the traits by chance coincidence in a few societies. (The definition of chance coincidence is here necessarily to be made in terms of probability theory, and at a specified significance level.) The second of these is the *undiffusional* association, by which I mean an association which does not reflect common historical origin; an undiffusional association can only exist between two traits at least one of which by the circumstances of the case *cannot* diffuse, *cannot* spread either by borrowing or migration nor persist while the differentiation of language into a number of new languages occurs (thus further multiplying instances of the association). The third type of causal associa-

[17] Raoul Naroll, "A Preliminary Index of Social Development," *American Anthropologist*, 58 (1956) 711 f.

tion I wish to distinguish I call (for want of a better term) a *semidiffusional* association. By a semidiffusional association, I mean one in which not only diffusional but also non-diffusional causes operate. Thus a semi-diffusional association spreads by diffusion. However, since other causes also are at work tending to produce the association, the associated traits tend to diffuse together. A society which for whatever reason decides to retain or adopt one trait is likely to retain or adopt the other also. For example, it is clear from Driver's studies that matrilineal descent and matrilocal residence are both traits which often spread by diffusion. But it is the opinion of Murdock, Wilson, Driver and many others, including the present writer, that a matrilocal, matrilineal society which for any reason—emphatically including the example of its neighbors—decides to drop matrilocal residence is likely to drop matrilineal descent as well.

In studying correlations, cases of traits associated in the predicted way I call "hits"; cases associated in some other way I call "misses". For example, in studying the association of descent and residence, Murdock and Driver conclude that the two traits are correlated: matrilineal descent is likely to be found with matrilocal residence, patrilineal descent with patrilocal residence and bilateral descent with neolocal residence. Any case in which these associations in fact occur would constitute a "hit"; but a case in which patrilocal residence accompanied matrilineal descent, or neolocal residence accompanied patrilineal descent, or the like, would constitute a "miss". If this correlation is a semidiffusional association, hits would tend to diffuse but misses would not. That is, the combination of matrilocal residence and matrilineal descent would very likely be borrowed together, or retained together over the centuries in the course of the fission of societies through migration or dialect differentiation. But the combination of matrilocal residence and patrilineal descent would not be equally likely to be borrowed together, or to be retained together over the centuries. On the other hand, if this correlation is not a semidiffusional association but a hyperdiffusional one, misses would tend to diffuse as readily as hits. This distinction, implied by the very definition of the two kinds of association, is the basis for one of the two solutions, the cluster test, presented below.

The present paper demonstrates the existence of a particular semidiffusional association. The reader may perhaps question whether either of the other two kinds actually exists. This paper does not attempt a rigorous demonstration that either does—no such demonstration is needed for its purpose. It is enough to state that in my opinion hyperdiffusional associations do commonly occur, for example, between bow ties and airplanes. However, I cannot think of any examples of clearly undiffusional associations.

The original concept of the present problem is that of the need for independence of cases. "In order to make a statistical method a success, it is essential that the phenomena counted must be independent of each other," wrote Boas.[18] To this, Kluckhohn added "Boas impales the attempt to verify

[18] Kluckhohn, *op. cit.*, p. 359.

sociological generalizations upon this dilemma but it is evident that the objection applies equally forcefully to both approaches. The sociologist assumes that the possibility of historical connection can be neglected, the historically minded ethnologist assumes that internal, functional associations can be neglected."[19]

The present paper presents a method of escaping between the horns of the dilemma. The basic logic involved needs explicit attention. As Kluckhohn also pointed out in his critique of 1939, the mathematics of probability theory have been given more attention by anthropologists than the underlying logic—and it is a logical problem we face here. There are of course three basic approaches to probability logic currently in use among mathematicians, each turning on a different concept of probability—the classical concept, the frequency concept, and the axiomatic concept.[20] I rest my argument on the classical concept. This has been formally defined by Laplace thus: "If an event can take place in n mutually exclusive ways, all equally likely, and if r of these correspond to what may be called 'success', then the probability of success in a single trial is r/n." This idea is best expressed by the familiar model: consider a jar containing a number (n) of spheres like ping-pong balls all absolutely identical in shape, size and other characteristics excepting only color—r of them are black, the others white. If the balls are thoroughly mixed and then a blindfolded person draws one ball out of the jar, the probability of the ball being black is r/n. That is the definition of the classical probability concept. When we say that an event has a probability of .05, we mean that it is as likely to occur as the blindfolded man is to get a black ball if there is one black ball to every nineteen white.

Where events being considered must occur in discrete units or bundles (or as the mathematician says, are discretely distributed) it is a relatively straightforward matter to work out correspondences between these discrete events and the model of a jar full of ping-pong balls. Where instead they can occur in magnitudes varying along a continual scale, like height or weight or distance (are continuously distributed), the use of integral calculus and the probability density concept lets us work out correspondences between such situations and the model of a jar full of ping-pong balls.

The various statistical tests which are used to calculate probabilities all can be related to the ping-pong ball jar model; the relationship is worked out mathematically and invariably involves certain stated mathematical assumptions. The logic of statistical inference involves inquiry as to the suitability of the mathematical model of the test being used. The test asks whether observed events can be explained by a given mathematical model. This question is the null hypothesis; if it is answered positively, the observations being tested are considered to lack statistical significance. For example, the chi-square test used by Murdock in *Social Structure* asks: would a random sample from a

[19] *Ibid.*

[20] John F. Kenney and E. S. Keeping, *Mathematics of Statistics, Part Two* (2nd Edition, New York: Van Nostrand, 1951) pp. 2-5.

universe of two independent and continuously distributed phenomena be likely to produce an association of the kind observed? The *t* test used by Whiting and Child in *Child Training and Personality* asks: would a random sample of two independent and normally distributed phenomena be likely to produce an association of the kind observed?

The key point is thus this: If an event being studied conforms in every way to the mathematical model of the statistical test being used, the result of a statistical test almost always must be to support the null hypothesis—to report the absence of a significant association, or a significant difference, or whatever. The point of the test is to establish the fact that the event being studied *cannot* plausibly be considered to conform to the mathematical model of the test.

It is then a logical and observational rather than a mathematical problem to explain the failure of the data to conform to the mathematical model. If ethnological observations are entirely independent of each other, then *ex hypothesi* neither historical nor sociological relationships exist among them and the only plausible explanation for apparent relationships is sampling error. Where a statistically significant result is observed, then *random* sampling error is discredited as an explanation for the apparent relationship. In an ideally controlled experiment, only two possible explanations for any relationship are permitted—the hypothesis being tested and random sampling error. But in ethnological statistical studies, other hypotheses are also possible. We cannot plausibly explain the correlations in Murdock's *Social Structure* or Whiting and Child's *Child Training and Personality* or in the University of California trait distribution studies as the result of random sampling error. That is what the statistical tests tell us and that is all that they tell us.

How can we explain the correlations in *Social Structure?* Critics have pointed out that they might reflect sampling biases (since the sample was not random); or that they might reflect errors in the data (random errors tend to lower correlations but observational biases might produce spurious correlations, as I have elsewhere demonstrated[21]); or that they might reflect inconsistencies in the unit of study. (While the mathematical model describes units identical in all respects except the trait being studied, variations in unit characteristics would matter only if they tended to produce a correlation of the kind Murdock observed. This would be the case, for example, if somehow the societies with traits correlated as predicted tended to be broken up into smaller units and thus counted several times while those with traits not so correlated tended to be lumped together into larger units. Conceivably, such a situation could escape the investigator's notice and thus deceive him with a spurious correlation.)

All these possibilities can be offered to explain the results of the Whiting and Child study; and another one as well—that the results might reflect

[21] Raoul Naroll, "Controlling Data Quality," Series Research in Social Psychology, *Symposia Studies Series*, Volume 4, National Institute of Social and Behavioral Sciences, September, 1960. Raoul Naroll, *Data Quality Control*, Chicago: The Free Press of Glencoe, in press.

deviations from normal in the distribution of the data being studied. While Murdock's statistical model does not involve normal distribution, that of Whiting and Child does.

The application to ethnological studies of probability theory needs to deal with all these possible explanations of the observed discrepancies between the results of the study and the statistical model. A study needs to show that its results cannot plausibly be explained by sampling bias; a method of controlled sampling, random in all respects except one or two specified biases like wealth of descriptive data, can meet this need by testing to see if the sampling bias tends to produce an artifactual correlation. But judgemental or quota sampling, however conscientiously carried out, can never eliminate the possibility that something the sampler failed to consider has introduced a bias. In his World Ethnographic Sample, Professor Murdock took into consideration many important factors—but he only thought about the things he thought about and failed to think about the things he failed to think about. A controlled sample is random with respect to the things the sampler fails to think about and biased only in known—and hence measurable—respects.

A study needs to show that its results cannot be explained as observational biases—whether of the informant, ethnographer or comparativist. Data quality control provides a proven method for doing so.

A study needs to show that inconsistencies in unit definition do not produce the observed correlations. This need can be met by defining units rigorously, so that the subjective judgement of the comparativist is not involved; several types of units will be needed; and the comparativist must control for unit definition bias by seeing if the relationship he is studying is found alike in all types of units, or not.

The present paper concerns itself with the one remaining difficulty which would exist if these other requirements had been met—discriminating hyperdiffusional from semidiffusional correlations. The tests here proposed can show that a statistically significant association cannot plausibly be explained as merely reflecting random sampling error or diffusion. What the best explanation then is remains a matter for further consideration. If these tests show that traits A and B are semidiffusionally associated, then we must presume that they are *somehow* causally linked. A may be the cause of B; B may be the cause of A; or they may be joint effects of some third factor.

The methods offered here are fairly simple, and inexpensive (*very* simple and inexpensive when compared with such techniques as factor analysis or latent structure analysis). They involve non-parametric statistics: mathematical models which do *not* make any assumption that the variables studied are normally distributed but only that they are continuous; each method uses a *statistic* which has been mathematically demonstrated to closely approximate a normal distribution for samples above a minimum size and for which tables of exact probabilities have been computed for samples below the minimum.

The methods here presented all rest upon the obvious fact that propinquity is usually a measure of diffusion. That is, the closer in space two societies are to each other, the more likely they are to resemble each other in any trait subject to diffusion. This is true whether the diffusion results from borrowing or migration and is the fact on which rests all studies of diffusion among peoples lacking written records. Obviously, people are more likely to borrow traits from their immediate neighbors than directly from more distant people; and obviously, societies which split up through migration or differentiation of dialects into several new societies are likely to be near each other and unlikely to be far distant. (This likelihood is far greater if we consider only trait distributions not borne by overseas Europeans after 1500 A.D., and accordingly, this study omits overseas Europeans from its consideration.) Of course, it is true that exceptions to this tendency are not uncommon: coffee spread by direct borrowing all the way across the Indian Ocean from Arabia to Java; there is a gap of something like a thousand miles between the southern Athapaskans and the main body of this language family; and so on. But the methods here presented permit frequent exceptions; they simply rely on the obvious fact that by and large diffusion is more likely to have taken place between nearby people than between distant ones.

The data used in this demonstration is gratefully taken from Murdock's "World Ethnographic Sample"[22] and the test of course assumes that his data is substantially free from observational bias (but evidence of random error by Murdock or the authors of his sources or their informants strengthens rather than weakens the results of the test, since random errors tend to lower correlations rather than to raise them.) The test likewise assumes that neither Murdock's unit definition nor sampling judgements tend to bias the sample in favor of the hypotheses here tested. (A comparison of Murdock's kinship data with Driver's on North American tribes on the track of the diffusion arc described below indicates that on the contrary Murdock tendend systematically to *over*-represent cases unfavorable to his "functional" hypothesis: such a result could be expected from his policy of including all special or unusual culture types and from his scientific concern not to permit his theoretical views to bias his sampling judgement.)

The method here described measures the propinquity of the tribes in the sample. To do so conveniently, it deals not with culture areas or continents as such but instead with long narrow strips—called *diffusion arcs*. Diffusion is measured along the arcs but not across them. I use here two diffusion arcs, one called the Cape Arc, the other the Island Arc. Each is 600 nautical miles wide and many thousands of miles long. The track line of the Cape Arc follows the great circles connecting the following points: Cape Horn—Cuzco—Panama City—Mexico City—Cape Prince of Wales, Alaska—East Cape, Chukchi Peninsula—Peking—Port Said—Cairo—Cape of Good Hope. The track line of the Island Arc follows the great circles connecting the following points: Great Blasquet Island, on the west coast of Ireland—Istanbul—Delhi—Singapore—Upolu Island, Samoa—Easter Island. All the tribes in Murdock's

[22] George Peter Murdock, "World Ethnographic Sample," *American Anthropologist* 59 (1597) 664-487.

World Ethnographic Sample whose centers as stated there lie within 300 nautical miles on either side of the track lines just defined are considered in this study; no others. A number of tribes so considered are excluded for reasons stated below.

The selection of these particular diffusion arcs is, logically speaking, entirely arbitrary. The logic of our method does not demand any particular arc or pair of arcs; it simply demands that we reduce the problem of measuring propinquity from two dimensions to one. We pick two arcs which as it were are cross-sections of the world's cultures. We do not assume that they constitute a representative sample or a random sample any more than a cross-section of an animal body constitutes a random sample of that animal's tissues. The method here proposed could be used with any other arcs which intersect each other at a reasonably large angle.

However, the arcs were not chosen casually. Rather, there were three prime considerations. First, it seemed to me that the arcs should be as long as possible, including as many distinct cultures as possible. Second, it seemed to me that the possibility of solidly-distributed diffusion waves from a single culture center being found duplicated in both arcs should be kept to a minimum. Third, it seemed to me that arcs should dissect known major diffusion patterns by connecting the margins of each continent with its major center of cultural diffusion around 1500 A.D. For these reasons, the arcs are believed particularly convenient for the study of diffusion.

The semidiffusional relationship which is tested in this study to demonstrate the method is one whose truth is already generally accepted—that there is correlation between the development of political organization and that of social classes. Murdock's column 14 classes social stratification other than slavery into five types, designated respectively *A*, *C*, *H*, *O* and *W* (see Table 1, below, for key to these symbols). For our purposes here types *A*, *O* and *W* are lumped; then type *C* is treated as level 3 of stratification, type *H* as level 2 of stratification and types *A*, *O* and *W* as level 1 of stratification. (I pay no attention to slavery in this study.) Murdock's column 15 classifies political organization into seven types (see Table 1): I treat type *S* as level 3 of political organization; types *M*, *L*, and *P* as level 2 of political organization; and types *A* and *O* as level 1 of political organization. Overseas Europeans are left out, for the reason already given. Type *D* (dependent societies lacking any political organization of their own) is generally treated as a case of no data, and omitted along with those tribes for which Murdock was unable to supply data. Also omitted are the Albanians, through an oversight not detected until too late, and the Rwala, which contain a typographical error in column 15 of the W.E.S. making it inconvenient to classify them. The study generally concerns itself with the remaining 192 societies in the diffusion arcs. The hypothesis tested is that level of political organization and social stratification as just defined are correlated. As will be expected from the earlier discussion, I shall call a "hit" a tribe with the same level of political organization as social stratification; I shall call a "miss" a tribe with differing levels: for example, the Yahgan, the

Chibcha and Aztecs are hits; the Cuna, the Lenca, the Cakchiquel, and the Comanche are misses.

The measure of propinquity used is distance along the diffusion arcs. Imagine each arc crossed by a succession of lines, each intersecting the center of each tribe and perpendicular with the track line of the arc. Two tribes on successive intersect lines are considered neighbors for the purpose of this study; two tribes whose intersect lines are separated by the intersect line of a third are not considered neighbors. Thus, as stated earlier, diffusion is measured only in the direction of the track, and not perpendicular to it. (If it is desired to measure diffusion in another direction, other arcs in other directions can be constructed readily.)

Table 1 lists the tribes in their order, giving cumulative distances in nautical miles of the points where their intersects cross the diffusion arcs; these distances are approximate, being taken from U.S. Air Force navigation charts[23]; but a number of distances were checked by spherical trigonometry and I am confident that the cumulative errors involved are under 3 % of the stated cumulative distance—usually under 1 %.

TABLE 1

DIFFUSION ARCS

(From Murdock's World Ethnographic Sample)

Explanation of Entries

Column 1 shows distance in nautical miles along the track of the arc from Tierra del Fuego (Cape Arc) and Great Blasquet Island, off the west coast of Ireland (Island Arc), to the point on the track nearest the location given in the WES.

Column 2 names the society and gives its reference number. The reference number shows the culture area in Murdock's World Ethnographic Sample followed by a decimal point and the number of the society within the culture area; for example "57.5 Yahgan" means that the Yahgan people are the fifth society listed in the 57th culture area in the World Ethnographic Sample "45.3 Comanche" means that the Comanche are the third society listed in the 45th culture area.

Column 3, taken from Column 15 of the World Ethnographic Sample, shows Political Integration and Succession types as given there. Key to abbreviations: A - Autonomous local communities, *i.e.*, politically independent local groups which do not exceed 1500 in average population; L - Little states, *i.e.*, political integration in independent units averaging between 10,000 and 100,000 in population; M - Minimal states, *i.e.*, political integration in independent units averaging between 1500 and 10,000 in population; O - Absence of any political integration even at the local level, *e.g.*, where family heads acknowledge no higher political authority; P - Peace groups transcending the local

[23] U. S. Air Force navigation and planning charts, 1:5,000,000, Lambert Conformal Conic Projection; two series of these were used, as available, the AP series and the GNC series. Great circle routes were worked out through the use of the Great Circle Sailing Charts of the U. S. Hydrographic Office; these furnish convenient gnomonic projections which can be applied to any land area simply by substituting any convenient meridian of longitude for the central meridian of the chart and relabeling the other meridians accordingly.

community where the basis of unity is other than political, *e.g.*, derived from reciprocal trade relations, defensive military agreements, or a common cult or age-grade organization; S - States, *i.e.*, political integration in large independent units averaging at least 100,000 in population.

Column 4, taken from Column 14 of the WES, shows Social Stratification as given there. Key to abbreviations: A - Formal age-grades without other significant stratification among freemen; C - Complex stratification into three or more social classes or castes (exclusive of slaves); H - Hereditary aristocracy or noble class differentiated from ordinary freemen; O - Absence of significant social stratification among freemen; purely political and religious statuses, *e.g.*, chiefs or priests, are not treated as classes; W - Wealth distinctions of importance, based on possession or distribution of property, without definite crystallization into hereditary social classes.

Cape Arc

1	2		3	4	1	2		3	4
0	57.5	Yahgan	O	O	6315	48.13	Zuni	A	O
60	57.3	Ona	A	O	6315bis	48.7	Jemez	A	O
200	57.1	Alacaluf	O	O	6320	48.8	Maricopa	M	O
555	47.4	Tehuelche	A	O	6345	48.10	Taos	A	O
965	57.2	Araucanians	A	W	6390	48.12	W. Apache	A	O
2535	56.4	Inca	S	C	6405	45.2	Cheyenne	M	O
2630	55.5	Piro	A	O	6415	48.5	Hopi	A	O
2735	55.1	Cashinawa	A	O	6420	44.12	Walapai	A	O
2875	55.2	Chama	A	O	6445	48.9	Navaho	A	O
3045	55.3	Cocama	A	H	6445bis	44.1	Havasupai	A	O
3095	55.19	Yagua	A	O	6540	44.6	Shivwits	A	O
3215	55.4	Jivaro	O	O	6600	44.11	Ute	A	O
3225	55.9	Witoto	A	O	6740	44.2	Hukundika	A	O
3465	56.2	Cayapa	A	O	6810	45.4	Crow	M	O
3600	56.3	Chibcha	L	H	6820	44.7	Shoshone	A	O
3905	51.4	Cuna	M	W	6945	44.5	Paiute	A	O
4085	51.5	Guaymí	M	H	7050	44.3	Klamath	P	W
4115	51.9	Bribri	M	H	7120	44.10	Tenino	P	W
4235	51.8	Miskito	M	H	7150	42.1	Alsea	A	H
4520	51.6	Lenca	A	H	7165	44.14	Wishram	P	W
4565	51.3	Chorti	M	H	7235	44.9	Sinkaietk	A	W
4665	51.2	Cakchiquel	M	C	7240	42.6	Puyallup	A	H
4735	51.7	Maya	M	C	7260	44.4	Kutenai	A	O
5135	50.8	Totonac	S	C	7335	42.8	Stalo	A	H
5215	50.1	Aztec	S	C	7340	42.7	Quileute	A	H
5255	50.7	Tarasco	S	H	7410	42.5	Nootka	M	C
5355	50.3	Huastec	M	C	7430	44.8	Shuswap	A	O
5975	49.6	Yaqui	A	O	7600	42.2	Bellacoola	A	W
5990	45.3	Comanche	P	O	7615	41.3	Carrier	A	H
6005	49.2	Opata	A	O	7855	42.4	Haida	A	H
6085	48.2	Chiricahua	A	O	7935	41.5	Kaska	O	O
6190	49.3	Papago	A	O	8030	42.1	Tlingit	A	H
6265	48.6	Isleta	A	O	8410	*42.3	Eyak	A	H
6290	48.1	Acoma	A	O	8795	41.11	Tanaina	A	H
6290bis	48.3	Cochiti	A	O	9845	23.2	Chukchee	A	W
6290bis	48.11	Tewa	A	O	10235	23.6	Koryak	A	W

1	2		3	4	1	2		3	4
11125	23.3	Gilyak	O	O	17640	9.11	Shilluk	S	C
12255	24.3	Ch'i-tan	S	C	17730	10.4	Dinka	P	W
12395	24.2	Chinese	S	C	17850	9.4	Bongo	A	O
13095	22.5	Monguor	M	H	17920	9.2	Banda	A	O
13325	22.4	Khalka	L	H	17980	9.1	Azandẹ	L	H
14415	22.3	Kazak	S	H	18090	9.9	Mangbetu	L	H
14890	22.6	Turkmen	L	H	18120	5.1	Babwa	M	O
14895	22.7	Uzbek	L	H	18150	1.2	Bambuti	A	O
15530	19.4	Georgians	S	C	18210	5.10	Poto	A	W
15585	19.1	Armenians	S	C	18630	3.5	Kuba	L	H
15665	20.4	Kurd	M	H	18765	5.6	Luba	L	H
15795	20.1	Babylonians	S	C	18945	3.2	Chokwe	L	H
16135	20.5	Lebanese	S	C	19045	3.6	Lamba	M	H
16245	20.3	A. Hebrews	S	C	19205	3.7	Lozi	S	C
16485	14.1	A. Egyptians	S	C	19230	3.3	Ila	A	W
16590	13.3	Siwans	M	W	19520	1.6	Kung	A	O
16750	14.4	Silwa	S	C	19630	2.1	Herero	A	W
17310	12.4	Kababish	L	W	19635	1.7	Naron	A	O
17545	9.5	Dilling	M	H	19690	1.3	Bergdama	A	O
17605	9.10	Mesakin	M	W	19905	1.4	Nama	M	W
17605bis	12.2	Fur	S	C	20160	1.9	Xam	A	O

Island Arc

1	2		3	4	1	2		3	4
50	17.6	Irish	S	C	4660	26.6	Oraon	M	C
375	17.3	English	S	C	4700	26.7	Santal	M	O
595	17.2	Dutch	S	C	4710	26.4	Ho	S	H
815	17.4	Prussians	S	C	5440	28.1	Andamanese	O	O
965	18.3	Czechs	S	C	5635	30.6	Selung	O	O
1195	18.5	Hungarians	S	C	5705	28.4	Nicobarese	A	W
1265	18.10	Serbs	S	C	6110	30.7	Semang	O	O
1405	18.1	Bulgarians	S	C	6130	32.2	Batak	A	O
1445	18.8	Rumanians	S	C	6150	30.4	Malay (Trengganu)	S	C
1605	15.2	A. Athenians	S	C	6345	32.9	Minangkabau	A	W
1735	20.6	Turks (Anatol.)	S	C	6380	32.6	Kubu	A	O
2145	19.7	A. Scythians	S	H	6850	32.4	Iban	A	O
2235	19.3	Cherkess	M	H	7330	33.6	Macassarcse	L	C
2325	19.6	Osset	P	H	7400	33.11	Toradja	A	W
2395	19.4	Georgians	S	C	7700	33.4	Ili-Mandiri	S	H
2415	19.1	Armenians	S	C	7810	33.2	Alor	A	W
2455	20.4	Kurds	M	H	7880	33.3	Belu	M	C
2845	21.3	Iranians	S	C	8160	33.9	Tanimbarese	A	H
3225	22.6	Turkmen	L	H	8250	33.5	Kei	A	O
3595	21.2	Hazara	M	C	8400	35.3	Kapauku	P	W
3615	21.1	Afghans	S	C	8445	35.10	Waropen	O	O
3670	21.5	Nuri (Kafir)	M	W	8825	35.4	Keraki	A	O
3780	25.3	Dard	L	C	8850	35.6	Kutubu	O	O
4010	26.1	A. Aryans	S	C	8880	35.11	Wogeo	O	O
4550	27.5	Gond	M	W	8890	35.5	Kiwai	A	O
4555	27.1	Baiga	A	O	8895	35.1	Arapesh	O	O

1	2	3	4	1	2	3	4
8955	35.2 Banaro	O	A	10360	38.3 Tismulun	A	W
8965	35.8 Miriam	O	O	10400	39.2 Tikopia	A	H
9195	35.9 Orokaiva	A	O	10420	38.2 Banks Is.	A	W
9265	35.7 Mailu	O	O	10435	38.1 Ambryn	A	W
9320	37.7 Nakanai	O	W	10935	38.8 Rotumans	M	O
9350	37.10 Trobrianders	M	H	11070	38.10 Nakaroka	M	O
9370	37.4 Dobuans	O	O	11075	38.4 Lau	M	H
9495	37.3 Kurtatchi	A	H	11555	39.8 Tokelau	M	O
9565	37.2 Siuai	A	W	11685	39.6 Manua	M	H
9565bis	37.9 Rossell Is.	M	W	12140	39.4 Pukapuka	A	O
9955	37.5 Malaitans	A	O	12800	40.4 Mangaians	M	H
9960	37.11 Ulawans	A	O	13155	40.8 Tahitians	M	H
9970	39.5 Rennell Is.	A	H	15485	40.1 Easter Is.	A	H

* After the paper was in press, it was discovered that the stated distance between the Eyak and Tanaina intersects on the Cape Arc was greatly in error. Beginning with the Tanaina and continuing through the Xam, all stated cumulative distances on the Cape Arc are 380 nautical miles too large.

A Diffusion Test

If these traits diffuse, they should tend to occur in clusters. True, any traits distributed at random occur in random clusters or bunches, but if these traits diffuse they should cluster more frequently than expected in a random distribution. The distribution of each level of social stratification, and of political organization has been individually tested for clustering by the "Wald-Wolfowitz" run test.[24] For example, in testing to see whether Level 3 of Social Stratification is diffused, we call every society on the arc at this level of Social Stratification an X, and every other tribe a Y. Each series of the same letter is called a run; in the sequence $XXYYYXYYY$ there are two runs of X and two runs of Y. Using the notation in Table Two (that of Mosteller and Bush), $m = 3$, $n = 6$, and $d = 2 + 2 = 4$. If diffusion did not occur, we would expect the X's to be scattered randomly among the Y's, with only as many runs as a random scattering would be likely to produce; the more diffusion of Level 3, the more concentrated will be the X's (and consequently likewise the Y's), and the fewer the *number* of runs. The results of this test, given in Table 2 show conclusively that these traits do tend to cluster far more than would be expected by random distribution, hence that they must presumably have been spread, at least in part, by borrowing and/or migration.

True, as William Kruskal has pointed out in a letter to the writer, such a clustering might logically also be explained by an undiffusional association

[24] Frederick Mosteller and Robert R. Bush, "Selected Quantitative Techniques," *Handbook of Social Psychology*, *op. cit.* 1: 321 f; Abraham Wald and J. Wolfowitz, "On a test whether two samples are from the same populations," *Annals of Mathematical Statistics*, 11 (1940) 147-162; Frieda S. Swed and C. Eisenhart, "Tables for Testing the Randomness of grouping in a sequence of alternatives," *Annals of Mathematical Statistics*, 14 (1943) 66-87.

TABLE 2

RUN TEST FOR DIFFUSION

Trait	m	n	d	$\bar{d}$	P
Social Stratification					
Level 1 (W, A, O)*	104	88	60	97.6	< .0001
2 (H)*	47	145	54	72.0	.0003
3 (C)*	41	151	39	65.5	< .0001
Political Organization					
Level 1 (A, O)*	98	94	51	97.1	.0006
2 (M, L, P)*	57	135	65	81.0	.0035
3 (S)*	37	155	35	60.7	< .0001

* For explanation of symbols in stub, see Table 1.

Caption: *m* = number of cases of type in question

n = number of cases of other types

d = actual number of runs

$\bar{d}$ = expected number of runs = $\frac{2mn}{m+n} + 1$

P = probability (one-sided) of random occurrence of so few runs, computed from the formula $\sigma_d^2 = \frac{2mn(2mn - m - n)}{(m+n)^2(m+n-1)}$; $z = \frac{d - \bar{d} + 1/2}{\sigma_d}$ and entering a table of area of the normal curve with z. Note that one uses such a table without the need to assume that the distribution of the underlying variable is normal. Wald and Wolfowitz show that no matter what this distribution is, the distribution of the runs tends toward normal and by actual computation Swed and Eisenhart show that the normal approximation almost never leads to error where *m* and *n* are each greater than 12 but not greater than 20; and the approximation gets even better as the number increases.

between the traits in question and some naturally clustering environmental feature, such as soil type or climate. Since the purpose of the present study is however to present a method for dealing with hyperdiffusional associations, the presumption that clustering as shown in Table 2 reflects diffusion is a conservative one; if the traits in question were both undiffusionally associated with soil type or climate, this would constitute a sociological law and not a mere historical accident. The final conclusion of this paper is that there is indeed some kind of sociological law at work; we do not identify it; perhaps environmental factors in their application to subsistence technology may indeed be the one—but that is not our problem here. The question of whether these traits have each spread from a single center of origin or have instead been independently invented two or more times does not concern us here either.

Implication of a Negative Result

If a comparatively small and widely scattered sample is measured by this test, a negative result (reporting no tendency to cluster) might well occur.

Such a result would not exclude the possibility of diffusion but would tend to show any association between the variables revealed by a statistical test (*e.g.*, by a chi-square test of a contingency table) is not to be explained as an artifact of diffusion, and could not be a hyperdiffusional association. It could be either an undiffusional association or a semidiffusional association.

If a complete study of all the tribes in a strip on which information can be had yields a negative result, diffusion is conclusively disproved. The presence of a few small clusters in such a strip would be explainable by mere random bunching. Any statistically significant association between two traits whose distribution is thus shown to be unaffected by diffusion must be an undiffusional distribution. However, it seems evident that all traits related functionally either to ecology, social evolution or value systems—all of which are known to be distributed in diffusion patches of the culture area type—will in fact have positive results.

Theoretically then "the WW run test," in conjunction with an ordinary statistical test of association can reveal the existence of an undiffusional association, distinguishing it from a hyperdiffusional or a semidiffusional one; but it does not seem likely that many such associations exist. Likewise, on a small well-scattered sample, these two tests might rule out the possibility that an association is hyperdiffusional.

A Sifting Test

John W. M. Whiting privately mentioned to me an unpublished study of his in which he rejected from his original sample one of each neighboring pair with identical results, in order to reduce the effects of diffusion. Such a procedure obviously would tend to reduce the correlations of the test for association; and attempts by me to put this method into practice on a modest scale invariably resulted in non-significant results.

The theory of the sifting test however did seem to have merit. True, the fact that two widely separated peoples have like traits does not necessarily rule out a connection through diffusion. But it does suggest that similar associations are not hyperdiffusional associations. The wide separation indicates that the traits, if not undiffusional associations, are semidiffusional ones—if we cannot say with confidence that these traits have not anciently diffused, we can say that the societies which bear them have clung to them despite considerable time and the example of neighbors with other traits. Where repeatedly, again and again, widely separated peoples cling to certain trait combinations, even though peoples in between have different trait combinations, hyperdiffusional association cannot explain the result. Some method following the line of reasoning of the Whitings ought then to be able to distinguish undiffusional and semidiffusional associations on one hand from hyperdiffusional associations on the other.

However, simply culling neighbors with like traits from a sample seems an inadequate procedure. One intervening example of another type offers a counter-diffusional force of undetermined and perhaps modest strength. Furthermore, in the diffusion arcs, it occasionally happens that tribes whose intersect lines are adjacent may be more distant from each other than tribes with a third intersect line between them. Some theoretical basis for sifting is needed which establishes a presumption that usually "functional" as well as "historical" factors are involved in the societies which survive the sifting process.

Such a basis exists. I have tabulated the rank order differences along the diffusion arcs of recurrences of each possible type of association. By rank order difference of recurrence is meant the interval measured in number of other societies between each instance of a type and the next succeeding instance of the same type. In a hyperdiffusional association, we would expect a unimodal frequency distribution of these rank order differences, with the mode at 1. That is, most often, the recurrent next succeeding instance of a given type would be its neighbor; next most often, the next succeeding instance would be the next tribe but one, and so on. In an undiffusional association, we would also expect a unimodal frequency distribution, but a vastly different one—the mode should be not at 1 but somewhere near m/n, where m = number of cases of the association in question and n = number of other cases. A semidiffusional association should partake of both types of distribution and consequently should have a bimodal distribution. Table 3 shows that such a distribution in fact occurs in the present sample for the traits studied. Consider the trough between the modes at a rank difference of 10. This trough suggests that some of the cases of lesser difference reflect the functional factor in the semidiffusional association (though most reflect the diffusional factor) while some of the cases of greater difference reflect the diffusional factor (though most reflect the functional). If we take this point as

Table 3

RANK DIFFERENCES BETWEEN SUCCESSIVE COMBINATIONS

This table exhibits the frequency of rank differences of successive combinations of like type. By rank is meant simply order of occurrence along the diffusion arcs (see Table 1). Example: the first society on the Cape Arc, the Yahgan, has Type O Political Organization and Type O Social Stratification; the second society, the Ona, has Types A and O respectively and thus is a combination of a different type; the third society, the Alacaluf, has Types O and O respectively, like the Yahgan; the fourth society, the Tehuelche, has Types A and O respectively, like the Ona; scoring:—Yahgan, no score since it is the first of its type; Ona, no score since it is the first of its type; Alacaluf, rank difference two, since it is the third society and differs in order of occurrence by two from the next preceding society of its type; Tehuelche, score two similarly. In this table have been included not only the tribes listed in Table 1 but also those tribes on the diffusion arcs with Type D—Political Organization omitted from Table 1. This table uses class intervals of two and five for convenience in presentation but the bimodal distribution here exhibited is by no means an artifact of the class intervals; class intervals of one, three, and four likewise display bimodality.

Rank Difference	Number of Societies	Modes
1-2	90	Mode #1
3-4	15	
5-6	12	
7-8	10	
9-10	2	
11-12	4	
13-14	3	
15-16	5	
17-18	0	
19-20	7	
21-22	2	Mode #2
23-25	0	
26-30	1	
31-35	1	
36-40	2	
41-45	2	
46-50	2	
51-55	2	
56-60	2	
61-65	2	
over 65	2	

our sift interval, we have a theoretical justification for supposing that we are losing about as many "functional" cases as we are gaining diffusional cases. Apart from this, fixing such a long interval reinforces the argument that traits which nevertheless remain in association though presented with so many contrary examples by intervening societies must have some tendency to diffuse together.

Accordingly, I sifted both arcs; once a trait combination of a given type occurred, I rejected all succeeding cases of a like combination not separated by at least nine unlike cases from its predecessor. (In this sifting, I treated each variety of each level separately; an AW combination was accepted even though it immediately followed an AO combination, both of which are at level 1.)

This sifting process left 63 survivors of the original 192 tribes. Each of these 63 tribes was separated by an unbroken interval of at least nine tribes of other types from the nearest other example counted of like type. A chi-square test of relationship between high and low levels of social stratification and political organization was made, as shown in Table 4; the result emphatically rejects the hypothesis that mere chance explains the association. This table indicates that on at least 43 separate occasions these traits were either independently invented in association or independently retained in association despite much counterdiffusional pressure from other traits; on only 20 occasions, less than half as many, was one trait adopted (or retained) without the other. This sifting test thus rejects the hypothesis that the association between political organization and social stratification is hyperdiffusional.

The sifting test does, however, have four weaknesses. None of them are

Table 4

SIFTING TEST

Political Organization	Social Stratification		Total
	High (C, H)*	Low (W, A, O)*	
High (S, M, L, P)*	27	14	41
Low (A, O)*	6	16	22
Totals	33	30	63

Chi-square (with Yates' correction) = 7.011
P = .004 (one-sided test)
Q = .675
Phi = .368

* For key to these symbols, see Table 1.

serious; it is easy to reject intuitively the assumption that the data of Table 4 could be an artifact of any or all. Yet they need to be mentioned. 1) Conceivably, two successive examples of like types, separated on the diffusion arc by at least nine intervening examples of other types, could be joined by a continuous distribution *outside* the arc. 2) The proportion of intervening examples of like types in the universe may differ importantly from the proportion in Murdock's sample. 3) Diffusion ripples spreading out from a culture center on or near the arc might duplicate distributions and associations on both sides (although if both sides survived the pressures of counter-diffusion of other types, this fact would strengthen rather than weaken the case.) 4) In designing diffusion arcs, it is important that parellel arcs be a considerable interval apart, in order not to duplicate results by counting diffusion bands twice. In practice, it is difficult to control this phenomenon unless the arcs are widely separated. (In the present example, the arcs cross in the Middle East; but as it happened the sifting process removed all but one of the duplicating examples—this duplication, the Turkmen, I deleted from the Island Arc.)

A Cluster Test

However, I offer a second test following an entirely different line of reasoning, which is free from all these objections. For this test, it does not matter how much diffusion occurs in tribes not in the sample, or not on the arcs, or how much duplication there is of diffusion patterns through spreading out of ripples from a diffusion center.

The cluster test concentrates on the peculiar character of semidiffusional associations. In an undiffusional association, neither hits nor misses diffuse; the association of traits occurs geographically at random—by definition. In a hyperdiffusional association, hits and misses both diffuse with equal facility. Only in a semidiffusional association is a difference to be expected between the diffusion rate of hits and misses. This difference is implied by the definition of a semidiffusional association, one in which traits tend to diffuse together. If such a tendency exists, hits should form large diffusion patches, misses only small ones. If on the other hand, the traits are simply accidental products of joint diffusion—hyperdiffusional associations—there is no reason why misses should not diffuse as readily as hits. The key variable becomes not the total number of hits and misses but their tendency to cluster. In a hyperdiffusional association, both hits and misses should have a high tendency to cluster; in an undiffusional association, neither should have a tendency to cluster; in a semidiffusional association, the hits should tend to cluster markedly more than the misses. In a WW run test scheme, I predict relatively fewer runs of hits than of misses. A test of this hypothesis is a test of the semidiffusional hypothesis; if there is no significant difference in the diffusion pattern, we are dealing with a hyperdiffusional distribution and the semidiffusional hypothesis is refuted. It seems not at all unlikely that some phenomena should reveal a highly significant difference between the tendency of hits to cluster and the tendency of misses to cluster—and yet, because of other factors not involved in the study, display a low overall association. Even so, a semidiffusional relationship would have been established, while a high association without a significant difference in this clustering tendency would in the presence of evidence that the individual traits diffuse constitute evidence of a high hyperdiffusional association. This test, then, is a test of the diffusion process itself and distinguishes hyperdiffusional associations from semidiffusional associations. (It is not applicable to most undiffusional associations.)

The basic variable is the expected number of runs, as computed for the run test ($\bar{d}$ in the Mosteller-Bush notation). Let this be computed for each type of miss, and compared with the actual number of runs (in computing these runs, of course, we distinguish the type being studied, which we call *X*, and all other tribes, whether hits or misses, which we call *Y*.)

For the purpose of this cluster test, the nine different possible combinations are classified as shown in Table 5. For this cluster test, each of the three types

Table 5

TYPES OF HITS AND MISSES

Political Organization	Social Stratification		
	Level 3 (C)*	Level 2 (H)*	Level 1 (W, A, O)*
Level 3 (S)*	H_1	E_1	E_2
Level 2 (M, L, P)*	E_3	H_2	E_4
Level 1 (A, O)*	E_5	E_6	H_3

*See Table 1 for explanation of symbols.

of hits (H_1, H_2, and H_3) are considered as well as each of the six types of misses (E_1, E_2, E_3, E_4, E_5, and E_6). (For this test, no distinction is made between the sub-types of each level; type W social stratification is treated as identical with type A and type O; this is done whether the combination is a hit or a miss and reduces the number of types of each to workable limits; it in no way biases the results).

Table 6 shows the results of this cluster test. The hits have a marked

TABLE 6

CLUSTER TEST OF HITS AND MISSES

Type	X	Y	d	$\bar{d}$	$d/\bar{d}$	rank	Mann- Whitney Test of Significance of Differences in $d/\bar{d}$ Ratio
Cape Arc							T = sum of ranks of less frequent case = 66
H_1	15	51	17	24.3	0.7	13	
H_2	17	50	19	26.4	0.72	11	$\bar{T} = \frac{m}{2}(m + n + 1) = 45$
H_3	51	42	33	47.1	0.702	12	$\sigma_d = \frac{mn(m + n + 1)}{12}$
E_1	2	57	5	3.96	1.26	1	
E_2	0		0		—	—	$\sigma_T = 7.746$
E_3	4	56	7	8.43	0.832	8	One-sided $P < .005$
E_4	14	46	27	22.4	1.2	2	
E_5	0		0		—	—	
E_6	11	52	15	19.1	0.785	10	
Island Arc							
H_1	17	40	12	24.9	0.481	14	
H_2	9	39	15	15.6	0.96	7	
H_3	31	33	27	32.8	0.825	9	
E_1	3	43	7	6.61	1.06	4	
E_2	0		0		—	—	
E_3	5	41	11	9.91	1.11	3	
E_4	8	39	15	14.3	1.05	5	
E_5	0		0		—	—	
E_6	5	41	10	9.91	1.01	6	

Explanation of Captions

Type = The nine theoretically possible combinations of the three levels of Political Organization and Social Stratification are labeled as shown in Table 5; for example, Type H_1 is a society at level three of both these traits. H_1, H_2 and H_3 are hit types, whose occurrence supports the hypothesis; E_1, E_3, E_4 and E_6 are miss types, whose occurrence fails to support the hypothesis (types E_2 and E_5, the two combinations of Level 1 and Level 3, never occur in this sample).

X = The total number of societies of the type in question.

Y = The total number of *runs* of societies of other types. The purpose of each line is to compute the tendency of each type to cluster, that is, to occur in runs; counting the runs of *other* types as single events eliminates *their* tendency to run from the computation of $\bar{d}$. This precaution seems wise theoretically; in the present problem if we do not take it but instead make $Y = N - X$, that is, make $Y =$ the total number of societies of other types, the final result is slightly more significant: $T = 67$.

$d =$ The total number of runs of X's and Y's. Example: $H_1H_1H_2H_3H_3E_1H_1H_1H_1E_1$. For H_1, $d = 4$; for H_2, $d = 3$; for H_3, $d = 3$; for E_1, $d = 4$.

$\bar{d} =$ The expected number of runs according to the Wald-Wolfowitz run test formula:

$$\bar{d} = \frac{2mn}{m + n} + 1 .$$

tendency to cluster more than the misses. This tendency is measured by the Mann-Whitney "*U*" test,[25] a non-parametric test of rank differences. It leaves no reasonable doubt that the misses tend to scatter more than the hits; the hits tend to cluster more than the misses; and this tendency is established by a standard which allows for the number of each type. That is, the test is not for how many clusters occur, but for the ratio between the observed number of clusters and the expected number, given the observed number of societies of the type in question and the observed number of other societies. Thus this test shows that the hits diffuse more readily than the misses; hence the association cannot be a hyperdiffusional association, and must be a semidiffusional association.

It has already been pointed out that the diffusion arc measures propinquity only in one direction and thus introduces a small amount of distortion by ignoring distances across the arc. This tendency has the effect of slightly reducing the number of clusters on the arc where diffusion is present; thus the true difference between the cluster tendency of hits and misses will tend to be slightly greater than that reported by this cluster test.

Discussion

If the association of traits is a sheer coincidence of common origin of two borrowing patches, there is no reason for the traits to have similar boundaries, and it is unlikely that the borrowing of one trait will stop where the borrowing of the other trait does. However, if traits are spread by migration patches rather than by borrowing patches, the limits of their distribution would tend to be the limits of the migration of the tribes. Now linguistic relationship is usually a measure of migration distributions. In the two diffusion arcs used here, if we can judge by the language map, there is practically no duplication of migration patches; the arcs cross in a region of considerable linguistic

[25] Mosteller and Bush, *op. cit.*, pp. 315-7; Colin White, "The Use of Ranks in a Test of Significance for Comparing Two Treatments," *Biometrics*, 8 (1952) 33-41, gives tables at two-sided .05, .01 and .001 significance levels for $N = 30$ and provides an empirical check on the closeness of the normal approximation and an alternative method of extending his tables.

diversity, with Indo-European, Semitic and other language families of the Caucasus region present; furthermore, the portions of the arcs adjacent to the intersection region differ substantially in language family: the Cape Arc has chiefly Turkic and Mongol to the northeast and Semitic to the southwest, while the Island Arc has an overwhelming predominance of Indo-European languages for about 2000 miles in each direction. Should an investigator use a series of parallel diffusion arcs which go through the same migration patch, the result of the cluster test could be misleading. To avoid this error, if neighboring tribes on the two parallel arcs have identical traits and belong to the same language family, the parallel clusters should not be counted twice. A good rule of thumb would be: there should be at least as many distinct clusters of each type of each trait as there are diffusion arcs.

Summary

To determine the nature of a statistically significant association between traits in a cross-cultural statistical survey, proceed as follows:

1) Group the societies by location in long thin strips. The diffusion arcs here used are examples with special convenience for certain purposes.

2) Use the Wald-Wolfowitz run test on each trait individually in turn to test for a tendency to cluster. *Positive results* on all traits involved in an association presumably require the rejection of the hypothesis of undiffusional association; positive results are usually to be expected. *Negative results* on any trait are rarely to be expected unless the societies in the sample are widely separated; they reject the hypothesis of a hyperdiffusional association.

3*a*) Step Two Positive: Use the cluster test to see if hits diffuse more readily than misses. It they clearly do, it is a semidiffusional association and hence involves a nomothetic relationship. If they clearly do not, it is presumably a hyperdiffusional association and hence probably involves an idiographic relationship. Alternatively, or as an additional check, the more cumbersome and less rigorous sifting test may be used: this requires an analysis of rank interval distribution and elimination of cases closer to preceding like case than the interval forming the trough between two modes of the rank interval frequencies.

3*b*) Step Two Negative: If sample used in step two involved minimal intervals between societies—that is, if all the societies on the strip were studied for which data is available and the data is substantially complete—a negative result for step two implies an undiffusional association; no further study is needed. If the sample used in step two did not involve minimal intervals, another sample might be studied which does; if this result is positive, the association is a semidiffusional association; if negative, it is an undiffusional association.

This paper demonstrates Steps 1, 2 and 3*a* for the association between complexity of political organization and social stratification and shows this to be a semidiffusional association. This demonstration establishes for the first time the hypothesis that this association is a nomothetic one, reflecting underlying sociological laws, and not an idiographic one, merely reflecting accidents of diffusion.

Acknowledgements

This paper represents the fruit of six years of analysis and trial-and-error. Much was done while a Fellow at the Center for Advanced Study in the Behavioral Sciences at Stanford, 1954-1955; and while at the Naval Ordnance Test Station, China Lake, California during the summer of 1959. I profited highly by discussions of this problem with Ralph Beals, Herbert Kelman, Clyde Kluckhohn, Robert H. Lowie, David Hays, Robert Redfield, and John W. F. Whiting. The paper was read in manuscript by Roy D'Andrade, Edmund Carpenter, Joseph B. Ford, A. L. Kroeber, William Kruskal, Thomas W. Milburn, George P. Murdock, Jerome Richfield and John W. M. Whiting; I am most grateful for their many valuable suggestions and criticisms. I am additionally indebted to Thomas W. Milburn, John W. M. Whiting and Frank Wilcoxon for special courtesies and cooperation which proved most valuable. Carolyn Huber did much of the work on Table 1. I alone am responsible for errors and shortcomings.

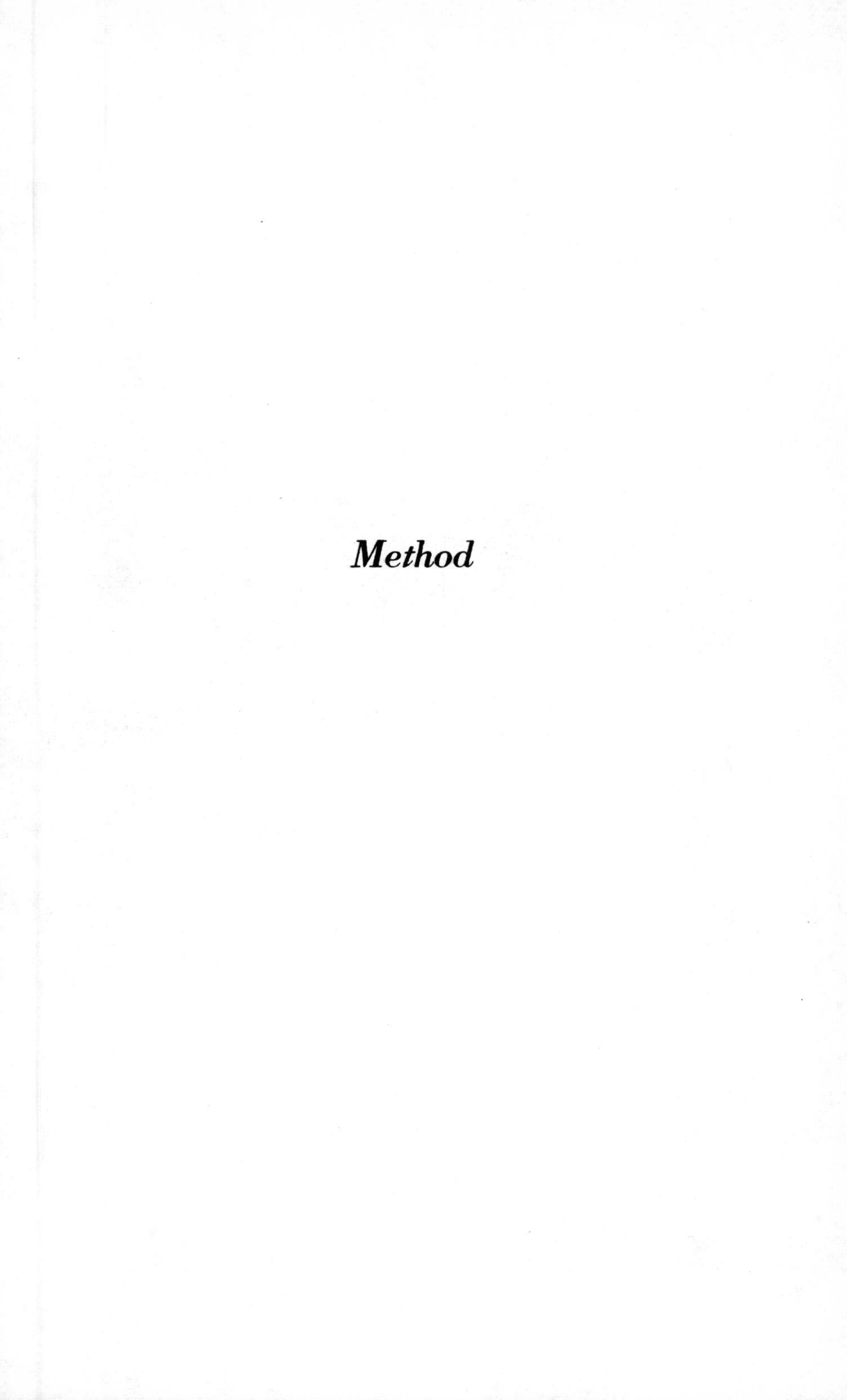

Method

A SAMPLE COMPARATIVE ANALYSIS OF MATERIAL CULTURE *

CLELLAN S. FORD

THE science of culture has as its general objective the systematic organization of the anthropological and sociological information now available and yet to be collected. This objective has many facets, some of which have been recognized as important while others have been neglected. Many notable attempts have been made to treat social phenomena in a scientific spirit, and some have yielded significant results. In certain sociological circles comparative cultural studies represent the dominant modern trend, while other students find their principal interest in historical studies of ethnic and culture-bearing groups. Some attempts have been made to apply statistical methods to cultural problems. Modern sociology, however, has apparently developed its general propositions, for the most part, on the basis of unanalyzed materials.

The natural sciences have proceeded by way of two general methods, namely, synthesis and analysis. By synthesis, data are organized to yield general theories. The theory or law thus developed presents an abstract description of a specific range of phenomena. It automatically becomes an hypothesis when an attempt is made to extend its validity beyond the original limits. Working in a reverse direction from this synthesizing of data, science has proceeded to analyze the facts substantiating the theories. Analytic treatment of the facts provides science with a more exact foundation for its generalizations. Faulty or inadequate theories may then be revised in accordance with the findings of analysis to yield satisfactory laws. If the study of culture is to become a full-fledged science, analysis presumably will play an equally important part in its development. As yet, however, the theories of the social scientists, despite their frequently glaring inadequacy, have seldom been subjected to refinement by analysis.

One such generalization is that the maintenance mores are basic. The facts show, it is contended, that the mores crystallizing out of

*Reprinted from George Peter Murdock (ed.), *Studies in the Science of Society* (New Haven, Yale University Press, 1937), pp. 225-246, by permission of the author and the publisher.

economic activities are the first to respond to changing conditions, and are the most influential in their reaction with the other mores. This theory, although doubtless true in the light of the evidence, is phrased in terms too general to be readily applicable. Practically no attempt has been made to analyze culture with a view to determining just how these changes and reactions take place. An attempt to analyze primitive material culture has seemed advisable as a first step in remedying this situation. Such a study should show, also, whether or not analysis is adapted to attacking the problems of culture. If recognized scientific methods are applicable anywhere to the data of sociology and anthropology, the field of material culture would seem to offer the greatest likelihood of success. When considered as one of the many intricate phases of culture, man's material adjustment appears to be comparatively free from the perplexing difficulties which seem so characteristic of other segments of culture. When, however, material culture is inspected in relative isolation, the apparent simplicity is transformed into complexity, and the problems encountered become so involved that it is even difficult to indicate clearly what is meant by "material culture."

Culture is primarily concerned with the way people act. The actions, then, of manufacture and use, and the expressed theories about the production, use, and nature of material objects constitute the data of material culture. In their relation to culture, artifacts and materials are to be classed in the same category as the substances, such as minerals, flora, and fauna, which compose the environment in which people live. Artifacts themselves are not cultural data, although, to be sure, they are often the concrete manifestations of human actions and cultural processes. The cultural actions of a people cannot even be inferred from them without extreme caution, for a number of reasons. Chief among these are the following: (1) instead of being a product of the culture the artifact may have been imported; (2) the process of manufacture is frequently not implicit in the artifact itself; and (3) the use or function of the artifact is not deducible from the object alone.

A careful investigation of man's actions with material things in any culture reveals that the complex processes described by the ethnographer are composed of actions which may be isolated as units. For example, the manufacture of pottery, treated in a single section by most ethnographers, is a combination of unit actions, each of which is specifically related to the others. One such unit type of action is the kneading of the clay. These individual actions may be visualized as the links in a chain of such actions, which, taken as a group, constitute the complex process of manufacture or use. Further consideration reveals that these unit actions play different kinds of rôles. Some serve only as necessary intermediate links between the raw material and the finished product. Such, for example, is the action of kneading clay in pottery making. Others are directly related to the physiological and psychological needs of human beings and represent the final links in a chain. Thus, for example, the cooking of food in a pot prepares materials directly for human consumption. Still other unit actions appear to combine the first two types; although serving primarily as links preparatory to other actions, they nevertheless, at the same time, satisfy directly some desire or need of the native. Such, for example, would be the final action which results in a decorated pot. Although primarily intended to enter into other actions as a utensil, and thus belonging to the first-mentioned category, the pot is itself pleasing to the maker and to other members of the society. Similarly a native, when binding an adz head to its haft, produces an ornamental lashing which has an æsthetic value. In this connection it is worth noting that some processes have as their result something which is ostensibly designed to assist in another action and yet which has no such function in the culture. Such, for example, would be a ceremonial adz.

Apart from the characteristics of actions which refer to their position within complex processes, other identifying features may be discerned which relate to the composition of an individual action. Close inspection of a number of unit actions reveals that each one is observable and describable in terms of: (1) purpose, (2) materials, (3) means, (4) method, and (5) result.

The *purpose* of the action is a part of the prevailing theory concerning the action; it may or may not be consciously expressed. The *result* is both *actual* and *theoretical*. By theoretical result is meant that which is believed to come about as the consequence of the action; it represents the fulfilment of the purpose. If the purpose is found achieved in the actual result, the action may be termed *rational.* If the purpose is found not to be achieved in the actual result, but only in the theoretical result, the action may be called *irrational* or *magical.* If the purpose is achieved neither in the actual nor in the theoretical result, the action may be called a *failure.* An action without a purpose is a *random action* and is not rational, although it may produce advantageous and desirable results. Whether or not the purpose is achieved in the actual result is a part of the judgment of the action which may be made on the basis of scientific investigation. However, even if the purpose stated by a native is demonstrated by modern science not to be achieved in the actual result, it is, nevertheless, extremely risky to posit that the action has no survival value. The action may be efficacious for reasons which might be overlooked by the scientist.

In a rational action, it should be noted, the theoretical result is identical with that part of the actual result which corresponds to the purpose. Oftentimes, of course, the actual result, besides achieving the purpose, includes other elements not covered by the purpose. These may be called *socially irrelevant results,* and they may or may not be consciously recognized as existing. This may be clarified by an example. When a tree is cut with an adz, a considerable portion of the kinetic energy or momentum of the moving tool is converted into sound upon contact with the wood. If the stated purpose of the native is to fell the tree, the sound thus produced is socially irrelevant. In many cases, as in this example, the socially irrelevant results are so obvious and striking that it is extremely improbable that they should be totally disregarded. The importance of noting the socially irrelevant results may be illustrated by the following example. In both Samoa and Fiji the bast of the paper mulberry is beaten on wooden anvils for the express purpose of so widening the bast that it will be suitable as segments of cloth. Sound is produced incidentally and is recognized by the natives to the extent that they keep time with their mallets, sometimes beating out complicated rhythms. This immediately suggests a connection with the wooden gong, which is used in both cultures. Indeed, it is quite possible that the wooden gong represents a specialized development growing out of the recognition of just such a socially irrelevant result as that involved in beating out bark cloth on a wooden anvil.

The *materials* may be defined as those substances which enter into an action and are found in the result. The *means* may be defined as that which enters into the process only to effect the result, and which is not found in the result. It is to be noticed that many substances commonly considered means are here classified as materials. Such is, for example, the sennit braid which enters into the action of securing an adz to its haft. Although commonly treated as the means, the sennit braid is here considered to be one of the materials entering into the action, the actual means being the hands. The confusion arises from the fact that the braid is the means by which the adz head is kept on the haft once the result has been achieved. It is in no sense, however, a tool effecting the original joining of adz and haft. *Method* refers to the way in which the means are applied to the materials in order to effect the result; it includes motor habits, techniques of manipulation, and scientific processes involved.

The substances which form a part of an action, either as materials, means, or results, may be characterized both by their properties and by their internal structure. Thus, for example, carbon monoxide gas may be described in terms of the properties which that gas has in its possible relationships with other substances, and also in terms of the number and type of atoms which compose its constituent molecules. For the purpose of this work it seems more logical and suitable to define substances by their properties. Reference to the cases will reveal the reason. If, for example, we find that the Samoan cuts wood with a species of shell, we should find ourselves burdened with an impossible task if we depended for our definition of the wood and the shell upon their respective molecular composition as determined by the chemist in the laboratory. Whatever descriptions of substances we make, therefore, if they are to be useful or even possible, must be primarily in terms of properties rather than of internal structure. The properties of matter are capable of logical classification according to four categories: form, composition, motion, and vibrational energy. By composition is meant the capacity of a substance for chemical reaction; vibrational energy is taken to include all wave phenomena such as sound, heat, and light. All matter is describable in terms of its properties and therefore in terms of its form, composition, motion, and vibrational energy. A certain wood used by the Fijians, for example, might be described, with reference to its form, as relatively hard, heavy, of a certain toughness and tensile strength, and of a certain shape. In respect to its composition, it might be described as susceptible to oxidation, destructive distillation, fermentation, and the like. As to its motion, the wood might be moving through the air, at a certain velocity and in a particular direction, in response to an impulse initiated by human muscles. Finally, the wood might be very hot, a factor of vibrational energy content. Much greater minuteness of description is possible, of course, but scarcely practicable for ethnological research.

Students of culture, generally speaking, have chosen to follow one or the other of two distinct courses in their consideration of material culture. The one course, elected by ethnographers interested in orienting the material culture within the total cultural framework, has been to group actions about certain central economic activities, such as hunting, fishing, food preparation, and agriculture. This has involved the description of complex processes in their entirety, and has resulted in concentration upon the seeming end-results of these processes and in an unduly sketchy filling in of the antecedent steps. The other course, while it has involved the analysis of complex processes into their component individual actions, has singled out technique for special emphasis, usually to the neglect of the other characteristics of actions. Technique, which is an element in what we have called "method," has proved particularly useful to anthropologists in historical research, especially in differentiating an action from, or identifying it with, a similar action in another culture. This emphasis upon technique has resulted in grouping man's actions with materials about the various arts and crafts, such as basketry, wood-working, weaving, and house-building.

There is, however, no *a priori* reason for believing that these are the only profitable ways of considering the data of material culture. Conceivably, for example, it might prove fruitful to classify the actions themselves, segregating them into groups essentially similar in kind. This method is recognized by the physical sciences as a valuable aid in discovering the natural relationships between actions. But the physicists and chemists, in describing the principles upon which a natural classification should be based, present them in a form suited to their own needs in making tests, analyses, and syntheses in the laboratory. They seem not to have concerned themselves with compiling an orderly classification of all the various "principles" recognized by modern science. Even did such a compendium of principles exist, it could not be assumed to be complete. Modern science—to give but one reason—has concerned itself almost exclusively with our own material culture, which is not necessarily all-inclusive. The principles isolated and described by natural science, moreover, are often characterized by a degree of complexity unsuited to our materials. For these and other reasons it was found impossible to construct a finite list of the principles, or types of actions, recognized by modern science, which could then be applied as a yardstick to the material culture of primitive peoples. Such a list can be worked out only as the result of a study such as this, not as a preliminary basis or starting point.

This and many other possibilities suggested themselves, and were tested and rejected, during the development of the method of classification presented below. Space is here lacking to explain them in detail and show why they were discarded. The method finally arrived at must suffice. That it is as yet clumsy, and possibly too involved, will be apparent. But its cumbersomeness is not to be overcome by the hasty elimination of the more obviously unwieldy portions. Refinement and simplification can be achieved only as changes are suggested in the course of its repeated application to the facts.

The significant features of the method are the analysis of complex processes into unit actions; the concentration upon general methods and means, disregarding technique; and the analysis of function into detailed specifications. In other words, processes are analyzed into relatively simple component actions. These unit actions are described primarily in terms of the general method employed to produce the result and of the precise functions which the result of each action exhibits in the culture. These functions are expressed in terms of *specifications*, that is, of the specific requirements set by the culture to which the result of the action must conform.

A Samoan mat, for example, might perhaps be characterized as something to sit or lie upon, or to cover certain parts of the body with. Such a functional description, however, disguises the fact that the Samoan mat is serviceable because it exhibits certain specific properties. The description does not expose the individual specifications to which the entire process of mat-making must represent an adjustment. The value of an analysis of function is readily seen when, by its use, such apparently unconnected articles as thatch roofs, mats, and clothing are found to be closely related. The specifications thus identify the specific requirements of the problem, which have been met in the solution. When articles are described in terms of the specific properties which they exhibit in a given culture, it becomes obvious that the actions whose results correspond to similar specifications bear a necessary relationship to each other. This has been superficially recognized in the past, principally because the results were often observed to be produced by similar techniques. Thus thatching and matting are treated together in works on material culture because the actions producing the results seem to be similar. That the actions need not be similar, however, is apparent from our own material culture.

On the basis of specifications of results, a classification of actions is made possible whereby all the actions, for example, which result in receptacles may be grouped together. These actions may then be differentiated within the group on the basis of additional specifications. Thus receptacles for liquids may be isolated as a special sub-group whose more detailed specifications require a more delimited method of production. Unless complex processes are analyzed into unit actions, one is likely to lose sight of the ramifications of a type of action, e.g., making a hole, throughout a culture. The analysis of processes into unit actions makes it possible to determine the distribution of any specific action throughout a culture and to discover how thoroughly the individual actions have been incorporated into the material culture of a people. Knowledge of the distribution of unit actions within a culture, taken in conjunction with the various actions invented or borrowed by the culture to solve the problems encountered by it, makes possible an objective comparison of diverse cultures with respect to their material adjustments. Furthermore, it may be possible eventually to compile in this way a finite list of the problems encountered and the solutions offered by all cultures.

An attempt to apply this method of analyzing material culture has revealed a number of defects and omissions in the existing descriptions of primitive peoples. Much valuable evidence which could be gathered by the field ethnographer has hitherto been generally neglected and omitted in ethnographical descriptions. For the analysis of material culture, among the most important items of information are the specifications to which the result of each unit action must conform in the particular culture. These are seldom expressly stated by the ethnographer. Consequently inferences must often be drawn about facts which the field anthropologist could have reported had he been aware that the information was important.

As one of the contributions of this study, the following outline has been prepared to indicate the specific information which should be included in a description of material culture.

In general, describe the various parts of each complicated process, not neglecting the precise functions of each resulting material. Describe in detail every process even though it seems to be nothing but a superstitious act. It is possible that the process may be based on some property of matter which is known only to the natives. Do not neglect any seemingly trivial steps of an action; make sure that no segment is left out of your description.

In particular, make sure that the following points have been adequately covered:

1. *Environmental factors.* Do not neglect any of the environmental factors which seem to be important to the natives. For example, note whether operations are carried on in the sunlight or in the shade; note whether warm or cool days are selected for a particular process; note whether muggy weather or clear days are correlated with the performance of a particular action.

2. *Purpose.* Do not neglect to determine, whenever possible, the purpose of each action. For example, determine why a yam is washed, why it is quartered before cooking, why it is cooked, and why it is placed in a basket after cooking.

3. *Motor habits.* Do not neglect any habitual motor habits that seem

to be identified with an action. For example, note whether the action of cutting or scraping is toward or away from the body.

4. *Technique.* Do not neglect the details of technique for each unit action. For example, note the technique employed in adding new strands in the manufacture of a rope as well as the actual braiding or twisting technique.

5. *Materials.* Do not neglect to describe in detail the properties of the materials of each action. For example, note the nature of the shells which are made into hooks and determine whether their surfaces are rough or smooth, whether the color is brilliant or dull, and whether or not they are likely to crumble or split.

6. *Means.* Do not neglect to describe in detail the properties of the means of each action. For example, note the nature of the water in the pools in which wooden bowls are soaked for seasoning purposes. Note in each instance the specific artifact or tool used. For example, do not state, merely, that a hole is bored without indicating that the means is a spiral shell.

7. *Result.* Do not neglect the many specifications which characterize each socially significant result. For example, do not make such a statement as "They put their mats in the sun to air" without indicating the precise specifications to which the mat must correspond after it has been treated in this manner. Do not neglect any socially irrelevant results that are obvious to the native. For example, if the native rubs a dart between two sticks so vigorously that heat is unmistakably produced, this should be recorded. If boring holes with a drill results in the obvious production of heat and sound these results should be included in your description.

8. *Personnel.* Do not neglect to state the precise qualifications of the individuals performing the action. It is important to know why it is that some individuals within the culture know how and actually do these actions whereas others do not. This may be satisfactorily determined by noting the qualifications characterizing those persons who are permitted or are able to perform the action in that culture.

Finally, review the description which you have made of each complicated process and make sure that you have not produced materials or means from nowhere. Each substance entering into an action has a history of actions behind it which should not be mysteriously concealed. For example, note the actions preceding the use of a coconut leaf as the material out of which a basket is made: how it is removed from the tree and transported to the site of operations. Also make sure that you have not assumed that a material or an action, since it bears a resemblance to a similar substance or action in other cultures, occupies a functional position in the culture which has not been justified by your observations. For example, do not state that the natives air wet bast to remove obnoxious odors unless it is specifically indicated by the native, either by word or deed, that the smell of the wet bast is obnoxious to them and that the displeasing odor is removed by the process of drying.

The method of analyzing material culture presented in this paper, it must be clearly understood, is strictly a cultural study. The specifications characterizing substances and artifacts are socially relevant and may be ascertained from the study of the part which that substance or artifact plays in the culture. Socially irrelevant specifications have already been discussed and, it will be remembered, are of importance to the cultural scientist only when they are of such a striking nature that the native is forced to recognize them. The findings of natural science, it is true, suggest tentative classifications and indicate possible specifications on the cultural level which are probably omitted in ethnographical reports. However, a description of function in the mechanistic terms of natural science is not, at present, directly usable by the cultural scientist. We are interested here in the properties of substances and artifacts as they are dealt with by the human beings of a society in solving the various problems which confront them. For example, it is not necessary to describe a wooden bowl from the point of view of the specific stresses and strains put upon it when liquids are placed within it, nor from the point of view that its various molecules will combine with oxygen in the presence of sufficient heat energy. For the cultural scientist it is sufficient to know that the wooden bowl is a receptacle which will hold liquids but which will not withstand the effects of fire and is, therefore, unsuited to cooking over a flame.

The analysis of function into specifications, it must not be forgotten, may be approached from at least two levels, namely, the physico-chemical and the physiologico-psychological. Since so little is known definitively concerning the latter, it must perforce be treated only very generally here and can be accorded by no means the importance which is its due. The following table presents the general methods and the specifications which form at present the culturally oriented basis for our classification of unit action types.

I. METHODS

A. *Moving,* wherein the result is motion

B. *Placing,* wherein the result is position (thus including conveying)

C. *Distorting,* wherein the result is a formal change without separation

D. *Separating,* wherein the result is a division or removal of parts

E. *Inserting,* wherein the result is one substance inserted in another

F. *Mixing,* wherein the result is one substance mixed with another

G. *Binding,* wherein the result is a unit of parts held together by a lashing or tying

H. *Interlacing,* wherein the result is a unit of parts plaited or woven together

I. *Cooking,* wherein the result is a substance changed by the application of heat

J. *Producing sound,* wherein the result is sound

K. *Producing heat,* wherein the result is heat

L. *Producing light,* wherein the result is light

II. SPECIFICATIONS

A. Physico-Chemical Specifications[1]

1. *Impediments,* wherein the result is adapted to restricting physical motion by virtue of inertia plus certain formal characteristics

a. Possessing the characteristics of a barrier

b. Possessing the characteristics of a support

c. Possessing the characteristics of a hole

d. Possessing the characteristics of a trough, i.e., permitting motion in at least two horizontal directions

e. Possessing the characteristics of a receptacle, i.e., restricting motion in all horizontal directions

2. *Machines,* wherein the result is adapted to producing physical motion by virtue of inertia plus certain formal characteristics

a. Lacking formal advantage

1. These specifications represent some of the problems solved by primitive peoples in their material adjustment from the physico-chemical point of view. The list is not complete nor is it more than roughly organized. This will be found to be even more true of the specifications listed from the physiologico-psychological point of view. Additions and organization will come, however, only as the specifications are found to be inadequate with reference to the data.

b. Possessing the characteristics of a lever
c. Possessing the characteristics of a wedge
d. Possessing the characteristics of a pulley

3. *Insulators,* wherein the result is adapted to restricting physical motion by virtue of inertia plus texture
   a. Porous to gas but not liquid or solid
   b. Porous to gas, liquid, and solid
   c. Porous to gas and liquid but not solid
   d. Impervious to gas, liquid, and solid
   e. Impervious to heat and light
   f. Porous to light
   g. Impervious to sound
   h. Conductor of heat
   i. Conductor of sound

4. *Weights.* Wherein the result is adapted to restricting physical motion by virtue of its inertia as a unit
   a. Easy to move
   b. Hard to move
   c. Moving
   d. Hard to stop moving
   e. Easy to move in some directions only

5. *Bodies,* wherein the result is adapted to resisting the motion of its parts in response to physical action
   a. Easy to change by separation
   b. Hard to change by separation
   c. Easy to change by distortion
   d. Hard to change by distortion
   e. Easy to change by separation but not by distortion
   f. Easy to change by distortion but not by separation

6. *Chemicals,* wherein the result is adapted to producing or resisting chemical action
   a. Chemically active
   b. Chemically inert
   c. Easy to change by chemical action
   d. Potentially active chemically
   e. Easy to change by chemical action in the presence of heat
   f. Hard to change by chemical action in the presence of heat

7. *Vibrators,* wherein the result is adapted to producing vibrational action
   a. Emitting heat
   b. Not suitable to produce heat
   c. Emitting light
   d. Not suitable to produce light
   e. Emitting sound
   f. Not suitable to produce sound
   g. Potentially capable of emitting heat
   h. Potentially capable of emitting light
   i. Potentially capable of emitting sound

B. Physiologico-Psychological Specifications

1. *Suitability for bodily consumption*
   - a. As food
   - b. As beverage
   - c. As stimulant
   - d. As sedative
   - e. As narcotic
   - f. As intoxicant
   - g. As medicine
   - h. As poison

2. *Suitability for human handling*
   - a. To move with the hands
   - b. To move with the feet
   - c. To hold with the hands
   - d. To hold with the feet
   - e. To carry
   - f. To hold with the teeth

3. *Attractiveness to the human senses*
   - a. To sight
   - b. To hearing
   - c. To touch
   - d. To smell
   - e. To taste

4. *Suitability for affecting animals and plants*
   - a. To bruise
   - b. To cut
   - c. To choke or strangle
   - d. To smother or asphyxiate
   - e. To burn
   - f. To poison
   - g. To blind
   - h. To deafen
   - i. To attract
   - j. To frighten
   - k. To stimulate
   - l. To narcotize
   - m. To favor growth
   - n. To discourage growth

The above-described method of analysis may now be illustrated by a sample comparative analysis of the material culture of Samoa and Fiji. For Samoa, the data are derived from Buck's excellent monograph.[2] For Fiji, the author is fortunate in being able to use information acquired in the course of his personal field work there as a Bishop Museum Fellow in 1935–36. Since limitations of space prevent a complete analysis of the material culture of the two island groups, we shall confine ourselves to "receptacles" as a representative example, noting its ramifications throughout the two cultures and how the two peoples solved the problem of retaining things.

A first list will catalogue the receptacles found in both Samoa and Fiji. Though the two techniques of production and the extent

2. Buck, P. H. (Te Rangi Hiroa), "Samoan Material Culture," *Bernice P. Bishop Museum, Bulletin 75* (1930).

of use may vary somewhat in the two cultures, these receptacles were found, upon analysis, to have been produced by the same general methods and to conform to the same specifications in both cases, and hence, for our purposes, they may be regarded as identical.

1. Barkcloth tent (used for smoking cloth)
2. Barkcloth mosquito tent
3. Pit for fermenting food
4. Pit for ripening bananas
5. Grave
6. Post holes
7. Planting holes
8. Coconut shell cup
9. Coconut water bottle
10. Wooden bowl
11. Wooden kava bowl with legs
12. Wooden basin
13. Wooden bailer
14. Bamboo water vessel
15. Dugout canoe
16. Plank canoe
17. Baskets
18. Fish traps
19. Fish nets
20. Fish enclosure
21. Pig enclosure
22. Bamboo rat trap
23. Bast strainers (for kava and turmeric)
24. Depressions on clubs for liming
25. Houses (dwelling house, cook house, eating house, yam storage house, temple)
26. Sheds (meeting shed, carpenter's shed, canoe shed)

A second list includes all the receptacles found in Samoa which are not present, so far as known, in Fiji or which do not exhibit the same specifications in the two cultures.

1. Breadfruit net-picker (a variation of the breadfruit picker which is found in Samoa at Fitiuta in Tau, "where the ground is covered with sharp pointed lava which would break the fruit if it fell to the ground" [Buck, p. 117], and which is not commonly used elsewhere, indicating that it is a specific development in response to local conditions)
2. Earth oven (although also present in Fiji, it differs there in its specifications; the Samoan earth oven is not hermetically sealed and is, therefore, porous to steam, whereas the Fijian earth oven is hermetically sealed with earth)
3. Fowler's hut (despite some evidence that fowling was also practiced in Fiji, the information as to the appliances used in this pursuit is too meager for identification)
4. Fowler's net (see 3 above)
5. Fowler's trap (see 3 above)

6. Coconut midrib vise (used in Samoa to hold tattooing comb during manufacture; no information obtainable from Fiji)

7. Coconut shell mortar (pottery bowl serves the same purpose in Fiji)

8. Coconut shell lamp (pottery lamp serves the same purpose in Fiji)

9. Sandal (a plaited receptacle for the foot to protect it from coral; the sandal is not found in Fiji)

10. Coconut leaflet toy canoe (a plaited toy for children not found in Fiji, where a canoe made of coconut husk fulfills the same specifications)

11. Sand bed for fish trap with coral sides (the disturbing of the sand during this operation is believed by the Samoans to create an attractive smell [puapua'i] which differentiates it from the same action in Fiji)

12. Fish house of coral (no artificial constructions of this sort are made in Fiji, so far as I know, although natural coral formations are carefully probed for fish)

A third list includes all the receptacles found in Fiji which are not present, so far as known, in Samoa, or which do not exhibit the same specifications in the two cultures.

1. Earth oven (see 2 of the Samoan list)
2. Pottery lamp (see 8 of the Samoan list)
3. Pottery mortar (see 7 of the Samoan list)
4. Pottery bowls (the subject of pottery will be discussed in detail below)
5. Pottery cooking utensils (see 4 above)
6. Sleeping mat (a double mat, made like a sleeping bag, is a variation not found in Samoa)
7. Turtle enclosure (an enclosure built in still tidal water to keep excess turtles; turtle fishing attained greater development in Fiji than in Samoa; there seems to be no obvious reason why the Samoan could not have developed a turtle enclosure had the need for one arisen, inasmuch as it is similar in all details to the fish enclosure found in both cultures)
8. Coconut husk toy canoe (see 10 of the Samoan list)

Comparison of the second and third lists reveals few differences of a fundamental nature in the receptacles of the two cultures. Only the occurrence of pottery in Fiji is found, upon careful inspection, to be of far-reaching importance. This might be expected from the general specification to which pottery utensils conform—a specification apparently not met by any Samoan utensil. For purposes of illustration a detailed analysis of the part which pottery plays in Fijian culture is presented below. Column I lists the specific uses of pottery utensils in Fiji; column II indicates how the same problem is met in Samoa; column III states whether or not the Samoan method is also used in Fiji, an asterisk denoting that it is an important alternative method in Fiji.

A. USES OF POTTERY IN THE PREPARATION OF FOODS

I	II	III
1. Boiling man, pig, turtle, fish	Earth oven	Yes*
2. Boiling yam, taro, kumala, breadfruit	Earth oven	Yes*
3. Boiling fermented material for bread	Earth oven	Yes*
4. Boiling banana, papaia, or tavioka for puddings	Earth oven	Yes
5. Boiling coconut cream sauce (for puddings, meat, fish, or vegetables)	a) Earth oven; in banana leaf package b) Hot stones in wooden bowl	a) Yes b) No
6. Boiling tavioka or arrowroot plain	a) Earth oven b) Hot stones in wooden bowl	a) Yes* b) No
7. Boiling squid, crab, eel, taro leaves	Earth oven; in banana leaf package	No
8. Boiling chicken	a) Earth oven b) Grilled on fire	a) No b) No
9. Boiling fish, squid, crab, eel, yam, taro, taro leaves, tavioka, or arrowroot with coconut cream	Earth oven; in banana leaf package	No
10. Boiling fish chowder, shellfish chowder	Absent	
11. Boiling tavioka or arrowroot, breadfruit, vutu, or the like before fermentation	Absent	
12. Boiling tavioka and arrowroot for flour preparation	Absent	
13. Boiling kumala with coconut cream	Absent	

The above comparison brings out the following points. The banana leaf package, together with the wooden bowl and hot stones, serves the purpose, in Samoa, of cooking liquids. The use of the earth oven for cooking solids in both Samoa and Fiji indicates that the method of boiling these substances in Fiji is not paralleled in Samoa. The use of a pot which may be placed directly on the fire thus adds to the methods of preparing foods in Fiji. This is brought out most clearly, perhaps, with reference to food preparation during voyages in canoes. The Fijian boils his food on ship board much as he does on land, whereas the Samoan is forced to depend on either cold or grilled food. Furthermore, there are some articles of diet which, prepared in Fiji with the aid of the pot, do not appear in Samoan food preparation. It is likewise interesting to note that the banana leaf package is used in Fiji. The hot stones and wooden bowl method is also used in Fiji for the preparation of pig fat and entrail pudding, which is customarily made while the pig is being cooked in the oven. Another point of interest is that the earth oven differs in the two cultures in accordance with their general patterns of cooking; in Samoa, where there is no true boiling, the earth oven is not hermetically sealed, while in Fiji, where boiling is the vogue, the earth oven is made impervious to the escaping steam.

B. USES IN THE PRODUCTION OF MATERIALS ENTERING INTO OTHER ACTIONS

I	II	III
1. Making pastes[3]		
a) Boiling arrowroot to make flour used as paste when mixed with water	Baked in oven to form cooked lump used for paste when dipped in water	No
b) Boiling taro to make flour used as paste when mixed with water	Absent	
2. Making dyes[4]		
a) Boiling manui leaves for hair dyeing[5]	Absent	

3. The over-ripe breadfruit paste commonly employed in Samoa is very seldom used in Fiji. The Fijians deem this paste too stiff for their purposes and use it only when other pastes are not available. On the other hand, the juice of the viscid berry of the tou (*Cordia aspera*) is used in both cultures.

4. The dye-producing processes which do not require cooking are identical in the two cultures, with but very few exceptions.

5. Fijian hair dressing with this and the following dye is designed to make the hair itself perfection without the use of wigs (although some of the latter were used in the old days by chiefs). The hair is made to stand on end by means of lime, kura, and manui. It is dyed red or black according to preference. The bush of the hair gives protection against the sun, conforms to the native ideal of beauty, requires utilitarian combs and thus obviates the desire for ornamental combs, requires elaborate care at night and thus makes pillows and headbands necessary, and reëmphasizes the sacredness of the head. Samoan hair dressing, on the other hand, involves the extensive use of wigs. Preparation of the hair itself is confined to slight bleaching with lime, primarily as a protection from the sun during fishing. The wigs are not dyed but are bleached with salt water and exposure in the sun. Ornamental combs are in vogue and utilitarian combs very scarce except for modern productions. The pillow is probably an importation, and no night headband is required.

I	II	III
b) Boiling kura bark for hair dyeing	Absent	
c) Boiling candlenut bark for black tapa dye[6]	Absent	
d) Boiling kura bark for red tapa dye	Absent	
3. Preparing materials either to alter color or to remove foreign substances		
a. Boiling coconut filled with salt water to decompose inner meat during production of water bottle.[7]	Filling with water and allowing to stand for a couple weeks	No
b. Boiling coconut husks, changing color (resulting in dark brown and black depending upon the maturity of the nut) and loosening interfibrous material	Steeping in water to soften interfibrous material, no change of color resulting	No
c. Boiling draudreka, an inferior voivoi or pandanus, to render it suitable as a mat material	Absent	
d. Boiling vau bast with drau ni tavola to produce black colored strips	Analogous process: pressing whole garment of ti leaves in mud of swamp	Yes
e. Boiling vau bast with kura bark to produce red colored strips	Analogous process: staining whole garment with red earth	Yes
f. Boiling voivoi (pandanus) with drau ni tavola after soaking in swamp mud, to produce black wefts[8]	Absent	
g. Boiling whale teeth in oil to age and color them	Absent	
h. Using hot shards to singe hair	Using lighted bark	No?

6. Fijian tapa is characterized by contrasting designs in red and black on a natural background; Samoan tapa, by soft contrasting shades of brown on a natural background. The same is true of the sennit designs of the two cultures.

7. The coconut water bottle is a more important utensil in Samoa than in Fiji. The reasons for this are two, both of them related to pottery. In the first place, the coconut water bottle is used in Samoa where pots serve similar purposes in Fiji. In the second place, the manufacture of coconut water bottles is facilitated in Fiji by pottery; an operation requiring two or three weeks for completion in Samoa is accomplished in a single day.

8. The black and natural contrast in plaiting so characteristic of Fiji is almost completely absent in Samoa, where the designs on mats are usually in two shades of brown, although an overlay of the black skin of the plantain is sometimes used. Connected therewith we find an elaboration of extremely fine plaiting in Samoa, which is absent in Fiji.

C. USES OF POTTERY NOT DEPENDENT UPON FIRE-RESISTING SPECIFICATION[9]

I	II	III
1. Water jar	Coconut water bottle	Yes*
2. Kava bowl, in which kava may stand or be brewed	Wooden kava bowl, in which kava is not allowed to stand for long lest the bowl become warped	Yes
3. Water pitcher, for pouring water into kava bowl during mixing	Dipping water from wooden bowl with coconut cup	Yes
4. Wash basin, in which hands are cleansed before mixing kava or eating	Pouring water over hands with a coconut cup	No
5. Lamp, burning coconut oil	Coconut shell lamp	Yes
6. Shard used for collecting soot of kowrie gum or candlenut	Stone used for same purpose	No?

We have now examined the receptacle and its ramifications throughout the cultures of Fiji and Samoa. Instead of comparing the methods of obtaining food or the plaiting techniques of the two cultures, we have made a cross-sectional comparison of the solutions offered by these cultures to the problem of retaining things. This analysis has exposed relationships hitherto unsuspected, demonstrating that the presence or absence of at least one type of receptacle may have far-reaching consequences. Regarding the methods of production and the specifications of the result, the great majority of receptacles in the two cultures are identical. The one difference elaborated in this paper illustrates the possible importance of dissimilar receptacles. The presence of pottery utensils in Fiji and the absence of these in Samoa has been seen to be surprisingly significant. The analysis shows, however, that the importance of pottery is not due to mere chance. Pottery utensils represent an important cultural difference because they offer a solution to the problem of cooking liquids directly over a flame—a problem not solved in Samoa. The fundamental difference between Fijian and Samoan material culture brought out here is not the absence or presence of pottery *per se;* it is the absence or presence of a solution to a specific problem. The specification to which the Fijian pot corresponds, namely, resistance to the effects of fire, is

9. It is important to note that all these uses of pottery in Fiji are paralleled by the use of comparable objects in Samoa.

not paralleled by any Samoan receptacle. Many contrasts between Fijian and Samoan material culture are hidden and mysterious until analytical study brings them together and demonstrates their dependence upon the presence of a single process.

Of the more striking contrasts between the two cultures, noted even by the casual tourist, a considerable proportion are directly traceable to pottery. The easily observable differences in cooking methods are obviously correlated with the presence and absence of pottery cooking utensils. Less obvious, but nevertheless demonstrable, is the dependence of the mode of hair dressing upon pottery. The Samoan, handicapped by the lack of a receptacle with fire-resisting properties, cannot parallel the waving, stiffening, and complex dyeing of the hair so characteristic of the Fijian. The Samoan, with his emphasis upon hair bleaching and the use of wigs, scarcely approximates the Fijian tonsorial art. The Fijian mode could not diffuse to Samoa without the accompanying diffusion of pottery or the independent development of a solution to the problem of cooking directly over a fire. The casual tourist also notes the differences between the two cultures in the colors and designs of tapa, mats, and sennit-work, and he tends to attribute these differences to fundamentally divergent ideals of beauty. This explanation seems less satisfactory, however, when it is realized that the Samoan could not, even if he wished, duplicate the contrasting black, red, and light brown designs so characteristic of Fijian art. Within his limitations, indeed, he has attempted to do so, e.g., by the use of an overlay of black plantain skin in mat-making and the blackening of ti leaf garments with swamp mud. But further conformity to Fijian design was not possible without the possession of pottery or a comparable means for the manufacture of the necessary dyes.

Purely technical studies of material culture or detailed investigations oriented within major cultural activities would not have exposed these relationships. Application of our method of analyzing material culture, however, demonstrates an integration of widely separated and apparently unrelated culture traits. Such an analysis dampens enthusiasm for oversimple diffusionist explanations of culture.

This method of analyzing material culture from the point of view of the problems faced and the solutions offered by a culture is presented here to suggest a profitable way of conducting research concerning man's material adjustment. The specifications of the adaptive solutions constitute a key to the approach to fundamental differences in material culture. Though susceptible to future refinement, the method promises to facilitate the comparative study of material culture. An objective classification of primitive peoples based upon the respective problems faced and the actions developed in the course of their solution is made possible. In addition, the method of analysis and characterization here developed is apparently useful in exposing significant functional relationships between various customs and methods, both material and non-material, within a particular culture. The precise interrelation of primitive material culture with religious, æsthetic, and social elaborations may be determined within a given culture and compared with that of another culture. Thus light may be shed on problems of diffusion; the true nature of cultural complexes may be ascertained; and the essential cultural differences between specific tribes may be exposed. Finally, at least one of the major hypotheses of cultural science, namely, that the economic or maintenance mores are basic, may conceivably be verified or revised by the continued application of this method.

The Processing of Anthropological Materials *

By GEORGE P. MURDOCK

I. INTRODUCTION

As the number of anthropologists increases and the range of their interests expands, the problem of keeping abreast of current theoretical advances is beginning to be sensed as serious. It pales into insignificance, however, compared with the problem of mastering the descriptive literature of our subject. Whether we are engaged in teaching or research, we repeatedly have need of acquainting ourselves with the ethnographic data pertaining to an area or a subject, and we are all acutely aware of how laborious and time-consuming this task must be if done well. New textbooks and current articles help to keep us up to date on trends in theory, but the descriptive literature accumulates at a rate far beyond the capacity of even the most industrious of us to keep pace.

In sheer bulk, the mass of descriptive material of interest to the anthropologist probably exceeds by several times that of all the rest of the social sciences put together. Psychologists, sociologists, economists, and geographers depend in the main upon the materials which they themselves have accumulated, but for anthropologists the data assembled by themselves constitute but a small proportion of the descriptive materials upon which they depend and must be augmented by vast quantities of information gathered by travelers, missionaries, government officials, artists, natural scientists, and historians, as well as by social scientists of several sister-disciplines.

Other social scientists concern themselves in the main only with the complex societies of the present and the historical past—perhaps a hundred all told. Anthropologists share their interest in these higher civilizations but also have an equal concern with the many simpler societies of the world, which probably number at least three thousand. The descriptive data of no other social science can even remotely compare in quantity with the wealth of ethnographic detail available on these thousands of peoples. For a comparable situation one must turn to such biological sciences as botany and zoölogy—fields with innumerably more practitioners and vastly superior research resources in the form of summary compilations and bibliographic aids.

This paper will deal with various aspects of the problem faced by all anthropologists in coping with the magnitude and diversity of their descriptive materials in teaching and research. It will be based primarily upon the experience of the Human Relations Area Files, its predecessor the Cross-Cultural Survey at Yale University, and such related undertakings as the Plains In-

*Reprinted from A. L. Kroeber (ed.), *Anthropology Today* (Chicago, University of Chicago Press, 1953), pp. 476-487.

dians survey at the University of Nebraska, the Navaho and Values projects at Harvard University, and the research on Mongolia and Tibet at the University of Washington. These various projects have in common not only a special awareness of the problems generally encountered by anthropologists in coping with their voluminous descriptive literature but also the specific objective of overcoming a number of them.

Since the development and methodology of the Human Relations Area Files have been fully described elsewhere (Murdock and others, 1950), it will be necessary here only to state that it is a co-operative enterprise of fifteen American universities (Chicago, Colorado, Cornell, Harvard, Hawaii, Indiana, Iowa, Michigan, North Carolina, Oklahoma, Pennsylvania, Southern California, Utah, Washington, and Yale), operating with the aid of foundation and government grants, for the assembly, translation, and classification of the descriptive materials of anthropology and for their reproduction in readily accessible form in files deposited at each of the member institutions.

II. CLASSIFICATION OF CULTURES

Every anthropologist who undertakes a regional or comparative study, as well as most of those who engage in field research, must make a decision as to the social groups which he will treat as cultural units. Will he, for example, select single communities, clusters of communities with essentially identical cultures, or groups bearing traditional tribal names? If the latter, will he follow native usage in regard to nomenclature or the practice of previous anthropologists, or will he define and name his groups according to criteria of his own? In any event he is likely to become acutely aware of the lack of uniform standards for the classification of cultures and the social groups which bear them. In this respect anthropology presents a striking contrast to botany and zoölogy, with their widely accepted systems of classification.

The Human Relations Area Files faces this problem whenever it initiates work in a new area. It must, before any processing begins, make a definitive decision as to which groups and cultures are to be segregated in separate files as essentially distinct and which are to be grouped in a single file as essentially only subgroups or variants of the same larger culture. Accumulated experience in making such decisions suggests the possibility, as well as the desirability, of establishing a uniform system for the classification of societies and cultures comparable to the systems used in the biological sciences for the classification of organisms. A tentative proposal to this effect is outlined below.

Two types of social and cultural units which have already attained wide acceptance may be adopted as starting points. The first is the local group or community—a band, village, or neighborhood—which seems to be the smallest social group to carry essentially a total culture and thus to parallel roughly the "subvariety" in biology. The cultural system carried by a community may be tentatively called a "local cultural variant." Its content, unlike the body of traits carried by such smaller social groups as families and voluntary associations, covers nearly the entire range of the existing culture, though it may be deficient in some areas, especially the political and economic, where the interdependence of communities produces phenomena identifiable only with some larger social group.

Also widely accepted is the concept of the culture area, which embraces the related cultures of different peoples inhabiting a defined geographical region. A culture area would appear to correspond in general to a "family" in biological classification. Between the established levels of the community and the region, of the local cultural variant, and of the culture area, it seems possible to set up three intermediate social and cultural levels roughly corresponding to the variety, the species, and the genus in biology, as in Table 1.

Admittedly, the degree of social integration and cultural similarity decreases progressively from the smallest to the largest of the above units, but the establishment of typical intermediate units is not necessarily more difficult in anthropology than in biology, especially since an element of arbitrariness is recognized as inevitable in any classificatory system. To avoid mere analogy, of course, the criteria employed must be genuinely appropriate to the processes of cultural change and differentiation.

TABLE 1

Culture-bearing Social Unit	Corresponding Cultural Unit	Analogous Biological Unit
Community....	Local cultural variant	Subvariety
Subtribe.......	Subculture	Variety
Tribe..........	Culture	Species
Nation........	Culture cluster	Genus
Region........	Culture area	Family

A cultural species will be called simply a "culture," and the people who bear it a "tribe." Occasionally, as in the case of Zuni pueblo, a culture is confined to a single community, so that tribe and community coincide. Far more commonly, however, numerous communities with only slightly differing local cultural variants are spread over a considerable geographical area. When a biological form similarly varies over geographical space, all its members are classed as a single species, however much they differ at the opposite margins of the area, provided that interbreeding regularly takes place between adjacent forms. Only when there occurs a geographical barrier or other break, separating forms which do not interbreed and thus vary around different modes, does the biologist classify forms into separate species.

In the realm of culture the equivalent of interbreeding is diffusion, and barriers to diffusion may be used to separate cultural species, i.e., distinct cultures. Unlike the situation in biology, to be sure, such barriers are only relative rather than absolute. Nevertheless, they seem to be fairly readily determinable. Mountain ranges and bodies of water across which communication is difficult and diffusion consequently slight or sporadic allow the processes of cultural change to produce variations around gradually diverging modes until the cultures on either side of the barrier assume markedly different forms. A similar result can be produced, in the absence of an actual barrier to communication, when adjacent geographical zones provide markedly different natural resources, so that distinctive modes of economic exploitation come into being and give rise to adaptive variations in technology, social organization, and other aspects of culture in the two zones.

Language differences likewise constitute a significant barrier to diffusion. Even in the same geographical area, a boundary between two mutually unintelligible languages may operate to retard diffusion sufficiently so that the groups on either side of the boundary gradually diverge around different modes until they come to possess genuinely distinct, though related, cultures.

There are, of course, other factors which inhibit cultural borrowing, but those of geography and language have probably been the most universal and important in promoting the differentiation of cultural species. We therefore propose to define a culture as including all local cultural variants exhibited by communities within a particular geographical area which speak mutually intelligible languages and have essentially similar forms of economic adjustment.

This conception of a culture, and of the tribe as its social correlate, coincides very closely with actual anthropological usage as this has developed through general consensus rather than explicit definition. One branch of anthropology, i.e., linguistics, has independently evolved a strictly comparable concept, that of a language, which is defined as the variant forms of speech over a geographical area where adjacent forms are always mutually intelligible although those at a distance may not be. The existence and apparent utility of this concept, based on strictly cultural considerations, in one division of our science suggest both the possibility of extending it to the classification of cultures in general and the probability that such an extension, far from being a mere analogy from biology, may have an inherent validity of its own.

If a culture be accepted as the anthropological equivalent, and a tribe as the sociological equivalent, of a biological species, the terms "subculture" and "subtribe" can be reserved for cultural units and social groupings intermediate, respectively, between a culture and a local cultural variant and between a tribe and a single community. If, for example, the Tsimshian of the Northwest Coast are regarded as a tribe, then the Niska, Gitksan, and Tsimshian proper may be considered as subtribes, each with its own subculture and each comprising a number of communities with local cultural variants representing cultural differences of a still lesser magnitude.

Political integration does not ordinarily complicate the problem of classification as long as it has not advanced beyond the tribal level. In some areas of the primitive world, as among the Plains Indians, political organization normally coincides with the tribe; in other areas, e.g., native Australia and New Guinea, each local community is politically autonomous; in still others, political integration commonly encompasses a number of communities, but only those of a subtribe, not of an entire tribe. Whichever of these situations prevails, the determination of social and cultural varieties and species usually presents no difficulties.

Wherever the accidents of political history have united peoples with different cultures under a single unified government, however, the problem of classification is complicated. Social unity exceeds cultural unity and gives rise to institutions, usually economic and often religious as well as political, which, though cultural, are not truly a part of the component cultures. Such cultural phenomena can be described and understood only from the point of view of a social group which embraces several tribes and for which we propose the term "nation." They form part of a cultural category larger than a single culture but smaller than a culture area—one for which the term "culture cluster" is herewith advanced. Wherever cultures have become interdependent through the political and social integration of the groups which carry them, the Human Relations Area Files has usually found it necessary to use the culture cluster rather than the tribe as the unit for classifying anthropological materials.

Situations of this type are common enough in complex modern societies, e.g., the French Canadians and British Canadians, the Flemings and Walloons in Belgium, and the several "tribes" of the Swiss nation. They also occur not infrequently on the primitive level. Thus the League of the Iroquois united into a single nation five tribes with distinct languages and cultures—the Cayuga, Mohawk, Oneida, Onondaga, and Seneca—and, in Uganda and Ruanda, Hima herders, Iru tillers, and sometimes also pigmy hunters are politically and socially united in a number of separate instances. A similar phenomenon is observable in caste societies like India. Even in a state which originally embraced only a single tribe and culture, social classes may differentiate with time to the point where class subcultures have really evolved into distinct cultures and would have to be treated as such if their bearers were not socially and politically integrated.

The standard classification of social groups and cultural systems proposed herewith is not so much an innovation as an effort to make explicit, with only minor reconciliations, a system of categories which appears to be implicitly accepted in essence by most anthropologists who have attempted to classify peoples and cultures in different parts of the world. It may be useful to call attention here to some of these regional classifications. The works cited below by no means constitute a complete compilation; they include only sources which the writer has had occasion to consult with profit in his own researches.

For the North American continent, the most comprehensive classificatory attempt is that of Kroeber (1939), to which Murdock (1941) may be considered a supplement. Useful regional classifications include Beals (1932), Johnson (1940), Kroeber (1925), Osgood (1936), Park and others (1938), Ray and others (1938), Sauer (1934), Speck (1928), Spier (1936), Steward (1937, 1938), and Swanton (1946).

For South America, all earlier attempts have been superseded by the classic work of Steward (1946–50), which Murdock (1951) has adapted to the specific use of the Human Relations Area Files. An unpublished map by John H. Rowe incorporates a number of useful corrections.

For Africa, the volumes of the "Ethnographic Survey of Africa," currently being issued under the general editorship of Daryll Forde, will, when complete, supersede all earlier work as definitely as does Steward's compilation for South America. The contributions which have already appeared include Forde (1951), Forde and Jones (1950), McCulloch (1950, 1951), Manoukian (1950, 1952), Tew (1950), and Whiteley (1950). On areas not yet covered by the Survey, there are useful classifications of the Khoisan and Southeastern Bantu peoples in Schapera (1930, 1937); of the Congo tribes in Czekanowski (1917–27), Maes and Boone (1935), and Van der Kerken (1944); of the tribes of Cameroon and French Equatorial Africa in Bruel (1935) and Tessmann (1932); of the Nigerian peoples in Meek (1931) and Talbot (1926); and of the Nilotes in Köhler (1950). Special attention should also be called to the noteworthy linguistic classification by Greenberg (1949–50).

For Asia, an area on which the writer has done comparatively little ethnographic research, he can cite as useful from personal experience only Jochelson (1928) and Embree and Dotson (1950) on the peoples of Asiatic Russia and Southeast Asia, respectively. In addition, he may mention Gerland (1892) as still, despite its age, incomparably the best ethnographic atlas; besides the Eurasiatic continent, it covers Africa, Oceania, and the New World.

For Oceania there are classifications of the Indonesian peoples in Kennedy (1942, 1945) and Van Eerde (1920); of the Philippine peoples in Beyer (1917) and Tangco (1951); of the aboriginal tribes of Australia in Tindale (1940); and of the Micronesian peoples in Murdock (1948). Polynesia presents few serious problems, but Melanesia and particularly New Guinea are still largely *terra incognita*. Rivers (1914) is still useful, but detailed analyses of restricted regions like that of Oliver (1949) on Bougainville in the Solomons are urgently needed.

III. GUIDES TO PUBLISHED SOURCES

Every anthropologist, when he undertakes to acquaint himself with a new culture for any scholarly purpose, faces a problem identical with that encountered by the Human Relations Area Files whenever the decision is reached to process a new body of cultural materials, namely, that of discovering the relevant published sources and of determining which of them are the most comprehensive, reliable, and basic. He may in some cases be fortunate enough to secure a recent book or article with a full and critical bibliography, but in most instances he must depend, first of all, upon general bibliographical compilations and secondarily upon notices and reviews in the anthropological journals to bring him in touch with publications postdating the available bibliographies.

The problem of discovering all the relevant sources and selecting the best ones is peculiarly acute in anthropology, as compared with the natural sciences, for a number of reasons. First of all, we lack almost completely the series of abstracts and periodic summaries that are common in other sciences. The only notable exception is *Social Science Abstracts,* which was published from 1929 to 1933 only. In the second place, general bibliographies, even when regional in scope, are practically useless to us, since they are rarely complete or selective and are seldom critically annotated or topically classified. Such resources as we have, in so far as the writer knows them and has found them genuinely useful, are enumerated below.

There are apparently no comprehensive ethnographic bibliographies covering the entire world, although the *Ethnologischer Anzeiger* (Köln) went far toward filling this need prior to World War II. In addition, several professional journals make an attempt to keep abreast of current publications on a world-wide scale through reviews, book notices, and lists of publications received. Outstanding among them are *Anthropos* (Fribourg), *Anthropologie* (Paris), and the *Zeitschrift für Ethnologie* (Berlin). The *American Anthropologist* (Menasha, Wis.), which at one time ranked with them, has lost most of its usefulness since it discontinued notices of periodical contributions in the second number of Volume LI in 1949. *Man* (London) and *Ethnos* (Stockholm) carry, in general, only book reviews.

For the New World there are comprehensive ethnographic bibliographies by Murdock (1941) for North America and Steward (1946–50) for Central and South America. Current publications are well covered in several periodicals. The *American Anthropologist* is still occasionally of subordinate use, but Americanists today must depend primarily upon the *BBAA* or *Boletin bibliografico de anthropologia americana* (Mexico), the *Journal de la Société des Américanistes* (Paris), and T. F. McIlwraith's annual lists of publications in ethnology, anthropology, and archeology in the *Canadian Historical Review* (Toronto).

For Africa there is a useful but inadequately organized comprehensive bibliography by Wieschhoff (1948), and the volumes of the previously mentioned "Ethnographic Survey of Africa" include excellent coverage of unpublished as well as published sources. Among regional bibliographies that by Schapera (1934) on South Africa is particularly noteworthy for its selectivity and analytical comments. Current publications are admirably recorded in *Africa* (London), which can be supplemented by consulting such other regional journals as *African Affairs* (London), *African Studies* (Johannesburg), *Bibliographie ethnographique du Congo belge et des regions avoisinantes* (Tervueren), *Congo* (Brussels), and the *Journal de la Société des Africanistes* (Paris). A recent venture of considerable promise is *African Abstracts* (London).

For Eurasia, unlike the continents previously considered, there is apparently no single comprehensive bibliography of anthropological materials. The researcher must depend upon regional compilations, of which that by Embree and Dotson (1950) on Southeast Asia is an outstanding example. As regards sources of information about current publications, the writer has had little recent experience, but journals which he recalls consulting with profit in the past include *Bulletin de l'Ecole française d'Extrême-Orient* (Hanoi), *Far Eastern Quarterly* (Lancaster), *Folk-Lore* (London), *Revue des études islamiques* (Paris), *Sociologus* (Berlin), *Transactions of the Asiatic Society of Japan* (Yokohama), and *Zeitschrift für vergleichende Rechtswissenschaft* (Stuttgart), and this list could certainly be considerably expanded by specialists in Asiatic cultures.

For Oceania, we have a fairly complete ethnographic bibliography by Taylor (1951) and the excellent compilation by Kennedy (1945) on Indonesia. Tindale (1940), though incomplete, is useful on Australia. Duff and Allan (1949) have compiled an invaluable selective bibliography specifically on the New Zealand Maori. Current publications on the Pacific area are most fully reported in the *Journal de la Société des Océanistes* (Paris). Other regional journals like *Oceania* (Sydney) and the *Journal of the Polynesian Society* (Wellington) unfortunately present at best only an occasional book review or bibliographical note.

The foregoing discussion of guides to the published literature of anthropology has concentrated upon the field of ethnography, since the writer is not sufficiently familiar with the aids available to linguists, archeologists, folklorists, and physical anthropologists to deal adequately with them. The subject should not be concluded, however, without mention of two important bibliographical aids which are accessible to American scholars, though not in published form. The Peabody Museum at Harvard University has an extraordinarily complete classified card index of anthropological materials for all areas of the world, the potential value of which is impossible to exaggerate. The Cross-Cultural Survey at Yale University has virtually complete bibliographies on some areas, including Micronesia, Formosa, the Ryukyu Islands, and the Amazonian basin of South America, and useful selective bibliographies on many other regions. Only in a few instances as yet have these been reprocessed for the Human Relations Area Files.

IV. LOCATION OF UNPUBLISHED SOURCE MATERIALS

Difficult as it may be to assemble the published sources on a new culture or area, even when one has access to a good library and is familiar with the bibliographical resources, this problem pales into insignificance compared with that of locating important materials which have not been published. Nearly every professional anthropologist in the world has unpublished field materials, often in usable manuscript form. Every university with an active anthropology department has unpublished doctoral and Master's dissertations with invaluable descriptive data. Every ethnological museum has files of manuscript materials, both old and new, which are often of the utmost importance. Missions in all parts of the world and administrative offices in colonial territories often have extensive archives of reports and ethnographic records assembled only for their own local use, with no thought of even eventual publication. Invaluable reports by early travelers and even full-length records of scientific observations often remain in manuscript form in certain parts of the world, perhaps especially in the literate countries of Asia, and are gradually accumulated in the libraries of private collectors. Unpublished materials in these and comparable forms probably equal in bulk, and perhaps in their potential usefulness to anthropologists, the entire body of published materials available in our best libraries.

Of this enormous body of descriptive data, only an infinitesimal fraction is accessible to any individual scholar, even if he makes every effort and utilizes the most modern of reproducing techniques. Short of a large-scale program for the systematic location, reproduction, and distribution of such materials, anthropologists must continue to work in complete ignorance of half of their actual descriptive resources.

V. UTILIZATION OF MATERIALS IN FOREIGN LANGUAGES

Even if he is able to locate all the published sources that he needs, and perhaps some of the relevant unpublished materials as well, the professional anthropologist is often unable to utilize them because of the diversity of languages in which they are written. As a trained scholar he can be expected to command three languages—usually English, German, and French—but somewhere between 20 and 25 per cent of world ethnography is in languages other than these. Much of the best literature on Central and South America is in Spanish. The principal sources on Siberia are in Russian, and on Indonesia in Dutch. A substantial amount of descriptive information on Brazil and Angola is in Portuguese, on Ethiopia in Italian, on Greenland in Danish, on the Belgian Congo in Flemish, on South Africa in Afrikaans, on the Finno-Ugric peoples in Finnish and Swedish, on the Ainu and Formosan aborigines in Japanese. If a scholar is to encompass the major sources on the Ruthenians he must command Polish, Ukrainian, and Magyar as well as German; for the Mongols he needs Russian, Chinese, Mongol, and Japanese. He may even require Latin to use the primary source on some tribes, e.g., the Mojo of Bolivia. In some instances literature in the vernacular, where missionaries have introduced literacy to an aboriginal people, is of major importance.

Rarely can a single scholar command all the languages needed to control the basic literature for any area. American anthropologists commonly underestimate this problem because of the fortunate accident that for native North America the overwhelming bulk of the ethnographic literature is in English and most of the rest in Spanish. Even German and French are rarely needed—the former for such tribes as the Cora, Quiche, Tlingit, and Totonac; the latter for the Otomi and some northern Algonkians and Athapaskans. With these four languages, plus Russian for the Aleut and Danish for the Greenland Eskimo, the ethnographic literature on the entire continent can be fully covered.

This fortunate situation, however, is duplicated nowhere else in the world. In South America, for example, no one language accounts for as much as one-third of the literature. English, French, German, Spanish, and Portuguese are all indispensable, while the chief Bororo source is in Italian, the major Carib source in Dutch, and the standard Mojo monograph in Latin, not to mention substantial works in Swedish and other languages. The situation is equally complex in Africa and Oceania, vastly more so in Eurasia.

The ideal solution to this problem would be a concerted effort to assure the translation of every important work in other languages into either English, French, or German, which are the three traditional vehicles of scholarship and each of which already has a volume of published ethnographic materials at least double that of any other language. In advance of the attainment of this ideal, the anthropologist has only two alternatives: (1) to acquire new languages as he needs them or (2) to arrange for the translation of needed materials in languages which he does not control. For those who choose the latter solution, the experience of the Human Relations Area Files warrants a word of advice. Since competent translators who are genuinely bilingual are rare, one is usually forced to choose between persons whose native language is that of the original text and native speakers of the language into which the translation is to be made, i.e., English in the present instance. Experience has demonstrated overwhelmingly the superiority of the latter class of translators as compared with the former.

VI. LOCATION OF SPECIFIC ITEMS OF INFORMATION

Many types of anthropological research involve assembling specific items of information on many cultures rather than the intensive study of a few. Among them are most comparative studies, analyses of trait distributions, and investigations of particular instances of diffusion. When other scientists approach anthropologists for information, they commonly seek data of this type. The same is true of government agencies in time of war or of peace; they may, for example, want to know about native reactions to strangers for the guidance of castaways or commandos, or about taboos which occupying troops must respect at their peril, or about native medical customs which might affect the success of a public health program.

When masses of ethnographic literature must be ransacked for specific items of information, the problem of locating the sources themselves is complicated by that of locating the information desired in the sources after they have been assembled. Indexes and tables of contents are frequently of little use. Often the entire literature must be combed almost page by page to make certain that important bits of data have not been overlooked—an immensely time-consuming task. Unless this were done for the Kwakiutl, to choose but a single example, a researcher interested in child-training techniques would miss essential information buried in the midst of a series of recipes for salmon-head soups, and one interested in kinship terminology would find practically nothing except in a work on the mythology of a neighboring tribe.

An unfortunate consequence of this necessity is that hundreds of anthropologists have laboriously combed the same standard ethnographies for different items of information but that the careful notes they have accumulated are rarely of use to anyone else. Another is that dozens of government agencies, at excessive cost, have excerpted masses of information about foreign countries on subjects of immediate pertinence but are no better off than when they started when it becomes imperative to know in a hurry some vital fact of previously unanticipated significance.

VII. CONCLUSION

The problems considered above, some of them hitherto insoluble and others only partially or inadequately solved, are common to all anthropologists and related social scientists. The Human Relations Area Files has made the basic assumption—possibly a rash one—that none of them is inherently incapable of solution and has sought to come to grips with all of them at the same time. Its program of resolution may be summed up as follows:

1. All the peoples and cultures of the world, historical and contemporary as well as primitive, are gradually being classified, on the basis of the criteria discussed above, into groups with distinctive cultures and culture clusters, for each of which a separate file of descriptive data will ultimately, it is hoped, be assembled and reproduced for all participant institutions. The first of a projected series of areal classifications of cultures, Murdock (1951) on South America, has already appeared.

2. With each completed file is included a full analytical bibliography, embracing sources not processed as well as those actually covered.

3. A special effort is made to locate and process unpublished as well as published materials and thus to make previously inaccessible source materials available.

4. All works in other languages are translated into English, but each file includes a photographic reproduction of the original text of all translated sources, so that scholars may readily make comparisons or, if they prefer, use only the original.

5. All materials are transcribed on cards and filed according to a standard system of topical classification, presented in Murdock and others (1950), so that all information on any desired subject for any particular society can be secured in a few moments. Though classified, data are never wrenched from their written context, for a complete set of notes is retained in page order (essentially an exact copy of the original source) in each file in addition to those distributed by topic. Finally, excerpts are rigorously avoided; when a source is considered worth processing, its content is reproduced in its entirety.

Any research involving the use of cultural or background materials from societies for which complete files have been assembled can be accomplished in an inconsequential fraction of the time required to do the same task by the ordinary methods of library research. Completely eliminated are all the labors of compiling bibliographies, physically assembling the sources, translating from foreign languages, and locating the precise information required. Research time can be concentrated almost exclusively upon productive scholarly operations rather than dissipated in routine "legwork." The potential gains can be illustrated by an actual test performed by the writer two years ago. Asked to prepare a paper on family stability in non-European cultures, he planned the research, examined the data on forty representative societies, and wrote the article (Murdock, 1950), all within a total elapsed time of 25 hours. Without the aid of the Human Relations Area Files he could not have turned out a comparable contribution in 25 full research days.

In addition to the scholarly problems adumbrated above, the Human Relations Area Files has had to cope with a host of technical questions, e.g., quality control in translation and classification, alternative systems of photographic reproduction, methods of duplicating pictorial materials, efficient techniques for sorting and filing, and the adaptability of punch-card systems. Not all the problems, either scholarly or technical, have as yet been satisfactorily solved, and constructive suggestions are welcomed.

BIBLIOGRAPHY

Beals, R. L. 1932. "The Comparative Ethnology of Northern Mexico before 1750," *Ibero-Americana*, II, 93–225. Berkeley.

Beyer, H. O. 1917. *Population of the Philippine Islands in 1916*. Manila: Philippine Education Co.

BRUEL, G. 1935. *La France équatoriale africaine*. Paris.

CZEKANOWSKI, J. 1917–27. *Forschungen im Nil-Kongo-Zwischengebiet*. 5 vols. Leipzig: Klinkhardt.

DUFF, R. S., and ALLAN, R. S. 1949. *Selected Bibliography of the Anthropology of New Zealand, 1900–1948*. Seventh Pacific Science Congress, New Zealand. (Mimeographed.)

EERDE, J. C. VAN. 1920. *Inleiding tot de volkenkunde van Nederlandsch-Indië*. Haarlem.

EMBREE, J. F., and DOTSON, L. O. 1950. *Bibliography of the Peoples and Cultures of the Mainland of Southeast Asia*. ("Yale University Southeast Asia Studies.") New Haven.

FORDE, D. 1951. *The Yoruba-speaking Peoples of South-western Nigeria*. London: International African Institute.

FORDE, D., and JONES, G. I. 1950. *The Ibo and Ibibio-speaking Peoples of South-eastern Nigeria*. London: International African Institute.

GERLAND, G. 1892. *Atlas der Völkerkunde*. (Berghaus' *Physikalischer Atlas*, Abteilung 7.) Gotha.

GREENBERG, J. H. 1949–50. "Studies in African Linguistic Classification," *Southwestern Journal of Anthropology*, V, 79–100, 190–98, 309–17; VI, 47–63, 143–60, 223–37, 388–98.

JOCHELSON, W. 1928. *Peoples of Asiatic Russia*. New York: American Museum of Natural History.

JOHNSON, F. 1940. "The Linguistic Map of Mexico and Central America." In HAY, C. L., *et al.* (eds.), *The Maya and Their Neighbors*, pp. 88–114. New York: Appleton-Century.

KENNEDY, R. 1942. *The Ageless Indies*. New York: John Day.

———. 1945. *Bibliography of Indonesian Peoples and Cultures*. ("Yale Anthropological Studies," Vol. IV.) New Haven.

KERKEN, G. VAN DER. 1944. *L'Ethnie Mongo*. ("Mémoires de l'Institut royal colonial belge," Vol. III.) Brussels.

KÖHLER, O. 1950. "Die Ausbreitung der Niloten," *Beiträge zur Gesellungs- und Völkerwissenschaft, Professor Dr. Richard Thurnwald zu seinem achtzigsten Geburtstag gewidmet*, pp. 159–94. Berlin: Gebr. Mann.

KROEBER, A. L. 1925. *Handbook of the Indians of California*. (Bureau of American Ethnology Bull. 78.) Washington.

———. 1939. *Cultural and Natural Areas of Native North America*. ("University of California Publications in American Archaeology and Ethnology," Vol. XXXVIII.) Berkeley.

MCCULLOCH, M. 1950. *Peoples of Sierra Leone Protectorate*. London: International African Institute.

———. 1951. *The Southern Lunda and Related Peoples*. London: International African Institute.

MAES, J., and BOON, O. 1935. *Les Peuplades du Congo Belge*. ("Musée du Congo Belge, Publications du Bureau de documentation ethnographique," sér. 2, "*Monographies idéologiques*," Vol. I.)

MANOUKIAN, M. 1950. *Akan and Ga-Adagme Peoples of the Gold Coast*. London: International African Institute.

———. 1952. *Tribes of the Northern Territories of the Gold Coast*. London: International African Institute.

MEEK, C. K. 1931. *Tribal Studies in Northern Nigeria*. London: Kegan Paul, Trench, Trubner & Co.

MURDOCK, G. P. 1941. *Ethnographic Bibliography of North America*. ("Yale Anthropological Studies," Vol. I.) New Haven. (A revised edition is now in press.)

———. 1948. "Anthropology in Micronesia," *Transactions of the New York Academy of Sciences*, ser. 2, XI, 9–16. New York.

———. 1950. "Family Stability in Non-European Cultures," *Annals of the American Academy of Political and Social Science*, CCLXXII, 195–201.

———. 1951. *Outline of South American Cultures*. ("Behavior Science Outlines," Vol. II.) New Haven: Human Relations Area Files, Inc.

MURDOCK, G. P.; FORD, C. S.; HUDSON, A. E.; KENNEDY, R.; SIMMONS, L. W.; and WHITING, J. W. M. 1950. *Outline of Cultural Materials*. ("Behavior Science Outlines," Vol. I.) 3d rev. ed. New Haven: Human Relations Area Files, Inc.

OLIVER, D. L. 1949. *The Peabody Museum Expedition to Bougainville, Solomon Islands, 1938–39.* ("Papers of the Peabody Museum of American Archaeology and Ethnology, Harvard University," Vol. XXIX, No. 1.) Cambridge.

OSGOOD, C. 1936. *The Distribution of the Northern Athapaskan Indians.* ("Yale University Publications in Anthropology," No. 7.) New Haven.

PARK, W. Z., *et al.* 1938. "Tribal Distribution in the Great Basin," *American Anthropologist,* n.s., XL, 622–38.

RAY, V. F., *et al.* 1938. "Tribal Distribution in Eastern Oregon and Adjacent Regions," *American Anthropologist,* n.s., XL, 384–415.

RIVERS, W. H. R. 1914. *The History of Melanesian Society.* 2 vols. Cambridge: At the University Press.

SAUER, C. O. 1934. "The Distribution of Aboriginal Tribes and Languages in Northwestern Mexico," *Ibero-Americana,* V, 1–90.

SCHAPERA, I. 1930. *The Khoisan Peoples of South Africa.* London: G. Routledge & Sons.

———. 1934. "The Present State and Future Development of Ethnographical Research in South Africa," *Bantu Studies,* VIII, 219–342.

———. 1937. *The Bantu-speaking Tribes of South Africa.* London: G. Routledge & Sons.

SPECK, F. G. 1928. *Territorial Subdivisions and Boundaries of the Wampanoag, Massachusett, and Nauset Indians.* ("Indian Notes and Monographs, Museum of the American Indian, Heye Foundation," ser. 2, Vol. XLIV.) New York.

SPIER, L. 1936. *Tribal Distribution in Washington.* ("General Series in Anthropology," Vol. III.) Menasha: George Banta Publishing Co.

STEWARD, J. H. 1937. "Linguistic Distributions and Political Groups of the Great Basin Shoshoneans," *American Anthropologist,* n.s., XXXIX, 625–34.

———. 1938. *Basin-Plateau Aboriginal Socio-political Groups.* (Bureau of American Ethnology Bull. 120.) Washington.

———. (ed.). 1946–50. *Handbook of South American Indians.* 6 vols. (Bureau of American Ethnology Bull. 143.) Washington.

SWANTON, J. R. 1946. *The Indians of the Southeastern United States.* (Bureau of American Ethnology Bull. 137.) Washington.

TALBOT, P. A. 1926. *The Peoples of Southern Nigeria.* 4 vols. London: Oxford University Press.

TANGCO, M. 1951. *The Christian Peoples of the Philippines.* Quezon City.

TAYLOR, C. R. H. 1951. *A Pacific Bibliography.* ("Memoirs of the Polynesian Society," Vol. XXIV.) Wellington.

TESSMANN, G. 1932. "Die Völker und Sprachen Kameruns," *Petermanns Mitteilungen,* LXXVIII, 132–40, 184–90.

TEW, M. 1950. *Peoples of the Lake Nyasa Region.* London: Oxford University Press.

TINDALE, N. B. 1940. "Distribution of Australian Aboriginal Tribes," *Transactions of the Royal Society of South Australia,* LXIV, 140–231.

WHITELEY, W. 1950. *Bemba and Related Peoples of Northern Rhodesia.* London: International African Institute.

WIESCHHOFF, H. A. 1948. *Anthropological Bibliography of Negro Africa.* ("American Oriental Series," Vol. XXIII.) New Haven: American Oriental Society.

CROSS-CULTURAL DOCUMENTATION

by Frank W. Moore

The accumulation of anthropological data—particularly professionally written ethnographic monographs—during recent decades has made possible large-scale comparative studies covering as many as two hundred different societies that are fairly well documented. This growing body of ethnographic literature permits the use of much more sophisticated sampling procedures than were possible in the past. But at the same time its very mass makes the search for data relevant to a particular study increasingly difficult.

The problem of procuring specific information from a body of literature, recognized today in all the major scientific disciplines, has given rise to a new field of research loosely termed "documentation" or "information retrieval." Not surprisingly, most of the efforts to meet this problem are concentrated in the physical sciences, particularly metallurgy and chemistry. The urgency of the problem is reflected in the literature on documentation, which has grown to such an extent that it now presents something of an information retrieval problem in itself.

In contrast to the older physical sciences where literally thousands of publications related to a given topic may exist, anthropology is still largely dependent for primary information on studies covering the many diverse features of a single culture or area rather than investigations of a particular aspect of culture. Studies of a specific cultural aspect are usually secondary sources, that is, interpretations of primary data. Consequently, the researcher interested in a cross-cultural study faces the problem of retrieving data buried in sources that also include much material irrelevant to his study. A subsidiary, but important, problem lies in the nature and diversity of anthropological sources. For example, few disciplines find significant data in such publications as the *Sarawak Gazette* of 1890. The researcher must look far beyond the professional journals and monographs. Much important material is contained in early travel accounts, missionary reports, governmental documents, and countless other non-anthropological publications, ranging far beyond the resources of any single library. A common notion to the contrary, the long hours of physical labor expended in searching out and securing the required works do not enhance scholarship: going through thousands of pages in search of items of specific information may broaden the horizons of the researcher, but only a fraction of the time spent is productive for the task at hand.

The four basic operational problems of retrieving information for large-scale cross-cultural studies are: (1) identifying the pertinent sources; (2) securing the sources; (3) retrieving the relevant data; and (4) reducing the data to a form suitable for manipulation.

The conventional information retrieval device for meeting the first problem, *identifying the pertinent sources*, is the bibliography. A bibliography, of course, serves merely to indicate the existence of certain works, although the identification of sources is facilitated if the bibliography classifies the sources by subject, or if it is annotated as to content.

The second problem, *securing the sources*, is complicated by the diverse nature of the basic source materials. The established routines of library searches and interlibrary loans are the standard solutions for this problem, however time-consuming and frustrating they may be.

Retrieving the relevant data has traditionally been facilitated by the book index. The basic flaw of the book index, however, is that universal classification forms are not used. The use of specific rather than general concepts renders the index relatively meaningless for most cross-cultural research.

The final problem, *reducing the data to a manipulatable form*, is usually solved by copying pertinent passages or paraphrases on index cards, although the development of portable copying devices has reduced this difficulty somewhat.

As long as research has only these traditional tools, it tends to be confined to "safe" subjects, those on which a good deal of investigation has already been done. Bold and imaginative ideas too often cannot be explored because of the time and labor involved merely in sampling data to determine whether a hypothesis warrants a full-scale research effort. Many researchers feel they cannot "afford" an idea that may not prove fruitful. An efficient retrieval device is perhaps more vitally needed for this preliminary sampling than for the actual substantive research. If there is preliminary assurance that the research will be profitable, the work will probably be done eventually no matter how formidable the task.

A further drawback of conventional retrieval methods is the near impossibility of verification and review of the results of large-scale comparative studies. Checking the results of works of this type involves the same problems of retrieval that faced the original researcher. Criticism, therefore, is often mere quibbling. Unable to challenge the over-all results on the basis of a review of the data, the critic can only object to those specific points with which he is familiar and hint darkly about possible methodological and theoretical deficiencies. Realistic and valid criticism of comparative studies depends on efficient retrieval devices.

The need for an information retrieval device to meet these and other problems involved in large-scale comparative studies was recognized long ago by Herbert Spencer, who made one of the first attempts at a systematic presentation of cultural data in the form of abstracts or summaries which were published, starting in 1873, in several volumes under the title of *Descriptive Sociology*. Spencer's objective (Spencer, 1873, p. iii) was to have "the facts collected and arranged for easy reference and convenient study of their relations, being so presented, apart from hypotheses, as to aid all students of social science in testing such conclusions as they have drawn and in drawing others." He further stated (p. iv) that "before there can be reached in Sociology, generalizations having a certainty making them worthy to be called scientific, there must be definite accounts of the institutions and actions of societies of various types, and in various stages of evolution, *so arranged* as to furnish the means of readily ascertaining what social phenomena are habitually associated [emphasis added]."

Spencer organized his materials both by culture area and by subject or topical categories, presenting much of his material in tabular form. His topical categories, while not covering all facets of human activity in enough detail, nonetheless proved the organization of the raw material of social science a feasible undertaking.

There were, however, two major flaws in his system: (1) the original data had been interpreted and reworked, and (2) the fixed format (books) precluded the addition of new data and the physical manipulation of the data at hand.

The next significant step toward an information retrieval system designed for wide application and general availability to researchers came in 1937 when G. P. Murdock and others at the Institute of Human Relations at Yale University founded the Cross-Cultural Survey.

The Cross-Cultural Survey,[1] was a program for indexing, reproducing, and cross-filing excerpts from primary sources in anthropological literature according to a series of universal categories. Physically, the system consisted of 5 × 8 slips filed behind divider cards bearing numbers corresponding to the category designations. All materials on a particular culture were filed in a single location. The system avoided, in the main, the basic objections to Spencer's system. The material was given in the primary form, although extraneous passages were omitted, and the use of individual slips permitted additions and changes at any time. The individual slips could also be physically manipulated and compared, thus materially reducing the need for notetaking.

It is of considerable interest to note that this pioneering effort at a retrieval system that would solve all four of the basic operational problems was made in the social sciences. Recognition of a similar need in the physical sciences came later and is only now becoming an important consideration.

Although the Cross-Cultural Survey provided data that was relatively free of editorial intervention, the researcher was not given the complete context. Of course, *any* kind of categorization or classification to some degree intervenes between the researcher and the raw data, but if the system can be fully described and understood, its effect on research will be only as great as the researcher allows it to be.

In 1949 a new interuniversity organization, the Human Relations Area Files, was founded to reproduce and distribute to participating institutions the files of cultural materials assembled by the Cross-Cultural Survey. Gradually the scope of the project was broadened to include refinement of the system and the creation of entirely new files of information based on recent studies. A fully revised system of universal cultural categories was developed and published.[2] All new materials were analyzed according to this manual. In 1953 a significant new reproduction process, Haloid Xerography, became available, making it practical for the first time to provide actual reproductions of the pages of original data, both published and unpublished. Since 1953 the file categories have contained, instead of abstracted passages, actual pages from the source, reduplicated to be filed under as many category headings as there are categorized subjects on the page.

The importance of this innovation is that editorial intervention between the original material and the researcher is reduced to the absolute minimum,

[1] Murdock, 1940.
[2] Murdock, *et al.*, 1950.

leaving only the application of the universal classification device. Even the effect of the classification is reduced by the fact that complete page-order copies of the original sources, in addition to the categorized pages, are provided for the convenience of the researcher who may not wish to use the classification except as an index.

Besides anthropological data in English, the files today also provide translations of works in other languages, as well as reproductions of the original foreign text. While most American scholars can usually read at least one or two languages besides English, translation represents another time-consuming operation in cross-cultural research.

An information retrieval system necessarily requires a universal classification system that the researcher must deal with. In the case of the Area Files this system (*Outline of Cultural Materials*) is oriented for use by social scientists. For example, there are nearly forty categories specifically covering various aspects of kinship and marriage, while the entire field of chemical engineering is covered by a single category. This situation, incidentally, points up the fact that the *Outline of Cultural Materials* is not a theoretical construct. It was arrived at empirically. This factor, discussed in the introduction to the *Outline,* should be considered by anyone who uses the system.

It should further be recognized that single categories, designed for universal application, will rarely, if ever, exactly fit the specific theoretical framework of a given research problem. It most cases the desired data will be included in two or more categories. The researcher should expect to plan a program for the inspection of various categories. For example, a comparison of co-operation in hunting societies with co-operation in farming societies would require the inspection of several categories besides 474 (*Cooperative Organization*). Relevant data might be found in categories covering magic, ceremonial, food quest, play, housebuilding, etc. Only activities clearly described by the original author as co-operative will be found in 474. This makes it necessary for the researcher to make his own inferences as to co-operative activities not identified or identifiable as such on the basis of the criteria explained in the *Outline of Cultural Materials.*

Efficient use of the Area Files as an information retrieval device involves a comparatively easy but basic reorientation. Scholars are accustomed to treating books and articles as the basic units of research, regardless of the total content of these sources. In using the Area Files as a source of documentation it is preferable to consider the various subject categories as the basic units. That is, the scholar learns to do research on his problem in terms of the appropriate category or combinations of categories. Once the documentation is completed, the sources of data can easily be identified in terms of authors and publishers in the conventional fashion.

The Area Files, like the Cross-Cultural Survey, are organized by culture area.[3] That is, the category subject headings (divider cards) are filed numerically under specific cultural units. Until 1954, a cultural entity was identified only by its more or less commonly accepted name as shown on each file slip. The first edition of the *Outline of World Cultures* (G. P. Murdock, 1954) provided a code for defining the cultural entities in a system of categories essentially comparable to the *Outline of Cultural Materials.* Although every effort has been exerted to make the cultural groupings

[3] For detailed information on the organization and use of the Area Files see *Guide to the Use of the Files,* New Haven, 1956.

meaningful cultural units, legitimate questions as to the propriety of certain groupings can be raised in many cases. Identification is made on the file slips themselves, not only of the major group involved, but of the subgroups as well, by means of headings inserted at the top of each page. For example, under the major heading Dhegiha, the various subgroups or tribes are identified as Kansa, Osage, Ponca, and Omaha. The researcher must decide whether he wants to use Dhegiha as his unit or one or a combination of the subtribes. In some cases it might be desirable to merge information from two or more files or to consider separating subgroups that are listed in a single file. In other words, the mere fact that a collection of file slips reposes in specific drawers does not lessen the responsibility of the researcher in making his own judgment as to what constitutes a meaningful cultural unit.[4]

How adequately the literature has been covered in the various files is also a problem that must be solved by the individual researcher. In some cases the files contain nearly all the available literature, while in others only a representative sample has been processed.

A further consideration in the use of the files is the reliability of the coding operation. Lack of materials in a particular category may indicate that the original sources failed to cover this point, or it may indicate that a coding error has occurred and the information simply has not been placed in the proper place.

Reliability studies at HRAF (Kay, 1957) indicate a high degree of certainty that materials will be found in the proper categories. The researcher, however, may not be satisfied with a high average of reliability and will want to make an independent search. The book index is always processed (category 116) to aid in the solution of this problem. In general, experience has shown that an excess of nonpertinent materials in each category is more likely to be the problem than absence of subjects belonging in the category.

Another pitfall for the researcher in certain cases in the past has been the matter of context. The degree to which it is possible to deal with discrete items taken out of context is difficult to determine and varies with the degree of complexity of the problem. Ingestion of food, for example, is a matter that may be dealt with without particular concern for the cultural context if the mere occurrence and frequency of the action is the only consideration. If the cultural elaboration of eating habits is to be considered, however, a wider context must be observed. Once again, the researcher himself must assume responsibility for contextual accuracy.

It is obvious that the principal danger in the use of an information system such as the Area Files is that the researcher will tend to rely too much on the givens of the system and suspend his own critical evaluation. The dangers lie, not in the device itself, but in the uses or misuses that are possible with the system.

An evaluation of an information system such as the Area Files must be made in terms of its potential utility to researchers. In these terms, the ability of the system to relay information from the original source to the researcher is the basic consideration. The Area Files must be rated high for lack of intervention between the researcher and the source material. Obviously, the system meets, to some degree at least, all four of the basic operational problems found in large-scale comparative research. The system

[4] See Murdock, 1957, for a discussion of sampling and culture unit problems.

is probably weakest in regard to the fourth problem (reducing the data to manipulatable form), since only the equivalent of book pages are available to the researcher. Further reduction of the material is left entirely to the researcher in line with the HRAF policy of not altering the original source material.

In the beginning, the Area Files suffered from a lack of resources to implement the system. Only recently, after twelve years of operation, has an adequate sample of about two hundred cultures been processed and made available. The existing files are now in process of being brought up to date with the addition of recent studies. The time lag between publication and the appearance of the materials in the files—a constant problem in the past—is gradually being eliminated.

A further problem is caused by the limited number of only about two hundred different cultural units to select from. The researcher must either content himself with a considerably smaller sample than two hundred or work with a preselected sample. The fact that information on any given subject will not be available in all files further limits the sample size.

The Area Files are today the basic operational tool for cross-cultural research in the behavioral sciences. Although in many cases the researcher must look beyond HRAF for supplemental information, the fact remains that the basic source material for cross-cultural studies is readily available through this system.

The prospects for a more advanced retrieval system than HRAF for comparative research are tied to the possibility of some sort of technological breakthrough in electronic computer storage devices. When large-scale storage in electronic memories becomes possible, the use of computers might lead to actual manipulation of the data without recourse to the human quantification of raw data. It must be emphasized, however, that even such a computer filled with the world's supply of anthropological facts could not do research. It would still be only a tool in the hands of the researcher. The responsibility for asking meaningful questions and making meaningful interpretations of the data to arrive at answers is, and will continue to be, the basic research problem.

BIBLIOGRAPHY

Human Relations Area Files. 1956. *Guide to the Use of the Files.* New Haven.

Kay, Brian R. 1957. "The Reliability of HRAF Coding Procedures," *American Anthropologist,* Vol. 59, pp. 524-527.

Murdock, George P. 1940. "The Cross-Cultural Survey," *American Sociological Review,* Vol. 5, pp. 361-370.

———. 1950. *Outline of World Cultures.* (2nd ed., rev.) New Haven: Human Relations Area Files.

———. 1957. "World Ethnographic Sample," *American Anthropologist,* Vol. 59, pp. 664-687.

Murdock, George P., *et al.* 1950. *Outline of Cultural Materials.* (3rd rev. ed.) New Haven: Human Relations Area Files.

Spencer, Herbert. 1873. *Descriptive Sociology: Or Groups of Sociological Facts.* New York: D. Appleton.

The Cross-Cultural Method *

John W. M. Whiting
Harvard University

The cross-cultural method utilizes data collected by anthropologists concerning the culture of various peoples throughout the world to test hypotheses concerning human behavior. Some of the hypotheses tested have been derived from theories of cultural evolution, others from theories concerned with the integration of culture, and still others, particularly in recent years, from theories of individual and social psychology.

The cross-cultural method was first used by E. B. Tylor (1889), who presented at the meetings of the Royal Anthropological Institute of Great Britain a paper entitled "On a method of investigating the development of institutions; applied to laws of marriage and descent." It is interesting that Sir Francis Galton, one of the fathers of modern statistics, presided at this meeting. Although the intent of the study was to support Tylor's particular view of cultural evolution, its importance was that in the paper and the discussion which followed most of the basic assumptions of cross-cultural research were touched upon.

It was not until twenty-five years later, however, that the method was again used and, as before, to test evolutionary theory. Hobhouse, Wheeler, and Ginsberg (1915) published a monograph in which the frequency of occurrence of certain social institutions was determined for each stage of economic development from lower hunters to advanced agriculturalists. Essentially similar (but more methodologically and theoretically sophisticated) studies followed after another lapse of nearly twenty-five years with Simmons (1937) and Murdock (1937).

In the last fifteen years, the cross-cultural method has not only become more popular but has changed in its theoretical orientation. It has drawn upon the theory of general behavior science rather than that of cultural evolution. Ford's (1939) study of the frequency of certain types of behavior presumed to be closely related to biological needs was the first to represent this change, even though it was concerned with the development of an appropriate conceptual system and the establishment of cross-cultural norms rather than with the testing of hypotheses. His later work (1945), and with Beach (1951), is also primarily conceptual and normative.

The first study to be published which was concerned with the testing of hypotheses derived from behavior science was that of D. G. Horton (1943). He used the cross-cultural method to investigate the relationship between the drinking of alcoholic beverages and anxiety, and showed that alcohol reduced inhibition in all societies unless special measures were taken to prevent it.

Murdock's *Social Structure*, published in 1949, represents a landmark in cross-cultural research. In this study he used a sample of 250 societies distributed over the world to test hypotheses concerned with the correlation between kinship terminology and other aspects of social structure; particularly, residence rules, the form of marriage, and rules of descent. He draws specifically upon behavior theory to explain the origin and generalization of the incest taboo.

Studies with a behavior science orientation, but of more limited scope than Murdock's, include B. B. Whiting's (1950) study of the relation between sorcery and social control, McClelland and Friedman's (1952) study of the relation between child training practices and achievement motivation, Wright's (1952) study of the relation between child training and aggression as expressed in folktales, and Barry's (1952) study of the relation between child training and certain formal characteristics of decorative art.

The most elaborate use of psychological theory in cross-cultural research is that of Whiting and Child (1953). In this study certain hypotheses relating to the Freudian mechanisms of fixation, displacement, projection, and the development of guilt are tested. The antecedent variables in this study consist of child-training practices, and the consequent variables consist of magical beliefs and practices concerning the cause and cure of illness. Thus, ethnographic data from primitive societies have

*Reprinted from Gardner Lindzey (ed.), *Handbook of Social Psychology* (Cambridge, Mass., Addison-Wesley, 1954), I ("Theory and Method"), pp. 523-531, by permission of the author and the publisher.

been used not only to test theories at the level of culture and society but also theories which are derived essentially from individual psychology.

It might be asked at this point why ethnographic material should be drawn upon to test psychological principles. Why not stick to materials gathered in one's own society, where the language and culture are familiar and where more adequate control of the process of data collection is possible?

The advantages of the cross-cultural method are twofold. First, it ensures that one's findings relate to human behavior in general rather than being bound to a single culture, and second, it increases the range of variation of many of the variables.

With respect to the first point, that of generality, one might ask questions such as the following: Is the Oedipus complex a universal phenomenon or is it peculiar to middle-class western Europeans? Does the relation between frustration and aggression hold in societies other than our own?

Since most social psychological studies are done within the framework of western European culture, one can never be certain whether the discovered relationships are valid for all mankind or whether they are an artifact of some limitation or special circumstance of the culture in which they have been discovered. An example will serve to illustrate this point. Sears and Wise (1950) found as a result of a study of a sample of eighty children living in Kansas City that there was a positive relationship between the age of weaning and the degree to which the infant gave indications of emotional disturbance. That is, the later a child was weaned the more disturbance he showed. This relationship reached the 1% level of significance.

One might ask whether this relation between age of weaning and emotional disturbance is a general human trait or whether it is peculiar to the culture of Kansas City. Anthropologists are all too eager to find exceptions to any rule. Thus, Beatrice Blackwood (1935) reports that the Kurtatchi of the Solomon Islands do not wean their children until they are over three years old and that Kurtatchi children show no signs of emotional disturbance. Does this single case disprove the rule? More than two cases, e.g., Kansas City and Kurtatchi, are needed to answer this question.

Fortunately, the data are available. Whiting and Child (1953) in a cross-cultural study of child training and personality collected material, on the same variables as those used by Sears and Wise, from a sample of seventy-five societies distributed over the world. Evidence was available so that judgments could be made for age of weaning and emotional disturbance for thirty-seven societies. The mean score for emotional disturbance on a seven-point scale for the seventeen societies in which the onset of weaning was at two years or less was 3.5, whereas the mean score for the twenty societies in which weaning took place later than two years was 2.8.

It will be seen from this that in this instance the Kurtatchi are not a single exception but are typical of a tendency for late weaning to result in low rather than high emotional disturbance and thus there really seems to be contradiction between the Sears and Wise findings and the cross-cultural evidence. If the methods of measuring these two variables are accepted as reliable and comparable in the two sets of data, one might conclude that different psychological principles were operating in Kansas City than in the rest of the world. Closer examination of the data, however, reveals a much more plausible explanation and illustrates the second advantage of the cross-cultural method, namely, that of increased range.

The effective range of age of weaning for the Kansas City sample was 0-7 months (only five of the eighty cases were later than seven months), whereas for the cross-cultural sample, with the exception of two cases, it was from twelve months to six years. Thus, there is practically no overlap between the two distributions and, as is shown in Table 1, the two findings complement each other to indicate a curvilinear rather than a linear relation between the two variables. Due to lack of range, neither study tells the whole story.

The preceding case illustrates that, with respect to the age of weaning at least, psychologists would be exceedingly hampered by lack of range in developing a theory of its effects which would be applicable the world over. There is considerable evidence that this lack of range is not restricted to the age of weaning. Thus, although much of the accuracy of measurement and experimental control generally found in psychological studies on individuals in our society is lacking in cross-cultural studies, this spread in the variables provides a useful check upon and supplement to psychological research.

Even though extreme cases on some variable may be found in our society, these are deviant from the cultural norms. In cross-cultural research the norm for a whole society is taken as a score. Thus no matter how extreme a case may be from our point of view, the individuals

TABLE 1

RELATION BETWEEN AGE AT ONSET OF WEANING AND AMOUNT OF EMOTIONAL DISTURBANCE SHOWN BY CHILD.

Comparable data from eighty individual children from Kansas City (Sears & Wise, 1950) and from thirty-seven societies (Whiting & Child, 1953) are presented.

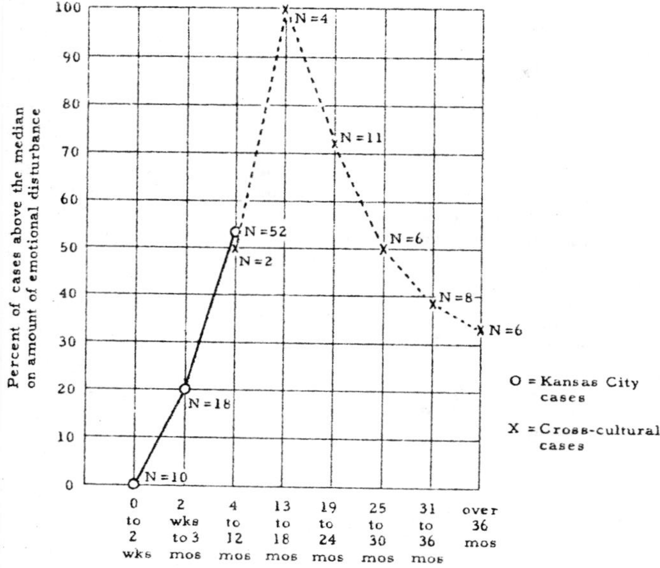

who manifest this behavior do not perceive themselves to be deviant. To return to the age of weaning, a Kurtatchi mother who does not wean her child until he is between three and four years old is doing just what other Kurtatchi mothers do. An American mother who nursed her three-year-old child, however, could not help but be aware that she was deviating from the usual practice — a factor which might have considerable effects on her and might therefore contaminate one's findings if one were interested in the consequences of late weaning rather than of deviant behavior.

Furthermore, the cross-cultural method, by studying cultural norms, holds individual variation constant. Psychological studies of individuals in a single society do just the opposite, in that cultural norms are held constant and individual variations are studied. A combination of these two methods should supplement and correct each other in the development of a general theory of human behavior.

Granted that the cross-cultural method is useful in that it provides an increased range for certain variables and a test for the generality of hypotheses, there are some basic assumptions involved in the use of the method which should be considered. First, the method rests on the assumption that the customs of a society are truly comparable to the habits of an individual. There are those who argue that culture is essentially independent of psychological laws. White (1949), for example, holds that there is a science, which he calls culturology, that concerns itself with the evolutionary development, diffusion and transmission of culture, and that the principles which govern these processes are on a different level of abstraction from that of psychology. Another view, represented by Ford (1939), Gillin (1948), Murdock *et al.* (1950),

Whiting and Child (1953), and Whiting *et al.* (1953), while recognizing the limitation which social interaction imposes upon culture, has defined a custom (the basic unit of culture) as a special case of a habit. Thus, the psychological principles which apply to habits should, by this definition, apply to customs.

To be more explicit, a custom may be thought to refer to the behavior of a typical individual in a given society. Thus, the Kurtatchi custom of weaning the child between three and four years of age, which has been referred to above, may be understood to refer to a typical or average Kurtatchi mother. Put in another way, the thirty-seven societies presented in Table 1 represent thirty-seven typical parents and their children, one in each of the thirty-seven societies. The problem of defining and measuring a custom in this way is discussed in detail in Whiting *et al.*, Chapter IV.

If one makes the assumption that a custom is the habit of a typical member of a society, then it becomes important to scrutinize the nature of ethnographic data and the methods by which they are collected. Were the societies chosen by anthropologists as large and complex as ours, to describe a custom would involve exceedingly elaborate sampling techniques, such as are described in other chapters of this handbook. It is the general practice of anthropologists, however, to study small and relatively homogeneous societies, or when large and more complex societies are studied, to limit the report to a single village or band.

My own experience with the Kwoma (1941) is not atypical of ethnographic practice. The Kwoma is a tribe situated in central New Guinea. The total population of some nine hundred people are divided into four subtribes. Each subtribe is in turn divided into sibs and each sib into hamlets. Except for a brief trip to the other subtribes and a few visits to other hamlets, virtually all of my observations were made on Rumbima hamlet of the Hayamakwo sib of the Hongwam subtribe of the Kwoma. Rumbima hamlet consisted of thirty-two adults and thirty-two children. Since my house was built in the hamlet and I lived there for nine months, the customs I report are concerned with typical people of various statuses within this hamlet. Whether the customs were representative of the Kwoma as a whole or of the Hongwam subtribe or of only the Hayamakwo sib I cannot say. For cross-cultural purposes, however, Rumbima hamlet — not the Kwoma — should constitute the case.

It is unfortunately the practice, as far as cross-cultural work is concerned, for anthropologists all too frequently to use in the titles of their monographs or articles some group larger than the one which they studied, just as I, myself, did. (*Becoming a Kwoma* rather than "Becoming a Rumbima.") This is misleading, for it suggests that the culture which they describe is representative of the larger group, an assumption which they are generally not warranted in making. Even more important, several ethnographers may each report on a given society but study quite different subgroups whose culture may vary to an unknown degree. If it were the case that one ethnographer described child-training practices in detail and another had a fine collection of folktales it would be very tempting, if one were studying the effect of child training on projective systems, to consider both reports to refer to a single case — tempting but dangerous. It is especially dangerous when the ethnography refers not even to a single society, but to a linguistic stock such as the Sioux or the Zulu.

Fortunately, anthropologists generally identify the group on which they actually gathered their material. This is usually in the introductory chapter. As a caution, to a novice undertaking a cross-cultural study — choose your sample from this identification and not from the title. An excellent discussion of this problem may be found in an article by Murdock (1953).

Although a small homogeneous society such as Rumbima hamlet presents no problem as far as sampling goes, it does raise a question of the stability of one's observation. Thus, in Rumbima hamlet only two children were being weaned during the nine months when I was present. Since both of these children were being observed I obtained a 100% sample of weaning practice at Rumbima in 1937. Two instances, however, do not provide a very stable measure. Individual variation in the two children could obviously introduce considerable bias. In fact, in the present instance, one of the children observed was quite sickly and his response to weaning may have been influenced more by this fact than by the actual age of weaning.

There is, however, an anthropological field technique that compensates to some extent for this defect. Anthropologists generally do not rely alone upon the observation of individuals or the questioning of respondents about their own experience, but they also use informants, who tell them what "the people" do (cf. Chapter 12). Thus, when I asked my Rumbima informants when they (the people of Rumbima) weaned their children, their answer represented not only the two children whom I saw but their opinion based upon all the children which they had observed being weaned. Although this greatly increases the number of individuals observed, it introduces another difficulty — that of the bias of the informant. Needless to say, this is a problem that is always with the social scientist who uses verbal report as a technique for gathering data. To minimize this type of bias, anthropologists generally check all information with a number of informants and they pay particular attention to instances of disagreement. They also check instances of disagreement between the statements of informants and their own, i.e., the anthropologists' observation. As an example of this last point, my Rumbima informants' report about weaning did not correspond to my observation of the sick child. When confronted with this fact, my informants agreed that this was due to the boy's illness.

In general, then, a reasonably reliable estimate of the typical behavior of people in small homogeneous societies or subgroups throughout the world can be made on the basis of ethnographic data.

There is another basic assumption, however, which underlies the cross-cultural method. This assumption is that customs can be compared from one society to another. There are many who argue that every culture represents a complex whole such that a custom which may look the same as a custom in another culture really means something quite different. This same problem is quite similar to that of the psychologist who compares individuals. Child psychologists express the same view when they insist on considering the "whole child."

It is, of course, true that any individual case, be it a person or a society, is unique and, as a whole, incomparable with any other individual case. Scientific investigation, however, is based on the assumption that attributes of the whole can be abstracted and compared. Thus it is said that no two snowflakes are identical, and yet it is also a valid statement that snowflakes are hexagonal, white, and will melt in temperatures above 32° Fahrenheit. Some investigators may be concerned with the beauty and intricacy of the crystalline pattern of each individual snowflake; others with discovering the general truths about snowflakes. Both are legitimate enterprises, although one might not think so if one listened to the heated arguments between proponents of these two approaches.

Those who are concerned with the description, explanation, or diagnosis of a single case generally use rather complex analytic units which combine a very complicated cluster of attributes or variables. Clinical psychologists are wont to speak of the Oedipus complex or the oral syndrome. Similarly, anthropologists in describing a single society speak of the political aspect, the religious system, the social structure, the economic institutions, or the ethos. These abstractions are so complex and multidimensional that they are of little use for cross-cultural research. If no further analysis is made, the ethos of one culture can scarcely be compared with the ethos of another culture. If one views cultures, or individuals, at this complex level of abstraction, one is left with the feeling that they are indeed unique and incomparable.

Comparison demands analysis into simple enough units so that certain attributes may be seen to vary along a single dimension. Comparative anthropologists, whether they have been concerned with historical or functional problems, have tended to use much simpler units of analysis than those who have been more concerned with the description of a single society. For example, Malinowski, concerned chiefly with a complete description of Trobriand culture, used the institution as his basic analytic unit, whereas Kroeber in his early historical comparative work used the concept of culture trait.

The concept of culture trait, although it is more promising than units of greater complexity, has, nevertheless, a weakness as far as testing hypotheses derived from psychological theories. It refers both to behavioral and material events. Cradleboards and methods of child care, spears and hunting techniques, drums and dance forms are all listed as culture traits. Cradleboards, spears, and drums are a different order of events from child care, hunting techniques, and dance forms. Principles of physics and chemistry apply to the former; principles of psychology and sociology to the latter.

The concept of a custom, discussed above, has the advantage of being both psychologically meaningful and simple. It is appropriate here to add to the definition of a custom, which has been defined above as a habit of a typical individual in a society, its essential attributes. They consist of (1) an agent or a subject (2) performing an act (3) in given circumstances. To distinguish a custom from an individual habit it is required that the agent, the act, and the circumstances be generally recognized as categories by the members of the society. Thus, the subject of a custom would be a mother or a farmer rather than Mary Smith or John Jones. Similarly, the circumstances and acts would be recognized categories such as "at dinner time" or "driving a car" rather than events that are relevant only to a particular individual or to some experimental setup. A unit with essentially these attributes was first suggested by Ford (1939), and developed by Murdock *et al.* (1950) and by Whiting and Child (1953).

Not only does the concept of custom have the advantage of simplicity but, since it is defined as a special kind of habit, psychological principles such as those of learning and extinction, generalization and discrimination, and motivation and conflict can be drawn upon to suggest hypotheses about culture. To do this, of course, customs must be measured in the same manner that habits are.

Many anthropologists agree that a culture can be analyzed into its component customs, but are still concerned about the comparison of customs across cultures. They point out that actions which are formally identical have quite different meanings in different societies. Belching may be complimentary or rude; thumbing the nose insulting or meaningless.

This problem is not so difficult as it at first seems. Cross-cultural comparison requires equivalence in meaning rather than formal equivalence. In other words, if customs are defined in terms of universal panhuman dimensions they can be compared across cultures. An insult is an insult whether it be accomplished by thumbing the nose, biting the thumbnail, or shouting "karaganda yikafa" ("little baby" in Kwoma). As Kluckhohn (1953, p. 517) puts it, ". . . biological, psychological, and sociosituational universals afford the possibility of comparison of cultures in terms which are not ethnocentric . . ."

Motives based upon social interaction such as aggression, dependence, affiliation, achievement, and the like provide a set of universal dimensions by which customs that are of particular interest to psychologists can be cross-culturally compared. McClelland and Friedman (1952), Wright (1952), and Whiting and Child (1953) have already used such a device in cross-cultural research.

But how does one go about doing cross-cultural research? What practical problems are involved? The method is not essentially different from any correlational study. The sample must be selected, the variables chosen, scales defined, judges trained, reliability established, care taken to prevent bias in judgments, etc. There are a few special precautions and some useful short-cuts, however, which should be mentioned.

First there is a precaution as to the choice of a sample. A criticism which has been applied to cross-cultural research ever since Tylor (1889) presented his pioneering paper is that of the independence of cases. These critics argue that if two societies derive from a common origin or have extensively borrowed from each other, they should not be counted as two instances but only as one. As Boas (1927, p. 120) stated it:

> In order to make a statistical method a success it is essential that the phenomena counted must be independent of one another. If a number of them go back to the same historical sources they cannot be considered as separate units.

Proponents of cross-cultural research consider this an extreme statement, and take the view that as long as two societies are politically distinct they are as independent as two individuals in a single society. This also is an extreme view. The problem is complex and not as yet completely solved. All empirical evidence so far supports the view, however, that Boas was overcautious. B. B. Whiting (1950) and Whiting and Child (1953) have each used somewhat different methods to correct for this possible error. B. B. Whiting checked her results by recalculating her major correlations on a sample which included only one society from each major culture area in the world. Whiting and Child used the technique of testing some of their hypotheses independently in each of the five continental and oceanic areas of the world.

Even though such corrective devices are available, one should bear the problem of independence of cases in mind in selecting the original sample. A simple precaution is to avoid using two cases which are known to have derived from a common origin within the recent past — that is, within such a short time that their cultures have not had a chance to change. A more cautious rule would require choosing no more than one case from a linguistic area in which the languages were still mutually intelligible. Still another method would be to get a fairly equal representation of cases from the five major areas of the world — North America, South America, Eurasia, Africa, and Oceania.

A second methodological precaution relates to the reliability of sources. The report of a traveler who has visited a society for a few days and writes an account of its culture clearly should not be given as much credence as the report of a trained ethnographer who has lived with the people for a year or more and learned to speak their language. To illustrate the type of report one sometimes finds in travel accounts, there is a persistent story told on the coastal towns of New Guinea by the Australian plantation owners to uncritical visitors. The story runs that there is a tribe of natives living in the interior who have long tails and live in houses on piles. In order to sleep comfortably at night, they have holes bored in the flooring through which they stick their tails. Unfortunately this makes them an easy prey to their headhunting neighbors who creep beneath their dwelling and tie knots in their tails before attacking. Clearly, there is considerable range in the reliability of sources and some assessment of sources should be made before using them.

A third precaution for a novice undertaking cross-cultural research relates to the *identification* of a society. This problem has already ben touched upon above in discussing the problem of sampling. In this context, however, it should be mentioned that the same society may be called by a different name in different sources. Thus the Teton tribe is also referred to as the Western Dakota and the Western Sioux.

A fourth precaution relates to the treatment of societies in which the variables under consideration depend upon a judgment of the presence or absence of certain beliefs or practices. Thus, the belief that animal spirits have the capacity to cause illness might be predicted to occur in societies with a high degree of aggression anxiety. Whiting and Child (1953), in attempting to test this hypothesis, found that this belief was reported to occur in thirty-eight out of their sample of seventy-five societies. In the remaining thirty-seven societies no mention of this belief could be found in the ethnographic sources. In none of these latter societies, however, was there the explicit statement that this belief was absent. This is by no means an unusual state of affairs. If ethnographies consisted of a listing of all the potential beliefs and practices which did *not* occur, as well as those which did, the bulk of the monograph would consist of negative evidence, since any one society has but a small fraction of the total number of customs that may be found throughout the world.

How should societies for which there is no mention of a particular trait be treated? Can it be assumed that the trait is absent if it is not mentioned, or should these societies be omitted on the basis of inadequate information? The latter solution is the more conservative and, as a rule of thumb, should generally be followed if both the antecedent and consequent variables depend upon the presence or absence criterion. Otherwise one may obtain a spurious positive correlation which reflects only differences in the adequacy of ethnographic coverage. That is, both traits would tend not to be reported more frequently in the poorly covered tribes than in the well-covered tribes. Such a spurious correlation will not result when at least one of the variables depends upon some variation in the degree of a trait rather than its presence or absence, and when such variation in degree does not depend upon the amount of information. To assume that no information means absence in such an instance, although it does not introduce bias, does, however, increase the amount of error variance, and for this reason should be avoided if possible.

The practice of always omitting cases with no information, however, often reduces the number of cases so that an adequate test cannot be made. To overcome these difficulties it is suggested, in instances where the presence or absence criterion is used, that a distinction be made between those societies in which no mention is made of a particular custom but the context in which such custom normally occurs is described in detail, and those societies in which the appropriate context is not described. The former can be scored as *inferred absence* whereas the latter can be scored as *not ascertainable* and the case omitted. Thus, for example, if one is interested in "bloodletting" and finds no mention of this practice in an ethnography which has a complete and detailed description of medical theory and therapeutic techniques, it could be fairly safely assumed that the practice was either absent or quite unimportant. If, however, there was no discussion of the medical practices at all, it would be much safer and more appropriate to omit the case.

Fortunately for cross-cultural research, many of the practical problems of selecting a sample, working up a bibliography, and identifying a tribe are greatly facilitated by the Human Relations Area Files. This is a cooperative enterprise among sixteen universities to collect and process the ethnographic material on a world-wide sample of societies. Processing consists of working up a complete bibliography of the major sources on a society, translating those which are in a foreign language, classifying or coding each paragraph according to a standard outline (Murdock, *et al.*, 1950), duplicating the paragraphs on 5 x 8 cards, and distributing them in the appropriate categories in a file. Each member university has a complete set of files. Of particular importance for the problems which have been discussed above is the fact that the files aim at world coverage, with each society carefully identified and each source evaluated. By using these files, a cross-cultural study can be done in a small fraction of the time it would otherwise take.

The selection of cases by the Human Relations Area Files has another advantage for cross-cultural research. The analysis of a sample drawn from these files will be available for the next study based upon the same or an overlapping sample. This is particularly valuable if the analysis includes scalar judgments done with due care for independence and reliability. For the information of those who may wish to take advantage of scores on numerous variables on overlapping samples, they are available in the following sources: Horton (1943), Murdock (1949), B. B. Whiting (1950), Ford and Beach (1951), and Whiting and Child (1953).

The following example will demonstrate the cumulative value of cross-cultural research based on overlapping samples of societies. Ford and Beach (1951, p. 219) report on the duration of the taboo restricting coitus following childbirth. Whiting and Child (1953, pp. 341-343) have a scale measuring the severity of childhood sex training on twenty-nine overlapping societies. On the hunch that the length of the taboo might be related to sex anxiety induced during the child-training process, these two variables were correlated. The results, presented in the following table, show that the societies with high sex anxiety are more likely to have long postpartum taboos than those with low sex anxiety.

Thus far, cross-cultural research based upon available ethnographic literature has been under consideration. There is, however, another method being developed that is of particular interest for psychologists. This method consists of gathering material in a sample of societies for the particular purpose of testing a hypothesis or a set of hypotheses. Such a method obviously cannot be undertaken by a single person. To learn a language, establish rapport, and adapt instruments and then gather material is a long and arduous task. For one person to gather material on enough societies for an adequate sample would take a lifetime or more. It is feasible, therefore, only through cooperative efforts.

An example of a cross-cultural study with the above type of orientation is the values project, "A Comparative Study of Values in Five Cultures," directed by Kluckhohn, Roberts, and Vogt of Harvard University. In this project five southwestern communities in the same environment but with differing cultures are being studied. As a part of the research design of this project, the same variables relating to an overall theory of values have been studied as they manifest themselves in each society.

This type of project not only has the advan-

TABLE 2

RELATION BETWEEN THE DEGREE OF SEX ANXIETY INDUCED DURING SOCIALIZATION AND THE DURATION OF THE POSTPARTUM TABOO RESTRICTING COITUS

	Duration of the post-partum taboo restricting coitus		
	A few weeks to a month	A month to a year	One year to three years
High sex anxiety	Manus Sanpoil Tanala	Chagga Chamorro Riffians	Abipone Azande Chiricahua Dahomeans Dobuans Kwoma Tiv Wogeo
Low sex anxiety	Chenchu Chewa Lamba Lepcha Marshallese Marquesans Murngin Siriono Witoto	Kwakiutl Hopi Thonga	Bena Lesu Trobrianders

tage of increasing the comparability of data gathered from different societies, but it also permits the testing and retesting of hypotheses based upon individual differences in a number of different cultural settings. For example, a number of hypotheses relating to techniques of child rearing and the internalization of moral values were tested on a sample of individual parents and children in each of three of these cultures by Faigin (1952) and Hollenberg (1952). This method bids fair to greatly increase the power of cross-cultural research, since a particular theory can be tested within a society at the same time that an additional case is being added to the cross-cultural sample.

In sum, then, the cross-cultural method, although it is still in its infancy, shows promise of being a useful adjunct to other research methods designed for the development of a general science of human behavior.

References

Aberle, D. F. The psychosocial analysis of a Hopi life-history. *Comp. Psychol. Monogr.*, 1951, *21*, No. 1.

Barry, H., III Influences of socialization on the graphic arts. Unpublished honors thesis, Department of Social Relations, Harvard Univ., 1952.

Blackwood, Beatrice *Both sides of Buka Passage.* Oxford: Clarendon Press, 1935.

Boas, F. Anthropology and statistics. In W. F. Ogburn & A. Goldenweiser (Eds.), *The social sciences.* Boston: Houghton Mifflin, 1927. Pp. 114-120.

Faigin, H. Child rearing in the Rimrock community with special reference to the development of guilt. Unpublished doctoral dissertation, Harvard Univ., 1952.

Ford, C. S. Society, culture, and the human organism. *J. gen. Psychol.*, 1939, *20*, 135-179.

Ford, C. S. A comparative study of human reproduction. *Yale Univ. Publ. Anthrop.*, 1945, No. 32.

Ford, C. S., & Beach, F. A. *Patterns of sexual behavior.* New York: Harper, 1951.

Gillin, J. P. *The ways of men.* New York: Appleton-Century, 1948.

Hobhouse, L. T., Wheeler, G. C., & Ginsberg, M. *The material culture and social institutions of the simpler peoples: An essay in correlation.* London: Chapman & Hall, 1915.

Hollenberg, E. Child training among the Zeepi with special reference to the internalization of moral values. Unpublished doctoral dissertation, Harvard Univ., 1952.

Horton, D. The functions of alcohol in primitive societies: A cross-cultural study. *Quart. J. Stud. Alcohol*, 1943, *4*, 199-320.

Kluckhohn, C. Universal categories of culture. In A. L. Kroeber (Ed.), *Anthropology today.* Chicago: Univ. Chicago Press, 1953. Pp. 507-523.

McClelland, D. C., & Friedman, G. A. A cross-cultural study of the relationship between child-training practices and achievement motivation appearing in folk tales. In G. E. Swanson, T. M. Newcomb, & E. L. Hartley (Eds.), *Readings in social psychology* (rev. ed.). New York: Holt, 1952. Pp. 243-249.

Murdock, G. P. Correlations of matrilineal and patrilineal institutions. In G. P. Murdock (Ed.), *Studies in the science of society.* New Haven: Yale Univ. Press, 1937. Pp. 445-470.

Murdock, G. P. *Social structure.* New York: Macmillan, 1949.

Murdock, G. P., *et al. Outline of cultural materials: 3rd revised edition.* New Haven: Human Relations Area Files, Inc., 1950.

Murdock, G. P. The processing of anthropological materials. In A. L. Kroeber (Ed.), *Anthropology today.* Chicago: Univ. Chicago Press, 1953. Pp. 476-487.

Sears, R. R., & Wise, G. W. Relation of cup feeding in infancy to thumb-sucking and the oral drive. *Amer. J. Orthopsychiat.*, 1950, *20*, 123-138.

Simmons, L. W. Statistical correlations in the science of society. In G. P. Murdock (Ed.), *Studies in the science of society.* New Haven: Yale Univ. Press, 1937. Pp. 495-517.

Tylor, E. B. On a method of investigating the development of institutions; applied to laws of marriage and descent. *J. anthrop. Inst. Gr. Brit. Irel.*, 1889, *18*, 245-269.

White, L. A. *The science of culture.* New York: Farrar, Straus, 1949.

Whiting, B. B. Paiute sorcery. *Viking Fund Publ. Anthrop.*, 1950, No. 15.

Whiting, J. W. M. *Becoming a Kwoma.* New Haven: Yale Univ. Press, 1941.

Whiting, J. W. M., & Child, I. L. *Child training and personality.* New Haven: Yale Univ. Press, 1953.

Whiting, J. W. M., *et al. Field manual for the cross cultural study of child rearing.* New York: Social Science Research Council, 1953.

Wright, G. O. Projection and displacement: a cross-cultural study of the expression of aggression in myths. Unpublished doctoral dissertation, Harvard Univ., 1952.

PROBLEMS AND PROCEDURES*

Stanley H. Udy, Jr.

DESPITE THE FACT that comparative analysis has long been recognized as a legitimate means of discovering sociological principles, its current popularity as a method of research is less than notable.[1] There are, moreover, some very good reasons for this evident lack of vogue. Comparative analysis not only presupposes a considerable number of descriptive studies in the area to be researched, but also presumes that such studies are of a sufficiently uniform theoretical and methodological persuasion to render comparable the data presented. Conditions in this regard seem particularly discouraging in the field of industrial sociology, owing not so much to a paucity of case studies, but rather to a lack of comparability between them. The student interested in general propositions about industrial work organization is therefore faced with a lifetime of countless field studies, not to mention attendant difficulties of securing access to observe in each case, before he can even begin to develop his major interest by this method.

Ironically enough, this situation does not entirely apply to the study of nonindustrial production. Over a period of several decades a considerable amount of ethnographic data has been amassed on nonindustrial cultures by methods which admit of at least some minimum degree of comparability. The relatively recent development of the Human Relations Area Files and their expansion to workable proportions have, moreover, made comparative studies of rather broad scope quite practicable.[2] In such ethnographic materials, the student of work organization finds a wealth of descriptive data pertaining to his field of interest and relating to a variety of cultural contexts. It was felt that an attempt to analyze such materials with a view to generalization

---

*Reprinted from *Organization of Work: A Comparative Analysis of Production among Nonindustrial Peoples* (New Haven, HRAF Press, 1959), pp. 1-9 (Chapter 1), by permission of the author.

would be of some value. All work, whether nonindustrial or not, has certain common general features about which surprisingly little is known. For example, although it is well known in a general way that work organization structure is determined both by its cultural setting as well as by the technological features of the work being done, very little is specifically known about which features of organization structure are determined by technology irrespective of cultural setting, and which features are on the other hand culturally variable irrespective of technology. Again, one may be quite sure that the pattern of rewards for work depends both on kind of organization as well as the broader cultural setting, but which specific aspects of rewards are determined by organization structure as opposed to general culture is far from clear. Clarification of such matters would not only add to the general fund of knowledge of social organization, but would also be relevant to the study of development of underdeveloped areas and to industrial sociology per se. Furthermore, cross-cultural analysis of organizational forms is useful in establishing extreme limits of possible variation of such forms, and hence useful in developing administrative and organizational theory in more restricted settings.

This monograph, then, is a comparative study of the various ways in which different kinds of work are organized among nonindustrial peoples in the production of material goods. Such production may be carried on either by individual persons or by collectivities, and is found in some form in every known human society. This study, however, will be concerned only with collectively organized production systems in nonindustrial cultures, and will place particular emphasis on three aspects of this subject: technology, organization, and rewards. Primarily, the analysis will explore specific interrelationships between these elements, in their broader social setting. Two very general hypotheses have guided the research; they will be set forth presently, together with a discussion of the sources of empirical data and the methods of analysis employed.

Basic Concepts and Methods

Production is defined as the purposeful alteration and combination of physical material until it reaches some desired empirical state. Physical activities performed in connection with production constitute *work*.

Any collective production system involves a technological process carried on by a production organization, with a reward system, in a social setting. The term *technological process* refers to the system of physical operations performed on the material, and *production organization*, to any social group manifestly engaged in carrying on one or more such processes, at least some of the time. Such a group may or may not have other functions as well; their range and nature is left as a matter for empirical determination. A *reward* is defined as any material object which accrues to an individual or group as an institutionalized consequence of participation in a production organization; a *reward system* is that pattern according to which rewards are allocated among members of the organization.[3]

All production organizations exist within some society, and may further prove to be fully contained by some subgroup within a society. In this sense, all production organizations, technological processes, and reward systems function within a *social setting*. No production organization is functionally self-subsistent; as a bare minimum, all are ultimately dependent on the social setting for provision of raw materials and recruitment of personnel.

Essentially, then, this study seeks to discover the principal ways in which technology, production organization, reward systems, and social setting are interrelated. Two general hypotheses have guided the research:

A. *The structure of any production organization is determined partly by the characteristics of the technological process which it is carrying on, and partly by the social setting within which it exists.*

B. *The structure of any reward system is determined partly by the characteristics of the production organization involved, and partly by the social setting, within limits imposed by features of the technological process.*

In the form stated, these hypotheses appear rather obvious. The problem is not to test their validity as such, but rather to discover the specific ways in which, and the specific conditions under which, one alternative possibility holds true as opposed to another. For example, the fact that production organization depends both on technology and social setting is well known, but little is known about which specific aspects of organizational structure depend on technology, which depend on the social setting, and what specific features of technology and social setting are involved. The primary analysis, then, will be of interrelationships between subcategories of these basic concepts, organized around the above two hypotheses.

For purposes of the present study, both technological process and social setting are assumed to be given, and are treated as independent variables. Actually, of course, the range of available technological processes is limited by social factors just as is the range of available organizational forms. Consideration of the relationship between technology and society, however, lies outside the scope of this work.[4]

The empirical basis of this study is a comparative analysis of 150 nonindustrial production organizations, as reported in the ethnographic literature. Any comparative social analysis of this type immediately encounters two rather difficult problems of method. The first is the question of independence of the units of observation, inasmuch as diffusion is often an unknown quantity. Each of the 150 sample organizations studied here was drawn from a separate society, under the assumption—not entirely realistic, to be sure—that production organizations in different societies constitute independent entities, while those in the same society do not.[5] Having thus at best "disposed" of this problem, one next faces the difficulty of securing a sample known to be unbiased. It is obviously impossible to select societies at random, owing to unevenness in the source materials. The expedient of consciously selecting societies distributed as evenly as possible over world culture areas was therefore resorted to, using the selection criteria set forth by Murdock, such that a roughly equal number of societies was chosen from each of the six major culture areas which he delineates.[6] To secure something approaching an even distribution within each area, the attempt was made to use no fewer than two and no more than four societies from each subarea. Beyond this, the societies chosen were those on which the material available seemed the most reliable and complete. The result was a "quota" sample of 150 societies roughly stratified by culture area, as follows:

AFRICA

Ashanti
Azande
Bemba
Boloki
Chagga
Chiga
Dahomeans
Dogon
Fang
Hottentot
Ila
Jukun
Kikuyu
Kipsigis
Lobi
Mbundu
Naron
Nuer
Nupe
Nyoro
Otoro
Sotho
Tallensi
Thonga
Tiv
Turkana
Zulu

CIRCUM-MEDITERRANEAN

Babylonians (2000 B.C.)
Bedouin
English (1100 A.D.)
Germans (medieval)
Hutsul
Kabyles
Lapps
Megrelians
Mzab
Osset
Riffians
Romans (Imperial)
Saxons (900 A.D.)
Somali
Songhai
Tigre
Tuareg
Wolof

EAST EURASIA

Afghans
Andamanese
Betsileo
Bhotiyas
Burmese
Burusho
Cambodians
Chinese (Shantung)
Chiru
Chukchee
Dard
Gilyak
Hazara
Iranians
Karen
Kashmiri
Kazak
Li
Malay
Maria Gond
Muong
Samoyed
Semang
Telugu
Thai
Tibetans

INSULAR PACIFIC

Aranda
Atayal
Belu
Bisayan
Buka
Fijians
Iban
Ifaluk
Ifugao
Kiwai
Maanyan
Macassarese
Malekulans
Mangaians
Maori
Marshallese
Mount Hagen Tribes
Murngin
Pukapukans
Samoans
Tahitians
Tikopia
Trobrianders
Wogeo
Yami

NORTH AMERICA

Aleut
Blackfoot
Coeur d'Alene
Copper Eskimo
Crow
Flathead
Haida
Havasupai
Hidatsa
Hopi
Iroquois
Kwakiutl
Maricopa
Menomini
Navaho
Ojibwa
Paiute (Northern)
Papago
Patwin
Penobscot
Popoluca
Sanpoil
Sinkaietk
Taos
Tarahumara
Tarasco
Tubatulabal
Winnebago
Wintun
Yaqui (Sonora)
Yokuts
Zuni

SOUTH AMERICA

Abipon
Apalai
Aymara
Cagaba
Caingang
Camayura
Carib (Barama River)
Cayapa
Cuna
Haitians
Jivaro
Mam
Nambicuara
Ona
Siriono
Tenetehara
Terena
Timbira
Trumai
Tupinamba
Wapishana
Yagua

From ethnographic sources on each of these 150 societies, material was abstracted on 426 clearly reported production organizations and classified according to the conceptual framework which will be developed as the discussion progresses. The Human Relations Area Files proved invaluable and were utilized whenever possible.

From these 426 cases, one case was drawn at random from each society, with the exception that the sample was stratified so as to include an approximately equal number of organizations of each of seven major technological types to be defined in the next chapter. This sample was utilized in all statistical tests unless otherwise specified.

Thus in the majority of instances conclusions are based on a sample of 150 production organizations representing 150 different societies. These conclusions are stated in the form of propositions, and are demonstrated by simple statistical procedures.[7] Detailed examples given in the course of verbal discussion, however, are not necessarily restricted to these 150 sample cases. Also, in all statistical tests, cases lacking data on the matters at hand were dropped; unless otherwise noted, this procedure did not result in an upset of the over-all distribution by culture area.

It seems necessary to point out that the methodological problems of observational independence and sample bias are in no way related to the use of statistical procedures, but are common to all studies of this type whether statistical procedures are used or not. Implicit in the statement of any general relationship reached through the examination of a number of cases by whatever method is the contention that the relationship observed did not occur by chance. The use of statistical procedures does nothing more than make this contention explicit and in itself introduces no additional problems or assumptions provided appropriate techniques are employed.

Wherever possible, the Human Relations Area Files were employed in gathering data, and their availability materially shortened the research task. With the aim of locating descriptions of collective production, the following categories, as set up in the Files, were searched:

22. Food quest
23. Animal husbandry
24. Agriculture
31. Exploitative activities
32. Processing of basic materials
33. Building and construction
342. Dwellings
46. Labor
47. Business and industrial organization

Categories 46 and 47 were used mainly as checks on the procedure, for in principle every form of organized work reported for the society will be at least alluded to in the data indexed under these categories. Generally, however, work is described in detail under the appropriate functional category. Any kind of work mentioned under categories 46 and 47 not described under any of the other categories above was investigated in detail by consulting whatever other category was appropriate.

Social influences alluded to in the material on production were then followed up by consulting the appropriate institutional category in the Files. The following institutional categories were consulted especially often in this connection:

59. Kinship
60. Family
62. Community
64. Government

Category 62, "Community," was always consulted as a matter of course, since it usually includes some information on all subgroups reported to affect life in the locality group. In many instances it contained all of the societal information needed; recruitment of membership and operational consequences of nonindustrial production systems do not as a rule extend far beyond the bounds of the locality group. Other categories, however, were consulted whenever the data indicated that it was appropriate to do so, including categories other than the ones listed above, such as those dealing with religious institutions and voluntary associations.

NOTES TO CHAPTER ONE

1. Perhaps the best-known recent example of the use of this method is Murdock, *Social Structure.* Also see Apple, "The Social Structure of Grandparenthood," *American Anthropologist,* LVIII (1956); Davie, *The Evolution of War;* Driver, *An Integration of Functional, Evolutionary, and Historical Theory by Means of Correlations;* Freeman and Winch, "Societal Complexity: An Empirical Test of a Typology of Societies," *American Journal of Sociology,* LXII (1957); Goode, *Religion among the Primitives;* Hobhouse, Wheeler, and Ginsberg, *The Material Culture and Social Institutions of the Simpler Peoples;* Levy, *The Structure of Society;* Lewis, "Comparisons in Cultural Anthropology," *Yearbook of Anthropology* (1955); Murdock, "World Ethnographic Sample," *American Anthropologist,* LIX (1957); Salisbury, "Asymmetrical Marriage Systems," *American Anthropologist,* LVIII (1956); Schuessler and Driver, "A Factor Analysis of Sixteen Primitive Societies," *American Sociological Review,* XXI (1956); Simmons, *The Role of the Aged in Primitive Society;* Sumner and Keller, *The Science of Society;* Whiting, "The Cross-cultural Method," in Linzey (ed.), *Handbook of Social Psychology;* Whiting and Child, *Child Training and Personality: A Cross-Cultural Study.* Many other older works in the classical "evolutionist" comparative tradition could of course be cited, such as Lippert's *Kulturgeschichte der Menschheit.* These earlier works, however, differ in many important respects from more recent efforts.

The only studies with which the author is familiar which deal with the cross-cultural analysis of work are Buxton, *Primitive Labour;* and Nieboer, *Slavery as an Industrial System.* Buxton's work is in the earlier "evolutionist" tradition, and stresses technology as such; it does not deal with organization specifically. On the other hand Nieboer's study—which, as one may imagine deals with "slavery" more than with "work"—may quite accurately be termed cross-cultural. Furthermore, this remarkable and impressive work is, in general, more "functionalist" than "evolutionist" in orientation, despite the fact that it was written in the late nineteenth century; for its time, Nieboer's approach was virtually unique.

2. For a discussion of the Human Relations Area Files see Murdock, *et al.*, *Outline of Cultural Materials.*

3. It would be highly desirable to consider certain nonmaterial items here, such as enhanced status. The attempt to do so, however, had to be abandoned owing to a lack of adequate cross-cultural data.

4. This subject has, moreover, been extensively treated in the literature. For only a few such examples see Forde, *Habitat, Economy, and Society;* Thurnwald, *Economics in Primitive Communities;* Viljoen, *The Economics of Primitive Peoples;* relevant sections of Hobhouse, Wheeler, and Ginsberg, *The Material Culture and Social Institutions of the Simpler Peoples;* and Cottrell, *Energy and Society.*

5. "Separate" societies were deemed to be those designated as distinct in Murdock, *Outline of World Cultures.*

6. See Murdock, "World Ethnographic Sample," *American Anthropologist,* LIX (1957).

7. The .05 level of significance was set as the criterion for rejections of null hypotheses, except in instances where not only the relationship itself but also the specific expectation that it would be very weak could be deduced independently from known facts. In such cases, null hypotheses were rejected at the .10 level.

INTRODUCTION TO STATISTICS FOR COMPARATIVE RESEARCH[1]

by Harold E. Driver

Many of the articles in this volume assume that the reader possesses some statistical sophistication. For this reason this introduction attempts to describe the more elementary statistical operations at a level that assumes only a knowledge of eighth-grade arithmetic and ninth-grade algebra. There are many useful techniques that may be understood and applied with only these simple tools, and knowledge of this rudimentary material is prerequisite to a fuller and deeper understanding of the theory of statistics.

Having given a course entitled Methods of Cross-Cultural Analysis for several years, the present author is aware that some graduate students in anthropology have either not mastered or have forgotten elementary arithmetic and algebra; and some of their post-Ph.D. teachers are not appreciably better qualified in these subjects. As a result, most of the generalizations made by cultural anthropologists are impressionistic rather than demonstrated by means of an explicit inductive technique. At the same time, such generalizations are probably correct, which is a tribute to the abilities of some anthropologists, such as textbook writers, to generalize about hundreds of peoples around the world. It is also evidence that many relatively high correlations actually exist in anthropology if they can be discovered with so little in the way of formal procedure. Because truths thought to be self-evident at one stage of knowledge may not appear to be so at a later and presumably more informed time, it is the duty of the scientific researcher to make his methods as explicit as possible and leave as little as possible to imagination and intuition.

Students are attracted to anthropology for many reasons, among them a distaste for laboratory procedures, an aversion to quantification, an interest in the exotic and bizarre, a thirst for adventure, and a desire to express one's own individuality. As a result of such factors, most ethnographic field reports are better representations of the uniqueness of the cultures they describe and of the personalities of the authors than of the comparative position of each culture in a culture area, a continent, the world, or in a temporal sequence. Of the thousands of field reports written in this century, no two of them package their data in the same manner; no two of them use the same table of contents or present their material in the same sequence; nor are any two indexed in the same way.

Quantitative statements in field reports, such as the frequency of any

[1]The author is indebted to Karl Schuessler for reading the entire manuscript and offering helpful criticisms, and to Gerald Slatin for computing the intertrait correlations in Table XVIII.

practice within a society under study, are relatively rare; and even when given, the quantitative categories of a number of field reports often do not match each other. For these reasons, the comparative ethnologist is usually compelled to reduce differences in frequency to the minimum number of categories, namely, presence and absence. This limitation is not a preference on the part of the cross-cultural statistician, who would much prefer multi-step scales, but is imposed upon him by the character of most of the reports with which he must work. For this reason, this introduction to comparative statistics will be limited to the presence and absence of attributes or qualitative variables, as the statistician calls such twofold variables.

The sample of data in Table I has been chosen to illustrate the procedures described in this article because it is small enough to make the methods transparent. The tribes represent a one-sixth sample of the tribes in the United States given on the map in the pocket at the end of this author's book (Driver, 1961, Map 38). The word *tribe* is used in this article to designate any culture-bearing unit suitable for comparative purposes; it does not mean that all such units necessarily have tribal organization. Such units are distinguished from each other principally on the basis of language and separate geographical location, but also on the basis of cultural and, more rarely, biological differences. Although such comparative units show great variation in level of culture, size of population, size of territory, etc., and are subject to the criticism that the cross-cultural researcher is mixing oranges, apples, and potatoes in his statistical operations, they are objective in the sense that each can be easily distinguished from every other such unit.

The 132 tribes, on the map mentioned above, whose territories lay wholly or principally in what is now the United States, were reduced to one-sixth of their number in order to obtain a sample of data that would fit conveniently on a single page. Each of the 132 tribes was listed alphabetically and then a single die was rolled vigorously for each one in alphabetical order. Every time the one-spot came up, the tribe was included in the sample. The sample is therefore strictly random with respect to the 132 tribes in the United States, but is not randomly chosen with respect to the whole continent, the world, or an infinitely large universe.

The word *trait* will be used here for any subdivision of culture suitable for comparative purposes. It includes culture elements or components, culture complexes or assemblages, and culture themes or other broader parts of total culture. Obviously, such terms are relative ones and are not sufficient in number to take care of all the variation in scope of form, use, function, and content that the researcher will encounter. For example, one might divide total culture into universals and nonuniversals (see Kluckhohn, 1953), the universals into weapons and nonweapons, the weapons into projectiles and shock (hand-held) types, the projectiles into bows-and-arrows and others, the bows into self and reinforced bows, the reinforced bows into "corded sinews tied on" and "uncorded sinews glued on," the arrows into single shaft and multiple shaft (foreshaft), the multiple shaft arrows into those with points of wood, bone, and stone, those with stone points into ground stone and chipped stone, and those with chipped stone points into innumerable classes. There are obviously no micro-units in cultures comparable to the phonemes in languages, nor larger units as objective as morphemes. There are, instead, an indefinite number of units in an indefinitely numerous hierarchy of classes within classes. The responsibility for choosing meaningful culture traits falls on the researcher rather than the statistician.

TABLE I. Comparative Data on Indians of the United States. From Driver, 1961, Maps 3, 21, 23, 31, 32. X, present; blank, absent.

		Alsea	Chinook	Comanche	Creek	Flathead	Fox	Havasupai	Hidatsa	Iowa	Jicarilla	Klamath	Missouri	Nez Perce	Omaha	Penobscot	Sauk	Shawnee	Takelma	Tubatulabal	Ute	Walapai	Wenatchi	Yakima	Total positive
		1	2	3	4	5	6	7	8	9	10	11	12	13	14	15	16	17	18	19	20	21	22	23	
Dominant subsistence																									
Fish	a	x	x																				x	x	4
Game	b			x		x	x			x	x		x	x	x	x	x	x			x				12
Wild plants	c																			x		x			2
Cultivated plants	d				x			x	x																3
Balance of game and wild plants	e											x							x						2
Dominant clothing materials																									
Hide and fur	f			x			x		x	x	x		x		x	x	x								9
Hide, fur, wild plants	g	x	x		x	x		x				x		x				x	x	x	x	x	x	x	14
Dominant non-cooking containers																									
Hide	h			x		x			x	x	x		x		x										7
Bark	i															x	x								2
Woven baskets	j	x	x		x		x	x				x		x				x	x	x	x	x	x	x	14
Post-nuptial residence																									
Patrilocal	k	x	x	x		x		x		x		x	x	x		x	x	x	x			x	x	x	16
Matrilocal	l				x				x		x										x				4
Bilocal or neolocal	m						x								x					x					3
Descent																									
Patrilineal	n						x			x			x		x		x	x							6
Matrilineal	o				x				x																2
Bilateral	p	x	x	x		x		x			x	x		x		x			x	x	x	x	x	x	15
Total positive entries		5	5	5	5	5	5	5	5	5	5	5	5	5	5	5	5	5	5	5	5	5	5	5	115

The traits in the small sample of Table I are actually complexes or assemblages, in that each could be further subdivided into a large number of details. They were chosen because their geographical distributions among Indians of the United States are virtually completely known and readily available on maps (Driver, 1961, Maps 3, 21, 23, 31, 32), and also because they are few enough in number to provide a simple illustration of method. These traits are, therefore, a selected sample, not a random sample from a larger list of traits.

In Table I the tribes are arranged in alphabetical order and the traits in an equally arbitrary order within five subdivisions which, with the exception of clothing, are universals. Clothing is a universal among Indians of the United States, however, and may be treated as such in this sample. Because each trait is the dominant form of a universal, each tribe can have only one variant within each universal; and because the five major categories are universals, each tribe must necessarily possess one variant of each. Therefore, each tribe has exactly five traits present; the remaining eleven are absent. In actual practice, the Yale school (e.g., Murdock, 1949) has operated mostly with traits that are members of universal categories, while the California school has utilized larger numbers of traits not grouped under universals, and fewer numbers of tribes.

The vertical alignments of presences and absences in Table I are called columns. Column number one contains the trait inventory of the Alsea tribe, column two that of the Chinook tribe, etc. The horizontal alignments are called rows. Thus, row *a* is "Dominance of fish in subsistence"; row *b*, "Dominance of game in the diet," etc. Two kinds of twofold comparisons may be made from Table I: one may compare any combination of two rows, such as those for "Patrilocal residence" (*k*) and "Patrilineal descent" (*n*); or one may compare any combination of two columns, such as those for the Alsea (1) and the Comanche (3). A comparison of two rows of traits is an intertrait correlation, sometimes referred to in factor analysis as *r* technique, irrespective of the numerical coefficient employed. A comparison of two columns of trait inventories is designated an intertribal correlation, sometimes labeled Q technique in factor analysis, again irrespective of the coefficient used.

Where large and representative samples are available, it is advantageous to compute correlations between pairs of trait distributions (rows) or pairs of tribal inventories (columns), or both. On the other hand, when samples are small and their representation of a larger universe questionable, it is better not to compute correlation coefficients, but to group the data in simpler ways. For example, we may compare the intertrait distributions of patrilocal residence and patrilineal descent by listing the tribes under the four possible categories thus:

TABLE II

		Patrilocal Residence Absent (−)	Patrilocal Residence Present (+)
Patrilineal Descent	Present (+)	Fox Omaha	Iowa Missouri Sauk Shawnee
	Absent (−)	Creek Hidatsa Jicarilla Tubatulabal Ute	Alsea Chinook Comanche Flathead Havasupai Klamath Nez Perce Penobscot Takelma Walapai Wenatchi Yakima

From Table II, it is obvious that many tribes with patrilocal residence lack patrilineal descent, while only two have patrilineal descent without patrilocal residence. These two categories are called the negative quadrants because they contain the negative instances. The positive quadrants are the ones in which both traits are present (upper right) or both traits absent (lower left). The number of tribes in the negative quadrants outnumber those in the positive quadrants, suggesting a negative relationship in this sample between the two traits. (This is due to a sampling error, as the relationship based on all 132 tribes is positive.) This kind of diagram has been used by Beatrice B. Whiting (1950, Tables I-IV), and by John W. M. Whiting and Irving Child (1953, Tables 4-8, 16, 18-21).

The next step in the direction of abstraction is the counting of frequencies in the four cells thus:

TABLE III

		Patrilocal Residence Absent (−)	Patrilocal Residence Present (+)	Total
Patrilineal Descent	Present (+)	2	4	6
	Absent (−)	5	12	17
	Total	7	16	23

Where considerable numbers of such raw frequencies are to be given, it saves space to present them in the following type of table:

TABLE IV

	a	b	c	d
Patrilocal Residence—Patrilineal Descent	4	2	12	5

where *a* is the number of tribes where both traits are present, *b* the number where the first trait is absent and the second present, *c* the number where the first trait is present and the second absent, and *d* the number of tribes where both are absent. Any number of such relationships may be expressed in this manner in the space of one or two (if the trait labels are lengthy) lines each.

The final step toward increasing abstraction is achieved by expressing the relationship of Tables III and IV with a single correlation coefficient or probability value. This will be described below.

Relationships between pairs of tribes may be tabled in the same manner as those between pairs of traits, thus:

TABLE V

		Alsea	
		Absent (−)	Present (+)
Comanche	Present (+)	Game diet Hide & fur clothing Hide containers	Patrilocal residence Bilateral descent
	Absent (−)	Wild plant diet Cultivated plant diet Balance of game and wild plants in diet Bark containers Matrilocal residence Bilocal or neolocal residence Patrilineal descent Matrilineal descent	Fish diet Hide, fur, wild plants for clothing Woven basket containers

Because trait labels tend to be more lengthy than tribe labels, this form of expression becomes more awkward than the former.

As above, the number of traits may be given for each quadrant:

TABLE VI

		Alsea		
		Absent (−)	Present (+)	Total
Comanche	Present (+)	3	2	5
	Absent (−)	8	3	11
	Total	11	5	16

Again, this information may be reduced to a single line for each pair of tribes:

TABLE VII

	a	b	c	d
Alsea-Comanche	2	3	3	8

The present author presented 120 relationships of this type on a single page (Driver, 1939, p. 430).

Clustering Multiple Relationships. The examples just completed are limited to ways of demonstrating relationships between combinations of only two traits or tribes at one time. For many purposes it is more meaningful to cluster larger numbers of traits and tribes in a single table. To some extent Table I shows all the interrelationships of both traits and tribes, but the scattered appearance of the positive entries leaves something to be desired. Because the tribal inventories contain only five traits each, it is probably easier to cluster the tribes first. This procedure is not entirely objective, but can be accomplished without much difficulty for small samples such as the one given here.

First copy each column on a separate piece of cross-section paper. Then take the first tribe in the list, the Alsea, and compare by inspection its trait inventory with that of every other tribe. It will be found that the Chinook (2), Wenatchi (22), and Yakima (23) have trait inventories identical with that of the Alsea (1). Now take a fresh piece of paper big enough for the entire distribution table and copy these four columns so that they are adjacent to one another as in Table VIII. Then select the next tribe on the list, the Comanche (3), and compare its trait inventory with that of every other remaining tribe. It will be found that no other tribe matches the Comanche (3) exactly, but that the Penobscot (15) and the Jicarilla (10) agree in all but one trait. Lay these three slips in a pile to one side. Then take the next tribe on the list, the Creek (4), and compare it with the remaining tribes not yet classified. It will be found that the Creek share no more than three traits with any other tribe and that they share three only with the Hidatsa (8) and Ute (20). Place these three tribes tentatively in a group. Continue this process until all the tribes have been allocated to some group. Then match each group as a whole with the first four tribes clustered, and copy that group which shares the most with the first group adjacent to it. It will be found that the Klamath (11) and Takelma (18) match each other exactly and differ in only one trait from the members of

TABLE VIII. Same data as Table I, but with clustering of tribes. X, present; blank, absent.

Tribes

Traits		Alsea	Chinook	Wenatchi	Yakima	Klamath	Takelma	Walapai	Nez Perce	Havasupai	Tubatulabal	Ute	Creek	Shawnee	Flathead	Comanche	Penobscot	Jicarilla	Iowa	Missouri	Sauk	Omaha	Fox	Hidatsa
		1	2	22	23	11	18	21	13	7	19	20	4	17	5	3	15	10	9	12	16	14	6	8
Fish diet	a	x	x	x	x																			
Game diet	b								x			x		x	x	x	x	x	x	x	x	x	x	
Wild plant diet	c							x			x													
Cultivated plant diet	d									x			x											x
Balance of game and wild plants	e					x	x																	
Hide and fur clothing	f															x	x	x	x	x	x	x	x	x
Hide, fur, wild plant clothing	g	x	x	x	x	x	x	x	x	x	x	x	x	x	x									
Hide containers	h														x	x		x	x	x		x		x
Bark containers	i																x				x			
Woven baskets	j	x	x	x	x	x	x	x	x	x	x	x	x	x									x	
Patrilocal residence	k	x	x	x	x	x	x	x	x	x				x	x	x	x		x	x	x			
Matrilocal residence	l											x	x					x						x
Bilocal or neolocal residence	m										x											x	x	
Patrilineal descent	n													x					x	x	x	x	x	
Matrilineal descent	o												x											x
Bilateral descent	p	x	x	x	x	x	x	x	x	x	x	x			x	x	x	x						

the first group. For this reason, copy their columns adjacent to those of the first group, as in Table VIII. Continue this process until all the tribes have been clustered approximately as in Table VIII.

After Table VIII has been completed, copy each trait on a separate slip of paper and group the traits in similar fashion, placing those with most similar distributions adjacent to each other. The final result should be a double clustering similar to that of Table IX.

The double clustering of Table IX reveals two major groups of tribes and three major groups of traits, separated by solid lines. The upper left major cluster contains twelve tribes, all of whom wear clothing made of hide, fur, and wild plants, use woven baskets as their principal non-cooking containers, and all but one of whom have bilateral descent. The nine tribes in the lower right major cluster all wear clothing made exclusively of hide and fur, and most of them have patrilineal descent, eat game as their principal diet, and use chiefly hide containers. Patrilocal residence is shared by a majority of the member tribes in both major groups. Two tribes, the Shawnee (17) and the Flathead (5), share three traits with each other, three each with the upper left major cluster, and two each with the lower right major cluster. They are, therefore, in limbo with respect to the other tribes in the sample. The major trait cluster in the middle consists of cultivated plant diet, matrilineal descent, and matrilocal residence. The Creek and Hidatsa both possess all three of these traits, but each at the same time shares two traits with the other two major trait clusters, and each shares at the same time three traits with tribes who are members of the two largest trait-tribe clusters. They, too, approximate a limbo status. In the last section, it will be shown how statistical measures can facilitate clustering.

CONVENTIONAL COEFFICIENTS AND PROBABILITY VALUES

When the quantity of data is too large to sort by mere inspection and the sample is thought to be reasonably representative of some universe, it is desirable to use a more compact form of expression of the covariation within it. Coefficients of association and correlation, and probabilities derived from chi-square, serve this purpose.

One of the most common such measures used is the coefficient of association proposed by G. Udney Yule and called Q after Quetelet, the nineteenth-century statistician. If we symbolize the two by two (fourfold) table thus:

	Absent (−)	Present (+)	Total
Present (+)	b	a	a + b
Absent (−)	d	c	c + d
Total	b + d	a + c	N

then the formula for Q is:

$$Q = \frac{ad - bc}{ad + bc}$$

TABLE IX. Same data as Tables I and VIII, but with clustering of traits as well as tribes. X, present; blank, absent.

Tribes

Traits		Alsea 1	Chinook 2	Wenatchi 22	Yakima 23	Klamath 11	Takelma 18	Walapai 21	Nez Perce 13	Havasupai 7	Tubatulabal 19	Ute 20	Creek 4	Shawnee 17	Flathead 5	Comanche 3	Penobscot 15	Jicarilla 10	Iowa 9	Missouri 12	Sauk 16	Omaha 14	Fox 6	Hidatsa 8
Fish diet	a	x	x	x	x																			
Hide, fur, wild plant clothing	g	x	x	x	x	x	x	x	x	x	x	x	x	x	x									
Woven baskets	j	x	x	x	x	x	x	x	x	x	x	x	x	x									x	
Bilateral descent	p	x	x	x	x	x	x	x	x	x	x	x			x	x	x	x						
Patrilocal residence	k	x	x	x	x	x	x	x	x	x				x	x	x	x		x	x	x			
Balance of game and wild plants	e					x	x																	
Wild plant diet	c							x			x													
Cultivated plant diet	d									x			x											x
Matrilineal descent	o												x											x
Matrilocal residence	l											x	x					x						x
Bilocal or neolocal residence	m										x											x	x	
Bark containers	i																x				x			
Patrilineal descent	n													x					x	x	x	x	x	
Game diet	b								x			x		x	x	x	x	x	x	x	x	x	x	
Hide and fur clothing	f															x	x	x	x	x	x	x	x	x
Hide containers	h														x	x		x	x	x		x		x

If we apply this formula to the data of Table III, the following results:

$$Q = \frac{(4 \times 5) - (2 \times 12)}{(4 \times 5) + (2 \times 12)} = \frac{20 - 24}{20 + 24} = \frac{-4}{44} = -.09$$

When applied to the data of Table VI, it yields the following:

$$Q = \frac{(2 \times 8) - (3 \times 3)}{(2 \times 8) + (3 \times 3)} = \frac{16 - 9}{16 + 9} = \frac{7}{25} = .28$$

The highest positive value of Q is 1.00, as illustrated by the following example:

TABLE X

		Alsea (1)		
		Absent (−)	Present (+)	Total
Chinook (2)	Present (+)	0	5	5
	Absent (−)	11	0	11
	Total	11	5	16

$$Q = \frac{(5 \times 11) - (0 \times 0)}{(5 \times 11) + (0 \times 0)} = \frac{55 - 0}{55 + 0} = 1.00$$

The highest negative value of Q is −1.00, as illustrated thus:

TABLE XI

		Hide and fur clothing (f)		
		Absent (−)	Present (+)	Total
Hide, fur, and wild plant clothing (g)	Present (+)	14	0	14
	Absent (−)	0	9	9
	Total	14	9	23

$$Q = \frac{(0 \times 0) - (14 \times 9)}{(0 \times 0) + (14 \times 9)} = \frac{0 - 126}{0 + 126} = -1.00$$

In both of the above examples, there were zero frequencies in two diagonally opposite quadrants of the two by two table.

One of the properties of Q is that the presence of a zero frequency in a single quadrant gives a value of unity. This is illustrated by the relation of the "Dominance of fish in the diet" (a) with "Patrilocal residence" (b).

TABLE XII

		Fish diet		
		Absent (−)	Present (+)	Total
Patrilocal residence	Present (+)	12	4	16
	Absent (−)	7	0	7
	Total	19	4	23

$$Q = \frac{(4 \times 7) - (12 \times 0)}{(4 \times 7) + (12 \times 0)} = \frac{28 - 0}{28 + 0} = 1.00$$

Although all the fish-eaters have patrilocal residence, all of the tribes with patrilocal residence do not subsist principally on fish. In other words, all the fish-eaters are included within the group with patrilocal residence, but the two groups are not identical in membership. Such a relationship of inclusion may be diagrammed as follows:

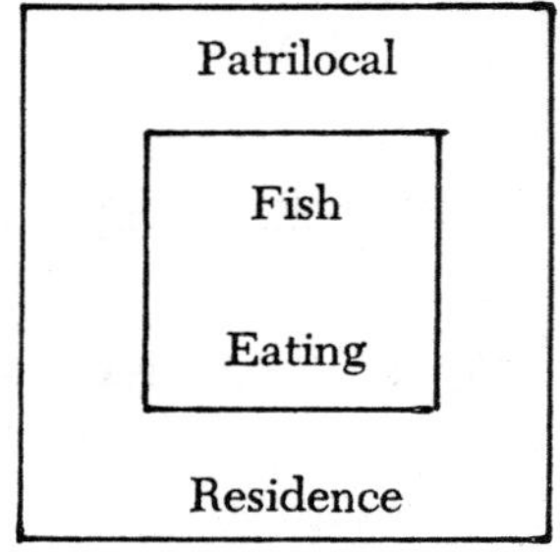

Forrest Clements (1931) ran into difficulty with his intertribal Sun Dance Q coefficients. Information on the Sun Dance of the Plains Ojibwa was scanty and consisted of only eight traits that were also present among many other tribes in the universe. In other words, the Plains Ojibwa inventory was included in that of many other Plains tribes. The result was a disproportionally high number of perfect positive associations between the Plains Ojibwa and the other tribes, and these in turn led to a dubious historical reconstruction.

Although this characteristic of the Q coefficient is generally regarded as a liability, it can become an asset if the researcher is looking for relationships of inclusion. More of this below.

Q is attractive to beginners because it is easy to remember and easy to compute, but actually its derivation is arbitrary and a precise probabilistic interpretation has only recently been given by Leo A. Goodman and William H. Kruskal (1954, p. 750). However, a chance relationship will always yield a Q of zero. For example, if you toss two coins a large number of times, the frequencies of heads and tails will approximate the following percentages.

TABLE XIII

		Large Coin		
		Tails (−)	Heads (+)	Total
Small Coin	Heads (+)	.25	.25	.50
	Tails (−)	.25	.25	.50
	Total	.50	.50	1.00

If you roll two dice a large number of times, the frequencies for the appearance of the same face on the two dice, versus other combinations, will approximate the following ratios.

TABLE XIV

		Red Die		
		Not one (−)	One (+)	Total
Green Die	One (+)	5	1	6
	Not one (−)	25	5	30
	Total	30	6	36

Both of these chance distributions will give a Q of zero.

Another measure for cross-cultural research is the Phi coefficient, which, in the same symbolism, is

$$\phi = \frac{ad - bc}{\sqrt{(a + b)\ (a + c)\ (b + d)\ (c + d)}}$$

Phi varies from plus one to minus one, as does Q, but the relationship of the two is complicated (see Mueller and Schuessler, 1961, pp. 242-52; and Driver, 1939, pp. 298-304). However, when the marginal totals to the right and below the two by two table are close to a 50:50 presence-absence ratio, the two measures are highly correlated with each other as Driver and Schuessler (1957, fig. 1) show. Under all conditions, except at zero and unity, Q gives a value greater in both positive and negative directions than that of Phi, as we shall see.

Applying Phi to the data of Table III:

$$\phi = \frac{(4 \times 5) - (2 \times 12)}{\sqrt{(6)\ (17)\ (7)\ (16)}} = \frac{20 - 24}{\sqrt{11424}} = \frac{-4}{107} = -.04$$

From the data of Table VI:

$$\phi = \frac{(2 \times 8) - (3 \times 3)}{\sqrt{(5)\ (11)\ (5)\ (11)}} = \frac{16 - 9}{5 \times 11} = \frac{7}{55} = .13$$

From the data of Table X:

$$\phi = \frac{(5 \times 11) - (0 \times 0)}{\sqrt{(5)\ (11)\ (5)\ (11)}} = \frac{55 - 0}{5 \times 11} = \frac{55}{55} = 1.00$$

From Table XI:

$$\phi = \frac{(0 \times 0) - (14 \times 9)}{\sqrt{(14)\ (9)\ (14)\ (9)}} = \frac{0 - 126}{14 \times 9} = \frac{-126}{126} = -1.00$$

From Table XII:

$$\phi = \frac{(4 \times 7) - (12 \times 0)}{\sqrt{(16)\ (7)\ (19)\ (4)}} = \frac{28 - 0}{\sqrt{8512}} = \frac{28}{92} = .30$$

It is apparent that relationships of inclusion, where there is a zero in a negative cell, do not yield perfect positive (1.00) Phi values. Here the two measures give the greatest contrast among the examples used. Phi agrees with Q exactly only where the distribution is one of chance and the correlation zero, and where all the cases fall in the two negative quadrants or the two positive quadrants and yield unity.

An obtrusive property of Phi is that it cannot reach unity unless the two sets of marginal totals at the right and below the two by two table are identical. Furthermore a zero frequency in the common presence quadrant will give a perfect negative correlation only when it is matched by a zero frequency in the common absence quadrant; for example:

TABLE XV

		Alsea		
		Absent (−)	Present (+)	Total
Hidatsa	Present (+)	5	0	5
	Absent (−)	6	5	11
	Total	11	5	16

$$\phi = \frac{(0 \times 6) - (5 \times 5)}{\sqrt{(5)\ (11)\ (5)\ (11)}} = \frac{0 - 25}{5 \times 11} = \frac{-25}{55} = -.45$$

In this example the Alsea and Hidatsa share no traits at all and are as different ethnographically as it is possible to be, yet their Phi coefficient is −.45, not −1.00.

The only perfect negative Phi value in our small sample is that between "Hide and fur clothing" (f) and "Hide, fur, and wild plant clothing" (g), Table XI.

$$\phi = \frac{(0 \times 0) - (14 \times 9)}{\sqrt{(14)\ (9)\ (14)\ (9)}} = \frac{0 - 126}{14 \times 9} = \frac{-126}{126} = -1.00$$

Perhaps the most important advantage of Phi over Q is that the former may readily be converted into a probability statement by way of chi-square if the sample is representative. However, it should be cautioned that chi-square should not be used when the expected frequency in any quadrant is less than five, no matter how carefully the sample has been chosen. The special formula for chi-square applied to two by two tables is:

$$\chi^2 = \phi^2 N$$

where N is the total number of cases. Applying this formula to the data of Table XII,

$$\chi^2 = (.30)^2 \times 23 = .09 \times 23 = 2.1$$

Chi-square for a two by two table may be converted to a probability figure by means of Table XVI. The derivation of this table is too complex to be included here, but larger tables of this type are standard in statistical textbooks.

TABLE XVI

Probability values of χ^2 for a 2×2 table.

P	.99	.90	.80	.70	.50	.30	.20	.10	.05	.02	.01	.001
χ^2	.00	.01	.06	.15	.46	1.07	1.64	2.71	3.84	5.41	6.63	10.83

A chi-square of 2.1 falls between the probabilities .20 and .10. This is interpreted in the following way: the probability of obtaining a chi-square of 2.1 or larger is less than .20. This brings us to the null hypothesis.

The null hypothesis asks this question: if the true correlation from all the cases in the given universe were zero, what would be the probability of obtaining, by an error of sampling, a value as high or higher than that obtained from the observed sample? In other words, sampling errors around a zero relationship can produce apparent correlations, and it is necessary to consider them in deciding whether an obtained correlation is likely to be real and not the result of a mere sampling error. Because Phi-square is multiplied by N to get chi-square, it is obvious that the larger the number of cases, the larger the chi-square and the lower the probability of obtaining such a chi-square by chance.

The theory on which chi-square and its derived probabilities is based demands a strictly random sample. Because such samples are rarely obtainable in cross-cultural research, chi-square has been abused more than any other statistical measure. To cite an extreme example, a recent paper by Spiro and Andrade (1958) computes a chi-square from eleven tribes not chosen randomly. This is faulty on two counts: the sample is not random, and the expected values in the two by two table cannot all be five or larger. We are not criticizing the utilization of eleven societies or fewer in a comparative study, but only the application of probability statistics to the data.

The concept of expected versus observed frequencies is best introduced along with the general formula for chi-square which is applicable to two by three, three by three, and larger tables:

$$\chi^2 = \Sigma \frac{(\text{O} - \text{E})^2}{\text{E}}$$

where Σ is the summation sign, O the observed frequencies, and E the expected frequencies. This formula is applied to the following data from Table I, and the expected (chance) frequencies are given in parentheses in each quadrant. The chance frequencies are too small to justify the use of chi-square, so that the example to follow is to be regarded only as illustrative and expository. For a more complete discussion of chi-square, see Lewis and Burke (1950).

TABLE XVII

		Hide containers		
		Absent (−)	Present (+)	Total
Hide and fur clothing	Present (+)	3 (6)	6 (3)	9
	Absent (−)	13 (10)	1 (4)	14
	Total	16	7	23

The expected frequencies are obtained by multiplying the marginal totals of each quadrant together and dividing by N, thus:

Upper right: $(9 \times 7) \div 23 = 63 \div 23 = 3$
Lower right: $(14 \times 7) \div 23 = 98 \div 23 = 4$
Upper left: $(9 \times 16) \div 23 = 144 \div 23 = 6$
Lower left: $(14 \times 16) \div 23 = 224 \div 23 = 10$

	O − E	(O − E)²	$\frac{(\text{O} - \text{E})^2}{\text{E}}$
Upper right:	3	9	3.00
Lower right:	−3	9	2.25
Upper left:	−3	9	1.50
Lower left:	3	9	.90
			$\chi^2 = 7.65$

Referring back to Table XVI, we see that a chi-square of 7.65 falls between the probabilities .01 and .001. Therefore, the probability is less than .01 that such a two by two distribution would occur by chance if the true relationship were zero. This is easily significant, and the inference is that if all tribes in the United States were correlated for these two traits, the relationship would be positive.

Now the relationship between Phi and chi-square will be checked by computing the latter the short way.

$$\phi = \frac{(6 \times 13) - (3 \times 1)}{\sqrt{(9)\ (14)\ (7)\ (16)}} = \frac{78 - 3}{\sqrt{11412}} = \frac{75}{119} = .63$$

$$\chi^2 = \phi^2 N = (.40)\ (23) = 9.2$$

This value of chi-square is higher than the first because we rounded off the expected frequencies to whole numbers in the first computation. If we had used two decimal places, the difference between observed and expected frequencies would have been 3.26, the squares of these differences 10.63, and the chi-square resulting from these figures exactly 9.2. If a larger number of cases were involved, the results from the two methods of computing chi-square would match more closely without resorting to decimal places.

Because of their mathematical relationship, Phi and chi-square make a better combination for most purposes than the Q and chi-square used by Murdock (1949) and S. H. Udy, Jr. (1959).

Without any knowledge of probability theory, anyone can check the probability of getting a chi-square of a certain value or higher from sampling errors by tossing two coins and recording the combinations of heads and tails in two by two tables. If, say, twenty tosses are made, the figures recorded, and this operation repeated about twenty times in as many separate two by two tables, the twenty chi-square values obtained will be close to those given in the probability table, Table XVI. Such probabilities have been checked empirically in classes in statistics many times.

For throwing light on problems involving evolutionary sequence, causality, and the concept of a necessary antecedent condition, a combination of Phi and Q is more meaningful than either alone. For instance, it seems likely that the Crow type of kinship terminology would arise only in a society that already had matrilineal descent. In this case, matrilineal descent is assumed to be a necessary antecedent condition for Crow kinship terminology and, according to theory, the latter should be found only where the former exists. Because Crow kinship appears later, not every society with matrilineal descent would be expected to have it. The expectable synchronic relationship is one of inclusion, with societies having Crow kinship terminology included among those with matrilineal descent but being less numerous. Under such circumstances Q would give a perfect positive relationship (1.00) and Phi a positive value less than perfect. By using both coefficients, the researcher can ferret out all the relations of inclusion in a large corpus of data. In practice, relationships of perfect inclusion are rare, but there are many that are nearly perfect. These would be indicated by high positive values of Q and values of Phi lower than would be obtained from marginal totals that were symmetrical (.50:.50) for both variables. For a discussion of the relations of correlation and causality, see Blalock (1960).

Our conclusion is that neither Q nor Phi, nor any other measure, is best for two by two tables under all conditions. Phi, however, has another advantage in that it is a form of Pearson's r to which more advanced techniques, such as factor analysis (Driver and Schuessler, 1957), may be applied. For a comprehensive collection and mathematically advanced discussion of other measures for cross-classification, see Goodman and Kruskal (1954, 1959).

SIMPLER MEASURES LESS DIRECTLY RELATED TO PROBABILITIES

The glottochronologists (see Hymes' review, 1960) have extensively employed a very simple measure to indicate the lexical relationships between pairs of languages. It is nothing more complicated than the percentage of cognates shared. The denominator is the total number of meanings (glosses) in the list, and the numerator the number of cognates shared by the two languages being compared. This idea is meaningful in comparative ethnology for tribe with tribe comparisons, but demands that the denominator be not the total number of traits but the total number of universal categories into which the traits have been packaged. The universals need be universal only within whatever area the investigator has chosen for his study. If the study is limited to a single culture area, then the major categories to be counted need be universal only in that area. If the frame is worldwide, however, they must be world universals.

Applied to the data of Table I, it is apparent that there are five such universal categories: dominant subsistence; dominant clothing materials; dominant non-cooking containers; dominant post-nuptial residence; and descent. The denominator, therefore, is five. The first two tribes, the Alsea and Chinook, share the same variants for all five universals, making their relationship 100%. The Alsea and Comanche (3), on the other hand, share only two traits in the list, which is 40%. The Alsea and Omaha (14) share none; their relationship is 00%. There can be no negative percentages, of course, so that the range of variation is 100% to 00%.

If and when someone gets around to correlating language and culture, it is advisable that he employ this measure of relationship between cultures, because it is what the glottochronologists have already used. Although no one has yet tackled this problem, it would seem that an ethnologist and an archeologist combined could work up a list of historically stable traits that change less rapidly than most culture traits, and are therefore appropriate for such a problem. Without getting involved in inferential chronology, it would be a simple matter to take the percentages of cognates shared by the members of a language family and compare them with the percentages of conservative culture traits shared. This could be done with nothing more original than the Pearsonian r or eta and the final conclusion of the study could be expressed in a single correlation coefficient.

In the 1930's, Kroeber and, to a lesser extent, the present author, experimented with a number of coefficients for intertribal comparisons. Most of these were of no value and reflected the lack of statistical sophistication on the part of those who "coined" them. One, however, has recently been independently rediscovered by the linguist Alvar Ellegard (1959). In the symbolism employed above,

$$r_n = G = \frac{a}{\sqrt{(a + b)\ (a + c)}}$$

Kroeber and Driver (1932) were the first to propose this coefficient, which they called G for geometric mean. Ellegard (1959, p. 138) labels it r_n. He also worked out a sampling error for it (*Ibid.*, p. 150).

A glance at the formula shows that it ignores *d* values, the common absences. Ellegard argues at some length that r_n is more meaningful than Phi as a measure of genetic linguistic relationship, and that its variation from .00 to 1.00 is a better expression of the similarities of languages than Phi with its negative and occasional zero values. When he applies r_n to the same Indo-European data intercorrelated by Kroeber and Chretien (1937), he finds it yields a classification that differs only in unimportant details from that of Kroeber and Chretien's Q_6, a trigonometric function of Phi. Q_6 was devised by Karl Pearson to correct Phi values upward (in both positive and negative directions from zero) to match more nearly those of Tetrachoric r, which he favored over Phi, but which was much more time-consuming to compute than Phi was at that time. For purposes of classification, Q_6 and Phi will give identical results under all conditions, because they are mathematical functions of one another.

Neither Ellegard nor Kroeber (1960) seems to be aware of the fact that all coefficients will yield parallel classifications as long as the marginal totals in the two by two tables are close to the .50:.50 ratio. As these ratios become more and more asymmetrical, the various coefficients give more widely divergent results until complete chaos is reached. This was demonstrated by this author in his Ph.D. thesis, written under Kroeber in 1936, and was later published (Driver, 1939, pp. 298-304). Asymmetry can become a serious problem, as this author found in his study, *Girls' Puberty Rites in Western North America* (Driver, 1941), where over half of the two by two tables were at least as asymmetrical as .80:.20 in at least one variable. In intertribal comparisons of the kind made by the California school from lengthy trait lists, the frequency in the common absence category was clearly relative to the size of the areal universe. If the areal universe included only two tribes, there would be no common absences at all. If it included three neighboring tribes, a few would show up, because each tribe would be certain to possess at least a few traits that the other two lacked. As the size of the areal universe and the number of constituent tribes increases, the number of culture elements increases and the number that falls in the common absences category increases, while those in the other three cells remain the same. The larger and culturally more variable the areal universe, the more the Phi and Q values are altered in the positive direction, because more and more traits fall in a positive quadrant, the *d* cell.

This can be illustrated from our small sample of Table I. If we extended the area to include all of North America, we would have to add *cotton* or *maguey fibre* to the list of dominant clothing materials, *pottery vessels* to non-cooking containers, and *avunculocal* to post-nuptial residence. Because all the tribes in the sample of Table I lack all three of these additional traits, they would fall in the *d* quadrant of every two by two table and thus alter Phi and Q coefficients in the positive direction. G (r_n) would remain unchanged. It should also be emphasized that the position of the zero value would change and some low negative values would shift to positive. For example, the Phi for patrilocal residence and subsistence on game, from Table I, is −.07. If we add three tribes which lack both of these traits to our sample, the Phi becomes +.10. If we add more tribes which lacked both of these traits, it will give a still higher positive value.

The kind of culture traits assembled by Murdock in his *Social Structure* (1949) and in his "World Ethnographic Sample" (1957a) would not increase in number very rapidly if the size of the area were increased from, say, North America to the world for intertrait correlations. The reason is that most of them apparently arise independently over and over again in area after area around the world. Therefore, intertrait correlations with Q and Phi, based on his data, would not change much after an area the size of a continent had been reached.

This would not be true for many other kinds of data. Localized assemblages, such as the Sun Dance, the Potlatch, and the Kuksu Cult, would show up as common absences in all the areas where they failed to occur, so that an expansion of such localized material would again load up the common absence (d) quadrant. A Phi correlation between the split profile in Northwest Coast art and the plank house would start out at a modest positive figure in northwestern North America and swell to almost unity when hundreds of common absences came up from other tribes in other parts of the world. This change would not take place for r_n (G). This re-emphasizes the conclusion reached with respect to Phi and Q above, that no one measure of relationship is best for all problems and all the kinds of data that conform to a two by two table.

SAMPLING

When the researcher confines his investigation to a restricted area, a restricted subject, and a limited time span, it is possible to include almost every people and almost every relevant culture trait within the given restriction. If, at the same time, he refrains in his text from extending his generalizations to other areas, other time periods, or other subjects, the problem of sampling is not serious. In actual practice, such exhaustion of evidence within a limited framework is seldom achieved; but it is possible to utilize all the known information, if time is cut off at some date in the past, and thus collect a sample complete enough to make it difficult, if not impossible, for a later investigator to add enough new information to seriously alter the relationships. For instance, the data employed by Driver and Schuessler (1957) included about 2,000 culture traits. Even though the trait sample was not strictly random, it seems unlikely that additional information would produce significant differences in the intertribal correlations based on late nineteenth-century information. Many other correlation studies done by the California school were similarly limited in area and time span.

The Yale school, in contrast, has generally aimed at worldwide intertrait correlations based on samples of from about 2% to 20% of the world's peoples. Some literate peoples have also been included in these samples, as in Murdock's "World Ethnographic Sample" (1957a), but the majority are nonliterate. If the total number of cases (peoples) for the entire world were known and the information sought was obtainable for all, a strictly random sample of 20% from a total of about 2,500 "tribes" would be more than ample for most purposes and a 2% sample would be sufficient to reveal high correlations within the original universe of 2,500 peoples. Because these ideal conditions are far from realized, worldwide cross-cultural studies face a perpetual sampling problem.

Generally speaking, the larger the sample, the greater is the probability of its being representative, but when the sample is not randomly chosen, increase in size may not improve it. On the other hand, if the researcher can demonstrate his own lack of bias in choosing his sample, the larger it is the more likely is it to be representative of a larger universe.

Some samples are necessarily biased by the very nature of the information sought. The best example of this predicament is that in which the glottochronologists find themselves. Their problem is to develop a method by which time depths of nonliterate languages can be inferred. But the only languages for which rates of change can be empirically (inductively) determined are the literate languages for which we have adequate documentary records. It is impossible to make any selection of literate languages which can qualify as a random sample of all languages, both literate and nonliterate. Therefore, the entire structure that the glottochronologists have erected rests on a blind faith in the uniformity of the rate of change for all languages. They may be correct, but they will never be able to prove their case by any legitimate brand of statistical inference. The wide acceptance of their results reflects the ignorance of many anthropologists in regard to the rules of statistical inference.

The technique of choosing the small sample of tribes in Table I was mentioned above. First, we collected a list of all the major tribes in the United States; then we rolled a die for each tribe and chose those for which a one-spot came up. Another simple random sampling technique requires the writing of the names of all the tribes in the universe (area) on uniform slips of paper or cards, and the mixing up or shuffling of the slips or cards before drawing the number desired in the sample. The Mexican National Lottery works on this sample principle. A huge, hollow sphere five or six feet in diameter contains a million or more small spheres the size of marbles, each with a number corresponding to that of a lottery ticket. The large sphere, which must weigh a ton or so, is rotated by a mechanical device to mix the marbles between successive drawings. A small opening at the bottom releases a single marble, the number of which is read by an employee and confirmed by a second employee to guard against dishonesty.

Coin tossing is another technique of random sampling. If the researcher desires a 50% sample, he may toss a single coin and choose those cases for which heads comes up. A 25% sample may be obtained by tossing two coins together and choosing the cases for which two heads appear. A 12.5% sample would result from occurrences of three heads from tossing three coins, and a 1-in-36 sample from the simultaneous appearance of the same face, say the one-spot, for two dice. Tables of random numbers, found in books on statistics, may also be used to select samples. All cases in the universe are numbered, as before, and those with numbers corresponding to those in the table of random numbers are chosen. These somewhat redundant examples of random sampling have been given because the statistical formulas most commonly used by cross-cultural researchers are geared to random sampling, and the researcher should have a clear idea of what it consists.

In practice, few comparative researchers have operated with random samples. Those of the California school have generally taken every tribe in the restricted area chosen for study. Stanislaw Klimek (1935) included every tribelet on which data was available within the boundaries of the present State of California, and his sample of traits, something over 400, included all the data he could get together in the time at his disposal. Forrest Clements (1931) and Driver and Kroeber (1932) correlated the table of Sun Dance data compiled earlier by Leslie Spier; it included all, or nearly all, of the tribes which had the ceremony, and the list of traits was the best that Spier was able to assemble at the time he wrote. The available data in these and other studies was so limited that no conscious attempt was made to sample it in any explicit way, although, of course, some selection was implicitly made.

The Yale school, in contrast, has been more conscious of sampling problems, because the task of assembling most of the data in the world or the nonliterate world on a given subject is enormous. The only instances of apparent random sampling that I have been able to find in the publications of this group are those mentioned by Murdock (1957a, 1957b). On page 250 of the latter paper, he says he used a "purely random selection" of ten societies each from Asia, Africa, Oceania, and native North and South America. In this same paper (p. 253) he mentioned two other samples, "one completely unselected and the other very carefully compiled to give equal representation to all the culture areas of the world." Because the concept of random sampling is so poorly understood by ethnologists and social anthropologists as a group, statements about it should mention the specific sampling device employed.

The two samples mentioned by Murdock (1957b, p. 253) consisted of 300 societies each, and were chosen to test the correlations published earlier in his *Social Structure* (1949). After over-modestly characterizing his sample in *Social Structure* as a half-hearted attempt, he summarizes the results of this sampling experiment. "While there were no serious upsets, the results from the selected and unselected samples were sufficiently divergent in enough instances to convince me of the imperative need of far more careful representative sampling" (1957b, 253). His "World Ethnographic Sample" (1957a) is his answer to this need, and on page 664 of this latter publication he again mentions the same smaller samples.

Because Murdock is by long odds the leading cross-cultural researcher and has selected the largest and best samples of their kind to date, it is with some hesitation that I offer any criticism at all of his samples. However, it should be kept in mind that his World Ethnographic Sample is selected to facilitate intertrait correlation studies aimed at demonstrating either multiple independent origins of like phenomena from like antecedent conditions, or multiple borrowings and integrations into clusters of functionally related traits. He therefore eliminates pairs and larger groups of peoples known to have recently diverged from a common cultural ancestry or to have had recent contact with one another. Such a sample is not appropriate for problems concentrating on acculturation, diffusion, migration, and all other kinds of contact-caused change. It is amazing that Naroll (1961) was able to demonstrate that geographical clusters, suggestive of diffusion, actually occur in Murdock's sample selected to eliminate most of them. Had Naroll chosen data from some of Driver and Massey's (1957) maps, the areal clustering would have been much more marked.

The sample of the Human Relations Area Files is a selected sample chosen to represent as evenly as possible thirty-one variants of four major subjects, plus language family. The major subjects are geographical environment, basic subsistence economy, descent, and political organization. Language family is included as an indicator of common history. Each of the thirty-one variants appears a multiple number of times among the approximately 200 peoples in the sample. The limitation of this sample lies in the implicit assumption that it will be representative of all other variants of all other cultural subjects. It implicitly assumes that all other aspects of culture will correlate positively or negatively with one or another of the thirty-one items in the list. Psychologists, working with samples of individuals from a single culture, that of the United States of America, have found as many as fifteen mutually uncorrelated factors in relatively small populations. It seems likely that there are a much larger number of mutually uncorrelated factors in the thousands of the cultures of the world and that no sample selected on the basis of representativeness for thirty-one variants can be representative for some much larger number such as 3,100.

It seems to this author that we haven't enough knowledge at present to select a world-wide sample for general comparative purposes, but that different samples must be obtained for different problems. Murdock's "World Ethnographic Sample" is indeed an admirable one for the problems he wishes to solve. Because the peoples chosen for all samples must be those which are the best known, it might be advantageous to try another approach. Why not select all those peoples in the world on which we have data that comes up to a certain standard of both quality and quantity? This would be partly subjective, but would be less so than the procedure mentioned above. It could be objectified by soliciting opinions of multiple specialists for every locality or area of the world. This should yield more than 1,000 cases. Let this be a kind of universe or parameter from which smaller samples for world-wide studies might be chosen by strictly random procedures. It would be up to the researcher to select randomly at least twice as many cases as he wished to work with, because the lack of relevant data would cut his random selection down to half or less after he had searched his sources. This proposal leaves less to human judgment and more to chance, in the technical meaning of that word. This is what all statistical coefficients demand. However, such samples would not necessarily be representative of all cultures from the natural history point of view; they would not necessarily include every species and variety of cultures and might leave out key peoples (comparable to the duck-billed platypus of biological taxonomy) which constitute important typological or evolutionary links. They would also fail to represent little-known areas and peoples.

Because no such supersample exists at the present time and would take considerable cooperative effort to construct, what is the individual researcher to do at present? There are several pragmatic suggestions. First, use someone else's sample, such as Murdock's or that of the Human Relations Area Files, in order to maintain impartiality on the part of the investigator. Second, choose as large a sample as possible. If you collect over half of the data in existence on your problem. it will push the next researcher pretty hard to find enough additional information to significantly alter your conclusions. Third, map as much of your data as your publisher will stand for. Worldwide correlations may obscure local clusterings of data which may show significant differences from one continent or culture area to another. Fourth, if differences in areas or time levels are great, test for significant differences from one area or time period to the next. Fifth, if your problem is so difficult or your time or money so limited that you can collect only a couple dozen cases, don't use any measure of correlation or probability at all, but limit yourself to the raw figures.

CLUSTERING LARGE SAMPLES WITH COEFFICIENTS OF INTERRELATIONSHIP

When samples are relatively large, with a hundred or more tribes or traits, clustering is facilitated by first computing one or two sets of intercorrelations. If the sample of Table I were enlarged to include all 132 tribes in the United States, sorting by inspection would be more difficult. The expedient procedure would be to intercorrelate the 16 traits. It would be possible to intercorrelate the 132 tribes, instead, or in addition, but with only 16 traits involved, this would hardly be worth the effort. If, on the other hand, the sample of Table I were increased by adding 100 more traits, bringing the total to 116, it would be more expedient to intercorrelate the 23 tribes. For most problems, the best procedure is to intercorrelate which ever set of variables is fewer in number. However, where both tribes and traits are about equally numerous and run to 50 or more each, it is often desirable to compute both sets of intercorrelations.

Because most universities now have electronic computer centers available to all researchers, the technique of assembling data for these machines will be briefly described. There are two kinds of work sheets. The first is a sheet on which all the tribes are listed and which is headed by a single trait. After all the data have been collected, such a sheet will give the distribution of this trait among all the tribes; it corresponds to a horizontal row in Table I. Each trait should be listed on a separate sheet of this kind, so that all the sheets combined give all the distributions of all the traits among all the tribes. The second type of work sheet is one on which the heading is a single tribe, and on which all the traits are listed. This work sheet corresponds to a vertical column in Table I. There should be one such sheet for every tribe, and collectively these sheets give all the tribal inventories in the sample. These two sets of work sheets are cross-classifications of each other, and normally a researcher works with only one set. Computing machines can automatically construct one set of sheets from the other set by means of punch cards. In the initial stages of research, it is not necessary to know the complete list of tribes or the complete list of traits; new ones may be added as the work proceeds. From the work sheets the information can be punched on cards for the electronic computer.

When the correlations are obtained from the calculating machine, they are normally in the alphabetical order of the tribes or the traits, as the case may be, because this was a convenient order for retrieving a desired tribe or trait from a stack of work sheets as the data were being collected by the researcher. After the correlations are obtained, it is desirable to cluster them so that the high positive values fall as closely as possible to the diagonal of self-correlations running from upper left to lower right, and so that the high negative values fall as far from this diagonal as possible in the upper right and lower left sections of the table. This is accomplished by placing the most highly positively correlated variables adjacent to each other in the new serial order being constructed, and by placing the most highly negatively correlated variables as far apart as possible in the sequence. Correlation methods are superior to the mere inspection of work sheets because they can handle much larger quantities of data. The amount of data they can classify is almost unlimited.

The intertrait correlations are arranged in this manner in Table XVIII. It is clear from this table that there are three major clusters of traits. These are the same trait clusters already displayed in Table IX. Within each of the two larger clusters is a smaller core cluster set off by broken lines. Wild plant diet (trait *c*) is the most isolated trait in the entire group. It shows only a slight tendency to correlate positively with the upper left cluster, and has all negative relationships but one with the traits in the other two clusters.

The intertribal correlations are shown in Table XIX. Because each tribe possesses exactly five traits, pairs of tribes may share five, four, three, two, one or no traits. These six possibilities are represented by six correlation values, each of which repeats over and over again in the table. From Table XIX, the tribes have been classified into two major groups, with two tribes in the center in limbo, as in Table IX. The two limbo tribes correlate in the middle positive range with each other and with nearly all members of both major groups. The upper left major cluster contains three minor clusters, two of them within a third one. The lower right major cluster contains only a single minor cluster.

Perhaps the most transparent example of this technique so far published is that of Stanislaw Klimek (1935). Klimek clustered intercorrelation tables of nearly 100 variables with no technique other than visual inspection. After he had obtained both sets of intercorrelations and clustered them in the above manner, he constructed a series of clustered distribution tables comparable to our Table IX.

A more recent example of clustering is that of Driver (1956). In this instance, only intertrait correlations were clustered and the original distribution table, which was 25 traits by 280 tribes, was not rearranged in clusters in the manner of our Table IX.

Forrest Clements (1954) was the first ethnologist to use a numerical cluster analysis technique. The results he obtained show little or no significant difference from those obtained by Driver and Schuessler a little later (1957) with a more precise factor analysis technique.

Clustering, either by inspection or by a more specific technique such as that of Clements, may be done with any coefficient. Factor analysis is limited to forms of Pearson's *r*, of which Phi is the most suitable for comparative ethnology. The assumptions underlying tetrachoric *r* do not fit ethnological data as well as those of Phi.

When large numbers of variables are intercorrelated, it is sometimes difficult to comprehend the relations of so many coefficients and to cluster them in a meaningful manner. In such cases it is possible to reduce the coefficients to a smaller number of factor loadings by factor analysis. So far this has been applied to only 16 variables (Driver and Schuessler, *Ibid.*), but may be applied to any number. The experience of psychology shows that intercorrelations among 100 or more variables often can be reduced to about 10% as many factor loadings.

With the appearance of factor analysis in the 1930's and of electronic computers a decade later, it is no longer correct to say that anthropology is data poor, that there are too many variables to intercorrelate. The largest computers can intercorrelate 400 variables in one operation. Such machines can ingest all of the data in Murdock's (1957a) World Ethnographic Sample or on Driver's and Massey's (1957) 160 maps and run off a complete set of intercorrelations in one continuous operation and, if desired, can continue on to a factor analysis. These techniques are now ahead of anthropological data and offer a challenge to the researcher to obtain larger and better samples.

BIBLIOGRAPHY

BLALOCK, H. M., JR. 1960. "Correlational Analysis and Causal Inferences," *American Anthropologist,* N.S., Vol. 62, pp. 624-631.

CLEMENTS, FORREST. 1931. "Plains Indian Tribal Correlations with Sun Dance Data," *American Anthropologist,* N.S., Vol. 33, pp. 216-227.

———. 1954. "The Use of Cluster Analysis with Anthropological Data," *American Anthropologist,* N.S., Vol. 56, pp. 180-199.

DRIVER, HAROLD E. 1939. *Culture Element Distributions: X, Northwest California.* University of California Anthropological Records, Vol. 1, pp. 297-433.

———. 1941. *Girls' Puberty Rites in Western North America.* University of California Anthropological Records, Vol. 6, pp. 21-90.

———. 1956. "An Integration of Functional, Evolutionary and Historical Theory by Means of Correlations," *Supplement to International Journal of American Linguistics,* Vol. 22, pp. 1-35.

———. 1961. *Indians of North America.* Chicago: University of Chicago Press.

DRIVER, HAROLD E. and A. L. KROEBER. 1932. *Quantitative Expression of Cultural Relationships.* University of California Publications in American Archaeology and Ethnology, Vol. 31, pp. 211-256.

DRIVER, HAROLD E. and WM. C. MASSEY. 1957. *Comparative Studies of North American Indians.* Transactions of the American Philosophical Society, Vol. 47, pp. 165-460.

DRIVER, HAROLD E. and KARL F. SCHUESSLER. 1957. "Factor Analysis of Ethnographic Data," *American Anthropologist,* N.S., Vol. 59, pp. 655-663.

ELLEGARD, ALVAR. 1959. "Statistical Measurement of Linguistic Relationship," *Language,* Vol. 35, pp. 131-156.

GOODMAN, LEO A. and WM. H. KRUSKAL. 1954. "Measures of Association for Cross Classification," *Journal of the American Statistical Association,* Vol. 49, pp. 732-764.

———. 1959. "Measures of Association for Cross Classifications. II: Further Discussion and References," *Journal of the American Statistical Association,* Vol. 54, pp. 123-163.

HYMES, DELL H. 1960. "Lexicostatistics So Far," *Current Anthropology,* Vol. 1, pp. 3-44.

KLIMEK, STANISLAW. 1935. *The Structure of California Indian Culture.* University of California Publications in American Archaeology and Ethnology, Vol. 37, pp. 1-70.

KLUCKHOHN, CLYDE. 1953. "Universal Categories of Culture," in A. L. Kroeber (ed.), *Anthropology Today*. Chicago: University of Chicago Press.

KROEBER, A. L. 1960. "Statistics, Indo-European, and Taxonomy," *Language*, Vol. 36, pp. 1-21.

KROEBER, A. L. and C. D. CHRETIEN. 1937. "Quantitative Classification of Indo-European Languages," *Language*, Vol. 13, pp. 83-103.

LEWIS, DON and C. J. BURKE. 1949. "The Use and Misuse of the Chi-square Test," *Psychological Bulletin*, Vol. 46, pp. 433-489.
(For criticism of this article, see same journal, Vol. 47, pp. 331-355, 1950.)

MUELLER, JOHN H. and KARL F. SCHUESSLER. 1961. *Statistical Reasoning in Sociology*. Boston: Houghton Mifflin.

MURDOCK, G. PETER. 1949. *Social Structure*. New York: Macmillan.

———. 1957a. "World Ethnographic Sample," *American Anthropologist*, N.S., Vol. 59, pp. 664-687.

———. 1957b. "Anthropology as a Comparative Science," *Behavioral Science*, Vol. 2, pp. 249-254.

NAROLL, RAOUL. 1961. "Two Solutions to Galton's Problem," *Philosophy of Science*, Vol. 28, pp. 15-39.

SPIRO, MELFORD E. and ROY G. ANDRADE. 1958. "A Cross-Cultural Study of Some Supernatural Beliefs," *American Anthropologist*, N.S., Vol. 60, pp. 456-466.

UDY, STANLEY H., JR. 1959. *Organization of Work: A Comparative Analysis of Production among Nonindustrial Peoples*. New Haven: HRAF Press.

WHITING, BEATRICE B. 1950. *Paiute Sorcery*. Viking Fund Publications in Anthropology, No. 15.

WHITING, JOHN W. M. and IRVIN CHILD. 1953. *Child Training and Personality: A Cross-Cultural Study*. New Haven: Yale University Press.

TABLE XVIII

Intertrait Correlations (Phi)

	a	g	j	p	k	e	c	d	o	l	m	i	n	b	f	h
a		.37	.37	.33	.30	-.14	-.14	-.17	-.14	-.20	-.17	-.14	-.26	-.48	-.37	-.30
g	.37		.82	.58	.35	.24	.24	.10	-.14	-.20	-.28	-.39	-.57	-.62	-1.00	-.66
j	.37	.82		.44	.14	.24	.24	.10	-.14	-.20	.10	-.39	-.31	-.62	-.82	-.82
p	.33	.58	.44		.40	.22	.22	-.32	-.42	-.24	-.32	-.17	-.81	-.42	-.58	-.40
k	.30	.35	.14	.40		.20	-.20	-.36	-.47	-.69	-.58	.20	-.14	-.17	-.35	-.28
e	-.14	.24	.24	.22	.20		-.10	-.10	-.10	-.14	-.10	-.10	-.17	-.32	-.24	-.22
c	-.14	.24	.24	.22	-.20	-.10		-.10	-.10	-.14	-.37	-.10	-.17	-.32	-.24	-.20
d	-.17	.10	.10	-.32	-.36	-.10	-.10		.79	.53	-.14	-.10	-.22	-.40	-.10	.10
o	-.14	-.14	-.14	-.42	-.47	-.10	-.10	.79		.67	-.10	-.10	-.17	-.32	.14	.20
l	-.20	-.20	-.20	-.24	-.69	-.14	-.14	.53	.67		-.17	-.14	-.26	-.10	.20	.29
m	-.17	-.28	-.10	-.32	-.58	-.10	.37	-.14	-.10	-.17		-.10	.40	.20	.28	.10
i	-.14	-.39	-.39	-.17	.20	-.10	-.10	-.10	-.10	-.14	-.10		.22	.30	.39	-.20
n	-.26	-.57	-.31	-.81	-.14	-.17	-.17	-.22	-.17	-.26	.40	.22		.57	.57	.35
b	-.48	-.62	-.62	-.42	-.17	-.32	-.32	-.40	-.32	-.10	.20	.30	.57		.62	.49
f	-.37	-1.00	-.82	-.58	-.35	-.24	-.24	-.10	-.14	.20	.28	.39	.57	.62		.66
h	-.30	-.66	-.82	-.40	-.28	-.22	-.20	.10	.20	.29	.10	-.20	.35	.49	.66	

TABLE XIX

Intertribal Correlations (Phi)

	1	2	22	23	11	18	21	13	7	19	20	4	17	5	3	15	10	9	12	16	14	6	8
1		1.00	1.00	1.00	.71	.71	.71	.71	.71	.42	.42	.13	.42	.42	.13	.13	-.16	-.16	-.16	-.16	-.45	-.16	-.45
2	1.00		1.00	1.00	.71	.71	.71	.71	.71	.42	.42	.13	.42	.42	.13	.13	-.16	-.16	-.16	-.16	-.45	-.16	-.45
22	1.00	1.00		1.00	.71	.71	.71	.71	.71	.42	.42	.13	.42	.42	.13	.13	-.16	-.16	-.16	-.16	-.45	-.16	-.45
23	1.00	1.00	1.00		.71	.71	.71	.71	.71	.42	.42	.13	.42	.42	.13	.13	-.16	-.16	-.16	-.16	-.45	-.16	-.45
11	.71	.71	.71	.71		1.00	.71	.71	.71	.42	.42	.13	.42	.42	.13	.13	-.16	-.16	-.16	-.16	-.45	-.16	-.45
18	.71	.71	.71	.71	1.00		.71	.71	.71	.42	.42	.13	.42	.42	.13	.13	-.16	-.16	-.16	-.16	-.45	-.16	-.45
21	.71	.71	.71	.71	.71	.71		.71	.71	.71	.42	.13	.42	.42	.13	.13	-.16	-.16	-.16	-.16	-.45	-.16	-.45
13	.71	.71	.71	.71	.71	.71	.71		.71	.42	.71	.13	.71	.71	.42	.42	.13	.13	.13	.13	-.16	.13	-.45
7	.71	.71	.71	.71	.71	.71	.71	.71		.42	.42	.42	.42	.42	.13	.13	-.16	-.16	-.16	-.16	-.45	-.16	-.16
19	.42	.42	.42	.42	.42	.42	.71	.42	.42		.42	.13	.13	.13	-.16	-.16	-.16	-.45	-.45	-.45	-.16	.13	-.45
20	.42	.42	.42	.42	.42	.42	.42	.71	.42	.42		.42	.42	.42	.13	.13	.42	-.16	-.16	-.16	-.16	.13	-.16
4	.13	.13	.13	.13	.13	.13	.13	.13	.42	.13	.42		.13	-.16	-.45	-.45	-.16	-.45	-.45	-.45	-.45	-.16	.42
17	.42	.42	.42	.42	.42	.42	.42	.71	.42	.13	.42	.13		.42	.13	.13	-.16	.42	.42	.42	.13	.42	-.45
5	.42	.42	.42	.42	.42	.42	.42	.71	.42	.13	.42	-.16	.42		.71	.42	.42	.42	.42	.13	.13	-.16	-.16
3	.13	.13	.13	.13	.13	.13	.13	.42	.13	-.16	.13	-.45	.13	.71		.71	.71	.71	.71	.42	.42	.13	.13
15	.13	.13	.13	.13	.13	.13	.13	.42	.13	-.16	.13	-.45	.13	.42	.71		.42	.42	.42	.71	.13	.13	-.16
10	-.16	-.16	-.16	-.16	-.16	-.16	-.16	.13	-.16	-.16	.42	-.16	-.16	.42	.71	.42		.42	.42	.13	.42	.13	.42
9	-.16	-.16	-.16	-.16	-.16	-.16	-.16	.13	-.16	-.45	-.16	-.45	.42	.42	.71	.42	.42		1.00	.71	.71	.42	.13
12	-.16	-.16	-.16	-.16	-.16	-.16	-.16	.13	-.16	-.45	-.16	-.45	.42	.42	.71	.42	.42	1.00		.71	.71	.42	.13
16	-.16	-.16	-.16	-.16	-.16	-.16	-.16	.13	-.16	-.45	-.16	-.45	.42	.13	.42	.71	.13	.71	.71		.42	.42	-.16
14	-.45	-.45	-.45	-.45	-.45	-.45	-.45	-.16	-.45	-.16	-.16	-.45	.13	.13	.42	.13	.42	.71	.71	.42		.71	.13
6	-.16	-.16	-.16	-.16	-.16	-.16	-.16	.13	-.16	.13	.13	-.16	.42	-.16	.13	.13	.13	.42	.42	.42	.71		-.16
8	-.45	-.45	-.45	-.45	-.45	-.45	-.45	-.45	-.16	-.45	-.16	.42	-.45	-.16	.13	-.16	.42	.13	.13	-.16	.13	-.16	

Appendix

HUMAN RELATIONS AREA FILES WORLD ETHNOGRAPHIC SAMPLE
(September 1961)

OWC Code Numbers and Name of Societies		Number of Sources	Text Pages
ASIA			
AA1	Korea	55	7,250
AD1	Formosa	37	3,000
*AD4	Formosan Aborigines	Sub File	
AE3	Sino-Tibetan Peoples	3	500
*AE4	Lolo	6	850
*AE5	Miao	9	750
*AE9	Monguor	1	150
AF1	China	84	20,750
AF12	North China	10	3,500
AF14	Central China	2	1,250
AF15	East China	3	1,500
AF16	Southwest China	7	3,125
AF17	South China	8	2,000
AG1	Manchuria	6	1,375
*AH1	Mongolia	8	1,375
AH6	Inner Mongolia	11	1,375
AH7	Outer Mongolia	3	375
AI1	Sinkiang	3	1,000
*AJ1	Tibet	26	7,300
AJ4	West Tibetans	23	2,875
AK5	Lepcha	8	1,000
AL1	Southeast Asia	5	2,000
AM1	Indochina	180	22,500
AM4	Cambodians	Sub File	
AM8	Laotians	Sub File	
AM11	Vietnamese	Sub File	
AN1	Malaya	90	7,750
AN5	Malays	Sub File	
*AN7	Semang	2	625
AO1	Thailand	38	5,500
AP1	Burma	30	5,000
AP4	Burmese	Sub File	
*AP6	Kachin	3	625
*AR7	Khasi	11	675
AU1	Afghanistan	74	8,750
AV1	Kashmir	6	2,125
AV3	Dard	4	625
AV4	Kashmiri	5	2,125
AV7	Burusho	4	1,000
AW1	India	54	16,000
AW2	Bihar	1	375

OWC Code Numbers and Name of Societies		Number of Sources	Text Pages
ASIA (continued)			
AW5	Coorg	1	375
AW6	East Punjab	2	1,250
AW7	Gujerati	4	750
AW17	Telugu	1	375
AW19	Uttar Pradesh	3	750
AW25	Bhil	5	1,000
AW31	Toda	6	1,250
AW32	Gond	8	2,000
*AX5	Vedda	1	700
AZ2	Andamans	3	1,000
AFRICA			
†F1	Africa	1	3,000
FA8	Bambara	4	1,150
FA28	Mossi	8	625
FC7	Mende	5	750
FE11	Tallensi	10	1,000
FE12	Twi	23	2,425
FF38	Katab	4	250
FF52	Nupe	5	1,200
FF57	Tiv	28	4,000
FF62	Yoruba	42	1,575
FH9	Fang	8	1,125
FJ22	Nuer	16	1,525
FJ23	Shilluk	28	925
FK7	Ganda	6	1,000
FL10	Kikuyu	8	1,450
FL11	Luo	18	350
FN4	Chagga	4	2,800
FN17	Ngonde	8	1,150
FO7	Azande	55	3,500
FO32	Mongo	9	775
*FO42	Rundi	8	1,100
FP13	Mbundu	5	750
FQ5	Bemba	9	850
FQ6	Ila	6	1,000
FT6	Thonga	2	1,125
FT7	Yao	11	550
FX10	Bushmen	11	900
FX13	Hottentot	14	1,550
FX14	Lovedu	4	450
FY8	Tanala	1	375

OWC Code Numbers and Name of Societies		Number of Sources	Text Pages
EUROPE			
E1	Europe	9	1,750
E16	Slavic Peoples	10	2,875
EA1	Poland	35	4,875
EB1	Czechoslovakia	102	8,250
EC1	Hungary	5	2,000
ED1	Rumania	7	1,375
EE1	Bulgaria	9	1,625
EF1	Yugoslavia	12	3,000
EF6	Serbs	2	750
EG1	Albania	8	2,125
EK1	Austria	3	1,750
EL1	Finland	2	500
*EP4	Lapps	3	1,000
ER6	Rural Irish	13	1,400
MIDDLE EAST			
M1	Middle East	72	15,250
MA1	Iran	72	7,000
MA11	Kurds	Sub File	
MB1	Turkey	3	375
MD1	Syria	13	2,250
MD4	Rwala	2	1,000
MG1	Jordan	25	3,125
MH1	Iraq	9	2,000
MI1	Kuwait	3	750
MJ1	Saudi Arabia	30	3,750
MJ4	Bedouins	4	1,000
MK4	Trucial Oman	3	375
ML1	Yemen	14	500
MM1	Aden	7	625
MM2	Hadhramaut	23	1,250
MO4	Somali	17	1,150
MP5	Amhara	10	1,075
MR14	Siwans	6	500
MS12	Hausa	16	1,200
MS25	Tuareg	6	700
MS30	Wolof	14	675
MX3	Rif	5	500
NORTH AMERICA			
NA6	Aleut	64	3,000
NA12	Tlingit	16	1,250
ND8	Copper Eskimo	16	1,875
ND12	Nahane	7	800
NE11	Nootka	17	1,400
NG6	Ojibwa	15	2,500
NJ5	Micmac	8	1,200
NH6	Montagnais	15	950
NL7	Historical Massachusetts	1	560
*NM7	Delaware	15	2,000
NM9	Iroquois	28	2,250
NO6	Comanche	10	1,000
NN11	Creek	3	750
NQ10	Crow	18	2,000
NQ12	Omaha	8	1,500
NORTH AMERICA (continued)			
NQ17	Mandan	10	1,300
NQ18	Pawnee	11	925
NR4	Plateau Indians	4	500
NR13	Northern Paiute	4	375
NR19	Southeast Salish	8	1,175
NS18	Pomo	22	1,200
NS22	Tubatulabal	4	200
NS29	Yokuts	16	1,100
NS31	Yurok	13	1,100
NT13	Navaho	150	10,000
NT14	Plateau Yumans	13	800
NT15	River Yumans	6	600
NT18	Tewa	15	1,300
NT23	Zuni	11	2,100
NU7	Aztec	17	1,900
NU28	Papago	15	1,500
NU31	Seri	6	500
NU33	Tarahumara	10	1,200
NU34	Tarasco	10	625
SOUTH AMERICA			
SA15	Mosquito	5	300
SA19	Talamanca	5	300
*SB5	Cuna	36	3,525
SC13	Goajiro	8	1,000
SD6	Cayapa	3	500
SD9	Jivaro	31	2,250
SE13	Inca	13	2,500
SF5	Aymara	8	700
SF21	Siriono	5	625
SG4	Araucanians	10	800
SH5	Tehuelche	6	600
SH6	Yahgan	3	1,700
SI4	Abipon	2	450
SI7	Mataco	4	600
SK6	Choroti	2	525
SM3	Caingang	4	400
SO8	Timbira	1	375
SO9	Tupinamba	26	1,250
SP17	Nambicuara	7	250
SP22	Tapirape	12	500
SQ13	Mundurucu	12	725
SQ20	Tucuna	5	300
SR9	Carib	1	500
ST13	Callinago	12	800
RUSSIA			
R1	Soviet Union	80	14,250
RB1	Baltic Countries	3	310
RB5	Lithuanians	12	1,650
RC1	Byelorussia	3	375
RD1	Ukraine	20	2,500
RF1	Great Russia	2	500
RG4	Estonians	3	625
RH1	Caucasia	7	2,500
*RI3	Abkhaz	2	300

OWC Code Numbers and Name of Societies		Number of Sources	Text Pages
	RUSSIA (continued)		
RL1	Turkestan	4	1,000
RL4	Turkic Peoples	3	1,375
*RQ2	Kazak	2	375
RR1	Siberia	2	750
*RU4	Samoyed	14	750
RV2	Yakuts	30	1,000
RY2	Chukchee	20	3,000
RY3	Kamchadal	11	875
*RY4	Koryak	5	1,250
*RX2	Gilyak	9	500
	OCEANIA		
OA1	Philippines	57	7,875
*OA5	Apayao	Sub	File
OA14	Central Bisayan	Sub	File
OA19	Ifugao	Sub	File
*OB1	Indonesia	6	1,125
OC6	Iban	15	1,100
OF5	Alorese	3	750

OWC Code Numbers and Name of Societies		Number of Sources	Text Pages
	OCEANIA (continued)		
OG6	Makassar	1	400
OI8	Aranda	39	2,875
OI17	Murngin	13	1,550
OI19	Tasmanians	1	500
OI20	Tiwi	9	500
OJ23	Orokaiva	4	650
OJ27	Wogeo	14	250
OJ29	Kapauku	3	700
OL6	Trobriands	21	3,000
OM10	Lesu	7	600
ON6	Buka	5	750
OO12	Malekula	3	1,000
OQ6	Lau	8	1,000
OR11	Marshalls	20	2,200
OR21	Woleai	40	2,500
OT11	Tikopia	19	1,875
OU8	Samoa	17	2,875
OX6	Marquesas	15	1,000
OY2	Easter Islanders	15	1,000
OZ11	Pukapukans	12	750

* Additional sources in process.

† Ethnographic summaries of African cultures prepared by George P. Murdock.

SUMMARY

Total number of Files available	220
Total number of source pages	400,000
Total number of sources in Files	3,180
Total number of file slips in each set (estimated)	2,000,000
Total number of source pages in OWC file	5,000